PITTSBURGH GLASS

1797–1891

A History and Guide for Collectors

PITTSBURGH

GLASS

1797–1891

A History and Guide for Collectors

⚲

Illustrated with photographs

⚲

LOWELL INNES

HOUGHTON MIFFLIN COMPANY   BOSTON   1976

Book design by David Ford

Portions of this book have appeared in *Antiques*.

Library of Congress Cataloging in Publication Data

Innes, Lowell.
    Pittsburgh glass, 1797–1891.

    Bibliography: p.
    Includes index.
    1. Glassware — Pennsylvania — Pittsburgh — History.
2. Glassware — Collectors and collecting. I. Title.
NK5112.I55   748.2′9148′86   76-25833
ISBN 0-395-20733-9

Printed in the United States of America

H 10 9 8 7 6 5 4 3 2 1

Midwestern Cased Glass.

Large cased pitcher of lead glass on an applied opaque base, ca. 1850. Polished pontil, unusually attractive handle with slight thumb-rest. Pitcher is made from three gathers of glass—a layer of amethyst on the inside covered with a layer of opaque white, then a casing of clear glass on the outside. George McKearin acquired the pitcher in 1946 in Adams County, Pa., and pronounced it definitely Pittsburgh. H. 9½″. D. of base 4½″. *Collection of the author.*

Large cased compote of lead glass on an applied clear stem and foot, 1850–1875. The bowl is made from three gathers of glass—a layer of opaque white on the inside covered by a gather of amethyst with milk white loopings, finally covered by a casing of clear glass. Shown in Plate 21, McKearin, *Two Hundred Years of American Blown Glass.* H. 8⅜″. D. of top 9⅝″. *The Corning Museum of Glass.*

For Ethelinda

Preface

The late Charles A. McClintock had an unbounded interest in glass, both as a scholar and as a collector. While president of the Historical Society of Western Pennsylvania in the years 1949–1962, he saw the need for a definitive work on Pittsburgh glassmaking and he set about to have it written. He took his idea to the Laurel Foundation, which agreed to provide grants to make the work possible, and he arranged for the Historical Society to serve as sponsor of the undertaking. As author, I wish to express my deep gratitude to those who conceived this project and encouraged me in its undertaking: Charles A. McClintock, the Laurel Foundation, and the Historical Society of Western Pennsylvania.

In addition, I am under a pleasant obligation to many other persons and organizations. The time period covered, 1797–1891, and the variety of the Pittsburgh product called for objective advice from specialists on techniques. I have been fortunate in my friends: the late James H. Rose on lacy glass, Jerome Strauss on cut and engraved, Helen McKearin on bottles and flasks, A. Christian Revi on late pressed glass, and Paul Hollister on paperweights.

The late Dr. E. R. Eller of the Carnegie Museum offered constant and invaluable help on the Pittsburgh area and its glass. Laura W. Watkins gave me a rare Pittsburgh circular. Helen McKearin generously loaned me notes she had compiled from early newspapers. Dr. Arthur Peterson aided with patent information. Thomas C. Pears III furnished family records and a rare Bakewell catalogue. The late William Frank and his son, James A. Frank, also offered family records for study and the James Frank collection of bottles for photographs. Charles R. Mitchell sent family letters recounting Dithridge glassmaking achievements. Walter M. Brainard made the facilities of the Westmoreland Glass Company available.

Cooperative treatment from many museums warmed my heart. At the Corning Museum of Glass, Paul Perrot (now at the Smithsonian Institution), Jane S. Spillman, and Robert H. Brill were always helpful. George O. Bird and Walter E. Simmons, Jr., at the Henry Ford Museum took on even the smallest tasks, as did Mary Glaze Seiler and Berry B. Tracy at the Metropolitan Museum of Art. At the Wadsworth Atheneum, Henry P. Maynard, now retired, and Graham Hood, now at Colonial Williamsburg, made routine work pleasant. Paul V. Gardner and C. Malcolm Watkins at the Smithsonian opened new vistas. Richard Carter Barret, former director of the Bennington Museum, by reading the manuscript, and David S. Brooke and Melvin E. Watts at the Currier Gallery of Art eased my labors. Milo Naeve, now at the Chicago Art Institute, directed me to important examples at the Henry Francis du Pont Winterthur Museum. John W.

Keefe, now at the Chicago Art Institute, suggested Pittsburgh material in the Toledo Museum collections. Lawrence S. Thurman, now curator of the Daniel Boone Homestead, made available record books from the Harmony Society at Old Economy. The list stretches on: Nancy O. Merrill at Sandwich, Charles F. Montgomery and Patricia Kane at Yale, David A. Hanks at the Philadelphia Museum of Art, David T. Owsley at the Carnegie Museum, and Daniel B [sic] Reibel, curator of Old Economy Village.

A book on glass depends on the quality of its photographs. The bulk of the pictures have been taken by Leo Sarnaki of the Carnegie Museum, Ray Errett of the Corning Museum of Glass, Charles Miller and Carl Malotka of the Henry Ford Museum, and Bill Finney of Concord, New Hampshire. Many others, though unnamed, also contributed their skills.

Staff members, past and present, of the Historical Society of Western Pennsylvania, have helped me tirelessly. Prudence Trimble, Mrs. Ruth K. Salisbury, and her daughter, Ruth Salisbury, Mrs. Helen M. Wilson and Mrs. Viola L. Altenburger were of invaluable aid in library research. Mrs. Geraldine Gempel carefully checked all the glass photographed from the Society and helped immeasurably in matching pictures to the text throughout the book. Thanks are due also to the staff of the Carnegie Library in Pittsburgh, in its Pennsylvania Room and its Science Room, and particularly to Catherine C. Hay in the Art Room. Librarians at the New York Public Library Annex, 521 West 43rd Street, worked patiently. Grace G. Stewart of Maryland shared her researches on Pittsburgh glass.

Extensive private collections of Pittsburgh and Midwestern glass assembled by members of the Early American Glass Club in Pittsburgh were made available for study and photography, as were collections of the late Dr. Florence Kline, the late John and Margaret Grossman, the late J. Robert Rodgers, the late Earl Dambach, and the late Robert and Harriet Carew. Theodore E. Kel-

ler of Cincinnati, William J. Elsholz and Walter and Vera Simmons of Detroit, and Dr. E. R. Eller of Pittsburgh contributed pictures of significant pieces of Midwestern glass. In the East, Dorothy Lee Jones and Ruth and Kenneth Wakefield have been gracious in sharing knowledge and photographs.

The following enthusiastic friends, collectors, historians, and students loaned prize possessions and helped me to explore the past.

Mrs. Woodward C. Adams, Mr. and Mrs. Holbrook G. Botset, Carleton Brown, Kenneth Burr, Robert J. Charleston, Barbara H. Chase, James E. Courtney, David M. Craig, Barry Curcio, Robert and Mary Campbell Eckhardt, Evelyn Evans, Carl U. Fauster, Regis F. Ferson, Edith Gaines, J. Nevin Garber, Charles B. Gardner, Clifton F. Giles, Jr., Mr. and Mrs. William M. Guthrie, Mr. and Mrs. John Heard, Justin B. Hickin, Mrs. Helen Carew Hickman, Michael Holt, Mrs. Thomas P. Jones, Jr., the late Mrs. Hugo Laughlin, H. Fred Mercer, George Michael, Mrs. Thomas G. Miller, Dorothy B. Neal, Lily Lee Nixon, Mrs. Ray Patterson, Dr. E. David Pollock, Mrs. Ann Reeder, Mr. and Mrs. Samuel Schwartz, John D. Strassler, Peter H. Tillou, J. Fuller Trump, Elaine Walker, the late Crawford Wettlaufer, Mr. and Mrs. Edward Whitney, Robert G. Wheeler, and Mrs. Elizabeth Ingerman Wood.

My friend Kenneth M. Wilson of the Henry Ford Museum, an authority on New England glassmaking, not only read the manuscript with meticulous care but also guided me through many pitfalls. His corrections were salutary, his suggestions constructive.

My editor, Robert C. Alberts, helped to organize the material with professional skill and showed unusual zeal and enthusiasm toward its publication.

Dr. Donald A. Shelley of the Henry Ford Museum advised and encouraged me constantly. His valuable help was my shield and buckler.

I cannot close without the highest accolade to my wife, Ethelinda, for a major job of typing manuscript and captions, no matter how many times they were changed. Her organization of lists of picture locations, of quotations, and of ownership of glass photographed has been painstaking. She has corrected me when I have been wrong, chided me when I have been dilatory, challenged me when I have been complacent. It is her book, too.

LOWELL INNES
SACO, MAINE

Contents

PART TWO

An Introduction to Pittsburgh Glass

My purpose in writing this work is to tell the history of glassmaking in Pittsburgh and its home county in the years 1797–1891. The story begins with free-blown glass and ends with late nineteenth-century art glass and novelty pieces. It begins with the founding of the second-oldest glasshouse west of the Allegheny Mountains when Pittsburgh was an eighteenth-century frontier town of a few thousand people; it ends with the merging of nine Pittsburgh companies into the giant United States Glass Company cartel, when Pittsburgh had become a metropolitan city and the largest of nineteenth-century American glassmaking centers.

Two important factors make such a history valuable. Nowhere else in American glassmaking can we study in a single locality the continuous production of glass from the simplest windowpane and the crudest bottle to the streamlined mechanization that could turn out perfect sets of pressed tableware or thousands of mechanically blown bottles. The Pittsburgh area offers a marvelous chance to observe changing techniques and to judge popular taste of nineteenth-century America. Every technique of American glassmaking was used there except the lily pad. More glass was made in Allegheny County than in any other single area of the United States.

The second factor is even more important to collectors and students. Nowhere can one pick up a volume devoted solely to the story of Pittsburgh glassmaking. As early as 1927, Rhea Mansfield Knittle in *Early American Glass* listed, in fifty-three chapters, major Pittsburgh factories with brief statements about their products. That there were only eight chapters about Pittsburgh and three about Wheeling shows the need for a work on glass of the Pittsburgh District.

In *American Glass,* first published in 1941 and in its twentieth printing in 1970, George S. and Helen McKearin gave full recognition to Pittsburgh work and its characteristic forms and related it to many of the earlier researches of Mrs. Knittle. Though the McKearins offered new perspective and honor to the achievements of Pittsburgh glassmakers, their basic points are separated and become diluted for many readers in such a monumental work. In *Two Hundred Years of American Blown Glass,* 1949, they paid discerning respect to Pittsburgh glass.

In view of the zeal with which Pittsburgh glass is collected today and the prices paid for early pieces, it is difficult to convince young dealers and collectors that only a few decades ago the glass was ignored by most, depreciated by many, and cherished by relatively few. Nor is this neglect surprising. The three eighteenth-century glass factories — Wistarberg, 1739–1780; Stiegel, 1763–1774; and Amelung, 1785–1795 — were proximal to the Eastern dealers, students, collectors, and museums. Though their production was limited, their styles were distinctive and closely related to the old countries from which workmen had come. Frederick Hunter's *Stiegel Glass,* 1914, guided Eastern collectors and collecting.

By 1926 Harry Hall White had begun his researches in the Midwest, publishing "Early Pittsburgh Glass Houses" in *Antiques* for November of that year. His article focused on off-blown ware, pattern-molding, and figured whiskey flasks. *Antiques* helped the Pittsburgh cause in March 1927 by carrying two articles on the famous Bakewell factory: "Concerning William Peter Eichbaum and Bakewell's" by Rhea Mansfield Knittle; and "The First Successful Flint Glass Factory in America" by the Reverend Thomas C. Pears, Jr.

Dr. Pears, grandson of an early member of the firm, John Palmer Pears, pictured family pieces — cut, blown, engraved, and pressed — that were fine enough to challenge Eastern factories. Dr. Pears also assembled quotations from travelers visiting Pittsburgh, each visitor uniting in his admiration and praise of Bakewell's. Pears, of course, mentioned that Bakewell's had made cut and engraved services for President Monroe in 1817 and President Jackson in 1829. He was equally proud of the silver medal won in 1825 at the Franklin Institute in Philadelphia for a pair of cut decanters. He did not point out that the New England Glass Company opened its doors in 1818 and Sandwich in 1825, long after Bakewell's was well established.

Mrs. Knittle's article about the first superintendent, William Peter Eichbaum, also showed the quality and background of Bakewell's products. She took up a more important point in her *Early American Glass* in discussing the attribution of a pair of dolphin candlesticks and matching dolphin and shell compote. A granddaughter of a superintendent of the Sandwich factory owned one set; a grandson of a member of the Bakewell firm (Thomas C. Pears, Jr.) owned another; and a third set belonged to the daughter of a woman who had bought them from the man who made them at the J. B. Lyon factory. The Bakewell owner did not wish his pieces to be called Sandwich; the Sandwich owner was indignant if hers were attributed to Bakewell; and the Lyon owner could not persuade her friends that Lyon made dolphins.

On this point Homer Eaton Keyes, the great editor of *Antiques,* gave farseeing advice as early as April 1927: "On the whole it seems probable that at various times, the same, or similar patterns were turned out by a number of unrelated and widely scattered concerns, which either copied each other's successful designs or else purchased their molds from moldmakers who impartially supplied all their clients with the same thing."

Mr. Keyes had been shown a McKee and Brothers 1868 catalogue and was keen enough to recognize its value in attributing pressed glass. As far as I can ascertain, this was the first time a Pittsburgh catalogue was published. This was the same catalogue that Ruth Webb Lee later used for plates in her *Early American Pressed Glass,* 1931. The title of Mr. Keyes's article, appropriately enough, was "By No Means Sandwich."

Mr. Keyes stimulated one of his contributors, Charles Messer Stow, antiques editor of the old New York *Sun,* to an interest in the attribution of pressed glass. Stow was lucky enough to find a second McKee & Brother catalogue, undated but probably 1860.* Following Keyes's lead, he wrote for *Antiquarian,* October 1929, an article titled, "Sandwich Glass that Pittsburgh Made." He said

Into the former classification [Stiegel] was dumped all the early blown glass and much of the glass that was blown into a mold. In the second [Sandwich] was placed all pressed glass, no matter what period it might have represented. Especially that form of glass called "lacy" was likely to be ascribed to Sandwich.

Thus Pittsburgh glass was being recognized by two careful Eastern scholars. Two years later,

* These two McKee catalogues now belong to the Corning Museum of Glass.

Ruth Webb Lee's *Early American Pressed Glass* included nine plates from the McKee and Brothers 1868 catalogue and thirteen from an undated Bakewell one (circa 1875). Since Mrs. Lee had no Eastern catalogue material, Pittsburgh emerged in the limelight in her book. It needed only a 1934 disagreement over a marked lacy creamer, *R. B. Curling & Sons,* to establish Pittsburgh as a rival for Sandwich in lacy glass. Dr. Charles Green, an authority on lacy, tenaciously insisted that the piece *had* to be Sandwich; but James Rose, who held that it was Pittsburgh, had done such extensive scholarly research on lacy cup plates and the background of Midwestern glass that the outcome was never in doubt. Advanced students and museum curators began to accept Pittsburgh glass. Dealers and collectors were hesitant for some years to come; they still liked Wistarberg, Stiegel, Sandwich, South Jersey, and Stoddard. The East Coast continued to believe in the cultural lag of the Midwest.

Pittsburgh had not yet become a magic name; these articles were only the beginnings. When scholars excavated and made important discoveries at various semirural sites of defunct Eastern glass factories, Pittsburgh glass again was ignored, this time by necessity. Its factories, concentrated in what had become a metropolitan area, had long since been replaced by new commercial buildings.

Finally, the Pittsburgh glass generally and generously found in the East was the later pressed tableware, which collectors felt was artistically inferior to their best Sandwich, New England Glass Company, or South Jersey pieces. Indeed it may have been, but the comparison was illogical and the judgment false.

Pittsburgh glass paid an artistic price for its commercial dominance in the 1870s and 1880s. Its makers capitalized on the lime glass formula originated in Wheeling in 1864 and developed in Pittsburgh, which took some of the weight and resonance out of pressed glass. They were more eager now to catch the attention of the public than to adhere to the higher tenets of design.

They suppressed the individuality of the blower in order to concentrate on mass volume, not always with an eye to discrimination.

Harper's Bazaar for January 26, 1878, crystallized an attitude toward Pittsburgh glass that has persisted:

All the glass in general use in America is manufactured in this country, while on the contrary, our products, especially pressed glass, are exported in large quantities to nearly all parts of Europe. Bottles are made principally in the state of New Jersey; New England produces some fine grades of glass, while Pittsburgh makes the lower grades of pressed ware.

The *Harper's Bazaar* editors did not know or did not care that eleven years earlier American glass manufacturers had selected the J. B. Lyon Company of Pittsburgh to represent their industry at the 1867 Paris Exposition. Lyon won a gold medal.

In scrambling for sales, Pittsburgh manufacturers brought out novelty pieces and naturalistic subjects (Atterbury's milk glass, for example, and Challinor & Taylor's Farm Yard Assortment). Critics considered such pieces undistinguished and inferior to the work of the better-known Eastern factories. As a consequence, a whole body of earlier work of sound artistic quality and high technical proficiency suffered in reputation, even though Pittsburgh had (and has) rich examples of free-blown, mold-blown, pattern-molded, lacy, and early pressed glass.

It is ironical that critical judgment has changed on pressed lime glass tableware and much of the art glass and novelty pieces. Taste has shifted to bring these into some artistic repute and give them respectable places in collections and in the history of American glassmaking and of nineteenth-century decorative art. James Laver of the Victoria and Albert Museum has given an acute analysis of what happens:

As we move forward in time the black patch of bad taste moves after us, separated from us by an almost constant number of years. There is, in short, a "gap of appreciation." A gap not in the competence of the artist craftsman but in our own minds.

It is a fascinating experience today to look back at the struggle of the serious scholars in the 1920–1950 period to persuade dealers, collectors, and other scholars to broaden their concepts of American glass and its sources. (It was far more fascinating to play a role in fighting that victorious campaign.) The Pittsburgh Chapter of the National Early American Glass Club sponsored, in 1940–1942, a rotating exhibit in a case at the Carnegie Museum; and for two weeks in October 1947, it arranged a showing of early American glass, with emphasis on Pittsburgh, at the Historical Society of Western Pennsylvania. Those two exhibits aroused local enthusiasm, but it was the Carnegie Museum Exhibition, April 1949–June 1950, that drew national attention to the variety and excellence of the Pittsburgh product. Some 890 pieces of Pittsburgh District glass were lent by one institutional and forty-three individual owners. The exhibit received wide coverage. The editor of *Antiques Journal* called it "the finest showing of early American glass that has ever been arranged for public exhibition," and he then reported that within three weeks of the April opening "there wasn't a piece of Pittsburgh glass to be found in the East." The catalogue, issued at $1, was reviewed generously by the *Sun*'s Charles Messer Stow, became something of a collector's piece, and is now virtually unobtainable at many times the original price.*

Leslie Buswell, a collector from Gloucester, Massachusetts, wrote me in 1949:

Since my visit to the Carnegie Museum last May, I have been thinking over what that splendid collection of Early Pittsburgh Glass means to the Museum itself

* Lowell Innes, *Early Glass of the Pittsburgh District, 1797–1890*, 56 pages, 45 plates. The catalogue and the Carnegie exhibit were accompanied by a four-installment article by the author on "Pittsburgh Glass" in *Antiques* for December 1948 and January, September, and December 1949.

and to those who take advantage of its educational values. . . .
American history can be studied from early examples of glass — especially in bottles, cup plates, wine glasses, and the individual designs acceptable to the purchasing public of the times.

Mr. Buswell raised a fundamental point. American history can indeed be studied from early examples of glass. At the same time, a serious student and collector must study glass in relationship to the technical, economic, and social conditions that shaped the industry. Often it is more important to tell why certain forms of glass were made than to theorize about attributions simply to please collectors. This is to say that the study of glass cannot be separated from the history of the time in which it was made.

I have attempted in this work to give something of the historic fabric against which the Pittsburgh glass industry wove its design: modes of transportation, trade routes, inflation, tariffs, imports, labor problems, fires (the bane of all glasshouses), and, finally, the reasons for the owner-management decision that there was need in 1891 for stable control in the industry in the form of a monopoly-cartel.

Pittsburgh and its antique glass lend themselves admirably to a treatment in which history, technology, and products complement one another. Allegheny County as a single unit of study concentrated an extraordinary amount of history in the ninety-four years covered by this volume. It was the national center of glassmaking throughout most of those years. It was at or near the scene of discoveries made within the industry that revolutionized American glassmaking, and of external developments, such as the use of natural gas as a fuel and of oil refined into lighting fluid, that revolutionized it again.

Part one of this volume concerns itself primarily with the story of Pittsburgh glasshouses in terms of their operations, technology, problems of production, and the history of the times. Part two is concerned with the products themselves. Interest in the two parts will vary according to the taste of the reader, but it should be pointed out that those whose interest is solely in glass products may find background material in the historical chapters that will improve their understanding and heighten their enjoyment of pieces made in the Pittsburgh District.

It is my hope that this work on Pittsburgh glass will open vistas to further study. Certainly there are opportunities and need for more research and writing. Countless examples remain to be examined and analyzed. The glasshouses are gone, but many of their records and catalogues remain. The manuscript papers of James O'Hara in the Historical Society of Western Pennsylvania and of Isaac Craig in Pittsburgh's Carnegie Library, liberally quoted in this volume, have never been thoroughly mined; they deserve to be used, annotated, and published in full. The trade magazine of the glass industry, *The Crockery and Glass Journal,* which supports much of the material in the later chapters of this work, is a rich mother lode for phases of glass operations and history after 1875. It has had relatively little use in the articles and books written on American antique glass.

In an article written in 1928, Rhea Mansfield Knittle said:

When the complete history of the early glass industry of the Pittsburgh District is some day written, it will form one of the most illuminating, surprising, and stimulating contributions to the manners and times of the formative period of our country which could be embodied in printed form.

I cannot, of course, claim or pretend to have produced a work that meets those high expectations. I do feel that I have written one that has long been needed. I hope that the reader will find it informative, entertaining, and useful.

PART ONE

CHAPTER I

Background and Beginnings

The principal articles constituting loading for the boats trading on the
Ohio and Mississippi are flour, whiskey, apples, cider, peach and apple
brandy, bar iron and castings, tin and copper wares, glass and cabinet work,
windsor chairs, mill stones, grind stones, nails, etc. . . . And the principal
articles brought up the Ohio in keel boats are cotton, lead, furs and
peltry, and hemp and tobacco from Kentucky.
— Zadok Cramer, *The Navigator; Containing Directions for Navigating
the Monongahela, Allegheny, Ohio and Mississippi Rivers; with an
Ample Account of These Much Admired Waters*, 1817

What conditions create and nourish a new industry? Raw materials, a product, and, of course, a market. A trained labor force and competent organizers. Transportation facilities. Capital, the seventh requirement, will normally come where the others are conjoined.

Pittsburgh, a frontier town of about 2400 people in 1797, was fortunate in the first four of the seven essentials. The product was glass. The immediate market was Allegheny County and its three neighbors in Southwestern Pennsylvania: Westmoreland, Washington, and Fayette counties — an area of 3400 square miles with a population (in the 1790 United States census) close to 65,000. It was a sizable and growing market in a nation of 3,000,000 people, and one that needed supplies. All but one of the raw materials for making glass were reasonably available. Courageous and farsighted organizers could raise capital and recruit skilled workmen from the East.

Transportation to and from the cities in the East was a problem but one that eventually turned into an advantage. For such a brittle commodity as glass, the freight rates over the mountains were prohibitively high. This meant that not much of the product could be shipped to the large markets in the East — but Pittsburgh's markets did not lie in that direction. It also meant that Pittsburgh was protected — even isolated — not only against competition from the Eastern glass producers but against the competition of English, Irish, and French imports.

In 1797, the year in which James O'Hara and Isaac Craig founded the first glass manufactory in Pittsburgh, Conestoga wagons were making regular trips from the East, the full journey requiring a month.* Even then, the great bulk of goods made the last part of the westward journey on packhorses from the points where many wagon trains stopped: Shippensburg or Chambersburg in Pennsylvania, Winchester in Virginia. A hundred pounds shipped to or from the East cost $5 or $6, and where the commodity was breakable it might

* The first stage service from Philadelphia to Pittsburgh was inaugurated in 1804. Coaches departed twice a week carrying passengers and mail.

cost $10. A ton of freight carried from Philadelphia to Pittsburgh in 1814, after the roads had been somewhat improved, cost $140, and drivers sometimes charged $250 a trip each way, when prices were not fixed. In that year 4055 wagons of four to six horses carried goods over that 300-mile route. The artist George Catlin wrote in an 1819 letter: "I saw on my route the 20 cents per acre land in Pennsylvania, so much talked about among our neighbors, but I cannot recommend it."* Since General Anthony Wayne's defeat of the last Indian resistance in Ohio in 1794, settlers had been pouring in at a phenomenal and increasing rate.

Pittsburgh, already known as "The Gateway to the West," was a natural point of transshipment, and as such it was a promising center for manufactures. Pittsburgh's larger market for glass included the entire Ohio Valley, a thousand miles southwestward to the mouth of the Ohio and on another thousand to New Orleans and the Gulf of Mexico. A shorter but active route led to the Great Lakes and the Canadian market: north up the Allegheny River to Frenchman's Creek, then to Waterford, then a portage of fourteen miles to Presque Isle, thus opening up the Great Lakes and Canadian trade. The third valley market developed later in the century: southward up the Monongahela River in the face of several rival glasshouses situated between Pittsburgh and New Geneva and Greensboro, Pennsylvania.

Pittsburgh's boat-building industry grew with the increasing importance of the downriver route. Schooners of 250 to 400 tons made the journey to New York by going down the rivers to New Orleans, around Florida, and up the East Coast. Flatboats, keelboats, and broadhorns were most numerous and carried most of the intertown short hauling. In two months in 1810–1811, 197 flatboats and fourteen keelboats descended to the Falls of the Ohio near Louisville. By 1794, two

* "Early Travel on the Ohio and Its Tributaries," *Michigan Historical Magazine,* Michigan Historical Commission 20 (spring-summer 1936): 153–161.

boats were plying regularly between Cincinnati and Pittsburgh, once every four weeks for each boat. An advertisement in the Pittsburgh *Gazette* for October 19, 1793, took a lofty tone:

The Proprietor of these boats having maturely considered the many inconveniences and dangers incident to the common method hitherto adopted of navigating the Ohio, and being influenced by a love of philosophy and desire of being serviceable to the public has taken great pains to render the accommodations on board the Boats as agreeable and convenient as they could possibly be made.

The proprietor assured safety against Indian attacks and a separate cabin for the men and the women. "Conveniences," he said, "are constructed on board each boat so as to render landing unnecessary as it might at times be attended with danger." Pittsburgh built a number of armed galleys, two of them named *President Adams* and *Senator Ross.* By an act of Congress in 1808, the city was made a port of clearance. In October 1811, the *New Orleans,* the first steamboat on the Western waters, built in Pittsburgh by Nicholas J. Roosevelt of New York, began a historic voyage to the Gulf of Mexico.

Clearly this water route would be of inestimable worth to glass manufacturers of the Pittsburgh District.

The Product and Its Uses

What did every house, frontier cabin, and public building need? Glass, of course, for windows. What did every household and tavern use? Drinking vessels and containers. What did every traveler carry? Bottles, of course, for whiskey.

Rye, barley, and corn were abundant crops, and the whiskey made from those grains was at once a basic beverage, a source of income, an article of barter, a medicine, a ration for the soldiery, and a medium by which hospitality and good will were extended. It was also a leading commodity of export over the mountains to the

1 *The Early Trade Route to the Great Lakes:* up the
Allegheny to Frenchman's Creek, then to Waterford, and
overland to Presque Isle (Erie).

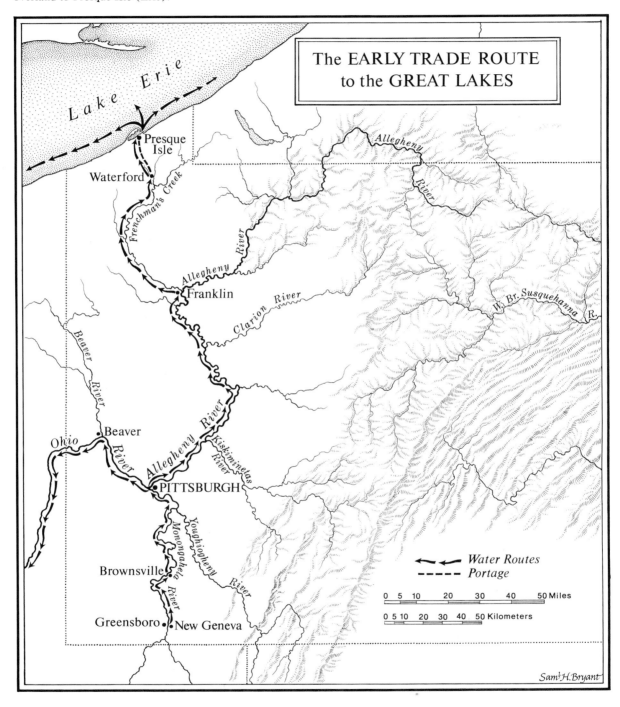

2 *The River Trade Routes:* the Allegheny and
Monongahela rivers forming the Ohio at Pittsburgh; the
Ohio and the Mississippi forming the great trade valley
down to the Gulf of Mexico. The Allegheny Mountains
stood as a trade barrier between the Eastern seaboard and
Western Pennsylvania.

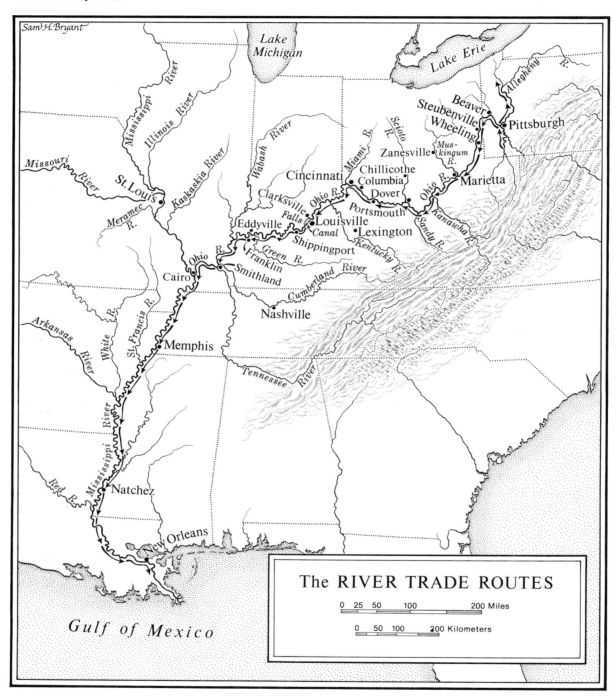

East and down the rivers to the Southwest.* One horse could carry four bushels of rye in casks and barrels in a pack train headed for Philadelphia or Baltimore, but in the distilled contents of two eight-gallon kegs it could carry twenty-four bushels. "Monongahela rye" was a choice drink in the Eastern cities, and it fetched there around $1 a gallon, twice what it sold for at home. Said one historian: "What a bank bill was at Philadelphia or a shilling at Lancaster, that was whiskey in the towns and villages that lay along the Monongahela."†

Stills were expensive and not many farmers could afford to buy one (a 100-gallon still was worth a 200-acre farm in Western Pennsylvania around 1800), but every settlement had its common distillery, often on the same stream or river as the gristmill and the sawmill.‡ Much later, with the heavier influx of settlers and the conversion of villages to towns and towns to cities, the larger commercial distilleries appeared. For storing and carrying their product, nothing could surpass bottles.

A study of early glasshouse records shows two standard products: window glass and bottles. The term "hollow ware," found in early letters and advertisements, is an overlapping one; today collectors think of it as jars, pans, bowls, tumblers, decanters, and even table pieces. Early in the nineteenth century, however, it included druggists' ware and often bottles of all shapes and sizes. Cut glass tableware was also produced in limited quantities, but pressed glass was not added until after 1825. Window glass and bottles, however, formed the backbone of the industry through the first half of the nineteenth century. A tax list on real estate in 1798 showed the number of windows and window lights in houses owned by Craig and O'Hara. Craig had thirteen windows and 183 lights; O'Hara had twenty-six windows and 560 lights. One can guess that the panes came from their own factory, though it had been running only a year. Because of the scarcity and cost of glass at this time, oiled parchment and animal skins were commonly used in windows.

The Home Area and the Market

In considering glass of the first half of the nineteenth century, we must adjust our present-day geographical conception of the term "Midwest." In the context of antique glass it is clearly limited to areas in three states: Western Pennsylvania, West Virginia, and Ohio. The West Virginia division centers on Wheeling and flows with the Ohio River. As late as 1870, the state of Ohio had only nine glass factories, so that we can legitimately accept "Midwestern," as applied to glass, to mean an area with Pittsburgh and Allegheny County as a focal point. It was bounded by the Allegheny Mountains on the east, stretched south up the Monongahela to New Geneva and Greensboro, reached down the Ohio past Wellsburg to Wheeling, and extended west as far as Zanesville on the Muskingum. Today we identify the forms that developed from interchange of workmen and influences in this Midwestern area by the generic term "Midwestern glass." Within this frame "Pittsburgh glass" has been individualized and given top rating.

The larger market for Pittsburgh glass included the entire Ohio River Valley — north up the Allegheny River, south up the Monongahela, south-

* "The use of whiskey was universal. The quality was good, the taste pleasant, its effect agreeable. Storekeepers kept liquor on their counters and sold it in their stores, and the women customers used it as well as the men . . . It was good for fevers, it was good for a decline, it was good for snakebites . . . It made one warm in winter and cool in summer. It was used at all gatherings. Bottles of it were set out on the table at christenings and at wakes." George Dallas Albert, *History of the County of Westmoreland, Pennsylvania* (Philadelphia: Everts, 1882), p. 171.

† John Bach McMaster, *A History of the People of the United States from the Revolution to the Civil War*, vol. 2 (New York: Appleton & Co., 1900), p. 189. Trade statistics for many years showed that glass shipments to the East were small.

‡ Leland D. Baldwin, *Whiskey Rebels* (Pittsburgh: University of Pittsburgh Press, 1939), pp. 26–28.

3 Free-blown pieces from early window glass and bottle factories. Though meant to be taken home by the glassworkers for gifts, most of the pieces were functional. These articles were exhibited at the Carnegie Museum by the Pittsburgh Chapter of the Early American Glass Club in 1941. Length of rolling pin: 17½″.

westward down a thousand miles to the Mississippi, even down another thousand to New Orleans and the Gulf of Mexico.

The Raw Materials

The essential raw materials for the manufacture of glass — fuel, silica, and potash — were plentiful in Western Pennsylvania. Wood was everywhere, and potash was formed from the burning of trees and vegetation. Deposits of silica in the form of sand and pulverized sandstone varied in quality. At first, coarse sand from Frenchman's Creek was used, but a somewhat better quality was later found on the Youghio-

gheny River near the mouth of Jacob's Creek, close to Belle Vernon.

Formulas for bottle and window glass were quite similar: silica, potash, and lime, except that for window glass, soda — alkali salt — often replaced potash to give greater clarity. Soda came from the Ohio territory and New York. Frequently, however, potash alkalized the mixture. In early times, the color of bottles and hollow ware hardly mattered. Iron oxides in unpurified silica. gave strong greens, while manganese produced ambers and browns.

By 1804 O'Hara and Craig had made attempts to produce clear flint glass. To silica and potash they added lead, niter, and glassmakers' soap —

black oxide of manganese, a decolorizing agent. Red lead was brought by water from the Illinois territory at a cost of ten dollars a hundredweight. Niter (saltpeter) was available from Kentucky. Later the use of metallic oxides gave early colored flint.

At the garrison towns potash cost only a shilling per bushel. André Michaux, a French visitor to Pittsburgh, wrote in 1802: "Expenses occasioned by clearing land are always covered by the produce of pearl ashes extracted from the ashes of trees and burned and that persons undertake to clear it on the sole condition of having the pearl ashes. This economy does not exist in the East."*

Though wood was plentiful, to insure themselves a supply of low-cost fuel O'Hara and Craig bought two lots of land on Coal Hill (Mount Washington) on the south bank of the Monongahela across from Pittsburgh's Point. Theirs was the first glassworks in the United States to use coal to heat the glass furnace.

The one raw material not readily available was the special kind of melting-pot clay needed to withstand high temperatures without cracking. Isaac Craig wrote hopefully on March 1, 1800, to James Naylor at Waterford:

Pray make enquiry of the settlers in your neighbourhood, for Clay, such as is used for melting pots at Glass Works — its colour is generally white inclining to blue, is free from sand, and when rubbed appears to have some of the properties of Soap, but is not fuzible by the strongest Heat — should Clay of that description come to your knowledge an experiment might be made as to its resisting a Strong Heat in your Smith's fire, the heat of which may be increased to the highest degree which may determine the quality of the Clay.†

* Dorothy S. Coleman, "Pioneers of Pittsburgh, The Robinsons," *Western Pennsylvania Historical Magazine* 42 (March 1959): 61.

† All extracts from James O'Hara and Isaac Craig letters quoted in this work are from the unpublished O'Hara manuscripts at the Historical Society of Western Pennsylvania in Pittsburgh and the unpublished Craig manuscripts in the Pennsylvania Room of Pittsburgh's Carnegie Library.

Naylor found no clay, and the seriousness of the problem is revealed in an O'Hara-Craig advertisement that appeared (to no avail) in the Pittsburgh *Gazette* on July 2, 1802.

ONE HUNDRED DOLLARS REWARD

Will be given for the first discovery of a bed or bank of Clay fit to answer the purpose of making Melting Pots for the Pittsburgh Glass Works, within one hundred miles of this place on the Monongahela, Allegheny, and Ohio rivers, and within ten miles of either river, to be determined by the Glass-makers, the Clay for this purpose is found in the beds of rivers or creeks, or in low lands, the best color is white, though white mixed with red or blue stripes will answer the purpose. Any person producing a specimen that will stand well in the fire, and the bed from whence it came appearing to contain fifty tons, shall be entitled to the above Reward from the proprietors of the Glass works.

Clay, in short, had to be imported from the East — from Delaware, from Bordentown or Burlington in New Jersey, or, if the highest quality was desired, from Holland, Germany, or England by way of an importing seaport such as Philadelphia or Baltimore. The high cost of the clay and of its transportation was a sharp thorn that the partners complained of frequently. The clay had to ripen before use; very cold weather was not a good time for forming the pots; and after a pot had been shaped, O'Hara wanted it to harden for six months. Planning against such contingencies was not easy, and time after time the operation stopped while men and managers waited for clay or for the pots to harden. If the furnaces were at full blast as much as eight months at a stretch, the manufacturers were elated. Not until the Missouri clay beds were opened in the middle of the nineteenth century could Pittsburgh expand its glass manufacturing efficiently and economically.*

* The following Craig-O'Hara letters are concerned with the problems of clay: Craig — August 14, 1798; April 4, August 24, October 5 and 18, 1799; March 1, 1800; O'Hara — April 19, June 11 and 24, July 5 and 30, 1805; December 11, 1806; April 28, May 12, June 12, 1807; August 31, 1811.

The Entrepreneurs

James O'Hara (1754–1819), trained in business methods in Liverpool, landed in Philadelphia in 1772. The next year, before he was twenty, he journeyed to Pittsburgh, where he invested capital with Devereaux Smith and Ephraim Douglas, who were engaged in Indian trade. Through the American Revolution, the post-Revolutionary frontier wars, and on until his resignation from the military in 1800, General O'Hara headed the services of supply of Western armies, of which Pittsburgh was the garrison center and chief depot for stores. In the manner customary to eighteenth-century quartermasters with lucrative army contracts, he accumulated a substantial amount of capital. This he invested and reinvested in an extraordinary variety and number of commercial enterprises: in a brewery, a sawmill, a gristmill, a tanyard, an iron foundry, and a branch of the Bank of Pennsylvania; in boat building, the fur trade, salt, land, and construction of houses (with bricks from the dismantled Fort Pitt). O'Hara's shrewdness, imagination, and method are suggested by his salt operation. In 1795, under the terms of his contract to provision the garrison at Oswego on Lake Ontario, he reserved the right of ownership in the empty barrels in which supplies had been freighted northward. These he filled with salt from the Onondaga works at Salina (Syracuse). He boated them westward across Lake Ontario and Lake Erie to the port of Erie (723 barrels in 1800; 14,346 in 1809), loaded them on carts for a rough fourteen-mile portage to Frenchman's Creek, and again placed them on boats for the journey down the Allegheny to Pittsburgh. There they sold for $4 a barrel, about half the price of salt brought over the mountains from Baltimore.

In 1797, O'Hara entered still another business. He recognized that the Western country needed windowpanes, bottles, and glass tableware. With his deputy quartermaster general, Major Isaac Craig (ca 1742–1826), he founded the Pittsburgh Glass Works on the left or south bank of the Monongahela River across from Pittsburgh.

During the Revolution, Isaac Craig rose from the rank of captain in the marines to that of major in the artillery. Henry Knox, Secretary of War in Washington's Cabinet, sent him to construct a new stockade, Fort Fayette, at Pittsburgh. Craig sensed the possibilities of that community as a control center for all Western trade and bought land that had originally belonged to the Penn family. He stayed on the grounds and looked after the glasswork operations when O'Hara was away.

In that same year, 1797, some sixty miles south of Pittsburgh, Swiss-born Albert Gallatin (1761–1849), member of Congress from Fayette County, started the New Geneva Glass Works. The folk tale of Gallatin's meeting with six German glass blowers headed westward has little documentary foundation. John Badollet, a friend and partner in Albert Gallatin & Company, wrote Gallatin from Greensboro in May 1797 to say that he, Louis Boudillon, and Charles Cazenove had been negotiating with six experienced Germans to start a glassworks. Gallatin and his brother-in-law, James Nicholson, joined the three and the partnership was completed in September 1797.* Helen McKearin has established that the first glass was blown at New Geneva in January 1798.

Isaac Craig stated in a letter to James Morrison, June 24, 1805, that it was a year after starting before he made glass. In a May 1805 letter to Craig Amelung he specified that his works had been improving for seven years. A third letter to John Kinnear at Natchez on November 23, 1799, bears out information in the two later ones: "I am sorry this ware is not of the first quality *as it is the product of the first attempt* . . . we shall shortly be able to supply your country with Glass Ware of the first quality." We can safely assume that Gallatin was producing

---

* Gallatin's future lay in politics, for he became a famous secretary of the treasury, reduced the national debt, and at the same time lowered taxes.

before O'Hara and Craig. The commercial products of both firms were window glass and bottles. These were two glasshouses of fewer than a dozen at work in the newly formed United States. They were the first of that industry west of the Allegheny Mountains.*

The Gallatin and the O'Hara-Craig factories were joined eleven years later by a company whose name was destined to outlive theirs. Benjamin Bakewell (1767–1844) came west in 1808 in search of business opportunities after his importing businesses in England and in New York had been disrupted by war and trade rivalries among and between England, France, and the United States. In Pittsburgh in 1808 he and several associates bought an undercapitalized glass company that had been newly formed by Edward Ensell and possibly another of James O'Hara's employees. Bakewell had no experience in glassmaking, but he was an able administrator and superb salesman. By his selection of craftsmen, his company was to produce glass that won the highest regard of buyers in the nineteenth century. The fine quality of his work challenged other early Pittsburgh companies. From them we have a tradition of glassmaking long recognized by twentieth-century collectors, scholars, and museum curators.

* In "The First Glasshouse West of the Alleghenies" (*Western Pennsylvania Historical Magazine,* September-December 1949), Dorothy Daniel advanced the theory that O'Hara and Craig started their house in 1795. The O'Hara and Craig letters, however, sustain the accepted date of 1797. Gallatin's New Geneva Glass Works preceded the Pittsburgh Glass Works by several months.

CHAPTER II

The Development of the Pioneer Glasshouses

Materials are very conveniently procured and the Glass Works situate on
the bank of a navigable river so near an extensive coal mine that one
old Horse is able to haul more than one hundred bushels of Coal per day
from the Coal pit to the Glass house. Our market is plentiful and cheap
and our Climate is healthy, and extensive prospects of Sales of glass ware.
— Isaac Craig to Edward Ensell, 103 Pearl Street, New York,
    April 18, 1801

As good businessmen, James O'Hara and Isaac Craig kept records of their correspondence and had their clerks write out or press copies of all letters for the company's letter books. The penmanship is sometimes undecipherable, but from the letters we get a picture of the economic problems of early glass manufacturers, of their business procedures, and of the social background against which they made and marketed their product.

In the first twenty-five or thirty years of the century, anyone with a little capital and the desire to beget a business was very likely to look on glass production, especially on the frontier, as a smooth and sure path to riches, and so might build a new glass factory or reclaim one that was standing idle. Businessmen and even skilled glass craftsmen could not envision all the costs and problems involved in setting up a glass manufactory. To build a shed for the melting furnace and annealing oven was merely a beginning. Raw materials had to be acquired, technical problems met, and the product distributed. Tools wore out

and major pieces of equipment broke down. The factory and its employees, wherever situated, needed at least the services of a gristmill, a sawmill, a carpentry shop, a blacksmith shop, and a general store.

It is somewhat of a paradox that so many underestimated both the skill required to be a glassman and the acumen and perseverance demanded of a successful operator. Many of the state governments were wiser: they recognized the skill of the glass blower by exempting him from military service except in time of invasion or civil insurrection.*

The Not-So-Ordinary Workman

The ever-present obstacle for glass manufacturers beyond the Alleghenies was getting and holding an adequate supply of labor, both skilled and unskilled, up the scale from apprentices through clay tramplers, pot makers, batch mixers,

* New York State Laws, 50th Session, 2nd Meeting, Revised Statutes, 1827, p. 165.

12

4 Milk pans blown of aquamarine window and bottle glass, 1797–1860. 1 — Ordinary size with graceful sloping shoulders. 2 — Many deep pans, holding a generous quantity, have been found. 3 — These show hasty and uneven workmanship. 4 — Of a rare size, these may be personalized pieces. *Ex coll. John J. Grossman.* The dates given in the captions should be considered suggestive rather than prescriptive.

furnace men, and master blowers to the superintendent himself. According to Deming Jarves, founder of the Boston and Sandwich Glass Company, some workmen lacked the skill for which they had been hired, some opposed the training of apprentices, and others were determined to limit the quantity of production by limiting the number of hours they worked. The most competent workmen, of course, often left to start their own operation.

From letters of the period we can assess the character of the ordinary glasshouse workman — at least as O'Hara and Craig saw him. He was dissipated, undependable, rebellious, and migratory. Some part of that reputation persisted for more than a century. General O'Hara wrote on January 18, 1806:

Charles Haines having forfeited all claim to indulgence by his constant practice of getting drunk and neglecting his business to the great loss and disgrace of the works, is discharged. . . . Boehl has also after many repeated abuses of his duty in being drunk in the composition room become unworthy of any confidence and is to be immediately discharged from this employ.

One of the O'Hara-Craig glass blowers disappeared in 1803, leaving some debts behind, and Craig sought an agreement with his competitor to have him barred from further employment. To James Nicholson, Gallatin's brother-in-law and partner at New Geneva, he wrote on August 4, 1803, in a fair spirit:

James Clarke disappeared, he is under agreement to blow for us under Fire now begun. . . . You will not employ him particularly as we have in all our transactions since the establishment of our works scrupulously avoided a Competition or rivalship with the Geneva Glass Works and have reason to expect a similar conduct on the part of the proprietors of your

5 A variety of forms in off-hand pieces blown of amber bottle glass, 1800–1860. Such articles were made in all early window and bottle glass factories throughout nineteenth-century America. These were exhibited at the Carnegie Museum in Pittsburgh in 1949. Height of handled bottle: 7¾″.

works but should this man be employed or retained in service contrary to our Expectations and I presume contrary to the mutual interests of both Geneva and Pittsburgh we shall be under the necessity of instituting suits in your County both for breach of contract and recovery of debts.

The owners longed for virtuous qualities in their workmen and often asked agents to send them sober, industrious Germans. They were reluctant to employ men with large families because they feared the effects of poverty among their employees when the works were shut down. "They breed like minks," Craig complained. O'Hara wrote, "Single men or men with very small families would be preferred for very obvious

reasons." On May 11, 1807, he promised Baker Johnson* "free privilege to make a garden for you and all workmen." Wages at his factory, he said, were the "best in U.S. . . . Our markets good — prices cheap — fair certificates of wage to look at." To Joseph Carson of Philadelphia he wrote on June 18, 1810:

When the fires are out the Blowers receive one dollar a day preparing for the next . . . and for other wares and window glass in proportion one-fifth of

* A resident of Fredericktown, Maryland, for whom Amelung inscribed and decorated a case of bottles in 1788 "B. Johnson." The Smithsonian, Corning and Winterthur each own a bottle.

the selling prices (whether it sells or not) for making. A few good blowers will be employed at my new works at the above prices for making to be paid weekly or as may be required. The Blowers shall be furnished with Dwelling Houses and the best coal fuel at their doors, all free from cost, and all traveling expenses paid from their places of residence to this place.

An English traveler observed the Pittsburgh workmen:

Journeymen in various branches, shoemakers, tailors, earn $2 a day. Many of them improvident and thus remain journeymen all their days. It is not, however, in absolute intemperance and profligacy that they in general waste their surplus earnings, it is in excursions and entertainments. Ten dollars spent at a ball is no rare result of the gallantry of a Pittsburgh journeyman.*

A later visitor from England was struck by the fact that the wage of an American mechanic, converted into English currency, would buy a Londoner thirty pounds of beef.†

Still another traveler described the location of the O'Hara-Craig works and how the workmen's houses clustered about it:

The opposite bank of the Monongahela presents to the eye a fine level bottom, well cultivated and settled, with a ridge of hills half a mile behind it, which gradually approach the river until immediately opposite the town, where rising abruptly at the water's edge, to the height of about five hundred feet perpendicularly, they take the name of the Coal Hill, from that fuel being formerly dug out of it for the use of the town, before pits were opened more convenient on this side of the river. It still supplies that coal for General O'Hara's glassworks, which, with the houses of the overseer and the workmen, forms a village at the foot of the hill on the river bank, immediately opposite the point where the spectator stands. . . .

* Morris Birbeck, *Notes on a Journey in America from the Coast of Virginia to the Territory of Illinois,* 3rd ed. (London: printed by Severn and Company for James Ridgeway, 1818), p. 42. A journeyman is one who has fully served his apprenticeship and is qualified to work at his trade in another's employ.
† Zadok Cramer, *The Navigator* (Pittsburgh: Cramer & Spear, 1811, 1814, 1817), p. 37.

Window glass of good quality and quart bottles are made at this manufacture, which with the rival one at New Geneva about sixty miles up the Monongahela supplies all the western country.*

Stiegel had set the pattern in the eighteenth century for corralling skilled and unskilled workmen: recruit them in England and on the Continent. O'Hara and Craig did not do so, perhaps because their resources were stretched too far, perhaps because none of their agents would risk the severe punishment they would receive if apprehended in that illegal activity. Benjamin Bakewell explored Europe, however, in search of workmen to serve special purposes in his production. His son, Thomas, traveled to England in 1815, the last year of the Napoleonic wars, and brought back a number of workers. Thomas Pears, his clerk, went to England the following year.† He found no workmen in England and in August proceeded to Paris, where he visited a bottle works and found its process surprisingly simple. "I know of only one difficulty in the way of getting these men," he wrote, "and that is the demand being brisk at present for wine bottles, for the armies destroyed so many that it creates an extra demand." He offered contracts for three, six, or nine years, with the option of being free from the engagement at the end of three years, with payment of passage and wages to begin with the signing of the contract. To one man he offered 3000 francs per year or one sou per bottle. He returned in October with one glass cutter and a case of glass, attributing his lack of success to a shortage of money, his prospects demanding so high a down payment that he would have had no way to pay their passage.

Pears made a second trip to France in 1818 on his own account, having left Bakewell's to found (in the same block) a factory to make black

* Fortescue Cuming, *Sketches of a Tour to the Western Country* (Pittsburgh: Cramer, Spear, & Eichbaum, 1810), p. 229.
† Pears had married Sarah Palmer, Bakewell's niece by his widowed sister.

bottles.* He obtained a quantity of special clay for his furnaces and signed up four blowers, four *garçons* (journeymen), two *gammains* (apprentices), and a Monsieur Farge, *contremaître* (foreman), to whom he agreed to pay 8000 francs a year. A cryptic comment in one of his letters seems to indicate that he smuggled these men aboard the ship disguised as ordinary workers. (One story is that they were disguised as bakers.) Such heroic efforts apparently were not customary among Western Pennsylvania glassmen. Pears's bottle factory failed and he returned in 1820 to Bakewell.†

Superintendent One: Eichbaum

The first superintendent of the O'Hara-Craig works was William Peter Eichbaum, a Saxon German who had learned his craft in France, worked there for the Court, fled the Revolution, and had come to the Forks of the Ohio after employment at Schuylkill Works in Philadelphia. The niceties of French cutting and engraving had not prepared him for American methods or Western Pennsylvania products, but he applied himself to the building of a glasshouse and an eight-pot furnace and to the production of greenish window glass, green or brown bottles for the O'Hara distillery, and the basic pieces of hollow ware. He succeeded to the extent that in the second year his employers leased the factory to him and a partner, Frederick Wendt, lately of Philadelphia. Craig wrote on October 4, 1799, to O'Hara, who was in Trenton:

Eichbaum, Wentz & Co . . . have delivered a considerable quantity of the most saleable Bottles and upwards of twenty boxes of Window Glass . . . At

* A glassmaker's term for dark amber bottles made of unpurified silica. Later the term may also have been applied to dark olive green, amethyst, or blue bottles.
† Thomas C. Pears III, "Sidelights on the History of the Bakewell, Pears, & Co. from the Letters of Thomas and Sarah Pears," *Western Pennsylvania Historical Magazine* 31, September–December 1948.

the same time have given me notice that they will deliver up the works at the end of their year — viz. 1st December next as not inclining to continue their Partnership but wish to continue on other terms either to work by the piece or by the month but as I don't consider myself fully authorized to decide on that point I have to request your opinion as early as possible. It is certain that *as good Window Glass can be made at our works as anywhere in the United States.* Sandstone of a superior quality has been lately discovered on or near the bank of the Allegheny about twelve miles from this place and I am in hopes that a white clay lately discovered near Fort Littleton will on proper experiment be found to answer for Pots. But our principal want is a man qualified to superintend the business and such a man I hope you have endeavoured to find.

O'Hara replied on October 18:

I have to observe that I am apprehensive the Glass Manufactory will not go on well the ensuing year under the direction of Eichbaum or any of the people engaged as his partners. I find that an implacable enmity exists between Eichbaum and Wentz, and that the latter has attached Phillis and Smith to him in such a manner that the former is treated with very little respect. Eichbaum told me the other day that Wentz and Phillis were determined to go to Albany soon after the expiration of their year and they themselves assure me that they never had any intention of leaving the works.

Eichbaum resigned early in 1800 but Wendt stayed on as foreman. Problems of technology as well as of personality arose. The company was competing for a government contract to make oversize windowpanes. Other American companies like the Boston Crown Glass Company capable of producing such glass were not interested or did not meet specifications. Eventually the contract was awarded to a foreign firm.

In 1800 Eichbaum left the superintendency to run a tavern. On May 15 of that year, the following advertisement appeared in the Pittsburgh *Gazette:*

WILLIAM EICHBAUM

Begs leave to inform the public that he has opened a house of entertainment at the sign of the Indian

Queen in Front Street near Market Street, where he shall use his utmost endeavor to give satisfaction to travellers and others who may please to call on him. N. B. He also wishes to acquaint the public that he follows the glazing business and cutting glass of any pattern.

When Bakewell began to produce flint (lead) glass in 1808, Eichbaum contracted to cut chandeliers for him, possibly specializing also in elaborate work on tumblers, decanters, and vases. Alexander Wilson, poet and ornithologist visiting Pittsburgh in 1810, described a chandelier he saw at Bakewell's, highly ornamented and perfectly transparent. It was sold to a Mr. Kerr, an innkeeper, for $300 and hung with its cascade of sparkling prisms in Ohio Masonic Lodge Number 113. Eichbaum's business seems to have prospered, for his son Arnold, who apparently assumed a management position, ran this notice in the *Gazette* for April 6, 1814:

WANTED IMMEDIATELY

Two Apprentices to the Glass Cutting Business. Boys of good character and reputable connexions, from fourteen to sixteen years of age, will find an eligible situation by applying to Arnold Eichbaum, Corner of Liberty and Fourth Streets. Boys from the country would be preferred.

William Eichbaum branched out into other activities in the town, starting a wire factory and holding office on a number of committees for civic betterment. His name appears on a commission appointed to study the slack water problem on the Monongahela, along with those of Benjamin and Thomas Bakewell, Morgan Robertson, and Alfred Curling. Each was a prominent glass industrialist.

Superintendent Two: Price

O'Hara and Craig proceeded to hunt for a superintendent to succeed Eichbaum. Craig wrote to O'Hara on August 15, 1800, to recommend William Price. Advertisements in the Philadelphia, New York, and Boston papers,

Craig thought, "would bring forth men of Abilities and Character." Lewis Reppert, who was in charge of Johnson's Glass Works in Maryland, was considered. "He was here some time in the summer assisting Phillis and Wentz," Craig wrote to O'Hara. "I presume you will recollect seeing him, he has two Brothers also Glass Blowers who are now at Albany, but who will also come to Pittsburgh if wanted, and Phillis assures me that Repart [sic] is so much esteemed by the glassblowers generally that he can bring with him any workmen he pleases."*

O'Hara and Craig employed William Price of Stourbridge, England, as their second superintendent in August 1800, apparently on the persuasion of Eichbaum and Samuel Hodgdon (the O'Hara-Craig agent in Philadelphia). The competitive blandishments of Scott & Beelen, a rival Pittsburgh company, failed to win Price away. Craig indicated to O'Hara in a letter of September 5 that Price had "offered to show us specimens of his abilities without any charge." Price introduced a series of improvements and experiments in the fall of 1800. The partners raised money for separate pots, for calcined potash (refined pearl ash), purer silica, at least $600 for buildings and equipment, and eventually for additional skilled blowers from the East and the Continent. Craig wrote to Aaron Aimes at Funks Tavern on Franklin Road in September:

Beg of you immediately to prepare about one hundred pounds of Pearl Ash and you are to observe that it is to be refined in the best manner, so that it may be perfectly pure as it is to be applied in the composition of Chrystal Glass by a man immediately from Lon-

* Lewis Reppert was a relative of George Reppert's, who was from the Amelung factory and was one of Gallatin's six original workmen. The Albany reference is mystifying, for it has been generally believed that all the Repperts worked for Johnson at the Frederick County works near Baltimore. There was a small factory at New Albany in Fayette County, Pennsylvania, established around 1812, and there was a factory in Albany County, New York from 1785 to 1792, and later from 1815 to 1823.

6 Glazed pottery pitcher presented to William Price by the Curling factory, 1828. Front: "Friendship's Gift to William Price," the American eagle. H. 7". *The Historical Society of Western Pennsylvania.*

don, and who is unable to make his first experiment until he receives a quantity of your Pearl Ash. I have therefore to beg of you to lay aside all other business that might prevent your immediate attention to it.

Price satisfied Craig that he had the skills requisite to produce glass called variously "white," "crystal," "lead," or "flint" glass; Craig wrote to O'Hara in Washington for support on his decision to proceed. They tried cut glass in 1804 and apparently experimented with blue flint. O'Hara wrote to Frederick M. Amelung the following May 26:

Two white glassmakers will be acceptable. We have tried this in the same furnace with the window glass with perfect success: the blowers were both Englishmen so dissipated that they became a great Nuisance.

And to Terence Campbell, a customer in Chambersburg, on March 14, 1806:

I do not make white glass yet in quantity. I will send you a package of small articles by first opportunity, the ware is better than the imported — the color — and quality is the same as the window glass. I shall make whiter in the course of the summer. I am pleased with your giving my glass a trial at Chambersburgh. . . .

The two excerpts establish an interesting point: flint glass was made in Pittsburgh, even if for only a brief time, before the date customarily accepted for that product — 1808 at the Bakewell factory.

Craig withdrew from the company in 1804, persuaded to do so, according to legend, by relatives who feared he would suffer financial ruin. Price left under a cloud early in 1805. O'Hara sent two angry letters on April 19, one to James Morrison in Lexington, Kentucky, in which he declared, ". . . owing to the perfidy of Price my Superintendent and Wendt the forman makes in plotting to abandon the works the large size glass is not made." The other was to Frederick Amelung, in which he complained, "Frederick Wendt, ignorant, obstinate and seditious is gone off down this river."

Price had had experience in England in production of brass, and in 1808 he opened a foundry, specializing in pipe and light articles of brass and iron and large crucibles for fusing brass and copper. Thenceforth he prospered and became a figure of some importance. Near his foundry he built an octagonal dwelling, later known as the "Round House," which occasioned considerable attention and comment. Anne Royall, visiting Pittsburgh in 1829, wrote:

At the southeastern boundary of the city on the Monongahela stands Kensington, or as it is commonly called, Pipe-town; deriving this name through one of its early settlers, an eccentric little gentleman still well known among all classes for his odd humour and the universality of his mechanical genius, Mr. William Price, who established a pipe manufactory there.*

* Anne Royall, *Mrs. Royall's Pennsylvania, or Travels Continued in the United States,* vol. 2 (Washington, D.C.:

7 Curling-Price pitcher. Side: Fort Pitt Glass Works and a view of early Pittsburgh. Cannon advertises Price's brass foundry. Rim border: conventional ceramic decoration, curlicues. *The Historical Society of Western Pennsylvania.*

But Price never forgot his background in glassmaking. In 1816 he entered a patent for an improvement in the composition of glass. (Since the patent office records were destroyed by fire in 1836, we cannot know the nature of the improvement.) And in 1827, he and Robert Curling, a former pot maker and clerk at Bakewell's, organized and operated the Fort Pitt Glass Works.

Price's colleagues at Fort Pitt Glass presented him in 1828 with a commemoration earthenware pitcher that shows their high regard for him and depicts his Round House,* a glass furnace in full blast, a cannon, and articles manufactured at his brass foundry (see Figures 6 and 7). The pitcher, an exciting find for anyone interested in the early history of Pittsburgh or its glass industry, is of the Staffordshire type, mealy yellow in color, with designs and the legend — "Friendship's Gift to William Price 1828" — fired in a

dark brown.* The classic American eagle, its wings spread, appears below the legend — one more use of a leading design element that was appearing on American whiskey flasks, touch marks on pewter, china bowls, handwoven coverlets, and carved corner cupboards.

Superintendent Three: Amelung

Frederick Magnus Amelung, son of the great John Frederick, left New Bremen after his father's factory failed. He established a small glassworks in Baltimore in 1799 and when that also failed, he traveled west to become O'Hara's third superintendent, carrying with him at O'Hara's request a complete set of molds.

Amelung's sojourn in Pittsburgh was shorter than Price's, lasting some four years, and apparently was unsatisfactory. We may assume, however, that in that time he gave O'Hara's workmen full knowledge of his father's techniques — techniques that were also in use at New Geneva and that would produce priceless pieces of American blown and engraved glass. John Frederick advertised "cut devices," but at present we have no cut pieces with definite attribution to that factory.

In the year of Price's departure and Amelung's arrival, O'Hara delivered himself of a frank and realistic appraisal of the operations of his glassworks. In answer to a query from James Morrison of Lexington, he wrote on June 24, 1805:

Your question on the probable expense of erecting Glass Works may be answered correctly . . . I was engaged one year before we made glass, the first bottle, a very ordinary one, cost me $10,000: this

---

privately printed, 1829), p. 53. Kensington lay between Smithfield Street and Second Avenue where it joins the Monongahela River diagonally.

* Lowell Innes, "William Price and the Round Church," *Western Pennsylvania Historical Magazine* 47 (October 1964).

* The pitcher belongs to the Historical Society of Western Pennsylvania. It came unheralded and unnoticed in 1961 as part of the otherwise undistinguished glass and china contents of a handsome cherry corner cupboard from the estate of Frances W. Lane. The pitcher is typical of early Ohio Valley pottery. Cramer's *Navigator* lists two Pittsburgh potteries as operating in 1810. Trotter & Company advertised in the Pittsburgh *Directory* of 1815, "Pitchers similar to those of the potteries of Philadelphia."

bottle was all the blast produced. Had the works pulled down and began in the new and continued from 1797 till my disbursements exceeded 32,000 dollars. Major Craig gave up his connection in them last year. There is no person concerned with me at present. I have not been able to reduce the balance due me by this manufactory under 30,000 dollars, exclusive of the fee simple property.

My works has not averaged 1,000 dollars worth per month with eight blowers perfectly supported.

Amelung endeared himself to many in Pittsburgh through his social graces, friendliness, and broad cultural interests. A visitor wrote:

Several unusual amateurs are associated here under the title of the Appolonian Society. I visited it by invitation at the house of Mr. F. Amelung the acting president. . . . I was particularly astonished at the performance on the violin of Mr. Gabler, a German employed at Gen. O'Hara's glasshouse.*

Amelung left in 1809 to manage a glassworks in the East. By 1810, O'Hara was writing to Joseph Carson in Philadelphia:

Enclosed you will have Frederick M. Amelung's note due on the 28th of October 1809 for $100. . . . Amelung manages the glass works down the Delaware, he is employed in endeavors to get my best glassblowers to desert my works. I wish you could get me two or three of his best.

Though the Pittsburgh Glass Works continued and flourished, Amelung was the last of the "name" superintendents whose identity is of interest to us. O'Hara continued to operate the factory until shortly before his death in 1819. A historian paid him this tribute in 1898:

The real industrial growth of [Pittsburgh] and its existence as a manufacturing center within the knowledge of Eastern cities must date from the establishment of this enterprise, not from iron foundries or

* Cuming, *Sketches of a Tour to the Western Country,* p. 65. Gabler was possibly John Christian Gabler, one of the glassblowers from New Bremen who joined the Gallatin venture at New Geneva. If not, certainly he was one of his relatives.

cotton mills. The fact that a man of such prominence would pour out his wealth to the extent of many thousands of dollars on an enterprise so difficult, hazardous, and unpromising must be conceded to have added immensely to the fixity and stability of Pittsburgh pioneer industries.*

How the Glass Was Sold

To the problems of getting raw materials, day laborers, and plant superintendents were added those of selling goods and collecting accounts in distant areas without a stable currency, a fast post, a developed system of banks and courts of law, or reliable transportation and travel. Craig lamented on February 28, 1798, in a letter to Presque Isle, near Erie, Pennsylvania:

Fraudulent means have been used in fabricating a voucher. Kean . . . asserts that he neither received payment nor was called upon to sign a receipt.

O'Hara to Morrison in Lexington on June 17, 1806:

I send Robert Campbell's bond. Do whatever you please with it. I sent it to you to prove that those swindlers who had formed a plan of Robbery were perjured. How else could you defeat the infamous judgment and execution obtained in Jefferson County by your appeal to the district court of the U.S. Your enclosed chancery bill must be another piece of infamous forgery or profound ignorance.

The problem common to many of these financial transactions rested in collectible accounts. O'Hara wrote to Lewis Sanders of Lexington, Kentucky, on June 17, 1807:

You have my amount and order against Frederick Heiss of Lexington for glass which he carried away in a very cavalier manner in May 1806. This man has obtained no credit from me, and when under way with his glass he promised to remit the amount by Mr. Surmall.

* Erasmus Wilson, ed., *Standard History of Pittsburgh* (Chicago: H. R. Cornell & Co., 1898), p. 198.

As the wartime financial squeeze approached, O'Hara lamented on July 5, 1811:

There are so many balances due the glass house that my capital is nearly exhausted. It has been necessary that my friends should pay these accounts to enable me to carry on the manufactory.

One such friend, to whom all lovers of early Pittsburgh glass are indebted for the helpful service, was the prominent lawyer James Ross, "a young man of grave and distinguished appearance,"* Federalist candidate for governor three times, United States senator (1794–1803), and a political power in Pennsylvania through the first four decades of the century.

One natural handicap of the industry brooked no control by man and allowed little room for planned preparation. Almost all Pittsburgh glass was sold in the West and South; it was shipped there by water, and the water was very often too high in the spring, too low in the summer, or frozen in winter. During the first forty years of the century, boats were at the mercy of such river hazards as submerged and floating logs (planters and sawyers), heavy sandbanks, rocks and shoals, and swift runs. The weather and the stages of the rivers limited the market and confined the plant to seasonal production. The O'Hara-Craig letters are full of apologies for and complaints about the difficulties of transport. July 27, 1798: "The rivers said to be lower at this season than ever known." September 29, 1799: "You will receive it before the river shuts." April 19, 1805: "The precarious state of the river may have delayed shipment." September 12, 1806: "Our waters are this day lower than they have been for thirty-five years and I believe since Noah, no craft of burthen can move." May 12, 1810: "We now have a rising of the waters." The first steamboat, the *New Orleans,* launched in March 1811, had to wait until October for the river to rise before leaving Pittsburgh. It waited some three weeks at Louisville to obtain a favorable stage of water.

* Leland D. Baldwin, *Pittsburgh,* p. 174.

The merchandising activities of these early companies were direct and unadorned. The company would ship its glass either with a salesman or, in most cases, directed to an agent in care of the boat master. If the glass was accompanied, it would be sold, bartered, or raffled at river towns. If destined for an agent, it would carry with it an invoice and a letter of detailed instructions.

Flatboats and keelboats carried glass not only to all the river settlements but also to points of inland distribution. For example, a privately kept account of Bakewell's written by Thomas C. Pears, Jr., contains a map indicating deep overland penetrations into Kentucky and Tennessee. A flatboat 15 or 20 feet wide and 50 or 100 feet long — not unlike a raft in appearance — could carry between 40 and 80 tons, including a cabin, livestock, poultry, crew, and passengers. Keelboats were long, slender, lighter in construction, more manageable and more suitable for shallower waters. The average keelboat load was probably less than thirty tons. New Orleans was a principal point of destination in the first forty years of the century; boats were generally sold there and the journey home made by sailing vessel around Florida and up the East Coast, or by horseback, or even by foot. The Pittsburgh *Commonwealth* observed sagely on November 5, 1806: "The people on the Western Waters are already becoming rivals to each other at New Orleans, and the Atlantic states are rivals to us all."

The first shipment of Pittsburgh glass down the Ohio set a pattern followed for some decades. Isaac Craig wrote to John Kinnear ("or in his absence the Contractor's Agent") at Natchez on November 23, 1799, the earliest documentation of Pittsburgh glass production:

Enclosed you will find an invoice of Glass Ware of Pittsburgh Manufactory delivered to James Farlan (who has in charge a large flat boat principally loaded with stores the property of the United States destined for several posts on the Ohio and Mississippi) and which he is to dispose of, at the several places he may have occasion to touch at — at the prices specified in the invoice — but in case he should be unsuccessful in sales he is to deliver it to you — which you will please to dispose of in the best manner, on account of James O'Hara and myself and if possible to cover 25/ per cent on first cost. I am sorry this ware is not of the first quality as it is the product of the first attempt. At present the Manufactory goes on well and we shall shortly be able to supply your country with Glass Ware of the first quality.

Almost a year later (November 3, 1800), Craig turned over forty boxes of window glass to Benjamin Cummins, boat master, who was to deliver them to his agent, James Naylor, at Waterford on the farthest reaches of Frenchman's Creek. The glass was intended for a merchant in Queenstown in Canada. Naylor would please receive them, have them transported by a safe conveyance over the fourteen-mile portage to Presque Isle. He was to request "the Acting Quartermaster or some other confidential person" to take charge of it "until a safe opportunity offers of sending it to its place of destination on the opening of navigation next spring." In the meantime, Naylor was at liberty to dispose of a part of it (amount not specified) "should there be a demand at your post or at Presqu'isle, at fourteen dollars per box."

Even then Albert Gallatin foresaw the dangers of competition. In rivalry with O'Hara and Craig and later with other Pittsburgh factories, he first suggested a ceiling of $14 for window glass. By 1804, in an unstable money market, a box of 100 square feet of window glass was being priced as follows: 7 by 9 — $11, 8 by 10 — $12, 10 by 12 — $13. Larger sizes ran as high as $22. Gallatin received no encouragement when he urged his associates to sell the popular sizes at the suicidally low figure of $4.50. He reasoned that future competition would thus be limited, but the others thought the present demands of the settlers would support high prices. In 1829, however, when he appeared before a congressional subcommittee, Benjamin Bakewell testified that 8 by 10 windows sold for $3.80 to $4 and the 10 by 12 size from $4.75 to $5. And Bakewell said that

the low price was due to domestic competition, not foreign imports. Gallatin's unorthodox ideas of marketing and his sound grasp of business were vindicated twenty-eight years later.

Be that as it may, New Geneva glass enjoyed popularity and a good reputation down the rivers and westward. On one occasion New Geneva triumphed gloriously over Pittsburgh on a hotly contested contract. The river town of Chillicothe, Ohio, ordered eight hundred 10 by 12 panes in 1801 for its courthouse — from New Geneva.

In Pittsburgh itself, glass of all kinds could be bought directly from the factory or from a merchant who might also be selling dry goods, home furnishings, and queensware (English cream-colored earthenware). Specialty shops had not yet developed. The small factories did much of their own selling, using the device of the weekly auction. Such methods bespeak small quantities and personalized transactions. One suspects that merchandise was often crafted to the taste of the buyer; that would account for variations in early blown and cut glass as well as differences in lines of early pressed of one pattern, such as scalloped edges, an extra star in the bottom, or added knobs on the stem.

A remarkable venture called the Pittsburgh Manufacturing Company was founded in 1819. (It is not to be confused with the earlier banking and insurance company of that name.) This was a cooperative group engaged in the wholesaling and retailing of products manufactured in Pittsburgh. A glassman, George Sutton, was elected first president. The cooperative advertised in the newspapers and frequently opened its warehouse for displays and public inspection. The warehouse, filled with furniture, glass, iron, and tinware for the home, cutlery and copperware and hundreds of other articles, must have been an exciting place to visit. The Harmony Society, after its return to the Ohio River at Economy in 1825, dealt many times with the cooperative. The Pittsburgh Manufacturing Company, operating before the trading practices of later cooperative ventures, stabilized the market and established good customer relationships. From such a group the move to distributors' warehouses, commission men, and manufacturers' agents was but a small step.

Glassmakers' societies knit the business ties more firmly. The Allegheny County Society for Protecting Agriculture and Domestic Manufactures was formed in 1820, with Thomas Bakewell and William Eichbaum serving on the committee to circulate subscription papers.

Efficiency in merchandising methods grew with the growing trade. One glass entrepreneur began to use the river as a means of advertising. The New York *Evening Post* for April 9, 1842, quoted this account from the Buffalo *Commercial Advertiser:*

A large flat boat is fitted up with furnace, tempering oven . . . in full blast every night, melting glassware, which is retailed . . . along the shore. . . . It hails from Pittsburgh and is owned by Ross & Co.*

The Adventures of a Traveling Salesman

The letters of Bakewell's Thomas Pears to his wife, Sarah, afford a remarkable view of the difficulties and hardships of selling glass along the rivers before the railroads began to appear in the 1840s.

Pears loaded a stock of glass on two keelboats, with twenty-five more boxes on a third vessel, and set out at the end of 1819 for a "trading voyage" down the Ohio. From Shippingport, Kentucky, he wrote on January 5, 1820:

The passage down the river to Cincinnati was more agreeable than I had expected. We had plenty of water and arrived in 15 days from Pittsburgh. Some part of the time the weather was excessively cold; but I did not suffer from it except one evening when I went in the skiff about 14 miles ahead of the boat to see if I could sell anything at Portsmouth. I came

* Helen and George S. McKearin, *American Glass* (New York: Crown Publishers, 1941), p. 604.

here in the steamboat, and it is well I did on account of forwarding the goods to Nashville, as the weather is now so extremely cold that if they had been delayed I doubt they would not have reached Nashville this winter.

I intended to have left here tomorrow, but I have been disappointed by a horse I had purchased on credit falling lame, and I have now another to seek, the purchase of which will probably take nearly all the money I intended to have sent to Pittsburgh.

From Cincinnati, May 7:

People may talk as they please of this Land of Promise, but as yet I have seen no place better than Pittsburgh. This of all others is at present the worst. They have two complaints here which I have never before found united — very little money and that very bad.

Mr. Bakewell seems pleased that I am here. He believes that I may do something in the selling line at Nashville and he has not been there. . . . It's quite useless travelling over the ground where he has been. The glass which he sold last fall and this spring is yet undisposed of, and money is so scarce people will not buy more.

Pears wrote from Smithland, Kentucky, that he had spent two days getting shipment of his glass to Nashville, finally placing all but the twenty-five boxes on two keelboats at a cost of 65 cents per hundred pounds. "Tell your uncle," he said, "that I have sold very little and collected as little." From Eddyville, Kentucky, he wrote on June 2:

Arrived here yesterday, having left the boat and footed it here, supposing it possible to sell some trifle. But like most of my expectations it has ended in nothing. I believe there is not 50 $ of glass in the place, and they are not very likely for the town to want much, — for it is like Smithland, a miserable hole. But if they wanted ever so much they have not the money to buy. . . .

One [keelboat] passed here last evening, and I expect the other every minute. Thomas Carr is on the first, and I go up in the other, except when I get out to walk on, that if I sell anything they may not be detained. Small chance as there is of selling anything, there is still smaller of getting at what one wants, unless it should be perchance on deck or in the bow;

and they really are afraid to stop lest the water should get so low they cannot cross the shoals. If I should ever make another trading voyage my boat shall be very differently arranged.
You cannot conceive the disagreeableness of a keel boat. No room to eat, drink or sleep but on deck, and of all the men I've ever seen boatmen are the worst. To say the best of it — it is purgatory.

Pears sold $50 worth of glass in Dover and bought a horse "with some sort of accoutrements for 115 $, worth more. Doing pretty well for such a rowdy place as that is." Pears sold $120 worth in Clarksville, cash on delivery, which he found "a more Christian like looking town than any I have seen lately." He made a sale of $113 at Franklin and Columbia, $150 in silver, the remainder in sixty days, and regretted that he could not find exchange paper to send home. "At Franklin it was St. John's Day, and here it's Court, and there is no hurrying them in purchasing, for money's so scarce that they part with it reluctantly." At Nashville he attempted to sell "a good deal of the fine glass" in several raffles but did poorly — "and now I cannot exchange my money but at an enormous premium."

Thomas Pears did make at least one more "trading voyage" in that territory, for he wrote his wife again from Nashville on April 13, 1821:

You want to know what I am doing. It is but little. I sell some glass and collect some debts and send the money to Pittsburgh as fast as I get it. . . . I have been well since I have been here, except for four or five days when I had such a pain in my back I could scarcely move. It took me as I was packing a box of glass.

Pears continued to sell for Bakewell until 1822, when he apparently became a company book-keeper. In 1825 he moved with his family to New Harmony, Indiana, to participate in Robert Owen's experiment in communal living. He returned to Pittsburgh and presumably to Bakewell's in 1826. He and his wife died of pneumonia within a week, as the result of moving back into their house too soon after the great 1832 flood. Three years later their son, John Palmer Pears, was made manager of the glasshouse. He stayed with the company all his life, dying as a senior partner in 1874.*

* Pears III, "Sidelights on the History of Bakewell.

CHAPTER III

The Rise of the Great Companies

This has been called a Pittsburg, a cut glass bill, local, partial in its
operations . . . In selecting articles worthy of national [tariff] protection,
none are more eminently deserving of it than those, the raw materials of
which are of no value for exportation; the conversion of which into articles
for use produces something out of nothing — turns into manufactures of
the greatest value and beauty the worthless produce of the earth — furnishes
a market for the productions of the farmer — gives employment not only
to laboring men, but boys who would otherwise contract habits of
idleness and vice.
In the days of our prosperity we have made to the amount of a quarter
of a million dollars worth in a year. It was so much money extracted
from the bowels of the earth by the labor of hundreds, adding to the
wealth and comfort of all within the sphere of its action.
— Henry Baldwin, congressman from Pittsburgh, to the House of
Representatives, April, 1820

Improvements in inland transportation took away
some of the delays and uncertainties of freighting
glass and reduced its cost tremendously. The Erie
Canal linking Buffalo and Albany was completed
in 1825. Its immediate effect was to reduce prices
for Eastern goods brought into Ohio — 50 percent for glass and iron. Its secondary effect was
to show Pittsburgh merchants that Ohio trade,
hitherto treated with indifference, had become
very desirable.

Pennsylvania's answer to the threatened loss of
trade was the Main Line Canal (1834) connecting Pittsburgh and Philadelphia. This waterway
reduced freight costs between the two cities more
than 50 percent. Not content with the Main Line
Canal, Pennsylvania and Ohio promoters joined
to construct the Cross Cut Canal from Beaver to
Warren (1839) to Cleveland, each state assuming

the cost for the mileage within its borders. In
April 1840, the length was completed — a canal
from Pittsburgh to Cleveland. The optimists believed that Buffalo and Erie would be icebound
while Cross Cut was still freighting.

In 1833 a merchant from Warren, Ohio,
bought 1400 boxes of window glass in Pittsburgh,
had it transported overland to Lake Erie, and
from there shipped it by water to Detroit and
Buffalo. Another merchant more accessible to the
lake bought 1900 boxes.* These men were sending back to Pittsburgh in payment, among other
shipments, 80 tons of cheese, 80 tons of pearl
ash, 400 to 500 barrels of whiskey, and inciden-
tals. Dealings with this Ohio group in the past
had exceeded this figure, so that the new canal
would expand Pittsburgh business.

* Pittsburgh *Gazette,* December 11, 1833.

TABLE showing the GLASS HOUSES in and around Pittsburgh, in 1857.

Style of Works.	Style of Firm.	Location of Office.	When established.	Who by.	Cupolas.	No. Pots.	Factor's.	Description of glass manufactu'd.
Birmingham..............	C. Ihmsen & Co.,............	No. 133 & 135 First st......	1810	C. Ihmsen..................	5	60	5	Green, blk & flint
Duquesne................	George A. Berry & Co.,......	" 92 " "......	......	Geo. A. Berry.............	2	16	2	Window.
Eagle,...................	F. Bobe,..................	" 135 Water "......	1853	Bobe & Albeitz...........	1	7	1	Vials, &c.
Empire, ...	Wm. M'Cully & Co.,........	" 14 & 16 Wood "......	1852	Wm. M'Cully.............	1	12	1	Window.
Fort Pitt,..............	Curling, Robertson & Co.,...	" 17 " "...	1830	Curling & Price,...........	2	21	1	Flint.
Mastodon,...............	T. A. Evans,..................	Birmingham	1855	T. A. Evans,..............	1	6	1	Flint vial.
Pennsylvania, ...	S. M'Kee,..................	No. 102 Second st..........	......	S. M'Kee & Co.,..........	3	26	3	Window & vials.
Penn.....................	Fred'k R. Lorenz,..........	" 63 Water "........	1796	Gen'l. O'Hara,..........	3	25	3	" "
Pittsburgh Flint,.......	Bakewell, Pears & Co.,......	" 33 Wood "........	1808	Bakewell & Page,.........	2	20	1	Flint.
Pittsburgh Vial,........	Wm. M'Cully & Co.,........	" 14 " ".........	1837	Wm. M'Cully	1	7	1	Vials.
Pittsburgh Glass,.......	A. & D. H. Chambers,........	" 117 Water "........	1841	Anderson, C. & Co........	3	25	3	Window & vial.
Pittsburgh Green Glass,...	E. Wormser & Co.,..........	" 22 Market "........	1847	Chambers & Agnew......	1	7	1	Green glass.
Pittsburgh City,........	Cunningham & Co.,..........	" 119 Water ".........	1850	Cunningham & Co........	2	15	2	Window & vials.
Phœnix,.................	Wm. M'Cully & Co.,........	" 14 Wood ".........	1833	Wm. M'Cully.............	1	5	1	Black bottles.
Sligo,..................	" " "......	" " " "........	1824	F. Lorenz..................	1	12	1	Window.
	Adams, Macklin & Co.,......	Ross & Water "........	1831	Adams, Macklin & Co....	2	20	1	Flint.
	Bryce, Richards & Co.,......	No. 41 Wood "........	1850	Bryce, M'Kee & Co......	2	20	1	"
	James B. Lyons & Co.,........	" 116 Water "........	1837	Parks, Campbell & Co....	2	20	1	"
	Ledlie & Ulam,..................	Market & Wood	......	Mulvany & Ledlie........	2	20	1	"
	F. & J. M'Kee,..................	No. 23 "	1853	F. & J. M'Kee..............	1	9	1	"
	Phillips & Best,...................	Try & Second sts..........	1840	Wm. Phillips..............	2	20	1	"
					39		34	

Another artery for Pittsburgh was the improved navigation on the Monongahela. The private Monongahela Navigation Company built toll dams (the first in 1841) so that the river was navigable at all times except when frozen. This route gave good access to the Wheeling-Baltimore trade carried over the National Pike. The least impressive canal in size and engineering may have been the narrow canal around the falls at Louisville. It eliminated much of the portage and transfer of cargo at that point.

The Ohio and the Mississippi trade was looming large in 1840. The Pittsburgh *Mercury* for January 31, 1838, reported the departure of 1764 vessels with 52,373 tons of cargo, 173 of them for short-haul deliveries on the Monongahela and Allegheny, 523 for Louisville, 109 for St. Louis, and 19 for New Orleans. The eventual destinations of much of the New Orleans cargo were New York, Bermuda, Mexico City, and Rio de Janeiro. The Pittsburgh *Gazette* for January 14, 1845, reported that the Allegheny wharfmaster

had collected wharfage on 132 steamboats, 78 keelboats, and 854 flatboats.

These improvements in transportation opened new markets for glass and at the same time projected the industry into a period of intensified domestic competition. The complex trade relationships set up by roads, canals, and rivers lasted until late in the century, even after the coming of the steam railroad to Pittsburgh and to Wheeling in 1852. Northern Ohio continued to use New York; Wheeling used Baltimore; Pittsburgh used Philadelphia. Yet by midcentury each of these paired communities had become a trade rival with the other.

Despite the newly opened lines to the East, Pittsburgh glass moved eastward only moderately. The Pittsburgh market still lay at home and in the West. As the market grew, as more efficient ways of shipping developed and freight rates dropped, the volume of Pittsburgh's glass production doubled and doubled again. Glass had been the city's sixth industrial product in 1810; it moved up to third within five years, and it remained third throughout those decades in which Pittsburgh became the nation's strongest force in heavy industry.

The Pittsburgh Glasshouses: 1797–1850

The O'Hara-Craig and the Bakewell factories were followed in the first half of the century by some twenty-five glass companies founded in the city, with thirty-five others in the Tri-State Pennsylvania–Ohio–West Virginia region. Some of the houses died a few months or a few years after their founding, for the rate of mortality among glasshouses everywhere was high.* The Pittsburgh factories, with their cheap fuel, burgeoning market, and geographical protection from Eastern competition, were more robust than the average, and many of them flourished, or at least survived, until late in the century. A few are still operating.

In reporting on a locality with numerous glasshouses, an analyst has two approaches. The historian and the economist are impelled to tabulate every factory, its products, its operators, and its longevity. The collector and some curators, however, dismiss factories whose products — such as window glass and ordinary bottles — are anonymous. They focus on examples of fine workmanship and artistic merit. The test of time has shown that glass of a high quality deserves such attention. In the Pittsburgh area we find a noticeable time division around 1850. Before this, free-blown and pattern-molded, cut and engraved, figured flasks, lacy and early pressed were produced by relatively few factories. Yet the quality was of the highest.

* The McKearins point out that in the years 1800–1830 there were ninety-odd glasshouses in the United States, but that the turnover was such and the genealogy so intricate that they were operated at various times by three times as many companies. The companies, in turn, had been formed by an even larger number of glassmen, merchants, and other businessmen. More than half the companies operating glasshouses failed between 1815 and 1820. *Two Hundred Years of American Blown Glass* (Garden City: Doubleday, 1949), pp. 54, 56.

9 Labor, materials, and acreage. Harris Directory of 1857.

These 34 Glass Factories are carried on by nineteen firms, who have employed in the factories—

1,982 hands, whose yearly wages are	$ 910,116.00

In the manufacture of Glass they consume

5,736 tons Soda Ash,	458,880.00
13,008 " Sand,	130,080.00
637 " Lead,	89,730.00
326 " Saltpetre,	65,200.00
7,035,000 feet of Lumber,	85,525.00
3,952 kegs of Nails,	10,856.00
161½ tons Bar Iron,	8,490.00
882 " German Clay,	2,646.00
2,820,668 bushels Coke and Coal,	141,024.40
276,500 Fire and common Brick,	3,450.00
3,173 tons Fire Clay,	6,346.00
5,299 cords of Wood,	15,897.00
238,940 bushels Lime,	47,788.00
4,160 barrels Salt,	7,280.00
442 tons Pearls,	66,300.00
1,514 " Straw,	13,626.00
40 " Castings,	2,000.00
90 " Willows,	12,600.00
Total,	$2,078,734.40

They run twenty steam engines, and produce

6,340 tons Flint Glass,	$1,147,540.00
561,600 packages Window Glass, 50 feet each,	1,123,200.00
131,700 " Vials, Bottles, Druggists' ware, &c.	329,250.00
80,000 Demijohns,	32,000.00
Total,	$2,631,990.00

To give some further idea of the extent of these manufactories, is enumerated below the real estate of one firm in the business. They have and use

10 acres of ground,	3 Lime houses,
3 Factories,	3 Mixing houses,
54 Dwelling houses,	3 Pot houses,
3 Cutting houses,	3 Packing houses,
2 Grinding mills,	4 Store houses,
3 Coal houses,	2 Box houses and shop,
2 Flattening houses,	1 Mould house,
3 Sand houses,	1 Blacksmith shop.

STAINED GLASS MANUFACTORY.
An establishment for the production of stained glass after the style of the ancient Gothic churches, and in modern patterns, is among

Between 1840 and 1850 we enter the expanding and mechanical period, a time when thirty-four factories operated in the city proper. Many of these continued to the 1890s through a period of fierce competition. They set styles for pressed glass, led the country in making lamps and chimneys, and achieved technical and artistic novelty, but they allowed designs to degenerate into glass for Montgomery Ward and Woolworth's. Therefore, two quite different eras must be outlined. The first era (1797–1849) is limited to a few factories, several of which changed owners or partners frequently. The second era (1850–1891), covered in chapter five, contains many factories with tremendous production. (In both periods several little-known factories are omitted.)

The *Pittsburgh Glass Works* was founded in 1797 by James O'Hara and Isaac Craig, the second company (by a few months) established west of the Allegheny Mountains and the first in Pittsburgh. It is notable for being the first to use coal for melting. It began with window glass and bottles and in 1800 advertised "glass of large sizes . . . for pictures, coach glasses, clock faces, and bottles of all kinds of any quantity . . . together with pocket flasks, pickling jars, apothecary's shop furniture and other hollow ware, the whole at least 25 per cent lower than articles of the same quality brought from any seaport in the United States." The company made a very limited amount of flint glass by 1804 and even advertised cobalt. To manufacture flint extensively would have required too great an expenditure of capital, so O'Hara and Craig kept to their basic lines of window glass, bottles, and hollow ware.

William Peter Eichbaum and Frederick Wendt leased the plant in 1798; the owners resumed control two years later. The firm is an example of what could happen to a good site. For one year, 1798–1799, the property was leased to William Peter Eichbaum and Frederick Wendt. O'Hara and Craig had resumed operations by the end of 1799, but Craig, fearful of the cost, withdrew in 1804. O'Hara continued the business until 1819, when Frederick Lorenz, Sr., leased the plant. He ran it till 1841. In that year William McCully, who had worked at Bakewell's, took over the lease, maintaining it until 1851. Then Lorenz, Thomas Wightman, and A. W. K. Nimick carried on for nine years. From 1860 to 1863 Fahnestock, Albree and Company tried a lease. Finally Lorenz and Wightman bought the factory, and it continued a long life of window glass and bottles. This is a familiar pattern for many glasshouses.

We shall relate it only when the product justifies the space.

Though the Historical Society of Western Pennsylvania has two pieces of clear lead glass attributed to O'Hara and Craig by family history, we cannot be certain from the heaviness and crude cutting that they came from the first attempt. We can give a high rating to two early historical flasks made under Lorenz management: G. Geo. Washington (*GI-7*) and G. G. Washington (*GI-8*).* Both carry the initials "F. L." on the reverse. Lorenz undoubtedly made other figured flasks, but many of like design lack identifying marks.

Bakewell was founded as Bakewell and Ensell in 1808 by Benjamin Bakewell and Edward Ensell, Sr., one of O'Hara's glassblowers. (Ensell withdrew within a few months.) It was the first American company to produce flint glass successfully, the first to sell a table service of glass to a President for use in the White House (Monroe in 1817, Jackson in 1829), and the first to earn an American patent for pressing glass (1825). As Bakewell, Page & Company it won honorable mention for cut glassware at the Franklin Institute's first exhibition (1824) and a silver medal for the best pair of cut glass decanters at the second exhibition a year later.

Bakewell as early as 1809 advertised in the Pittsburgh *Gazette* conventional decanters, wines, and tumblers. What is remarkable in the advertisement is that it names butter and sugar basins with covers, cream jugs in assorted colors, egg-cups, cruets, and mustard pots. We can only guess at what they were as we judge shape, metal,† and colors of early free-blown glass.

After the tariff battle of 1824–1825 waged by Henry Clay and Henry Baldwin, Bakewell pro-

---

* Reference numbers here and following, prefaced by the G designation, refer to George S. and Helen McKearin's "Charts of Flasks," in *Two Hundred Years of American Glass*, pp. 512–82.

† Modern glass students frown on the use of "metal" for "glass."

10 Letter of commendation to Bakewell from the Franklin Institute, 1824.

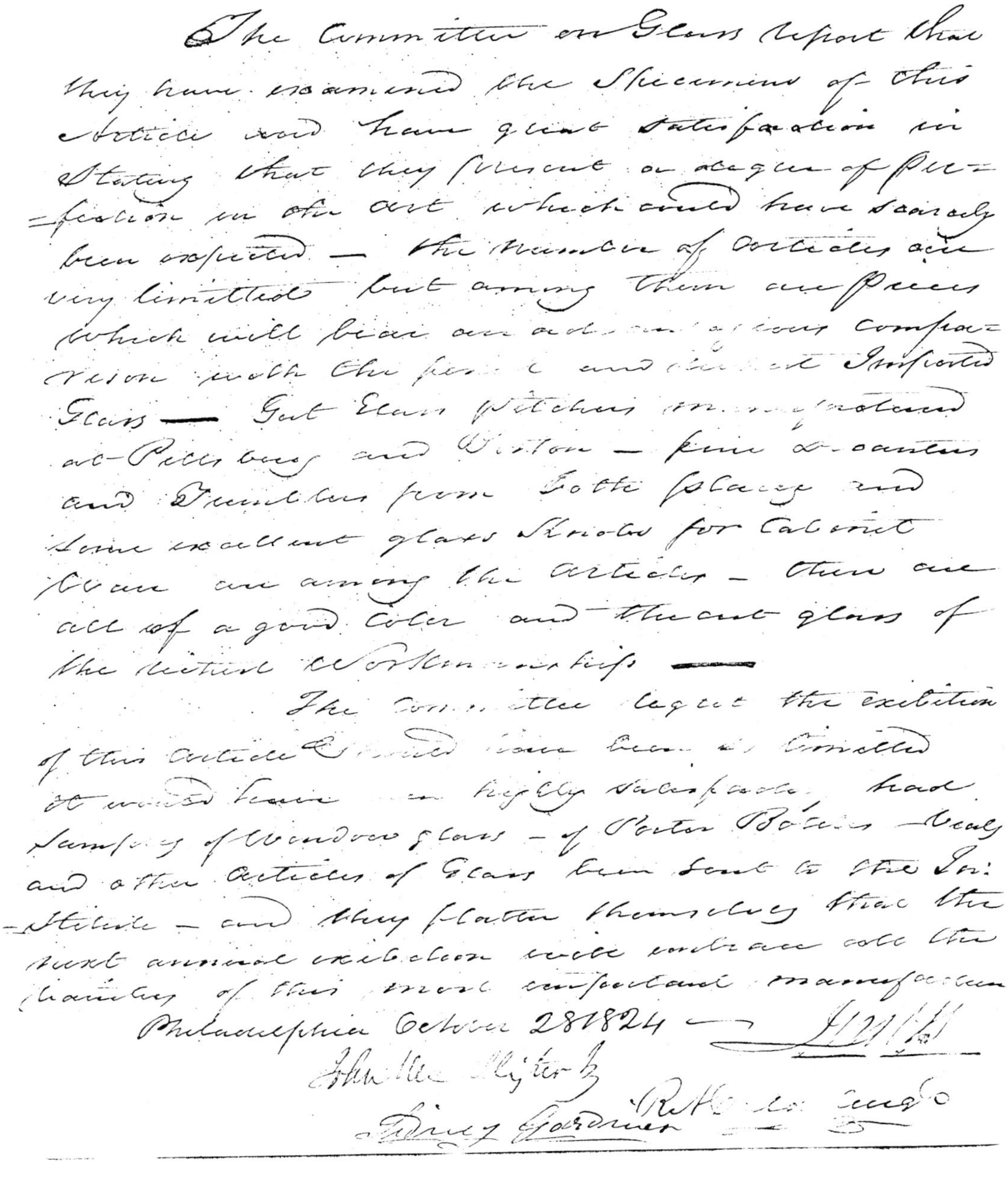
The Committee on Glass report that they have examined the Specimens of this Article and have great satisfaction in stating that they present a degree of Perfection in the art which could have scarcely been expected — the number of articles are very limited but among them are Pieces which will bear an advantageous comparison with the finest and best cut Imported Glass — Cut Glass pitchers manufactured at Pittsburg and Boston — fine decanters and Tumblers from both places and some excellent glass knobs for Cabinet Ware are among the articles — these are all of a good color and the cut glass of the best Workmanship —

The Committee regret the exhibition of this article should have been so limited it would have been highly satisfactory had samples of Window glass — of Porter Bottles — Vials and other articles of Glass been sent to the Institute — and they flatter themselves that the next annual exhibition will embrace all the varieties of this most important manufacture

Philadelphia October 28 1824 — [illegible]

[illegible]

11 Award of silver medal to Bakewell for the best pair of cut decanters, conferred by the Franklin Institute in 1825.

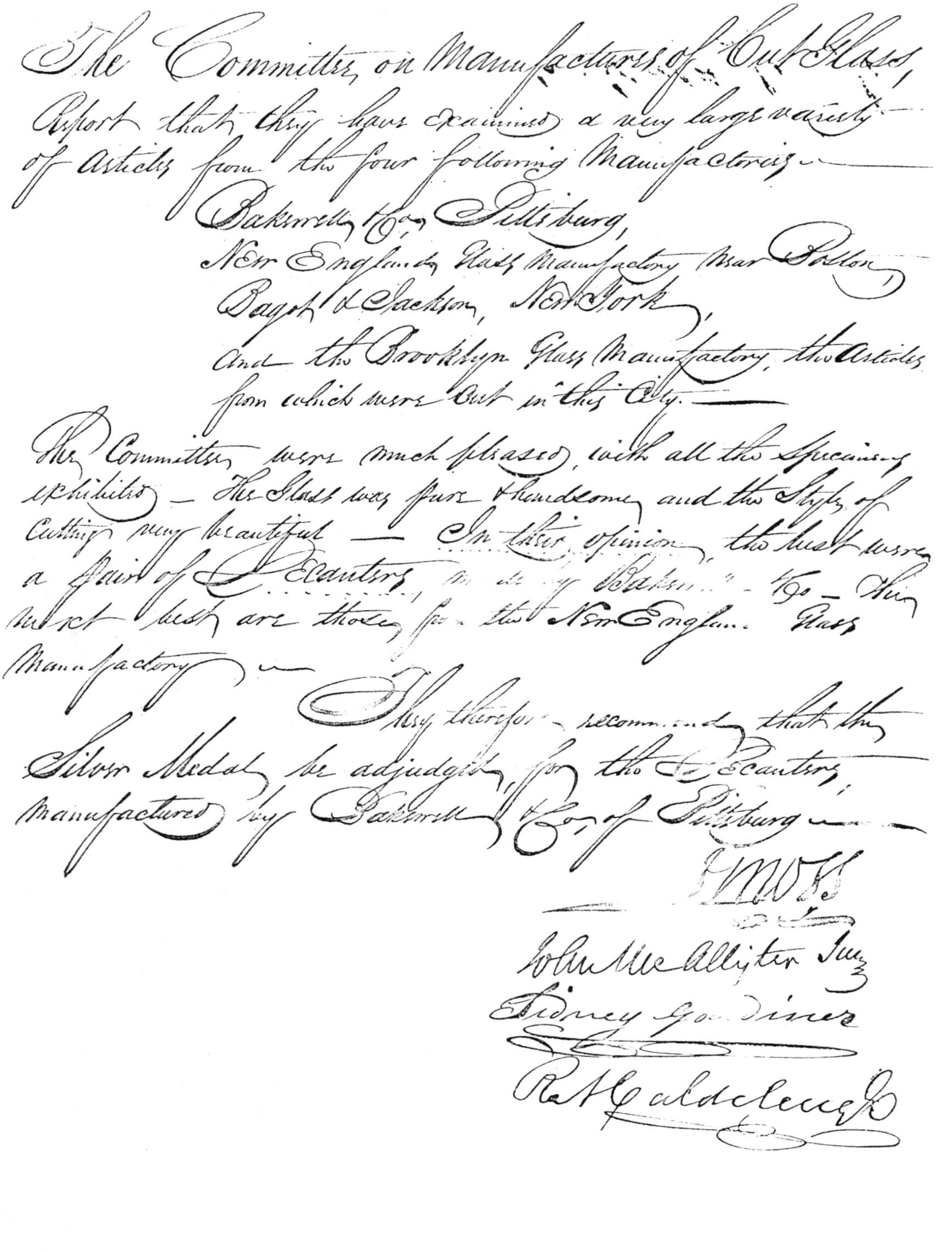

The Committee, on Manufactures of Cut Glass,
Report that they have examined a very large variety
of Articles from the four following Manufactories —
    Bakewell & Co, Pittsburg,
    New England Glass Manufactory near Boston,
    Bayot & Jackson, New York,
    And the Brooklyn Glass Manufactory, the Articles
    from which were Cut in this City. ——

The Committee were much pleased, with all the Specimens
exhibited — The Glass was pure & handsome, and the Style of
Cutting very beautiful —— In their opinion, the best were
a pair of Decanters made by Bakewell & Co — The
next best are those from the New England Glass
Manufactory —

    They therefore recommend that the
Silver Medal be adjudged for the Decanters,
Manufactured by Bakewell & Co of Pittsburg —

                                    John McAllister Jun
                                    Sidney Gardiner
                                    R H Galdcleugh

12 Pint flask, *The American System GX21*, obverse, aquamarine, nonlead, ca. 1825. Early paddle-wheel steamboat moving to the right, narrow flag to the left from the bow. Large American flag from the mast behind the smokestack. The legend above the boat reads "The American"; it curves and continues under the boat with "System." This commemorates the efforts of Henry Baldwin and Henry Clay to pass a protective tariff bill. *The Corning Museum of Glass.*

13 Pint flask, reverse. Large standing sheaf of rye encircled by the words *"Use Me But Do Not Abuse Me."* Around the inscription are 27 small dots, possibly representing stars. Imperfect rectangle under the sheaf. Herringbone edges, plain lip. No. 388 GX21 in McKearin *American Glass. The Corning Museum of Glass.*

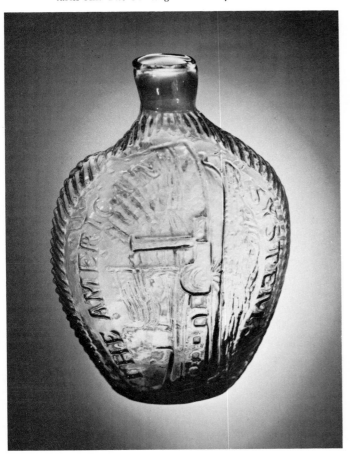

duced one of the most sought-after commemorative flasks — "The American System" (*GX-20*).

Marked pieces can show evidence of changing partnerships and help modern students to date a piece, as attested by two scroll flasks marked "B.P.B." (Bakewell, Page, and Bakewell — 1824–1832). A pressed tray with a scroll border marked "Bakewell & Anderson" indicated a change in partnership (1832–1836). When John Palmer Pears entered the concern in 1836 it became Bakewell, Pears & Company.

In 1825 Bakewell employed sixty-one hands with twelve engravers and ornamenters. In these figures we understand why the commercial production of copper wheel decorated glass has come to be associated with Pittsburgh. The journalist Anne Royall admired the Bakewell greyhound tumbler. Today we note its style relationship to and influence on other engraved tumblers of the period (see pages 119–24).

When lacy glass became popular in the 1830s and 1840s, Bakewell marked two lacy panes; one of them, combining Classical and Gothic styles, is a tour de force. We surmise that Bakewell also produced other lacy panes found in the area as well as many unidentified lacy pieces.

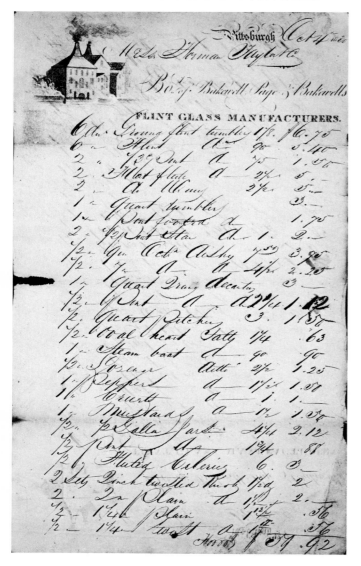
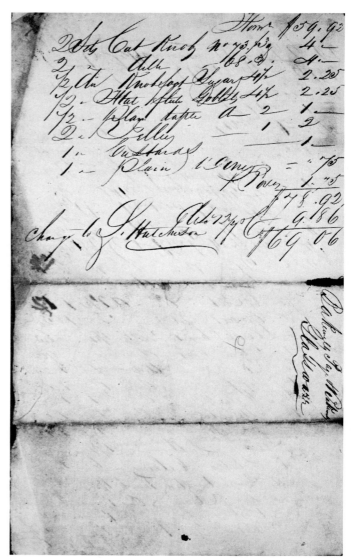

Bakewell caught the public fancy in the late 1870s with two well-designed compotes: a frosted dolphin stem supporting a shell bowl and a Rebecca at the Well stem with a frosted ribbon bowl. All these various techniques and styles show the scope of a factory that ran from 1808 to 1882 and won acclaim in all these fields. We should remember with admiration that this factory balanced its quality with utilitarian glass. The 1876 Centennial Committee spoke of the company's "moulded tableware, druggists' bottles, perfumers' wares etc. of ordinary qualities of forms and metals." Bakewell, Pears & Company succeeded because it recognized the need for utility as well as quality.

Its growth from 1808 to 1882 is normal: one eight-pot furnace increasing to two ten-pot furnaces with greater capacity than the old ones; forty-odd hands increasing to 125. What is extraordinary is the wise management that in the space of one city block — Ninth and Tenth streets at Bingham Street on the South Side — brought together all the essential steps in making and selling glass. The family ownership set standards recognized throughout the glass world. When other factories suffered from the strikes of 1877–1879, Bakewell's showed a flexibility that kept their labor force loyal and their factory open. *The Crockery and Glass Journal,* December 30, 1875, declared: "There is no house in the U.S. at the present day, whose reputation is more firmly established for turning out first class goods."

Ensell, Wendt and Company was founded in 1810 in Pittsburgh's Birmingham (South Side) district as the region's second flint glasshouse. The founders were Edward Ensell, Sr., Bakewell's original partner; Frederick Wendt, formerly associated with O'Hara and Craig; and Charles Ihmsen, who had come from Baltimore. First known as Ensell, Wendt & Company, the concern became Ihmsen, Wendt & Company soon after its founding. The company produced mainly window and bottle glass, though it undoubtedly made hollow ware. In 1812 the firm became Beltzhoover,

Wendt & Company and in 1836 the Pennsylvania Flint Glass Works. By 1850 the company had become Young, Ihmsen & Plunkett. Finally it was merged with other Ihmsen ventures in 1855 as the Ihmsen Glass Company.

This Charles Ihmsen record does not account for the engraved decanter at the Corning Museum of Glass depicting the naval battle between the Hornet and the Peacock (*140*). Family history establishes that Charles Ihmsen engraved it about 1813. * He may have bought a blank and had it engraved, for we have no advertisements of clear flint from the early Ihmsen partnerships.

The importance of Ihmsen's work for collectors today is centered in the *Pennsylvania Flint Glass Works,* run by Thomas I. Whitehead, Christian Ihmsen, and William Phillips. They advertised cut, plain, engraved, and flint pressed glassware. Up to this time no Ihmsen advertisement had mentioned more than bottles and window glass. Many hitherto unattributed Pittsburgh pieces may have come from this factory operation. The so-called Ihmsen sugar bowl (*327*) would also fit the time sequence (see pages 302–3).

Several Ihmsens were variously connected with Pittsburgh glassmaking. One who has left an interesting achievement is William, who leased a factory at Williamsport, Pennsylvania, around 1826. He made the Agriculture flask (*GII-10*). Obverse it shows "W. Ihmsen's" above an eagle standing on an oval frame; below it "Glass." On the reverse "Agriculture"; below it a sheaf of rye and tools of the farmer, celebrating an agrarian society (*202* — see also pages 207, 211).

The *Stourbridge Flint Glass Works* was established in 1823 by John Robinson, an English glassman, to make plain and cut flint glassware. Though the company's production in 1825 was valued at $22,000 — less than half that of Bakewell's — it rivaled Bakewell in quality. The Robinson cut decanter at the Historical Society of Western Pennsylvania would have lent grace to

* Helen and George S. McKearin, *Two Hundred Years of American Blown Glass,* p. 286, Plate 83.

any English or Irish table of the period. The betrothal tumblers (79), on loan to the Historical Society of Western Pennsylvania by Miss Lily Lee Nixon, are worthy rivals of the Bakewell greyhound. The engraved baskets of flowers on them are attractive but restrained and are more personal than the greyhound. The panel cutting follows the best traditions.

John Robinson is famous for several early flasks, including General Washington marked "J.R." (GI-6) and General Jackson marked "J.R." (GI-66). A scroll in shades of amber, citron, or amethyst is marked "J.R. and S" (GIX-42). One like it in aquamarine or amethyst contains the inscription "J.R. & Son" (GIX-43).

Robinson also made lacy boat salts similar to those produced at Sandwich and marked to honor Lafayette. These he marked "J. Robinson & Son Pittsburgh" or merely *Pittsburgh* without the firm name (309). Collectors today prize them, especially those in fiery opal, amethyst, and cobalt. We feel certain he must have made other excellent pieces of lacy glass. The soda glass semi-lacy plate marked "T. & J. Robinson Pittsb^G" (264) is of inferior glass and is poorly designed. Robinson, an inventive glassman, may have been experimenting. We know he had registered the third patent issued for pressing knobs.

John Robinson, Sr., died in 1836, but his sons, Thomas and John, Jr., kept on with Alexander W. Anderson as partners until the works closed in 1845.

The *Fort Pitt Glass Works* was launched on a long career in 1827 by Robert B. Curling and William Price as a producer of flint glassware. Born in England, Curling applied for citizenship in 1816 and qualified five years later. The 1815 Pittsburgh directory lists him as a pot maker at Bakewell's. He had risen to a clerk's position when he left to form his own company with Price, whom O'Hara and Craig had engaged in England twenty-five years earlier to serve a stormy period as their second superintendent.

By 1828 Price had dropped out and Curling's

two sons, William and Alfred B., joined the company, the name changing to R. B. Curling & Company. When Morgan Robertson became a partner in 1834, the name became Curling, Robertson & Company, remaining so until 1857, though the sons retired in 1840. Advertisements indicate that the factory made flint glassware of every description — molded, cut, and pressed. The company reported a capital of $30,000 in 1832. Twenty men were then receiving from $5 to $20 a week, while sixteen boys were receiving $1.50 to $3.50, with steady work day and night.

Henry Ringwalt was a limited partner in Curling, Robertson & Company between 1852 and 1857 and possibly longer, though his continued connection is not clear (see page 308).

The Fort Pitt factory, like Bakewell's, was a family affair. The products were similar. A pair of fine cut decanters (91), given to Pittsburgh's Carnegie Museum by Mrs. Edward C. Albree in 1946, had been presented to Martha Curling in March 1848 when she married George Albree. The workmanship is reminiscent of styles of the Irish factories. The lacy creamer (257) — marked "R. B. Curling and Sons" — verifies the production of lacy glass in Pittsburgh. Like Bakewell, Curling made lacy panes, for one marked "Curlings & Robertson" has been recorded. Today the Curlings are more widely known for cup plates: the Fort Pitt eagle and the well-designed group (Lee and Rose, *American Glass Cup Plates*, Nos. *210–217*). One of these, No. *216C*, has appeared as the base of a compote. In the late 1850s, Fort Pitt Glass Works, advertising in the *Directory 1856–57*, pictured standard pressed patterns such as Waffle and Bulls Eye, Flute, and Colonial. Also pictured was a lacy sugar bowl with weak stippling. The same bowl was advertised in a New England Glass Company catalogue about 1868, and it was produced also at Sandwich, in handsome colors. Curling, like Bakewell, sold druggists' wares and bottles. Their extensive products have not yet been thoroughly identified.

Edward Dithridge, who had joined the com-

15 Advertisement of Curling, Robertson & Co. (Fort Pitt Glass Co.) in the 1850 Fahnestock's *Pittsburgh Directory*.

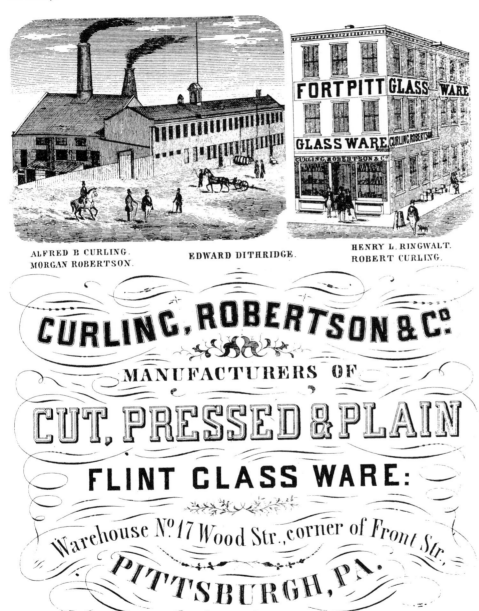

ALFRED B CURLING.
MORGAN ROBERTSON.

EDWARD DITHRIDGE.

HENRY L. RINGWALT.
ROBERT CURLING.

pany as a glassblower, became the sole proprietor in 1863. He was succeeded by George Dithridge and three others. Dithridge discontinued making tableware after 1863 and concentrated on chimneys and lighting ware. Edward Dithridge, Jr., who had bought a factory at Martins Ferry, Ohio, in 1881, moved to New Brighton, Pennsylvania, in 1887. There he manufactured cut and engraved glass of good quality. He also sold lead crystal blanks to many cutting and engraving companies, gaining a well-deserved reputation. The factory closed about 1900.

Union Glass Works was established in 1831 at Etna on the Allegheny River above Pittsburgh, as a producer of flint glassware. The founders were Henry Campbell and John Hay (who had founded the Union Flint Glass Works in Pittsburgh two years earlier, not to be confused with Union Flint Glass Works, in Kensington, Pennsylvania). John E. Parke replaced Hay in 1834 and the company became Parke & Campbell. When Thomas Hanna entered the company around 1837, the name became Parke, Campbell & Hanna.

Not much is known about the product of this company except for a marked and dated cup plate — "Union Glass Works, Pittsburgh 1836." Each of the octagonal sides is numbered one to eight. In the Corning Museum of Glass Exhibition of 1954, James Rose assigned an octagonal, 6⅜-inch lacy plate (Lee, No. *427*) to this factory. The plate, carrying a complicated hairpin design, is of heavy flint glass and brilliantly stippled (*266*). Rose based this attribution on cap ring pattern and cup plate analogy. It is interesting to note how many times small or short-lived Pittsburgh factories have made fine pieces of glass but how little recognized are their general lines.

Birmingham Flint Glass Company was founded in 1832 by William O'Leary, glass cutter, and Patrick Mulvaney, apparently a cabinet maker, as a producer of plain, cut, and pressed flint glass. The company became Mulvaney & Ledlie (James

E. Ledlie) in 1845. The Historical Society of Western Pennsylvania has on display a large panel cut bowl on a plain stem. The amethyst border overlay dresses up the plainness of the design and gives a pleasing touch of color. George Hogg bought it in 1846 for his daughter-in-law, Mrs. George Hogg, Jr. After 1850 the company was operated by two other companies, Ledlie & Ulam and Ihmsen and Ulam. It closed in 1860.

S. McKee and Company, a bottle and window glass factory, was established in 1842 by Samuel and James McKee. It built a new factory in the 1840s, and in 1886, the last year of record, was operating three furnaces for producing window glass and one for green glass. Before its extensive window glass production, S. McKee marked a beautiful aquamarine heart-shaped scroll flask (*GIX-26*). Another unmarked but similar scroll is also considered McKee's work (*GIX-27*).

Chambers, Agnew and Company, a bottle and window glass factory, was established in 1842 on Brownsville Road just beyond the city's southern limits. The founders were John Agnew, who had been apprenticed to William McCully in 1833 when he was fourteen, and Alexander Chambers. The name became John Agnew & Company in 1854 when Chambers withdrew.

Most of the flasks, bottles, and jars marked "A. & Co." were manufactured after 1850 and thus belong to the group in the second half of the century. Flask and bottle factories flourished under the demand of the West and the Midwest for flasks with symbols of the nation and the outcome of the Civil War — Eagle, Union, and Clasped Hands, and Dove of Peace.

Alexander Chambers and his brother, David, built a factory in 1852 which they called Pittsburgh Glass Works. Alexander stayed with Agnew for two years. Then the two brothers entered a period of great activity until 1875.

The Agnew company was operating as Agnew & Company as late as 1886.

The *Pittsburgh City Glass Works* was established in 1845 on Water Street as a bottle and window glass company, the founders being Wilson Cunningham and George Whitten Jackson. George Duncan worked for the concern for a few years around 1849. The name became Cunningham and Ihmsen when it was owned by Dominick Ihmsen and three members of the Cunningham family. It became Cunningham & Company around 1875 and D. O. Cunningham & Company by 1886, the last date of record. In 1867–1868 the company was advertising window glass, druggists' glassware, and convex glass for parlor windows, churches, and public buildings. The generalizations about Agnew and the Chambers brothers are also true of Cunningham: similar products and frequent change of personnel.

Bryce, McKee and Company was launched in 1850 by the McKee brothers and James Bryce, who had entered into an apprenticeship at Bakewell's at the age of fifteen. The company produced pressed flint tablewares, lamps, apothecary glasswares, and bottles. When the McKees withdrew, the name was changed to Bryce, Richards & Company. The concern showed pressed and cut tablewares at the 26th Exhibition of Franklin Institute in 1858. In 1865, the name became Bryce, Walker & Company, and in 1886 Bryce Brothers. The factory was moved to Mount Pleasant, Pennsylvania, east of Pittsburgh, in 1889. Two years later the company joined the United States Glass Company cartel.*

The record shows that the Pittsburgh factories possessed a stronger hold on life than did those in the East. Most of them had histories like that of the O'Hara-Craig venture: leasings, changes of partners, and often change of products. Bakewell's, an exception, continued from 1808 to 1882 under a family name and partnership. Another family venture (Beltzhoover, Wendt & Company) was operated by the Ihmsens from about 1812 to 1895. The ubiquitous William

* For much of the information in this sketch of companies for the years 1797 to 1850, I am indebted to the "Chronological Chart of American Glass Houses" compiled by George S. and Helen McKearin in their *American Glass.*

THIS INDENTURE Witnesseth,

That .... by and with the consent of his .... as testified by .... signing as a witness hereunto, hath put himself, and by these presents doth voluntarily, and of his own free will and accord, put himself as an apprentice to .... to learn the art, trade and mystery, and after the manner of an apprentice, to serve .... from the day of the date hereof, ... During all which term, the apprentice, his said masters faithfully shall serve, his secrets keep, his lawful commands every where gladly obey. He shall do no damage to his said masters nor see it done by others, without letting, or giving notice thereof to his said masters. He shall not waste his said masters goods, nor lend them unlawfully to any. With his own goods, nor the goods of others, without license from his said master he shall neither buy nor sell. He shall not absent himself, day nor night, from his said master s service, without leave; nor haunt ale-houses, taverns, or play-houses; but in all things behave himself as a faithful apprentice ought to do, during the said term. And the said master s shall use the utmost of their endeavours to teach, or cause to be taught or instructed, the said apprentice, in the art, trade, or mystery of a .... and procure for him sufficient meat, drink, lodging and washing, fit for an apprentice, during the said term of ....

And for the performance of all and singular, the covenants and agreements aforesaid, the said parties bind themselves each unto the other, firmly by these presents. In Witness whereof, the said parties have hereunto set their hands and seals.—Dated the .... day of .... in the year of our Lord One Thousand Eight Hundred and ....

Sealed and Delivered in presence of

ALLEGHENY COUNTY, ss.

THE above done and acknowledged before me, a justice of the peace in and for said county, the day and year above written.

McCully, after apprenticeship with O'Hara and with Bakewell, really picked up speed after the middle of the century and managed the Phoenix, the Sligo, the Empire Glass Works, and the Mastodon Works conjunctively (see Appendix, page 481). The site of the Fort Pitt Glass Works was variously occupied from 1827 to 1900. That, too, remained a family business of the Curlings, at least until the middle 1860s.

"Hard Times" in 1819 and 1837

The growth of the Western glass industry was, by the standards of the time, prodigious and rapid, but it was not achieved without travail and pain. Commercial development on the frontier, then near the frontier, and finally in an established manufacturing area was linked inseparably with the problems of money, credit, and general business conditions, as well as with those of transportation and technology.

Glassmen everywhere — no less in Pittsburgh — were always conscious of two regressive threats to their prosperity and growth. One was the cycle of intermittent "hard times" — the money panic or depression that was just ending or the one that was about to begin. The other was the pressure of foreign imports — of English, Irish, or French glassware that was often of superior quality and design and was almost always sold at a lower price.

The severe depression that followed the unpopular 1812–1814 war with England was felt grievously by Pittsburgh glassmen. At the end of 1817, the Pittsburgh glass factories were producing less than one fourth of their normal flint glass output. Between 1815 and 1819, the worst years, employment in Pittsburgh glass factories dropped from 169 to 40 workers, and annual output from $235,000 to $35,000.*

The quarrel between President Jackson and

Nicholas Biddle, president of the (second) Bank of the United States, over the bank's right to a national charter helped to precipitate the panic of 1837. That marked another low point for Pittsburgh merchants. They were said to have had in February 1837 some $10 million in debts on their books that they could not collect.* James Dick in Pittsburgh wrote to his brother, David, in Meadville on April 26, 1837:

At present we have quantities of money in the shape of Ohio Bank notes that we cannot use. . . . I fear your [pearl] ashes will not bring over 7 cents as we have had no more offers to buy at 7½ cents and none of the glass men will purchase any more than they can get along with.

Conditions were still bad as late as 1842. Dick wrote to his brother on March 3:

I hope you will be able to rub along until you get your Pearl Ash to Market. The prospect of making sales then in the Spring is dull and I think you will be obliged to send part of yours to New York. Bakewell's are unwilling to make contract for any, but I think I will buy some in the Spring.†

As the century developed and as banks and commercial credit became more stable, curtailment in Pittsburgh glass production became less severe.

The Curb on Glass Imports

After the War of 1812, England adopted a hostile commercial policy of subsidizing its manufactured products, including glass. She often shipped glass as ballast so that it could be sold in volume well below cost; as a result, business activity on the East Coast, other than the import trade, was prostrated. Though low-priced English glass was not flooding their markets, Pittsburgh glassmen were adversely affected. Any section

---

* McKearin, *Two Hundred Years of American Blown Glass,* pp. 58, 59, 61; Wilson, *Standard History of Pittsburgh,* pp. 204, 214.

* Wilson, *Standard History of Pittsburgh,* p. 171.
† The Dick letters are at the Crawford County Historical Society, Meadville, Pennsylvania.

that takes raw materials in exchange for finished products and uses the surplus to get cash with which to pay debts in the East — as Pittsburgh and the Midwest were doing — is vulnerable at any time, and especially in a time of crisis. Easterners had to call in the credit they had extended to Pittsburgh merchants. The Pittsburghers, in turn, could not support the optimistic loans or credits they had extended to other merchants in their area or to down-the-river buyers. Since barter rather than specie payments had governed their proximal and river trade, they were caught in a crippling business squeeze in 1819 and again in 1837.

The harm done by a flood of surplus goods dumped on young industries in an immature country produced two results. It generated in Congress a system of protective trade legislation, and it created in the public a feeling of loyalty to domestic manufactures.

Walter Lowrie of Beaver, Pennsylvania, who was elected to the U.S. Senate in 1818, had offered a resolution to the Pennsylvania Senate two years earlier:

The citizens of this state have already embarked extensive capitals in manufactures, particularly in iron and glass, woolen and cotton goods. But the large and unprecedented importation of foreign articles has given a shock to our infant manufactures, unprotected as they now are by discriminating duties.

"Discriminating duties" was a phrase coined and used by Senator Henry Clay, later John Quincy Adams' protection-minded Secretary of State (1825–1829). Clay was the exponent of the "American System" — a patriotic philosophy that called for tariff protection of domestic industries; a strong national bank; a program of improvements that included building of roads and canals, improvement of harbors, and clearing of the river channels; and economic integration of the whole country.

The leading legislative spokesman for the western glass industry was Henry Baldwin, a 1797 Yale graduate, a prominent Pittsburgh lawyer and politician, romantic enough to have fought a duel with pistols over a girl in his youth. He was elected to the House of Representatives in 1818 and there became chairman of the powerful new standing Committee on Manufactures. He was a strong supporter of Henry Clay's and his American System; some historians believe that Baldwin himself originated the term to describe the proposed system of tariff protection. In 1818 he helped to increase the duty on cut glass to 30 percent ad valorem. Two years later he delivered an eloquent oration in Congress in defense of a bill that called for payment of import duties in cash and the raising of tariffs from 20 to 100 percent on nearly all articles manufactured in Pennsylvania (see page 25). The bill passed the House but was defeated in the Senate by one vote. The Tariff Act of 1824 raised the rates to a level somewhat more modest than those called for in the earlier bill, but still high enough to gratify Western Pennsylvania protectionists.

Baldwin was a hero to his home business community; he may be the only two-term congressman in history to return to his hometown to receive a thirteen-gun salute, a welcoming delegation headed by the mayor, and a great banquet tendered by the manufacturers. Benjamin Page presided and made a speech at one such dinner in August 1824 at which Baldwin received his portrait painted by James R. Lambdin and ringing toasts were drunk to "Henry Clay and the American System." It may have been on that occasion that Bakewell brought out one of its most sought-after flasks, The American System (*GX-20* — see pictures *12, 13,* and pages 209–10). The flask has the letters "B. P. & B." (Bakewell, Page & Bakewell, organized in 1824), and since Clay and Baldwin were feted in Pittsburgh the same year, it is logical to assume that the flask came out after Congress passed Clay's protective measure.

The 1828 "Tariff of Abominations" raised the duty rates so high that a reaction set in. Benjamin Bakewell's testimony before a congressional committee on January 17, 1828, was surprisingly moderate.

Question: Are further protecting duties essential to sustain you against foreign competition in your branch of manufactures?
Bakewell: I think not.

Bakewell reported that in 1808 he had sold half-pint tumblers at $2 per dozen, at $1 per dozen after the currency of the state became settled, and now at about 81 cents per dozen. Quart decanters, he said, had dropped from $6 a dozen to $2.25 in the twenty years; wine glasses from $1.50 a dozen to 75 cents. He said that a comparative price reduction had taken place in window glass, though his factory did not produce it.

Question: Is window glass manufactured extensively at Pittsburgh and what is the price per box of one hundred square feet, of the sizes 8 by 10 and 10 by 12 of Pittsburgh manufacture?

Bakewell: It is. The price per box of 8 by 10 is from $3.80 to $4. That of 10 by 12 is about from $4.75 to $5.

And Bakewell went on to say that the low price was due entirely to domestic competition. Gallatin's economic thesis of twenty-eight years earlier was substantiated.

Asked once again if window glass (and by implication the other glass products) required further protection, he stated unequivocally that an increase in duty would not help a situation caused entirely by domestic competition.

Pittsburgh glassmen, indeed, were now chiefly concerned with domestic rather than foreign competition. The depression was over, the solid companies had entrenched themselves, and Pittsburgh was emerging as the most important glass manufacturing center in the United States. A new technical development, moreover, had just been introduced in Pittsburgh that meant almost a new glass industry.

CHAPTER IV

Technology and Industrial Growth

They [Bakewell's] have introduced a fashion of stamping figures on glass
while it is warm, also moulding glass which is done neatly in the same way
metal is cast.
— Anne Royall, *Mrs. Royall's Pennsylvania, or Travels Continued
in the United States,* 1829

During the yeasty economic and technological changes of the nineteenth century, many improvements in the glass industry centered in the Pittsburgh District. Three developments that took place there — between 1825 and 1875 — revolutionized methods of producing glass, increased production, and broadened market demand.

The Breakthrough in Pressed Glass

The first and most striking advance took place in mechanical production. Virtually all glass before 1825 — window glass, bottles, flasks, vials, hollow ware, and tableware — was produced by a skilled artisan who took a gather of molten metal on the end of a hollow rod and blew and shaped the product, either by free-blowing or by blowing it into a mold. But on September 9, 1825, John P. Bakewell took out a patent for an improvement in pressing glass (furniture knobs) — the first known American patent for pressed glass. In this method, the molten glass was dropped into a mold the exact size and shape of the finished knob. A plunger operated by a lever drove the glass in the mold against a receiving die. The end product was perfectly and uniformly shaped, and at a fraction of the time and cost that would have been re-quired to blow the product into an open or closed mold.

Much has been written about the first American patents for pressed glass. In spite of the fact that some Easterners and collectors still believe that Deming Jarves of Sandwich originated pressed glass in this country with his patent for "Improvement in the Mode of Pressing Melted Glass into Molds," December 1, 1828, the very title proves that he was a follower. Six other patents for knobs and pressing predated his.* Bakewell was incontestably the first. Enoch Robinson and Henry Whitney of Cambridge, Massachusetts, followed on November 4, 1826, with a patent for pressing glass, the validity and originality of which were contested by "powerful Pittsburgh parties," presumably the Bakewells. Helen McKearin concludes after a scholarly study that the 1826 Robinson and Whitney patent produced the first practical glass knob.† The New England Glass Company, she found, com-

* 1825, B. Bakewell, Pittsburgh; 1826, E. Robinson and H. Whitney, Cambridge; 1827, J. Robinson, Pittsburgh; 1827, two patents, P. Dummer, C. Dummer, and J. Maxwell, Jersey City; 1828, B. Bakewell, Pittsburgh; 1828, D. Jarves, Sandwich.
† "The Case of the Pressed Glass Knobs," *Antiques* 60, August 1951.

16 Five lacy knobs marked "Bakewell's Patent," 1825–1835. Nos. 1 and 4 boat salts are marked "J. Robinson & Son Pittsburgh," 1835. *Ex coll. John J. Grossman.*

plained in the Philadelphia Court of Equity in 1829 that its patent had been infringed. It won the contested suit but was able to pin the guilt of infringement only on the Union Glass Company, Kensington, Philadelphia. By 1832, Bakewell was advertising in the Pittsburgh *Statesman* that it had exclusive rights west of the Alleghenies to manufacture knobs under the New England Glass patent, thus establishing a contractual relationship.

The first Bakewell knob seems to have had a square shank on the base that would require cutting into the face of the drawer. The Jarves knob used a round glass peg on the base, threaded, about an inch long. Neither was as efficient as the Whitney and Robinson device: a metal pin run through a hole in the knob, capped on the face, and held fast inside the drawer by a nut.

In an age when technological discoveries developed slowly, those in pressing glass spread with

amazing speed. Within five years of Bakewell's patent, many companies were pressing glass mechanically — simple articles like cup plates, bases of lamps, candlesticks, small dishes, and bowls of compotes. Soon the technique improved to include creamers, sugar bowls, lamp fonts, and large plates and bowls.

Perfection of the Lime-Soda Formula

Pressed glass was a towering contribution to the glass industry, but it was matched by a second development hardly less dominant in its effects. This was the discovery of a working formula to produce an improved lime-soda glass. William Leighton of Hobbs, Brockunier in Wheeling, West Virginia, finally earned success in 1864 by substituting bicarbonate of soda for the previously used carbonate of soda or soda ash. We do not know the exact amount of lime or other chemicals that may have been employed. The new product was almost as clear as lead glass and much less costly to make.

There was nothing new about lime-soda glass made with carbonate of soda. It had thrived from the very birth of the first pieces of glass produced on the Mediterranean shores. In London around 1675 the English found that glass with a lead-oxide content had better clarity, brilliance, and resonance and a softness better suited to cutting. Thenceforth the two formulas traveled side by side. No one should disparage the early soda formula: it was undoubtedly used by the Venetians, by Stiegel's workmen, by Amelung, and by their descendants or apprentices in some of the most vivid colorings not only in American nineteenth-century flasks but also in the fine examples of pattern-molding in the Midwest.

We should digress here to clear up the clouds in which advertising and loose application have enshrouded the term "flint glass." The Irish and the English had taken the word "flint" from the use of ground flint stones instead of silica sand. Then it was applied as well to glass with a lead content. The term "double flint" appears in many early American bills and letters; students believe that this meant glass of the first quality. Lead glass had clarity and weight, and it had resonance when struck. Since good lime-soda glass could be as clear as lead glass, and since, given an object of the right shape, it could ring when struck, later manufacturers of pressed and blown lime-soda glass easily took to misusing the words "crystal" and "flint" in describing their wares.

Glassmen further confused the issue by making flint a synonym for clear or white glass. After 1864, companies that made lime-soda glass or used a very weak lead formula called themselves dealers in flint glass tableware or used the word flint in the company name. Advertisers also seized on the word crystal to describe pressed tableware. The semantic suggestion of the word takes us right back to the qualities of true lead glass: heavy, clear, resonant, and brilliant.

The Crockery and Glass Journal tried (November 2, 1882) to clarify use of the different terms. When the English spoke of flint glass, it said, they meant that it contained lead. The French and Belgians used the word crystal to describe glass with a high lead content. The Germans complicated matters by loosely applying crystal to all clear glass, regardless of its lead or nonlead content. The confusion of terms freed American advertisers to lean heavily on the word crystal in speaking of glass made under the lime-soda formula. Manufacturers of tableware, bottles, lamps, and lamp chimneys also used the word flint too generously. "German flint," appearing as a trade name less frequently, could attract the buying public. The words flint and crystal have plagued collectors — far more, in fact, than they have plagued glass manufacturers and contemporary antique dealers. The careful modern collector uses the term flint to mean only glass with a lead content.

The English brought the lead formula into balance in the seventeenth and eighteenth centuries and deserve credit for the magnificent glass that graced the tables of the titled and the wealthy. In the New World, the tradition of using lead or flint glass continued for engraved and cut pieces. Up until 1830, even with the acclaim and achievement of the Bakewells and of John Robinson's Stourbridge Glass Works, flint glass was a luxury product in the Midwest. Certainly Pittsburgh itself could not absorb its own complete production.

Sooner or later a cheaper substitute had to be found both for flint glass and for lime-soda glass made in the old method. The times and the market demanded increased production and reduced manufacturing costs. The substitute was found through a basic but simple change in formula. The expensive chemical compound carbonate of soda was replaced with inexpensive bicarbonate of soda — baking soda — and slight adjustments were made in the proportion of lime. Glass from that mixture cooled and became rigid much more quickly than lead glass. The new lime-soda glass was lighter in weight, just as durable, just as clear, and could be as brilliant. Since it was lighter, cooled more quickly, and was easier to handle, production was stepped up and freight costs were lowered. It lost in weight, luster, and resonance, the three qualities that delight most modern collectors. Even the youngest, newest beginner today has two questions: Is it flint? Will it ring?

Perfection of the lime-soda process is credited to William L. Leighton, Sr., who in 1863 left his position of many years as superintendent of the New England Glass Company works to take charge of production at Hobbs, Brockunier & Company, Wheeling. There he devoted himself to experiments in search of the new formula, succeeding in 1864. A loyal Pittsburgh historian, however, attributes the discovery to John Adams, one of the great figures of Pittsburgh glass. According to this account:*

In 1851, Adams, Macklin & Co. established a factory at the corner of Ross and Second streets, for making flint glass. Shortly after the formation of this firm, Mr. Adams began a series of experiments to demonstrate the practicability of the use of lime as a substitute for lead in making table ware, with a view to cheapening the cost of its production. This was an important "new departure" in the glass making, resulting in making Allegheny County the controlling centre in table ware. The cost of lead made an important item in the cost of its manufacture, and the substitution of lime, it is apparent, would at once reduce it.

Adams began his experiments about 1850, and though he was several times on the point of abandoning his attempt, "he persevered to the crown of success."

While for a few years lime glass . . . suffered in comparison with lead or flint glass . . . continued practice and improved knowledge in the use of lime has resulted in the production of "lime glass" of as

great beauty as the old flint glass, of which little is now made, except for the purpose of making "cut glass" or druggists ware, for which lead or flint is requisite, owing to its greater weight and ductility.

At this time, or perhaps shortly before, William Phillips, of Phillips & Best, also began a series of experiments in the use of lime in the manufacture of glass, but does not seem, from the recollections of the glassworkers, to have been successful. Thurston concludes that the glass trade of Allegheny County is indebted to John Adams for that great advancement in the processes of its manufacture.

It is reasonable to believe that Leighton's perfected formula of 1864 came gradually through trial and error and that the trade carried word of Adams' earlier researches from Pittsburgh to Wheeling. Perhaps the two men worked in friendly cooperation. At any rate, the new formula was available to all, and it was an immediate success. The many concerns around Pittsburgh and Wheeling were happy with it; as long as the glass retained its clarity, they were quite willing to relinquish weight and resonance.

As the population beyond the mountains increased and the Western country became more stable, pressed tableware came into wider use even before 1864. Pressed glass with a high lead content superseded some of the cut and engraved and free-blown glass that earlier had served as status symbols. With lowered prices under the lime-soda formula, the industry saw a "democratization" of its products. Lowered production costs resulted in a flood of inexpensive tableware, allowed more money to be spent on molds, increased the number of patterns, and ushered in a wide use of color. These new products came within the economic reach of almost every American.

The New England Glass Company, however, was reluctant to cheapen its glass by giving up lead, and so it stayed doggedly with flint glass. The Boston and Sandwich Glass Company accepted the lime-soda formula but did so too late

* George H. Thurston, *Allegheny County's Hundred Years* (Pittsburgh: A. A. Anderson & Son, 1888), p. 188.

to save itself from failure.* The dominant strength and vitality of the glass industry was swinging to the Midwest before 1864. The lime-soda formula, coupled with a major new development in fuel, sounded the warning knell for the East.

The Revolution in Fuel

There were two revolutions in the nineteenth century in the fuel the glass industry used for its melting pots and annealing ovens, and both were generated in Pittsburgh. The first began in 1797 with the use of coal to replace wood. O'Hara and Craig had set up their factory on Coal Hill (now Mount Washington) opposite Pittsburgh's Point and founded the industry because of the plentiful supply of good coal.

The second revolution began in August 1859, on Oil Creek, one-half mile south of Titusville, Pennsylvania, when E. L. Drake brought in the first successful oil well. The vast oil fields of Western Pennsylvania also contained rich deposits of natural gas. Gas strikes came with or instead of oil, to the disgust of the operators, who for many years burned off the by-product gas as useless.

Gas manufactured from coal had been used for street lighting in Pittsburgh since 1837, but natural gas, when discovered in quantity, was considered impractical and dangerous. And yet there were many reasons for gas to supplant coal. It occupied no storage bin and left no ashes. It was cheap and the flame could be regulated and shaped. It did not mar the color of the glass in the annealing oven as did sulfur fumes from coal and coke. It did not require tightly covered pots or tall smokestacks. And it extended the life of the pots.

The first Siemens gas furnace in the United States had been constructed in Pittsburgh in 1863 by Park, McCully & Company for refining copper.

* Professor Frederick Norton of the Massachusetts Institute of Technology has studied Sandwich fragments scientifically and found no evidence of lime-soda use in the more than 2400 pieces he tested.

The Rochester (Pennsylvania) Tumbler Company apparently was the first of the glass manufacturers to foresee the value of natural gas for all phases of its heating operation. It began to drill a well on its own property in 1874. When the well was brought in, gas served to illuminate, to fuel the pots and glory holes, and to heat and temper the annealing ovens. The beginnings were small and progress slow. The rank and file glassworkers were skeptical. Somehow the well filled in; the undismayed owners ordered a deeper boring. At 950 feet they struck gas and pronounced it good. They sank a second well to a depth of 1000 feet, got two barrels of oil a day along with a considerable volume of gas, and predicted at the end of 1876 that they would soon be using natural gas exclusively.*

In Pittsburgh, as practical a glassman as John Adams was willing to gamble on the future of gas. With William Doyle, Thomas Atterbury, David Challinor, John McCutcheon, and Joseph Finch — the first four of them glassmen — he proposed to bore a well in the vicinity of Tenth Street. The group thought 1600 feet would be deep enough to prove or disprove the presence of gas, and they expressed a willingness to put up $4000. They reckoned that each furnace, glory hole, and annealing oven used $200 worth of coal weekly. The project came to nothing, but it pointed a way that was followed in later events. Adams, who had installed a French Ragot gas furnace at Adams & Macklin, estimated that the fuel saving could be up to 50 percent, with a sizable reduction in the time of the melt.

In 1877, Philip Arbogast, a famous furnace designer,† improved the heating and combustion of the glory hole — the small furnaces requiring higher heat than the melting furnaces, used for

* *The Crockery and Glass Journal,* August 26, 1875.
† His furnaces were noted for the purity of the metal produced in their pots. He is supposed to have built the largest furnace in the country for Challinor & Taylor. He built two others almost as large for the Sandwich Glass Company.

fire polishing or in reheating and shaping partly finished pieces before they reached final form. A tube from the grate passed through the center of the lower part of the pot. Arbogast added lateral tubes on each side of the opening into the main chamber and allowed a draft of fresh air to heat the chamber near the top. The smoke around the laterals was met by a jet of hot air or gas and entirely consumed, so that flames in the glory hole might be free of smoke. This efficient use of fuel improved the glass by doing away with discoloration. The Bryce-Walker concern introduced the Arbogast improvement and gave its approval.

Evan Jones, a pot maker at Wightman, set out to improve the direct heating of the pots. Planning a furnace of six pots, he devised upright flues at each of the four corners. Over each pot he placed a gather and a blowhole so that the melting and blowing furnaces would be combined. Each was given a greater fire surface — seventeen inches with a diameter of fifty-five inches. The melting time of a pot was cut by that arrangement from fourteen or fifteen hours to eight or nine.

In 1879, Campbell-Jones reported that the old-process coal furnaces could be satisfactorily changed to gas. The heat generated made a saving of four hours in the overall process, in addition to the expected gains in time of melting and in fuel costs. The company announced that it would apply the process to a flattening department of a window glass factory to melt the glass there.

Despite these developments, the use of natural gas spread in the industry for a time with remarkable slowness. By 1880, only 21 out of 348 American melting furnaces were burning gas.* Two years later, however, a U.S. Chamber of Commerce report accepted the gas furnace as an efficient and economical industrial machine. *The Crockery and Glass Journal* for January 3, 1884, declared, "It may be set down as an exceedingly

* Warren G. Scoville, *Revolutions in Glassmaking,* (Cambridge, Mass.: Harvard University Press, 1948), p. 29.

probable event that every flint factory in Pittsburgh will be using natural gas in the annealing lears and ovens before the lapse of six months." Many factories began to use the closed time during the Christmas lull — normally applied to stocktaking — for preparing to change to gas. The Duncan factory promised that it would make the change as soon as the weather permitted.

With this promise of extensive industrial use, pioneers in developing new gas wells became numerous. When the Fuel Gas Company brought in more wells in the Murraysville area east of Pittsburgh, one source said that forming gas companies had become a mania. The Fuel Gas Company was given the exclusive right to bring natural gas by means of pipes to the city. All the glass manufacturers and many iron and steel producers became exercised over this decision and signed a petition of objection. (Basically they wanted free enterprise.) The Chamber of Commerce promised to act to have the unsatisfactory law of 1874 repealed. By the turn of the century, most glass companies that were accessible to gas and had the capital to install the equipment had changed over.

Once again the Eastern factories — especially those in New England — were faced with a fuel handicap. By 1860, only one major American factory was still burning wood; the others had converted to coal, often brought in by rail from distant coalfields. By 1880 their Western competitors were burning a still more efficient fuel — one that they would not have in quantity for another generation or more. "Gas," said *The Crockery and Glass Journal* on May 8, 1884, "is helping to boom glass manufacture in Pittsburgh and making it harder than ever for outsiders to successfully compete against her."

A New Market . . . a New Means of Transport

The discovery of oil had a stimulating effect on the glass industry; it was the source of a new fuel for illumination, "kerosene." Glass lamps and glass chimneys gave the industry a whole new market and a new range of products. Pittsburgh's chimney business alone in 1878 reached a yearly value of $600,000. Some 790 hands produced 16,200,000 chimneys. To pack the output of just nine factories, 725 tons of straw were required. Pittsburgh boasted that it made all the flint glass chimneys produced in the United States and four fifths of all others. Not far away, Acme Glass of Steubenville persisted in its claim that it was the largest chimney house in the country. A. Thierry & Company of South Brooklyn advertised in 1875 that *it* was the largest; the following year it failed.

A further development, rail transportation, worked a change almost as deep and lasting as pressed glass, lime glass, a new manufacturing fuel, and a new product, lamp chimneys. The railroad came into Pittsburgh in December 1852 and into Wheeling a few weeks later. Eastern markets were now open to the Western producers.

The Pennsylvania Railroad penalized Pittsburgh at first with discriminatory rates. The cost of a hundred pounds of freight from Pittsburgh to New York in 1858 was $1.23; from Columbus, Ohio, to New York, $1.15; from Cincinnati, $1.25. The railroad excused this discrimination on the ground that to lower rates from Pittsburgh in proportion to those from points farther west

would deprive the road of the power to meet its liabilities. Equitable charges finally came into effect, and Pittsburgh glass could move eastward in large volume.* Pittsburgh agencies had existed in Philadelphia and Baltimore and appeared in Boston in 1870. Wholesale houses multiplied. Manufacturers' agents traveled with a speed, comfort, and certainty of arrival time that agent Thomas Pears, in his keelboat, on his horse, and on foot, would have been overjoyed to share.

It is worthy of note that the Pittsburgh glass then generally and generously found in the East was the later tableware, the production for the larger populace — pressed lime-soda tableware. To Eastern collectors of Sandwich and New England Glass products, this alone represented Pittsburgh glass, and it met with their artistic disapproval.

* George H. Thurston, *Allegheny County's Hundred Years* (Pittsburgh: A. A. Anderson & Son, 1888), p. 194.
In 1863–1864, the thirty-four glass factories in Pittsburgh shipped the following:

	Window Panes — boxes	Glassware (tableware) — boxes
East	11,633	141,646
West	233,037	308,009

CHAPTER V

New Companies and Discoveries in Pressing

The highest skill, the most perfect machinery, and economy in expenditures
are the things which control the market and bring success.
— *The Crockery and Glass Journal,* January 4, 1877

Western Pennsylvania glass factories before 1880 had few of the characteristics of large-scale production and improved mechanization typical of glass manufacture in the last two decades of the nineteenth century. Too often we think that with the issuance of Bakewell's pressed glass patent in 1825 the industry flowered soon after into large-scale production. In truth, the day of the artisan and the small shop prevailed for some fifty years longer, at least until 1880. Manufacturing techniques, though improving steadily, required batch operations, handicraft production, and highly skilled labor. Warren Scoville, in *Revolutions in Glassmaking,* estimates that around the middle of the century a typical plant would employ from thirty to seventy workers, would be capitalized at $20,000 to $40,000, and would produce in value from $20,000 to $60,000 annually. The ten-pot furnace was still very much in use, but after 1860 the pot capacity of each unit increased to 2500 or 3000 pounds, while the number of weekly meltings doubled. In the seventy years between 1810 and 1880, Scoville says, ordinary furnace production must have increased more than seventy times.

These generalizations in size, capitalization, and output are not applicable to the few "giant" companies of the period — Sandwich and New England Glass, for example, or the Dyottville works in Philadelphia. Nor were they typical of the larger companies in Pittsburgh. Five manufacturers there — McCully, the McKees, F. R. Lorenz, the Chambers, and the Ihmsens — were each working three or more different factories in 1857. (By technical definition, a factory is a certain number of pots, varying from five to twenty, under the same roof or in connected buildings.)

There had not been many corporate organizations, except perhaps to raise money. Individual families and partnerships flourished, but companies failed or reorganized in hard times. Too often bookkeeping under such circumstances was erratic and individualized. When glass factories went into big business, family records fell out of style. The way had been paved — not in the East but rather in Pittsburgh and the Midwest.

Annual Pittsburgh glass production had dropped from $1,260,000 in 1836 to $1,000,000 in 1850, but in the next ten years, despite the panic of 1857–1859, it more than doubled ($2,075,000). In 1857 in Pittsburgh, nineteen companies were working thirty-four factories. Fourteen of the factories made window glass; eleven made bottles, vials, hollow ware, and lamp chimneys; and nine made pressed flint tableware. The newer factories — those founded in the years 1836–1857 — held approximately the same product ratio.*

The Pittsburgh Glasshouses: 1850–1891

Since its founding in 1808, Bakewell's had represented quality glassmaking and had brought wide fame to Pittsburgh. When John Palmer Pears joined the firm in 1836 it was the undoubted leader among Pittsburgh glasshouses operating in the first half of the century. It continued as a force in the second half by turning out first-class goods. That Bakewell's was now the oldest glasshouse beyond the Alleghenies, that it had already had a distinguished record, that it had been a family enterprise since its beginning, would have had little bearing if it had not kept abreast of technology and the market. Like most other factories of this period, it owed its financial life to producing commonplace daily necessities: tumblers, other drinking vessels, decanters, lamp chimneys and globes, lanterns, drugstore furniture, candlesticks, bowls, and limited pressed pieces. It was not as large as several of its rivals, employing around 125 men. It had suspended manufacturing operations briefly during hard times in 1840. After the fire of 1845 that destroyed much of Pittsburgh's "Golden Triangle" section, it rebuilt on the same location but moved to the South Side in 1854. Otherwise the company was busy in what must have been a well-balanced glass establishment.

Bakewell's occupied the entire square between Ninth and Tenth streets, with offices and warehouses fronting on Bingham Street, the factory facing the Monongahela River. Unlike most other glasshouses, Bakewell's was built of brick in a handsome and substantial manner. The glasshouse proper, a large square building, encompassed two ten-pot furnaces, each of much greater

* Catherine E. Reiser, *Pittsburgh's Commercial Development, 1800–1850* (Harrisburg: Pennsylvania Historical and Museum Commission, 1951), p. 203.

capacity than the old ten-pot units they had replaced. In time a third pot was added. The potting room was in the cellar. After 1860, when Thomas Coffin of New Hampshire established the first Pittsburgh glass pot factory in a stable on the South Side, manufacturers no longer had to bear the expense of stocking clay and constructing pots. In what was a sizable forward step in the industry, they could now call, instead, on such a supplier as Coffin's and get pots at an average price of only $38. Thenceforth the Bakewell room for making and storing pots was a past advantage rather than a present necessity. The lehr for annealing and the mixing room were on the first floor, and on the second the cutting and engraving room, the packing room, and the mold shop.

Two large iron-clad warehouses flanked the commodious offices and showroom. Here were stored and exhibited crystal and flint tableware, bar and apothecary shop furniture, gas and kerosene globes and chimneys, lantern glass, and every description of other blown and pressed pieces. Many of the leading Pittsburgh glassmen had got their start and served an apprenticeship at Bakewell's, among them Robert Curling, James Bryce (apprenticed at age fifteen — see page 37), John Adams, Thomas Evans, and Daniel Ripley.

During the costly strike of 1878, Bakewell's was one of two Pittsburgh factories whose pressers did not all walk out. The owners had shown an understanding of the workers' point of view, and enough men stayed on the job to keep the factory running. Bakewell's showed a quiet and restrained behavior toward the losing strikers and rehired wisely and fairly. They respected the skill and experience of their old-time employees.

Thomas C. Pears III of Pittsburgh owns a Bakewell catalogue from about 1875 that shows the types of glass one should expect in this period. His father left this note:

My father marked shortly before his death the following patterns as among the oldest ones made by Bakewell, Pears & Co. for many years: Argus (Thumbprint), Leaf (Loop), Lotus, Pitt Diamond (similar to Smocking), Prism, Mellon, Thistle.

The factory closed out business in 1882.

Among the score or more of glass companies established in and around Pittsburgh after 1850, the following made a lasting impression in the industry and, with the strong companies founded earlier (see chapter three), they will be referred to frequently in later pages of this work.*

Though James and Frederick McKee had been in the glass business before 1850, they did not establish their own factory, *McKee and Brother,* with James Bryce till 1850. They separated from Bryce in 1854 under the style of McKee and Brother for the manufacture of flint glass tableware, lamps, apothecary glassware, and bottles. When Stewart McKee joined the firm in 1864, "Brother" was changed to "Brothers." They became the largest of the Pittsburgh tableware factories, running two furnaces and employing 160 hands with a payroll of $2000 a week. This is a particularly interesting factory to students because we have three of their catalogues to study: an undated one, probably 1859 or 1860, at the Corning Museum of Glass; a dated 1864 one in the author's possession; and one at Corning dated 1868.†

A careful study can be made of lamps and globes from the three catalogues and interesting relationships with Eastern pressed tableware can be established. Each catalogue emphasizes one of the patterns. In 1860 a conservative grouping of

* In compiling these brief accounts of Pittsburgh glasshouses operating after 1850, I have been aided greatly by George S. and Helen McKearin's *American Glass,* Albert Christian Revi's *American Pressed Glass and Figure Bottles* (New York: Thomas Nelson and Sons, 1965), and Minnie Watson Kamm's Pitcher Books (Grosse Pointe Farms, Mich.: privately printed, 1939–1953).

† Ruth Webb Lee used this last catalogue for cuts in her *Early American Pressed Glass,* 36th ed. (Wellesley Hills, Mass.: Lee Publications, 1960). Significant articles based on two of these catalogues have been written by Homer Eaton Keyes and Charles Messer Stow.

Crystal led the way. We are not surprised to see Excelsior, Mitre Diamond, Comet, and Leaf (Loop) in a few examples. In 1864 many more patterns and pieces are pictured. Ribbed Leaf (Bellflower) is given four pages — single and double vine, evidently a new pattern. Sandwich collectors have long claimed this pattern, but the McKee catalogue offers the only documentary evidence yet found. Stedman, Excelsior, Eugenie, and Crystal fill single pages, but every once in a while a miscellaneous page contains one or two pieces of those patterns. Sprig (Ribbed Palm) occupies two pages.

In 1889 the McKees established a factory in Jeannette, Pennsylvania. They joined the National Glass merger in 1899 but resigned from it in 1903 and continued operating. McKee has been a strong and active company throughout its life and is currently operating as a division of Thatcher Glass Manufacturing Company in Jeannette.

James B. Lyon & Company, The O'Hara Glass Company, and The *O'Hara Glass Company Ltd.* were prominent in the period from 1850 to 1891, which could well be designated "the pressed tableware period." From 5 percent production in 1825, tableware rose to 45 percent of glass manufactured. No better representative of the growth period can be found than James B. Lyon & Company. Entering the glass business in 1848 with William Wallace, Lyon occupied the old Union Glass Works of Hay and Campbell. The firm became James B. Lyon & Company about 1853. An unpublished 1861 catalogue (in the author's possession) lists three names at the top of the cover — James B. Lyon, William O. Davis, and Alex. Lyon. They named the factory the O'Hara Glass Works, probably in honor of James O'Hara's first venture in 1797. Though Lyon exhibited cut glass at the Franklin Institute in 1858, he boldly set forth to specialize in pressed tableware. This was a departure, for most factories hedged in their advertisements: blown, cut, molded, pressed. Deming Jarves praised the company's pressed ware in highest terms in 1865 and complimented it on its labor relations: "Great credit . . . is due this firm for their success in overcoming difficulties well understood by glass-makers, and doing away with the prejudice of the skilled blowers, who naturally were not inclined to put the new and more mechanical process of manufacturing glass on a par with the handicraft of the old. Lyon & Company also excel all other American firms in large ware for table services as well as in the more delicate objects of use."*

American manufacturers honored Lyon by selecting his firm to represent the whole industry at the Paris Exposition of 1867. The French gave him a handsome medal for his workmanship and nine years later he won another at the Philadelphia Centennial. We cannot be certain whether W. O. Davis was a limited partner or merely the superintendent. He was, in either case, one of the most knowledgeable glassmen in the area. His many patents show that he knew the mechanical phase as well as problems of design and management. The Portland Glass Company, after a disastrous fire in 1867, persuaded Davis to come to Maine, where he designed the famous Tree of Life and patented Loop and Dart. There he struggled vainly against the economic odds of fuel costs, transportation of raw materials, and high mortgage interest.

In the Tariff Parade of 1878 in Pittsburgh, the O'Hara Works had 275 men and 75 boys, the largest delegation of all nineteen factories represented. Yet by 1886 O'Hara was operating only one furnace. In 1875 the firm name was changed to the O'Hara Glass Company Ltd. They joined the U.S. Glass Company in 1891 as Factory L.

The 1861 catalogue throws new light on patterns made at the O'Hara Works. In general they are plain, following geometric figures and linear curves with a marked relation to cut glass. The O'Hara Loop and the standard Leaf or Loop

(329, 330) afford opportunity to compare with the Eastern Loop. Lyon showed two versions of Crystal (329, 372), which should be compared with McKee's. We can expect popular patterns like Huber, Palace (Waffle and Thumbprint), and Cincinnati (Honeycomb), but we have new ones: Genella, Star, Reeded, Wreath. These were made in limited forms, for they are not often found. Having been familiar with later Crystal Wedding and Pennsylvania (Hand), we should look at the 1861 patterns with new understanding.

The Lyon firm held its reputation throughout the period. In its issue of December 14, 1882, *The Crockery and Glass Journal* wrote, "There is not a house in the United States that excels the O'Hara Glass Co. in the manufacture of pressed glass (equal to cut glass). Its line of toilet bottles has taken the trade by storm." The company had also built up a large export trade.

Adams, Macklin and Company eventually became *Adams and Company*. John Adams, a native Pittsburgher, was apprenticed to Bakewell's at an early age. In 1846 he was making as little as $116 for a six-month period. What he learned in practical experience, however, was invaluable. He joined Macklin in 1851 to establish a factory on the site of John Robinson's old Stourbridge Flint Glass Works at Ross and Second streets. Ten years later Adams branched out for himself and moved to the South Side. Beside registering many patents, he experimented toward the lime-soda formula and may have been more instrumental in helping to perfect it than he has ever been credited for doing. His factory made pressed tableware and nearly every article currently demanded in glass, but soon he also began to specialize in lamps.

The Crockery and Glass Journal felt that his patterns would be standard for years. When modern collectors think of Wildflower, Plume, Gypsy (Baltimore Pear), Palace (Moon and Star), and Thousand Eye, they must agree. He frequently advertised German Flint Glass, believ-

* *Reminiscences of Glass Making,* 2nd ed. (Boston: Eastburn's Press, 1865), p. 95.

ing perhaps that it was an honest way of making lime-soda glass accepted by the public. In one of his advertisements in *The Crockery and Glass Journal,* 1875, the fine print below the heavy black letters tells us, "The Pittsburgh and Birmingham Street Cars leave the Union Depot, Central Hotel, and Monongahela House and Pass the works every ten minutes."

Uncle John Adams, as he was affectionately known in the trade, was highly respected and a friend to everyone. As president of the Western Flint and Lime Glass Protective Association, he helped management to appreciate the value of ties with the Pottery Association and to work out procedures to meet labor problems. Like several other large Pittsburgh companies, Adams & Company built a thriving export trade, particularly to South America.

Around 1861 his company could vie with the McKees. It became one of the largest in the Pittsburgh area, its plant covering some two acres with five buildings, two furnaces, twenty-three pots, more than 200 hands, a weekly payroll of $2000, and an annual volume of $200,000. By 1878, however, he was employing only 150 hands with a weekly payroll of $1800. It was a natural shrinkage, not an indication of weakness. Adams died in 1886, but the company continued the name until it merged with the United States Glass Company as Factory A.

The Excelsior Glass Works was founded in 1856 by Francis and James Plunkett as a producer of window glass and glassware. The name became Wolfe, Plunkett & Company in 1859 when Wolfe entered the company. It was soon taken over entirely by Wolfe, Howard & Company. A second factory set up in 1863 under the name Excelsior Flint Glass Works produced flint glass chimneys. Though it advertised glassware earlier, it could not have produced much or we should have examples. A. C. Revi does not list the factory in his extensive and excellent *American Pressed Glass.* Excelsior was commended for chimneys and silvered glass reflectors at the 1876 Centennial. The company was still operating after 1886.

The Crockery and Glass Journal for February 1875 listed nine chimney factories operating in Allegheny County. Three claimed to be using lead in their formulas, for this stipulation was stated in an advertised discount they had agreed upon. Dithridge and Company on the old Fort Pitt Company site had been admonished by Dithridge senior on his last day, "Never change the formula" (see Appendix, page 483). The Excelsior Flint Glass Company was running thirty-five shops with 300 men and boys. In addition to chimneys it made a renowned line of silvered reflectors. The principal product of the Keystone Flint Glass Works was chimneys with crimped tops. Before 1890 they had made a record of 4,500,000 chimneys in twelve months. In 1875, however, they were proud of working eleven turns a week with 160 workers, the largest number of turns ever reached up to that time.

Six other factories, using a modified lime formula, advertised handmade chimneys. Challinor and Hogan were noted for their thoroughness and financial stability. They boasted of one twelve-pot furnace as the largest in the country. They had installed a new gas furnace and added five new glory holes. They were the first to use the patent crimper, which aroused so much labor trouble. Evans, Sell & Company, which afterward became Evans & Company and was known as the Crescent Works, prided themselves in 1890 on turning out 60,000 chimneys daily. A workman could finish 250 to 300 chimneys in one turn. The Duquesne Glass Company, Penn Glass Company, and Frank Plunkett and Company all specialized in chimneys. These firms changed ownership frequently, but essentially the same men continued in chimneys. Plunkett and Ihmsen began in 1878 and in addition to chimneys made ring and specie jars.

A great many tableware and window glass factories also manufactured chimneys as a separate line. Adams and Company, for instance, was advertising molded chimneys. McKee as early as 1864 supplemented its tableware catalogue with lamp chimneys. By the last quarter of the century, when specialization was well under way, bottle and vial factories like B. L. Fahnestock and M. W. Sackett and Company carried extensive lines of chimneys. We should expect William McCully, who owned five factories,* to manufacture chimneys widely. Nevertheless only one page in his 1875 catalogue is devoted to them. McCully concentrated on window glass, bottles, and jars. Pittsburgh, however, was still the largest center of lamp chimney manufacture in the country.

Campbell, Jones and Company was established in 1865 on the site and in the buildings of Shepherd (Shepard) Company, founded two years earlier at Twentieth and Mary streets. The principal stockholders were James W. Campbell, Jenkins Jones, and John F. Loy. They operated one ten-pot furnace with 125 men.

Dalzell withdrew to form his own company, Dalzell Brothers and Gilmore. In 1886 the style of the parent company became Jones, Cavitt & Company, Ltd., continuing till 1895. The firm did not join either the U.S. or National cartels.

The quality of its product varied. At one time it is spoken of as a fine grade of crystal-clear soda-lime glass. Probably this was used in Mary B. Campbell's Currant, 1871, and Jenkins Jones's Dewdrop with Star, 1877. (Incidentally, the lamp in this pattern carries the patent date.) *The Crockery and Glass Journal* often spoke of the firm's very cheap goods. This would appear in a few sets but more consistently in novelties like the Wheel Barrow, the Whisk Broom, and the Rose Sprig Sleigh. A plate with stars or pearls developed for the Central and South American markets carries "Give us this day our daily bread" in Spanish. Probably Jones designed this piece. In

* Green Vial factory, Twenty-Second Street; Phoenix, a black bottle factory; Sligo and Empire, Carson Street, South Side; and The Mastodon, Twenty-Eighth and Railroad.

1880 they manufactured Pillar, a pattern made by Bakewell much earlier. The pattern soon took the lead in popularity. Jones, Cavitt & Company tried paperweights unsuccessfully. Their Garfield Memorial Plate, 1881, however, was well received. We are likely to remember the company because a woman, Mary B. Campbell, was an excellent designer and an important person in planning. A fine Pittsburgh mold maker, Henry Franz, also often worked for them.

Doyle and Company was founded about 1866 by William and Joseph Doyle and William Beck. Within two years it had moved to Tenth and Water streets. Though Doyle was essentially a pressed tableware factory, it apparently tried novelties and other lines: jelly glasses, cruets, toys, and a well-advertised Centennial Salt. This piece was an accurate representation in crystal of the cracked Liberty Bell. The top in white metal had "Centennial U.S." inscribed upon it; the letters were perforated to allow shaking out the salt. The interior cavity was smaller at the bottom than at the top to prevent caking. Their ABC and motto plates also became popular. In 1876 they sold 20,000 toy sets. Twelve thousand toy cups and saucers went to the Springfield Vermont Industrial Works, a true cooperative venture. One of its many branches of manufacturing was toys — a good example of how far Pittsburgh glass traveled.

Doyle operated a ten-pot furnace and employed ninety hands. A fire at the factory in 1878 crippled the firm with a loss of $8000 to $10,000 in spite of its insurance. Soon after this they were taken over by the Phoenix Glass Company of Philipsburg (Monaca), Pennsylvania. Doyle retained its name and operated at a different location till 1889. It was joined to the U.S. Glass Company in 1891 as Factory P.

The *Cascade Glass Company* was founded in 1859 by Johnson, King & Co. The company became King, Son & Company in 1869 under the ownership of William S. and Alexander King. After 1880 it was renamed King Glass Company.

It operated two ten-pot furnaces with from 100 to 110 workmen at its home plant on 18th Street on the South Side. In 1884 it bought the burned factory of the Crystal Glass Company in Bridgeport, Ohio. Nevertheless, King kept offices and works in Pittsburgh.

The Corning Museum of Glass has a Cascade Glass Company catalogue that is probably from about 1876. A. C. Revi in his *American Pressed Glass and Figure Bottles* has pictured generously from it, so that students may profitably study a glass catalogue of the period.* One notices immediately the emphasis on plain surfaces: Mitchell ware, Plain ware, and Centennial. With eighteen copper wheel engravers and numerous designs available, King was using good business sense. It is surprising to see the number of earlier patterns recurring only in individual pieces or in the conventional table arrangement of four pieces: Argus (Thumbprint), Huber, Crystal, and New York (Honeycomb). Collectors today will associate the King factory with Floral (Bleeding Heart), Union (Banded Buckle), Gothic Ware, Jewel, and Frosted Ribbon with Double Bars.

The catalogue does not explain a fluted molasses can that was first pressed upside-down, then had its bottom reheated and closed quite according to the principle of "cut and shut." Nor does it indicate that King did a thriving business in store jars: Solid Ring-Plain and Prism, Blue and White. The children's pieces are interesting, and the novelties were adequate to help sales.

The firm exhibited at the Centennial and joined other major Pittsburgh factories in entering the U.S. Glass Company in 1891 as Factory K.

Atterbury and Company, proprietors of the White House Factory, was established in 1858 or 1859 under the style of Hale, Atterbury & Company. By 1867 James S. and Thomas B. Atterbury had taken control. The Atterburys were probably most instrumental in advancing patents

* See also *Pennsylvania Glassware, 1870–1904* (The Pyne Press, Princeton, New Jersey, 1972) pp. 17–44.

on joining the parts of glass lamps; their Eureka and Boss lamps were steps toward producing a lamp pressed in one operation. Their factory soon became one of the country's leading producers of opaque white (milk) glass. They seemed to be the only ones interested in opaque cameo designs like Rock of Ages, Three Graces, and Fish centers of clear oval platters. In other pieces, lamps particularly, they combined opaque and clear.

The company made a wide variety of glass articles in addition to pressed sets: novelties, bar goods, jellies, and animal figures. At the 1876 Centennial they won an award for lime glass lamps, chimneys, and globes. In December 1879 they moved to a new factory said to be one of the largest in the country, though they operated only an eleven-pot furnace and employed about 125 hands. The new lot at First and Carson streets had a 200-foot frontage and ran back 700 feet to the river. They claimed the offices would be the finest in the country.

A revolving lehr had been designed by T. B. Atterbury and a newly patented teaser (stoker) was in operation. The brothers had long shown themselves to be practical and imaginative inventors, taking out in the years 1862–1897 a total of 110 patents, 79 for manufacturing improvements and 31 for design.

The brothers, conscious of the need for catchy and contemporary designs, advertised that twelve artists from France and Belgium were engaged in designing and decorating their ware. Apparently the Atterburys were in a strong financial position, for they never saw the need to join either the U.S. or National mergers.

Joseph Richards and William T. Hartley established their factory in 1869 at the corner of Pride and Marion streets, Pittsburgh. They manufactured tableware, lamps, and bar furniture. Apparently they did well with perfumery ware, for this appears in their advertisements more markedly than in those of other Pittsburgh factories.

They operated one ten-pot furnace with 110 workers. After twelve years they moved to Tarentum, Pennsylvania. They exhibited successfully at the Centennial, and in 1891 they joined the United States Glass Company merger as Factory E.

Among their many patterns, two are of great interest to students: Thousand Eye (Daisy) and Loop and Dart with Diamond Ornaments. Adams & Company had already produced its version of Thousand Eye, the marked difference being the knobbed finials or the fan on the Adams version, and the scalloped tops and bases, whenever possible, on Richards and Hartley's.

On May 11, 1869, William O. Davis patented Loop and Dart with Round Ornaments for the Portland (Maine) Glass Company. Annie W. Henderson patented Loop and Dart with Diamond Ornaments on June 1, 1869, for Richards and Hartley. It hardly seems possible that she had borrowed and adapted the Davis patent in that short time. Richards and Hartley also produced Leaf and Dart, a related pattern.

Challinor & Taylor, Ltd., was founded in 1866 on the South Side under the name Challinor, Hogan Glass Company. The company moved to Tarentum in 1884, there producing tableware, bar goods, lampshades, and specialties and novelties in colored glass. Two years later it was operating one ten-pot furnace with about 110 hands. Most of the patents were issued to David Challinor, who is famous for Mosaic (Marble or Slag) glass patented in June 1886. The firm also concentrated on opaque white, opaque turquoise, and opaque amethyst. Brown, green, and black can also be found. Its tableware patterns were more numerous than those of its rival, Atterbury, and its novelties were many and varied. The firm joined the U.S. Glass Company in 1891 as Factory C. Soon afterward the factory burned and was not rebuilt.

The company has not received full credit for the artistic quality of its plates, bowls, and compotes, which often surpass the Atterbury products. Atterbury was well ahead in the amount of opaque white marketed, and for a long while many of the Challinor-Taylor pieces were attributed to Atterbury. Today the pinwheel plates with painted decorations are eagerly sought: Morning Glory, Field Flowers, and Trumpet Vine. Lattice-edged plates like the Trumpet Vine show how Challinor-Taylor could handle this form. Their compotes seem as stiff and conventional as the Atterbury ones. The six-paneled Daisy and Tree of Life bowl with three panels of Daisy and three of Tree of Life indicates a willingness to experiment. They advertised that they would make Amberine. Students have not yet verified that they tried that line, but the firm certainly began a fashion in Mosaic. We should remember them for more than their Mosaic and the numerous novelties like Farmyard assortment and covered animal dishes.

Frank Challinor owns two paperweights made by his father, Charles Challinor, in the 1880s. Charles learned the trade at Gillinder's in Philadelphia. Paperweights have been found in recent years in the Tarentum area; the finest is on a standard that repeats the design of the weight in smaller form.

The *Crystal Glass Company* was founded in 1868 by David, William, and J. M. Bennett. *The Crockery and Glass Journal* calls them good old English stock. They operated two ten-pot furnaces and employed eighty hands. They were strictly a pressed tableware factory, though they may have made a little molded glass and had an adequate line of bar ware. They promoted their Crystal Jelly Tumbler with great zeal, claiming that the glass cover could be airtight when used with an adhesive. J. M. Bennett had devised this. They exhibited at the Centennial Exposition. In 1882 the company was reorganized and moved to Bridgeport, Ohio. There disastrous fires in 1886 and 1902 limited their growth.

Mrs. Minnie Watson Kamm, in *A Fourth*

Pitcher Book (pp. 5, 6), attributes Pinafore (Actress) to the Crystal as well as to the La Belle Glass Company. The actresses chosen had been well known throughout the country.*

David Bennett patented in 1874 a plain design similar to Mitchell ware. At the same time he patented plain pieces with circular bands of reeding, on the order of Prism.

Ripley and Company was founded in 1866 by Daniel C. Ripley, George Duncan, and four others at Tenth and Washington streets. Ripley left in 1874 when the company became George Duncan & Sons (see below). Ripley, who held many patents, established a new company under his name at Ninth and Bingham streets on the South Side.

The firm operated one ten-pot furnace with hands fluctuating between 110 and 120. It was said to have the largest engraving department in the country, employing thirty to forty skilled craftsmen. The variety of its products indicates initiative and imagination: tableware, lamps, confectioners' ware, sample bottles for oil and other liquids, druggists' ware, many kinds of jars, even the Egyptian, jelly glasses and tops, flytraps, and Easley's Patent Lemon Juice Extractor. Ripley registered four important patents among others: one, a procedure for pressing tops on blown bodies; two, one for pressing articles for different uses in one mold; three, the Bride's or Marriage Lamp; and four, the Baptismal bowl.†

Ripley's exhibited at the 1876 Centennial, but the real growth came later. They devised sharp pressed patterns that imitated cut. The raised and plain surfaces could be stained and the color

baked on, so that the piece would seem to be cut and flashed. Around 1890 Ripley was regularly advertising on whole pages in *The Crockery and Glass Journal*. He would always have something to take the public eye like sets named for states — Idaho, Wyoming, Dakota, and Montana. When Idaho came on the market, Ripley specified a fifty-piece set — plain or engraved. That gives documentary evidence of the size of pressed sets. What he meant by one-half-gallon tankard sets in Idaho, Roanoke, and Montana is uncertain.

For twenty years D. C. Ripley, as president of the Western Flint and Lime Glass, was a power in glass circles. He was one of the moving forces in formation of the U.S. Glass Company in 1891, which his firm joined as Factory F. His son, Daniel C. Ripley, Jr., became its first president. The Ripley group was still a member of the cartel in 1904.

George Duncan and Sons was established in 1874. George Duncan had been working in glass in Pittsburgh since 1849, and he became associated with Ripley in 1865. When that partnership was dissolved in 1874, Duncan formed his own firm with two of his four sons, George and James, and with his son-in-law, Augustus H. Heisey. They operated in the old Ripley works at 10th and Carson streets, South Side. The number of hands fluctuated between 122 and 150. Two ten-pot furnaces were usually fired. At the Centennial they were commended for lime glass tableware.

Some time after 1886 the firm became Duncan and Heisey. Heisey, who had the reputation of being the best salesman on the road, had previously worked for King and Son. The company joined the U.S. Glass Company in 1891 as Factory D. Though Heisey became sales manager for the U.S. Glass Company, both he and the Duncans withdrew from the cartel and started a new factory at Washington, Pennsylvania. This operated for a long while as the Duncan Miller Glass Company. Heisey started the famous factory that bore his name in Ohio in 1895.

Duncan and Sons was fortunate to have John

---

* Sugar	Milk pitcher & Butter dish
Kate Claxton	Fanny Davenport
Lotta Crabtree	Lillian Adelaide Neilson
Spooner	*Cake stand*
Mary Anderson	Annie Pixley
Maude Granger	Maude Granger

† March 17, 1868 — pressed tops on blown bodies; October 20, 1868 — several glass articles of different use in one mold; February 8, 1870 — a baptismal font; June 14, 1870 — a marriage lamp.

Ernest Miller as designer and superintendent. It is believed that William O. Davis joined the organization after the Portland (Maine) Glass Company ceased operation in 1873. Miller's Three Face and the Pittsburgh Tree of Life and Heisey's Shell and Tassel gave the firm great strength. Today Amberette adds to their reputation. In the seventies and eighties we constantly find references to French style and later to imitation cut in such words as "A plain goblet just completed by Duncan will compare favorably with the best French shapes." They also made handsome and serviceable beer and ale glasses, cruets, pitchers, and molasses jugs with metal tops. Throughout the eighties their lines were replete with novelties, usually in the basic Daisy and Button pattern: slippers and shoes, hats, chairs, and coal hods. Duncan was an early producer of what we call stained ware. They designated it as a handsome line of hand-painted ware and were very successful in production of ruby. In 1886 James E. Duncan left for the West Coast on a sales trip to remain six or seven weeks, so we know that their business was good.

A great deal was made of the death of George Duncan, Sr., in 1877, with references to his rise to success by honest toil, industry, and prudence. The real accolade, however, was "a sturdy and true friend of the working man."

Bryce, McKee & Company; Bryce Richards & Company; Bryce, Walker and Company; and Bryce Brothers — all four firms center on James Bryce, who was brought from Scotland to Philadelphia in 1818 and went to Pittsburgh in 1819. On December 1, 1827, at the age of fifteen, he was indentured to Bakewell, Page and Bakewell for a period of six years. He evidently stayed on as a journeyman for about eight years. After the panic of 1837, when the glass companies began to curtail operations, Bryce tried the grocery business for a while. He then returned to the craft he had been taught, working for Mulvaney and Ledlie in 1845.

He joined Fred McKee and his brother, Robert Bryce, to form Bryce, McKee in 1850. Four years later the style was changed to Bryce, Richards and Company. In 1865, when William Walker entered the partnership, the firm became Bryce, Walker and Company. Walker left in 1882 and it became Bryce Brothers. They exhibited at the Franklin Institute in 1858 and at the Centennial. The firm joined the United States Glass Company in 1891 as Factory B.

A. C. Revi in *American Pressed Glass* attributes more than fifty patterns to the Bryce firms by 1890. Like its rivals, it produced several good naturalistic patterns: Strawberry, Thistle, Grape Band, and Curled Leaf. Modern collectors recognize Bryce styles in Jacob's Ladder (Maltese or Imperial), Ribbon Candy, and Roman Rosette.

In 1896 Bryce Brothers established a factory at Mount Pleasant, Pennsylvania, which became a subsidiary of Lenox china in 1970.

Bryce, Higbee & Company was established in 1879 by John Bryce, a brother of James, who was a partner in Bryce, Walker & Company. John Higbee (a salesman of Bryce, Walker & Company) and Joseph A. Doyle (of Doyle & Company) were the other partners of the new firm. In 1879 it was operating one furnace with about 100 men. Its production had increased by 1886 to two furnaces with twenty-one pots. It manufactured a heavy volume of tableware, decorative objects, and lighting goods. It probably sold to Montgomery Ward. The company changed its name around 1900 to J. B. Higbee Glass Company and moved to Bridgeville, Pennsylvania, south of Pittsburgh. At that time it expressed its individuality by impressing a tiny raised bee on the inside base of pressed ware. "H" was on the left wing, "I" on the body, and "G" on the right wing. Collecting would be easy if more companies had marked their pieces as fancifully as this.*

Tibby Brothers was established on June 19, 1866, at the corner of Twenty-Second and Smallman streets; it later built a factory at Sharpsburg.

* Today an accurate reproduction is being advertised.

Three brothers, John, William, and Matthew, formed the partnership primarily to make bottles and vials of all sorts. Even as late as 1893 their catalogue read *Flint Bottle Manufacturers*. It was a good example of a progressive manufacturing operation.

Situated on the Allegheny River six miles above Pittsburgh, the Tibby factory in Sharpsburg was one of the city's three so-called "rural" glasshouses, the others being Bryce, Higbee at Homestead on the Monongahela and Lindsay & Company at Chartiers on the Ohio. Tibby was working ten pots in 1873. In 1879 its operations covered four acres of ground and its number of pots had doubled. It employed 180 hands, paid them $4800 a month, and had annual sales of $180,000 — a remarkable record for a company specializing in bottles, vials, and druggists' wares. In April 1879 it filled an order for a Chicago customer — 700 gross of four-ounce drug bottles. The "rurals" could save money by "teaming," connecting their shops to a railroad line by spurs or sidings. Bryce, Higbee estimated that it saved $2000 a year by such jointure and $1000 a year in taxes by operating outside the city limits.*

The 1893 Tibby catalogue identifies five kinds of bottle lips, and it names fifty-three different bottles according to their function and shape, with accompanying pictures. Two standard flasks (Union and Shoo Fly) are advertised, but neither one is figured. Nevertheless, two statements about molds cause a collector to wonder: (1) "We give special attention to Private Moulds and are always glad to quote prices, whether we secure orders or not," and (2) "Iron moulds furnished at a cost from eight to thirty dollars." Many of the regular Tibby bottles undoubtedly could be furnished with lettering.

The *Rochester Tumbler Company* was established in 1872 in Rochester, Pennsylvania, twenty-five miles northwest of Pittsburgh at the confluence of the Ohio and Beaver rivers. The main administrative and sales office was strategically located in Pittsburgh, the hub of nineteenth-century glassmaking. Too little has been written about the Rochester Tumbler Company, which was among the first to take the risk of specializing in the mass production of one product (tumblers) and to make all its manufacturing operations self-sustaining. It scored outstanding successes in both respects.

It was a cooperative undertaking guided by fourteen top men, six of them from the J. B. Lyon works. Henry C. Fry, the company's first president, had been an employee of Phillips & Company before the Civil War, had failed in two later ventures, and had become superintendent of Lyon's O'Hara factory in 1869. Glassmen had hardly dared to specialize, preferring to hedge and vary their products, but Fry, besides being a personable executive and an astute employer, was an innovator. His sole product was pressed tumblers. In its first years of production, the company made 120 different styles of tumblers and turned out 200,000 pieces every six days.

Rochester received both a commendation and a medal at the Centennial. By 1877 the company had developed nearly 300 different patterns, and other firms were beginning to learn it was more profitable to buy their particular patterns from Fry than to manufacture them in their own factories.

The plant covered two and a half acres with twelve structures. The main building contained two ten-pot furnaces with a capacity of 4000 pounds of glass at a melt. The working force quickly grew from 175 to 310. The company had its own sawmill and shop for fabricating shipping boxes and a machine shop for making molds and repairing tools and machinery. The workmen fashioned the pots of Missouri clay, Fry having adopted it in place of the German clay first used. A Ragot Patent Furnace for making gas from coal was replaced by two gas wells on the property (see page 45).*

* *The Crockery and Glass Journal,* September 25, 1879.

* Sources of material on Rochester Tumbler Company: *The Crockery and Glass Journal,* August 26, September 16, October 14 and 21, December 23 and 30, 1875; May

THE ROCHESTER TUMBLER COMPANY.

OFFICE, 231 LIBERTY STREET,   **·   ·   ·**   **PITTSBURGH, Pa.**

Works at Rochester, Penn.

MANUFACTURERS OF TUMBLERS EXCLUSIVELY.

We Make all the Well-Known Styles of

TABLE & BAR TUMBLERS,

COMPRISING

More than 175 Different Patterns.

Our Goods are the Recognized STANDARD among the Trade and are Sold by Leading Houses both for Home and Export Trade.

Capacity of Works, 200,000 Tumblers every Six Days.

Fry managed to avoid three of the common complaints of labor: seasonal layoffs, night work, and irregularity of payment. He paid his men in acceptable currency every two weeks, choosing Tuesday — not Saturday — as payday to avoid Blue Monday absenteeism and to help his workmen save their money by staying away from the weekend bars. He resolved to have only daylight hours of work so that employees would have time for study and self-improvement. Workmen could count on fifty weeks of work every year; the company gave continuous employment except for six weeks in 1873. Fry insisted that there was no

need for harsh discipline in his plants, but when a wave of strikes disrupted the industry and the economy, he dismissed forty-two of his men who belonged to labor organizations and expressed an unalterable determination to engage no union men.

Fry was not averse to taking as manager the same action his forty-two men had taken as employees. On July 1, 1876 — a depression year — his company and A. J. Beatty & Sons of Steubenville issued a joint statement:

All old lists and special prices are hereby cancelled. On or after this date new price lists *without any favored prices* will be published. Common one-third and one-half pint tumblers have been too low. Our factories, the bulk of whose products are tumblers, have united to set a modest advance to cover costs. Hitherto no real value has been fixed. With agents

18, November 16, 1876; July 5, August 3, September 27, December 13 and 20, 1877; August 15, 1878; June 29, September 4 and 11, 1879; December 14, 1882; January 26, 1884; December 1, 1887; January 19, 1888.

and customers making their own prices they have demoralized trade and destroyed confidence.

Fry and Beatty predicted that chimney manufacturers would follow the same course and make a combine.

The Fry-Beatty strategy and returning good times had a beneficial result. A third furnace was added and the company was turning out 25,000-dozen tumblers per week and was shipping 50,000 packages yearly. Such success required an active sales force, and Rochester devoted more time, study, and money to the development of foreign trade than any other firm in the Tri-State area. In 1879 a salesman spent six months in Australia, where he was given large orders by reason of the excellence and superior styles of the wares. Sales records show orders from South America, Canada, the West Indies, Japan, Germany, and the British Isles. The company in 1879 filled its eight hundredth order for Great Britain.

The Rochester Tumbler Company added a new department in 1888 for the exclusive manufacture of blown flint tumblers. The addition of an eleven-pot furnace brought the total to five furnaces with fifty-seven pots and a working force of 600. It was the largest factory of its kind in the world. A rival, John Oesterling of the Central Glass Company in Wheeling, praised their pressed workmanship: "They were as thin as a sheet of paper and as clear as crystal, also destitute of any mold mark."* Some pressed tumblers after a good fire polishing could also put modern collectors on the wrong track, so we should not assume that all Rochester tumblers looked like conventional pressed pieces.

In 1899 Rochester joined eighteen factories to form the National Glass Company of Pittsburgh, a rival cartel to the U.S. Glass Company. Henry C. Fry became its first president.

* The Crockery and Glass Journal, February 22, 1877.

The Mold Makers

A necessary auxiliary to a large, growing, and healthy glass-producing center is the presence of mold-making companies. In the first quarter of the century, when free-blowing and pattern-molding were predominant, a few stronger factories set up modest mold-making departments. Ordinary factories, on the other hand, bought their molds or borrowed or swapped them. The popularity of pressed glass after 1850 and the competition to catch public favor forced the large factories to include fairly adequate mold departments. McKee, Adams, Lyon, Duncan, Atterbury, and others would have been severely handicapped without an opportunity to produce their own designs and, better yet, to keep them secret until they could be advertised. By 1875 the demand for new patterns had become so great that firms had to have much of the work done by outside shops. In 1860, even before this increased demand for pressed glass, five metal-mold shops were working under 334 male hands, turning out a product valued at more than $100,000.

Washington Beck, the most famous of the foundry owners and probably better known throughout the world for his inventions than any other Pittsburgh glassman, shipped molds and presses to Canada, to all the European glassmaking countries, and even to Japan. Awarded nine patents in his field, he seems to have been more honored abroad than at home, for it is next to impossible to find much source material on him.

Pittsburgh supported two other mold-making concerns — Andrew Thompson & Company and P. Smith & Company on First Avenue near Wood Street. Single mold makers, often unrecorded, plied their trade among Pittsburgh factories. Henry Franz, located at 1908 Wharton Street, was listed in the Pittsburgh City Directories from 1872–1889 as a "Mould-maker." Late in 1889 the firm of Franz & Braun at 69 South 20th Street made flint and bottle glass molds. In the East, Homer Brooke at 38 Vesey Street in New York seemed to have more extensive patronage than A.

Walters and Anthony Kribs, both companies in Brooklyn, and Charles Yockel in Philadelphia. In 1884, Stephen Hipkins, Jr., an experienced mold maker, opened a factory at Martins Ferry, Ohio. His mold shop soon became the largest in the Midwest. All these men pretty well controlled the manufacture of molds and presses.

When business conditions began to improve around 1878, Midwestern mold makers and press manufacturers were pushed to the limit. Washington Beck contracted to furnish five presses for a factory at Wheeling, was at work on three for McKee, and shipped four iron presses to manufacturers in France of the same model he had supplied to Gillinder & Sons in Philadelphia. P. Smith & Company was filling orders from California, Illinois, and New Jersey. By 1886, improved working methods had reduced the number of hands in Pittsburgh's four surviving mold-making factories to seventy, though the value of the product had risen to almost $175,000. When we relate a single mold to the relatively few specimens normally pressed into it before it was discarded, the mold and its maker take on a great significance in the industry. The concentration of mold-making establishments in Pittsburgh indicates clearly how designs must have originated there and circulated not only in the Midwestern Tri-State region but throughout the country as well.

The slow and costly manufacture of a mold usually followed this sequence: make a plaster of paris or wooden mold, decide on the number of parts and how they will fit together, and produce an iron cast of the mold in all its model parts. (At this time cast iron or steel was being used for pressed glass.) The design might be on the plunger; if it was on the mold itself and was not too elaborate, it might be engine-turned. The delicate traceries and details of lacy glass were chipped by hand on the mold — a long, painstaking, and expensive process. The parts of the mold, from two to twelve in number, were interconnected by powerful hinges.

We should always think in terms of three or more molds in use, rather than one. While one mold was in operation, another was being heated and one was being cooled. Pressing machines seemed to be of two sizes — one for pieces of glass put together from two parts pressed separately, such as lamps, candlesticks, vases, and compotes, and one from much larger single pieces.

Mechanical and Design Patents

An obvious way to determine regional glass activity is to examine records of the U.S. Patent Office. After the disastrous fire at the Patent Office in 1836 we have a good picture of what was happening in the glass industry. In 1842 and thereafter, patents were differentiated as mechanical and design. A mechanical patent ran for seventeen years; a design patent for three and a half, seven, or fourteen years. Design patents for glass were not used widely until the sixties, probably because the restricted patent time could be short and because a slight alteration in the design enabled the pirating firm to escape litigation.

Many mechanical patents embodied very slight changes and improvements. Each new one generated others. Any student of the Patent Office is immediately impressed by the number of patents from Pittsburgh and by the quality and importance of each advance. No comparable concentration of glass patents exists for any other American locality.

Several key patents were related to the operation of the press. W. O. Davis, superintendent of the J. B. Lyon factory, registered two. The first, registered on January 31, 1854, controlled the direction of force by means of the side lever and a toggle joint. The second, on August 25, 1863, assured a vertical movement of a steam-operated piston, the rod, and the plunger. Thus a troublesome unevenness in the lip of tumblers and like pieces would be avoided. In 1864 Frederick Mc-Kee and Charles Ballinger worked out the use of steam as applied to the piston rod of the plunger

18 This amber stopper mold embodies the principle of pressing ten stoppers at once. In order not to waste glass, the matrix was made into a usable bowl (right). 1850–1870. *Stopper: 2½". Wadsworth Atheneum, Hartford, Edith Olcott van Gerbig Collection.*

so that the rod could rise while the plunger remained still. Jonathan Haley devised a reciprocating plunger that would adapt itself automatically to variations in the quantity of glass in the mold (May 13, 1873). Washington Beck's patent on May 4, 1875, perfected the steam press by using atmospheric pressure in combination with a movable plunger. Water from condensation in pipes previously had caused an unevenness of timing in the stroke of the plunger. This had injured molds and produced imperfect pieces. Beck's patent promised a regularity of plunger stroke.

Though William Gillinder was based in Philadelphia, his patented blowpipe should be mentioned for its relation to the plunger. Registered on December 5, 1865, the patent claims the blowpipe would aid in making articles with press-molded handles. The tool combined the functions of blowpipe, plunger, and snap clamp. The workman could press a blank and blow it into a desired shape in one operation.

Molds, of course, were important to the operation of pressing. In the early years of pressing they probably were discarded when the scale could not be cleaned and when the hinges became worn. Washington Beck, Henry Feurhake, and William Wuth patented four methods for cleaning molds (October 28 and November 13, 1879). In September of the same year Beck and Feurhake patented an "Improvement in Processes of Preparing Glass Molds." This patent contains a thorough discussion of treating molds for the various steps in the different ways of etching and

19 D. C. Ripley's patent, Mar. 17, 1868. Pressed top
and handle to be applied to the blown body.

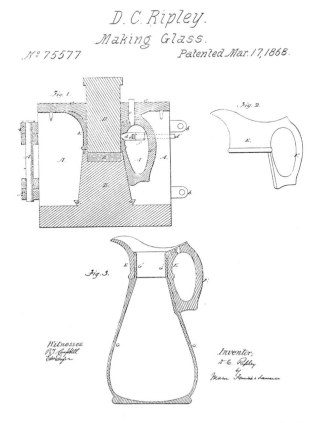

D. C. Ripley.
Making Glass.
Nº 75577 *Patented Mar. 17, 1868.*

ornamenting glass. (A detailed study of this
patent appears in part two, chapter seventeen.)

Manufacturers, however, were more interested
in increasing production than in the niceties of
decoration. Hiram Dillaway of Massachusetts
pointed one way in which the mold could help: a
ten-stopper mold patented May 21, 1841. The
stoppers were connected radially to a flat matrix.
Years later, Daniel C. Ripley of Pittsburgh
formed the matrix into a bowl so that there would
be no wasted glass when the stoppers were broken
off. Ripley also devised a mold that would press
three articles at once: a lamp handle, a lamp foot,
and a glass stopper (October 20, 1868). He
registered another patent for pressing the top of a
pitcher in a mold and then attaching it to a blown
base. The Atterbury brothers and James Reddick

improved on that by showing how pressing and
blowing could be accomplished in one operation
(June 30, 1868). Five years later they perfected
their own patent (June 17, 1873). Philip Arbogast registered a similar method in 1882.

William King of the Cascade Glass Company
carried Dillaway's patent in another direction. In
his 1871 patent application for "Improvement in
Machines for Operating Glass Molds," he ex-
plains:

My invention consists in the construction of a revolving block, carrying a number of glass molds, and
certain devices for revolving such a block so as to
bring and hold the molds consecutively in such position that a plunger, operating in connection with such
devices, shall descend therein and form an article of
glass-ware, and of certain devices for delivering the
article after it is formed.

By December 1872, King added two improvements that allowed flexibility in tipping and tilt-
ing. The principle of the revolving block carrying
a number of glass molds foretold mechanized production.

David Barker patented a way in which the
same mold could be used for different designs
(June 3, 1879). Working with a mold without a
design, he constructed it so that it could hold print
blocks for figure ornament on the outer side of the
ware. Such print blocks were removable or interchangeable, but the same mold could always be
used.

Another revealing phase of patent development
centered on the making of a pressed lamp in one
operation. Thomas Bakewell Atterbury, James
Seaman Atterbury, and James Reddick accounted
for the important steps in joining base and font:
the Atterbury Eureka lamp on September 29,
1868, and the Atterbury Boss lamp on August 29,
1876. D. C. Ripley and John Adams contributed
greatly to the efficiency of lamp-making with related and basic patents. The Atterburys, however, deserve the attention.

Arthur G. Peterson of De Bary, Florida, who

20 J. S. & T. B. Atterbury's patent, June 30, 1868. It formed in one operation a glass lamp (or other piece) with a blown body and pressed handle.

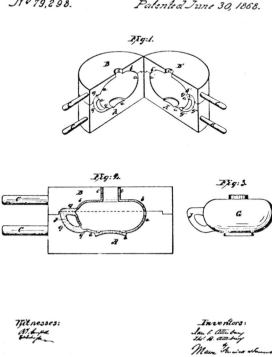

has made extensive studies of patent records, writes that the Atterburys could claim 110 different patents. One patent, June 1868, No. 79,298 (*20*), facilitated blowing and pressing of bowl and handle in one operation (in one mold), lessening the need for hand manipulation and reducing cost. They devised a mold with the lower portion for pressing and the upper for blowing. The purpose was to make and protect ornamental designs or figures between two plain surfaces of lamp pegs (bowls). Since the inner and the outer surfaces were smooth, "no chance exists for dirt to fill in the ornaments nor of the fluid in the vessels destroying the effects on the eyes. . . . Therefore articles less difficult to clean are produced at less expense." Thomas Atterbury also designed a pedestal for a lamp or stemmed glass-

ware. It consisted of a woman's head and shoulders suitably draped. Gossip thought she might be Jenny Lind, but she resembles more the Goddess of Liberty. This pedestal never caught public fancy as much as Ripley's Bride's or Marriage Lamp.

Even today the Ripley Marriage Lamp (June 4, 1870) is eagerly sought (*21*). It is a double font lamp: "a mold having a central cavity for the insertion of a center piece stock or stem and two or more side communicating cavities in which to blow simultaneously onto such centerpiece. . . . a corresponding number of lamp bowls." Between the two bowls a round cavity can hold matches. The lamp offers various color combinations: opaque blue fonts, connecting panel and match holder of clam water color, and base of opaque glossy white. The Marriage Lamp in principle followed Ripley's patent (February 1, 1870) of a stem or base for various articles of glassware that was suitable for use as a candlestick. A week later he registered a baptismal font using this base with two branching candlestick arms and a cuplike bowl in between for the baptismal water (*22*).

Pittsburgh glass manufacturers had as much at stake in making chimneys as in perfecting lamps. As early as 1861 Edward Dithridge of the Fort Pitt Glass Company patented an oval lamp chimney. The elliptical body was elongated and the bottom edge flattened to rest firmly on and to be locked to the burner. From this patent manufacturers could foresee sales value by varying shapes and in crimping or pearling the tops. Within fifteen years one chimney factory advertised forty different shapes for the plain unadorned lamp chimney. By 1875 both Adams and Atterbury were advertising molded or pressed chimneys, since pressing was more inexpensive than blowing. Atterbury's patent specified a seamless chimney. To avoid the handwork of crimping and final shaping of a chimney, three inventors patented mechanical flaring and crimping machines: T. Atterbury in November of 1875, Paul

21 Clam-water, pressed religious candlesticks with pewter sockets. Marked "Ripley & Co. Patnd Pending." Design Patent No. 3834, Feb. 1, 1870. H. 10⅞".
Collection of the author.

Ripley Marriage Lamp, opaque blue fonts with joining match holder in clam-water. Base shiny opaque white. Marked "Sept. 20, 1870." H. 12″ to top of lamps.
Collection of the author.

Zimmerman a few weeks later, and W. H. Maxwell in January of 1876.

Beside all the basic patents that advanced the industry technically, we should note two that might be called novelties. Actually, they were attempts to do in pressing what skilled workers carved by hand and by acid in cameo overlay. Benjamin Bakewell, Jr., patented a process called "Double Glass" on September 29, 1874. The large fruit bowl marked on the bottom "B. P. & Co. Patd. Sept. 29, 1874" shows that two layers of different colored glass could be fused by pressing.* The lower part of the bowl is a layer of fluted fiery opal. Out of this rises a clear inner layer to complete the piece. The Bakewells may have got the idea from an Atterbury and Reddick patent of March 4, 1862, which used two layers of glass like inner petals of a flower. The Atterbury technique of using two colors of glass fused became popular in their Three Graces, their Rock of Ages, and their Fish plates. Usually the center medallions are of opal or transparent blue glass. A. C. Revi calls them Atterbury's pressed cameo glass.

Glassmen were eager for increased efficiency and they obviously studied other patents assiduously. That is why so many different patents orbited about one process. Inventive changes also opened the way for independent, unattached workmen as well as for those employed by a single company. It was not uncommon for a man working at one factory to assign a patent to another company, which may have meant that he had been working on his own time with financial help from the outside. Charles Ballinger, for example, worked for McKee Brothers, David Barker for Crystal Glass, Feurhake for Washington Beck. Nothing prevented a Pittsburgher from selling his patent in another area or to another firm. J. Ernest Miller, a stalwart of the Duncan factory, sold at least one of his patents — a design

* Lowell Innes, "Pittsburgh White and Clear and the Bakewell Patent," *Antiques* 79, June 1961.

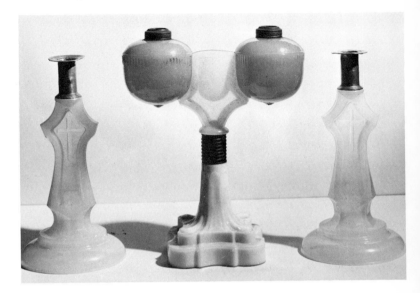

22 Ripley Baptismal Font in clam-water. This shows the ingenuity of using a candlestick stem for the shaft of a font. The cover for this font is missing. Design Patent No. 3954, marked "Feb. 1870." H. 13¾″ to top of candlestick arm. *Collection of the author.*

23 Four pieces of Star and Buckle showing an important step in manufacture. The same mold could be used for each one. In the case of the lamp and the spill holder, bases had to be added. Tops of the creamer, lamp and cruet had to be fashioned and shaped. 1865–1875. *Ex coll. John J. Grossman.*

of waved lines extending around the ware — to Sweeney, McCluney & Company of Wheeling.

No manufacturer, moreover, needed patent permission to use the same mold to produce different forms. Four pieces from the extensive and fine collection of Pittsburgh glass of the late John J. Grossman show the ingenuity of early pressed glass workers (*23*). The cruet shows clearly the original mold. The spill or spoon holder was sheared off and worked. The creamer had its top widened and the pouring lip drawn out after it was reheated. The font of the lamp was closed for the brass collar. Then the font was wafered to a standard base. The applied handles on cruet and creamer show that it was an early pattern even if we did not lift the pieces and ring them for lead content. A casual glance would identify the

pattern as Sandwich Star and Buckle. Stars in this mold carry seven points instead of Sandwich's eight. The Grossman pieces were found in the Pittsburgh area.

"Cut and Shut"

One technical device contributed greatly to the pressing of glass during the last quarter of the century — and to the confusion of collectors in our own time. Glassmakers called it "cut and shut." The three stages of the operation can be seen in the illustration of the pressed cruets from the Westmoreland Glass Company (*24*). The cruet is pressed upside-down with the plunger going through the knockout piece inside the top. After the cruet is pressed, it is snapped up on the bottom, and the top is warmed in, lipped, and finished. Then another warming-in boy holds the top in a specially made snap tool with a portion cut out to hold the handle and the rest to fit the snout. While it is held by this tool the bottom is warmed-in, closed, and finally cut shut (*24*).

In the case of a cruet, all the pressed patterns can be used, since, except for the work on the lip and cutting the bottom shut, the plunger and the mold belong to pressed glass technique. Any number of students, dealers, and collectors assume that such a cruet is blown, because the base usually shows a little depression, a small roughish knob, or what looks like the end of a curlicue. This abortive pontil mark has led to the misconception. An extensive study of cruets with pressed designs on the globular part will show evidence of cut and shut.

In an essay in the August 1936 *Hobbies,* J. Stanley Brothers, Jr., discussed this method of pressing an article that was smaller at the top than at the bottom.* He generalized that the plunger, always a cone and always smooth, had to be sent into the mold and withdrawn without difficulty. The large and heavy bar decanters, which reveal no mold seams, needed additional treatment. A cylinder — tapered wider from the top to the bottom — was inserted between the interior of the mold and the plunger, a requirement that became necessary in forming the shape of this particular type. The mold ring could be opened after the pressing, the cylinder removed, and then the article lifted out. Sometimes the pontil rod held pressed pieces for shaping or other work, so that the presence of a pontil mark is not an infallible sign of blown workmanship. The true test of that would be an examination of the inner surface, for in every blown molded piece there must be a concave-convex relationship as the molten glass follows designs in the mold.

A small amber toilet bottle pictured in the O'Hara, Ltd., catalogue, ca 1876, No. 500, was made by this method. Observing then the num-

* "Some Interesting Mechanics of the Glass Industry."

ber of pressed pieces in demand, in which the bottom was considerably larger than the top, upside-down pressing and cut and shut methods enabled glassworkers to form such pieces with efficiency. I doubt if a single factory or man has the sole right to claim this technique. O'Hara Glass Company, however, patented a fluted molasses can on November 2, 1876, that was obviously made by the cut and shut technique.

King, Son and Company also profited from the procedure, for in November of 1876 they spoke of a mold for a new fluted molasses can pressed in the same style as an O'Hara decanter. The neck of the can is upside-down and, of course, considerably smaller than the bowl. The plunger leaves the bottom open. It is stuck up and heated over. Finally the bottom is closed in by the finisher. A molasses can like this must not be confused with the Star and Concave piece shown in the 1860 Ringwalt catalogue (*332, 371*). The Star and Concave has been blown molded: this is shown by the softness of the lines and the indentations inside the can where the air pressure has forced the glass into the intaglio designs of the mold.

New Companies and Discoveries in Pressing 67

Patents multiplied for each important area of glass manufacture through the second half of the century. Some discoveries like Davis's side lever and toggle joint, Beck's perfecting of the steam press, King's revolving block, and Feurhake's granular mold surface were major advances. Though the improvements in many patents appear to be slight, the cumulative effect advanced the industry progressively. The results were improved quality, the production of glassware for all segments of the growing American market, and steadily lowered prices.

In 1854, diamond goblets sold for $2.33 a dozen. The price rose during the Civil War, but in 1874 the same goblet sold for 78 cents a dozen and in 1888 for 30 cents. The following table tells the story of relatively high initial prices, higher prices during wartime, and sharply reduced prices through postwar depression and boom. During the period shown, the industry made wage increases totaling 30 percent.

	1854	1864	1874	1880
Pressed saucers (dozen)	$ .40	$ .72	$ .25	$ .16
Tumblers (dozen)	.66	1.30	.55	.37
Wine glasses (dozen)	1.25	1.75	.50	.30
Lamp chimneys (dozen)	1.75	3.25	.50	.24
Window glass (boxes of 50 feet)	3.50	3.75	—	1.80

The lesson of all this to the glass scholar and serious collector is not the miracle of the American competitive system nor the certification of Pittsburgh as the center of the nineteenth-century glass trade. It is, rather, what these findings show us about the glass itself. Study of patents and of company histories establishes dates for pattern popularity and throws a revealing light on how glass was made, decorated, and marketed.

CHAPTER VI

"Half the Glass in America"

"As nearly as can be ascertained one-half of the glass factories in the United States are located at Pittsburgh, where there are forty firms engaged in the manufacture of glass, who run sixty factories producing the various descriptions of green, window, flint and lime glass, employing over four thousand workmen, and producing between four and five millions' worth of glass."
— William H. Egle, *An Illustrated History of the Commonwealth of Pennsylvania,* 1876

The Great Fire of April 1845, started by a washerwoman who left her fire unattended, destroyed one third of the city of Pittsburgh and two thirds of its wealth. Twenty squares of the city's most valuable property — fifty-six acres containing nearly 1000 buildings — were ruined. The Bakewell factory was lost. Once before, in 1840, Bakewell's had been closed in a period of financial stringency. After the 1845 fire they relocated on the South Side, long a center of Pittsburgh glass manufacturing.

In a curious sequence, Dr. David Alter, a physician, chemist, physicist, and inventor "of inquiring and ingenious mind," salvaged a piece of flint glass from the Bakewell ruins and from it ground a prism. He used the prism in conducting experiments in spectrum analysis that led in 1853 to what is known in physics as Kirchoff's Second Law.*

One of the structures destroyed by the fire was

* Thomas C. Pears, Jr., "The First Successful Flint Glass Factory in America," *Antiques* 11, March 1927. Anders Angstrom made the same discovery in Sweden independently and almost simultaneously. Alter's prism is in Pittsburgh's Carnegie Museum.

the Monongahela House, Pittsburgh's finest and most famous hotel, built only five years earlier. A new and even better hotel was erected on the same site, overlooking the Monongahela River at the northwest corner of Smithfield and Water streets. Colonel Crossan, the proprietor, developed a flourishing trade in tourists and commercial travelers. Rooms cost from $2.50 a day, and all guests were entitled to the same fare (in the vernacular of the trade, were "fed the same"). Six Presidents stayed there, including Lincoln on the way to his first inauguration, and Henry Clay, King Edward VII as Prince of Wales, and Jenny Lind. Manufacturers and businessmen met there in emergency session in June 1863, during the Gettysburg campaign, and agreed to suspend business operations and put their employees to erecting defenses against the expected assault from Confederate forces.

The Monongahela House was the regional center for trade exhibits, fairs, salesrooms, and banquets throughout sixty years of the century. We are apt to think of manufacturers and drummers staying at a hotel only two or three days, but in the 1870s and 1880s they stayed for weeks and often for a month. John Dobson, active in the glass trade in Baltimore, said that the Monongahela House appointments were far ahead of anything he saw at Delmonico's in New York. Since the offices of many Pittsburgh glasshouses were nearby, the hotel served as a focus for the Western Pennsylvania glass trade.

Probably the largest exhibition at the Monongahela House took place in July 1889, when twenty-four glasshouses showed their wares: eleven from Pittsburgh, eleven from Ohio, one from Maryland, and one from Indiana.* After a fire in December 1889, the hotel was refurbished, but unfortunately it never seemed to regain its former glory.

The U.S. Potters Association held its second annual banquet there on January 6, 1876, with officers from the Western Flint and Lime Glass Protective Association present for the first time as honored guests. The menu was Lucullan and the toasts were both eloquent and numerous. John Adams, president of the Glass Association, offered the second regular toast: "The Glass Manufacturers as a kindred art." He gave the statistics of his industry and declared that the interests of the two associations were identical — in customers, in tariff problems, and in the vagaries and injustices of the bankruptcy law. The third regular toast was drunk to "Our Organ," *The Crockery and Glass Journal,* and the fourth to "Our brethren in England and elsewhere — as honorable competitors we respect them, but in their efforts to evade the legal and honest payment of duties they deserve censure and forfeit our respect."

At the other end of the state, Philadelphia had been bustling with preparations for its International Centennial Exposition marking the one hundredth anniversary of the founding of the Republic (see chapter nineteen). Pittsburgh industrialists decided to precede it with a fair of their

* *The Crockery and Glass Journal* wrote on July 24, 1890: "Everyone is talking about the display of rich colored glassware shown at the Monongahela House by the Northwood Glass Company of Martins Ferry, Ohio, and that of the Buckeye Glass Company."

own. The Pittsburgh Industrial Institute held a monthlong exposition in October–November 1875, with premiums totaling $50,000 in value — the largest, reported *The Crockery and Glass Journal* (September 30, 1875), "ever offered at any first exposition ever held in America." The Pennsylvania Railroad put up 50,000 posters at its own expense along its road and advertised excursion tickets at half rates. The Pittsburgh *Herald* revealed that merchants from all the other great cities would visit the fair. When J. S. Keating, chairman of reservations, received more than 150 acceptances from editors, a large press room and telegraph office were set up.

A building 150 feet wide and 600 feet deep was erected in an incredibly short time at the remarkably low cost of $50,000. From the outside it resembled a large watering-place hotel, appearing from its rows of windows to be three stories high. Within it was a single enormous hall with a broad gallery on all four sides, where were shown extensive displays by 372 exhibitors. Products of a city known for its heavy industry were prominent: sheet iron, tin plate, forgings, block coal, tools, boilers, steam engines, pneumatic gas machines, firebrick, ore crushers, a steam hammer, a breech-loading cannon, and gunpowder. Some of the other exhibits — fire hydrants, burglar alarms, squeeze washing machines, a mechanical writing machine, photographic equipment, and a water elevator — foreshadowed an approach to the conveniences of the twentieth century. Pittsburgh had long been known for its whiskey, segars and segar boxes, and these were displayed handsomely, as were products for which it was becoming known: vinegars, celery sauce, and tomato catsup (soon to be renamed ketchup).

One week before the exposition was to open, *The Crockery and Glass Journal* warned, "The Wheeling glassmen will . . . make a desperate attempt to carry off Pittsburgh's glass trade. It behooves our glass men to stir themselves and throw off their apathy toward the aims and ends of the Exposition and take the place that rightfully belongs to them." The Wheeling companies apparently did not exhibit at all, but close to seventy other glasshouses in the area displayed their wares. Those from Pittsburgh proper included:

Bakewell, Pears and Company, glassware
Evans, Sell and Company, lamp chimneys
Excelsior Flint Glass Company, flint glass
King Son and Company, glassware
McCully and Company, window glass and glassware
O'Hara Glass Company, pressed glass
Richards and Hartley Glass Company, crystal tableware
Thomas Wightman and Company, glass and glassware.

These companies represented glass specialties:

John T. Gray, glass signs
L. E. Haid, ornamental glass signs
S. S. Marshall and Brother, stained glass in sash
Lampell and Coutrie, fancy glass blowers
Charles Mathews, Mexico, N.Y., fancy glass blowers
W. W. Barker, picture and looking glass frames
J. J. Gillespie, mirrors and decorations.

One Pittsburgh company, E. D. Weyburn, listed as a manufacturer and dealer, was praised for such a variety of wares that one must conclude that it commissioned some of its pieces; otherwise it would have held an important position in the industrial history of Pittsburgh glass. Weyburn is little known as a manufacturer, though he did register a patent on February 14, 1878, for a bottle stopper that would fit any bottle. The Pittsburgh *Daily Post* wrote on October 20, 1875:

In the glassware department, Messrs E. D. Weyburn & Co., of No 90 Smithfield Street, display the line of goods which they manufacture and deal in. Their stock in general consist of lamps, oils, and lampgoods, together with fine cut engraved, decorated and pressed flint and foreign glassware. They also make a specialty of table glassware and fancy bottles, goblets, etc. for bars. Their display embraces some

of the finest specimens of glassware to be seen at the Exposition, and they will run a lively tilt with all competitors in this line.

The *Post* also praised J. J. Gillespie, a firm long known to and patronized by Pittsburghers. Their embellishment of the exhibition consisted of "marble mantels, pier glass, a large parlor window, and pictures from their gallery adorning the walls."

Fires and Floods

A constant hazard of fire always faced glass manufacturers. In July 1878, the Ihmsen Glass Company lost $8000 through fire originating in the straw of the packing room. The Doyle factory burned soon afterward at a loss of $10,000. Fortunately the firm was well covered by insurance. In April 1879, fire destroyed the Cunningham and Company blowing house and so weakened the main cupola that it fell. The damage threw eighty men and boys out of work and caused a loss estimated at $10,000. In May the Alexander King factory was almost leveled, at a loss estimated at $75,000. Insurance rates on glasshouses were particularly high. Perhaps that is why the Phoenix plant at Philipsburg was insured for only $80,000. When the factory burned in 1884 the owners claimed a loss of $130,000, not even reckoning the $100,000 or more in business that would be lost.

Consequently glass manufacturers at Pittsburgh took it very hard in 1884 when the Monongahela and the Allegheny rivers swelled into the worst flood since 1832. It seemed unfair that nature, too, should conspire against them. Sixth Street became navigable, and boats also plied on Penn Avenue up Wood Street to First. For thirty-six hours the only communication between Allegheny City and Pittsburgh was by way of the Fort Wayne Railroad Bridge. At Oakmont near the Hulton Bridge, the Agnew Company escaped. Across the river but much nearer Pittsburgh, Tibby's at Sharpsburg was badly damaged, and J.

T. and A. Hamilton shut down. William McCully also suspended work. Atterbury's slight loss of $500 was hardly comparable to Abel, Smith and Company's $2000 and McKee's $10,000, losses serious blows to each. A. & D. H. Chambers was completely submerged, as were the Pittsburgh Clay Pot factory and the Rochester Tumbler Works. Wightman's was only half covered. Apparently King and Son, Bryce, Ripley, and Ihmsen escaped.

The Great Pittsburgh Glass Show

The Pittsburgh Exposition Society, founded in 1875 to provide a center for the exhibition of Pittsburgh goods, built several large halls on Killbuck Island at the mouth of the Allegheny River and then, in 1889, an enormous Exposition Hall along the Allegheny at the Point. The new hall was a tremendous success, entering into the social and commercial life of the area to a degree hard to comprehend today. Pittsburgh glass manufacturers had not made full use of the earlier buildings and were chided for indifference to the opportunity for display. Ripley and Company constructed an ingenious model building 15 by 12 by 16 feet high entirely of saltcellars for the 1889 fall fair, but it was apparently the only glass company present.

The attitude changed when the new hall went up. A Glass Manufacturers Exhibit Company — an incorporated concern — was formed.* The group wished the public to see and understand all phases of glass production, not merely to look at finished articles; and to that end they erected, on the river side of the hall, over an area of almost 3000 square feet, a full-scale operating glassworks. It boasted an eight-pot melting furnace, two glory holes, an annealing oven extending thirty-five feet, gas for fuel, wide aisles for public viewing, and the region's first stack built with

locally made enameled firebrick. (Heretofore all enameled firebrick used in Western Pennsylvania had been imported from England.) The plant was operated in such a manner as to show the product of each of the glasshouses involved.* Viewers watched every step of manufacture: filling the melting furnace pots with the batch; gathering, molding and pressing; blowing bottles and chimneys and fashioning novelties; annealing the finished pieces in the lehr; cutting; engraving; and readying the finished pieces for the sales counter. The public was advised that the cutting and engraving machines could be used for made-to-order designs, names, mottoes, or personal sentiments promptly executed on purchased pieces.

A pamphlet on the Pittsburgh Exposition described these marvels, and *The Crockery and Glass Journal* added its praise, declaring that the glassworks attracted more attention than anything else shown, with thousands of fascinated spectators seeing the inside of a glassworks for the first time.† All did not go smoothly, however, for the men refused to work on Saturday afternoons. The managers explained that Saturday was the time of largest attendance, that the plant was both a public and an industry benefit in education and advertising, and that it was not being run for profit — indeed, they expected to lose money. The men replied that the other glass factories were shut down on Saturday afternoons, and that was that.

The success of the Exposition Glass Works led the way to an annual glass exhibition; it in turn became the famous Pittsburgh Glass and Pottery Show, set up each year primarily for company

---

* D. C. Ripley was president, Thomas Evans was secretary, and R. E. Woods treasurer. Directors were Ripley, Evans, Woods, A. A. Adams, George A. MacBeth, Paul Zimmerman, James Duncan, and J. T. Hamilton.

* The companies operating the Exposition Glass Works were Ripley, Adams, George Duncan, Thomas Evans, George A. MacBeth, Dithridge, and J. T. & A. Hamilton. Dixon, Woods Company, contractors and builders of glasshouse furnaces and supplies, erected and completed the glassworks in every detail.

† Gillinder had set up a similar demonstration at the Philadelphia Centennial. The success of two such glassworks undoubtedly inspired the Libbey model plant at the Columbian Exposition in 1892 and the National Glass Company plant at Buffalo in 1903.

buyers and manufacturers' agents, some of whom stayed in the city as long as five or six weeks of each year to conduct their business. Pittsburgh was a most strategic location for both pottery and glass, and the yearly exhibit survived as an industrial institution past the middle of the twentieth century.

Pittsburgh at its Peak

Joseph D. Weeks, a special agent of the federal government, came to Pittsburgh in the late 1870s to assess the glass industry there for the 1880 census. A rule of thumb estimate had been made every ten years from 1790 on, but his 1880 assessment, drawn up with the full cooperation of the city's glass industrialists, was more accurate and more nearly complete than any of its predecessors. His *Report on the Manufacture of Glass* really sums up a century of American glass manufacturing.

The Weeks findings clearly established Pittsburgh and Allegheny County as the country's most important nineteenth-century glass manufacturing center. He wrote:

Pennsylvania stands first as a producer of glass in the United States, its percentage in value being more than three times that of any other state. About 65 per cent of this amount is credited to Allegheny County. . . . At present census . . . Allegheny County stands first as a glass making center.

No other county was treated with as much detail, and no other county could show a comparable growth. In 1880, Allegheny County contained virtually one fourth (24.17 percent) of the nation's glass establishments of all kinds. It had 27.6 percent of all the glass capital invested. It was producing 26.8 percent in value of the nation's glass products.

Weeks paid an ultimate compliment when he drew up comparisons of the formulas used in different countries and allowed Pittsburgh to stand for the United States' formula. His main headings read:

Window glass	Pittsburgh	French	English	
Flint (lead)	Pittsburgh	English	French	
Flint (lime)	Pittsburgh	Bohemian	French	
Bottle	Pittsburgh	French	English	Belgian

For the entire country, Weeks listed 211 separate glass establishments divided like this: 58 window glass, 56 green glass (bottles, hollow ware, druggists' ware), 91 glassware (pressed and luxury table glass) and 6 plate glass. He listed 51 glass establishments for Allegheny County divided this way: 12 window glass, 9 green glass, and 30 glassware. The 51 factories operated 85 furnaces, 797 pots, and in 1880 produced glass to the value of $5,668,212. They employed 6053 persons, including 4442 males over sixteen, 141 females over fifteen, and 1470 "children and youths." They paid $2,686,425 in wages.

Surprisingly, the greatest growth in the industry had come, not in window glass and bottles, but in tableware. Window glass had been around 70 percent of the total national output of glass earlier in the century; now it had fallen to 24 percent. Tableware had been only 5 percent; now it was 45 percent. Bottle production had remained relatively about the same. Shaping and finishing bottles and tableware demanded more labor and less capital per worker than window glass. Their factories employed twice as many workmen as did the window factories.

Despite labor trouble and strikes, the glass business was booming in the year Weeks made his researches and wrote his report. Bakewell, Pears revealed that its orders were more plentiful than they had been for the past five years. Between November 1878 and September 1879, Atterbury added fifteen hands, Adams fifty, and Doyle ninety-five. Pittsburgh's South Side factories were now all connected with their jobbers by telephone, and railroad spurs had been placed beside the loading docks. Workmen were clamoring for no break between spring and fall trade — an indication that the industry had moved toward a full year of work.

The Pittsburgh factories were operating nationally. An ordinary company like Richards and Hartley had salesrooms in Boston, Philadelphia, New York, Baltimore, and Montreal. The Baltimore firm of George and Johnson, manufacturers' agents in glass and earthenware, advertised for six factories: O'Hara Glass Company Ltd.; King, Son and Company; Campbell, Jones; Adams; Plunkett; and Challinor, Hogan. O'Hara Glass Works ran ads in New York and Philadelphia, and one of its partners was sent to take charge of the Boston Sample Room. The Chicago room had to be content with a general agent. (*The Crockery and Glass Journal* for July 27, 1876, reported that a prominent South Side glass manufacturer had the entire detective force of Buffalo looking for his agent, who "so far has sold $50 worth of glass, spent $200, and has been having a high old time for almost two weeks.")

Pittsburgh not only extended its glassmaking activities into communities around the city; its capital was available for factories in more distant Midwestern towns: New Brighton, Beaver Falls, Philipsburg, Massillon, and Steubenville. These were sending in encouraging reports of brisk trade.

The city's glass manufacturers had always worked the foreign markets, but now they were doing so with added skill and thoroughness. South America proved a rich territory — witness the bread plate produced by Campbell, Jones, with the inscription "Give us this day" in Spanish. *The Crockery and Glass Journal* announced on July 3, 1879, that it would produce a Spanish-American edition of 5000 copies.

Labor Trouble

The last quarter of the century was marked throughout the nation by strikes and frequently by violence. The glass industry in Pittsburgh, though it escaped the excesses of labor-management strife, was a part of that pattern.

Glass production, prices, and profits declined in the 1873–1879 depression. In June 1875, the Western Flint and Lime Glass Protective Association (organized the year before) unanimously resolved "that it would be advisable to stop production for two months during the summer." The curtailment, the Association felt, would reduce stock by at least $400,000 and enable member-manufacturers to get better prices when the fall trade opened. The move intensified the already strained relations between owners and workers and led to some fifteen years of intermittent strikes, lockouts, work slowdowns, and dismissals for union activity.

The immediate goal of nine tenths of the men was shorter hours at the same or better pay, but there were other related issues. The workers, union and nonunion, complained of uncertain periods of employment, of frequent shutdown of furnaces, and of the increased use of labor-saving machinery. They looked with disfavor on European workers who were skilled but who accepted lower wages. Union workers complained of the unwillingness of owners to deal with all-union representatives and of the owners' unwillingness to allow workers a voice in selection of the molds.

The Crockery and Glass Journal for October 24, 1878, reported the bitterness on the capitalists' side. Manufacturers felt aggrieved that unions claimed the right to dictate to employers who should be hired and fired. Relations of employer and employee are well defined: one pays, the other works: "We fail to see where the worker acquires the right to issue orders to the man who furnishes him the means of living in return for his labor. . . . We are not ready to surrender the control of our business affairs into the hands of Communists and Socialists."

The manufacturers pointed out that they were now paying out 43 percent of the value of glass in wages, and a reduction in number of turns (moves)* would further increase their costs. No branch of labor, they said, was better paid than glassworkers, and no glassworkers were better paid than those in Pittsburgh. Ordinary laborers

* A move lasts six hours.

frequently received twice as much as laborers in other comparable factory operations, and a truly skilled man might earn one-third to two-thirds more than those skilled in other crafts.* The number of working months were being lengthened, so that only six to eight weeks in the summer were now inactive. The twelve-hour day had been shrinking since 1840, and from 1870 on, three skilled blowers and four helpers were assigned to each pot. Piece-rate wages, greater specialization, and more healthful working conditions were stabilizing the industry. Nevertheless, flint glass workers wanted the number of turns reduced from eleven to nine.

As early as 1873, a local union of window-glass manufacturers had engineered a small but troublesome strike. Discontent reached a peak in January 1877, and ten of nineteen Pittsburgh factories were idle. By August the window-glass strike had swept the country and three quarters of the seventy-five factories had closed, putting more than 25,000 men and boys out of work.

A strike of chimney workers called in October 1877 was long and painful, lasting twenty-one months. The new crimping machine triggered it. Normally a workman would make 250 chimneys at a turn (six hours). With the crimper he could readily make 500. Though hands were willing to use the machine, they rebelled at making more than 250 unless they were given an increase in pay for the additional chimneys. The manufacturers refused because this would prevent them from increasing production and keeping costs down. Factories making pressed tableware leaned over backwards to help the strikers. Blowers at the Crystal Glass Works struck because the company had a large order for lantern globes. The men considered this an infringement on the chimney strikers.

According to the terms of the settlement, the wage rate was set at $1.83 a turn, a slight reduction; workmen would make 300 chimneys in a turn; and eight instead of six men would make up

* Scoville, *Revolutions in Glassmaking,* pp. 30, 33.

a shop (one working team). Both the patent crimper and the opener could be used. Results were that owners reduced their manufacturing costs better than 35 percent; Pittsburgh kept its supremacy in lamp chimneys; and in the post-strike rush to fill back orders, blowers were earning $3.66 a day — an increase of $3 for the six-day week.

When a strike of the Glass Pressers Union (that is, the workers in tableware) was threatened, *The Crockery and Glass Journal* warned that any extended work stoppage would also hit producers of coal, sand, soda ash, pots, and molds, and that it would be an economic blow that could lose Pittsburgh its supremacy in the production of pressed glass. Some $100,000 in wages and buying power would be lost in the payrolls of the ten largest companies that would be involved.*

A strike, nevertheless, was called in November 1878, and of thirteen pressed glass companies in Pittsburgh, only two were operating. (The James B. Lyon O'Hara Works and Bakewell, Pears were not struck; they had a special agreement with their workmen.) A number of the factories continued or resumed operations, mostly with new, green hands. The strike was settled in August of the following year. The men agreed to return to work at rates set by the Glass Association shortly after the strike began. Work was to be paid for by the piece instead of by the turn, and the manufacturer was to have full management control of his establishment. *The Journal* reported, "The manufacturers show a quiet, dignified behavior in

* Hands and payroll were:

	Hands	Weekly Pay Roll
Atterbury & Company	110	$1300
Adams & Company	150	1800
Doyle & Company	100	1200
Duncan & Sons	130	1500
Crystal Glass Company	80	1050
McKee Brothers	160	2000
Bryce, Walker & Company	130	1400
Campbell, Jones, & Company	125	1350
Ripley & Company	110	1200
Richards & Hartley	110	1300

their victory. . . . Green hands will not be turned away but retained." Returning employees would be used to make up new shops. By the first week of October, all window glasshouses and all pressed ware and chimney houses were in full operation. "For once," *The Journal* said, "there is peace on the South Side."

The settlement did not end or much diminish the continuing economic warfare between employers and workers. In June 1879, the gatherers at Dithridge's and Duncan's struck again. Two months later warming-in boys at Richards and Hartley's tried their strength. Soon afterward the finishing boys in lamp chimneys went out on strike. The brevity and failure of these strikes eased conditions temporarily but did not solve the problems. In 1884, crimping boys at Fort Pitt idled the factory and seventy-five workmen. A costly walkout was called and lost by tableware workers in 1887–1888. Many of the strikes seemed to catch fire from each other. They were badly managed and revealed a lack of cohesion among different unions. The larger glass unions, in fact, were plagued in the seventies and eighties with splinter groups and with financial and management problems.

Strikes often caused a shifting of experienced workers. Eastern hands were glad to receive higher wages in the Midwest. *The Journal** records that sixty-five glass blowers from New York arrived in Steubenville to take the place of strikers. In February 1878, twenty-nine Pittsburgh glass blowers and tending boys left for Saint John, New Brunswick. Fifteen bottle blowers moved to Saint Louis. As early as 1877 *The Journal* had estimated that more than 1200 workers would go elsewhere, that they were willing to work for less money until the strike was broken.

The chimney factories of Challinor, Hogan & Company and Evans & Company moved to Chicago in 1878 because of labor troubles. There they joined under the name of Hogan, Evans &

* *The Crockery and Glass Journal,* October 11, 1877.

Company. On their return to Pittsburgh in May 1879, they again operated as single factories. Even with the desertion of these firms, the 1200 figure seems high. All strikers feared the training of green hands, which ultimately might block their employment after the settlement, so they were apt to remain near their work bases.

Even then, however, certain small victories presaged a strong union movement whose demands would carry weight and whose power would spread throughout the industry. Fifteen Pittsburgh window glass companies agreed to pay the union $1 for every box over forty-eight produced in one week. When McKee & Brothers, Jeannette, employed a glassworker from Rochester, New York, who could not produce a union card, 200 men and boys walked out; the company immediately discharged the man. Blowers at Thomas Wightman & Company's green glass factory struck when the company introduced molds belonging to an Eastern factory whose hands were on strike; the molds were withdrawn and work resumed.

The Gigantic Tariff Demonstration

While recrimination and demands were being exchanged and two segments of the industry — window glass blowers and chimney men — were on strike, all forces joined hands to participate in a massive all-industries parade and demonstration on the need for higher protection. Though U.S. tariff policy seemed favorable to the Pittsburgh District, it did not protect against European glass made by workmen who were paid lower wages.*

* In the 1870s a U.S. consul to Belgium reported that that country's glassworkers were receiving $56 to $65 a month while those in Pittsburgh and Ohio were receiving $80 to $100. The pay differential, on the other hand, was to a considerable degree offset by superior American productivity. An American visitor to England noted that it took five factories there to produce what three could produce in the United States (Scoville, *Revolutions in Glassmaking,* p. 34.)

Testifying before a House Ways and Means Committee in 1890, George A. Macbeth listed current duties: on soda ash 23 percent, carbonate of potash 20 percent, lead two

There was no problem on pressed glass, for total imports of that product in 1878 were only $38,000, while Pittsburgh alone exported $860,000 worth. The foreign competition hit hardest in cut glass. Foreign-made cut glass goblets sold at $1.75 a dozen in American markets; troubled American manufacturers were paying their cutters alone $3 a dozen. American cutting for wine glasses at a cost of $2.50 a dozen precluded any profit, since foreign prototypes could be had for 60 cents a dozen. Pittsburgh manufacturers who cheapened their product were several times accused of sending their wares to New York and having them brought back as imported goods.

Some 15,000 persons — more than 3000 of them glassworkers — rode or marched in the giant tariff parade and demonstration on February 14, 1878.* In several cases the number parading

---

cents a pound, German pot clay 30 percent. The immediate effect of the tariff, he said, was that American glassmakers paid $79.63 a ton for materials that in Germany cost $40. To increase customs duties on materials merely increased the cost of glass the American manufacturers wished to export in competition with cheap foreign glass.

* Twenty-one Pittsburgh glasshouses and their hands were listed as participants:

Adams & Company	203
Atterbury	125
Bakewell, Pears	125
Bryce, Walker	175
Campbell, Jones	150
A. & D. H. Chambers	250
Crystal Glass	50
Cunningham & Ihmsen	200
Dithridge Glass	150
Doyle	—
Duff & Campbell	125
G. Duncan & Son	150
King & Son	75
S. McKee	250
O'Hara Glass Works	275 men
	75 boys
Phillips	150
Frank Plunkett	100
Richards & Hartley	110
Ripley	75
Stewart, Estep	100
Wolf, Howard	125

represented almost all of those employed. Those from Adams & Company carried framed glassware labeled "High tariff, home industry, and no monopoly." The Bakewell, Pears contingent, led by Thomas Pears, wore glass badges and carried a banner that read, "Low tariff, low wages; no tariff, no work." The McKee display, one of the most dramatic, showed two glass cylinders eighty inches long and thirty-six inches in circumference surmounted by elegant wreaths reading "We give light" and "Give us the dollar of our daddies." Plunkett's banner was simple and straightforward: "Protection is the life of the glass trade."

The Rise of an Industrial Giant

Joseph Weeks's 1880 *Report on the Manufacture of Glass* excluded Pittsburgh from production of one glass product. Plate glass, a new branch of the industry, was then being made in modest amounts by short-lived factories in Missouri, Indiana, Kentucky, and Massachusetts. A Pittsburgh company that was to become a giant of the industry entered this unstable plate glass manufacture in 1883.

Government commerce reports state unequivocally that not one piece of plate glass had been made in this country up to 1880 without loss to the manufacturer. As late as 1874, American plate glass was the color of straw. The French, who had started with straw-colored plates, had now advanced to the color of fairly clear water, but the quality of their product was often defective. A quantity sent to Pittsburgh in 1874 to be bent was so inferior that when heated it developed blisters. An editorial in *The Crockery and Glass Journal* asked on October 24, 1878, "Why is not plate glass made in this city? This is certainly the best point in the country on account of cheap fuels, freight, etc., and is the natural location for glass manufacture. As it is, Pittsburgh is getting plate glass from foreign countries or New Albany or Jeffersonville in Indiana."

The New Albany plant, across the river from

Louisville, had been started in 1864 by John B. Ford, Civil War captain, as a producer of window glass, mirrors, and bottles. At this time Ford was well on his way to a fortune as merchant, manufacturer, inventor, and shipbuilder. In 1869 he ordered three costly machines from England for rolling and polishing glass — the first polishing machine of its kind in America. Ford believed that the way to make flat glass was to run a ribbon of molten glass between rollers, then to cut and polish it. Since the market for plate glass was limited, he insisted that more uses should be found for it and that plate glass should be made on a large scale.

In spite of medals from the Indiana State Board of Agriculture for polished plate glass and window glass (1872), Ford was forced to sell his business. The panic of the 1870s and loans he had made to friends undid him. When he sold his Star Glass Works in 1873, it employed 165 hands with wages of $75,000 and production of $250,-000. Soon afterward he tried glassmaking twice but was unsuccessful.

Around 1880, he received some $17,000 for a sewer pipe of rough glass he had invented with Pittsburgh's Washington Beck, its purpose being to make easier the detection of pipe stoppage. He used the money to buy an eight-acre farm at Creighton, on the Allegheny River twenty miles northeast of Pittsburgh, and there to found with New York capital the New York City Plate Glass works. Through the efforts of Ford and a new partner, John Pitcairn, president of the Pennsylvania Railroad, the name was soon changed to Pittsburgh Plate Glass Company.

The company grew at a phenomenal rate. It built factories at Ford City and Tarentum; it installed 1356 incandescent lights to illuminate the Creighton plant and four electric motors to move raw materials and finished glass about the factory. Many of the technical advances stemmed from Ford's idea: Don't buy it if you can make it.

In 1890, Captain Ford declared, "Now we fill orders from the largest blocks down to little country stores. . . . Twenty years ago [the price] was $4 a square foot. Now it is .75 to $1 per square foot. The larger the square the bigger the profit. . . . The demand comes from all parts of the country. The demand for Pittsburgh plate is always large."*

On Founders Day 1891, he expressed his deep satisfaction that there had never been a strike in one of his enterprises and that his plate glass company had become seven different plants. Feeling a responsibility for sharing his success, he set up funds for educational opportunities and community projects. The company Ford founded, still headquartered in Pittsburgh, still a major producer of plate glass, is now PPG Industries. It has expanded to worldwide operations and in 1970 its glass sales alone exceeded $450 million.

By 1886, Pittsburgh could well claim that it was making one half of the glass being used in the United States. It employed more than 6000 hands, used some 12,000 tons of soda ash annually, and produced glass products valued at $7 million. Its fifty-nine glass companies controlled seventy-five factories. The tableware manufacturers made a proud claim for their wares — a claim the other Pittsburgh glass producers undoubtedly agreed with and echoed for their own products. "The articles turned out by these companies are not surpassed in looks, design or beauty by any other establishments of the kind within the United States."†

No other American glass center, obviously, could equal the continuous span of operation of Pittsburgh and Allegheny County, or the amount of wares produced. None could show greater sustained versatility in its craftsmanship.

The chapters that follow describe the products of this industry in Pittsburgh and of the major companies involved. The chapters begin with free-blown, cut, and engraved glass of the earliest

---

* *The Crockery and Glass Journal,* October 16, 1890.
† *The Crockery and Glass Journal,* August 17, 1882.

years; they end with the rise of art glass as its creators rebelled against the tons of mechanically pressed glass then being produced. No exact cut-off date for each chapter can be given. Every student of nineteenth-century glass knows that pattern-molding began early and has continued through our time, that bottles and flasks have had an equally long life span, that pressed glass includes several categories. The chapters have been arranged, therefore, on the time basis of popular demand and of those technical changes within the industry that advanced production. Each technique is described and illustrated particularly as related to the mainstream of glassmaking. We have individualized Pittsburgh glass, but we have recorded its inheritances from the past and its kinship to glass from other countries and from other American localities.

PART TWO

CHAPTER VII

Free-Blown Glass of the Pittsburgh District

Wishing to try every method that may promote the improvement and
economy of my Glass manufactory I send Mr. George Cochrane to you
for a sample of the sand used at the Geneva works, being informed that
it is clearer than the bank sand that I have been using. Mr. C. is prepared
to have a boat load brought down (with your permission). Any advice or
assistance you may be pleased to give him shall be acknowledged by your
old friend, James O'Hara.
— O'Hara to Thomas Clare, November 21, 1806

In considering glass of the Pittsburgh District, we must remember that glassmaking was one of the oldest crafts and that no factory of that district (or of any other America area) was ever free from the influences and techniques of the past. As W. A. Thorpe put it in his introduction to *English and Irish Glass,* "When [the nomad artist] comes among strange people and to strange places, where nature affords him different materials from those of his own country, he suffers a change and unlearns his native art in teaching it to others."

Out of this fusion, many types of glass developed that are recognized today as "Pittsburgh," that name including, to the scholar, all the establishments in Southwestern Pennsylvania, Eastern Ohio, and West Virginia. There were many nomad artists in the early years. Bakewell's Eichbaum was a German who had learned glass blowing and glass cutting in France. Gallatin's Baltasar Kramer had worked at the Stiegel plant before the American Revolution and then for Amelung. O'Hara's Price had learned his craft in England. The Robinsons were Scots. Bakewell's great cutter and engraver, Jardelle, was French. In early free-blowing, the artisan and his tools moved frequently, if only for short distances. His knowledge and his stylistic individuality worked twice. They stayed with the factory he had just left, and they traveled with him to the factory to which he went.

Color

In any early glassmaking district that specialized in window glass and bottles, the modern collector can expect to find only rare examples of free-blown pieces that seem at all related to the clear, elegant tableware of the mid-nineteenth century. Nearly all such free-blown pieces through the first quarter of the century were strongly colored. The change from the unpurified greens and browns of window and bottle glass to the shining elegance of clear flint glass, either cut or engraved, was never really accomplished until well into the nineteenth century.

The simplest formula for bottle glass was silica, lime, and potash. The formula for window

25 Free-blown functional pieces from the Pittsburgh and the New Hampshire areas, 1815–1860. 1 — Olive amber jar, Stoddard or Keene, New Hampshire. H. 9½″. 2 — Early traveler's flask, olive amber — heavy base and sheared neck. Originally in wicker casing with side loops to hold a shoulder strap. Pittsburgh, ca. 1815. H. 10 1/16″. 3 — Amber funnel, Stoddard, New Hampshire. 4 — Amber rolling pin, Pittsburgh. L. 14″. 1 and 3, *Currier Gallery of Art, Manchester, N.H.* 2 and 4, *Collection of the author.*

glass was silica, lime, and potash or soda. District glassmakers took their workable sand or sandstone (silica) wherever they could find it. And some years passed before they learned how to purify it economically and effectively. Consequently, the glass was a natural green where iron oxides prevailed, brown where manganese was also present. Intermediate olive ambers resulted from varying proportions of those two minerals. Bottle factories were commonly called "green glass factories," though their products might range in color from the palest amber green to an almost opaque brown. Many of the known products of the Pittsburgh District appear in different shades of green, but somehow collectors have applied the term "Monongahela River glass" to the heavy bowls and other pieces of dark brown color. There is little justification for the term's use.

It is always puzzling for a new collector to have authorities assign a color to clear glass. Early formulas for clear flint were never perfect and unforeseen impurities frequently gave a tinge. The smokiness of Amelung, for instance, has become somewhat a byword. Paul N. Perrot, former director of the Corning Museum of Glass, has written, "This decanter has a slight greyish cast often found in the Pittsburgh area."* The collector should not be upset if his Pittsburgh piece has a yellowish or bluish cast, for among the Pittsburgh free-blown pieces I have seen, there are more yellowish pieces than those of any other tint. A very smoky Pittsburgh pitcher with betrothal initials is dated 1852, long after Amelung. Sometimes too much manganese in the formula gave an amethystine tint. Early glass was also always in danger of being aquamarine. If the collector consults a color expert and sets his clear piece against a really white background, he will understand why clear glass is described as having color tinges; it was made in an age before true quality control. And no collector should be wor-

* Paul N. Perrot, "Glass: English, Irish, or American?" *Antiques* 79, March 1961.

26 Green glass from the Monongahela District, 1797–1850. 1 and 5 — Cylindrical bottles with ring collar, drawn-up necks, and high-kick pontil. 1 — H. 9". *Ex coll. Mrs. Paul Craig.* 2 and 3 — Witch ball and vase. The short stem, low bowl, and long flaring neck foreshadow later, more graceful vases. H. 16". *Collection of Dr. E. R. Eller.* 4 — Tumbler — *The Gallatin, Kramer works. The Historical Society of Western Pennsylvania.*

ried if the color of his pieces does not fit any of the generalizations given here.

Window Glass

Two main, basic glass products were manufactured in the Pittsburgh District from the first, and they remained dominant products as late as the 1860s; other articles were really a sideline not always produced commercially or profitably. Of these two — window glass and bottles — window glass was clearly the more important. Most early glass factories made bottles, but none or few made bottles exclusively. Joseph D. Weeks, writing a government report on the industry, could not discover one Pittsburgh factory devoted wholly to bottles before 1837, finding only "a record of a vial works and a black bottle factory, the only one of its kind in the western country."*

* Joseph D. Weeks, *Report on the Manufacture of Glass, Including a History of Glassmaking in the United States,* 10th Census (Washington, D.C.: Government Printing Office, 1880), p. 85.

In a letter from Thomas and Sarah Pears to Anne Pears Murphy on January 18, 1819, there are references to an ill-fated black bottle project started by Bakewell that year in a small building on Water Street opposite the main factory. His great-grandson, Thomas C. Pears III of Pittsburgh, thinks the panic and near bankruptcy of the Second U.S. Bank was a reasonable cause for its failure.* Bottle manufacturing became a distinct branch of the industry around 1837, with an increasing number of factories devoted solely to that product. "The custom of using the corner pot for bottles," Weeks wrote, "is now entirely discontinued in this section." (The story of free-blown bottles and flasks is covered in chapter eleven.)

From O'Hara's letter to Terence Campbell in 1806 (quoted on page 18), we have clear evidence that the early window glass was greenish and that it was used interchangeably for bottles. The late Earl Dambach, collector and student of early flasks, had a piece of green cullet† from Perryopolis, on the Monongahela above Pittsburgh, found at the site of the New Boston factory there. It shows the pane divisions very clearly. The layers are so superimposed that it is evident that several fragments of panes rested on each other in the cullet pile. Dates of the New Boston factory ran from 1816 to 1837, but window glass operations were rapidly expanding in the 1820s. The green tinge probably continued into the 1830s in pioneer windows.

In making window glass the workman had a choice of two techniques: the crown and the broad (or cylinder). In the crown method, he blew a broad bubble on his blowpipe, after which it was transferred to a pontil rod and reheated. Then it was rapidly rotated to spread it by centrifugal force to a flat disc, called a table or crown. Finally it was knocked off the rod and placed in an annealing oven. This flat disc could reach a diameter of four feet, and diamond or rectangular panes could be cut from it. The bull's eye or thickening would appear only at the point where the rod had been attached.

In the broad glass method (sometimes called German, cylinder, or roller or sheet glass), the workman blew a long cylindrical bubble. One workman boasted that he could blow a cylinder or roller weighing sixty-five pounds. Glasshouses often maintained a swing pit for such large rollers at the mouth of the furnace, or else the blowers stood on elevated platforms. The ends of the cylinder were cracked off by encircling them with either a hot wire or a thread of glass, then applying an iron tool dipped in cold water. The resulting cylinder was split lengthwise by a wetted iron and placed in a flattening oven where it could soften and be flattened into a sheet with the aid of a wooden tool fixed to an iron rod. When cooled, the sheet was cut to the desired sizes with a diamond. The original cylinders were shaped like the jars so popular and useful in every pioneer home.

Pittsburgh District factories used the broad (cylinder) method from the very beginning. It persisted in this country until late in the century, when the new technique of drawing glass into sheets in a continuous process was introduced.

The early letters contain frequent references to diamonds as cutters. One of the more interesting is that written by James O'Hara to Captain John Davidson in Washington on December 4, 1809:

Enclosed you will find three diamonds in a quill to try an experiment with your lapidary agreeable to advice by your last letter. These have never been used. No cut could be found in them (i.e., they did not cut glass), should you succeed in getting them made useful on reasonable terms considerable will be sent down. All we have been using since 1798 are on hand out of repair. Repair them if reasonable cost. You will confer a singular favor by purchasing one dozen or as many new diamonds as you can order under that number and send them by mail. I cannot go on without them.

---

* Pears III, "Sidelights on the History of the Bakewell, Pears & Co.," pp. 64, 65.

† Broken or waste glass gathered for remelting.

27 Green and amber milk pans, 1797–1830. 1 and 2 — More sophisticated and of later shape. 3 — Heaviest of the Pittsburgh area pans. Bought in this century at a second-hand shop on lower Fifth Avenue. D. 6″. 4 — Fairly typical shape of early pans. D. 10″. 1, 2 and 4, *The Historical Society of Western Pennsylvania. 3, Ex coll. Mrs. Paul Craig.*

Hollow Ware

Our knowledge of the exact original meaning of the term "hollow ware" is limited to those articles that are mentioned and priced in the early business correspondence.* Tumblers, jars, pitchers, decanters, and wines are listed frequently, but I have not noted an advertisement for glass milk pans (27), a common household article, until 1860 in the H. L. Ringwalt catalogue. Druggists' wares and chemical equipment probably fell within the meaning of the term. From time to

* The few early advertisements for free-blown glass are too general to be of much use.

time O'Hara was requested to custom-make "electrical vessels" for laboratory use. He wrote to Lewis Sanders in Lexington, Kentucky, in April 1810:

I presented your patterns for electrical vessels to the glassmakers here and they decline any engagements in this line.

On December 29, 1809, he wrote to Joseph Carson of Philadelphia, who sent on specifications from a Dr. Samuel Belton:

Vessels of various forms and sizes are made at my works with great facility and I have no doubt of being

28 Free-blown pieces, 1797–1840. 1 — Light green milk pan from Western Pennsylvania. 2 — Dark-green hat, a whimsey. D. 4½". 3 — Green inkwell, applied petaled foot. H. 2". (From Annie High Estate, Nicholas Township, Fayette County, Pa.) 4 — Amber tumbler, possibly Ohio. H. 3". 2, 3, and 4, *The Historical Society of Western Pennsylvania*. 3 and 4, *Gifts of J. Harry Gorley*.

29 Early pitchers from the Pittsburgh-Monongahela District, 1797–1830. 1 — Green bulbous with short neck and heavy short handle. 2 — Dark green footed on short spreading base. Bulbous with cylindrical neck. H. 7¼". 3 — Aquamarine creamer, eighteenth-century shape, on *flat* applied base. H. 5¼". 1, 2, *The Historical Society of Western Pennsylvania*. 3, *Gift of J. Harry Gorley*.

able to make anything in this way that the doctor may order with proper explanation.

But seven weeks later he wrote:

. . . Dr. Belton's figures which my glassblowers decline undertaking being apprehensive that they cannot please in accuracy. The patterns will be returned soon as required.

O'Hara's reservations on hollow ware as a standard product were shown in his December 29 letter to Carson:

I can say nothing respecting a limitation until I am informed of the special requisition. I don't wish to engage extensive in any kind of hollow ware at present but any communication that may be received on the subject in confidence shall be retained or returned with perfect purity. The prices for glass for chemical experiments may be quoted as follows:

½ Pints	12½ ¢
Pints and Quarts above	25¢
[more than] qts. & 1 gallon	25¢ per quart
all above gallons	20¢ per quart
Solid glass by the inch or pound	

It is tantalizing to think of all the early greenish pieces that workmen must have blown for home use or as a whim. The Gorley case at the Historical Society of Western Pennsylvania contains three exceptionally fine pieces of green free-blown glass. When George Kramer, son of Johann Baltasar Kramer (who had worked for both Stiegel and Amelung), left New Geneva, Pennsylvania, in 1818 or 1819 to travel farther west, he carried with him glass to barter for necessities. His granddaughter, Mrs. Martha Ellen (Herron) Emerick of Oxford, Ohio, sold these family treasures in her ninety-third year to Dr. Parke G. Smith. Falling under this family attribution are a flip glass (height 5", diameter 4½", bottom 3"), a green tumbler (height 3½"), and a green bowl (diameter 7½").* In the same case from Fayette County, Pennsylvania, is a folksy green inkwell

* Neil C. Gest and Dr. Parke G. Smith, "The Glass-making Kramers," *Antiques* 35, March 1939, 118–21.

on a petaled foot. Plain free-blown green tumblers are off the market now, obtainable perhaps when a collection is dispersed and then only at a high figure. There is only one known fine example of an early green pitcher, proof condition and authenticated from the New Geneva District; it belonged to the late Dr. Paul Stewart, president emeritus of Waynesburg College, and is on view at the Waynesburg Museum. However, milk pans — the vessels in which milk was placed to form a layer of cream — are still reasonably available in all shapes and sizes. The Ringwalt catalogue for January 1, 1860, carried this advertisement:

Milk Pans. (These are preferable to all others. Glass being a non-conductor, milk will keep uninfluenced by storms or climate.) Per dozen $3.00 to $4.50

Collectors always tend to give the earliest possible date to any piece of free-blown window glass or hollow ware — as, indeed, they do to any other antique piece of indeterminate age: porcelain, pewter, silver, buttons, furniture, or whatever. In being honest with ourselves, we should keep three things in mind. Most of the glass factories went through relatively short life cycles. The craftsmen were migratory, and their skills and styles, as well as their tools and molds, traveled with them. And the techniques of making free-blown glass have varied little for hundreds of years. Except for its greater oxidization, a bowl from the Elbert Eli Farman Roman Collection at the Carnegie Museum looks very much like an 1850 Pennsylvania milk pan. The birth date of our primitive-looking piece, therefore, is not necessarily around 1800. Many of the other early American glass factories followed the manufacturing cycle of the Pittsburgh area. Consequently, jars, tumblers, bowls, and pans from different areas may possess the same sort of likeness we find in the Roman bowl and the Western Pennsylvania milk pan.

Any discussion of early free-blown glass of the Pittsburgh District — or, indeed, of the United

30 Gallatin-Kramer–type aquamarine milk pan, 1797–1840. Purchased from the Moore family of Fairchance, Pa. H. 4½″. D. 10″. *The Henry Ford Museum.*

31 Gallatin goblet, ca. 1800. Green bottle glass. Hollow stem on flaring foot. The silver medal enclosed was probably awarded to Albert Gallatin in Switzerland. Goblet was purchased from a descendant of Charles A. Mestrezat, a relative of Gallatin. H. 9⅛″. *Collection of Jerome Strauss.*

Free-Blown Glass of the Pittsburgh District   89

32 Functional pieces of clear lead glass shown at the Carnegie Museum Exhibition of 1949–1950. 1 — Pitcher has an unusual band around the shoulder. H. 8". 2 — Vase has an unusual double bulbous bowl. 3 and 4 — Cruet and sugar bowl show an affinity of shape and applied base. 1810–1840.

States — must include the Gallatin goblet owned by Jerome Strauss (*31*). Blown of medium green bottle or window glass, the goblet stands on a hollow stem above a flaring foot. A silver medal encased in the stem was probably awarded to Albert Gallatin when he was a schoolboy in Switzerland. (Such medals were commonly given for scholastic excellence.) The goblet descended through Charles A. Mestrezat, a relative of Gallatin's. There is enough similarity between the Gallatin goblet and a green goblet brought from New Geneva to Ohio by descendants of Johann Kramer to link the two pieces to the New Geneva Glass Works and to the Kramer style.*

* For further comment on the Gallatin goblet, see McKearin, *Two Hundred Years of American Blown Glass*, Plate 69; Jerome Strauss, "Another Gallatin Glass," *Antiques* 36, August 1939; and Gest-Smith, "The Glassmaking Kramers."

The transition from window glass to bottles was smooth and fast in the early factories, since both were made of the same green and brown utilitarian glass. The further transition from bottle glass to the beautiful clear flint hollow ware and tableware was painful, slow, and expensive. The fact is that the market and demand for unadorned clear flint — plain sugar bowls, pitchers, and celerys — did not equal that for cut and engraved glass. Plain clear could not compete with cut and engraved as a status symbol, and those solid citizens who could afford to buy plain clear flint (as opposed to the green and brown functional glass) tended to buy cut and engraved pieces that emulated Anglo-Irish glass. The business experience of Bakewell and Company illustrates this estimate of the market.

Bakewell, which began in 1808 as the nine-

33 Hurricane candlesticks or shades set on heavy stems and bases, 1810–1840. Origin uncertain. H. 9¼". *Ex coll. Mrs. Paul Craig.*

34 Blown candlesticks of lead glass, 1810–1825: 1 and 3 — Bulbous candleholder joined to stem and base by wafers and knops. Shaft is hollow. H. 10½". 2 — Short bowl for oil or a candle. Double knops on stem. Generous bases on all pieces. *Ex coll. John J. Grossman.*

teenth century's first purely commercial flint glasshouse, advertised in the Pittsburgh *Gazette* for May 17, 1809, the following products:

Decanters of quart and pint size, of common or best double flint glass, either plain or ringed (collared) of half-pint and gill sizes, of common glass, plain or ringed.

Wineglasses, common and best

Wine coolers

Water decanters

Goblets of pint, half-pint, and gill sizes, of common and best double flint glass

Tumblers of quart, pint, half-pint and gill sizes, of common and best double flint glass

Jelly and syllabub glasses

Cups of quart, pint, half-pint and gill sizes

Egg cups

Butter and sugar basins with covers and cream jugs, assorted colors

Cruets and mustard pots

Finger cups

The products listed cover an extraordinarily wide range of household articles. Decanters, wines, and tumblers were to be expected, but jelly glasses and eggcups, butter and sugar basins with covers, cream jugs in assorted colors, cruets, and mustard pots — these made an impressive variety for a flint factory only a year old. All were free-blown; the phrase "assorted colors" so implies, even if some of the other pieces were cut. We may question whether there was heavy or even substantial volume in many of them. We know that O'Hara and Craig had not been eager — certainly not hasty — in trying to develop clear glass for hollow ware. We know that through the first ten years of its existence, Bakewell had to fight for its life in getting first-quality sand and pot clay, in finding skilled and experienced workmen, and in solving the production problems caused by the uncertainties and high costs of shipping. We know, too, that Bakewell added green glass to its established line in 1811, thus apparently revealing the difficulties of a house that had limited itself to flint glass. And we know that in 1825, a fairly

35 Pair of unusually bulbous free-blown whale oil lamps, 1810–1825. Note the knop joining of stem and the folded rim on base of right lamp. H. 9". 1, *Ex coll. Mrs. Paul Craig.* 2, *The Historical Society of Western Pennsylvania.*

prosperous year, Bakewell employed sixty-one hands and twelve engravers and ornamenters. That high ratio indicates clearly that unadorned free-blown white flint could not compete with cut and engraved glass as a status product. As soon as clear glass became cheaper, of course, the demand for it increased. Free-blown clear continued to be made throughout the century — which is one reason why it is so exceedingly difficult to date.

Three articles appear to have been produced in free-blown plain white flint in generous quantities: tumblers, wine glasses, and decanters. A study of the ledgers of the Harmony Society* bears this out. Next in frequency were salts — plain, oval, footed, and engraved. Common inkwells and eggcups followed, but it is difficult to be certain that these were of clear flint. If all the Harmony Society bills had specified a particular glasshouse, the evidence would be fairly definite as to the kind of metal used. Instead, purchases were usually made through wholesalers: Pitts-

* The Society lived at Harmonie, Pennsylvania, 1804–1815; at Harmonie on the Wabash in Indiana, 1815–1825; and at Economy, Pennsylvania, 1825–1905.

burgh Manufacturing Association, Park & Company, Isaac Bean & Joseph McFerren, and John Robinson (not the glass manufacturer), to mention a few.

In isolating bills directly from Bakewell and T. Robinson & Son, we are on firm ground in assuming quality and true clarity. Many of the articles named in the bills, however, were cut or engraved. Ordinary free-blown tumblers ran from 45 cents to $1 a dozen, decanters from $1.25 to $4 a dozen — rather clear evidence of what students have often surmised: that a company like Bakewell dealing in flint would have had two grades of glass — one sold mainly on price, the other on quality. In looking over bills for cut and engraved glass, we again find two qualities and two prices.

An Observer of Early Glassmaking

Anne Newport Royall (1769–1854) was an assertive advocate of women's rights and a sharp-tongued observer of life in America, as shown in her ten volumes of travel and comment. She visited Pittsburgh in 1828 and spent considerable time at Bakewell's, the showplace for all travelers who came to the city. She described the manufacture of tumblers in a superior piece of early industrial reporting:

But *Bakewell's* is the place; whoever wishes to see the blowing of glass done with ease and dispatch let them visit his glass house. It stands in the city on the bank of the Monongahela and the furnace has been in blast five years! that is, it has never been out. When a crucible breaks, they have a machine by which it is taken out of the furnace, and another one, which is always ready, put in. But the first thing that struck me here . . . was the appearance of the men of which there were but few; two only finished the pieces after they were blown by the boys, of which there were several. These boys, as well as the two gentlemen, who were entirely entitled to the epithet, if ever men were, are for skill and expedition unequalled.

Mrs. Royall had called the day before but was told that the blowers were not working. She was told at what time she might return the next day.

Almost at the entrance of the house, I was suddenly surprised by a gentleman sitting on a bench with a back to it and a sort of arm at each end, raised about half way to his breast, supporting a stick laid across it. The bench was about three feet in length; across these arms lay a piece of iron, if I recollect about the size of a walking cane; on the end of this stuck a tumbler partly formed, which he shaped by turning the iron very fast, by the assistance of a large pair of shears, which he ran now and then into the mouth of the glass, and turned it round, the glass being pliant, as if to widen it and put it into shape. This he did with one hand, while he kept turning the tumbler backwards and forward very fast with the other hand: but most of the time he turned it with both hands, or rolled it rather as we do a rolling pin in making pastry. He soon finished the glass by which time the boy who attended him brought him another similar piece of iron, and taking the first off laid this in the same place. The operation is so quick that I could scarcely believe my own eyes that it was reality — it may be supposed that the whole process was rapid when he makes 600 tumblers per day! The glass when brought to him is a hollow oblong, and the moment he receives it, rolling all the while, he clips what is to be the mouth of the glass with the shears, which brings it even; after this it is soon in shape. The mouth expands as he rolls it round.

Mrs. Royall described the artisan as one of the finest-looking men in Pittsburgh and neatly dressed. She was "riveted to the spot" by the ease and inimitable grace that accompanied his movements, his fine countenance and soft black eyes, "all bedecked with smiles of ineffable sweetness."

At length, upon looking up, I saw another man, which I took to be his brother, from a resemblance, which proved to be the case. He was employed in the same way at decanters, and was still more interesting in his appearance. He made 240 decanters per day! They informed me they had been employed in the same way for ten years! if I do not mistake. The proprietor has a good right to be proud of these men! they must be worth their weight in gold. Everything was neat, and in place: the whole presenting one of the most astonishing sights of regularity and skill I ever beheld.*

* Royall, *Mrs. Royall's Pennsylvania,* p. 110.

Two facts stand out: the men produced at the amazing rate of 600 plain tumblers and 240 plain decanters a day, and they had been doing it for ten years.

Clear free-blown pieces are less numerous today than we might expect. The quotation from Anne Royall indicates that tumblers and decanters were expendable. It gives further evidence that sugar bowls, pitchers, pans, and vases were not then being made in the same numbers as drinking vessels; that in the first part of the century, unadorned clear was not valued for its beauty or as a token of status; and that cut, engraved, and colored glass held the vogue.

Pittsburgh and the Ohio Valley, however, were comparatively rich in clear free-blown glass. I am acquainted with no other area that has yielded to twentieth-century collectors as many clear free-blown pitchers, sugar bowls, and plain vases. The shapes of such pieces are distinctive. Variations in form exist but are not strong enough to persuade the collector that he has a piece from another district. (I am not including plain blown

Free-Blown Glass of the Pittsburgh District   93

37 Four Pittsburgh pieces of lead glass showing several characteristics, 1815–1840. 1, 2, and 3 — Bulbous shape, predilection for applied bases. 2 — Funnel base. 1 and 4 — Tooling rims of pitcher. Reeded and hollow handles. H. of No. 4 8″. 2 and 3 — Galleried rims, domed covers, knop finials (flat finials also). *The Historical Society of Western Pennsylvania*. 1 and 4, *Violet Swem Brendel Fund*. 2 & 3, *Anna Moody Browne Fund*.

wines, flips or ringed decanters in this generalization.) If we could tabulate all the present available specimens of clear free-blown glass from the major Eastern glass areas, we should be surprised at how far short they would fall in numbers below those from the Midwest.

To Identify and Authenticate

When it comes to identifying and authenticating free-blown pieces, we are forced to depend on technique, shape, the quality of the glass, and geographical distribution. Gregor Norman-Wilcox accepts none of these factors as constant when he tries to set up criteria for attributing old glass.* He even questions family ownership — and quite rightly, for a vase owned in Manheim, Pennsylvania, is not necessarily Stiegel, and a tumbler that "has always been in the family" may have been acquired in 1890. Any criterion can be discredited, but unless we assemble and correlate bits of evidence, we will remain in a state of suspended equivocation until some genius sets up a sound law of relativity in glass attribution. Rhea M. Knittle may have been pointing in that direction when she made the acute observation that we ought to categorize glass, not by factories, but by techniques.

* Gregor Norman-Wilcox, "On Attributing American Blown Glass," *Antiques* 36, August 1939, 72–75.

38 Three Pittsburgh pieces of lead glass, 1815–1840. Similar characteristics. Note short baluster stem on No. 3. H. at handle 8¼″. *The Historical Society of Western Pennsylvania.*

Over the years, however — without being highly scientific about it, and allowing for inaccuracies — we have come to recognize certain shapes as belonging to blown glass of the Pittsburgh area, presupposing that the metal is of heavy and clear flint. Such attributions originally depend on geographical location, the finds appearing along the river arteries of travel:

The blown pitchers with generous bowls and heavy handles (sometimes hollow) have high shoulders and strong lines — rather cylindrical until they curve into the neck. An unobtrusive touch of individuality sometimes appears, such

as a flat thumb-rest at the top of the handle where it joins the body of the pitcher or cruet. This is a slight depression, not the thumb-latch seen so often in earlier Continental and South Jersey pieces.

The plain simplicity of the unadorned clear pitcher is often enhanced by tooling at the rim. The pouring spout is always funneled strongly. Enough of the earlier pitchers take their shapes from the decanter to express an affinity to the Irish.* If they are footed, the bases are generally flat and sturdy.

* M. S. Dudley Westropp, *Irish Glass* (Philadelphia: J. B. Lippincott Company, 1921), plate XVII, XXII, XXV.

Free-Blown Glass of the Pittsburgh District　　95

39 Cobalt sugar bowl on low funnel base with folded rim, 1820–1840. Note the narrow galleried rim and low domed cover. Flat finial. H. 7¼". *The Henry Ford Museum.*

41 Amber vase with threaded top and witch ball. Fashioned by Lewis Kaufman at McCully's Sligo Factory, 1861. Total height 9½". Such vase ornaments were also made in South Jersey, Connecticut, and New Hampshire. *The Historical Society of Western Pennsylvania.*

40 Free-blown and pattern-molded creamers, 1820–1840. 1 — Amber. Shape found in the Tri-State District. Folded rim, wide pouring spout, heavy handle. H. 6½". 2 and 3 — Cylindrical body, long neck, folded rim. No. 2 is amethyst. No. 3 is cobalt, pattern-molded, twelve ribs. H. 4¾". Note similarities of shape and handles in relation to bodies. *The Historical Society of Western Pennsylvania. 1, Anna Moody Browne Fund; 3, Gift of J. Harry Gorley; 2, Ex coll. Robert H. Carew.*

42 Amber creamer with clear handle on plain base, 1820–1840. Attributed to South Jersey, Not unlike Midwestern pieces that employ two colors. H. 5". *Yale University Art Gallery, Mabel Brady Garvan Collection.*

43 Cobalt sugar bowl with opaque white finial and opaque rim, 1820–1840. H. 6". The relation of bowl to base, the low height, white finial, and rim indicate possibility of English manufacture. *The Henry Ford Museum.*

The most distinctive sugar basins with pear-shaped bowls remind us of Stiegel. The galleried rims and domed covers look like Irish pickle jars.* The shape has grown familiar through several exquisite sugars, in cobalt or amethyst, in museums and private collections. The original bubble (parison) from the blowpipe became the bowl. Sometimes it was squeezed down for a wider basin. No one can ignore the significance of the bubble as an artistic and functional shape in all Midwest sugar bowls.

All the bases sturdily support any weight given them. Baluster and single-knopped stems are vigorous rather than graceful; the so-called funnel base is a good example. With fat bowls and heavy bases we think in terms of the Low Countries; then a double-domed cover and neat finial remind us that this is the New World and that we may expect variations even to infrequent flat bases like those of South Jersey. The globular cracked-off finial and the flat-tooled finial appear most often, the cracked one probably being the earlier.

Because the prevalent baluster stems follow normal variations, a collector likes to draw relationships to earlier glass. At the same time he observes many strong plain stems, even sometimes the wafer and less rarely the knop. He should never lose sight of the fact that Pittsburgh artisans seemed to be impelled to apply a foot. These bases, which range from the flattest of the Jersey types, reach an unusual height in the funnel base of the green milk pan (Color Print No. 3, item 2). One should not expect petaling or tooling. For the most part the lines of stems and base were smooth and fluid. Even the folded rim harmonizes.

These points cannot be stressed too strongly: First, many free-blown pieces were simply the product of individual workmen, proud of their skill and striving to express a creative urge. Second, in such instances the achievement fits into

* Westropp, *Irish Glass*, plates XXII, XXIV.

44 Cobalt and clear vase on baluster stem, applied base. H. 9¼". Blown in Pittsburgh by Thomas Bovard ca. 1830. *Collection of the author.*

45 Free-blown clear vase with a rim of blue applied to a flaring scalloped top. The neck is decorated with a double band of blue. The globular part of the vase is blue. The applied plain stem ends in a flat circular foot also trimmed with blue. It is a showy and attractive piece, ca. 1850. H. 12¼". D. of top 6⅜". D. of base 5". *The Henry Ford Museum.*

46 Impressive collection of Pittsburgh-Midwestern glass, 1800–1860, displayed at the First Midwest Antiques Forum at the Henry Ford Museum in 1960. Note the green and white looped sugar bowl and the opaque white and red creamer. Various techniques: free-blowing, pattern-molding, pillar-molding, and casing, Height of opaque vase 9″.

the technical pattern of the surrounding area, and often of other areas as well, with the signature (figuratively speaking) of its creator. Third, since the piece is free-blown, it is timeless, unless documentary evidence establishes a date.

A pair of amber vases with the threaded tops and the matching witch balls (*41*) represent all the points here suggested. Miss Emma Hammersmith attests that her uncle, Lewis Kaufmann, fashioned them at McCully's Sligo factory in 1861. Kaufmann, who is buried at the Mount Oliver Cemetery in Pittsburgh's South Side, was born on December 2, 1850, and died on May 26,

1887. Kaufmann was eleven in 1861. If family tradition is to be believed, his skill was highly developed at that age. (Perhaps the gaffer who blew the pieces let the boy assist him.) The Sligo factory, primarily a window glass house, was taken over by William McCully in 1851. Theoretically, the glass color would be clear or aquamarine. Such amber vases with attendant witch balls were blown at the bottle houses up and down the Monongahela River in the first quarter of the nineteenth century as well as at comparable factories in New York State and New England. So we have in these vases and balls the timelessness of free-blown pieces, the uncertainty of family history, the interrelationships of form and technique, and finally the divorce between the normal factory product and that of one of its workers.

Many clear celerys, open and covered compotes, and footed bowls were being made by the middle of the century. Blue and amethyst gave eye appeal to the bowls, but the vases really challenged the blowers. Deep cobalt, amber, and amethyst could appear at any time. The blower undoubtedly began with clear vases of classic simplicity on knopped, wafer, or baluster stems. In their directness, these vases were analogous to decanters. Collectors seem to have undervalued them for two reasons: such shapes were made throughout the century and could be examples of late workmanship, and engraving, gadrooning, pattern-molding, and color have consistently lured American collectors away from the clear and the unadorned. Not content with one color, Pittsburgh workmen emulated South Jersey glasshouses not only in using double colors for the same piece but also in loopings and draggings. The Bovard vase (*44*) dramatizes a cobalt bowl; the Ford Museum vase (*45*) with the ruffled edges of blue employs the color as a trim in rings and around the base. Wheeling equaled Pittsburgh in liveliness and gaiety when it fabricated the blue, pink, and opaque white of the vases with scalloped tops. Such vases, probably made in quantities in the 1870s, presaged the striving for color and new art forms that bloomed in the following decade. In passive acquiescence, we allow every vase with looped colors and a somewhat bulbous bowl where it meets the stem to be attributed to Bakewell, just as dealers and collectors tend to attribute latticinio pieces to Nicholas Lutz.*

The colored or looped powder horn matched

the colorful vases as another mantel ornament. Originally a glass horn was blown with a wide mouth, like those animal horns used to hold powder for the early muskets and rifles. Then the orifice was closed and the horn became a legitimate ornament. Finally, horns in striking color combinations and of impressive size were mounted like looped vases on clear standards (*47*). All sorts of whimsies appeared in brightly colored hues, honest cousins of the paperweights. Much more impressive are the loopings of white on green as found in the Crawford Wettlaufer

---

* A letter from F. L. Hills of the Phoenix Glass Works, South Boston, March 29, 1870, to Nicholas Lutz in Pittsburgh establishes that Lutz had worked in Pittsburgh before going to Sandwich.

48 Sugar bowl of clear lead glass looped with opaque white, 1830–1850. Bulbous bowl, wide domed cover, flat finial, galleried rim of average height. On clear applied base with folded rim. A rare and excellent piece. H. 7½″. *Ex coll. Robert H. Carew.*

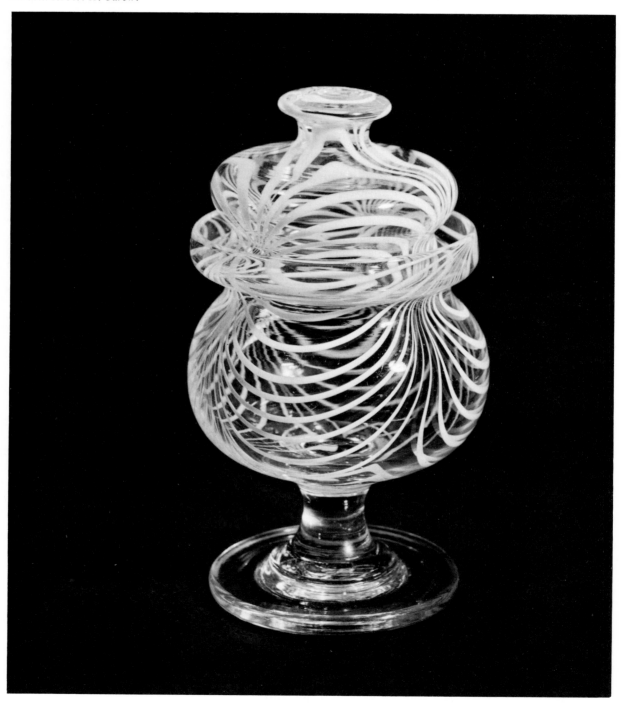

49 Clear vase, ca. 1850, with opaque white loopings, scalloped top, applied ring at lower part of bowl. Baluster stem joins applied base. Such vases, often called Bakewell, were also made at other factories in the Pittsburgh-Wheeling area. H. 8¾". *Ex coll. Robert H. Carew.*

50 Free-blown clear vase with an applied band of fiery opal at the rim. A thick application of fiery opal covers the globular part of the vase. The baluster stem and foot are clear. Ca. 1850. H. 6⅜". *Ex coll. J. Robert Rodgers.*

51 Colored vases with significant shapes and bases, 1830–1860. 1 — Green. Family history points to Cunningham factory. H. 8″. 2. and 3 — Cobalt and clear. Typical baluster stems. Bulbous and ringed shape of bowl is characteristic of the area and of earlier style. Scalloped rims are Victorian. No. 3. H. 8½″. 4 — Ruby and clear. Wide hollow base belongs to earlier time. H. 8″. 1, *The Historical Society of Western Pennsylvania, Violet Swem Brendel Fund.* 2 and 3, *Collection of Dr. E. R. Eller.* 4, *Collection of Jack Strassler.*

52 Unusual clear and light blue ale glass, 1850–1860. Loopings end in an abortive lily pad. The hollow stem and base are pattern-molded, joined by a wafer. The base is pattern-molded with a folded rim. H. 11″. *The Historical Society of Western Pennsylvania, Gift of Charles A. McClintock.*

sugar bowl in the Ford Museum Forum (1961) group picture (*46*), the Carew bowl (*48*) and vase (*49*), white on clear, and the Rodgers vase (*50*), fiery opal and clear.

A challenging relationship is set up by the impressive sugar bowl with double covers from the extensive Melvin Billups collection in New Orleans. This bowl, attributed to Bristol, with its white loopings on green, could be an elder and larger brother of the Wettlaufer bowl, which is assigned to the Midwest. No one pictures a pioneer workman bothering to fashion, even whimsically, two covers for the same bowl. The Carew bowl and the Rodgers vase, put beside the two sugars with their graceful and delicate loopings, have a strength and primitive quality the others lack. Shape and individuality of the Midwest are retained, even though the technique of combining colors came much earlier than many of the two-toned pieces, which date from the 1860s and 1870s.

Special mention must be made of the unique tall goblet that belonged to Charles McClintock, banker, glass enthusiast, and active president of the Historical Society of Western Pennsylvania from 1930 until his death in 1963. Though it

seems to me a controversial piece, Jerome Strauss and George McKearin have pronounced it a Pittsburgh product (*52*). The pale blue loopings are curved upward in thickenings of the glass, almost like abortive lily pads. Pittsburgh glassmakers used varied American techniques, but I know of no other example where they used the lily pad form. The hollow ribbed stem, wafered at the top and base, has a great deal of strength. The base

53 Blown pieces illustrated in undated Bakewell, Pears catalogue, ca. 1875, p. 40. *Collection of Thomas C. Pears III.*

with a folded rim of blue also carries the molded ribs. These two parts of the goblet bespeak England and the Continent. Would it be heresy to say that the tone of the whole vessel reminds me of the work done by De Cordova at the Union Glass Company of Somerville, Massachusetts, and by Tiffany on Long Island?

As the production of pressed glass increased in volume, the demand for free-blown (and particularly for flint) fell off. The lime-soda formula of 1864 (pages 42–45) cheapened the manufacture of pressed glass while at the same time enabling the manufacturer to retain the appearance of lead crystal; its effect was to push free-blown flint into the narrow corridors of luxury. The middle class could buy a matched set of the new pressed ware for table appointments and never give a second thought to any possible question of inferior quality. In the days of widespread use of pressed glass, only those of discriminating taste and determined mind would care to display pieces of the best flint — in other words, to stand against popular choice.

The O'Hara Glass Company Ltd. catalogue (probably 1876) shows what happened to the earlier Midwestern shapes of blown glass. Now

the pioneer strength has been lost. Handles are stuck on at the top. Stiffness has replaced earlier fluid lines. The variety of articles has narrowed, and clear flint has become more commonly utilitarian: fishbowls, candy jars, ordinary hollow ware (*53*).

Bakewell was the first flint glass factory in America, and it has left more records — scanty as they are — than any other flint glass factory except the New England Glass Company and the Boston and Sandwich Glass Company. Its name gained luster from its advertisements and from the admiring comment of scholars. But Bakewell was no more the sole Midwestern manufacturer of the free-blown flint glass discussed here than Sandwich was the sole producer of pressed glass in New England. To understand the full significance of the statements in these pages in which the name Bakewell appears, the reader must generalize; he should say to himself, "This could be McKee, or Ihmsen, or Robinson, or Curling, or McCully." No one should be upset if he sets his heart upon a piece from one of these factories and finds that it differs from other pieces in its class. The variant is the delight of the glass collector's heart.

54 Free-blown nonlead creamer inscribed "C.F. to M.H.F. 1851." Strong smoky tinge to glass. Caspar Freeling evidently fashioned it for his bride, probably after hours at a window glass factory. H. 5¼". *Collection of the author.*

55 Clear free-blown sugar bowl, ca. 1840. H. 10". Unique treatment of wafered and banded finial. Shape of bowl and applied rings are reminiscent of sugars by Thomas Cains of South Boston. Blown by James Lee of the Robinson factory when he later worked in New Jersey. *The Historical Society of Western Pennsylvania, Gift of Miss Lily Lee Nixon.*

56 Lattice basket meant to hold a glass bowl, ca. 1850. These pieces represented a tour de force. Fashioned by Nicholas Kunzler, Pittsburgh. *Collection of J. Nevin Garber.*

Free-Blown Glass of the Pittsburgh District   107

CHAPTER VIII

Cut Glass

At Page and Bakewell's glass warehouse I saw chandeliers and numerous articles of cut glass of a very splendid description: among the latter a pair of decanters cut from a London pattern the price of which will be 8 guineas. It is well to bear in mind that the demand for these articles of elegant luxury lies in the western states. The inhabitants of eastern America being still importers from the old country.
— Henry Bradshaw Fearon, *Sketches of America*, London, 1818

The style of early free-blown Pittsburgh glass held a natural relationship to the New Geneva and other Monongahela River factories. It held a relationship even to some of the Eastern factories, since some of the gaffers had come from the Stiegel and Amelung houses. In addition to this interrelationship of styles, the glass also reflected the local influences of the place and of the people.

Cut glass, on the other hand, was utterly divorced from local influences. In this product, the pioneer glass manufacturer was not seeking to satisfy the functional need for windows, bottles, and tableware. He sought to set up domestic production that would rival established art forms and meet the competition of the European importers. To do this, he had to match or excel the fine cut glass of the English and Irish. Such was the intent of the Pittsburgh area houses that set out to manufacture cut glass products. The results were unexpected and advantageous on several levels.

Cut glass sold well at the prosperous towns along the rivers and competed well at New Orleans. Though cut glass was bought for table and social use, it also created a proud display and gave aesthetic enjoyment. Ordinary citizens were likely to own "the poor man's decanter" — green or amber bottles (with or without handles) and flips (oversize tumblers). Some of them perhaps owned free-blown decanters of undecorated clear glass. But those who could afford it were satisfied with nothing less than cut or engraved flint glass.

There was also tremendous advertising potential in the design and sparkle of handsome and obviously expensive pieces. O'Hara and Craig had shipped their first window glass to Natchez in 1799, but then and thereafter no one was excited over such useful but pedestrian products. Samuel Jones's directory* in 1826 emphasized the difference:

The glass of Pittsburgh and the points adjacent is known and sold from Maine to New Orleans. Even in Mexico they quaff their beverages from the beautiful white flint of Messrs. Bakewell, Page and Bakewell of our city.

Then, too, flint and cut glass attracted visitors and acclaim because of the high degree of techni-

* Samuel Jones, *Pittsburgh in the Year 1826* (Pittsburgh: Johnson & Stockton, 1826).

cal proficiency required. A friendly Osage chief thought the glass blower who applied a handle to a pitcher must have communion with the Great Spirit. With something of the same feeling, Pittsburghers conducted visitors to Bakewell's, and probably to Robinson's, as to a monument of pride. Famous visitors brought attention and prestige to the operation. Gift pieces and awards dramatically demonstrated that the quality of workmanship was beyond simple copies of English strawberry diamonds and Irish flute panels. Against these evidences, the stiffest sceptic was convinced that cut glass from Pittsburgh, far from being a "local" product, deserved comparison with the best from abroad and at home (see Appendix, page 485).

Thus two significant facts about Pittsburgh glass, not always fully accepted, are established: its relationship to Irish and English cutting and its advertising value as a symbol of status, as proof of the skill of Pittsburgh glassmakers, and as evidence of the independence of manufacturers beyond the Alleghenies.

The Attribution of Cut Glass

It will be remembered that the technique of free-blowing lent itself to anonymity, because the same steps in manufacture had been followed at least since the first century A.D. The same was true of cutting, which had changed little since its development on the continent and in England and Ireland during the eighteenth century. A heavy blank of flint glass was blown. On it a design was traced. A rougher made the first deep cuts by means of a wheel (of iron or stone) grinding on an abrasive (of wet sand or emery). An artisan might complete the cutting by tracing the more delicate lines. Then the smoother polished the article with wooden wheels using pumice, rouge, or a like agent. Always the workman held the piece above the cutting wheels and the polishing wheel.

Cutters often received higher wages than blow-

58 Pitcher and compote in the Anglo-Irish tradition, 1815–1835. Strawberry diamonds and fans. Pitcher has panels at base and on shoulder. Linear cutting around the neck and under the lip. Compote has reeded base. H. 7⅞″. *The Henry Ford Museum.*

59 Typical Pittsburgh pieces of 1820–1835. The decanter is similar to the President Jackson glass of 1829 (different stopper). Note the circle or roundel and fan appearing on the tumbler and decanter. These pieces were shown at the Carnegie Museum Exhibition in 1949. *Picture courtesy of* Antiques.

ers and felt themselves above other workmen. Most of them remain anonymous, nevertheless, and recorded patterns for early cut glass are sparse, partly because of a fire in 1836 in the U.S. Patent Records Office.* We would expect, therefore, to meet the same obstacles that prevent the exact attribution of free-blown glass. Fortunately, this is not so. Cut glass was cherished for its early value, beauty, and scarcity, because of the honors it had received, and because it was so

* To realize what a student can do when factory records are available, see Westropp, *Irish Glass,* plates X through XIV.

often a gift presented on a special occasion. Therefore, even if we lack records with which to allocate exact patterns to their factories of origin, we do have many cut and engraved pieces with detailed family histories. From these we can often construct a framework of theory that is strong enough to bear the weight of scholarly examination.

Attribution is complicated by the fact that not all glasshouses did their own cutting; many sent their blanks to outside cutting rooms. Some experts did the cutting for several factories on their own premises. William Peter Eichbaum, a Ger-

man trained in France, was probably one of these for a time. Alex Jardelle, whose fame burgeoned after he cut and engraved the two presentation vases for Lafayette in 1825, set up his own shop before he joined Bakewell. There must have been other such cutters — anonymous now because their careers were short or because they were absorbed into the cutting rooms that substantial factories added to their facilities. Thus it is clearly unwise to attribute an early piece of cut glass to a single factory simply because it follows a certain design. Irish, English, and even French designs, moreover, were followed throughout the century and at first were commonly interchanged. No individual factory could keep a monopoly on design.

As early as October 13, 1817, the Pittsburgh *Mercury* told of a practical joke that demonstrated the uncertainties of attribution of glass pieces. A traveler — one who apparently considered himself an authority on glass — called on Benjamin Bakewell to examine his work. He was shown a tankard that Bakewell's son had selected in London as a pattern or specimen of the best English glass and the best cutting. "The gentleman looked at it, examined it slightly, and said that it was very good for American, but not equal to the British."

The increase in the number of factories producing cut tableware after Bakewell in 1808 adds to the cloudiness obscuring specific attributions. The Pittsburgh *Commonwealth* for August 20, 1809, wrote of two flint glass houses making tumblers, wine glasses, decanters, and other pieces to the value of $30,000 annually. One of these may have been the short-lived factory that belonged to George Robinson and Edward Ensell and later was sold to Bakewell. Thomas Clinton Pears of Bakewell's remembered that a single ledger of his company for 1814 carried a $14,000 profit on $32,000 in sales. It is doubtful, therefore, that the unknown factory was much of a competitor for Bakewell, Page and Bakewell.

Down the river at Wellsburg, Isaac Duvall opened a plant in 1815 and later sold cut pieces of high quality. John Robinson began production in Pittsburgh in 1823; Robert Curling and William Price were operating in 1827; and Hay and McCully (Union Flint Glass) began in 1829. In Wheeling, Ritchie & Wheat (1829) and M. & R. H. Sweeney & Company (1831) followed hard upon the Pittsburgh glassmen in excellence of workmanship if not in quantity. Three other Pittsburgh factories conclude the list: O'Leary, Mulvaney & Company, 1832, afterward Mulvaney & Ledlie; Whitehead, Ihmsen & Phillips, 1837; and Parke, Campbell & Hanna, 1837. All these companies

61 List of cut table glass bought by President James
Monroe from Bakewell, Page & Bakewell on Nov. 14,
1818. *The National Archives.*

62 Letter of acknowledgment of payment by the government for the President Monroe glass, 1818. Note date of payment, 1818.

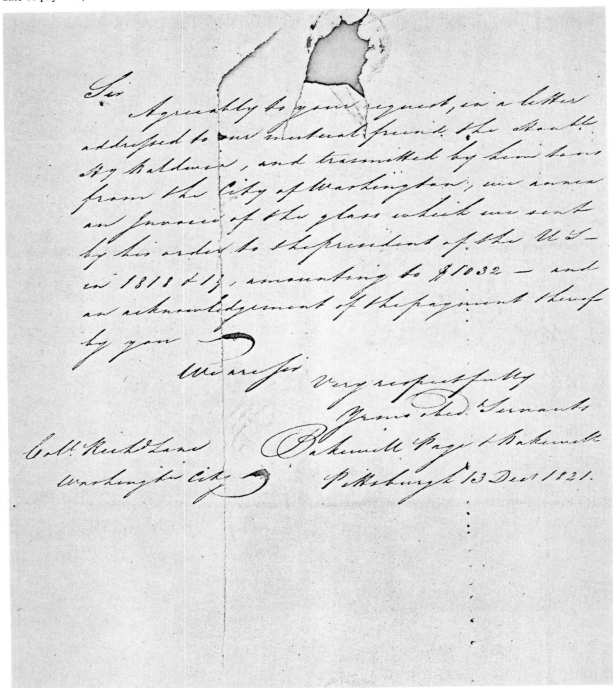

63 This is an imperfect example of the two vases presented to Lafayette on his visit to Pittsburgh and to the Bakewell factory in 1824–1825. *H. 32¼". The Yale University Art Gallery, Gift of Mrs. Alicia Bakewell Shaffer, daughter of William G. Bakewell.*

their products were fairly well and widely known. Examples of their work still exist.

Four Developments of Importance

Four outstanding, indeed, historic occurrences in the annals of Pittsburgh glass involved cut glass and the prestige of its sale in high places.

1. *The Monroe service.* In 1817, in his first year as President, James Monroe made a tour of the Western states to encourage domestic manufactures and discuss plans for major internal improvements. In Pittsburgh he visited the Bakewell factory. Benjamin Bakewell presented him with what the press described as a pair of "elegant" cut decanters. Monroe, in turn, ordered for the White House a service of decanters, wine glasses, tumblers, oval dishes, and salt dishes. The glass was double flint cut in the Colonial-Ashburton style by Alex Jardelle in his best manner, the arms of the United States being part of the design, with engraved grapes and leaves as a lesser decorative element.

Fortunately, the National Archives in Washington yielded a list of the individual pieces. A conservative assumption based on the list would be that the glassware was rather plain. The editors of the Pittsburgh *Mercury* on November 10, 1818, glowingly lauded the pieces as

. . . a splendid equipage of glass . . . exhibiting a brilliant specimen of double flint. . . . The glass itself must have been selected with great care, or the spirited proprietors must have made considerable progress in their art, for we have seldom seen any samples so perfectly pellucid and free from tinct [tint]. Upon the whole we think the present service equal, if not superior to the elegant Decanters presented to the President when he passed through Pittsburgh last year. . . .
We cannot forbear congratulating Messr. Bakewell and Page on this occasion; their meritorious struggles are at length crowned with partial success; may the policy be adopted by our government be such as, at no very distant day, to insure that reward which their urbanity, enterprise and industry merit, and may "the glass that sparkles" on the President's board operate

advertised flint tableware, and all except Hay & McCully carried the word "cut" in their advertising pieces. These were substantial factories and

64 Itemized list of table glass ordered by President Jackson for the White House in 1829. *The National Archives.*

Invoice of Sundry Glass furnished the President of the United States by Bakewell Page & Bakewells Pittsburgh.

Box

№10044	12 doz richest cut Tumblers .. 20/ 240.		
	Box .50		240.50
10045	6 pr cut decanters to match 28/ 168.		
	5 doz „ Wines .. to D. 18/ 90.		
	Box ... „ 50		258„50
10047	1 Elegant cut Centre Bowl & Stand 40.		
	2 „ D Smaller D ả 30. 60„		
	Box - .. „.50		100.50
10048	6 Cut floating Island dishes 15/ 90.		
	Box .50		90.50
10426	7 doz cut Wines to match 18/ 126.		
	6 doz „ Clarets D ... 20/ 120.		
	Box &c .. „ 50		246.50
10443	6 pr Cut pint decanters D.20/ 120.		
	3 pr D. Celeries to match 20/ 60.		
	Box & Coop &c „ 50		180.50
10445	6 pr Cut Pitchers to match . 30. 180		
	6 pr Salts & Stands ... 10 60.		
	Box &c - .. „ 50		240.50
1087.	2 pr 11 Inch Cut dishes to Match 20/ 40.		
	2 pr 9 In D D 15. 30		
	2 pr 7 In D D . 12 24		
	Box „ 25		94.25
			$1451.75

P.T.O.

65 Greyhound tumbler at left, ca. 1828, was presented by Benjamin Bakewell to William Reynolds of Meadville, Pa. Anne Royall described the Greyhound tumbler in *Mrs. Royall's Pennsylvania,* 1829. H. 3¼". *The Historical Society of Western Pennsylvania, Gift of Mrs. John Reynolds.*

Greyhound tumbler at right, ca. 1830, has shallower engraving; cut finger flutes at base instead of diamonds and panels on Reynolds tumbler. *The Historical Society of Western Pennsylvania, Gift of Henry King Siebeneck.*

as a talisman on our representatives to stimulate them to unremitting exertion in favor of manufactures.

2. *The Franklin Institute Decanters.* In 1824, Franklin Institute in Philadelphia held its first exhibit of domestic manufacturers. Bakewell displayed a selection of cut glass and won an honorable mention. The following year it entered a pair of decanters cut by Jardelle and won the first prize, a silver medal, in competition against the New England Glass Company, Jackson & Baggett of New York, and the Brooklyn Flint Glass Company. The Philadelphia Museum of Art has a decanter similar to the Bakewell prize one pictured in the McKearins' *American Glass,* plate 50, no. 4. They were like the splendid decanter Bakewell later presented to Henry Clay Fry of the Rochester Tumbler Company and subsequently of the Fry Glass Company of Rochester, Pennsylvania — now in the Corning Museum of Glass (see pages 138–39).

3. *The Lafayette vases.* In 1825, the Marquis de Lafayette, then in his sixty-eighth year, made a triumphal tour of the United States and in Pittsburgh visited the Bakewell factory. There he was presented with a pair of commemorative vases cut and engraved for the occasion by Jardelle, showing the American eagle on one and Lafayette's chateau at La Grange on the other. Lafayette generously pronounced the Bakewell products equal in fineness to Baccarat.

The Lafayette vases reveal the tribulations involved in achieving perfect pieces of cut glass. Mrs. Alicia Bakewell Shaffer, daughter of William G. Bakewell and niece of Lucy Bakewell Audubon, happened to visit the Yale University Art Gallery in the early 1950s. She expressed the wish at that time to give to the museum what her family had always called the Lafayette jar. It seems that one vase of the pair cut for Lafayette was flawed. A new pair was cut. William G. Bakewell bought the one perfect vase from the first pair. It descended to Mrs. Shaffer, somehow becoming broken and mended in the process. The mended vase can be seen today at Yale. The pair actually presented to Lafayette are supposedly at the Palace of Versailles Museum, though Paul Perrot of the Smithsonian Institution was unable to find them there.

4. *The Jackson service.* In 1829, President Andrew Jackson paid $1451.75 for an extensive table service of Bakewell glass, again cut and engraved by Jardelle. The service included bowls, celerys, salts, vases, and a complete range of decanters, cordials, wines, and champagnes. Apparently these pieces, like those bought by President Monroe, have disappeared into the limbo of past Presidents' belongings, for an inquiry addressed to the White House in 1947, in the administration of Harry Truman, brought an expression of regret that none of the Monroe or Jackson pieces remained.

Except for the Franklin Institute decanters, none of these four widely acclaimed pieces generated styles or established designs that continued as individualized patterns. We shall do well, therefore, to consider a number of authenticated pieces of Pittsburgh cut glass that illustrate a mode or indicate a trend — several examples of which have come down to us with a solid family record.

The Greyhound Tumblers

In the author's *Early Glass of the Pittsburgh District, 1797–1890* (1949), the following quotation appeared, taken from *Mrs. Royall's Pennsylvania, or Travels Continued in the United States.* Mrs. Royall was describing the Bakewell factory in Pittsburgh:

The engraving is very neatly done, indeed surpassing any I have seen in the country. . . . The ware is also high, $5.00 a tumbler.
The patterns are mostly obtained from Europe, and the pattern executed when I was in, for beauty and taste, was exquisite, particularly a greyhound with its head erect as though looking at something and though not an inch in length it was perfect and entire, the eyes, ears, nose being life itself.

In 1949, no Bakewell greyhound tumbler was known. Indeed, collectors and scholars for several decades had lamented their absence. Then one of those odd things happened: two greyhound tumblers appeared within a relatively short time.

A dealer in Clinton, Wisconsin, read the Royall quotation and informed the Carnegie Museum that he had a greyhound tumbler. Could it be one of those described by Mrs. Royall? The piece was examined, and Henry King Siebeneck of Pittsburgh bought it in 1949 and presented it to the Historical Society of Western Pennsylvania. At that time it was an interesting item for study, because it was the first greyhound tumbler to appear and because of the excellent workmanship (65). Jerome Strauss, a world authority on drinking vessels, examined it. He expressed moderate interest and indicated to me that the piece revealed strong French influence.

There the matter stood until 1956, when quite unexpectedly Mrs. John E. Reynolds of Meadville presented a greyhound tumbler to the Historical Society (66). With it came a declaration that Benjamin Bakewell had presented it in the middle of the nineteenth century to her father-in-law, William Reynolds. Bakewell had told Reynolds that the piece was one of the first eight tumblers of that design made years earlier in his factory.

Jerome Strauss examined the Reynolds tumbler with enthusiasm and pronounced it of as fine workmanship in cutting and engraving as he had seen. Both pieces are on view at the Historical Society. We have the Anne Royall quotation with a date, the authentication of the Reynolds piece, and the suggested relationship to Continental Europe in the Siebeneck piece. Jardelle may have done the work, but the cutting and engraving on the Siebeneck tumbler seem less strong than those on the Reynolds piece.

One strength of the Reynolds tumbler lies in the balance of design; the greyhound and the pedestal with doves are emphasized without blossoms and leaves distracting the eye. Another strength is the band of cut diamonds above the

68 The reverse of No. 67 carries a fringed shield with a crudely engraved "C." The shield rests on a cluster of leaves out of which a leafy branch rises on each side. The tumbler was probably a presentation piece or one of a set.

69 Cut and engraved tumbler with a greyhound chained to a pedestal surmounted by a two-handled vase. Doves on vase are ready for flight. On the opposite side, initials are framed by floral sprays with a beautifully executed crowning circle. A band of cut diamonds tops the flutes at the base like those on the Reynolds Greyhound (No. 65). H. 3⅜″. D. 3⅛″. *The Henry Francis du Pont Winterthur Museum, Gift of Mrs. E. du Pont Irving.*

70 Framed initials on tumbler shown in No. 69.

71 View of doves and greyhound on tumbler shown in No. 69.

short base flutes. They seem to give the tumbler weight to rest well on the table. Finally, a graceful floral band below the rim of the tumbler completes the design. We know that the greyhound had appeared before that time on Continental glass. Whatever the origins of the Siebeneck tumbler, its high quality of workmanship is apparent. As for the Reynolds tumbler, it is one of the most exciting of all authenticated pieces of cut and engraved Pittsburgh glass.

A glass collector can rarely find such documentation and family history as that revealed by the greyhound tumbler presented by Benjamin Bakewell to William Reynolds. Anne Royall's description of seeing such a tumbler made guides us in judging other tumblers fashioned in the same mode.

An engraved tumbler in the collection of Mrs. Ray C. Patterson of Slippery Rock, Pennsylvania, resembles the Siebeneck greyhound strongly. Finger flutes at the base carry a frosted band partway around the tumbler similar to the design on the Siebeneck one. A large daisy rises stiffly from two plumelike leaves on both tumblers. Roses and leaves also rest on the frosted band.

Marked differences appear in the conventional pedestals and the decorated bands at the top. The band on the Patterson tumbler contains a series of tuliplike blossoms. The one on the Siebeneck greyhound is more traditional: an upper line with dots, a lower line with half circles, but in between

a continuous line of diagonals. The pedestal on the Patterson tumbler is crosshatched with a dot in each diamond. It is the only one of the American tumblers that does not have a solid pedestal. A dove hovers over the two resting on the pedestal.

Evidently this tumbler was a presentation piece or one of a set, for the reverse carries a somewhat crude fringed shield with an engraved "C." The shield rests on a cluster of leaves out of which a leafy branch rises on each side. In spite of minor differences, the two tumblers are related in form and design.

The Henry Francis du Pont Museum at Winterthur, Delaware, has a more elaborately engraved tumbler with the greyhound chained to the pedestal. Other design elements are very similar to those on the Reynolds tumbler (65). A decorated double-handled vase rests on a truncated block rather than on the conventional pedestal. Two birds hover above it. No decorative band graces the top. Around the initials, however, are graceful festoons worthy of Amelung engraving. The base of the tumbler has short flutes below a band of large cut diamonds. Though the detail of engraving is not like that on the authentic Reynolds greyhound, the flute and diamond arrangement is almost identical on both. The underside of both tumblers is rayed.

A greyhound tumbler, hitherto unstudied, was first published by N. Hudson Moore in *Old Glass.**

* *Old Glass, European and American* (New York: Frederick Stokes Company, 1926), Figure 221, p. 368.

72 Cut and engraved tumbler of colorless lead glass, probably Pittsburgh, ca. 1830. A couchant greyhound looks at two birds. Four large plumelike sprays of leaves with daisy blossoms alternate with short stylized ferns. There are ten broad cut flutes around the base. Large polished pontil. H. 3⅛″. D. of rim 2⅞″. *Philadelphia Museum of Art.*

74 Cut and engraved tumbler in the style of the Greyhound tumblers, ca. 1830. Rayed oval with initials of the owner. Floral sprays from pedestal and oval. Cutting on base finger flutes. Top engraved band cut with inverted V's. H. 3⁵⁄₁₆. *Smithsonian Institution.*

It was assigned to the Kensington Glass Works of Philadelphia, perhaps because it was found in the Philadelphia area, perhaps because it is owned by the Philadelphia Museum of Art. The Philadelphia tumbler, beside picturing a greyhound couchant, carries flutes patterned like those on the Reynolds and the Winterthur tumblers. Though it lacks the pedestal and the doves that the Siebeneck and the Patterson have, it shows two birds with wings spread. It is different in that it lacks a decorative band at the top and has a polished instead of a rayed pontil. Its individuality is best shown by the bunches of plumelike leaves with small daisy blossoms. Where designs on all the other tumblers give a feeling of circularity, this one with upright stylized flowers and ferns carries the eye upward. Undoubtedly it belongs to America and probably to Pittsburgh.

The engraved American tumbler of the first quarter of the nineteenth century merits detailed study.

Some Tumblers Related to the Greyhound

Several other cut and engraved tumblers of the period, though without exact family or factory attribution, suggest relationships to the five greyhound tumblers that are worthy of study.

In 1952, two years after the Carnegie Museum Exhibition of Pittsburgh glass, Malcolm Watkins of the Smithsonian Institution sent a photograph of an engraved tumbler asking if it belonged to the greyhound group Anne Royall had described. It has no greyhound, but certain other design elements seemed to be related to the Siebeneck tumbler, particularly in the pedestal with winged doves on it. Both pieces have similar flowers and decorative bands around the top. Where the Siebeneck tumbler has finger flutes around the base, the Smithsonian piece has shorter and wider flutes not quite reaching the bottom.

In 1969, Mrs. Lee Renner of Isabella, Missouri, inquired if her family tumbler belonged to the Bakewell group. Like many of the others, it has the winged doves resting on a pedestal (76).

76 Cut and engraved tumbler in the style of the Greyhound tumblers, ca. 1831. Two doves with wings spread on a pedestal. Engraving is simpler than that of the Greyhounds, particularly in the grapes and leaves on the sides. Engraved band at top is a primitive design. Finger flutes at base are unusually high. Base rayed. H. 3⁵⁄₁₆". *Collection of the author.*

77 Opposite side of No. 76. Shield with date 1831 and initials "TN" (Thomas Norton), of Wheeling, W. Va.

78 Cut tumbler recently used to advertise White Horse Whiskey. Strawberry diamonds and roundels with rays. Attributed by advertisers to the reign of King George II (1727–1760).

79 Matching Betrothal tumblers given Charlotte Barker by James Lee, 1830–1835. Engraving pattern is conventional but restrained and attractive. This is an outstanding example of American workmanship. H. 3½".
The Historical Society of Western Pennsylvania, Collection of Miss Lily Lee Nixon.

The band at the top is merely a series of engraved dots divided by seven larger polished circles. Such a stiff and conventional pattern is much less pleasing than that on the greyhound tumblers. Instead of flowers and festoons, the decoration consists of grapes and leaves. Finger flutes around the base are longer and narrower than those of any other; they most closely resemble those of the Siebeneck tumbler. The underside of the base is rayed like the Winterthur and Reynolds pieces. Mrs. Renner reports that "T.N." in the shield stood for Thomas Norton, her grandfather, who lived for a time in Wheeling, West Virginia. So this could be a Wheeling tumbler and the date 1831 fits well with the greyhound period.

Having seen the Renner tumbler, Kenneth M. Wilson of the Henry Ford Museum became interested in a comparison and sent photographs to Robert Charleston of the Victoria and Albert Museum. Without actually seeing the tumblers together, Mr. Charleston was willing to express the opinion that the Renner tumbler, despite its strong English influence, could well be American.*

A tumbler made in England in the early nineteenth century owned by the Royal Scottish Museum of Edinburgh, and pictured in R. A. Robertson's *Chats on Old Glass*† (plate 34, no. 2), is worth examining because of the relationship it bears to the American pieces. It reminds us anew that the Anglo-Irish influence on cut and engraved glass in America was particularly strong during the first quarter of the century. The English tumbler has finger flutes cut at the base like several of the others. Only the English and Patterson tumblers have a crosshatched basket to support the

* A cut tumbler with all the earmarks of early Pittsburgh has for several recent years been pictured in advertisements for White Horse Scotch Whisky. It was purchased from Plummer's of New York City and is attributed by them to England of the rule of George II (1727–1760). Tumblers like this of nineteenth-century manufacture have appeared frequently in American collections.
† New York: Dover Publications, 1969, p. 93.

birds. The engraving on the English piece is more sophisticated and better balanced than that on the Patterson and Renner tumblers. The band around the top combines movement and stability in the line of ferns resting on two bands of stars.

The Betrothal Tumblers

Closely related to the greyhound tumblers in function and execution is a pair of charming betrothal tumblers produced by the Robinson factory (79). These are on loan to the Historical Society of Western Pennsylvania by Miss Lily Lee Nixon, descended from James Lee, who cut and engraved the pair at the Robinson factory in 1835. James had been apprenticed to Robinson in 1826 at the age of fifteen (80). His father, John, born in Inverness, Scotland, in 1780, may not have been proficient with his pen, but several original letters from his two brothers — one a physician in London, the other a schoolmaster and later a wealthy merchant in Philadelphia — show that the family was educated far above the average. James Lee one day saw Charlotte Barker walking down the street, told his family that he meant to make her his bride, arranged a meeting, and made his prediction come true. The tumblers were his betrothal present. The white rose was for Charlotte, born in Yorkshire; the thistle was for his own Scotch inheritance.* These betrothal tumblers from the Robinson factory rank with the Bakewell greyhound in execution and design.

Father Rapp's Tumbler

Old Economy, an early nineteenth-century community on the Ohio River below Pittsburgh, now a restored museum complex, was the third and final home of the German pietist-celibate

* An interesting account of the Lee family by Lily Lee Nixon may be found in *Pennsylvania History,* Journal of the Pennsylvania Historical Association XXI, No. 2, April 1954, 145–52.

80 James Lee Indenture at the Robinson factory, Dec. 25, 1826.

81 Tumbler cut and engraved for Father George Rapp, leader of the Harmony Society at Old Economy, Ambridge, Pa., ca. 1840. Elaboration of design indicates later production than Nos. 65 and 79. It is possibly a Bakewell piece. H. 3½″. *The Pennsylvania Historical and Museum Commission, on exhibit at Old Economy.*

82 Cut and engraved vases (H. 9″) and covered sugar (H. 7⅛″) used by the Harmony Society at Old Economy. Ca. 1840. Design is even more elaborate than that of No. 81. *Pennsylvania Historical and Museum Commission.*

group, the Harmony Society. In changing from an agrarian to an industrial organization, it became so productive and so financially powerful that the Pittsburgh newspapers often attacked it as monopolistic, especially in the areas of raw wool and manufactured cloth, including silk. Notables from all over the Western world visited Old Economy.

The Great House of Old Economy, built in 1830, now displays an elaborately cut and engraved piece known as Father Rapp's tumbler (*81*). It is rightfully so called because of the engraved "R" on the shield and the intricately entwined rose, which Father George Rapp (1757–1847), spiritual head of the Society, many times used as a mystic symbol. (In his sermons he gave it the qualities of beauty, happiness, and Christian love.) The tumbler was on loan for many years from Anderson C. Bouchelle of New Smyrna Beach, Florida. The Pennsylvania Historical and Museum Commission bought it from him in 1965.

Circumstantial evidence persuades us to assign the piece to Bakewell's and to date it in the 1830s. A firm friendship as well as a business relationship existed between the Rapps and John Palmer Bakewell. Because of recorded purchases of glassware from Bakewell's, it is not unrealistic to assign the tumbler to that factory. Furniture, silver, and glass were all of high quality (Garrett of Philadelphia made the silver) and all glassware and silver were in daily use in the Society's Great House. On the other hand, no actual sales record for the tumbler can be found, and the elaborateness of the cutting would imply that a set of such pieces would be exceedingly costly. This lends credence to the Society's long-standing assumption that the Rapp tumbler was a single piece made to commemorate Bakewell's admiration for Father Rapp.

The Society died out and was dissolved in 1905. John S. Duss, one of the last trustees, moved many of the better furnishings of the Great House to Florida. Through Mr. Bouchelle, many

83 Cut and engraved sulphide tumbler with bust of Washington, ca. 1824. Base panels surmounted by a band of strawberry diamonds and tall fans. Engraving limited to a band of leaves at the top and bordering the initials "FCW." H. 3⁵⁄₁₆". *The Corning Museum of Glass.*

of the pieces have found their way back to Old Economy — including that fine example of American workmanship in glass in the second quarter of the century, the Father Rapp tumbler.

The quality of all the tumblers described really depended on the engraving. Such pieces combining techniques of cutting and engraving can be included in this section as a guide to the student.

We may recapitulate with several established points on these American tumblers. All originated in Western Pennsylvania, Philadelphia, or Maryland. All except the Siebeneck have heavy bases. All carry initials except the Reynolds and the Philadelphia ones. We may conclude that engraved tumblers, excluding the Rapp tumbler, with cut bases, with stylized designs, and with initials for ownership were popular and cherished possessions; they were gifts or proud possessions of a well-established family. Enough similarity in style of cutting and engraving relates these tumblers to each other, and yet through individuality of design and quality of engraving, each is set apart. Knowing that cutters and engravers

worked individually as well as under factory supervision, we theorize that such table pieces represented a popular style of the 1820s and 1830s. The date "1831" on the Renner tumbler warns us that we cannot cut off a technique or a vogue in a given year. The only one of the greyhound family to be definitely attributed is that reported by Anne Royall. Benjamin Bakewell gave one of these to William Reynolds of Meadville. Whether Jardelle engraved it we shall never know. In spite of the English or French influence that may have engendered it, we believe that the Bakewell influence blossomed in other American tumblers of this group.

The De Witt Clinton Medallion

Sulphide bust tumblers bear a direct relationship in cutting to the Siebeneck and Reynolds greyhound and the Lee betrothal pair, even though they add political implications to their artistry. Medallion portraits of Washington, Franklin, Jackson, Lafayette, and Clinton appear in the base of such tumblers. Cutting rather than engraving usually governed the design. Also called a "cameo incrustation," such a portrait was prepared separately and was made of materials requiring a higher degree of heat for fusion than the glass in which it was to be encrusted. The medallion was introduced into the bubble of glass, which was then collapsed when the workman drew out the air.

We know that the Clinton tumbler was made to celebrate the occasion of Governor De Witt Clinton's visit to Pittsburgh in August 1825. "De Witt Clinton was here," Benjamin Bakewell wrote in a letter on August 6, "and ordered some glass. We had a very respectable company to dine with him and I think stand fair for Pennsylvania, Jersey, and York to start with [politically] in 1829. Thomas has sent you a Clinton tumbler."* The

* Thomas Clinton Pears, Jr., "Visit of Lafayette to the Old Glass Works of Bakewell, Pears & Co.," *Western Pennsylvania Historical Magazine* 8, October 1925, 195–203.

84 Cut and engraved De Witt Clinton sulphide tumbler, ca. 1825. Only engraving is the initials "DWC." Circular cut rings above and below a series of four panels of finely cut diamonds. H. 3¼". D. 3". *The Henry Ford Museum.*

86 Base of the Washington tumbler, ca. 1824. *Ex coll. J. Robert Rodgers.*

85 Base of a Washington tumbler, ca. 1824. *Ex coll. J. Robert Rodgers.*

87 Cut punch cup or handled mug, 1820–1835. Straight sides are more unusual than barrel-shaped cups. Attractive handles give such cups appeal. Strawberry diamonds and roundels with fans. H. 3⅜". *The Corning Museum of Glass.*

88 Variety of patterns in cut tumblers of the Pittsburgh area, 1815–1835. No. 4, H. 3½". *Collection of Dr. E. R. Eller.*

pictured tumbler (*84*) is one of a pair given to the New York Historical Society in 1884 by Alfred De Witt, whose father, Peter De Witt, received two from Mrs. De Witt Clinton. The celebration for Governor Clinton included a twenty-four-gun salute, the launching of a ship named for him, a businessmen's luncheon with complimentary toasts, a Masonic dinner the same evening, and a tour of Pittsburgh's manufacturing plants.* Clinton, of course, strengthened his political fences during his stay, for he had just come from a successful tour in Ohio.

An advertisement that appeared in the Pittsburgh *Gazette* of March 11, 1825, and intermittently for the next eighteen months, strengthens

* Lowell Innes, "Governor Clinton Comes to Pittsburgh," *Western Pennsylvania Historical Magazine,* September 1961.

the belief that cameo incrustations were occasional pieces. Demand for them evidently waned. In addition to their very complete assortment of plain, molded, and cut glass, Bakewell, Page and Bakewell had for sale at reduced prices Lafayette and medallion tumblers, ornaments, etc.

Cups, Mugs, and "Lemonades"

In our century a good many well-designed and tastefully cut mugs have been found in Pennsylvania. The modern collector, happy in such finds, has assumed that these were used for strong alcoholic drinks. A postscript to a letter written in 1811, however, indicates that they were also used for more genteel beverages. On July 19 of that year, James Miller wrote from Pittsburgh to his sister in Detroit:

I have sent little Ephraims fawns, their names are Fanny and Dick, their food is bread and milk, sweet apples, clover and almost anything a lamb or sheep will eat. You may let them out to play, they won't run away, they will follow you anywhere. I have also sent a small box of glass made in this town. Lemonadeglasses. 1 punch ladle, 7 glass teaspoons, one sugar tube for brother Ephraim. I send them as curiosities as they were all made here.*

To us the word "glasses" does not convey the meaning of punch mug, and it does not do so here, even with the juxtaposition of a punch ladle. Their word for glasses was usually "tumblers," and today we are beginning to believe that the small cut mugs may have been called "lemonades."

A Draft of Decanters

A decanter was a highly prized piece in the early decades of the nineteenth century. Decanters were needed to help the exchange of social amenities. Clear glass of heavy flint, engraved and cut, was a prized possession; it marked social standing and was handed down as a family heirloom. For some years the pioneer families of substance wanted the white flint decanter cut in the accepted mode of the English, the Irish, or the Continental styles of the eighteenth century.

The ledgers of the Harmony Society are informative in certain respects: the time bought, the pieces in demand, and a general identification, such as "Fluted Wines." The glass collector, however, cannot picture the shape or the cutting. When the Society bought through a middleman, the price of the article tells us whether it was free-blown or cut and engraved. Extrinsically decorated decanters, for example, cost from $5 to $8 a dozen; plain decanters, even though ringed, cost no more than $3.50 a dozen. The Society ledgers show what a lively and steady business Bakewell and the other Pittsburgh glasshouses must have carried on in flute cut and engraved drinking vessels from 1813 to the 1830s. A typical entry reads:

June 29, 1825 — Bot of Bakewell, Page & Bakewell

16	gross	Claret Bottles at $10	160.00
1	dozen	Fluted Wines	2.50
1	"	Flute, Ring & Glory	3.50
1	"	Fluted tumblers	1.75
1	"	Burnsyke cut	3.50
1½	"	Egg Cups at 1.00	1.50
1		Lamp Glass & mounts	5.00
18		Boxes at 25 cents	4.50
			182.25

Three Pittsburgh decanters are worthy of extended consideration:

1. The Robinson decanter (*89*). A heavy decanter with pillar cutting is now on view at the Historical Society of Western Pennsylvania. It was given by Mrs. John B. Sellers of Pittsburgh, who was a direct descendant of John Robinson, proprietor of the Stourbridge factory, near Ross and Second streets, Pittsburgh (1823–1845).* She had inherited it from the Misses M. and E. Wightman, also descendants.

The piece is not typical of most of the early Pittsburgh cutting; it is, in fact, much more reminiscent of the heaviness in design we like to think is characteristic of the English and Irish glass of the period. The rounded pillars appear fairly often in Waterford designs. A pair of decanters at the Henry Francis du Pont Winterthur Museum, presented by Albert Gallatin to E. I. du Pont, carry the same artistic feeling of heaviness (*90*). Could Gallatin have ordered the pair from Pittsburgh? A collector would be hard put to find another cut piece from the Pittsburgh District that would convey the same feeling of heaviness as that of the Robinson decanter.

2. The Curling matched pair (*91*). When Martha Curling married George Albree in March 1828, the bride's father, Robert B. Curling, gave them two matched decanters cut in twelve panels. These undoubtedly represented the finest flint

* From the Benson John Lossing Papers in the Burton Historical Collection, Detroit Public Library.

* Dorothy S. Coleman, "Pioneers of Pittsburgh—The Robinsons," *Western Pennsylvania Historical Magazine* 42, March 1959, pp. 55–57.

89 Heavily cut decanter, left, 1823–1830, from the Stourbridge Works of John Robinson. Long terraced neck. Pillar and diamond cutting with flutes at the base. Elaborate rays on base. Heaviness and all-over design show Anglo-Irish influence. H. 11″. *Presented to the Historical Society of Western Pennsylvania by Mrs. J. B. Sellers, a direct descendant of Robinson.*

Engraved decanter, right, 1825–1840, with Daisy and Leaf design, presented by Benjamin Bakewell to Ellen Murdoch, a young nurse in Pittsburgh. This is an important piece in that it established an engraved design from the Bakewell factory. H. 8½″. *The Historical Society of Western Pennsylvania, Gift of Miss Ellen M. Watson.*

90 These cut decanters in the Anglo-Irish tradition are thought to have been given by Albert Gallatin to E. I. du Pont. Pillar cutting and small strawberry diamonds. The treatment of the mushroom-shaped stoppers is unusual; stoppers may not be original. The decanters are shaped like No. 89. Ca. 1820–1830. *The Henry Francis du Pont Winterthur Museum, Gift of Mr. and Mrs. E. du Pont Irving.*

91 Decanters given to Martha Curling on her marriage to George Albree, Mar. 1828. Plain fluted surfaces with cut rings and lines. R. B. Curling & Sons, Fort Pitt factory. H. 10½". *The Carnegie Museum of Pittsburgh, Gift of Mrs. Edward Albree.*

92 Cut pieces with popular Pittsburgh designs, 1820–1840. The decanter has strawberry diamonds with fans and roundels with rays. The pitcher is cut in the vesica pattern. These pieces were exhibited at the Carnegie Museum show in 1949. The decanter and the celery were presented to Henry C. Fry by Benjamin Bakewell. H. of vase 8". Nos. 2 and 3 now owned by *The Corning Museum of Glass.*

glass and the most skillful workmanship the newly organized glass company of R. B. Curling & Sons could command. In 1946, Mrs. Edward C. Albree of Long Island, whose husband was a direct descendant of R. B. Curling, presented the decanters to the Carnegie Museum, Pittsburgh.

The pair of decanters apparently are the first cut ones to turn up with an unquestionably authentic Curling record. It is an exciting experience to discover cut glass pieces made by a company hitherto known only for its pressed glass products. Still, no one can fit the two decanters into an established pattern or an evolving art form. For one thing, the records of Pittsburgh cut glass have been fragmented and are centered largely in the Bakewell factory. For another, patterns and designs in cut glass were consciously imitated, so that an American decanter may appear to be Irish, English, or Continental.

The triple rings around the collars of the two Curling decanters, for example, were popular at Cork and the other Irish factories. So, too, were the handsome mushroom stoppers. The cut panels, on the other hand, were so common that it would be pointless to attempt to attribute them. And the symmetrically bulbous shapes are thoroughly characteristic of the first half of the nineteenth century, even though triangular shaped decanters were common during early years. The two pairs of cut bands around the body are pleasantly unusual and indicate a frank attempt by the craftsman to break the monotony of an accepted pattern. Ordinarily it was off-blown glass that was adapted more quickly to change and experiment.

It is surprising that none of the recorded Bakewell decanters match the Curling pair, though we can still hope for documented evidence to come.

3. The Bakewell decanter (*92*) was presented by Benjamin Bakewell, along with a celery vase, to Henry Clay Fry of Rochester, Pennsylvania. Fry, who had long been in the Pittsburgh glass

trade, was founder of the Rochester Tumbler Company and later of the Fry Glass Company. The two Bakewell pieces presented to Fry exemplify a cut design — strawberry diamond, roundel, and fan — that in the trade have come to be called Bakewell (though the design did not originate in Pittsburgh or with Bakewell). The English strawberry diamond with fan on the celery vase is repeated a great many times in Pittsburgh and elsewhere. To attribute these pieces to a given factory, one needs stronger assurance than pattern alone — such as the typically Midwestern heavy knop on stems of sugar bowls and vases and the general shape of decanters, celerys, and compotes — and perhaps a bit of comfort also from geographical location. We cannot count heavily on location, however, as Bakewell had distribution centers in Wheeling, Lancaster, and Philadelphia and agents in the field. As early as 1839 they had added a retail store on Main Street in Wheeling to supplement their commodious warehouse.

A Ubiquitous Decanter

Early advertising has given rise to some confusion on the design of cut decanters. Wide use was made of the picture of a single decanter — one with a center ring of roundels above and with bands of English strawberry diamonds below (*93*). Helen McKearin, who supplied me with several advertisements of this decanter, conjectures that the design may have been a symbol for those manufacturers of cut glass who did their own cutting. We have found the same picture of the same decanter in six different publications.*

* Pittsburgh *New Statesman,* April 23, 1823, New Stourbridge Flint Glass Works (John Robinson); New York *Commercial Advertiser,* December 7, 1824, Jackson & Baggett; Wheeling *Gazette,* December 19, 1829, Wheeling Flint Glass Works (Ritchie & Wheat); Pittsburgh *Gazette,* September 18, 1829, Fort Pitt Glass Works (R. B. Curling & Sons); Pittsburgh *Mercury,* May 12, 1830, Fort Pitt Glass Works; Pennsylvania *Daily Chronicle,* July 1, 1831, Richard S. Risley's Glass Cutting Factory, Philadelphia.

93 *Pittsburgh Statesman,* July 3, 1824. Robinson advertisement of the cut decanter that so many other factories also pictured.

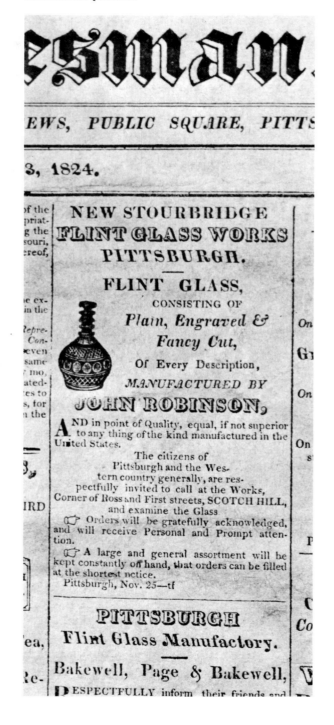

94 Small compote cut in strawberry diamonds with fans, 1835–1845. Diamonds are separated by large roundels with rays. All forms of the design are larger and coarser than earlier forms. Rim notched, base rayed, heavy knopped stem. This is the only compote of this small size the author has seen. H. 5¾″. D. 6¹⁵⁄₁₆″. *Collection of the author.*

95 Unrecorded cut lamp, strawberry diamond and fans and roundels with rays, ca. 1845. The single knop of the stem is decorated with cutting. The pressed base is reminiscent of those used in the eighteenth century. The size of the bowl poses a question as to the illuminating fluid used. H. 7″. *Collection of Dr. E. R. Eller.*

Richard C. Barret, former director of the Bennington Museum, has found the decanter pictured in the Waterford, New York, *Reporter* for September 19, 1826. Such widespread use of a single cut design is indeed a sobering warning against claiming a design for any one factory.

Roundel, Bulbous Stopper, and Applied Base

Collectors and students who insist on attributions often use a single specific example in an effort to establish a generalization. That is a risky course that can lead to error, but let us use it tentatively and with reservations for three design features commonly found on Pittsburgh decanters: the roundel, the bulbous stopper, and the applied base.

The roundel — or, if one prefers, the circle, punty, or *Kugel* — is very closely associated with Pittsburgh cut glass (*94*). Dorothy Daniel expressed the belief in *Cut and Engraved Glass 1771–1905* that William Eichbaum, because of his German origins, originated the *Kugel* in Pittsburgh. Certainly it has appeared frequently on Pittsburgh pieces other than decanters: in wines, tumblers, punch cups, compotes, celerys, and the very handsome sugar bowl owned by Barbara Chase of Pittsburgh — one of a group of strawberry diamond, fan, and roundel pieces (*96*). Rare examples are the pair of peg lamps in the collection of Theodore E. Keller in Cincinnati and a pair of magnificent blown and cut lamps in the

COLOR PLATES

1. (Frontispiece) *Midwestern Cased Glass.*
   Large cased pitcher of lead glass on an applied opaque base, ca. 1850.
   Large cased compote of lead glass on an applied clear stem and foot, 1850–1875.
2. Free-blown dark green bulbous pitcher on a short bell-like base, non-lead glass, 1800–1825.
   Free-blown amber milk pan with wide bowl and folded rim, non-lead glass, 1800–1850.
3. Free-blown green cruet or handled bottle, non-lead glass, 1800–1825.
   Free-blown green milk pan on high funnel base, non-lead glass, 1800–1850.
   Free-blown green tumbler, non-lead glass, 1797–1850.
4. Cobalt bowl pattern-molded in 16 ribs, 1800–1850.
   Light green goblet on knopped stem, patterned in a 16-rib mold, 1797–1820.
   Unusual clear ale glass with light blue loopings, ca. 1860.
   Free-blown cobalt sugar bowl of lead glass, typical Midwestern form often assigned to Bakewell, 1815–1845.
   Free-blown cobalt creamer of lead glass, 1815–1845.
5. Pattern-molded amethyst sugar bowl of lead glass, 12 ribs, 1815–1845.
   Pattern-molded amethyst cruet of lead glass, 16 ribs, 1815–1845.
   Pattern-molded amethyst creamer of lead glass, 12 ribs, 1815–1845.
6. Amethyst cup plate with elongated leaf forms, 1830–1835.
   Octagonal plate with a basket of flowers in the center and Midwestern anthemia on the shoulders, 1830–1835.
   Purple blue salt marked *Pittsburgh*, ca. 1830.
   The famous marked *Fort Pitt* eagle cup plate from Curling's Fort Pitt Glass Works, 1830–1835.
7. Pillar-molded vase in deep amber with 8 ribs, 1850–1870.
8. Swirled pillar-molded pitcher in a beautiful shade of amethyst, 8 ribs, ca. 1850.
   Small pillar-molded cobalt decanter, 8 ribs, 1850–1875.
9. Cobalt pressed vase, lead glass, Ashburton variant, ca. 1860.
   Fiery opal pressed vase of lead glass, ca. 1860.
10. Amber and milky amber candlesticks, ca. 1850.
11. Opaque turquoise candlesticks, non-lead glass, with pewter insets, ca. 1875.
12. Pair of opaque greenish white candlesticks, non-lead glass, with pewter insets, ca. 1875.
    Candlestick in peacock green with hexagonal socket and base, ca. 1850.

Color Plate 2

Free-blown dark green bulbous pitcher on a short bell-like base, non-lead glass, 1800–1825. H. 7¼″. *Ex coll.* **Dr. Florence Kline.**

Free-blown amber milk pan with wide bowl and folded rim, non-lead glass, 1800–1850. A form popular in the Tri-State District. *Collection of The Historical Society of Western Pennsylvania.*

Free-blown green cruet or handled bottle, non-lead glass, 1800–1825. Folklore has attributed it to the Brownsville, Pa., District. Its unusual shape gives it strength through simplicity.

Free-blown green milk pan on high funnel base, non-lead glass, 1800–1850. This type of base was popular in the Pittsburgh District. H. 7⅜″. D. 8¾″.

Free-blown green tumbler, non-lead glass, 1797–1850. Such tumblers were produced as salable items at both window and bottle glass factories.

Collection of the author.

Cobalt bowl pattern-molded in 16 ribs, 1800–1850. Bowls like this were made in England as well as in America.

Light green goblet on knopped stem, patterned in a 16-rib mold, 1797–1820. Originally from Uniontown, Pa., it was presented to the Historical Society of Western Pennsylvania by Mrs. Alan S. Davison, a direct descendant of Jane Free Turner, the first owner. It is probably a Gallatin-Kramer product, though of a rare shape.

Unusual clear ale glass with light blue loopings, ca. 1860. Loopings end in an abortive lily pad. Hollow stem and base are pattern-molded, joined by a wafer. The pattern-molded base has a folded rim. H. 11″.

Free-blown cobalt sugar bowl of lead glass, typical Midwestern form often assigned to Bakewell, 1815–1845. Pear-shaped bowl, high domed cover with flat finial—usual galleried rim. Bowl set on heavy applied base.

Free-blown cobalt creamer of lead glass, 1815–1845. Typical Midwestern shape. Tooled rim and generous applied ear handle.

The Collection of The Historical Society of Western Pennsylvania.

Color Plate 5

Pattern-molded amethyst sugar bowl of lead glass, 12 ribs, 1815–1845. Short footed applied base. Domed cover pattern-molded with flat finial. Galleried rim. Bowls of this type have long been attributed to Bakewell. H. 6½".

Pattern-molded amethyst cruet of lead glass, 16 ribs, 1815–1845. Free-blown ball stopper, hollow handle. A popular form in the Midwest but very rare in amethyst. H. 8½".

Pattern-molded amethyst creamer of lead glass, 12 ribs, 1815–1845. Rim tooled, hollow handle. This creamer and the sugar bowl were prized possessions of the late Dr. Florence Kline of Pittsburgh. H. 5⅛".

Collection of the Henry Ford Museum.

The amethyst cup plate belonging to the No. 170 group is numbered 171 by Lee and Rose because of its larger center circle, 1830–1835. The conventionalized leaf forms are more elongated than on other plates in the series, and there is no rope band next to the serrations. This plate is one of six found in Oxford, Ohio, and purchased in August 1943 by the late George C. Cannon, well-known cup plate collector. After his death the plate was bought in 1966 by William J. Elsholz, so this rarity has been in the hands of only two collectors during a span of thirty-three years.

Octagonal plate with a basket of flowers in the center and Midwestern anthemia on the shoulders, 1830–1835. The bull's-eye serrations are rare on such a plate, and

the moonstone color makes it unique. (The tiny black spot is an unmelted impurity in the batch.) D. 7⅜".

Purple blue boat salt marked *Pittsburgh* from the Stourbridge Flint Glass Works owned by J. Robinson and Son, ca. 1830. L. W. and D. B. Neal in *Pressed Glass Salt Dishes of the Lacy Period 1825–1850* term it very rare in this color. BT 2.

The famous marked *Fort Pitt* eagle cup plate from Curling's Fort Pitt Glass Works, 1830–1835. Lee and Rose, *American Glass Cup Plates,* No. 676B. It is very rare in this beautiful dark blue.

Collection of William J. Elsholz.

Pillar-molded vase in deep amber with 8 ribs, 1850–1870. Unusual stem with bulbous knop just below the bowl. A very heavy piece. Though most pillar-molded pieces were made in clear, color was used effectively in this technique. H. 10¼". *Collection of the author.*

Color Plate 8

Swirled pillar-molded pitcher in a beautiful shade of amethyst, 8 ribs, ca. 1850. Hollow applied handle with a skillfully ended flattened crimping. An example of fine workmanship. H. 8¾".

Small pillar-molded cobalt decanter, 8 ribs, 1850–1875. The pewter stopper serves as a jigger. Shape is unusual for American pillar-molding.

Collection of the Henry Ford Museum.

Cobalt pressed vase, lead glass, Ashburton variant, ca. 1860. Formed in a two-part mold. Eight panels end in scallops. Stem has seven panels. Pontil mark indicates vase was fire polished. H. 8". *Collection of the author.*

Fiery opal pressed vase of lead glass, ca. **1860. Prism** pattern—McKee and Brothers. Rim has 18 scallops. Design of stem was used frequently by James B. Lyon and other Pittsburgh manufacturers. An excellent example of early pressing. H. $9^{15}/_{16}$". *Collection of William J. Elsholz.*

Amber and milky amber candlesticks, ca. 1850. **These** came with pewter insets. H. 9½" and 10". *Collection of Theodore E. Keller.*

Opaque turquoise candlesticks, non-lead glass, with
pewter insets. They are called the Thistle pattern in the
Bakewell, Pears catalogue, ca. 1875. *Collection of Mr.
and Mrs. Walter E. Simmons.*

Color Plate 12

Pair of opaque greenish white candlesticks, non-lead glass, with pewter insets. They are Thistle pattern in the Bakewell, Pears catalogue, ca. 1875.

Candlestick in peacock green with hexagonal socket and base, ca. 1850. Though the color is not usual in Midwestern pressing, the shape differs from that of Eastern sticks.

Collection of the author.

96 Champagne glasses and sugar bowl cut in strawberry diamonds with fans and roundels with fans. Goblet is strawberry diamond with fans. Sugar bowl, bulbous and with a domed cover, is decorated with the same pattern. Finials are cut to match the rayed base. H. 8⅛". Pieces are 1820–1830. Champagnes and goblet, *Collection of Dr. E. R. Eller.* Sugar bowl, *Collection of Barbara Chase.*

Garvan Collection at Yale. We dare not assign all cut pieces with the roundel, of course, to the Bakewell factory simply because most of the pieces seem indigenous to Pittsburgh, nor because collectors and students in other regions do not ordinarily find the design in their early cut glass. Helen McKearin found an Eastern advertisement that spoke of the rising sun. It could be the roundel with rays above it.

The bulbous stopper on cut decanters is a sign — but not incontestable evidence — of Pittsburgh origin. It may be plain with unadorned cut circles or bull's eyes; it may carry strawberry diamonds with fan; or it may even have the individualized strawberry diamond with circle and rays found on so many Pittsburgh pieces. That is not to say that seaboard American factories may not have used the bulbous stopper. It is extremely rare, however, in Europe. In *Irish Glass,* Dudley Westropp pictures the mushroom, the wheel, and the plain cut stopper for Irish decanters, but not one bulbous example. Hugh Wakefield shows only one bulbous stopper in his *Nineteenth Century British Glass.* It is almost impossible to find such pieces in English antique shops.

The third example, decanters set on bases, is

97 Peg lamps for pewter candlesticks cut in the strawberry diamond design with fans and roundels, 1820–1835. H. 4″. D. 2⅞″. *Collection of Theodore Keller.*

98 Cut decanter, 1820–1840, in conventional strawberry diamonds and roundels with rays. Flute cutting from neck to body. Design on bulbous stopper. H. 10½″. *The Henry Ford Museum.*

less certain evidence of origin. From the middle of the nineteenth century on, Irish, English, and American cut claret jugs consistently rested on a well-designed base. The regular table decanter, however, never seemed to need the addition of a base or foot. Yet in the Pittsburgh District, footed decanters appear, cut in the coarse strawberry diamond pattern. One suspects that this was a carryover from the Pittsburgh predilection for a substantial foot on free-blown pieces.

Other cut motifs possible to find are crosshatching, sheaf, vesica, and small diamonds. It is well for us to compare the Corning sugar bowl (*100*), the Barbara Chase bowl (*96*), and the Irish example (*101*) to note the relationships and to observe how such relationships can intermingle.

The Middle Period

The Curling decanters may have been a forerunner of the Middle Period in American cut glass, when American taste shifted to a liking for planes, flutes, panels — the sort of design the

99 Cut decanter, 1830–1845, similar to No. 98 except that it lacks roundels on body. These appear on bulbous stopper. Decanter is set on a plain base. H. 10⅞″. *The Henry Ford Museum.*

100 Sugar bowl cut in the strawberry diamond and fan pattern, 1815–1825. Hollow knopped stem on undecorated base. Domed cover. Galleried rim and general shape are characteristic of the Pittsburgh District. The cut and patterned cover adds quality to the bowl. H. 8⅝″. *The Corning Museum of Glass.*

101 Irish bowl, ca. 1835, called a pickle jar by Westropp. Shaped like Midwestern sugar bowls. Cut design is more restrained than the Pittsburgh strawberry diamonds, fans, and roundels. Knopped stem, domed cover, and galleried rim are noticeable. Deep corrugations on rim and the cut circles on cover and finial are not frequent in America pieces. H. 7″. *Collection of the author.*

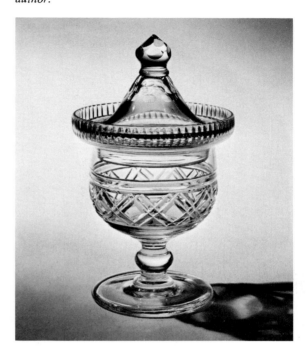

102 Cut and engraved sugar bowl in an unrecorded pattern, clearly in the Anglo-Irish tradition, ca. 1820. The rayed finial on the cover, the short, tiny, cut panels around the rim of the bowl, and the polished pontil would lead to an Anglo-Irish attribution. The general shape of the piece, however, and the sturdy stem and heavy stepped base bespeak Pittsburgh. H. 7¾″. Diameter of bowl 4⁵⁄₁₆″. *Collection of the author.*

103 Cut sugar bowl in variation of strawberry diamonds and linear diamonds with square panels, ca. 1830. In spite of its squat appearance, this piece has the general characteristics of Midwestern bowls. Excellent detail on cover. H. 6½″. D. 4¼″. *The Henry Ford Museum.*

Sweeneys and Ritchie & Wheat did so well at Wheeling. The Robinson decanter with pillars and plane surfaces carries the same artistic feeling, but the design influence apparently was negligible. Clearly the strawberry diamonds and bull's eyes from the Bakewell factory, now grown rather coarse, enjoyed longer popularity.

Another forerunner of the Middle Period could be the Masonic decanter exemplifying the Irish tradition transferred to American soil. It was found in the Pittsburgh area, and although the initials of the owner ("G.W.H.") have not been identified, the cutting fits the decisive and well-executed manner characteristic of the Pittsburgh factories. The McKearins' *American Glass* shows one like it (plate 51, fig. 3) and attributes it to Pittsburgh. Westropp's *Irish Glass* pictures two variations, both with fine cutting and arches (plate XVIII), and a third decanter assigned to Waterford that could well be an exact prototype of the Pittsburgh decanter. The design and cutting of the two decanters — Irish and Pittsburgh

— could be interchanged without anyone's being the wiser, but the Irish piece was blown in a mold, the ridges being clearly apparent around the base. The affinity of Irish and Pittsburgh pieces has already been noted in the shape of the Innes sugar bowl (pages 140–42), which Westropp calls a pickle jar.

We see in three decanters (*108*) a departure from the established patterns we have been talking about. More interesting than the elaboration and deep cutting is the cometlike peacock eye design that became exceedingly popular in lacy glass and in pressed sets (Comet and Horn of Plenty). Perhaps all variations of it should be called Comet, for in 1835 Halley's comet flashed across the sky and gave inspiration to imaginative designers. The comet variation was possibly an expression of rebellion against the standard strawberry diamond and fan and the other constantly used, conventionalized patterns. In any case, it did not presage the cut glass styles that followed. The impressive Mulvaney Ledlie open

105 Champagne glass and five wines typical of the Pittsburgh area, 1815–1840. Note the wafered stems and the emphasis on the roundel and rays. Height of champagne 7″. *Collection of Dr. E. R. Eller.*

compote with the amethyst border overlay is a truer guide to the Middle Period (*109*). George Hogg bought this compote in 1846 for his daughter-in-law, Mrs. George Hogg, Jr. Perhaps the plainness of the piece eventually defeated its own purpose and contributed to the waning popularity of cut glass.

The Brilliant Period and the Decline

The "all-over" decoration of the last twenty years of the century — which Dorothy Daniel named "The Brilliant Period" — followed the earlier comet design. Many of us have seen and remember family pieces of earlier days — wedding presents, perhaps — of fine workmanship in cutting but of a too-busy design to suit us.

The waning popularity of cut glass was predicted by John Ruskin's dictum that cut glass — all cut glass — was "vulgar." It was foreshadowed as early as 1876 in the Philadelphia Centennial Exhibition. Of the Tri-State companies exhibit-

ing, not more than one-fourth offered examples of cut ware. In *Allegheny County's Hundred Years,* George H. Thurston praised the Phoenix Glass Company of Philipsburg "for reviving the production of cut glass as a manufacture of Pittsburgh."

The making of cut glass had died out in Pittsburgh and for fifteen or twenty years the trade in that line had passed to the East, chiefly to the New England states. In 1885 the Phoenix Co. began the making of cut glass globes and in 1886 the cutting of tableware. In consequence Pittsburgh is again a cut glass market, as other firms are following in the lead of the Phoenix Co. . . . Today there is no finer cut glass made in the world than is produced at Pittsburgh.*

Mr. Thurston's loyalty notwithstanding, cut glass did not revive in Pittsburgh, and well before the 1876 Centennial celebration the New England Glass Company was generally accepted in the American trade as representing the highest quality metal and the best designs in cut glass.

* Pittsburgh: A. A. Anderson & Son, 1888, p. 191.

106 Small pint decanter, ca. 1850, cut in panels or flutes. Characteristic of the middle period of American cut glass styles. Probably Wheeling. H. 11″ to top of the stopper. *Collection of the author.*

107 Masonic decanter in the Irish manner, 1815–1835. Identical decanter is pictured by Westropp in *Irish Glass,* except that the American version was not blown into a low-ribbed mold as was the Irish version. H. 10½″. *The Corning Museum of Glass.*

108 Cut decanters in Comet design (Halley's Comet) are set on bases, 1835–1850. All have cut bulbous stoppers. H. of pair 9″, of single piece 11″. *Collection of Dr. E. R. Eller.*

109 Heavy compote cut in panels or flutes, 1845–1850.
Amethyst overlay. Mulvaney and Ledlie Glass Co.
H. 8½″. *The Historical Society of Western Pennsylvania, Hogg Family.*

A government pamphlet on the Centennial expressed a curiously modern and sophisticated viewpoint:

From widely-sundered nations are here shown wares so similar in form and ornament that they might readily pass for the production of one maker so far as these points are concerned. While in a wider sense this unification may lead to broader thought and higher art it certainly has no slight disadvantage, in causing the loss, or partial loss, by disuse, of national and individual modes of expression.*

One final caveat must be made on dating both cut and engraved glass. We are inclined to assign too early a date to fine American examples. Collectors know that early cut patterns like strawberry diamonds, plain diamonds, and flutes were made over a long period of time. They persist, however, in claiming the earliest dates possible for their own favorite pieces. Furthermore, there were relatively few companies producing cut glass before 1830 and their product was expensive. The dates of the Bakewell greyhound, the Curling decanters, and the Renner tumbler persuade us that we should gracefully change many of our recorded statements about early cut from the first quarter of the nineteenth century to the second quarter.

Thirty years ago, one student and collector, then a Pittsburgher, expressed himself somewhat unreservedly on the merits of Pittsburgh cut glass:

It is impossible to leave the subject of early cut glass without remembering the unequaled record of Pittsburgh before its great rivals, the Sandwich and New England Glass Companies, got fully under way. If we were to read all the early guidebooks touching on Pittsburgh, we should be overcome with pride for the excellence of her cut product.†

* The U.S. Centennial Commission 1776–1876, *International Exhibition 1876,* Vol. III, Francis A. Walker, ed. (Washington, D.C.: Government Printing Office, 1926) p. 504.
† Lowell Innes, "Glass Cut at Pittsburgh," *Carnegie Magazine* 20, June 1946.

110 Celery cut with roundels and fans, ca. 1830. Large compote cut in a single row of strawberry diamonds and fans, 1815–1825. The scalloped shell edge gives the bowl an appearance of not being as early as it really is. A very rare piece. H. 7¾″. D. 11½″. *Collection of Dr. E. R. Eller.*

111 Celery, left, plain cutting, 1825–1835, ovals and sheaves. H. 8¼". Celery, right, 1815–1825, cut in strawberry diamonds and fans. H. 8½". Rim is scalloped with shells. Note the stiff cylindrical form of the bowl. Goblet is conventional strawberry diamonds and fan. H. 5". *Collection of Dr. E. R. Eller.*

112 Celery and compote cut in the Sheaf of Wheat pattern, 1825–1840. This pattern was also used in the East. Heaviness of knops on both pieces is noticeable. H. of compote 6⅛". *Currier Gallery of Art, Manchester, N.H.*

113 Four pieces in the Sheaf of Wheat pattern, 1825–1840. Bulbous shape of the rare pitcher and its base foreshadow changing style. Diamond decoration on edge of rim and notches on the handle are slightly incongruous. H. of pitcher 7". *Currier Gallery of Art, Manchester, N.H.*

114 Four candlesticks that seem related in bases and in heaviness. 1 and 4 — flute cut with pewter insets, 1815–1830. 2 and 3 — pillar-molded, 1825–1840, H. 11⁹⁄₁₆". All four have the same bulbous socket. Nos. 2 and 3, *The Historical Society of Western Pennsylvania.*

115 Plate, strawberry diamonds and fans, ca. 1850.
The center is rayed. Sugar bowl, strawberry diamond
and crosshatching. Tumbler, band of diamonds with
rays, 1825–1840. 1 and 2, *The Historical Society of
Western Pennsylvania.* 1, *Gift of Mrs. Douglas Stewart.*

CHAPTER IX

Engraved Glass

The engraving is very neatly done, indeed surpassing any I have seen in this country.
— *Mrs Royall's Pennsylvania, or Travels Continued in the United States,* 1829

Many of the pieces described in the preceding chapter bear one decorative technique only — that of a cut pattern on the glass. Many of them bear two techniques, cutting and engraving, for both frequently appear on the same piece. The Monroe White House service was primarily cut glass, with the engraved grapes and leaves an added embellishment. The same was true of the Jackson service.

When supplementing the technique of free-blowing with copper wheel engraving, the engraver was freed from the stiff tradition of cut designs, because even minor cutting is rare on these pieces. In the Pittsburgh District, one frequently finds pattern-molded examples used for copper wheel engraving. In such pieces — sugar bowls, celerys, pitchers, and vases — one gets the feeling that engraving was of paramount interest to the artisan and the buyer. Tumblers and wines, however, may carry both cutting and engraving.

The task of analyzing Pittsburgh's engraved glass would resolve itself if we could definitely classify fourteen designs to Pittsburgh houses, as Frederick Hunter attempted to do in his work on the Stiegel factory.* Unfortunately, patterns of engravers were not consistent enough to form

many and rigid classifications in the Hunter fashion. Conventionalized patterns, of course, had existed before Stiegel's factory operated and continued after it failed, probably with the normal adaptation and change of design that characterize any evolutionary art form. It is more important for us to note the generally shallow engraving found on many of the Stiegel-type pieces. Stiegel workmen probably used copper wheels, as did the Pittsburgh engravers and the master, John Frederick Amelung.

At the Amelung operation, an additional factor lightens the problem of identification. Amelung specialized in presentation and occasional pieces inscribed to particular people or groups. Many of those pieces used the same design again and again — a wreath pattern around the inscription or legend. The McKearins are so impressed by the repetitive use of the pattern that they frequently use such expressions as the following: "The bowl of the goblet is ornamented on each side with a typical Amelung engraved foliated and floral wreath," and, "a foliated and floral scroll in typical Amelung style is engraved on the cover."*

The McKearins, of course, stress the depth and

---

* Frederick William Hunter, *Stiegel Glass,* reprint (New York: Dover Publications, 1950).

* *American Glass,* pp. 105, 108.

authority of Amelung engraving and accord him and his workmen top place in copper wheel engraving on American glass. Pittsburgh houses followed Amelung's tradition in firmness and depth of line rather than the light and shallow engraving of what we now call Stiegel-type glass.

Cutting and Engraving: Some Differences and Distinctions

Before discussing individual pieces, we should consider the basic differences between cutting and engraving. The main distinctions lie in the size of the wheel (smaller for engraving but ranging in size from one eighth of an inch in diameter to four inches) and in the handling of the glass during the process. In cutting, the artisan held the blank above the wheel, which was iron or stone in the first operation, then wood for smoothing. In copper wheel engraving, a much more difficult technique, the engraver held the blank under the wheel as he worked and brought it up to the wheel. Anne Royall described the process in 1828 on a visit to the Bakewell factory. After a tribute to the surpassing quality of the engraving, she said:

This is done by means of a turning lathe and a great number of copper wheels, some of these so small as to be scarcely perceived by the naked eye. A hole being placed in the lathe, the spindle is thrust through the wheel and after being rubbed with oil and emery, the engraver applys his foot to the step of the lathe and the glass to the copper wheel. When he has finished one figure on the front of the engraving, he takes off the wheel and puts on another, sometimes twenty before he is finished. The machinery of these lathes is costly on account of their exactness some cost as high as $50.00. The ware is also high, $5.00 a tumbler.*

The glass lapidary and the engraver have always been proximal, not only in technique but often in actual business. Beyond the Alleghenies in early times the two were frequently inter-

changeable. In April 1813, for example, Richard James, operating on Third Street between Grant and Smithfield streets in Pittsburgh, listed himself as lapidary and glass engraver.*

Engraved glass is more individualized than cut and in the first half of the century was less often produced in quantity as a commercial product. In 1773 Stiegel hired a Lazarus Isaac as "a letterer and flowerer." That tells us pretty well what would be ordered: initials and dates and scrolls, foliated wreaths, or vintage. More elaborately but less frequently we find symbols (war, masonry, trade) and genre scenes or places of importance.

Compote and Celery: A Matched Pair

Hitherto we have adhered to cut and engraved pieces with family or factory histories. Now we must set sail on the uncharted sea of association. An unusual engraved compote and matching celery vase lend themselves to this embarcation.

The compote (*116*) has a heavy twisted (*wrythen*) stem of a type used by both the Silesians and the Irish, and a deep folded rim at the base as well as at the top. The piece, bought from Gerald Patton at Duncansville, Pennsylvania, and now in the author's collection, was reputed to be Pittsburgh.

George McKearin and Jerome Strauss examined it at some length, and all were frankly puzzled. Mr. Strauss was inclined to assign it to the eighteenth century. Everyone agreed that its glass — double flint — limited it to England, Ireland, the East Coast, or Western Pennsylvania. The engraving, which overflows the leaf pattern in several places, led Dorothy Daniel to consider it a rare example of the early use of acid.† Experienced glass students today believe, however, that the copper wheel engraver simply overran his design. Two spots on the inner circle look sus-

* A further distinction is made in chapter eighteen between engraving and etching. Etching did not find widespread use until the last decade of the nineteenth century.
† Dorothy Daniel, *Cut and Engraved Glass*, p. 65.

* Royall, *Mrs. Royall's Pennsylvania*, p. 124.

116 Copper wheel engraved compote with folded rim and base, 1805–1815. Heavy Silesian type or *wrythen* stem. Wide blunt leaves with stiff veining. Between the leaves is a stylized flower, erect, with two narrow leaves. Engraving is somewhat crude. Probably Pittsburgh. H. 6⅞″. D. 9½″. *Collection of the author.*

117 Cut and engraved celery vase, left, 1825–1835. The leaves on the bowl and the flowers between are similar to those on compote in No. 116 but are more skillfully executed. Shape of vase is characteristic of Pittsburgh area. H. 8¾. Opaque white vase with deep red rim, ca. 1850. Scalloped top. The New England Glass Co. used this shape with more graceful lines and a more slender stem. H. 8¾″. *Collection of the author.*

piciously like this error. The stiffness and regularity of the pattern, the high lead content, and the weight of the glass do bespeak early manufacture.

Several years passed, and then in 1947 in Pittsburgh I was astonished and delighted to come upon a matching celery vase (*117*). Its shape and its heavy stem — really a shortened baluster — are so typically Western Pennsylvania that by association we can now theorize that its companion piece, the compote, also belongs to Western Pennsylvania. The engraving on the celery vase is finer than that on the compote, and there is no bleeding at the edge of the leaves. On the compote the leaves are truncated, so that the center of the bowl is clear. This is quite different from the leaves of the celery, which are completely formed. At the base of each leaf the engraver has placed a tiny bisected circle. Between the bottom of the leaves, inverted tulips alternate with the circles. The leaves on both pieces are shaped and veined similarly. Another likeness on both is the upright stem and blossom found between the tops of the leaves. Though the celery may not have as high a lead content as the compote, no one looking at the two can doubt a family relationship.

A Sequence of Three-Leaf and Daisy

We are on much firmer ground when we consider the copper wheel daisy and three-leaf design, which students and collectors have long assigned to the Pittsburgh District.* In an 1847 presentation piece we now have proof that the Bakewell factory used the copper wheel engraving of the leaf and daisy (*89*). J. P. Bakewell gave this piece, a decanter, to a young nurse named Ellen Murdoch. Though it has an encircling top border of sprays that seem a bit more elaborate than decoration on companion pieces, they are not out

* W. A. Thorpe, in *English and Irish Glass* (London: The Medici Society, 1927), plates 48 and 53, shows the same kind of leaf and blossom on earlier pieces than the American, but not together on the same piece.

of relationship to the basic design. Three free-blown pieces carry the daisy and three-leaf design (*118*). The sugar bowl on a heavy applied base has the gracefully domed cover and the generous fullness of other Pittsburgh bowls. The cream pitcher also fits the Pittsburgh style. The heavy celery (*119*) is probably an example of that type of free-blown commercial ware most frequently found without adornment.

The lamp (*119*) is a puzzler. A very astute student of American glass, on seeing it for the first time, thought the base might have been made at Sandwich and sent in a shipment to Pittsburgh. That is hardly likely. One accepts with good grace the joining of a blown bowl and a pressed base if one agrees with my opinion that many of the so-called early engraved pieces were actually made in the second quarter of the century when pressing was current. Another example of the design, owned by the Metropolitan Museum of Art, is found in the bulbous sugar bowl on a heavy knopped stem (*120*).

Three more pieces complete our sequence of three-leaf daisy engraving design. The Ford Museum owns a Pittsburgh pitcher pattern-molded with twelve short-base panels (*121*). Another piece with twelve panels is a handsome open compote (*122*). It is set on a typical funnel base; both base and bowl have deep folded rims. The clear metal with a good lead content enhances both the lines of the piece and the decoration with brilliance and dignity. At Corning, an even more exciting piece with this decoration is a three-mold-blown celery in the baroque pattern (*123*). (Further comment on these two is given in chapter ten on pattern-molding.) Many more specimens undoubtedly exist with the same design. Was this the most popular of all the Pittsburgh patterns? Probably! Was it the work of one engraver? Quite unlikely! It is hard to be objective when one has for some years lived with and looked at a number of these pieces, each a different functional article and each unmistakably proclaiming its Pittsburgh origin.

Variations on the Three-Leaf and Daisy

Another copper wheel pattern very much like the three-leaf and daisy is the long single leaf set at an acute angle, so that the eye movement from leaf to daisy and daisy to leaf gives a rhythmic feeling of waves. Six examples provide an impressive exhibit of this variation. One is a decanter owned by the late Mrs. John J. Grossman of Pittsburgh (*124*). Another is a pitcher in the Historical Society collection at Pittsburgh, unusual because of its double row of decoration (*125*). The Ford Museum owns a sugar bowl (*126*) and Corning a paneled celery set on a flat base with the same graceful engraving (*127*). The McKearins picture a compote in *American Glass* (plate 49, no. 5). Justin B. Hickin of Cuyahoga Falls, Ohio, had a choice little cream pitcher that climaxes this group (*129*). In studying the three-leaf and single-leaf daisy patterns we realize that copper wheel engraved pieces in Pittsburgh were straight commercial wares. In many of the early Eastern factories, cut and engraved pieces of similar quality were limited to individual order.

Another variation of the three-leaf and daisy pattern did not blossom; it carried three circles (probably representing grapes) instead of the daisy. It is shown on the Corning Museum sugar bowl (*130*). Still another variation is that with graceful feathery leaves springing from an even vine circling the sugar bowl, this one at the Historical Society in Pittsburgh (*125*). To break any possibility of monotony, the engraver in four places inserted circles in place of the blossoms. Both of these pieces belong stylistically to the Pittsburgh or Tri-State manner. If they were plain pieces without engraving, they still would be recognizable as Midwestern.

The Ford Museum decanter (*131*) and heavy-footed tumblers from the same type of mold are not necessarily Pittsburgh pieces. The decanter, blown into a shallow but sharply ribbed mold, has copper wheel engraved leaves shaped similarly to

118 Copper wheel engraved pieces from the 1949 Carnegie Museum Exhibition, 1815–1845. Vintage decanter and wine are later than the others. Creamer H. 6⅞″ and sugar H. 7³⁄₁₆″ are patterned in the Three Leaf and Daisy seen on the decanter (No. 89) that Benjamin Bakewell gave to Ellen Murdoch. Quart decanter shows a variation of the pattern. *Picture courtesy of* Antiques.

119 Bakewell pattern on blown font of lamp, 1835–1845. Pressed base on quatrefoil plinth, fluted on inside. H. 10⅞″. Bakewell design on the celery is excellently executed, 1815–1835. Heavy base and knop indicate early workmanship. Glass has a yellowish tinge. H. 8⅝″. *Collection of the author.*

120 Bakewell pattern on early sugar bowl, 1815–1835. Note the narrow galleried rim and flat finial on cover. H. 7³⁄₁₆″. *The Metropolitan Museum of Art, Rogers Fund, 1936.*

121 Bakewell pattern on 12-paneled pitcher, 1815–1835. H. 7″. Tooled rim and hollow handle. *The Henry Ford Museum.*

122 Bakewell pattern on large 12-paneled compote set on a funnel base, 1815–1835. Generous folded rim and base. H. 6¼″. D. 9½″. *Collection of the author.*

123 Bakewell pattern on three-mold baroque celery vase, 1815–1840. Vases like this have been found without copper wheel engraving. H. 9⅛". *The Corning Museum of Glass.*

124 Variation of Bakewell pattern on quart decanter, 1815–1840. Daisy and Single Leaf in wavelike motion. Plumes and floral sprays. Left, vine swags and blossoms. Right, vine leaves and berries, 1820–1840. *Ex coll. John J. Grossman.*

125 Sugar with circular sprays of leaves and berries, 1820–1840. High galleried rim, double domed cover, heavy knop stem. H. 7½″. Pitcher with two lines of single daisies and leaves in a wavelike motion, 1820– 1840. Pitcher is 12-paneled. The hollow handle ends in a good ridged ear. *The Historical Society of Western Pennsylvania, Michael L. Benedum Fund.*

126 Clear sugar bowl with copper wheel engraving of leaves and berries, 1830–1845. A typical Pittsburgh shape with galleried rim, domed cover, and flat finial. The base is pressed in the Midwestern Hairpin design. H. 7″. *The Henry Ford Museum.*

127 Twelve-paneled celery on flat applied base, 1820–1840. Single Daisy and Leaf in wavelike motion. From the base of each leaf rises a graceful floral spray. Below the Leaf and Daisy design are simple swags. H. 7³⁄₁₆″. *The Corning Museum of Glass.*

128 Pattern-molded vase of clear lead glass, ca. 1835–1840. The 10 panels are of uneven size. Heavy knopped stem on clear blown base. Copper wheel engraving, Flower and Leaf, as found on many Pittsburgh paneled pieces. H. 9″. *Collection of the author.*

129 Engraved creamer on flat applied base, 1815–1835. Heavy threading at the neck. Well-shaped reeded ear handle. Single Daisy and Leaf in a wavelike motion. Spray of berries above and below main design. A fine piece. H. 5″. *Ex coll. J. B. Hickin.*

130 Typical Pittsburgh bulbous sugar bowl on heavy knopped stem and base, 1820–1840. Engraved in Three Leaves and Berries pattern. H. 7⅜″. *The Corning Museum of Glass.*

131 Decanter blown into sharply ribbed shallow mold, 1820–1840. Engraving somewhat like the Bakewell pattern, but the leaves are smaller. Sprays of berries spread thinly give a lightness to the pattern. Though this type of mold was used on other Midwestern pieces, the decanter could be Eastern or European. H. 10½″. *The Henry Ford Museum.*

132 Clear pattern-mold creamer blown in a short, deeply incised 16-rib mold. The piece is clearly Midwestern in form and treatment of the handle. Tumblers from this same type of mold have been found in the Tri-State District. *Collection of Dr. E. R. Eller.*
Clear vase from a similar mold, 1825–1840. The heavy wafered stem has appeared on early vases from the East as well as from the Midwest. H. 8″. *The Historical Society of Western Pennsylvania, Violet Swem Brendel Fund.*

133 Engraved pitcher of typical Midwestern shape, 1815–1835. High shoulders. Daisy and Two Leaves with graceful berry sprays. Band of leaf sprays below the rim. Twelve panels, hollow handle. H. 5¹³⁄₁₆". *The Corning Museum of Glass.*

134 Engraved pitcher with excessive decoration, 1820–1840. Love knots, leaf sprays, stylized flower growing from the swag between the love knots. Leaf spray around rim. H. 5⅝". *Yale University Art Gallery, Mabel Brady Garvan Collection.*

those of the Bakewell pattern and arranged somewhat the same way. The arrangement of the berry sprays, however, is quite different from that on Pittsburgh pieces. The Ford Museum has tentatively assigned the decanter to the Eastern United States. We know that the shallow-ribbed mold was used for many pieces of Midwestern glass. This ribbed mold bears a relationship to that used in the Irish decanters, even though it is more sharply incised.

Further Variations

When we move from the flower and leaf to the flower and spray, we encounter all sorts of variations — a disunity, but not a dissonance, of design. The blown or the pattern-molded pieces carrying the design remain constant, however, to the traditions of Midwest styling. A commendable example is the Corning pitcher blown into a shallow twelve-paneled mold (*133*). Why the artisans thought so many twelve- or thirteen-paneled pieces needed copper wheel embellishment is an open question. The corresponding pitcher from Yale's Garvan Collection (*134*) demonstrates clearly how love knots, sprays, looped vines, and stiff flowers can be altogether too busy. The Corning pitcher has a stylized band of leaf-and-berry below the rim. On the body of the pitcher the main design of daisy and two-leaf with sprays gains its strength from the many stiff petals of the daisies. The design of the sugar bowl from the Garvan Collection, though busy, emphasizes the panels and avoids monotony by generous crosshatching in the center of eight surrounding circles (*135*).

The two-quart pitcher shown here (*136*) has the fern border and light festoons frequently found on gadrooned vases. Its lack of fullness of engraving may indicate that in many commercial wares, engraving was only a step away from unadorned free-blown ware. The decanter shown with it is an even better evidence of that possibility. The Innes pitcher (*137*), quite reminiscent

135 Engraved sugar bowl with band of leaves broken by a circle of eight berries with a latticed center, 1820–1840. Twelve panels. Stem has wafer knop, short galleried rim, high domed cover with flat finial. H. 7½". *Yale University Art Gallery, Mabel Brady Garvan Collection.*

136 Decanter with a simple engraved oval around the word "Spirits," 1815–1840. H. 9". Such a free-blown, three-ringed decanter is timeless. The engraving may have been executed long after the decanter was made. The trick pouring stopper belongs to the 1850s and 1860s. *Collection of Dr. E. R. Eller.* Two-quart pitcher, 1815–1840, engraved with swags and stars. High shoulder, short neck, small pinched lip. A band of ferns is engraved below the rim. *Ex coll. Robert H. Carew.*

137 Bulbous pitcher engraved in unusual geometric pattern, 1815–1835. Band of leaf sprays below folded rim. Heavy reeded handle. H. 6". *Collection of the author.*

of Irish blowing and engraving, shows how well the conventionalized designs we have seen scattered over all these pieces can be joined in a simple geometric pattern lightened by graceful sprays around the throat of the pitcher. The design avoids artistic redundancy, all the while making use of abstract figures.

Smaller pieces like tumblers, wines, creamers, and salts usually carry smaller individual decorations. The Garvan and Corning pitchers show the two most commonly used designs.

One of this group, a salt (*138*), is worth special notice for its family history. It was bought from two nieces of James Nicholson, who was Albert Gallatin's brother-in-law and was associated with him in the glass business. The salt, paneled with simple border decoration, was reputed to be a present from Pittsburgh glassmen to Nicholson. If true, belief is fortified that Pittsburgh used the panel mold, and the point is driven home that paneled pieces had become popular blanks for copper wheel engraving.

The largest engraved piece here pictured, except for the two-quart pitcher, is a handsome paneled and engraved compote on a heavy hand-pressed base (*139*). The festoons and tassels recall the gadrooned and engraved celery vases whose home factories ranged from Philadelphia to Baltimore to Pittsburgh. The pressed base reminds us of eighteenth-century English and Irish compotes and candle holders supported on hand-pressed bases. The owner, the late J. Robert Rodgers of Slippery Rock, Pennsylvania, an early and knowledgeable collector in Western Pennsylvania, was firmly convinced that it had been made at the Amelung factory. He based his belief on the fact that he could find similar patterns of engraving on accepted Amelung pieces. That pattern-molded glass came from that factory has been definitely established by the Corning-Smithsonian excavations at the Amelung site in 1962 and 1963. No pressed bases, however, were found among the fragments, and the Rodgers compote has a pressed base. There is reason to claim it for Western Pennsylvania, since the com-

138 Conventional engraved designs, 1815–1840.
Paneled salt and goblet are rare. Salt belonged to James
Nicholson, brother-in-law of Albert Gallatin, and may
have been a gift to him from Pittsburgh glassmen.
H. 2⅞″. No. 4, *The Historical Society of Western
Pennsylvania, Violet Swem Brendel Fund.*

139 Large compote on pressed base, ca. 1820, probably
Pittsburgh. Engraved with festoons knotted at the joining
with a hanging tassel. Twelve panels. Pressed base like
those used in the late eighteenth century. H. 6½″.
Tumbler, left, has engraving somewhat matching the
compote. Wine, right, on cut base. Bowl of wine is cut in
panels, Continental, 1815–1835. *Ex coll. J. Robert
Rodgers.*

140 The Ihmsen Hornet and Peacock Decanter (over two quarts) from Birmingham Glass Works, by Charles Ihmsen, ca. 1813. Depicts a naval engagement off the coast of South America, Feb. 24, 1813, in which the *Hornet* sank the *Peacock* in less than fifteen minutes. McKearins' *Two Hundred Years of American Blown Glass,* Plate 83. *The Corning Museum of Glass.*

pote is flint and most Amelung pieces are not flint — and since many other paneled and engraved pieces have Pittsburgh affiliations. The late James Rose pointed out very acutely that this large compote is not American in shape. In any case, the engraved wine glass with the cut base shown beside it in the picture appears to belong to the Continent, possibly to France.

Celery Vases

We must not leave copper wheel engraving without an admiring look at the engraved and gadrooned celery vases. The one with the nearest Pittsburgh connection is pictured in the Mc-Kearins' *American Glass,* Plate 48, Figures 5 and 7. It descended from the Richardson family of Maysville, Kentucky, who shopped regularly in Pittsburgh and often visited glasshouses there. This is a very handsome engraved vase with the two eagles resting on a classic column. Sprays and blossoms adorn an encircling band. Demand for such vases must have been heavy and the production high, for most museums and advanced collectors own examples. Patterns of engraving on some of them follow Pittsburgh styles, while others seem to follow Amelung and the East.

Decoration varies from the simplest and barest of festoons to the most elaborate engraving. Attribution is largely a matter of guesswork and hair-splitting.

Genre scenes rarely turn up, and we must conclude that they may have been too demanding of commercial time and talent. We must be content with eagles, greyhounds, perhaps a ship.

Some Economics of Engraving

The ledgers of the Harmony Society show that engraving was fairly common on tumblers, wines, and decanters; even salts were decorated in the early years. Prices of quart-size decanters ranged from $5 to $8 a dozen. Wines were fairly constant at $1 or $1.25 a dozen. Salts, probably more of a luxury table item, cost $2. The earliest ledgers (1812–1813) indicate rather clearly that engraving was then used very sparingly. After 1817, however, it seems to have found wide use. Prices eased somewhat as the years progressed.

Pittsburgh glass factories reached a wider market by offering different price levels of flint glass, but it seems apparent that they maintained the level of cutting and engraving and reduced their price by using two qualities of glass. Price and quality of imported glass were two points that sorely irritated glassmen. English and Irish exporters were never as particular about the quality of glass they sent to America — some of it second or third rate — as they were of their production for the home market.

One puzzling contradiction on the Harmony Society list for 1827 must remain unanswered. Medallion tumblers are priced at 50 cents each, whereas one dozen Flint and Figured tumblers bought of Bean & Butler are priced at $7. We may assume that these must have been Medallions, but we do not know. Perhaps they were elaborately engraved. Bakewell, Page and Bakewell were advertising medallion tumblers at reduced prices in the Pittsburgh *Gazette* for March 1825.

In conducting the commercial production and

141 Engraved sugar bowl with American Eagle in flight, 1815–1825. The finial knob and baluster stem belong to Pittsburgh, as do the flat finial and wafered stem. *Ex coll. Crawford Wettlaufer.*

142 Engraved "Wine" decanter with American Eagle, Stars and Shield, 1815–1835. Somewhat similar to No. 141. *The Corning Museum of Glass.*

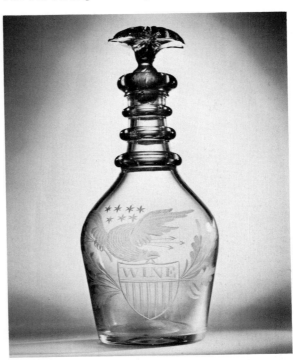

marketing of engraved ware, the manufacturers might all too easily have let engravers debase their craft for quick returns. This obviously did not happen, for copper wheel work done in the Tri-State area in the first half of the century compares favorably with early Irish, English, and Continental pieces. The work deserves an especially high rating on the scale of American glass manufacture for execution and design. For added evidence of this, examine the Ihmsen Hornet and Peacock decanter (*140*), the Crawford Wettlaufer eagle sugar bowl (*141*), and an *E Pluribus Unum* and Free Trade decanter at Corning. An interesting comparison may be made between the eagle on the Corning "Wine" decanter (*142*) and that on the Wettlaufer bowl.

In addition to actual examples that have survived the perils of more than a century, we have the testimony of those contemporaries who visited the factories and saw the work in its own time and place. One of the most eloquent of these was Thomas Green Nuttall, who wrote in 1821:

I went through the flint-glass works of Mr. Bakewell, and was surprised to see the beauty of this manufacture, in the interior of the United States, in which the expensive decorations of cutting and engraving (amidst every discouragement incident to a want of taste and wealth) were carried to such perfection.*

After the midcentury, acid etching and the sand blast flourished because of their reduced cost, but copper wheel engraving was and still is a praiseworthy part of American glassmaking. At one moment there is something passive about the art. The engraver waits for his customer's directions. But the art can be dynamic when the craftsman, impelled by the achievements of men or stirred by the beauty or dignity of a place, records them for posterity. There is always something poetic as the engraver striving for beauty of line releases his spirit and speaks with symbols.

* Thomas Green Nuttall, *A Journal of Travels into the Arkansas Territory During the Year 1819* (Philadelphia: Thomas H. Palmer, 1821).

143 Engraved pitcher with elaborate festoons and knots, 1820–1840. Stylized flower rising from bottom of festoon. Band of leaves below rim. Twelve panels. H. 6⅝". *The Corning Museum of Glass.*

144 Engraved pitcher with festoons, 1815–1825. Sprays of leaves circumscribe the shoulder and the neck. High shoulder and heavy handle bespeak early workmanship. *Ex coll. Crawford Wettlaufer.*

146 Large engraved compote with frieze of flowers and leaves, 1820–1840. Design rather primitive. Heavy stem with wafer knop. H. 6½". D. 8¼". *Toledo Museum of Art, Gift of Edmund Drummond Libbey.*

145 1 — See figure 67. 2 — Engraved decanter with pattern-molded stopper; ca. 1835. Each of the three rings consists of triplicate rings. Graceful swags ending in lovers' knots form half circles marked by small roundels. Between the swags are a stylized flower and several stars. 3 — Engraved deep bowl on an applied base, ca. 1835. It may be the bottom part of a covered sugar. The rim seems galleried and is feathered. Single daisies separated by three pairs of leaves encircle the bowl. Both these pieces could be European. *Ex coll. J. Robert Rodgers.*

147 Engraved creamer with large leaves and four berries (or petaled flowers), 1820–1840. Fine leaf sprays above and below the featherlike band on neck. Design is out of proportion. H. 4⅛″. *The Corning Museum of Glass.*

148 Engraved creamer with leaf motif, 1815–1835. Featherlike band around neck. Rim tooled. On a flat applied base. H. 5″. *Toledo Museum of Art, Gift of Edmund Drummond Libbey.*

149 1—Engraved celery with festoons and flowers. Featherlike band below rim. Superimposed gadrooning at lower left of bowl from a 20-ribbed mold. Double knopped stem. H. 9″. 2 — Sugar bowl and 3 — Celery fashioned in the same technique but not engraved. Such celerys were made in Philadelphia, Maryland, and Pittsburgh. All pieces 1820–1840. 1 and 3, *The Historical Society of Western Pennsylvania.* 2, *Collection of Dr. E. R. Eller.*

150 Whimsy — a fireman's trumpet engraved with a floral wreath. Inscribed "Presented to David M. Lyle of Philadelphia by Harry Tatnall of Pittsburgh" and "John Steen, Maker, Pittsburgh, Pa." (Lyle was a chief engineer of all volunteer fire companies of Philadelphia from 1860–1867.) H. 19⅔″. *The Corning Museum of Glass.*

CHAPTER X

Pattern-Molding: "The Apotheosis of American Glassmaking"

You are right in procuring the molds, I wish to have them complete.
— James O'Hara, Pittsburgh, to Frederick M. Amelung,
    Baltimore, July 30, 1805

Pattern-molding flourished in eighteenth-century America at the Stiegel and Amelung factories. Though both of those ventures had short lives, their influence on nineteenth-century American glassmaking was strong and persistent. When Pittsburgh began to use the technique is doubtful. We feel certain, however, that workmen at Gallatin's New Geneva plant were producing pattern-molded pieces from soon after the inception of the factory in 1797. Pittsburgh probably followed suit.

Since pattern-molding was then more than two thousand years old, we are surprised that techniques of its manufacture have been obscured and that we must theorize from meager records. Present-day usage has broadened the term to include work not properly within an exact definition. Only the products remain to speak for themselves. They are of such quality that one authority has called them "the apotheosis of American glass making."*

Glassmakers began early in the nineteenth century to make increasing use of the highly flexible technique. The artisan inserted his gather of hot glass into a mold that had an incised design of ribs, diamonds, or panels. The mold — either a hinged or a solid-dip mold — was approximately one-third to one-half the size of the piece to be finished.

The artisan blew his bubble to fill the mold, then withdrew it and continued to blow, expanding the piece to the desired size. He used the methods normally used in free-blowing: reheating and shaping; and he used the customary tools: chair, blowpipe, pontil rod, marver, pucellas, shears, and calipers. In the finished piece the pattern had softened under the enlargement and sometimes melted into the whole. The mold marks were gone (unless a hinged mold had been used). The inner and outer surfaces had a corresponding design — that is, a protuberant diamond on the outside of the piece would have a depressed diamond on the inside.

This was the technique that has come to be known as "pattern-molding." The glass took its pattern from the mold but demanded of the individual artisan the techniques and skill and judgment of free-blowing. Strictly speaking, this was "mold-blowing," but purists apply the term pattern-molding only to those pieces made in molds smaller than the size of the finished piece. Today

* George S. McKearin, "Ohio and Midwestern Glass," *American Collector* 9, November 1940, 12–14.

the distinction has become blurred. Collectors rather loosely call pattern-molded all blown articles that have taken the design from the mold. Therefore we must admit that mold-blown articles taking their pattern from the mold are pattern-molded. Our purpose in grouping them, and in including several variations that were little used in the Pittsburgh District, is to enable the beginning student and the new collector to study them in relationship to each other.

The Problems of Identity

Pattern-molding is as old as glass blowing, and it may appear in any country. Baron Stiegel's workmen favored it before the American Revolution, for Stiegel aimed to beat the English and Continental manufacturers who were exporting to the United States. He visited Bristol and traveled the Continent, wooing artisans to bring their skills, and perhaps their molds, to his enterprise in the New World. His designs and shapes — except for the diamond daisy and the daisy in the hexagon — had prototypes abroad. Pattern-molding flourished at Manheim and New Bremen; it crossed the mountains to New Geneva; it floated down the Monongahela to Pittsburgh and down the Ohio to Wellsburg and Wheeling; it traveled overland through Kent and Mantua to Zanesville in Ohio.

Remembering that many factories on the Monongahela bloomed and died in the first half of the nineteenth century, no collector should particularize and attribute his pattern-molded gem to one factory, unless he has a very solid provenance. He must also accept the fact that city factories like those in Pittsburgh and Wheeling cannot be excavated for a scientific study of fragments. The mobility of workmen and ideas and molds was such that the problems of identity are more difficult, perhaps, than those of any other modern art form. The collector may own a beautiful Christmas tree light patterned in Venetian diamonds but made in Bristol, England. He may

have a sunken-paneled flip glass with shallow engraving blown and decorated on the Continent. He may have a swirled bottle pattern molded at Pittsburgh or in Ohio. He may have an exquisitely colored salt blown in the expanded diamond pattern but made in the first quarter of the twentieth century at the Pairpoint factory in New Bedford, Massachusetts. The widespread interchange and similarity of techniques should not detract from the worth of the early pieces, nor from the pleasure the owner takes in them. American glassmakers in accepting traditions of color and form from the past were free to use and to adapt them. The orthodoxy of the products carried forward an earlier artistry, so that America could inherit, enjoy, and bequeath its beauty.

Mold-Blowing—A Forerunner of Three-Mold Blown

Mold-blowing, under our enlarged definition, was found early in the Boston factories. In this method, the artisan blew a very heavy bubble into a full-size mold. (Full-size does not necessarily mean large; the pieces most often found are the attractive, geometrically patterned "Cambridge" salts.) The gaffer needed extra breath to force the bubble into contact with all parts of the mold. When that action was completed, he kept on blowing until the thin bubble burst and fell away. After the piece had been annealed, the rough edges of the rim left by the "blowover" process were ground and polished to finish it. Occasionally the rims were further decorated by a serrated design. The walls of such pieces invariably were thick — so thick that the insides of the salts showed no reverse pattern. A fold of glass at the corner or along the inside edge of the bowl, plate, or salt helps the student to recognize it as a mold-blown piece. Designs of this type consistently used diamonds, ribs, fans, and sunbursts. The first advertisement of molded fan ends salts (Boston *Commercial Gazette,* October 4, 1819) ap-

151 Sapphire-blue creamer patterned in a 12-rib mold, 1815–1835. This is a magnificent piece. H. 5⅛″ at handle. *The Corning Museum of Glass.*

peared only one year after the New England Glass Company opened its doors.*

The technique apparently was not used in the Pittsburgh area, for scarcely ten pre-three-mold blown pieces have appeared there, and those have little evidence of a Pittsburgh source. It is surprising that the glassmakers of Western Pennsylvania did not seize upon this form of mold-blowing as an addition to their pattern-molding. The products were durable and manufacturers could copy patterns of Anglo-Irish cut glass, then being shipped to the United States. This less expensive method of production stimulated American glassmaking. In this technique the molds were sometimes of one piece, sometimes of three.

Three-Mold Blown

Three-mold blowing is closely related to mold-blowing in design and appearance, largely because of the prevalence of the diamond and sunburst patterns. The gaffer's bubble was thinner than that used in the early mold-blown New England Glass Company's products; therefore, the glass flowed into the hollows of the pattern, appearing as protuberances on the outside of the finished piece. Wherever there was a protuberance, there would be a corresponding hollow on the inside. The molds, formed in hinged sections (usually three vertical sections), were the same size as the finished piece, except in those instances where the gaffer made bowls and celery vases from the decanter molds, or fashioned tumblers, salts, and pitchers from inkwell molds. Such products, of course, needed manipulation after removal from the mold.

Three-mold blown was produced most widely at Sandwich and at Keene in New Hampshire and in Connecticut and New York, but Pennsylvania and Ohio factories manufactured it in limited quantities. The pieces were a successful, cheaper

imitation of the imported cut glass most in demand. The patterns were geometric, baroque, and arched.

The early historical flasks were made by a similar method. Mold-blown pieces have a pleasing softness in the outside contours that suffers not at all from the loss of sharper design. This was a highly commendable form that met market demand at a cheaper price and provided attractive decorations and uniform size of containers. From the number of existing examples of three-mold blown, we may judge that a great deal of it was manufactured in this country, probably between 1815 and 1845.

The mold used in this method had two, three, four, or more vertical hinged sections, but the trade still calls any piece so produced by the name three-mold blown. The ridged mold marks commonly found on the outside of *pressed* glass products, when tripartite, are sometimes confused with three-mold blown. Pressed pattern glass, which swept the country from the 1840s on, is fashioned by a mechanical plunger squeezing the honeylike hot glass against the mold pattern. The inside surface of any pressed piece is completely smooth, carrying no pattern relationship to the outer surface as nearly all mold-blown glass does. Today, thanks to the good direction of those who have written on American glass, collectors seldom claim pressed pieces as three-mold blown.*

Harry Hall White, a zealous student of American glass, conducted excavations of early factories at Kent and Mantua in Ohio, at Vernon in New York, at Keene in New Hampshire, and at Coventry in Connecticut. By correlating his fragments with locally owned glass, he established that the three-mold technique was practiced in those five communities. His pronouncement about Pittsburgh in his article "Early Pittsburgh Glass Houses" came years before he had made

* Lura Watkins, "An Antecedent of Three-Mold Glass," *Antiques* 36, August 1939, 68–70.

* See, for example, Helen McKearin, "Fictions of Three-Mold Glass," *Antiques* 16, December 1929; Lura Watkins, "An Antecedent of Three-Mold Glass"; and Harry Hall White, "Pattern Molds and Pattern-Mold Glass," *Antiques* 36, August 1939.

152 Pint molasses can, ca. 1860. Blown-molded, Star and Concave pattern, Britannia top, applied hollow handle. Shown in the 1860 Ringwalt catalogue and the 1861 Jas. B. Lyon & Co. catalogue. An almost identical piece appears in the 1864 McKee Brothers catalogue, the difference lying in the diamonds. In the Ringwalt and Lyon pieces, each diamond contains a star. The McKees named theirs "Diamond." This is a good example of how a design could be altered slightly, yet the successful design of the original could be retained. Height to top of handle 8¼". *Collection of the author.*

Molasses can, 1860–1880. Blown-molded but unpatterned with an applied solid handle. The can is of a typical shape. *Collection of Dr. E. R. Eller.*

these various excavations. Nevertheless his assumption is a reasonable one:

At just what year the three mold blown decanters were first made in Pittsburgh, there is no definite record; but it is safe to state that communication with eastern manufacturers was sufficiently close to allow the making of three mold pieces in Pittsburgh shortly after their eastern production, say 1815 or 1820. I am confident that this will be proven by subsequent investigation.*

 * *Antiques* 10, November 1926, pp. 363–68.

Examples of three-mold decanters, castor bottles, and tumblers are so rare in Pittsburgh, however, that we may conclude that these were not in heavy production in the Pittsburgh factories. What owner of what collection can confidently announce, "This is an example of Pittsburgh three-mold"? How many dealers are claiming this technique for their glass of the Tri-State region? A baroque celery at the Corning Museum is a shining exception; it is assigned to Pittsburgh largely because of its engraved design — the three-leaf and daisy.

Oddly enough, after the Eastern demand for three-mold had waned, Pittsburgh manufacturers were blowing syrup jugs ("molasses cans") into full-size molds. Examples are the star and circle piece pictured in the Ringwalt catalogue of 1860 (*152*) and the rose baroque. Even if Pittsburgh glassmen passed over the opportunity of producing geometric decanters and flip glasses, among others, they did indeed employ the technique.

From 1925 to 1950, practically every new England dealer had for sale articles fashioned in the three-mold technique. With the greater output of the Pittsburgh area factories, it is logical to conclude that they would have produced a comparable number of pieces for a receptive market. We may say that probably not more than 5 percent of the total American production of three-mold blown glass was made in the Pittsburgh area. This is a crude estimate based on the availability of three-mold blown pieces in Tri-State antique shops during the same period.

Broad Sunken Panels

A cousin of three-mold blown, broad sunken panels, reminds us of the past perhaps more definitely than do other forms of mold-blown glass. They do so because of the direct relationship between the eighteenth-century continental flip glasses and the so-called Stiegel-type found so often in American collections. We may recognize relationships, but at the same time we should be chary of claiming sole right to a family line. The sunken panel has an honorable past extending from the shores of the Mediterranean to the banks of the Ohio (*154*).

With an open decanter mold to work from, the artisan could shape a sugar bowl, a pitcher, a compote, a celery dish, an oversize ale glass. These 12- and 13-paneled pieces have been attributed to Philadelphia, Baltimore, and Pittsburgh. I can speak only for the last. One fact stands out: unlike the scarcity of three-mold blown in the Tri-State area, there is a normal

plenty of the paneled pieces. They will be referred to in these pages as a characteristic of the Pittsburgh District.

We may make several generalizations. The panels — generally 12 or 13, rarely 9 or 10 — are short and continue under to the base of the pontil mark (*156*). Pittsburgh glassmen embellished many of the sunken panel pieces with their typical copper wheel engraving designs. Most of the sunken panel pieces were of clear lead glass. Once in a while a blue rim was added. A few exceptions appear on plate *158*.

In view of the range of colors found on the Stiegel-type paneled vases (now attributed to the New England area), the absence of color on the Pittsburgh pieces is odd — not that any relationship exists between the two. On the Stiegel type, the panels run up the body of the vase; also, the shape of the vases has no prototype among the

154 Creamer, lead glass, 12 short panels, 1815–1840. High neck, tooled rim, strap handle feathered at base, well shaped. H. 5″. Sugar bowl, lead glass, 10 panels, 1815–1840. Flat applied base, narrow galleried rim, well-domed cover with folded rim, flat finial. Paneling on small sugars and creamers is rare. Overall height 6″. *Collection of the author.*

variety of Pittsburgh paneled items. In his New England source theory, based on geographical location, shape, and color of vases, George Mc-Kearin established the middle of the nineteenth century as the logical time for manufacture of many of the vases.* The point appears to be a valid one. Paneling seemed to have been popular in Pittsburgh at that time, though it had flourished earlier during the 1830s and 1840s. After pressing glass became well established, paneled bowls and compotes were joined to plain and lacy pressed bases. Their shapes, too, belong to the second quarter of the century, so that the time of

* "A Study of Paneled Vases," *Antiques* 36, August 1939, 60–63.

production of paneled pieces in New England and in Pittsburgh would synchronize. In Pittsburgh, most paneling was on clear rather than on colored pieces, and it is found on other forms as well as on vases.

Rib-Molding

It is difficult to understand why so few pattern molds are available today for study, considering that pattern-molding flourished at Pittsburgh and New Geneva, and considering that it had a popular rebirth in the midnineteenth century at numerous Ohio factories. Only three old pattern molds have been found. Harry Hall White discovered these in the possession of a Mr. Ralph Ross of

155 Clear compote patterned in a 12-paneled mold, 1820–1845. The open folded rim has an unusual amethyst edge. The hollow bulbous stem is on a flat applied base. Though paneled pieces were made in New England, the generous proportions of this compote bespeak Pittsburgh. H. 8″. *The Henry Ford Museum.*

156 Pitcher, 1815–1840. Lead glass, neck tooled, hollow handle, 12 short panels. Note similarity to No. 154. H. 7¼″. *The Corning Museum of Glass.*

157 Bowl, 1820–1840. Lead glass, 12 panels, on applied sloping foot, folded rim. H. 4½″. D. 8½″. *The Historical Society of Western Pennsylvania, Anna Moody Browne Fund.* Sugar bowl, 1830–1845. Lead glass, 12 panels on pressed Lacy base, Midwestern Hairpin pattern. The bowl has a galleried rim, narrow domed cover, well proportioned with a broad flat finial. H. 7½″. *The Historical Society of Western Pennsylvania, Violet Swem Brendel Fund.*

158 Three pieces of lead glass with cobalt rims, 1815–1835. 1 — Monteith or salt, 10 panels, stem knopped, base applied. 2 — Engraved tumbler unpatterned. Copper wheel decorations, Odd Fellows symbols. 3 — Paneled bowl on short funneled base with folded rim. Though the cobalt rim was used in England and on the Continent, these pieces seem quite American. *Ex coll. J. Robert Rodgers.*

159 1 — Clear large ale bowl with 12 short panels, 1820–1845. Hollow hourglass stem on an applied base connected by two wafers. H. 10⅞″. 2 — Clear pint decanter patterned from a 16-diamond mold, 1820–1845. This is a mystery piece, for none like it has appeared. It clearly belongs to the rebirth of pattern-molding in the Midwest. H. 7⁵/₁₆″. 3 — Paneled sugar bowl shown in picture 154. H. 6″. *Picture courtesy of* Antiques. *Collection of the author.*

McClellandtown, Pennsylvania. They had belonged to the Gallatin-Kramer New Geneva venture. They were of brass or bronze, and two were ribbed molds with 16 and 20 ribs each, one with diamonds and flutes at the base.* They are now in the collection of the Corning Museum of Glass, along with a sherbet blown in the 20-rib mold and a small wine glass or cordial blown in the 16-rib mold at a Pennsylvania factory about 1910. Since the height is only five inches and five and three-quarters inches, it is quite evident that the finished pieces were expanded. The third, a diamond mold, illuminated the manner in which most of the American pattern-molded diamond pieces were made. Apsley Pellatt indicated in 1849 in *Curiosities of Glass Making*† that many of the earliest diamond pieces (from the third century on) were fashioned from a ribbed mold, the workman pinching the ends of the ridges together evenly to form diamonds. That was accepted in 1849 as an ordinary method, though Pellatt also spoke of modern brass molds with diamonds already formed. This particular New Geneva diamond mold has 16 short ribs at the bottom of the mold, 16 diamonds in the top row, and 16 rows of diamonds in all. The mold persuades us that American glassmen did not often fashion diamonds by the more cumbersome method of pinching ribs.

The scarcity of pattern-molded diamond or ogival patterns in the Pittsburgh area is surprising. Mr. White's New Geneva diamond mold has been the basis of a theory built on a fact, which is never admissible in law. There was indeed a mold, but we cannot accept the theories that it was used widely, or that diamond patterned pieces found in the Pittsburgh District (though not necessarily derived from this particular mold) must be from Pittsburgh or the New Geneva factory.

Mrs. Knittle in 1931 pictured a marvelous blue diamond pattern molded sugar bowl that looked suspiciously like the Zanesville ten-diamond bowl.

* McKearin, *American Glass,* p. 25 and plate 46.
† Published by David Bogue, London, 1849.

She declared that it had been bought in Pittsburgh in 1824, that it remained in one family until 1930, and that it was probably Bakewell.* A decanter with 16 diamonds (*159*), bought in the Pittsburgh area and in the author's collection, could with equal likelihood be a Pittsburgh piece. It was fashioned of clear lead glass, not the kind of metal found in Ohio pattern-molded objects; while it has the right number of diamonds for the New Geneva mold, it is too large to be associated with that mold. The McKearins' *American Glass* pictures two 18-diamond sugar bowls (plates 52 and 79).

Ribbed specimens of pattern-molding far outnumber every other kind. On the evidence of Mr. White's excavations at Mantua, Zanesville, and New Geneva, and of the examples that exist in the Midwestern area, we may say that the number of ribs on nearly all pieces is 8, 12, 15, 16, 18, 19, 20, 24, or 32. There are exceptions. The Smithsonian Institution owns a small tumbler that, in view of its appearance and technique, may well have been the offspring of the ribbed vase with the swirled top, yet it was patterned in a 14-rib mold instead of the conventional 15. The Metropolitan Museum of Art owns two low-footed bowls in cobalt and amethyst with 14 ribs. Studying these, we would be hard put to establish marked differences between them and the amethyst bowl in the Corning Museum (*160*) that by general agreement is attributed to Pittsburgh. We must confess that no actual mold record for Pittsburgh or Wheeling exists.

Attribution of Ribbed Pieces

It would be foolhardy to accept any set number of ribs in identifying Pittsburgh or Midwestern glass. Certainly we must not disregard Mr. White's findings, which identify the Zanesville houses with 24 ribs and 10 diamonds; New Geneva with 16 and 20 ribs and 16 diamonds; Man-

* "American Glass Sugar Bowls," *Antiques* 20, December 1931, 344–48.

160 Pattern-molded amethyst bowl on heavy applied sloping foot, 1815–1840. Twelve ribs, folded rim. This undoubtedly could have been made into the bowl of one of the so-called Bakewell sugar bowls. H. 2⅞₁₆″. *The Corning Museum of Glass.*

161 Pattern-molded, cobalt-blue bowl on low applied base, 1815–1840. Twelve ribs. H. 2¾″. D. 5¾″. *Collection of William J. Elsholz.*

tua with 16 and 32 ribs and 15 diamonds; and Kent with 24 ribs. Individual differences in the base of the molds, ribbing, a terminal ring around the pontil, and other distinctions help us to identify place and factory. On the other hand, complete dependence on such features without regard to geography, family history, and shape and color of the object under study is not a good enough surety bond. Workmen were migrant and may have carried their favorite molds from one factory to the next, legally or otherwise. Different factories undoubtedly bought molds from the same maker. James O'Hara in 1805 asked Frederick M. Amelung to procure for him the molds "complete." He had just settled with Amelung to come from Baltimore to his new factory in Pittsburgh. Was Amelung to buy a set of molds to ship or carry west with him? From whom? Or was he to bring the molds he was then using? What these molds were remains shrouded in obscurity. Possibly they were molds that had belonged to his father's factory.

In the Pittsburgh district proper we can usually expect pieces with 8, 12, 15, 16, 18, and 20 ribs and the 24-rib hinged mold. The late James Rose believed that Pittsburgh could also claim 19, 25, and 32 ribs. He made the interesting point that many of the early 24-rib bottles in cornflower blue and olive yellow have turned up in Eastern Ohio near the river. Students today, influenced by Zanesville's 24-rib pieces, have rather accepted them as Zanesville. The magnificent amethyst sugar bowl and matching pitcher at the Ford Museum (color plate no. 5) have twelve ribs. The charming little clear cream pitcher that was a wedding present to the wife of Dr. David McCarrel of Hickory, Pennsylvania (*162*), carries only eight. The most common Pittsburgh mold patterns are 8, 12, and 15 ribs. Sugar bowls of a bulbous shape as the pitcher occur in cobalt, amethyst, green, and amber. The twelve-ribbed ones (*163*) have come to be called Bakewell bowls, though no apparent documentary sanction exists for the attribution.

162 1 — Creamer of lead glass, pattern-molded in 15-rib mold, 1815–1840. Typical Midwestern shape. H. 5¼". 2 — Sugar bowl matching the creamer. The high domed cover with a knob finial off center, and the unusually wide drawn-out base, seem to set it apart from its mate. H. 7". 3 — Creamer of lead glass, pillar-molded, 8 ribs, ca. 1845. 1 and 2, *Ex coll. Robert H. Carew*. 3, *Collection of the author*.

163 Pattern-molded pieces in blue, 1815–1840. 1 — Tumbler, 20 ribs. 2 — Creamer, 12 ribs. 3 — Sugar bowl, 12 ribs, flat base, domed pattern-molded cover with flat finial. H. 7¼". 4 — Bowl, 20 ribs, short sloping circular foot. *Ex coll. J. Robert Rodgers*.

164 1 — Greenish tumbler, 1800–1820. Blown in a 16-rib mold from one of the glasshouses near Brownsville, Pa. In spite of the faintness of the ribs, it is a charming piece. H. 3⅝″. 2 — Light green goblet on knopped stem patterned in a 16-rib mold. It originally belonged to Jane Free Turner, wife of Alexander Turner of Uniontown, Pa., a veteran of the War of 1812. It was presented to the Historical Society of Western Pennsylvania by Mrs. Alan S. Davison, a direct descendant. This, too, is probably a Gallatin-Kramer product, though of a rare shape, 1797–1820. 3 — Unpatterned vase holding a witch ball, light green glass. Glassblowers made such whimsical ornaments for the delight of friends and relatives. The belief still lingered that witch balls kept away evil spirits and brought good luck, also that they purified the air. 1820–1850. H. 8″. *The Historical Society of Western Pennsylvania: 1 and 3, Gift of Charles A. McClintock; 2, Gift of Mrs. Alan S. Davison.*

Rhea Mansfield Knittle commented on a similar piece in an article on "American Glass Sugar Bowls." (Most of the bowls pictured in the article were Midwestern.) She accepted the fact that pattern-molded pieces may be later than modern collectors like to think.

Attribution is not completely definite. Probably the type was blown at several of Pittsburgh's houses — Bakewell, Lyon, McKee — and at the Wheeling–Martins Ferry works of Barnes, Hobbs and Company. It is a typical trans-Allegheny form, may antedate 1835, and may be earlier than 1865.*

James Rose made the point crisply in the early 1960s in a personal letter not then intended for publication:

At last report ——— —— still has his amethyst sugar bowl. No nibbles. And I see no reason why these bowls and creamers can't be Curling. They're his

* P. 345.

165 1 — Green jelly glass, 1797–1805, blown in a 24-rib mold. Folded rim, heavy quality of glass, and the uneven shape indicate an early piece, probably Gallatin-Kramer. A very scarce item in any early glasshouse. H. 2½″. 2 — Light green tumbler patterned in a 20-rib mold. This was once the property of John Davenport, postmaster of New Geneva, Pa., by appointment in 1812. It has all the characteristics of Gallatin-Kramer glass, 1797–1820. H. 5⅛″. 3 — Green bulbous bottle patterned in a 19-rib mold, 1800–1845. Such bottles were blown everywhere in the Tri-State District. The author remembers seeing a man bring a chip basket filled with them into the shop of Theodore Strott in Chester, W. Va. 4 — Green glass jug patterned in a 24-rib mold, 1800–1845. Once the property of Armstrong Porter, Luzerne Township, Fayette County, Pa., a Revolutionary War soldier. Though pattern-molded jugs are rare, the unpatterned bulbous bottle with a handle might be found at any early factory. H. 5¾″. *The Historical Society of Western Pennsylvania;* 1, 2 and 4, Gift of J. Harry Gorley.

color range, you know. I don't know of any proof that they're Bakewell, do you?

We are still waiting for documentary proof that will establish these bowls as Bakewell.

Four ribbed pieces owned by the Historical Society of Western Pennsylvania, each with a convincing family ownership, take us to New Geneva. The 16-rib short-stemmed goblet or bowl on a ribbed knop came from Uniontown (*164*). Mrs. Alan S. Davison of Pittsburgh presented it to the Society; it had originally belonged to her great-grandmother, Jane Free Turner, wife of Alexander Turner, a veteran of the War of 1812. Their daughter Rebecca married George Paull of

Uniontown; their son, Mrs. Davison's father, used the bowl as a drinking vessel for cream. The green color is quite characteristic of the Gallatin-Kramer products at New Geneva.

A light green tumbler (*165*), blown in a 20-rib mold, was once the property of John Davenport, postmaster of New Geneva by appointment in 1812. This piece and two others are in the Gorley case of glass presented to the Society in 1957 by Mr. and Mrs. J. Harry Gorley of Uniontown. The green glass-handled jug and the heavy, rather crude dark green jelly glass, both fashioned in a 24-rib mold, are unusually scarce items (*165*). The jelly glass is another of the pieces George

166 1 — Cobalt bowl patterned in a 12-rib mold, 1815–1840. The bowl has not been expanded enough to absorb the ribs. 2 — Cobalt sugar bowl patterned in a 12-rib mold, 1815–1835. This type of sugar bowl has been attributed to Bakewell. 3 — Cobalt mug patterned in a 16-rib mold, 1815–1840. The difference between the molding of No. 1 and No. 3 lies entirely in the workman's intention. *Ex coll. J. Robert Rodgers.*

Kramer took to Oxford, Ohio, and were sold by his granddaughter to Dr. Parke Smith.

From the same type of mold we see the handsome and appealing amethyst open bowl owned by Corning (*160*). Resting on an applied circular foot, it has 12 ribs and was obviously expanded. Undoubtedly a Pittsburgh piece, it has been tentatively assigned to Bakewell, Page and Bakewell, as well it should be if the undocumented theory is accepted that sugar bowls with 12 or 15 ribs emanated only from that factory. Mrs. Ray Patterson of Slippery Rock owns a mate to it in cobalt. Both are good examples of the judgment and skill demanded of the artisan in the fashioning. One English authority says of such pieces:

Sometimes the ribs were started by incisions in a mold, but the vessel was delivered when its shape and size were only half complete. Inflation was continued after delivery and so the ribs were embodied in the surface of the vessel.*

The 12-, 15- and 18-rib cruets — many with hollow handles — are more standard articles of pattern-molding assigned by general agreement to the Pittsburgh District. They are very desirable collectors' items in cobalt and amethyst. They indicate how the artisan must combine judgment gained from experience and a skill in shaping dependent on his visual imagination. One glass historian has written:

Often . . . at an earlier stage of manufacture, the parison is given a pattern of ridges and furrows or "corrugations" by being blown into a cylindrical or tapering mold of that form. The vessel is afterward fashioned into its final shape by free blowing and

*W. A. Thorpe, *English Glass,* 2nd ed. (London: Adam & Charles Black, 1949), p. 16.

167 1 — Clear cruet patterned in a 24-rib mold, 1815–1840. Stopper patterned in 6 panels — a fine example of skillful workmanship and good design. Such cruets belong to the revival of pattern-molding in the Tri-State District. The unmelted piece of silica shows the lack of quality control. H. 9". *Currier Gallery of Art, Manchester, N.H.*

2 — Clear cruet patterned in a 20-rib mold, but swirled in being worked, 1815–1840. Hollow handle seems a bit large for the narrow cylindrical body. Acorn stopper allowed the workman to show his skill, even if it is too heavy. H. 7½". *Collection of the author.*

168 Pale green pitcher patterned in a 20-rib mold, 1815–1835. The high shoulder and bulbous shape represent one Midwestern style. The workman on this pitcher overblew after removing the piece from the mold. Excellent photography has emphasized the ribs much more strongly than would be seen in a glance. One of the tests of good pattern-molding is to know when to stop blowing in order to get perfect lines. H. 5⁷⁄₁₆″. *The Henry Ford Museum.*

169 Left: Aquamarine bottle swirled, patterned in a 24-rib mold. The faint ribs show overblowing. The collared neck places it probably in the middle of the century. H. 11″. Right: Globular aquamarine bottle patterned in a 16-rib mold, 1815–1845. Strong ribs show under-blowing. Lip rolled or folded. H. 7½″. *Collection of the author.*

170 Clear covered sweetmeat bowl, 1820–1840. Patterned in 14-rib mold with the correct cover, even though this is patterned in a 20-rib mold. Cover has an unusually deep apron. Bowl is on a heavy baluster stem, which marks many Pittsburgh pieces. Stem applied to a flat-shouldered base. H. 8″. *The Henry Ford Museum.*

171 Two-part wooden ribbed mold, modern, made to show how pattern-molding was done. Vase, 1820–1840, is pattern-molded with 15 ribs. On slight baluster stem. Flat base. Swirling was achieved by trundling the rod on the arms of the glassmaker's chair. H. 8⅝″. *Collection of the author.*

modeling and the corrugations which it receives from the mold expand or contract according to the contours of the vase.*

We could just as well read "cruet" or "pitcher" for the word "vase." The Pittsburgh and Midwestern pieces show how all this has to be captured in a very few minutes, and how a hollow handle must be applied at precisely the right time without causing a fire crack at its base. How many cracks at the base of handles have broken the hearts of zealous collectors! (No lover of old glass, of course, will lift any piece by its handle.)

An aquamarine pitcher at the Ford Museum is a good example of the judgment demanded of the artisan. This Midwestern gem was expanded too much and too long, so that the ribs, instead of being an integral and strong part of the decorative design, are barely discernible. The bulbous part and the neck must be held to the light to see the pattern-molding. We may note another example of overblowing, but without the same artistic loss, in a 16-ribbed tumbler in the collection of the Historical Society of Western Pennsylvania (*164*). A Brownsville, Pennsylvania, piece, this was once owned by the late Dr. Florence Kline. The tumbler has an unusual color — faint amber with too much of a greenish tinge to be called straw. Smaller than the Ford Museum pitcher, the tumbler has shorter ribs; hence the strength of the lines around the base carries the eye to the gradual tapering off. The late Charles A. McClintock gave his glass collection to the Historical Society of Western Pennsylvania, where the tumbler may be seen today.

Swirling

The ribs (or corrugations) on the mold, of course, are always vertical. If the artisan wishes to fashion the ribs into a curve (swirl) or S shape, he twists the piece sharply while it is still on the

* D. B. Harden, *Roman Glass from Karanis* (Ann Arbor, Mich.: University of Michigan Press, 1936), p. 19.

172 Reddish amber pattern-molded jug, 1815–1830. Fashioned in a 10-diamond mold used by Zanesville. H. 5″. Light amber pattern-molded jug, 1815–1840, fashioned in a 24-rib mold. Swirl to the left is unusual. Both of these pieces come from Ohio. *The Corning Museum of Glass.*

blowpipe. The action is called "trundling," and the blower usually does it by rolling his pipe on the arms of his chair while the bubble is still warm. He holds the end of the pattern-molded gather with a tool to achieve the twist. The clear Pittsburgh vase shows the marked swirl at the top; beside it is a hinged wooden mold with ribs — a prototype of the kind of mold used in the area (*171*). The fact that only part of the ribs curve proves that swirled pieces were always blown into a ribbed mold and are a form of ribbing. We speak of swirled pattern-molded glass only when the swirl is completed from top to bottom of the piece. This vase, swirled within three inches of the rim, clarifies the technique.

It is the fashion today to call every swirled piece Zanesville, because Harry Hall White found such convincing fragments of swirled pattern-molding and because in recent years examples of swirled bottles have been found chiefly in the Ohio area. Mr. White illustrated his 1926 article, "Early Pittsburgh Glass Houses," with the types of ribbed and swirled bottles assigned today to Ohio. At that time he considered them Pittsburgh and would undoubtedly still hold to the opinion that they could belong to the Pittsburgh-Monongahela area. It is unlikely that pattern-molding of this sort would have reached Ohio without pausing at the many river valley factories.

A swirled aquamarine pan (18 ribs) in the Gorley case at the Historical Society of Western Pennsylvania, attributed to Amelung by the dealer who sold it to Mr. Gorley, is clearly New Geneva–Gallatin–Kramer (*174*). An amber swirled pan (20 ribs) owned by the late Mrs. Paul Craig of Pittsburgh, bought near Tarentum on the Allegheny River, has a family history (unreliable as many such word-of-mouth histories may be) of having been made in Pittsburgh. The late G. David Thompson, noted collector and connoisseur of modern art, had a strong interest for a time in Midwestern glass. He once reported that he had owned a swirled bottle similar to that shown with the small pan (*175*) and that the

bottle carried a paper Pittsburgh label. It is unfortunate that he did not retain and record that evidence, for it would have conclusively expanded the area of manufacture of such pieces. We should note that the small pan and the bottle were fashioned from the same mold. Once again we must accept the demonstrated truth that an artisan could achieve many different results, even though he started his piece in the same mold.

Many swirled pieces have been found from New Geneva to Pittsburgh to Wheeling, though not in numbers comparable to the Ohio locations. All these pieces persuade us to generalize that nonlead window and bottle glass was frequently pattern-molded in the eighteenth-century tradition even beyond 1850. We lack advertisements of pattern-molding because bottles and hollow ware were standard forms from which pattern-molded pieces were made. These two commercial products generated profit through fast production, while pattern-molding required more time for manufacture. Without doubt, though, swirling stimulated sales of bottles through novelty and eye appeal. The wide color ranges possible also helped to popularize the technique. No factory

173 1, 3, and 4 — A group of pattern-molded bottles that today would be assigned to Ohio, 1815–1840. In shape and technique they might have been found along the three rivers or in Ohio. No. 4 would certainly qualify as a Stiegel-type of expanded diamonds. 2 — Wide bowl in light green patterned in an 18-rib mold and then swirled. Wide folded rim. The donor, the late J. Harry Gorley, attributed it to Amelung. It is safer to attribute it to the Monongahela River houses, Pittsburgh or Ohio, 1797–1840. D. 8″. *The Historical Society of Western Pennsylvania.*

174 1 — Light green footed creamer, free-blown, 1797–1810. Purchased from descendants of the Hoge family, who lived near the first Gallatin factory at New Geneva. H. 5⅜″. 2 — Bowl patterned in an 18-rib mold. D. 8″. 3 — Handled jug patterned in a 24-rib mold. H. 5¾″. 4 — Small, green glass inkwell, free-blown, with applied petaled foot, 1797–1803. Bought from a family of Nicholson Township, Fayette County, Pa., near the first Gallatin factory. The piece shows the pride of skilled glassmakers in creating an attractive whimsy that is functional. D. 2¾″. *The Historical Society of Western Pennsylvania, Gift of J. Harry Gorley.*

175 Light green, flask-shaped bottle and small pan patterned from a 24-rib mold but swirled in the fashioning, 1815–1845. These two pieces show how the same ribbed mold can be used as a starting point for two quite different articles. The late G. David Thompson once saw a flask like this one with a Pittsburgh label on it, though modern collectors would call it Ohio. H. of flask 6¾". D. of pan 5⅞". *Collection of the author.*

records have yet been found to tell us how long pattern-molding was profitable or how much such molded articles cost. We are fairly certain that the ordinary globular bottle — today called Zanesville — was a major commercial product. Many of the early swirled pieces of other shapes were fashioned by workmen who wished to show their skill and to escape routine. There is an affinity between them and the craftsmen of art nouveau in the nineties who were expressing their individuality in equally fine pieces, using the same technique.

Broken Swirls — Swirls Cut by Ribbing

Another design derived from pattern-mold ribbing is the broken swirl. The blower trundles the piece until all the ribs are swirled (*177*). He then reheats it, reinserts it into the mold, withdraws it, and expands it. The second impression, its swirls cut by faint ribbing, reveals an ingenious and attractive design. More broken-swirl pieces have been found in Ohio than in Pittsburgh. The Historical Society in Pittsburgh has a superb clear flip glass in this pattern. The Henry Ford Museum has a green quart pitcher without a handle said to have come from the Gallatin-Kramer works. Though the reeded handle has been broken away, this is excellent study material.

Pillar-Molding — Hotel, Bar, and Riverboat Glass

The scarcity of some designs of pattern-molding in Western Pennsylvania is compensated for by the large number of pillar-molded pieces produced at Pittsburgh. By its sturdiness and pleasantly rounded lines, pillar-molding possessed a dignity inherent in middle-class America. Examples of pillar-molding turn up today anywhere along the great valley from Pittsburgh to the Gulf of Mexico. Dealers, collectors, and authorities unite in declaring that these pieces belong to Pittsburgh.

176 1 — Clear bowl patterned in a 16-rib mold, 1815–1845. Not common in clear glass. D. 6". 2 — Clear quart pitcher patterned in an 18-rib mold, 1815–1845. Deep-folded rim, graceful hollow handle. The metal is brilliant and the swirling adds distinction — a tour de force of pattern-molding because the excellence of the pitcher does not depend on color. H. 7½". *Collection of the author.*

Pattern-Molding: "The Apotheosis of American Glassmaking"   193

177 Bluish green pitcher patterned in a 24-rib mold, 1815–1845. The broken swirl is achieved by trundling the rod after the piece has been removed from the mold the first time. It is then reheated and reintroduced into the ribbed mold; thus the swirls are broken by the lines of the ribs. H. 6⅞". *The Corning Museum of Glass.*

Apsley Pellatt described the process of manufacture some 120 years ago:

The metal is first gathered upon a rod in the ordinary manner, except that the first gathering should be allowed to cool to a greater degree of hardiness than usual. The second coating should be pressed into the mold as hot as possible that the exterior coating only shall be acted upon by the pressure of molding, and that the interior shall preserve its smooth circular area.*

Pellatt called it "patent pillar molding" and described the fire polish given by remelting of the surface of the glass after it has left the mold. He spoke of pillar-molding as one of the greatest modern improvements, but he admitted that the Romans had practised that technique.

We are inclined to believe that Pittsburgh glassmen used extra-deep ridges for their pillar-molded glass. Fire polishing was undoubtedly an integral part of the process. Pellatt compared the heavy ridges with the sharpness of refraction gained from the edges of cut glass, and he concluded that cut glass was superior. Nevertheless, the low cost of production (which he mentioned) and its clarity and durability made this type of pattern-molded glass a favorite on the frontier.

Just when pillar-molding became popular in the region is hard to say. A beginning date might be set in the late 1830s, but it flourished around the middle of the century and later. We know from the McKee catalogues of the 1860s that it was being produced then. We believe that it persisted into the seventies. Illustrations in catalogues of English glasshouses of the seventies support this opinion. Pellatt's *Curiosities of Glass Making* in the author's possession carries Frederick L. McKee's name on the flyleaf and the date 1850. This is hardly evidence that McKee's cruets (we should rather call them decanters, with the pewter slip stoppers holding a jigger) derive from the designs in Pellatt's book. Two of the

* *Curiosities of Glass Making*, London, pp. 104–5. No evidence has yet been adduced to show that Pellatt visited Pittsburgh or even came to America.

178 Pattern-molded clear flip glass in a finely executed broken swirl, 1815–1840. A rare example of this technique in clear lead glass and in this tumbler form. Found in the Pittsburgh area. H. 6". *The Historical Society of Western Pennsylvania.*

179 Five examples of pillar-molding from an 8-rib mold, 1835–1870. 1 — Clear sugar bowl on flat applied base with pointed domed cover. 2 — Well-designed clear cruet with unusual ball stopper. H. 8½″. 3 — Tall heavy amber vase on hollow baluster stem on an applied base. 4 — Cobalt cruet, triangular shape with a pewter jigger for a cover. H. 9¼″. 5 — Cobalt creamer. All these pieces were made for table decoration as well as for use. Carnegie Museum Exhibition, 1949–1950. *Picture courtesy of* Antiques.

180 Four pieces of clear pillar-molding, 8 ribs, 1835–1870. These represent ordinary design and a few years ago were collectible at reasonable prices. There is a marked heaviness in each piece — a characteristic that made them suitable for hotel, bar, and riverboat use. The term "riverboat" has persisted. 1 — Triangular decanter with pewter jigger. The top is dressed up with 2 rings and 6 panels. 2 — Open compote with folded rim and heavy baluster stem on a flat 2-layer base. The bowl has been fire polished, and the ribs are drawn out well. 3 — An early vase without the scalloped top that marked later pieces. Baluster stem on flat applied base. H. 8⅞″. 4 — Pitcher with tooled rim and hollow handle. More pitchers, pillar-molded, are found like this one without the applied base than with it. *Carnegie Museum Exhibition, 1949–1950.*

American pillar-molded decanters in the McKee catalogue (1864) do resemble the English pieces somewhat in shape. Their bulbous shoulders taper down to a wider base. Collectors have been apt to call such shapes English. The pinched pillars and crude triangular shape of some of the others are not so typical of the English work.

Two kinds of pillars exist in Pittsburgh area products. One is the heavy flowing pillar that bespeaks two insertions and, in the best decorative tradition, has a characteristically heavy, double-dipped and fire-polished rib. The other is the narrow pillar that stands out sharply and looks almost pinched, indicating that it was blown into a deeply cut mold. The number of ribs runs consistently to 8 or 12, occasionally 9. Some ribs can be so light that we are uncertain how to classify them. It is sometimes a most fascinating puzzle, in fact, how to draw the line between conventional pattern-molding and the obvious pillar ribs. The line of demarcation is as uncertain as that between prose and poetry, because they so often overlap at a common point. The small blue creamer (*179*) is a good example. In Pittsburgh proper it would be called pillar-molded; others would more probably call it pattern-molded.

The Historical Society of Western Pennsylvania has an open pillar-molded compote with heavy fire-polished pillars; it was a gift from the Bakewell family of Sewickley, Pennsylvania (*182*). That should not persuade us that all Bakewell pillar-molded pieces were so made, or that all McKee pieces had narrow, less pleasing ridges.

Quite possibly other areas than Western Pennsylvania made pillar-molded glass. In recent years a good many small pillar-molded decanters have come in from Canada, perhaps imported from England and Ireland (*183*). Lura Watkins believes that the New England Glass Company and possibly the Union Glass Company of Somerville, Massachusetts, may have produced pillar-molding.

Pillar-molding lent itself so well to the use of color (*184*) that the overwhelming number of clear pieces may surprise us, until we remember the high regard for clear lead glass in cut and engraved, and recall that manufacture of pillar-molded glass was primarily a commercial, not an artistic venture. We have few purely decorative pieces like vases, while utilitarian pieces abound: decanters, open compotes, cruets, pitchers, and tall covered candy and drugstore jars. Sugar bowls are more rare and are almost never found in color (*188*).

The two predominant colors, dark blue and amber, are occasionally lightened by a green, an opaque white, an amethyst, or a yellow decanter. Some of the tall, slender colored bottles were made into the twentieth century, when they became barroom and soda fountain accessories. Bottles, cruets, vases, open compotes, and pitchers (*190*) were likely to be chosen if color was to be used in the manufacture. A throwback to the eighteenth century were the decanter bottles and covered drugstore jars with a candy stripe of blue running down the pillar — objects that have fascinated generations of children. Sometimes, for the sake of novelty, the artisan combined other techniques with pillar-molding. Examples are the heavy opaque vase in the author's collection (*191*) and the Ford Museum's opaque white cruet cased with clear glass, on a clear foot, with a clear handle (*192*).

This type of glass fitted admirably our Western ways. It made a stunning display, and even the late Victorian vases possess charm. Its sturdiness and sparkle helped it to grace hotels, store windows, barrooms, riverboats, and even domestic sideboards. It was found on every elegantly appointed paddle-wheel boat that plied the Western rivers. The brilliance of pillar-molded glass, its resonance, the weight contributed by a good proportion of lead, attracted those buyers who felt an urge to add splendor to their homes or commercial establishments. It pleased them; it pleases us even against the background of today's skeleton-like functional design. We may say the same of the other shapes and forms and techniques in our rich inheritance of pattern-molded works of art.

181 Clear pillar-molded tumbler, ca. 1850, skillfully and attractively worked by trundling and fire polishing. Eight ribs. H. 3 1/16". *The Henry Ford Museum.*

182 Clear, pillar-molded, open compote on high baluster stem on a flat terraced base, 1835–1870. That this piece was given by Mrs. Donald Campbell Bakewell should not lead collectors to assume that Bakewell was the sole producer of pillar-molding. H. 9 1/8". *The Historical Society of Western Pennsylvania.*

183 Pillar-molding, 1835–1870. 1 — Clear pillar-molded cruet with Britannia cover. The flat applied base and the broad hollow handle give it authority. H. 10". 2 — Large clear covered compote on baluster stem with a flat applied base. H. 12 1/2". 3 — Blue triangular decanter with a heavy ring between the shoulder and rim. English glassmakers favored this design. H. 11". *The Historical Society of Western Pennsylvania: 1, Gift of Charles A. McClintock; 2, Gift of the Downey Family; 3, Violet Swem Brendel Fund.*

184 One of the finest pieces of American pillar-molding known, ca. 1850. Glowing amber enhances the well-proportioned vase. Hollow stem on flat base. H. 11 5/8". *Ex coll. Dr. Florence Kline, The Corning Museum of Glass.*

185 Clear pillar-molded pitcher on heavy applied base, ca. 1850. Solid handle. H. 7". *The Wadsworth Atheneum, Hartford, Edith Olcott van Gerbig Collection.*

186 Two unusual examples of clear pillar-molding joined to typically Midwestern pressed bases, 1840–1870. Lamp, probably for coal oil, is rare in pillar-molding. H. 7⅜". Plain vase with folded rim. H. 9¾". *Collection of Dr. E. R. Eller.*

187 1 — Early clear pillar-molded candlesticks with pewter insets, ca. 1835. Double-ringed tops on hollow bulbous shafts. Flat applied bases. H. 9½". 2 — Tall covered jar with knob, finial baluster stem on applied terraced base, ca. 1850. Such jars were used in store windows to advertise merchandise. H. 17½". 3 — Vase swirled at the rim, ca. 1845. Plain short stem on terraced base. H. 8⅜". *Ex coll. John J. Grossman.*

188 Unusual clear pillar-molded sugar bowl, ca. 1835. It takes the shape of Midwestern pattern-molded and free-blown sugar bowls rather than that of other pillar-molded sugars. Shortened baluster stem on flat terraced base. H. 7½". *The Wadsworth Atheneum, Hartford, Edith Olcott van Gerbig Collection.*

189 1 — Amber pillar-molded cruet with Britannia top. Squat bulbous bowl and the heavy applied base limit its style quality. 2 — Amethyst pillar-molded pitcher with ringed neck and heavy applied handle. The cylindrical shape, without any attempt by the maker to vary the form, gives it a heavy, awkward look, 1845–1875. *Ex coll. J. Robert Rodgers.*

190 1 — Blue pillar-molded creamer. H. 6″. 2 — Clear pillar-molded sugar, 8-rib mold. H. 10″. 3 — Opaque white creamer shaped to a broad base. Pillars are narrow, almost like pattern-molded ribs, 1835–1870. H. 5½″. 1 and 3, *Collection of Dr. E. R. Eller.* 2, *The Historical Society of Western Pennsylvania.*

Pattern-Molding: "The Apotheosis of American Glassmaking"   199

191 Pillar-molded vase cased, clear over opal, ca. 1850. A clear stem and applied base. Nearly all cased pillar-molded pieces are directly functional; consequently, this form is rare. H. 10⅝". *Collection of the author.*

192 Cruet, 1845–1870. Cased clear over opaque white. Pillar-molded in 8 ribs, pewter cover. Clear handle and applied clear base. This cruet is excellent evidence that the Pittsburgh area cased glass, though actual documentary proof has not yet been unearthed. This is a typical Midwestern cruet. H. 9⅞". *The Henry Ford Museum.*

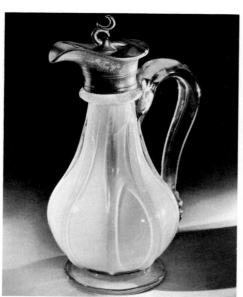

193 Pillar-molded pitcher, cased clear over opaque white, 1845–1870. Handle also cased. Pitcher set on a clear base. H. 8". Pillar-molded creamer, cased clear over opal, 1845–1870. Handle cased. The ribs are lighter than those on the pitcher. *Ex coll. Crawford Wettlaufer.*

194 Opaque white pillar-molded vase, 1845–1870. Metal unusually hard and shiny. Bulbous bowl rising in graceful proportions to a flaring rim. Shortened baluster stem on broad terraced base. H. 8½". *Plate No. 51 in the McKearins' Two Hundred Years of American Blown Glass. Collection of the author.*

195 Clear pillar-molded salt, ca. 1845. Pewter top and applied base. This charming early piece establishes the fact that all pillar-molding does not have to be large and heavy. H. 2¼". *The Wadsworth Atheneum, Hartford, Edith Olcott van Gerbig Collection.*

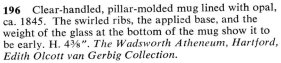

196 Clear-handled, pillar-molded mug lined with opal, ca. 1845. The swirled ribs, the applied base, and the weight of the glass at the bottom of the mug show it to be early. H. 4⅜". *The Wadsworth Atheneum, Hartford, Edith Olcott van Gerbig Collection.*

197 Clear pillar-molded compote with cobalt rim, ca. 1870. Inverted baluster stem on heavy applied base. This is a late piece, and may possibly be English. It lacks the simplicity and directness of earlier pieces. H. 9¾". *The Henry Ford Museum.*

Pattern-Molding: "The Apotheosis of American Glassmaking" 201

198 Characteristic examples of pattern-molding. 1 — Amethyst Stiegel-type perfume bottle, diamond diapering. Late eighteenth century. H. 4″. 2 — Cobalt Stiegel-type sugar bowl, diamond diapering, late eighteenth century. Though these bowls were also made in England, this one seems American in shape and workmanship. H. 6″.

3 — Amber chestnut-shaped flask patterned in a 10-diamond mold, Zanesville, 1815–1830. 4 — Cobalt three-mold blown creamer, G III-24. New England, 1815–1840. *The Historical Society of Western Pennsylvania, Michael L. Benedum Fund.*

199 1 — Clear creamer patterned in a broken swirl from a 16-rib mold, 1775–1835. The long neck and the bulbous part at the bottom are characteristics of the Stiegel-type shape. H. 4″. 2 — Child's amethyst decanter patterned in a 16-rib mold. H. 4½″. 3 — Cobalt baptismal bowl, diamond diapering, small applied base, late eighteenth century. H. 2¾″. D. 4¼″. 4 — Cobalt creamer patterned in a 14-rib mold. Knopped stem joined to a truncated base. First quarter of the nineteenth century. H. 3⅝″. *The Historical Society of Western Pennsylvania, Gift of J. Harry Gorley.*

202   Pittsburgh Glass — 1797–1891

200 Heavy turquoise opalescent broken-swirl pitcher on an applied base. Nonlead glass. The pushed-up lip would seem to make the spout impossible to pour. The handle finished at the top shows that the pitcher belongs to the 1870s. Handle and foot deep clear green. H. 8⅛". *The Henry Ford Museum.*

201 1 — Aqua goblet, double application of glass in a 24-rib mold. Attribution uncertain. 2 — Pale green milk pan patterned in a 20-rib mold, 1815–1835. Clearly Tri-State area. 3 — Free-blown green inkwell on heavy base, 1799–1815. 4 — Green bottle patterned in a 16-rib mold but made according to the German Half Post method. Attribution uncertain. *Ex coll. J. Robert Rodgers.*

CHAPTER XI

Bottles and Flasks

[Whiskey] was the indispensible emblem of hospitality, and the
accompaniment of labor in every pursuit; the stimulant in joy, the solace
in grief. It was kept on the counter of every store, in the corner cupboard
of every well-to-do family. . . . The minister partook of it before going
to church . . . and after he came back. At home and abroad, at
marryings and buryings, at house-raisings and log rollings, at harvestings
and huskings, . . . it was the omnipresent beverage of old and young,
men and women; and he was a churl who stinted it. To deny it
altogether required more grace or niggardliness than most men could
command, at least for daily use.
— *Centenary Memorial of the Planting and Growth of Presbyterianism
in Western Pennsylvania and Parts Adjacent,* 1876

With the steady growth of the population, the isolated cabins of the Midwest became part of villages, and villages became towns. Both had distilleries and breweries, and these required containers to hold their product. Wooden kegs and pottery jugs, though made in volume, could not keep up with the demand. There was a need for bottles — the ideal container for liquids and liquors. To meet it, scores of bottle-glass factories sprang up in and around Pittsburgh and in the other communities along the rivers. Their purpose was to produce articles of everyday use and homely service. Any thorough student or serious collector of American glass who examines Midwestern bottles and flasks in museums or in discriminating private collections marvels at the beauty, the sound artistic quality, and the high technical proficiency of these pieces.*

* "Excepting only the finest of the Stiegel perfume or pocket bottles, the flasks and bottles produced in Mid-

We dare not even guess at the millions of bottles and flasks that left these manufactories for local use, for the river and Western trade, and even for distant distilleries. The O'Hara-Craig letters quoted in chapter three contain many references to price lists, sizes, and various destinations. The Harmony Society ledgers reveal later in the century substantial purchases of bottles for their superior brands of whiskey, beer, brandy, wine, and cider.

The word "flask" appears as early as June 29, 1800, in an advertisement in the Pittsburgh *Gazette:* "Bottles of all kinds and in any quantity may be had together with pocket flasks, pickling jars, apothecary shop furniture or other hollow ware." This was the year in which Eichbaum and

western glasshouses operating during the first half of the nineteenth century have never been excelled and seldom equalled, in America or elsewhere, in colors and delicacy of molded design." McKearin, *American Glass,* p. 439.

Wendt rented the O'Hara-Craig works. The wording of the notice leads us to believe that the advertised flasks were smaller and flatter than the ordinary bottle, which naturally took its shape from the bubble at the end of the blowpipe (not necessarily round). Unlike the so-called "chestnut" bottles, flasks had shorter uncollared necks.

Early free-blown bottles were functional, low in cost, and generally had little individuality other than color. They were expendable and therefore have not come down to us in large numbers. Most of the early bottles we see were blown from one gather of glass, not from the two-gather German half-post method, and most were not even shaped by clay dip molds. Travelers' bottles and some of the spirit containers were cracked or whetted off the blowpipe, then finished sometimes by shearing and being fire-polished. The olive amber travelers' flask (*25*), once encased in straw, is a good example. The weight of the glass toward the bottom of this bottle, a frequent characteristic, indicates early and crude workmanship.

Early bottles became collectors' items in the 1920s, and in the past decade they have soared in value, or at least in cost. One of the collectible items in the Pittsburgh District has been the so-called Gallatin bottles — aquamarine to dark green, bulbous for the most part but sometimes cylindrical with a high-kick pontil. The first few came from descendants of the New Geneva families and undoubtedly were blown at the Gallatin works. These, however, were used as examples for eager collectors, and every pale green bottle in the district was called Gallatin. The shape and the metal, nevertheless, are typical of all early factories. Such bottles were called "the poor man's decanter." Often an applied handle was added to the bottle.

Prices for the early bottles furnish an interesting comparison. Black or very dark brown bottles apparently were prized more highly than ordinary green. (Certain materials are better preserved in dark glass.)

Free-blown bottles were rarely made in the technique of the German half-post method. The workman probably used an open dip or dish mold to help him produce vessels of at least an approximately correct measure — gill, half pint, pint, or quart. The mold would have been formed of clay, wood, or iron. The increasing demand for accuracy in measurement of content limited the large-scale free-blowing of bottles. What part pattern-molding played in this development is uncertain. Just as in the case of unpatterned bottles, one cannot expect the pattern-molded ones to be a completely accurate measurement. The size of the mold would not be a sure guide. The number of ribs in pattern-molded bottles was usually 12, 15, 16, 18, 20, 24, or 32.

The absence of any price lists on pattern-molded bottles, the complete lack of descriptive advertising, and the greater skill and longer time required to fashion such bottles persuades us that production of such ware was limited as compared with the production of free-blown bottles. The colors are so rich that sometimes we can theorize that a factory turned to pattern-molding when it had a vivid batch of metal. Colors ran from clover honey to a glowing amber that often almost turned to red, from the most delicate pale green at one end of the scale to a deepening emerald at the other, and with all shades of olive-amber in between the greens and the ambers. Cobalt and amethyst are so rare as to be much sought after. The patterns glorified the colors. Whether or not pattern-molding bore any relationship to the color mixture, we can be sure that the American consumer discarded free-blown bottles and saved pattern-molded bottles for their interesting beauty, whether in design, or color, or both.

Pictorial-Historical Flasks

A fascinating field for any collector of glass is the pictorial-historical whiskey flask, which recorded in sculptured mold and blown glass great names and events and famous symbols and mottoes of our early history. Many of the pictorials

O'Hara-Craig Price List 1804   1806   1810
                                                      (J. Carson, June 20, 1810)

		1804	1806	1810 Green	1810 Black or Dark Green
Hollow Ware					
Gallon Bottle, per doz.		$4.00		.80	4.00
½ gallon	” ”	2.40		.48	2.40
Quart	” ”	1.60	.60	.32	1.60
Pint	” ”	1.20			1.20
Porter & Claret	” ”	1.33⅓			
Pitchers					
Gallon	” ”			1.20	
½ gallon	” ”	4.00		.80	
Quart	” ”	3.00		.60	
Jars					
Gallon	” ”	4.90		.96	
½ gallon	” ”	3.00		.60	
Quart	” ”	2.00		.40	
Pint	” ”	1.33⅓		.30	
Tumblers					
Quart			2.67 (in 1808)		
Pint			1.67		
½ pint			1.00		
Flasks					
Pint			1.20		
Decanters					
Quart			3.00		
Pint			2.00		
½ pint			1.50*		

* Sources of compilation: Knittle, *Early American Glass,* p. 214; O'Hara-Craig letters: J. Carson, Philadelphia (June 20, 1810, prices), James Kelly, Cynthia, Kentucky (July 7, 1808, prices of tumblers), Terence Campbell at Bedford, Pa. (April 1, 1806, prices of tumblers, flasks, and decanters).

were commemorative. They flourished from about 1815 to the early 1860s. They were hand-blown into full-size, two-part, hinged molds.

We may estimate that the Pittsburgh-Monongahela-Wheeling District produced about one fifth of the early pictorial-historical whiskey flasks — those dating before the Civil War. The calculation, admittedly rough, is based on charts of flasks in the McKearins' *American Glass.* In the classification of 398 flasks there are 60 unidentifiables as to factory source. The remaining 338 were assigned to 63 factories — definitely, probably or possibly — of the Pittsburgh region. A good many of the 60 unidentifiables, however, show such similarity to this assigned group that its total might be appreciably enlarged.

Competition to catch the public favor in pictorial flasks appears to have been quite keen. Nine well-defined areas competed against the Pittsburgh-Monongahela District:

Maryland: Baltimore

Eastern Pennsylvania: Philadelphia (Dyottsville, Kensington)

Connecticut: Coventry, East Manchester, New London, Westford, West Willington

New York: Albany, Lancaster, Lockport, Mt. Vernon, Saratoga

Kentucky: Louisville

202 Flasks (1824–1840) by Frederick Lorenz (Nos. 1, 2, and 4) and William Ihmsen (No. 3). 1 — Aquamarine G. Geo Washington, G. I-7. 2 — Light green G. G. Washington, F L, G I-8. 3 — Green Ihmsen's Agriculture, G II-10. 4 — Aquamarine Eagle, half pint, F L, G II-15. *Ex coll. L. Earl Dambach.*

New Hampshire: Keene, Stoddard

Ohio: Kent, Mantua, Ravenna, Zanesville

New Jersey: Bridgeton, Fislerville, Glassboro, Hammonton

West Virginia: Wheeling, Wellsburg

Naturally, the flasks most sought after today carry the name of the factory owner or the mold maker, or, like Bakewell's "American System," mark a special occasion. We are concerned here only with bottles and flasks of the Pittsburgh District. It would be well to begin with the generalizations that may be made about Pittsburgh examples and then examine those pieces most respected by students and most eagerly sought after by collectors.

In shape, most are a symmetrical ovoid. In color, they range from aquamarine to a dark green, most of them being a light green. The few amber flasks show a deep tone. Some are of clear glass, but a very few come in blue or amethyst. A novice will seize on the beads on the two edges of the flask as a ready means of identification. Such beads arranged in pairs give a horizontal ribbed effect not unlike some of the true horizontal bars found on the sides of many Eastern flasks. On the early Pittsburgh-Monongahela historicals the beads are usually in double rows, sometimes bisected by a riblike line. One "extremely rare" Washington portrait pint flask (Group I–No. 5 in the McKearins' tables) has three rows of beads. Nevertheless, several important early Pittsburgh flasks have smooth sides: Ihmsen's "Agriculture" (*G 11–10*), F. Lorenz's "G. G. Washington (*G 1–8*) and "Eagle" (*G 11–15*), and B. Kimber's "Washington" (*G 1–13*).

Before 1850, Pittsburgh glassmen preferred to glorify national heroes, to follow political campaigns, and to seize on national slogans. The American eagle, symbol of courage, indepen-

203 Pittsburgh-Monongahela flasks (1823–1840) in the Robinson manner: 1 — Aquamarine Scroll, no legend. G IX-44. 2 — Aquamarine General Washington. G I-6 (Laird S.C. Pitt). 3 — Olive yellow General Jackson. G I-66. 4 — Aquamarine Scroll. J. R. & Son. G IX-43. *Ex coll. L. Earl Dambach.*

204 Two unmarked flasks and two from Bakewell (1824–1840), Page & Bakewell 1824–1836: 1 — Amber Inverted Cornucopia, half pint, G II-11. 2 — Yellow green Eagle, possibly Louisville, but shows influence of Pittsburgh-Monongahela. G II-24. 3 — Clear-violet tinge, American System. G X-20. 4 — Aquamarine Scroll, B. P. & B. G IX-39. *Ex coll. L. Earl Dambach.*

dence, and idealism, frequently formed the reverse decoration. The cornucopia, expressing the fruitfulness of the new country but also possibly carrying a religious symbolism, was not used as frequently on Pittsburgh flasks as on those of the East.

Many of the later scroll or violin flasks made extensively up and down the Ohio River can be assigned to Pittsburgh on the strength of the "J. R. & S." (John Robinson & Son) or the B. P. & B. (*Group IX–38* in aquamarine and *G IX–39* in many colors). Since the Bakewell, Page & Bakewell partnership existed from 1824 to 1832, we gain an idea of the approximate time during which scrolls were produced. McKee (*G X–26*) is also indicated as a major producer of scroll flasks.

Of the portrait flasks, John Robinson of the Stourbridge Flint Glass Works, Pittsburgh (1823–1830), produced several of the most desirable. A very rare "General Washington" (*G 1–6*) carries John Robinson's initials in an oval beneath an eagle (*203*). Below the eagle appears "Laird sc. Pitt," and at an illuminating stroke we are privileged to meet with an identification common in painting, sculpture, and porcelain, but rare in glass. This was the mold maker Joshua Laird, who applied for a patent on a glass-blowing machine in 1832, who presumably flourished in the glass trade before that date, and who must have designed many of the other early flasks found in the Pittsburgh District. That "sc." (sculpsit) tells us that Joshua Laird was proud of his work and wanted his name associated with it. We like to think that he designed the horizontal beaded edges that grace many of the early flasks of the Pittsburgh-Monongahela District.

Laird's marked "General Jackson" pint (*G 1–66*) is equally well known and rare. The two flasks show the American eagle on the reverse side with nine six-pointed stars, a breast shield of seven bars, three arrows in a thunderbolt in the right talon, an olive branch in the left talon, and a laurel branch in the beak. Another "Jackson"

pint (*G 1–64*) is so much like the marked piece that McKearin assigns it, also, to Robinson. A pint scroll, rather corset-waisted, carries the letters "J. R. & Son" (*G IX–43*). Since this is a more vivid color — dark amethyst — than the earlier ovate flasks, it is much sought after. Another scroll carrying "J. R. & S." — one half pint only — is decorated with a large anchor (*G IX–42*). A third half pint (*G IX–41*) is so similar to it that McKearin assigns it to Robinson also, though it is unmarked. Several other scroll flasks echoing the pattern but not the color clearly belong to the Pittsburgh-Monongahela District.

After the death of James O'Hara in 1819, Frederick Rudolph Joachim Lorenz, who had learned the craft at O'Hara's works, leased the O'Hara plant until he could buy it. His famous marked pint flask, "G. G. Washington" (*G 1–8*), carries on the reverse side the eagle standing on an oval with the initials "F. L." inside (*202*). Lorenz marked two other flasks: a pint with "G. Geo Washington" in a half circle above Washington's bust, with the eagle and stars on the reverse (*G I–7*), and a vertically ribbed half pint with an eagle, sun rays pointing at its head, with the filled cornucopia on the reverse side (*G II–15*).

One of the most famous of the Bakewell commemorative flasks, the "American System" (*G X–20*), discussed on pages 39 and 210, has a side-wheel riverboat on one side, with the U.S. flag, stiffly flying, encircled by the legend, "The American System" (*204*). On the reverse side, a sheaf of rye is encircled by the warning "Use me but do not abuse me." Since one flask has the letters "B. P. & B." (Bakewell, Page & Bakewell, organized in 1824) and since the flask celebrates passage of the protective tariff act of 1824, it is safe to assume that it commemorated Henry Clay's visit to Pittsburgh and the banquet tendered Henry Baldwin for his congressional support of the tariff bill. Other flasks with the riverboat and the words "American System" have come to light but as yet have not been attributed by the McKearins. Helen McKearin suggests that Joshua Laird may

205 Flasks (1822–1840) by Benedict Kimber showing a departure from ribbed sides: 1 — Aquamarine Cornucopia, half pint, G II-16. 2 — Yellow green Washington (B.K.), G I-13. 3 — Aquamarine Eagle (B.K.), G II-3. 4 — Yellow green Eagle (unattributed), G II-5. *Ex coll. L. Earl Dambach.*

have made the original mold and sold copies to other glasshouses, for one "American System" carries the initials "B. M." under the steamboat. Bakewell marked two half-pint violin scrolls (*G IX–38* and *39*) with "B. P. & B." They are similar except for a slightly broader medial rib and a more circular base in G IX–39. Several other violin flasks, unmarked, have strong likenesses to the marked Bakewell ones but have been given no factory attributions by the McKearins. The charming scroll flask in *G IX–39* has appeared in light and dark blue, in brilliant yellow and green, in moonstone with a greenish tint, and in the conventional aquamarine. Scroll flasks from the Pittsburgh-Monongahela District consistently show a wider and more appealing range of color than do the early historicals, probably because they were manufactured when color control was less of a problem.

No portrait flask has yet been assigned to the Bakewell factory, but a bill from the Pittsburgh Manufacturing Association leads us to an interesting speculation. It is dated February 13, 1827, is found on page 190 of the Harmony Society ledgers, and reads:

4	boxes 8/10 window glass		4.00
4	doz. qt. bottles	87½	3.50
3½	doz. pint do	65½	2.19
2	doz. Washingtons	75	1.50
4	" flint ½ pt tumblers	90	3.60
1	" Engr. Salt		1.00
1	" Pillar do		1.50
1	" barrel wines ea 1 & 1.25		2.25
4	" Medallion Tumblers	50	2.00
	Box		.25

Store at Vincennes

The four-dozen flint tumblers, the engraved salt, and the four dozen medallion tumblers were all Bakewell pieces. Could the two dozen "Washingtons" also have been flasks of that manufacture? The tantalizing possibility is as close as anyone has ever come to finding that Bakewell made an historical flask besides "The American System."

Benedict Kimber, one of Amelung's workmen,

acquired the Bridgeport Glass Works on the Monongahela and there made a notable contribution to the Washington pieces. On a pint flask (*205*) the name "Washington" curves above a three-quarter bust (*G 1–13*). On the reverse appears the ubiquitous eagle with the sun's rays terminating in 13 stars; it stands on an oval that contains the initials "B. K." Kimber operated glass factories near Brownsville in 1822, in 1837, and in the middle 1840s.

These four companies — Robinson, Lorenz, Bakewell and Kimber — pretty well set the tone and quality for early historical flasks in the district. We should also mention the "Agriculture" fashioned by William Ihmsen, who in 1826 had leased the Williamsport Glass Works in Monongahela City (*202*). On one side an eagle with the conventional three-arrow thunderbolt in its talons stands on an oval containing the word "Glass." The name "W. Ihmsen" appears at the top of the circle above the eagle's head. On the reverse is the word "Agriculture" with scythe, sickle, pitchfork, rake, and plow bordering a sheaf of grain.

John Taylor & Company of Brownsville made outstanding Adams and Jackson flasks for the 1828 presidential campaign (Andrew Jackson versus John Quincy Adams) and continued their production well into the 1830s (*206, 207*). A fine but as yet unattributed flask celebrates William Henry Harrison and his cider barrel campaign. Down the Ohio, flasks were fashioned in Wellsburg by McCarty & Torreyson and in Wheeling by Knox & McKee, Wheat & Price, and Wheeling Glass Company. Samuel McKee placed his name on an interesting scroll flask (*G IX–26*). It carries a heart-shaped frame with scrolls, with an eight-pointed star in a diamond above it. At the top of the design is another star.

Gradually the designs became simpler, smaller in relation to the whole bottle, and less pronounced. We look at an eagle in the early period and see that its strength, its fierceness, and the arrows clutched in its talons are as important as the flask itself. After 1850 the eagle does not stand out so prominently above the surface; it seems more benign and less dominant. Manufacturers were nearing an early form of streamlined production and did not want expensive molds that demanded skill in design and elaborate detail. The shape of the flask changed from the squat ovoid to become flatter, longer, with higher and wider shoulders, with a narrower base, and with smooth sides.

The Snap-Case Method

The snap-case method of manufacture appears to have come into use around 1850. The earlier flasks always showed a pontil mark at the base. The two-part mold was opened and the flask was affixed to and held on a pontil rod while the gaffer, after cracking or whetting the bottle from the blowpipe, fashioned the collar. In the snap-case method, on the other hand, there was no need for a pontil rod, for the bottle, if not completed in the mold, was held on a pair of long, springlike pincers. (A few snap-case bottles, nevertheless, do show a pontil mark, probably because they were attached to a pontil for special fire polishing.) All the early flasks were fire polished. We need only to feel the smoothness of the surface design to realize the value of fire polishing.

The Collar

We now approach the time and technical development when the collar became a part of the bottle — at first as an applied band, later as the ridged or tooled collar we know today. Too many amateur collectors like to date a flask or bottle by its collar or mouth. We know for the following reasons that such practice is undependable.

The commonly used term "sheared neck" for collar is misleading and not traditional.* Glass

* See Harry Hall White, "The Story of the Mantua Glass Works," *Antiques* 26, December 1934 and February 1935.

206 John Taylor Co. of Brownsville, Pa., fashioned a fine Monongahela River flask — a campaign advertisement of 1828. Obverse: Aquamarine John Q. Adams. G I-62. *The Corning Museum of Glass.*

207 John Adams, Eagle reverse. G I-62. *The Corning Museum of Glass.*

208 An unattributed William H. Harrison Campaign Flask typical of earlier workmanship. Portrait bust marked "Wm H. Harrison," ca. 1840. G I-63. Aquamarine. Obverse. *The Corning Museum of Glass.*

209 Log cabin, plow, cider barrel. Reverse of picture 208. G I-63. *The Corning Museum of Glass.*

210 Three beautiful Scrolls (1824–1840), all marked:
1 — Amethyst J.R. & Sons (Robinson). G IX-43. 2 —
Aquamarine S. McKee. G IX-26. 3 — Aquamarine
B.P. & B. (Bakewell, Page & Bakewell). G IX-38. *The Corning Museum of Glass.*

211 Pikes Peak and Post–Civil War, 1859–1875. 1 —
Amber Union and Clasped Hands. 2 — Green Eagle.
3 — Aquamarine Pikes Peak. 4 — Amber Pikes Peak.
Ex coll. L. Earl Dambach.

212 Variations of the Pikes Peak Flask (1859–1875)
(more than forty variations). 1 — Influence of the Army.
2 — A regular colonist-miner. 3 — Old Rye — a satire
on the get-rich-quick irresponsible adventurer. *The Henry
Ford Museum.*

artisans themselves spoke of "whetting" or "cracking" off the neck — that is, separating the tube of glass that connects the bubble (in this case, the body of the bottle) to the blowpipe. The other end of the bottle was held on a pontil rod, while the tube or connection at the blowpipe was chilled by a cold iron and cracked off. Then the pontil held the rough mouth to the fire for smoothing and finishing. The same routine was followed when the workman whetted off — that is, when he touched the connecting tube with the tip of a moistened tool or a wire sustaining a drop of water.

The lips or mouths of early pictorial flasks and scrolls were finished by chilling and whetting, then by fire polishing, but the technique had existed long before the first quarter of the nineteenth century and persisted afterward. The ridged or tooled neck so popular after the middle of the century required greater handwork, which is perhaps the reason it was so late in developing. A pair of shears with a solid cylinder on one blade held the inside of the neck while a shaped block on the other was rotated on the outside of the neck to set the kind of collar — heavy, rounded, smooth, or rolled like those of the modern pop bottle. There were several types of finishing tools; the one described was used before 1843. It is understandable that early flasks would be whetted or cracked off and the lip smoothed merely by fire polishing. It is understandable, too, that a more sophisticated society would expect a definite and finished roll. Yet the same type of flask may sometimes appear with a smooth, fire-polished neck and then again grooved and with the heavy roll. It is for this reason, among others, that the generalized dating of a flask or bottle by its collar is far from infallible.

Bottle workers around the time of the Civil War developed a new technique that reduced or eliminated the need of fire polishing. Decades earlier they had used hardwood for molds, but these had charred away under the strong heat. Helen McKearin does not believe that wooden molds were used for pictorial flasks. Copper and brass molds were expensive and melted at a lower temperature than molten glass. Cast-iron molds were rough even when new and soon became coated with carbon. But a mold fashioned of chilled iron had a smooth surface, and sprinkling the mold with water enabled the blower to turn the bottle as he blew. Fire polishing for smoothness was more common in early flasks and bottles than has generally been thought; the chilled iron mold, by reducing the amount of fire polishing and still delivering a smooth product, was an outstanding improvement in technology.

"Pike's Peak" or "The Western Traveler"

One of the most popular flasks between the early portraits of national heroes and the flood of pictorials that came with the Civil War was the Pike's Peak flask (211). As the result of historical circumstances, it stands as a good transitional piece between the early historicals and the post–Civil War "Union and Clasped Hands."

Zebulon Pike was a daring young lieutenant who in 1806 had been selected by Governor James Wilkinson of the Louisiana Territory to explore the Arkansas River and basin. Pike never climbed the peak later named in his honor, but his expedition sighted it and he drew its profile. He was killed in action as a brigadier general in the War of 1812. Counties in Illinois and Missouri were named for Pike, and since a flood of adventurers moved through them in the Gold Rushes of 1849 and 1859, any gold seeker headed for California in 1859 was called a "Pike's Peaker." The migrants, generally poor and ill-equipped, lent themselves to caricature by artists, and flask makers joined in the fun.

The Pike's Peak flask depicts a walking traveler with his "budget" (sack or bag with its contents) hanging at the end of a stick. A tall hat and, on some bottles, a walking stick or umbrella, give him a degree of respectability (212). Above his head is the legend "For Pike's Peak." Below his feet may be a raised oval containing the words "Old Rye" or no inscription at all. On the reverse an eagle with half-opened wings holds a wavy ribbon in its beak. In some versions the eagle rather than the traveler stands over the oval, which encloses the factory name or location. Often enough, however, both sides bear the raised oval, and yet both ovals can be blank. In the larger bottles the eagle generally faces right; in the smaller bottles it often faces left.

A few of the Pike's Peak flasks were blown in the earlier manner, handled with a pontil rod, and finished without a collar; most, however, have a collar and no pontil. Some with collars show evidence of pontil handling, with a dark rough circle that was worked after the rod was given a thin glazing of glass.* The modeling of both figure and eagle is of a simplicity of design that foreshadows later mass production. Many of these flasks, in fact, are so unevenly shaped that the workmen seem to have been striving for numbers rather than quality.

Many of the flasks were marked with the names of Pittsburgh houses, among them Cunningham & Company, McCully, A. & D. H. Chambers, and Arsenal Glass Works. Peaks were undoubtedly made in Wheeling, Louisville, and the Ohio factories. Since most have been found in Ohio, Kentucky, Indiana, and points westward, collectors conclude — as they did with pattern-molded free-blown bottles — that the Pike's Peak flask was an Ohio product. And still, with one probable exception, no flask with any factory or place label other than Pittsburgh has yet turned up.

The exception is a flask marked "Ceredo." The late Earl Dambach of Pittsburgh unearthed the fact that Ceredo, a town in West Virginia, presumably named for the Roman goddess of agriculture, had a large gristmill, a flour mill, a carriage factory, a match factory, a saltworks, and a glass factory. This is circumstantial evidence that the lone, marked Pike's Peak was made there, but it must serve until a better explanation is given.*

Dating the flasks must be done in general terms. The flood of emigrants in the second Gold Rush wave in 1859 points to that as the year of origin. Certain factories whose names appear on some flasks fit that date. One of them, A. & D. H. Chambers, had broken away from Chambers, Agnew & Company. Its price list in 1866 recorded what doubtless were Pike's Peak and Union patterns as follows:

½ pint Eagle, new style, 6 doz. bxs per gross								$ 7.20
1 pint "	"	"	"	"	"	"	"	9.60
Quart "	"	"	"	"	"	"	"	12.00

Its 1872 pamphlet indicated a rise in prices:

Plain Pike's Peak and Union Patterns

¼ pint	6 doz bxs per gross	$10.00
½ "	" " " " "	12.00
1 "	" " " " "	16.00
Quart	" " " " "	24.00*

* Harry Hall White, "Glass Monuments to Zebulon Pike," *Antiques* 22 September, October 1932.

Another marked Pike's Peak came from Cunningham, a prolific producer of the late type of flask. That company had operated the Pittsburgh City Glass Works in 1849 and was organized as Cunningham & Company in 1875.

The long life of the Pike's Peak flask is extraordinary, especially in view of the fact that after

* The earliest American pontilist had the assistant dip the pontil rod in molten glass and then apply it to the bottom of the bottle, where it adhered. In the later technique, the assistant placed a bar iron pontil rod (heated, of course) against the bottle. Apparently a chemical change took place with the touch of bare iron on the glass. Eventually, when oxygen worked on the point of contact, ferric oxide developed and the contact area would remain discolored — anything from a reddish brown to black. Popular jargon among bottle collectors has given this a name that is quite incorrect: graphite pontil. (See "Empontilling: A History," by Dr. Julian H. Toulouse, *The Glass Industry,* Part 1, March/April 1968.)

* C. W. Thomson, "History of Ceredo and Kenova" (an unpublished paper in the Huntington Public Library, West Virginia, 1959).

213 1 — Golden amber Union and Clasped Hands flask, pint. "C.I. & Sons" on banner in eagle's mouth on reverse (Charles Ihmsen & Sons, Pittsburgh). G XII-20. 2 — Bluish aquamarine Union and Clasped Hands, pint. "F. A. & Co." beneath cannon and flag on reverse (Fahnestock, Albree and Company, Pittsburgh). G XII-40. 3 — Aquamarine calabash bottle with Union and Clasped Hands on obverse and Eagle on reverse. A large pint. Possibly A. R. Samuels, Philadelphia. G XII-43. 4 — Aquamarine Union and Clasped Hands flask with "Old Rye" on obverse and "A and D H C" and "Pittsburgh" on reverse. Quart. (A. and D. H. Chambers, Pittsburgh). 5 — Aquamarine flask, pint. Girl on bicycle on obverse and Eagle and "A & D H C" on reverse. All flasks 1860–1880. *The Corning Museum of Glass.*

214 Late Post–Civil War flasks: 1 — Light amber
Union and Clasped Hands on obverse. Eagle with Shield
and "E. Wormser & Co., Pittsburgh, Pa." on reverse.
(The "o" of "Co." is outside of border.) 2 — Aquamarine
flask similar to picture 1. *Collection of James A. Frank.*

the Civil War it was competing against the late American eagle and the "Union and Clasped Hands." It has been estimated that between 100 and 150 different versions of the Union and Clasped Hands are reasonably collectible. Probably close to a hundred of the "Double Eagle" exist. We are certain of forty versions of Pike's Peak. The McCully catalogue of May 1, 1875, advertised Union and Clasped Hands, Eagle, and Pike's Peak.

Post–Civil War Flasks

There are innumerable variants for the three most popular post–Civil War flasks: the eagle, double eagle, and Union and Clasped Hands. Usually these variants can be identified by or related to the parent design from which they branch. A number of Pittsburgh pieces are among the most appealing. Cunningham and

Ihmsen marked its double eagle "C. & I." William McCully, who also favored the double eagle, placed "William McCully, Pgh. Pa." in one oval and left the other oval blank. E. Wormser & Company placed an eagle and shield and its name on the reverse; on the obverse, it showed clasped hands and a shield with 13 stars and the word "Union." A Frederick Lorenz–marked Union flask has "F. L. & Co.," the shield and clasped hands on one side, and an eagle, a scroll, and "Pittsburgh, Pa.," on the other.

A quart is extraordinarily elaborate in detail (*215*). An Indian with a bow and arrow shoots at a bird perched in one of two trees. Behind him stands a dog. Below is "Cunningham & Co. — Pittsburgh, Pa." On the reverse side an eagle flies toward the right with a ribbon in its beak. It stands on a shield in which waves a very stiff American flag. The shield rests on a monument with 13 pillars, a boat, and two sheaves of rye. Vines ascend each side of this arrangement and the word "Continential" (sic) stretches strongly across the base.

A mystery flask — at least it has puzzled Stephen Van Rensselaer and Helen McKearin — is a marked Pittsburgh quart with Union and Clasped Hands bordered by a floral vine. Underneath the hands appears "L. F. & Co." On the reverse an eagle facing right with a ribbon in its beak surmounts an elongated shield enclosing "Pittsburgh, Pa." No known Pittsburgh company answers to those initials. A normal response would be to say Lorenz, Fahnestock, but those two names were separated by a time gap of some years and as far as we know never partnered any flasks. Charles Flaccus and William Frank, two flask and bottle manufacturers, fit the time period and the character of the product, but the "L" is inexplicable.

A Little-Known Glasshouse of Peculiar Merit

William Frank and Sons* is an interesting fac-

* John P. McMaster, *Manufactures of Pennsylvania* (Philadelphia: Galaxy Publishing Co., 1875), gives a report of the Frank and Wormser operations with biographical facts about the Franks.

215 Post–Civil War flasks (1860–1880): 1 — Dark amber Eagle, pint. Midwestern, probably Pittsburgh. G II-93. 2 — Yellow green Eagle, pint. G II-112. Obverse: Cunningham & Co. Reverse: Glass Manufacturers. 3 — Aquamarine flask with Union and Clasped Hands and Compass on obverse; Flying Eagle and H & S (Haught & Schwerer, Brownsville, Pa.) on reverse. Quart. G IV-39. 4 — Aquamarine flask, Eagle and "Continential" on obverse; Indian shooting bird and "Cunningham & Co Pittsburgh Pa." on reverse. Quart. G II-142. 5 — Olive green Union and Clasped Hands. Quart. Midwestern. G XII-10. *The Corning Museum of Glass.*

216 Flasks (1858–1876) from the Wm. Frank & Sons factory. 1 — Aquamarine, quart, Union and Clasped Hands. "Wm. Frank & Sons, Pitts." Reverse, Flag and Cannon. 2 — Dark amber, pint, Union and Clasped Hands. "Wm. Frank & Sons, Pitts." Reverse, Flag and Cannon. 3 — Light amber, pint, plain flask. Flat shoulders, patented internal threads, glass stopper. Obverse "W. Frank & Sons," reverse "Pittsburgh, Pa." 4 — Aquamarine, half pint, Union and Clasped Hands. "W.F. & Sons." Reverse, Eagle with Shield. *Collection of James A. Frank.*

tory on two scores: it made some exceptionally fine bottles and jars, and it has had little written about it. In 1854 William Frank joined his brother-in-law Ephraim Wormser in the glass business. Probably he was somewhat a silent partner until 1858, because he owned a dry goods store and was also operating in an oil firm. Wormser's withdrawal in 1866 dissolved the partnership, but both families kept on manufacturing glass.

One of the best-known Frank flasks is the Union and Clasped Hands and a heart-shaped shield with the company's name on one side and a cannon with flag and six cannonballs on the other. The quart shows 10 balls. Both sides carry 13 stars and "W." or "Wm. Frank & Sons, Pitts." One pint model has 14 stars. The pints vary the size of the Union and the Clasped Hands; when the one is large, the other is small.

Fahnestock & Albree made this cannon reverse (*213*), and altered the obverse slightly: clasped hands, heart-shaped shield, and an oval panel with "F.A.& Co." and a branch on each side with

"Union" and 13 stars. Lorenz and Wightman, successors to Lorenz & Buchanan, stamped "L. & W." on the bottom of a pint Union and Clasped Hands and left the two raised ovals blank. On this flask the clasped hands are on top of a squarish shield, while lines below run vertically as though they were the stripes of a flag. Stars and vines border the arrangement. On the reverse side an eagle flying to the right carries a ribbon in its beak.

Another well-known Frank flask is the Union and Clasped Hands on one side and, on the reverse, a small eagle with spread wings and a ribbon in its beak, perched on a conventional shield (*216*). The different colors of marked Frank flasks indicate greater variety than we expect from the ordinary manufacturer of marked green flasks in the 1860s and 1870s. We find an interesting color spread in the pints — aqua, green, a rich blue, and dark and light amber. No blue has appeared in the quarts. Great-grandsons of the original William Frank today own pints in sapphire blue, pale green, and dark amber, and a

217 Functional bottles of the period. (1858–1876).
1 — Aquamarine, half pint, medicine bottles. Label: "Spirits of Camphor." Bottle: "Pittsburgh, Pa." on one side, "W. Frank & Sons" on reverse. Flat shoulders, patented internal threads with glass stopper. 2 — Medium dark amber bottle, square cross section. Sides are plain. "Wm. Frank & Sons" and "Pitts" (in mirror image on bottom, i.e. "ᴢɈɈiꟼ"). 3 — Dark amber calabash-style bottle. "Wm. Frank & Sons" on bottom. 4 — Aquamarine preserving jar. Wax sealer with groove in lip to take tin lid. "Wm. Frank & Sons, Pitts." on bottom. *Collection of James A. Frank.*

quart in very light amber. A yellow quart has been seen in New York state.

That Pittsburgh glassmen sought ingenious devices for improvement is attested by an amber pint with absolutely no decoration on either side, with the legend "W. Frank & Sons" on one side and "Pittsburgh, Pa." on the reverse (*216*). Each side has a flat panel running from base to heavy neck. Inside the neck are internal threads for a screw stopper. An aquamarine half pint, plain except for "W. Frank & Sons" on one side and "Pittsburgh, Pa." on the other, has a glass screw stopper with the label "Spirits of Camphor" and the words "Drug Store" and "West Va." The names of the store and town are obscured by age. On August 6, 1872, Himan Frank, son of William, received two patents: No. 130207, a tool for Forming Bottle Mouths, and No. 130208, a Bottle Stopper.

The late William K. Frank of New York, grandson of the original William, remembered hearing his father, Isaac, relate how Henry John Heinz, founder of the H. J. Heinz Company, used to buy a dozen bottles at a time from the company. According to the story, Heinz, who was a boy at the time, used the bottles to put up and peddle a product grown in the family garden in Sharpsburg, a suburb of Pittsburgh. From the Heinz family history comes the information that young Heinz bought bottles for packaging his first commercial product, horseradish, using clear instead of green glass to show that his root was of high quality and not mixed — as was the custom — with a filler of leaves, wood, and turnips.

The Frank operations are enlightening in several respects. The company name was originally Pittsburgh Green Glass Company, operated by Wormser, Burgraff & Company. In 1857, William Frank, Ephraim Wormser's brother-in-law, entered the business and the name became E. Wormser & Company. It was changed the next year to the Frankstown Glass Works, probably

218 1 — Dr. Henley's California IXL Bitters. Reverse plain. Mold-blown at the Frankstown Glass Works, 1858–1876. Sheared lip below which is a crude applied ring. On the base "W. Frank & Sons Pitt." Medium aqua, H. 12". 2 — J. C. Buffum & Co., Pittsburgh, Pa. Reverse, "W.F.," probably for William Frank, as similar Buffum soda bottles have other Pittsburgh glass factory names in the same place. Buffum was a large bottler. Mold-blown at the Frankstown Glass Works, 1858–1876. Medium aqua. H. 6¾". *Collection of James A. Frank.*

because William Frank owned large holdings in the area of Pittsburgh bearing that name. (This was not the city's present Frankstown District but lay between the Monongahela River and the present Second Avenue.)

Wormser and Frank jointly bought more than three acres of land for the glassworks. From this association extending from 1858 to 1876, two series of marked flasks have emerged: those of William Frank & Sons and those of E. Wormser & Company or Wormser Glass Company. Possibly two factories — Frank and Wormser — were operated on the same acreage, for in 1866 Wormser deeded to Frank his interest in the Frankstown Glass Works. Frank, with his two sons, Himan and William, took over the company. The capacity of the works steadily increased and in 1873 a new factory was erected. A gas furnace patented by Himan Frank enabled them to save in fuel and in soda consumption without diminishing production.

Unfortunately on June 11, 1874, the works were entirely destroyed by fire at a loss of $80,000, only partially covered by insurance. They erected a new plant ten weeks after the destruction of the old on land owned by Wormser, adjoining his home, a site just a short distance west of the site of the old Frankstown Glass Works. They broadened their lines of amber and green bottles for druggists as well as continuing flasks and bottles for liquor. *Manufactures of Pennsylvania* states that there were seventeen houses at the new site for the partial accommodation of their 120 hands, "the works being probably among the best arranged and most complete in the country."

Nevertheless, William Frank gave up all his interest in the glass company in 1876. Since jars and flasks marked with the Frank name continued to appear, the two-factory theory might seem to be valid. Wormser's factory supplied double-thick glass windows in the State of Ohio building at the Centennial in Philadelphia in 1876.

219 1 — "A Brandy" is hand lettered in gold on white paper with red and black shading with gold colored oval border. Glass label is cemented over paper and fits the embossed panel. Reverse plain. Mold-blown at the Frankstown Glass Works, 1858–1876. On the base "Wm Frank and Sons Pitt." Deep amber, presumably a "back bar bottle." Up to 1971 it was displayed on the boat *Robert E. Lee River Queen* (not the original) at St. Louis. H. 11½". 2 — Plain mold-blown wine or brandy bottle with typical wide lip and ring. On the base deeply embossed "Wm. Frank and Sons Pa." ca. 1858–1876. Usually the marking is "Pitt" instead of "Pa." Heavy amber. H. 10¾". *Collection of James A. Frank.*

220 Marking on the base of bottle, No. 219 right.

221 Wm. McCully & Co., established 1830, catalogue, May 1, 1875. Page 44, popular flasks over a long period extending from 1859 on. *Collection of the author.*

44

FLASKS.

Eagle Style.

½ Pint Flasks, Eagle. New Style, 6 doz. box. ℔ gro. $12 00
1 "   "   "   "   6 "   "   16 00
Quart "   "   "   6 "   "   24 00

Union Style.

½ pint Flasks, Union............6 doz. boxes, ℔ gross, $12 00
1 "   "   "   ....6 "   "   16 00
Quart "   "   ....6 "   "   24 00

Pike's Peak Style.

½ pint Flasks, Pike's Peak,.....6 doz. boxes, ℔ gross, $12 00
1 "   "   "   .....6 "   "   16 00
Quart "   "   .....6 "   "   24 00

Plain Style.

½ pint Flasks, Plain Style,...6 doz. boxes, ℔ gross, $12 00
1 "   "   "   ...6 "   "   16 00
Quart "   "   ...6 "   "   24 00

"Shoo Fly" Style.

½ pint Flasks, Shoo Fly Style, 6 doz. bxs. ℔ gross, $12 00
1 "   "   "   "   6 "   "   16 00
Quart "   "   "   6 "   "   24 00

We have a set of "Shoo Fly" Moulds—½ Pint, Pint and Quart—with opening on one side for inserting name of a person or firm, and business address, or any device required, at the low price of Fifteen Dollars for three sizes. Die prepared for either one, separately, six dollars. No additional charge for the Flasks.

Wormser did not establish another factory of his own until 1882.

The Wormser designs were consistently Union and Clasped Hands, with the eagle, ribbon, shield, olive branches, and arrows on the reverse (*214*). Instead of the oval at the bottom of the obverse side, a rectangle with turned points at each corner encloses "E. Wormser & Co., Pittsburgh, Pa." The "Pa." is sometimes omitted. Of the Wormser product Rhea M. Knittle says in her *Early American Glass:*

With no reservations or exceptions the finest metaled and molded flasks I have ever seen are two quart whiskey bottles marked E. Wormser & Co., Pittsburgh, Pa. The pattern on each is the rather common obverse, Union and Clasped Hands; reverse, Eagle in flight above panel. But the metal is almost as thin as insufflated glass, and the design stands out in bold relief, the glass seems to shimmer in both natural and artificial light — one is citron, the other is ultramarine blue.*

* Pp. 346–47.

Even making allowances for possible enthusiasm and recognizing that workmanship varied on flasks blown into a two-part mold, it is clear that little-known Pittsburgh factories did indeed turn out top-quality results in their commercial production of bottles and flasks.

COLOGNE & POMADE BOTTLES.

COLOGNE BOTTLES.

2 ounce,	French Colognes,	5 gross boxes,...	℔ gross,	$	3 50
4 "	" "	3 "	...	"	4 50
1 "	Fiddle,	5 "	..	"	2 75
2 "	"	3 "	...	"	3 25
1 "	Vase,	5 "	...	"	2 75
2 "	"	3 "	...	"	3 25
1 "	Diamond,	5 "	..	"	2 75
2 "	"	3 "	...	"	3 25
4 "	"	2 "	...	"	4 00
2 "	Gothic,	3 "	...	"	3 25
4 "	"	2 "	..	"	4 00
2 "	Hock,	3 "	...	"	3 25
2 "	Virginia Hock,	3 "	...	"	3 00
4 "	" "	2 "	...	"	4 25
2 "	Boston,	3 "	...	"	3 00
6 "	"	1 "	...	"	5 00
1 "	" Colognes,	5 "	...	"	2 75
No. 1,	Wreath, 3/4 oz.	5 "	...	"	2 25
No. 2,	" 1 "	3 "	...	"	2 50
No. 3,	" 1½ "	3 "	...	"	3 00
No. 1,	Arch,	5 "	...	"	2 75
No. 2,	"	3 "	...	"	2 75
2 ounce	Fancy Tapers,	3 "	...	"	3 50
2 "	Oval Fluted,	3 "	...	"	3 25
3 "	" "	2 "	...	"	3 25
4 "	" "	2 "	...	"	5 50
1 "	Circassian	5 "	...	"	2 75
2 "	"	3 "	...	"	3 25
3 "	"	2 "	...	"	3 25
¼ "	Oriental,	5 "	...	"	2 75
2 "	"	3 "	...	"	3 00
4 "	"	2 "	...	"	4 00
8 "	"	1 "	...	"	5 50
2 "	Toilet Cologne,	3 "	...	"	3 25
2 "	Ear of Corn,	3 "	...	"	3 25
1 "	Mosaic,	5 "	...	"	2 25
2 "	"	3 "	...	"	2 75

..........per cent. discount off above prices, cash.

38

Patent Medicine Vials, &c.

Bateman's,...	5 gross boxes,	℔ gross,	$5 00
Turlington's,...	5	"	"	4 50
Peppermint,...	5	"	"	4 50
Haarlem Oil,...	5	"	"	4 50
British Oil,...	5	"	"	4 50
Bear's Oil, (small,)...	3	"	"	4 50
Godfrey's,...	3	"	"	5 00
Opodeldoc, (large and small,)...	3	"	"	5 00
Liquid Opodeldoc,...	3	"	"	5 00
Lemon Acid,...	5	"	"	4 50
Calcined Magnesia,...	1	"	"	5 00
Red Ink, (sq. or octagon,)...	3	"	"	4 50
Genuine Essence,...	5	"	"	5 00
Balsam of Honey,...	3	"	"	4 50
London Mustard,...	1	"	"	5 50
Cayenne,...	1	"	"	4 50
Durable Ink,...	5	"	"	4 50
Dalby's Carminative,...	3	"	"	4 50
Nerve and Bone Liniment,...	3	"	"	5 00
One Ounce Vermifuge,...	5	"	"	4 50
Varnish Bottles,...	5	"	"	4 50
Stoughton's,...	5	"	"	4 50
Pomatums, 1¾ oz. fancy flut.,	2	"	"	5 50
Plain Macassar Oils,...	3	"	"	4 50
3 oz. Blueing, or Oval, L. N.,..	3	"	"	6 50

Common Long or Pedlers' Vials.

Narrow Mouths.

½ and 1 ounce,...	5 gross boxes,...	℔ gross,	$4 50
2 ounce,	5 "	...	"	5 00

..............per cent. discount off above prices, cash.

Camphor and Snuff, Ink and Unguents

It is easy to think and write only of those bottles and flasks used to hold spiritous liquors and to neglect or overlook their other uses. We must not forget that bottles were also used to hold camphor and snuff, unguents and ink, toilet waters and medicine, mustard, milk for nursing babies, and blacking for stoves. Pittsburgh never seemed to produce the elaborate pressed perfume and toilet bottles that grace the Sandwich Museum and have been assigned with equal certainty to the New England Glass Company. It is obvious, however, that Pittsburgh workmen blew

PRICE LIST OF

· B. L. FAHNESTOCK & CO.'S PROPRIETARY ARTICLES,

The Most Celebrated Medicines of the day, put up in a style of unequaled neatness, from original designs; entirely different from any other remedies now in the market, and sold at prices that afford ample remuneration to dealers.

		Retails.	Dozen.	Gross.
B. L. Fahnestock's	Vermifuge, - - - -	$ 25	$ 1 50	$17 00
"	Worm Pastiles, - - - -	25	1 50	14 00
"	" " in Glass, - - -	25	1 75	16 00
"	Compound Cathartic Pills, (Sugar Coated,) -	25	1 50	16 00
"	Sarsaparilla and Blood Purifier, -	1 00	8 00	84 00
"	Bronchial and Lung Syrup, Large, -	1 00	7 00	78 00
"	" " " " Medium, -	50	3 50	40 00
"	" " " " Small, -	25	1 75	19 00
"	Eureka Liniment, Trial Size, - -	25	1 75	19 00
"	" " Large -	1 00	7 00	78 00
Mucilage.	- - - - - - -	25	1 75	19 00
Sing's Itch Ointment,	- - - - -	25	1 75	16 00
Dr. R. A. Wilson's Pills, (Plain,)	- - - -	25	1 50	17 00
"	" (Sugar Coated,) - - -	25	1 60	18 00

many of those molded bottles in the Midwestern patterns that for a long time were attributed to Stiegel. Bottles for cologne and pomade were later described in the McCully catalogue of May 1, 1875.

Less glamorous but more useful were the medicine and drugstore chemical bottles. The early physician carried a leather satchel containing bottles as tiny as a little finger, graduated upward in size and probably very much the same in the third quarter of the century as they had been in the first. "Drugstore furniture" included glass show jars, funnels, retorts, mortars and pestles, tubing, and bottles for tinctures, oils, extracts, and prescriptions. By 1875, certain factories were advertising homeopathic prescription bottles, long and fluted in shape. Page thirty-eight in the McCully catalogue gives a good cross section of the wide use of bottles for the apothecary.

Two celebrated names in drug annals were B. L. Fahnestock & Company, proprietors of the celebrated Fahnestock Vermifuge (*224*), and B. Page, Jr. & Company, makers of Boerhave's Holland Bitters. This remedy for the thirsty attained an astonishing sale among the Germans settled in Pennsylvania. The medicinal drinks all carried enough alcohol to stimulate the patient and lead him to the happy conclusion that the tonic was curing his illness.

The American patent medicine bottle furnishes as many trails to follow and prizes to be shot down as does the whiskey flask. Collector and student alike marvel at the manufacturers' ingenuity and imagination and the great variety of unrelated ailments a single medicine was supposed to cure. Pittsburgh manufacturers stood high in the quality of medicinal bottles and flasks produced.

Wm. McCully & Co. catalogue, May 1, 1875. Pages 48 and 49, variety of bottles and current uses. Note page 49 reference to clay and iron molds. *Collection of the author.*

48

Black Bottles, Demijohns, &c.

RED OR AMBER COLOR.

Superior in Style and Finish to any Imported.

Wine or Brandy Bottles.

4's to gallon, new style,			...............1 gro. bx. ⅌ gro.	$17	00
5's	"	"	...............1 " "	16	00
5's	"	"	bulb neck, 1 " "	16	00
6's	"	"	.... "	14	00
7's	"	"	.... "	13	00
8's	"	"	.... "	12	50
10's	"	"	.... "	12	50
12's	"	"	.... "	12	50

Schnapp Bottles.

Quarts,...............1 gross boxes,.......⅌ gross,	$16	50
5s to gallon,...............1 " .... "	16	50
6s " ....1 " .... "	16	50
6s " paneled,...1 " .... "	16	50
Pints,...............1 " .... "	12	00
6s to gallon, paneled on three sides,.......... "	16	50

Bitter Bottles.

Bulb Neck, or Boker's Bitters, qts. 1 gro. bxs. ⅌ gro.	$16	50
" " " pts. 1 " "	12	50
½ Cask, (Barrel Shape,)............................... "	16	50
Kimmel Bottles,............................... "	18	00

Inks, Black Glass.

Pints,...............⅌ gross,	$11	00
Quarts,............................... "	17	00

Lager Beers.

Quarts, holding 6s to gallon, extra heavy and temp.	$16	50
Pints, " 12s " " "	13	50

..............per cent. discount off above prices cash.

49

Handled Jugs, Red Glass.

Pint Jugs, handled, ovals,...............per gross,	$25	00
Quart " " " .... "	30	00
" " " round,............... "	30	00

Demijohns, Heavy and Uniform. Handled and Covered.

Quarts, holding the quantity,...............per doz.	$6	00
½ Gallon,............... "	9	00
Gallon,............... "	12	00
2 Gallons,............... "	15	00
3 Gallons,............... "	18	00
4 Gallons,............... "	19	20
5 Gallons,............... "	21	60
Pocket Flasks, covered, pints,............... "	5	00
1 gal. Macerating Jars, wide mouths, 2 handles, "	15	00
2 " " " " " "	18	00

HOCK WINES.
Ruby Color.

Hocks, 5s or 6s, to gallon, Clay Mould,... ..⅌ gross,	$20	00
" half-size, " " ...... "	16	50
" 5s or 6s, to gallon, Iron " " ...... "	18	50
" half-size, " " ...... "	15	50

OLIVE CLARETS.
French Style, 20 to 22 ounces.

Olive Clarets, Clay Mould,.. ....⅌ gross,	$20	00
" " Iron " .... "	18	50

PORTER BOTTLES.

Quart, heavy,...............⅌ gross,	$20	00
Pint, " .... "	13	50

SCOTCH ALES.
Bulb Neck.

Quarts,...............⅌ gross,	$16	50
Pints,............... "	13	50

...........per cent. discount off above prices, cash
4

Flasks for an unidentifiable mixture called Shoo-fly were quite common in the 1870s. Page forty-four of the McCully catalogue, in fact, gives Shoo-fly flasks as much importance as the Eagles and Unions. Shoo-fly — a mixture of molasses and brown sugar used in baking — could not possibly have flowed in such quantities as to demand commercial flasks. Could it have been a brown sugar syrup? A fly poison? Helen McKearin and Kenneth Wilson think the name designates the kind of bottle used rather than any one product contained therein. Charles Gardner agrees and has furnished an old letter from Maring, Hart & Company of Bellaire, Ohio, dated October 8, 1886, that pictures a Shoo-fly flask. It has the same flat side panels and high ribs on the edge as those advertised in the McCully catalogue. It is surprising that such a plain bottle has been competing in price and popularity with the more picturesque Eagles and Unions. An interesting point in the Maring, Hart advertisement is the use of the word "flint." Commercial bottles of the mid and late nineteenth century certainly did not carry any high lead content. After the suc-

226 Wm. McCully & Co. catalogue, May 1, 1875. Page 58. *Collection of the author.*

228 Wm McCully & Co., established 1830, catalogue, May 1, 1875. Page 45, early type of preserving jar. Pages 46 and 47, improvements in preserving jars. *Collection of the author.*

58

MISCELLANEOUS.

1 ounce, Carmine Ink,	5 gro. boxes, ℔ gr.	$2	25
2 " " "	3 " "	2	75
Citrate Magnesia Bottles,	½ " "	10	00
Oval Nursing Bottles, new style,	½ " "	6	50
Glycerine Bottles,	½ " "	8	50
Oil Sample Bottles,	½ " "	6	00

FLASKS—White Glass, Oval Style.

½ pint, 6 dozen boxes,	per gross, $	5	00
1 " 6 "	"	7	00

FLASKS—Shoo Fly Style.

¼ pint, 6 dozen boxes,	per gross, $	4	20
½ " 6 "	"	5	00
1 " 6 "	"	7	00
Quarts, 6 "	"	10	00

Mustard Barrels.

4 ounce, Ground Tops,	℔ gross, $	4	25
6 " " "	"	5	25
8 " " "	"	6	75
6 " French, New Style,	"	6	75

.... per cent. discount off above prices, cash.

Shoo Fly Flasks, Glass Stoppers.

½ pint, 6 dozen boxes,	per gross, $	11	00
1 " 6 "	"	13	00
Quarts, 6 "	"	20	00

NET PRICES.

Ground Stoppered Bottles.

½ ounce, Lubin Extract,	℔ gross, $	6	00
1 " " "	"	6	00
½ " Night Blooming Cereus,	"	6	00
1 " " " "	"	6	00
½ " R. S. Prescription Vials,	"	6	00
1 " " " "	"	6	00
2 " " " "	"	8	00
3 " " " "	"	9	00
4 " " " "	"	9	00
6 " " " "	"	10	00
8 " " " "	"	10	00
12 " " " "	"	12	00
16 " " " "	"	15	00

45

FRUIT JARS.

—◆◆—

M'CULLY'S

Standard Fruit Jar,

GROOVE RING,

WITH TIN CAP & WIRE COMPLETE.

Quarts,	℔ gross, $	9	00
½ Gallon,	"	14	00

.........per cent. off above prices.

227 The shape of the standard Shoo Fly Flask. Maring and Hart Letterhead, 1886. *Courtesy of Charles B. Gardner.*

cessful lime-soda formula of William Leighton was established in 1864, manufacturers still persisted in calling the product "flint" — doubtless an advertising strength. As late as 1894, Agnew & Company of Hulton, near Pittsburgh, was offering Shoo-fly flasks. The Olean Glass Company of Olean, New York, showed the same type of flask on its letterhead as that advertised by Maring, Hart (*227*).

Advertising of glassware to the trade was be-

46

DICTATOR

SELF-SEALING

FRUIT JAR!

METAL TOPS.

Quarts,.................................℔ gross, $16 00
½ Gallon,................................ " 22 50

Discount,........off above.

GLASS TOPS.

Quarts,.................................℔ gross, $20 00
½ Gallon,................................ " 28 00

Discount,.........off above.

Simplicity! Cheapness!! Reliability!!!

THE

THREE ESSENTIAL POINTS

COMBINED IN THIS JAR.

NO NECESSITY FOR BUYING HIGH-PRICED

SCREW TOP JARS,

THE

"DICTATOR"

Combines all their Good Points, and sold 25 per cent. less.

47

W. W. LYMAN'S

Patent Improved

SELF-SEALING

FRUIT JARS.

Quarts, Tin Cap,...............per gross, $25 00
½ Gallon, " .... " 30 00

.... ..per cent. discount off above prices.

We offer special inducements for large buyers on above Jar.

This is one of the most Reliable Jars that is offered to the Trade, and with the New Opener, which is furnished without charge, any child can Unseal the Jar.

We are the Exclusive Manufacturers

FOR THE

WESTERN COUNTRY.

coming more common with the improvement in freight transportation and consequent increase in interregional competition. William McCully advertised in the catalogue of May 1, 1875:

Iron Moulds for every description of Green and Black Bottles can be furnished at an expense of from 10 to 25 dollars. For Flint Glass Vials and Bottles from 20 to 50 dollars.*

* McCully catalogue, p. 41.

Preserving jars were often marked with the factory name: Frank, Cunningham, Ihmsen, McKee, Wormser, A. G. Wks L. (Arsenal Glass Works, Lawrenceville). The Historical Society of Western Pennsylvania owns preserving jars marked William Frank & Sons; S. McKee & Co.; The Hero-INE (Cunningham & Ihmsen); John Agnew & Son A, Pgh., Pa; Union Fruit Jar; and A. & D. H. Chambers. Though Mason jars were adver-

229 Iron mold and bottle made therefrom ca. 1880. Fahnestock factory. *Courtesy of Mr. John J. Heard and the late Mrs. Heard.*

tised in the Ringwalt catalogue of 1860, they were a small item then compared with their popularity at the outset of the increase in canning in 1875.

One might almost think that 1874 Pittsburgh manufacturers foresaw the Prohibition era when the following trade descriptions were released to the December 26, 1874, issue of *The Crockery and Glass Journal:*

For the benefit of temperance travelers, we give the following information about the bottle business. For the coming season pocket flasks are to be the leading novelty and already sample designs are showing for Western and Southern manufacturers, indicating thin flat concave bottles to wear comfortably in hip pockets of pantaloons; broad thin flat rim, short-necked bottles to go inside breast pockets; long narrow octagon-shaped flasks to fit small and specially made pockets in overcoats, just back of the usual breast pockets. Then there are bottles of yellow earthenware, made to represent in shape and color memorandum books and red morocco colored glass flats from 1 to 2½ inches in thickness in various lengths and breadths designed to represent the bottom lining of a traveling bag.

In spite of the individualized shapes referred to in the quotation, bottles were becoming standardized and less decorated. In November 1877, Cunningham & Ihmsen shipped 1600 gross of beer bottles (230,400 pieces) in a full barge to the Anheuser Busch Brewery in St. Louis. These were blown by workmen, but four years later mechanical air pressure began to supplant the use of human lungs. Mechanization came to the manufacture of bottles in 1896 and was advanced by the Michael Owens machine in 1903, which fathered all modern streamlined production of bottles.

Advancing technology brought high-speed mass production, lower costs, and an absolutely uniform product of high quality, but it sacrificed those elements that excite the scholar and collector: individual beauty and creative variety in shape, color, and design.

CHAPTER XII

The Joining of Pressed and Blown

Soon after the introduction of [flint glass] into this country, a very great
improvement in the mode of manufacture was introduced. . . . Pellatt
in his admirable work on glass alludes to the American invention in only a
few words and passes it by as but of slight importance, but it has brought
about a very great change, and is destined to exert a still greater; in
fact it revolutionized the whole system of flint glass manufacture simply by
mold machines for the purpose of pressing glass into any form.
— Deming Jarves, *Reminiscences of Glass-Making,* 1865

Often when an established method of production is failing to meet the volume demand, a new technology develops to solve the problem. Thus the fabrication of glass pieces by an artisan with a blowpipe began to be replaced in the late 1820s by the dramatic new technique of pressing. Dropping a gather of glass into a mold, ramming a plunger into the mold by hand or mechanical means, forcing the glass into the shape and design pattern, and withdrawing a finished piece — this was not only a simpler, cheaper, and faster method, it made possible the production of many types and shapes.

Naturally, the parallel production of blown and pressed glass, with the slow decline of the first method and the rise of the second, resulted in articles made by both methods. No one has yet tackled this subject as a unit in American nineteenth-century glass, because it stretches from the mists of the past to the uncertainties of the present. We accept without question the existence of drinking vessels and candlesticks, lamps and bowls, compotes and vases, which combine parts that are pressed and blown. The pieces have puzzled us as to time of manufacture, but not enough of them exist to make glass students feel they represent an important phase of commercial production or industrial development. The students, therefore, have not researched and reported on this anomaly of production and have usually dismissed blown and pressed pieces as "transitional." They are a good deal more than that.

Our approach here will be to look at early pieces from the Pittsburgh District that embody both pressing and blowing. In doing so, we should remember that up to 1850 — in spite of twenty-five years of pressing glass in molds — blowing more than held its own in general manufacture. Its decline after 1850 was rapid in relation to the total national production of glass, and pressed glass easily outstripped the older method.

We encounter two theories about the earliest pressed pieces. The late James Rose held that early pressing lasted briefly and then passed quickly into the lacy period of elaborate design and intricately cut molds — in short, that lacy pieces made up a major part of early pressing. The present writer believes that the earliest

230 Pair of clear compotes, pressed bowl and blown base, 1830–1845. Bowl rayed in center, double rings on the shoulder. Cap ring large scallop, point, small scallop, point. Fine quality of heavy lead glass. H. 4½″. D. 8¼″. *The Corning Museum of Glass.*

pressed designs were geometrically plain, perhaps even crude; that production of these plain pieces persisted; and that lacy glass developed later than has generally been accepted.

Both theories are involved with the fact that pressed glass — some form of pressed glass, at least — commonly appeared in the feet of various articles imported into this country in the last quarter of the eighteenth century. Deming Jarves spoke of these in 1865 in his *Reminiscences of Glass-Making,* in an apparent reversal of his earlier statement on pressed glass printed at the head of this chapter: "Fifty years back the writer imported from Holland salts made by being pressed in metallic molds [and bowls and candlesticks from England] with pressed square feet, rudely made, somewhat after the present mode of molding glass."* Though there may have been a

* Jarves, *Reminiscences,* pp. 93–94.

few dissenters, it is now generally agreed that the Americans were the first to develop mechanically pressed glass as we know it. Our concern in this chapter is with the style of pressed-and-blown pieces as well as with the approximate dates when they were made.

Collectors, dealers, and some students have steadfastly held that a piece with pressed feet or base and blown top or stem is among the very earliest of pressed-and-blown articles. Because we can find blown candlesticks with pressed bases — simple, direct pieces — it is assumed that they must be early. Undoubtedly the fact that a candlestick is an early lighting device influences that judgment. But it is just as possible that American pieces with pressed tops and blown or tooled bases may have been made as early as those with pressed bases. The theories meet in a pair of compotes with blown or tooled bases and pressed rayed bowls (*230*). If we accept the reasonable possibility that the bowls may have been made in one of the earliest pressings, then we may assume that the compotes were earlier than those that often appeared with lacy cup plate bases (*231*).

Such bases attributed to the Fort Pitt–Curling factory usually appear in Lee and Rose's *American Glass Cup Plates* Nos. 216-C and 217, rarely in Nos. 183 and 184, in the round rather than in the octagonal form. Cup plates seem to date the compotes around the middle or the late 1830s. Certainly it is a neat way to attribute, for no one can logically expect the Fort Pitt factory to sell its pressed bowls and cup plates to factories down the Ohio for further work. The purchasing factory would have to attach a blown base to the pressed bowl or a baluster stem to connect the pressed bowl to a cup plate base. That is not practical business.

Four such small compotes in the discriminating collection of William J. Elsholz of Detroit furnish an interesting study. All the pressed bowls and cup plate bases are joined by a hand-formed baluster stem — a popular standard in the Midwest. The bowls furnish a contradiction: they are incipient lacy, but they have all been fire polished, though fire polishing would be the quickest way to blunt the sheen of true lacy stippling. Three of the patterns are Roman Rosette, the fourth a band of diamonds, then a plain double-fluted band, all the bands radially joining the center of the bowl. Two of the Roman Rosette bowls carry a Fort Pitt cup plate (Lee and Rose, No. 216-C). The compote with the band of diamonds and clear glass carries the same plate (Lee and Rose, No. 216-C), for its base.

We can be fairly secure, therefore, in believing that all three are products of the Fort Pitt–Curling factory. The fourth compote, a Roman Rosette Pattern, has cup plate No. 498 for its base. Rose states that the origin of No. 498 is uncertain. From the relationship of pattern and form we can without temerity assign it also to the Curlings (*234*). The rims of the four compotes present two interesting designs: beaded bull's eyes on the diamond and plain compote and a scalloped rim with arch points between on the other three. The bowls show a consistency of sizes: 5 ¾ inches, 6⅛ inches, and 6⁹⁄₁₆ inches. The glass, too, has resonance, weight, and clarity — qualities that usually belong to Pittsburgh-pressed pieces until after the middle of the century.

Pressed bowls were often not attached to any base, though we may find the same bowl joined to a baluster or knopped stem on a blown or tooled base. An example is the shoulder-paneled one in cobalt (*233*). The Currier Gallery of Art in Manchester, New Hampshire, owns a small cobalt bowl matching in pattern the compote with the band of diamonds alternating with the plain double-fluted band.

The persistence of that design is well shown by the pressed bowl on the pressed base in the Bennington Museum (*234*). Though such an all-pressed bowl does not technically belong in this chapter, it appears here to serve as a lesson for collectors: the appearance of an early design is not always proof that the piece carrying such a pattern is necessarily early.

Pressed-and-Blown Candlesticks

Candlesticks throw little light on the problem of dating. They merely emphasize the plainness and solidity of Midwestern pressing. The round and the square bases of the two pairs from the Historical Society in Pittsburgh illustrate this generalization. Both are crowned by double knops with deep sockets; in one pair the socket expands into an attractive bubble. The single stick on the square base from the Society (*236*) seems a bit short for grace, but it carries an interesting hollow ogee figure between base and socket. The base with inside paneling seems plain when compared with that of the single clear candlestick from the Ford Museum, whose square base appears elaborate with reeding and an easy curve between the corners (*237*). Again the deep socket appears;

231 1 — Compote pressed in the Roman Rosette pattern and fire polished to achieve even smoothness. Blown stem, heavy knopped. H. 4¼". 2 — Cup plate, No. 216C, Lee and Rose, *American Glass Cup Plates*. 3 — Compote with pressed bowl and cup plate base joined by blown knopped stem. A product of the Fort Pitt factory. H. 4¼". Ca. 1835. *Collection of the author*.

232 1 — Cup plate, Lee and Rose, No. 217A. 2 —
Compote pressed in diamond panel, alternating with a
double, plain panel. Base, cup plate, Lee and Rose,
No. 216C. H. 4¼″. 3 — Similar compote on blown base
with a knopped stem. Product of the Fort Pitt factory,
ca. 1835. *Collection of Dr. E. R. Eller.*

233   Three compotes with pressed bowls and blown
bases, 1835–1850. Heavy knopped stems. 1 — Cobalt
pressed bowl. The bowl of a compote was often sold as a
bowl. D. 6½". 2 — Clear footed compote. Pattern
matches No. 1. 3 — Compote shown in No. 230. Note
teardrop in the stem. 4 — Compote shown in No. 232.
Carnegie Museum Exhibition, 1949–1950.

234   Compote, similar to No. 232, with bowl joined to a
pressed base consisting of 6 panels, 1840–1850. H. 4¼".
*Bennington Museum, Bennington, Vermont, The May K.
and Joseph W. Limric Collection.*

235 Two pairs of clear lead candlesticks with blown tops and pressed bases, 1830–1845. 1 and 4 — Long socket with pewter candle holders. Double knopped stem. Bases paneled, similar to a pressed form used on Midwestern compotes. H. 7½". *The Historical Society of Western Pennsylvania, Violet Swem Brendel Fund.*

2 and 3 — Narrow socket enlarged below into bulbous form. Double knops join socket and stem. Square bases terraced by three circular rings. This square base was used in both the East and the Midwest. H. 9". *The Historical Society of Western Pennsylvania, Anna Moody Browne Fund.*

1 — Candlestick, long socket with pewter candle holder. Shown in No. 235. *The Historical Society of Western Pennsylvania, Violet Swem Brendel Fund.* 2 — Lamp of clear lead glass. Blown font cut in a pattern of strawberry diamonds and roundels with rays — a pattern favored by Pittsburgh factories. Base of font is cut in panels and shoulder of font is notched. Pressed base with small pyramids. Stepped-up platforms ridged to match corners. Variations of this base were used in the East, ca. 1835. 3 — Early clear lead candlestick, ca. 1830. Generous socket joined by ring wafers to a hollow ogee bowl and to a square paneled pressed base. The joining rings at top and base of ogee bowl create an unusual design. The panels above the square pressed base are wider and shallower than those used by the New England Glass Co. H. 8⅝". *The Historical Society of Western Pennsylvania, Gift of Mrs. Thomas C. Wurts.*

the craftsman catches our eye with an upright elongated bubble joining the major parts. At both connecting points the conventional wafer has become nine circular rings. They look as though the artisan had trailed his glass to tie up each joining with a winding of string.

A single clear candlestick from the Garvan Collection at Yale is related to both of these pieces in its bubble between socket and base stem (*238*). Its base is also square with curving lines between the corners. The marked difference occurs in the four steps of the terraced base.

A pair of clear candlesticks from the William J. Elsholz collection has many similarities to these

237 Early clear lead candlestick, ca. 1835. Wide and deep blown socket with pewter inset. Main shaft of candlestick is an inverted bubble. This is joined to the socket and base by circular rings that look like windings of thread. Square pressed base with rounded corners and curved sides between them. A series of ridges inside the base gives the appearance of reeding. H. 10⅝". *The Henry Ford Museum.*

238 Clear lead candlestick, ca. 1835. Deep socket joined to an inverted bubble by knop of three circular rings. This blown top is joined to a pressed stem and base by a similar knop. The square base is curved between the rounded corners and four stepped-up levels rising to a 6-ribbed stem that joins the base of the bubble. Possibly Eastern. H. 10⅜". *Yale University Art Gallery, Mabel Brady Garvan Collection.*

pieces (*239*). Where the socket joins the stem we have five circular rings like those on the Ford stick. At the union of base and shaft, however, the workman has compressed these to form a ridged knop. These sticks have three knops between socket and base like the pair from the Historical Society with two knops. The square

base is curved like that on the Ford stick; the inside of the base is ridged to give the appearance of reeding; and, as on the Garvan stick, the base is terraced into three tiers. All these points of similarity tell us how much skilled glassworkers depended on each other as they adopted and altered traditional styles.

239 Blown and pressed candlesticks of clear lead glass, ca. 1835. Bottom of sockets threaded. Stem triple knops joined to the base terraced wafer. Base shows an affinity to that of No. 237. H. 8⅝". *Collection of William J. Elsholz.*

240 Clear lead candlestick with long socket joined by a clear three-ringed knop to a hollow cobalt shaft, 1835–1845. The shaft, in turn, is joined by a cobalt three-ringed knop to a pressed clear hexagonal base by means of a hexagonal wafer. This base has appeared on completely pressed candlesticks, such as No. 394, described in Rose, *The Story of American Pressed Glass of the Lacy Period, 1825–1850. The Henry Ford Museum.*

241 Lead candlesticks of a dark olive green, 1835–1845. The pressed bases reach to the blown sockets, which are short with a wide lip above a vaselike bubble. The bases are hexagonal panels with four graduated shoulders. The pressed design is typically Midwestern. H. 9⅛". *Collection of William J. Elsholz.*

Color always produced interest. Another single stick from the Ford Museum catches the eye with a large cobalt bubble elongated somewhat downward to meet the base *(240)*. The shoulder bubble extends beyond the clear wafers at the socket contact, whereas the cobalt wafers touching the base retain a strength of design lost at the juncture of the socket.

242 1 and 2 — Pair of clear lead candlesticks on a rare pressed base, 1830–1835. Long sockets ending in a ringed wafer knop. Three rounded knops form the stems and are joined to the bases by a heavy ring wafer knop. Pressed bases of bell-like shape heavily ridged to match the wide border at the bottom of the candlestick. The bell part of the base is bisected by a circular ridge.

H. 9⅛". 3 — Clear lead candlestick, blown top on pressed lacy base called Midwestern Hairpin, 1830–1835. 4 — Cobalt candlestick. Blown socket and stem consisting of two rounded knops. Hexagonal base rises gracefully to meet joining wafer, 1835–1845. H. 8¼". *Collection of Theodore E. Keller.*

The Elsholz candlesticks (*241*) — a queer, greenish, smoky amber — represent the hexagonal base not very common in the Midwest. The pyramidal bases remind us by analogy of later pressed McKee and Bakewell examples. If we lined up all these candlesticks and the later pressed pieces, the similarities would persuade us of the relationship.

Blown Candlesticks with Lacy Bases

James Rose's theory that lacy pieces were a major part of early pressing is best supported by the blown fonts and many lacy bases of lamps, but it is also sustained by the candlesticks. A pair from the collection of Theodore Keller of Cincinnati shows a reasonable progression (*242*). Looked at from a distance, the bell-like base with

243 Pair of clear lead candlesticks on an unusual pressed base, ca. 1835. Blown socket is decorated with six rings. The shaft consists of four rounded knops joined to the pressed base by a broad wafer. Base is heavily ridged. Circular dots are reminiscent of bull's-eye cap ring found on many Midwestern lacy pieces. At right, interior of base. *Collection of Carleton Brown.*

a series of ridges has the spirit of stippling because of the repetitive effect. The base rim, a series of little upright cylinders, borders the edge almost like a Pittsburgh bull's-eye cap ring. These sticks, too, have deep sockets, three knops, and wafers that become an integral part of the design. Comparing these bases with the hairpin stippled base beside them, we see how they could represent a step from the unadorned, plain base toward the delicate tracery of a true lacy piece.

Carleton Brown of the Ford Museum owns a pair of candlesticks with bases that have the same ridgelike quality as the Keller sticks, except that they are flatter (243). Four knops instead of three join the top and base. A recent acquisition of the Ford Museum is a heavy celery vase decorated by copper wheel engraving of the single undulant leaf and the daisy (244). The unusually heavy pressed base is closely related to that on the Brown sticks. This vase is an especially interesting piece also because of the molded ridges at the bottom of the bowl.

In mentioning the hairpin lacy base so common to the Pittsburgh area, we must point out that the term is used too loosely. The true hairpin design found on so many handsome Eastern lacy pieces (plates, bowls, shell dishes, compotes) is more delicate than the lancets or darts on Midwestern lacy (245). These lancets on plates alternate; one clear, one stippled. On the notable Midwestern lacy casket and on many bases, the lancets are clear with a stippled border. At the top, where two touching lancets have curved away from each other to a point, the resulting space is dotted with a flowerlike medallion. In general, lacy bases of the Midwest follow this design rather than the more elaborate and better-patterned New England hairpin. In nomenclature, however, no distinction has been made; the Midwestern version is also called hairpin.

By analogy we assign to a much later period the pressed bases of the pair that matches the lamp (246). True, the Roman Rosette design of these pressed bases matches that on the com-

244 Copper wheel engraved vase on a heavily ridged pressed base, ca. 1835. Vase has been patterned in a short ribbed mold. Engraved design is Daisy and undulant leaf with sprays of berries. The pressed base is closely related to that on the Carleton Brown candlesticks (No. 243). Possibly a unique Pittsburgh piece. H. 8". *The Henry Ford Museum.*

245 Clear lead candlesticks with very deep sockets and a short stem of two rounded knops, ca. 1835. Heavy circular wafer joins a lacy base, called Midwestern Hairpin. These interesting sticks seem foreshortened. H. 7¼". *Collection of William J. Elsholz.*

The Joining of Pressed and Blown 243

246 Three lead pieces with identical lacy Roman Rosette bases, 1835–1850. This pattern appears on the Grossman compotes shown in Plate XVI, No. 354, Rose, *The Story of American Pressed Glass of the Lacy Period, 1825–1850.* 1 and 3 — Candlesticks with deep sockets, pewter insets, and short stems consisting of two round knops joined to the pressed bases by wide circular wafers. H. 7¾". 2 — Using the same pressed base, a workman has fashioned a bulbous whale oil lamp font with pewter wick holder. Note that he raised the font above the base by a lengthened stem so that the light would be stronger. H. 7¼". *Collection of Theodore E. Keller.*

pletely pressed compotes owned by the late Mrs. John Grossman, and pictured in Rose's *The Story of American Pressed Glass of the Lacy Period 1825–1850,* Plate XVI, No. 354, which are obviously later. If we did not have this information, we would take it for a later piece on the evidence that larger diamonds had replaced the stippling, that several parts of the surfaces were completely unadorned, that coarser patterns of the geometric figures of the design had left the delicate intricacies of old lace, and that the stippling was engine-turned — all signs of later manufacture.

All these Midwestern blown-top and pressed-base candlesticks seem to have the deep generous socket and symmetrical knops on the stems. Any departure from the knops uses the bubble in different forms to effect a union between base and socket.

An atypical piece from the Corning Museum of Glass* proves the futility of any attempt to set up

* James H. Rose, *The Story of American Pressed Glass of the Lacy Period, 1825–1850* (Printed in the Netherlands for the Corning Museum of Glass, 1954), Plate XVII, No. 366.

247 Three whale oil lamps with pressed bases characteristic of the period 1835–1845. 1 — Paneled font on elaborate pressed lacy base. Note the series of dots at the bottom edge of the base, clearly Midwestern style. 2 — Undecorated blown font on a base similar to that shown in Picture 235, Nos. 2 and 3. Base could be Eastern. 3 — Bulbous blown font on knopped stem joined to Midwestern lacy Hairpin base. *Ex coll. John J. Grossman.*

a time sequence for pressed-and-blown candlesticks. This specimen, though carrying the double knop and the ridged wafers like the early sticks, has a pressed socket obviously designed to imitate early cut glass patterns. The octagonal stepped-up base offsets the heaviness of the socket.

Pressed-and-Blown Lamps

Early whale oil glass lamps were far less numerous in the Midwest than along the Eastern seaboard. The Pittsburgh *Gazette* for December 12, 1844, lists 75,237 kegs, tierces, and barrels of lard and 2636 barrels of lard oil imported by way of the Ohio River. Much of this undoubtedly served as fluid for lighting. Lamps for whale oil seem to follow the kinds of bases appearing in the candlesticks, as shown in three typical pieces (*247*). As in the candlesticks, the wafers joining font and base are emphasized and are part of the design. This becomes an interesting point when we think of later wholly pressed candlesticks. By then the artisan intended to make the joining wafer disappear. He did so with blown fonts and

248 Pair of clear lead Pittsburgh whale oil lamps on plain pressed base, 1835–1840. Blown font of unusual triangular shape. Brass collars and wick holders. Design of base has not appeared on other Midwestern pieces. A mark of Midwestern lacy was the table rest. Easily noticeable are the table rests on the right corner of each lamp. Well proportioned and well designed, they speak well for the maker. H. 9¾". *Collection of the author.*

249 Camphene lamp, cut, blown, and pressed, 1835–1850. Font is unusually small. Decorated by strawberry diamonds with fans. Below the font and several heavy wafer knops is a second but false font that serves as a stem. Below its base wafer is a square base with curved sides and rounded corners. The interior of the base is pressed in fine ridges that reflect lines. (See Nos. 237 & 239.) H. 13¼". *Yale University Art Gallery, Mabel Brady Garvan Collection.*

pressed bases of lamps of the 1860s and the 1870s until the metal connection of the two parts was perfected. Our consideration here, however, is with the forerunners of the midcentury product.

The Grossman lamp (*247*) and the Keller one (*246*) — with their early blown bowls on later-style pressed bases — would seem to refute my generalization that the hairpin base with bull's-eye cap ring was earlier than the coarsely designed bases on the three Keller pieces (Roman Rosette). Here we have an almost identical font with a hairpin base on a single knopped shaft. The fixture on the Keller lamp may be earlier than the neater one on the Grossman lamp. A logical explanation, however, may be that the hairpin base was most popular and persisted over a long period of time, so that the lamp could still be later. To repeat once again, hard and fast rules cannot be laid down in assigning early glass, and the contradictory qualities of handworked pieces add to their charm and desirability.

Another puzzler is the pair of Pittsburgh-type lamps with the unadorned wavy square bases (*248*). From a distance one might think the bases are duplicates of the hundreds of thousands of pressed kerosene lamps that graced miners' and steelworkers' homes in the late 1870s and are still being made. Careful observation, however, reveals little knobs under the base rim — table rests common to many lacy Midwestern plates and bowls. The plain base, moreover, though uneven in surface, has a good lead content. The curves and flutes seem anachronistic. Not many matched pairs of Pittsburgh early blown-and-pressed lamps exist, so it behooves us not to be too critical. There is an obvious affinity of design between these lamps and the base of the Ford Museum candlestick with the cobalt bubble (*240*).

Inevitably we find cut fonts in the so-called Bakewell pattern — strawberry diamonds with roundels edged with rays (*95*). One example (*236*) has a magnificent stepped-up base with little pillars at each corner. A companion from the Garvan Collection at Yale (*249*) lacks the corner finials of the lamp in picture *236* and has a plainer base. The shape of the font is very similar; the cutting carries the strawberry diamond and fan and the roundel with rays. In this lamp the use of joining wafers to extend markedly beyond the stem as well as the hollow part of the stem between the two wafers establishes an artistic relationship with the early pressed-and-blown candlesticks. In shape and plainness the heavy base allies itself to the bases on the matched Pittsburgh pair. A lamp at the Corning Museum similar in shape and cut design has been attributed to the Union Flint Glass Company of Kensington, near Philadelphia.

In addition to cut fonts we find those with typical Pittsburgh copper wheel engraving. An impressive font (*119*) shows the stiff but strong three leaves and the daisy, the same pattern as that on the decanter Benjamin Bakewell presented to Ellen Murdoch in 1847 (*89*). The reeding on the stem of the base and the plain round flanges on the bottom itself speak of an earlier date. This possibility is quite in keeping with our knowledge that copper wheel engraving flourished as early as 1818 and continued through the turn of the century.

That the joining of pressed-and-blown techniques persisted is clearly shown by the lamp with the pillar-molded font (*186*). It is rare to find a pillar-molded font and doubly rare to find it on a pressed base. Without depending on the brass collar, one could assign this lamp to the 1850s or

1860s, on the form of the pressed base. In a Bakewell, Pears catalogue of the 1870s an Icicle compote carries a similar base. Also, the Pressed Block open compote pictured in Ruth Webb Lee's *Early American Pressed Glass* (Plate 12, No. 2) is closely related. Mrs. Lee says that a member of the Pears family bought a plate of the Block pattern at the old factory in 1853. For the most part, the McKee and O'Hara factories used straighter paneled bases or sharper paneled knobs. The nearest that McKee comes to the pressed base of the pillar-molded lamp is found in his 1864 catalogue on a so-called Cracker Bowl in the Crystal pattern. An O'Hara (or McKee) covered compote in the Loop pattern (*400*) at the Historical Society in Pittsburgh also has that kind of base. Pillar-molding as a technique flourished around the middle of the century.

Compotes, Bowls, and Vases

Compotes, bowls, and vases can probably run early pressed-and-blown lamps a good race in numbers produced. Though we see some of the same lacy and plain bases, time changes are more easily discerned on the bowls. An eighteenth-century type of pressed base is found on the magnificent paneled and engraved bowl from the Rodgers collection discussed on page 166. The square base supporting the paneled bell-like section is joined to the bowl by a short unadorned cylinder instead of the knops and balusters we are more accustomed to. With the graceful floral festoons and the eighteenth-century base, it is no wonder that Mr. Rodgers always considered his piece an example of Amelung's work.

Another outstanding blown-molded paneled example is the superb clear sugar bowl at the Corning Museum of Glass (*250*). (There is a similar one at the Historical Society in Pittsburgh.) It rests, however, on the familiar lacy hairpin base. A mate to it from the Ford Museum has more elaborate engraving, long and heavy leaves with clusters of seven berries (*126*). We find this base occurring almost as frequently as the plain baluster stem and plain circular base, though the conventionality and heaviness of the baluster better fit the general run of Pittsburgh pieces — free-blown, pattern- and pillar-molded, and even the pressed-and-blown type under discussion. It was used particularly on pressed plates and shallow bowls that could be given a foot or made as completely functional pieces just as they came from the mold (*233*).

Another widely used pressed base is square with extended round corners (*251*). Above the square base, graduated circles, ordinarily three in number, rise toward the shaft, a gracefully shaped pedestal that joins the ring of wafers in the case of a lamp and the bowl itself in the case of an open compote (*251*). The shaft of the pedestal may have six, seven, or eight flat panels. Later on, the panels swelled to round ridges with a stodginess not as attractive. Pittsburgh has no claim to priority on the square type of base; it also appeared in New England. The character of the copper wheel engraving on some of the bowls and on the blown lamp font, and the fact that many pieces with such pressed bases have been found in the Tri-State area, assure us that it was an accepted Pittsburgh product. Besides, a completely pressed small compote — a Pittsburgh product — indicates that the base also served later manufacturing processes (*252*). It is much easier to find an all-pressed compote with such a base in the Midwest than along the Eastern seaboard.

The collector must not be led astray by pieces that have been fire polished. Pressed bowls on baluster or plain stems were often reheated to soften the lines and edges of the pressed bowl, so that the smoothness would at first sight seem to belong to a free-blown compote.

Pressed-and-blown vases pose none of these interrelated problems. They did not have the variety of designs found in candlesticks and lamps. And there was little contradiction in time between tops and bases. The vase cut in panels at the Historical Society in Pittsburgh (*252*) — at-

251 Three clear blown pieces of lead glass, 1840–1850, are joined to the same pattern of pressed base, also used in the East. This base has appeared before on a lamp, No. 247, and a candlestick, No. 235. 1 — Small compote with folded rim and cut decoration. Swags and cinquefoils are major design, but below the rim is a border of slanting finger flutes. 2 — Whale oil lamp. Font is rather narrow with a high shoulder and a small cavity for oil. 3 — Large compote decorated by copper wheel engraving in a simple vintage pattern. Leaves and fruit encircle the bowl. *Ex coll. John J. Grossman.*

252 1 — Vase of heavy lead glass, first quarter of nineteenth century. Bowl cut in panels so that it looks to be pressed. Heavy knopped stem on blown base. Attributed by Dorothy Daniel to the O'Hara-Craig factory. H. 9⅞". *The Historical Society of Western Pennsylvania.* 2 — Pressed compote on pressed base, 1850–1870. (See Nos. 235, 247, and 251 for the use of the same base.) Bottom of bowl is rayed and shoulders are decorated by a series of parallel lines in groups of three. Cap ring is large scallop and small scallop. H. 4". *Collection of the author.* 3 — Celery vase pressed in panels, then fire polished and expanded at the top into scallops, 1860. Blown base with baluster stem. *Collection of Mrs. Woodward C. Adams.*

253 Fiery opal pressed bowl that has been fire polished to simulate blown glass, 1850–1860. Pattern is Colonial, possibly McKee. H. 4⅞″. *The Henry Ford Museum.*

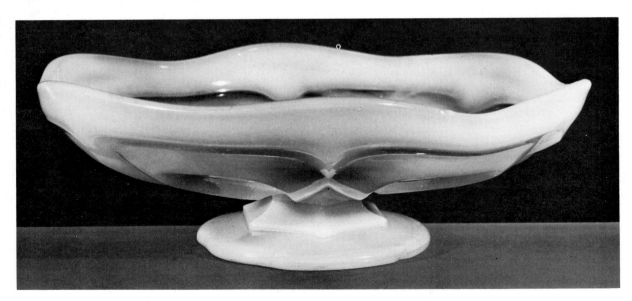

254 Fiery opal pressed bowl that has been fire polished to simulate blown glass, 1860–1870. Design used by Bakewell. H. 2⅞″. D. 9⅜″. *The Corning Museum of Glass.*

255 1 — Fiery opal Ashburton sugar bowl, pressed, ca. 1860. H. 7½″. 2 — Fiery opal celery vase pressed into panels, ca. 1860. Rim expanded and flattened into scallops. Vase rests on clear base joined by a short baluster stem. H. 8½″. 3 — Pressed fiery opal candlestick on hexagonal base, ca. 1865. 4 — Pressed fiery opal goblet, Argus (Thumbprint) ca. 1865. Bakewell, Pears & Co. 5 — Pressed fiery opal lacy bowl in the **Roman Rosette** pattern, ca. 1840. D. 6½″. This design was used in the East as well as in the Midwest. 1 and 5, *The Historical Society of Western Pennsylvania, Gift of Henry King Siebeneck. 2, The Historical Society of Western Pennsylvania, Michael L. Benedum Fund. 3 and 4, Ex coll. John J. Grossman.*

no! see p 336-7. this is Cincinnati or Honeycomb

256 Fiery opal celery vase, pressed into 6 panels, ca. 1865. H. 8⅝". It matches No. 255–2, except for the blown opal stem, which is more triangular than the baluster. *The Henry Ford Museum.*

tributed to O'Hara's early works — does not belong in this discussion, but since it bears such a close artistic relationship to the later vase in the same plate, it can indicate how styles develop. The second vase has a pressed bowl that has been fire polished (*252*). Both set well on heavy baluster stems. An outgrowth of these two is the fiery opal vase designed along the same lines, though it is lighter in body and stem (*255*). One would expect to find various early colors in such an attractive shape. Three museums and two private collections have such a fiery opal vase, but I know of no example of cobalt, green, amethyst, or amber pressed tops in plain panels on clear baluster bases. Why was an obviously commercial product limited to fiery opal?

In addition to assembling pictures of pressed-and-blown pieces, this chapter has other purposes that are less clearly evident. In one piece, the time of manufacture depends apparently on the character of the blown part, in another on the design of the pressed part. We must often fall back upon comparison. The previously stated generalizations, which are obvious when one looks at the pictures, may sometimes include English or Continental pieces. Like the baluster stem, the pressed base establishes a direct relationship with the Eastern coast. Many of the blown fonts and bowls merely restate the glassmakers' practice and design handed down from generation to generation. The value of cup plate base as a source of attribution for the patterns of pressed bowls is inestimable.

An interesting generalization may be made about the numbers of pressed-and-blown compotes and lamps. The Midwest seems to outstrip the East in variety of lacy compotes with blown or tooled or pressed bases, and the East shows greater variety of lacy bases for blown lamps. The East probably used lacy bases earlier than the West.

In spite of all the qualifications and hedging applied to the pieces in these pages, there is something of solidity, freedom, freshness, and courage in most of the pressed-and-blown articles. The striving of the pioneer underlies their creation — a promise of a society that would need, use, and cherish them would take root in the Midwest. At the same time, these pieces continue traditions of the craft — traditions much more permanent and far-reaching than those of any mere geographical locality.

CHAPTER XIII

Midwestern Lacy

> Though lacy glass was produced in an era when excessive decorative elaboration was the rule, it almost invariably represents a just sense of the inherent quality of glass as a material and a remarkably sound taste in adjusting patterns at once to the capabilities of the machine and to the nature of the substance employed. Later, and in other localities, this rule was less carefully observed.
> — Homer Eaton Keyes, "Museum Examples of Sandwich Glass," *Antiques,* July 1938

Lacy glass began somewhere, some time, in the late 1820s as an imitation of cut glass, but with its flexibility and complexity of form it at once outstripped the rigidity of cut designs. Lacy also began as a decoy to divert the eye from the grayness of early glass and to cover the wrinkles caused by uneven cooling, by imperfections in the process of pressing and by the mold itself. Stippling, hand-done or engine-turned, was a decorative requirement. Since the "all-over design" had the appearance of crocheting and the joining of medallions in old lace, the name developed naturally. The brilliance and reflection of light from many surfaces, the increased refraction, and the sparkling return of light from whichever vantage point all helped to elevate lacy glass over pieces that served ordinary functional requirements. It earned an honored position on the sideboards and tables of the well-to-do and of those who wished to own a beautiful piece of glass.

The riddle of who made the first lacy glass may some day be solved, but for the present we must resort to theory. The French have a claim, for the Baccarat factory 210 miles from Paris was operating in 1822. The following year it had 327 workmen and a product worth 800,000 francs, and by 1830 it had begun to press glass. The Val St. Lambert factory in Belgium began operations in 1825, and its first catalogue issued in 1829 declared that articles *"moules à la presse"* were of a metal just as brilliant as that from Baccarat, though of coarse stippling. Both these houses sold through the same agent, Launay, Hautin & Cie. of Paris. Launay's 1840 catalogue listed Baccarat, St. Louis, Choisy le Roi, and Bercy as exhibitors. This common sales channel has confused attribution on many of the midcentury Continental pieces. For many years, French and Eastern American lacy glass were subjects of debate about origin, design, pattern, and precedence, for Sandwich often seemed related to French lacy in design and brilliance.

Sandwich is believed to have been the largest single producer of the glass, and for a long time the collecting and dealing public called most lacy "Sandwich." They were not particularly interested in Continental lacy, to which they gave the generic name "Baccarat."

Lacy was made possible by and grew out of the development of pressed glass. Much of the early pressed glass was lacy, and the Sandwich claim to precedence rested on the belief that American mechanics and the product of pressing preceded and surpassed the efforts of England and the Continent. The first American patents for pressed glass, for making bureau knobs, were as early as 1825–1829 and seemed to carry the design and spirit of lacy.

American collectors, dealers, and glass scholars ignored Midwestern lacy until the 1930s, and when they finally acknowledged its existence, they called it a late arrival of crude, provincial appearance. Though they did not say so aloud and may not have even realized it, they invariably thought in terms of a cultural lag between the Eastern shore and the wild regions on the far side of the Alleghenies.

Pittsburgh and the Midwest had some rather remarkable advantages in the later stages of this debate. For one thing, it was a Pittsburgh factory that submitted that first patent for pressing bureau knobs in 1825, the year Sandwich opened its doors. For another, more marked lacy pieces have been found in the Pittsburgh area, clearly attributable to Pittsburgh area factories, than in any other United States locality. Bakewell marked many knobs, a tray, and two windowpanes. Fort Pitt Glass Works (Curling) marked a creamer, a cup plate, and a windowpane. Stourbridge Flint Glass Works (the Robinsons) marked several boat salts and a plate. Union Glass Works (Parke and Campbell) marked and dated an 1836 cup plate. John and Craig Ritchie in Wheeling marked a pane "J and C Ritchie." Since they were in partnership only in the single year 1833, we have a key date for that mold, even if it was used subsequently.

The paucity of marked pieces on the whole Atlantic seaboard is in strong contrast. New England Glass Company marked a salt (not a true lacy piece) and a lamp. Sandwich put its name on the Lafayette boat salts. Providence Flint Glass Works, 1831–1833, marked a salt. Jersey Glass Company, in Jersey City, marked a nonlacy salt.

In the face of such evidence, the battle for recognition of Midwestern lacy has long since been won. With the foregoing evidence one would think that the Midwestern and the French lacy would have merited a more careful study. The informed public may still think in terms of a nineteenth-century cultural lag between East and Midwest, but it now less frequently calls every piece of lacy "Sandwich." Scholars have been writing about the quality and the identification of Midwestern lacy, and Midwestern examples no longer struggle for artistic consideration.

If there was an outstanding leader in the debate, it was James H. Rose, who established and defended Midwestern lacy glass. Dr. Charles Green had written an article for *American Collector* titled "Sandwich Made First Lacy Glass." In it he said that the marked Curling creamer "was very likely made at Sandwich as a commercial sample in an effort to sell under Curling's name a side line to add to the more commonplace product the Curlings were able to make."* Mr. Rose answered the challenge in the September 20, 1934, issue with "Lacy Glass Also From Fort Pitt." Speaking for the McKearins, the Knittles, and Albert Marble, dean of cup plate collectors, he showed how lacy cup plates and salts had clearly come from Pittsburgh factories. The following sentence establishes Mr. Rose's objectivity: "Speaking for my colleagues, I can say that we would much rather call a piece of lacy glass *Sandwich* than to admit grudgingly that it may have originated at almost any one of a great many Midwestern factories of which we know little or nothing."† The *American Collector* for October 4, 1934, carried an answer to Mr. Rose: "Dr. Green Still Champions Sandwich."

What a difference twenty years can make in knowledge and attitude! In 1954, Mr. Rose or-

* July 26, 1934, pp. 1, 7, 11.
† Pp. 2, 11.

257 The Curling Creamer, the only known lacy creamer from the Midwest, is marked on the bottom "R.B. Curling & Sons Fort Pitt." Changing company partnerships would indicate 1829–1832. Baskets of fruit, flowers, and leaves are below the band of geometric forms. The pressed handle may have been used after Deming Jarves' patent for pressing handles. One of three known specimens. H. 4⅛". *The Corning Museum of Glass.*

ganized an exhibition of American Pressed Glass of the Lacy Period at the Corning Museum of Glass. He prepared a scholarly catalogue on lacy glass for the exhibition; it serves as a guide on that subject. Needless to say, Midwestern lacy receives equal time today.

Some Sources of Design

In the early years of lacy production, no glass was being pressed in Ohio. Pittsburgh, Wheeling, and the river environs of each center represent the term "Midwestern" as applied to lacy. (No records of patenting lacy patterns have ever been found.) Students are still occupied in isolating the unmarked Wheeling product. The interchange of workmanship up and down the river valley and the similarity of products, not only in lacy but also in free-blown and pattern-molded, blurs fine geographical distinctions. Such distinctions actually seem of less importance than the product turned out by the whole region.

In pressed glass, prime responsibility for the pattern, shape, form, and artistry shifted from the blower to the artisans who designed and cast the mold. Mold makers (not always straight glassmen) began by adapting the patterns of lace, but they very soon made use of the arch and windows of Gothic church architecture, the columns and pediments of the Greek revival, and designs in the

258 Symbolic use of patriotic forms (eagles and shields) gives strength to this large plate, 1830–1835. The 214 series of cup plates (Lee and Rose, *American Glass Cup Plates*) has centers matching that on this plate. Mr. Rose assigned the 214 group to Curling's Fort Pitt factory. D. 8". *Ex coll. John J. Grossman.*

instruction books written by the great cabinet makers. One mold maker used the designs found on the library and great room ceilings and walls of Kenmore, the Fielding Lewis home in Fredericksburg, Virginia.* Someone designed a plate using the pattern on the ceiling of the Park Theater (1822) in New York. One Midwestern lacy pane carries a simple, stylized rose medallion; a church tower in Owego, New York, has a similar flower. Other designers drew heavily on the patterns of wallpaper of the eighteenth century and later.

It was long believed that the design of a Sandwich vegetable dish had been copied directly from a Meissen dish. Walter Simmons of Detroit decided to find out. He simply wrote to the German factory and asked, and he was told that the Germans had copied the design from Sandwich.† Less well known are the various Staffordshire borders that were transposed into shoulder designs for cup and toddy plates. Regardless of who and which came first, the basic point is that there was indeed a relationship between the design on fine glass and the design on earthenware and porcelain tableware. Some scholar might well write a thesis on the sources of lacy design. He might begin by searching out the relationships of that design to the work of Benjamin Latrobe, Thomas Bulfinch, and Samuel McIntyre.

Guideposts for Attribution and Understanding

In analyzing lacy glass, we should note identifiable characteristics. Even so, Eastern and French lacy will creep into the exposition. Lacy cup plates and salt dishes, which in one respect are separate categories, will be used for analogy

* "Kenmore," *Antiques* 53, April 1948.
† Meissen dishes found in corresponding patterns in lacy glass: Meissen Vegetable dish — Ruth Webb Lee's *Sandwich Glass Handbook* (Northboro, Mass.: privately printed, 1947), Plate 152; Meissen Butterfly tray — Lee, Plate 95, 10″ size; Meissen plate — McKearin, *American Glass,* Plate 132, No. 1; Meissen compote — Lee, Plate 119, bowl, Plate 138, stem and foot; Meissen bowl — Lee, Plate 96, center of lower row.

and comparison. Three illuminating areas for attribution and understanding are: (1) the cap ring, (2) the character of design, and (3) the forms of the pieces produced.

Cap Ring Designs as Evidence of Origins

Rose presents line drawings and diagrams of molds for pressed flat pieces or open bowls (*259*) in the Corning Museum Catalogue. To oversimplify the process, we may say that the earliest pressing operation was like working a potato ricer. The molten glass was dropped into the press, the handle was brought down, and the glass was compressed into the desired shape and pattern. Guessing the exact amount dropped into the mold required skill and judgment — so much of it that some inventive glassman got the idea of adding a cap ring to the mold. That accomplished two things: it controlled the evenness of the outer rim of the piece being pressed, and it eased the problem of overfilling and underfilling. The ring may have been the subject of Phineas Dummer's Cover Plate of 1827 or may have developed from it.*

The French were likely to eschew the cap ring, folding the edges or allowing the design to flow to the edge. Generally they placed their pattern on the base mold. In American lacy glass, on the other hand, manufacturers could press their pieces upside-down with a challenging emphasis on the cap ring as well as press them conventionally with the pattern on the base mold. James Rose has given an admirable description of how an uncomplicated form like a cup plate was pressed.† The base mold shapes the surface of the plate. The cap ring presses the edges of the plate with the rim pattern. The actual design of the cup plate is on a die slipped beneath the plunger and attached to it.

The mold principles for hollow pieces and deep bowls were more complicated because of the additional divisions of the mold. We get some idea of

* *The Story of American Pressed Glass,* p. 14.
† Lee and Rose, *American Glass Cup Plates,* pp. 28–30.

259 Schematic drawings of mold structure and press operation in the manufacture of cup plates and flat pieces like larger plates and ordinary-sized bowls. The molds for hollow pieces were hinged and more complicated, but the operational principles remain the same. *Rose, The Story of American Pressed Glass of the Lacy Period, 1825–1850. The Corning Museum of Glass.*

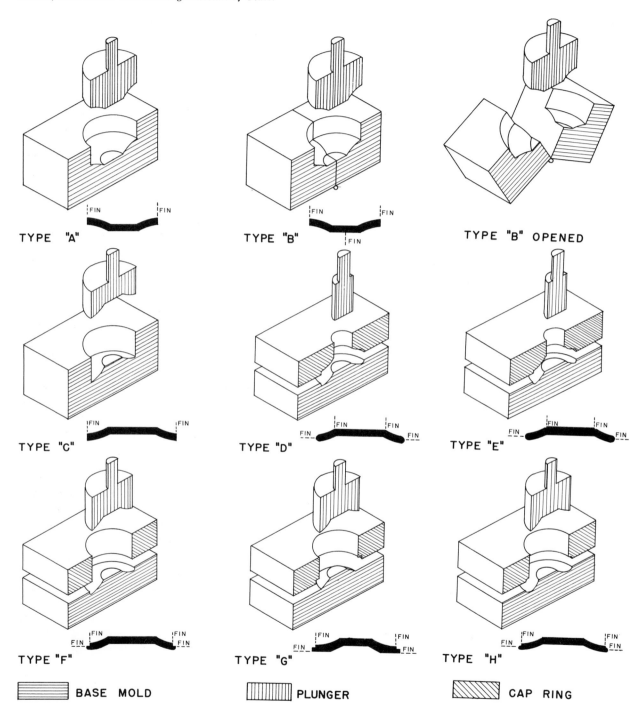

TYPE "A" TYPE "B" TYPE "B" OPENED

TYPE "C" TYPE "D" TYPE "E"

TYPE "F" TYPE "G" TYPE "H"

BASE MOLD   PLUNGER   CAP RING

the value of a pattern mold in a letter Deming Jarves wrote to Captain William Stutson on June 23, 1828. "Be careful no one gets a clay impression from the new mold," he wrote, and then, "Better take the plunger away." Apparently glasshouses were pirating molds and obviously Jarves' plunger bore such a close relationship to the main shaft that its loss would be costly.

A consideration of these technicalities leads directly to a study of the patterns of cap rings used, so that their designs may serve as guideposts for attribution. Pittsburgh and the Midwest employed varied cap rings, sometimes intricate, more often flamboyant. Frequently the rings became a part of the basic design of the piece. Sandwich and other Eastern manufacturers liked unobtrusiveness, with the result that many of the Eastern cap rings were regular and similar and did not bespeak individuality.

Bull's-Eyes, Scallops, and Some Relatives

For years, scholars have accepted the plain bull's-eye cap ring as evidence of Midwestern origin. James Rose identified more than fifty varieties of cup plates edged with 34 bull's-eye serrations or with a ten-scallop rope rim and plain rope. When we add different cup plates that bear 30, 36, 40, 45, or 48 bull's-eyes, we begin to lose count. All have been assigned to Pittsburgh and the Midwest.

Another fairly common design long accepted as Pittsburgh or Midwestern is a 6-inch plate in the shell pattern with a twelve-pointed star in the center and twelve smooth circles or roundels on the shoulders. It has twelve dots or table rests on the underside of the ring, where it meets the shoulder. On this plate, 48 bull's-eye serrations make up the cap ring. Sometimes the plate is finished as a bowl 1¼ inches deep, but the decorative devices and the number of rim eyes remain constant (260). The popularity of the plate was such that the pottery people in the East Liverpool-to-Wheeling area copied it in light tan Rocking-

ham ware (260). The Henry Ford Museum owns such an example.

The centers and the shoulder designs of this plate should not be confused with two other related plates, each 4¾ inches in size and with 38 bull's-eye cap rings (261). One of these, item 2, a toddy plate, has six roundels on the shoulder rim, six cinquefoils, and six other cinquefoils in the center, which is a circle surrounded by twelve short heavy rays. Six heavy table rests support the plate. The other plate carries 14 small roundels in the shoulder tied together by curved fish-shaped stippled motifs. At the outer border of the center, 14 fans fall between 14 table rests. The center consists of a graceful sunburst of 14 rays bordered by 14 small roundels or circles. It is interesting how the first plate holds to 6- and 12-design elements, while the other is consistent with 14.

The 6-inch Midwestern plate (260) with the 48 bull's-eye serrations occurs with two other cap rings. One cap ring has deep scallops or flanges separated by correspondingly smaller ones; the other has long flattened scallops separated by a short point, a smaller scallop, and then another short point. From the similarity of design on all three plates (262), we can add these last two rims to the Midwest roster. Such evidence is invaluable in helping to attribute other lacy pieces of different forms which carry those two cap rings.

The second cap ring on those three plates — large scallops or flanges with corresponding small scallops between — occurs rarely. The McKearins attribute to the Midwest an unusual 5⅞-inch plate with the same cap ring (*American Glass,* Plate 142, No. 2). The center has a variation of the peacock eye, while the shoulders are crowded with foliated scrolls, vines, and swans in sharp contrast to the spare, classic center design.

Among the cup plates, Lee and Rose attribute one with a similar rim to the Fort Pitt Glass Works (*American Glass Cup Plates,* No. 214-B). Mr. Rose designated two cup plates with the large and the small scallop as products of Curl-

260 Popular Pittsburgh designs for lacy plates and bowls, 1830–1840. 1 — Shells and circles design. Bull's-eye cap ring is evidence of Pittsburgh manufacture. D. 6″. 2 — Pottery copy of same plate. *The Henry Ford Museum.*

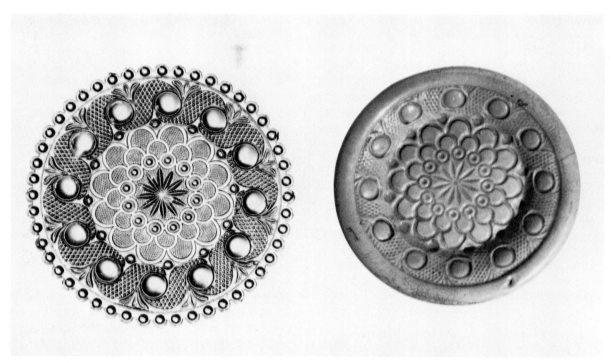

261 Two plates, closely related to the popular design of No. 260, 1830–1840. 1 — Shoulder has cluster of dots instead of trefoil. Rayed center and shoulder each have 14 roundels. D. 4⅞″. 2 — Six large roundels on shoulder are separated by cinquefoils instead of fish-shaped (stippled S) scrolls. Six table rests appear as dots. D. 4⅞″. *Collection of the author.*

262 Identical 6-inch plates in Shell and Circle pattern with different cap rings, 1830–1840. An example of the importance of the cap ring as evidence for attribution. 1 — Large scallop, point, small scallop, point. 2 — Large scallop, small scallop, found in Pittsburgh pieces. 3 — Bull's-eye cap ring accepted as Pittsburgh establishes probable attribution of Nos. 1 and 2. D. 6″. *Collection of the author.*

ing's Fort Pitt Glass Works (Nos. 535-A and 676-B). We should digress here to confess that the rim analogy among and between cup plates, 4- and 6-inch plates, and larger plates is at best a loose one. Mr. Rose shrewdly pointed out that the relative measurements of scallops between the two categories necessarily must be different.

Several cup plates, usually called the Log Cabin and Cider Barrel, commemorate the presidential campaign of William Henry Harrison. Mr. Rose considered the origin of No. 592 in the group uncertain, but the Midwestern implications and the analogous cap ring would weigh the scales in the favor of the Midwest.

The deceptiveness of such analogy can be seen by looking at Lee and Rose Nos. 336 and 506, which also carry similar rims of large and small scallops. The first has 16 large scallops, the second 22. Curling's cup plates (Nos. 535-A, 676-B, 214-B, and 217-A) consistently show 20 large scallops and, of course, the flat shoulder characteristic of Curling and Midwestern pressing. Nos. 336 and 506 may have Midwestern characteristics but certainly not from any Curling analogy. When comparing cup plate with cup plate, however, or 6-inch plate with 6-inch plate, the student has every right to make attributions with assurance.

A rare 6-inch plate formerly owned by Louise Esterly of Reading, Pennsylvania (*263*), offers an exciting analogy, because it carries the same rim with large and small rounded scallops alternating. This piece was first pictured in Rose's catalogue of the Corning Museum Exhibition, Plate XX, No. 21. The center has a busy geometric design, the shoulders a stiff version of the hairpin. The coarseness and crudeness of the heavy rim lead one to believe that it is fairly early. Its affinity to cut glass, moreover, bespeaks the beginnings of lacy. The scarcity of examples of this particular plate may be a tribute to the good taste of the manufacturer. Collectors of Eastern lacy would need only a glance at it to assign it with a smile to the Midwest.

The third cap ring of the three identical plates also has many relatives. A cup plate somewhat similar to it comes from the Fort Pitt factory (Lee and Rose, No. 183-A). The identical rim, however, appears on a controversial J. & T. Robinson lime-soda plate that lacks all semblance of laciness except in the center. The Robinson firm, which had started in 1823, became a partnership

263 Rare plate pressed in a geometric pattern in the center. A stiff version of the Hairpin on the shoulder, ca. 1835. The cap ring matches No. 262–2. Illustrated 1954 Corning Exhibition catalogue No. 421. D. 6″. *Ex coll. Louise Esterly. The Corning Museum of Glass.*

264 Plate marked "T & J Robinson Pittsbg." ca. 1835. The Robinsons operated the Stourbridge Flint Glass Works between 1830–1836. Poor stippling and decadent design make the plate seem much later. D. 5⅝″. *Collection of the author.*

around 1830 and continued with various combinations of partners until 1845. The plate is finished crudely and the unadorned shoulders seem out of tune with the too-busy center. Is it a very early plate? Or is it a decadent, cheap, late example of the decline of the true lacy?

Another specimen of the scallop–point–smaller scallop–point–scallop rim design is the well-known pair of lacy heart plates that the McKearins attribute to Wheeling (*American Glass,* Plates 162, Nos. 1 and 3). These plates, unlike most Midwestern lacy, come in beautiful shades of dark green, smoky green, and light clear green. The rims of the marked Robinson, the small Pittsburgh, and the Wheeling heart all carry 14 large scallops, and when the rims are matched the points and small scallops fall correctly and satisfyingly into place. Are these all Robinson plates? More probably we have the same mold maker, perhaps one from Pittsburgh. The Pittsburgh District is still the only attribution we may permit ourselves. Still, matching this cap ring can give a collector a feeling of comfortable assurance.

We can see an example of this scallop and point cap ring in the common arch and square plate (*265*). The shoulders, a series of identical arches, have no stippling except for a faint semblance in the spandrels. This abortive stippling alternates with a quatrefoil. The center, with a background of real stippling, presents a square made up of sixteen small squares — a checkerboard of alternating plain and stippled squares. Judging from the scantiness and coarseness of the stippling, a collector would call this a late plate. Its appearance in varied colors helps to confirm that opinion.

Before we discuss other Midwestern cap rings, we should count the bull's-eyes on 4½-inch plates: 38 for the lancet and oak leaves; 38 for the shell circles and roundels; 38 for the cinquefoils and roundels. The size of the bull's-eyes often controls the numbers but not the size of the plate. The well-known thistle and drape 7-inch plate with dull stippling has 54 eyes (McKearins,

265 Four typically Midwestern lacy pieces, 1830–1845, shown at the Carnegie Museum Exhibition, 1949–1950. 1 — Rectangular dish with large anthemion on the sides and double cinquefoils touching a diamond in the center. 7⅛ x 4¾". *Collection of Dr. E. R. Eller.* 2 — Octagonal compote with leaf and lancet bowl and oak leaf center. Showy cap ring with 8 large circles at the points and 3 smaller ones between on each side. Base is Roman Rosette. Midwestern lacy compotes are quite rare and this is an excellent example for study. H. 4⅛". D. 7³⁄₁₆". *Ex coll. John J. Grossman.* 3 — Shell and Circle plate already shown, No. 262. 4 — Later geometric plate with inferior stippling. Arches on the shoulder and 16 squares in the center. Cap ring matches No. 262–1. D. 5⅞". 3 and 4, *Collection of the author.*

266 Identical plates with different cap rings, ca. 1835. 1 — Unique geometric plate in octagonal form. The cap ring has a series of small scrolls with larger completed ones at each of the 8 corners. Between and above the corner scrolls is a small star. Cup plates No. 183B, 184, and 185 (in Lee and Rose, *American Glass Cup Plates*) have similar rims. These cup plates were found in Pittsburgh. Rose assigned this plate to Hay & Campbell, Union Glass Works, Pittsburgh. D. 6⅜". 1954 Corning Exhibition Catalogue, No. 427. 2 — The matching plate of inferior metal carries the familiar bull's-eye cap ring, so that if we had no other evidence we should reasonably adduce that No. 1 belonged to the same factory and location. D. 6⅛". *Collection of the author.*

267 Unstippled octagonal plate with a stippled cap ring found on early pieces. Rayed center represents a design used widely in the 1840s. The simplicity of the plate and the stippled cap ring contradict in time the rayed center. D. 6⁵⁄₁₆. 2 — Octagonal deep dish of heavy metal with the only decoration a center design of a 6-petaled flower. From this radiate 6 graceful plumelike cinquefoils, 1835–45. D. 7⅛". *Collection of the author.*

American Glass, Plate 144, No. 1). The geometric 6-inch, which matches the octagonal with the intricate cap ring, has 52 eyes against 48 on the usual 6-inch plate (*266*). All pieces referred to except the 7-inch plate have plain rims and eyes without stippling. Large octagonal dishes 9 inches by 6½ inches with 64 eyes seem in proportionate agreement to the whole design and, in fact, to a design relationship already established in other pieces. Smaller compotes 5½ and 6⅞ inches have only 50 eyes.

Variations in numbers of bull's-eyes are not consistent. One of the challenges of studying early glass lies in variants and unanswerable questions. The bull's-eye cap ring with stippling, for instance, appears on a nonlacy plate (*267*), and it borders the Elsholz basket of flowers plate (*American Glass,* Plate 143, Nos. 2 and 4). The puzzling plate is absolutely plain except for a fine sunburst in the center and two rings around the inner circumference before the cap ring. Why should a plain plate be embellished with one of the standard lacy Midwestern cap rings? Is it an example of early pressing marked by plain geometric figures? Or was it fashioned when lacy was going out of style, with use of a lacy period

268 A favorite device of mold makers was to repeat the same design in several sizes, ca. 1835. 1 — Cup plate No. 203 (Lee and Rose, *American Glass Cup Plates*). 2 — Octagonal plate. D. 6½″, with rose in the center and anthemion on the shoulders. Cap ring circles with point serration between. 1954 Corning Exhibition catalogue, No. 359. 3 — A 5-inch plate of the same design. Cap ring scallop and point. 1954 Corning Exhibition catalogue, No. 355. *Collection of the author.*

269 1 — Unrecorded oval tray, ca. 1835. Shoulders have 8 arches, each bisected by a stylized flower with fleurs-de-lis on each side near the tops of the arches. At each end of the tray a thistle with branching leaves represents a popular Midwestern design. These figures are found on some octagonal vegetable dishes with bull's-eye rim. Center shows a large clear lancet with stippled ones on each side. At either end 3 clear roundels are separated by stars. A rope edge forms a table rest. Scallop and point cap ring. L. 5⅜". W. 7⅞". 2 — Salt dish, ca. 1840, top size 2¾" x 2⅛". In Neal's *Pressed Glass Salt Dishes*, this model (GA 3) with arches and circles is attributed to the Pittsburgh area. Pictured in *Antiques*, August 1971. *Collection of the author.*

270 Small oval tray with shoulder designs like No. 269, ca. 1835. Center shows wide use of the roundel or circle (18 bordering the oval). Ten-petaled flower in the center with a fleur-de-lis on each side. Tray rests on a rope edge. Cap ring has small scallop with tiny point between, L. 6", W. 4½". *Antiques,* August 1940. *Collection of the author.*

cap ring? It can well be an example of early pressing, but if we study the sunburst design as it appears in cup plates, we must confess it was a pattern of the midcentury and later. The combination of a cap ring that graced many more elaborate and earlier plates creates an artistic anomaly because of the absence of stippling. Such a rim, with its 40 bull's-eyes surrounded by coarse engine-turned stippling, is not out of place on the octagonal riverboat plate, but seems a far cry appearing on the clear, unglamorized sunburst plate. A realistic conclusion would be that the cap ring was used over a long period. Possibly it paralleled somewhat the longevity of the hairpin base, which we can find on late and almost decadent Princess Feather bowls.

Let us return for a moment to the clear bull's-eye rims, 52 eyes, without stippling, found on the imperfect geometric plate (*266*). Its counterpart, an eight-sided plate shown with it, bears an even outer rim. At each corner of the eight sides is a round protuberance. Under the protuberance gleams a tiny six-pointed star. On the underside of the rim running all the way around is a series of scrolls. Where the extra width of the rim occurs at each corner, two large and perfectly formed scrolls — almost figure eights with dots in each loop — run lengthwise. Where the rim narrows within each side, curving lines simulate scrolls. Certain cup plates have similar rims (*American Glass Cup Plates*, 183-B, 184-B, and 185). Several of these have been found in Pittsburgh. James Rose tentatively assigned the octagonal plate to Parke & Campbell, Union Glass Works, Pittsburgh (*The Story of American Pressed Glass of the Lacy Period*, No. 427, p. 115). The inferior quality of the round geometric with bull's-eye serrations (No. 431 in the same catalogue) and the superior brilliance and weight of the octagonal counterpart establish the lack of quality control in the factory. We are interested, of course, in the fact that another Midwestern cap ring has been added to the list.

These two plates prove that Midwestern de-

271 Octagonal plate with Ohio River steamer with two flags, 1830–1835. Rope edge border of this center has two elaborate scrolls between the rope edge and the circle where the shoulders rise. Four anthemia decorate the shoulders. Four stylized acanthuses stand between the anthemia. The cap ring consists of small roundels

with a larger one at each corner. Between these clear roundels are stippled points. Below this rim are 8 flattened triangles. D. 6⅛". Shown in McKearins' *American Glass,* Plate 143, No. 1. *Collection of William J. Elsholz.*

On the rims of each of these plates there are 30 scallops. Does the matching of 30 scallops mean that the pieces were made at the same factory? Not necessarily. The molds may have been bought from the same mold maker, or they may have traveled between different factories. A number of cup plates with the scallop and point rim have been attributed to Pittsburgh and Wheeling without any consideration of the rim. The cup plate matching the 4½-inch rose plate (No. 203 in *American Glass Cup Plates*) carries 24 scallops. The rose anthemion and the eagle acanthus belong to this group. The oval tray with the large scallops separated by points (*269*) has 36 large scallops compared to 18 found on the 6-inch Esterly plate. The smaller oval tray with essentially the same cap ring has 42 smaller scallops. A collector can be fairly safe in expecting Midwestern characteristics of design where the scallop and point rim appear. Sometimes the point serration may be stippled.

signers could handle a geometric pattern that covers the whole surface and yet, because of its excellent proportions, cannot be called "busy." Perhaps the lines are bolder than those on comparable Eastern plates, but the strength is that of a frontier culture.

Scallop and Point and Table Rests

A favorite Midwestern cap ring was the scallop and point. Two important 4½- and 4⅞-inch plates with such a rim are the rose and anthemion and the eagle and acanthus, on which the acanthus extends under the center to form table rests (*268*). Midwestern manufacturers evidently considered table rests a protection for lacy pieces, and they may be considered an indication of Midwestern pressing. Usually they are little more than round dots that show through the center as eyes. Occasionally, as in the 4⅞-inch toddy plate with the cinquefoils mentioned above, they may become protuberant knobs.

The Flat Roundel

The most showy cap rings of all the Midwesterns are the roundels with a stippled point between. On octagonal plates, the Fulton and riverboat and the Oak Leaf and Lancet, we find 32 undecorated flat circles, dramatic enough to take one's eye momentarily away from the center and shoulder designs (*271*). The Grossman compote on a pressed base carries the same rim with an identical number of roundels (*265*). On all octagonal bowls and plates we find 32. The Corning Museum's Midwestern eagle plate, in which the acanthus ends at the center ring, has 48 roundels (*272*). Otherwise, it duplicates in design the smaller plate that has the acanthus running into the center and forming table rests (*273*).

The rare vegetable dish from the Historical Society of Western Pennsylvania has a rim closely related to these roundels (*274*). The thirty on the vegetable dish are much larger, without the border stippling between. A series of unstippled wavy

272 Octagonal plate, 1830–1835, with eagle, shield, arrows in the center surrounded by 13 blossoms, each held in its own circle. Acanthuses on the shoulder do not extend into the center as in No. 273. Thirteen fleurs-de-lis stand between the acanthuses. Cap ring — small clear circles with stippled points between. D. 7½". *The Corning Museum of Glass.*

273 Rare 5-inch circular plate showing the eagle with shield and arrows, 1830–1835. Thirteen acanthuses on the shoulders continue into the center of the plate and form table rests on the underside. Cap ring, scallop and point. *Collection of the author.*

274 1 — Scrolled eye plate with typical shell and circle center surrounding sun rays, ca. 1835. Each of the eyes forms a table rest. Fifteen stylized flowers border the plate and give it a classical air. Bull's-eye cap ring. D. 9⅛". Shown in McKearins' *American Glass,* Plate 145. *The Historical Society of Western Pennsylvania, Anna Moody Browne Fund.* 2 — Oval dish, 1830–1835, with a center design of a line of 11 roundels bisecting the small shells and circles. Table rests are clearly evident. Shoulders consist of arches divided by a single flower. Fleurs-de-lis and thistles in the spandrels. The cap ring represents the largest of all roundel rims with stippled points between. Only one other example is known. L. 10". W. 6⅞". Shown in the 1954 Corning Exhibition catalogue, Plate 15, No. 351. *The Historical Society of Western Pennsylvania, Violet Swem Brendel Fund.*

275 1 — Peacock eye compote with large eyes forming the upstanding rim. Two clear sections separate the stippled forms on the shoulder. The lower part of the bowl is divided into 6 triangular sections with small diamonds. The base is the Midwestern Hairpin. H. 3⅝". D. 5¾". 2 — Oval dish described in No. 274. A good chance to compare roundel rims and to see slight variations that frequently occur in lacy. 10 x 6⅞". 3 — Whale oil lamp with blown font on pressed Midwestern Hairpin base. H. 9". All pieces ca. 1835. 1 and 3, *Collection of Dr. E. R. Eller.* 2, *The Historical Society of Western Pennsylvania.*

276 Oval dish, 1830–1840, with an unrecorded version of the peacock eye, the eyes forming the rim of the dish. The 16 clear circles around the center design are characteristically Midwestern. Possibly unique. L. 8¹⁄₁₆". W. 5½". *The Henry Ford Museum.*

lines rises to a point of serration between the large roundels. In Dr. E. R. Eller's small compote, the large unadorned circles form the end of a peacock eye and touch each other, rimming the bowl with the curve of upper circles (Rose, *The Story of American Pressed Glass of the Lacy Period,* Plate XVIII, No. 384). They are an integral part of the design, not a cap ring in the true sense, but on first sight they would appear to be blood brothers to the rim of the vegetable dish.

A Midwestern bowl from the Ford Museum (Corning Museum catalogue, No. 380) uses these large circles as the top of peacock eyes. Here again we have the completion of the bowl design, not a true cap ring. The circles occur in series of fours, separated each time by a set of smaller

277 Three coarsely designed Midwestern lacy plates, 1840–1850. 1 — Rope edge found in Midwestern cup plates. Here it is scalloped. Double rope edge also borders the center section. Large 4-pointed star with coarse stippling centers the plate. This plate is also found with a plain rope edge. D. 6". 2 — Three circular bands hold contrasting designs: roundels and blossoms, a garland of leaves, and fleurs-de-lis alternating with stylized blossoms. At the center of the plate 6 fleurs-de-lis are entwined with six roundels. The cap ring forms large scallops. D. 6¼". 3 — Four thistles, a favorite form in Midwestern lacy, radiate from each other in the center of the plate. Branches with leaves come from the same center. Eight heavy dots around the center section form table rests. The cap ring is large scallop, small scallop, point, small scallop. D. 5¼". Note similarity of design to No. 161, Lee and Rose, *American Glass Cup Plates. Ex coll. John J. Grossman.*

circles. The compote and the bowl are reminiscent of the Sandwich Peacock Eye and Comet designs.

The rope edge that occurs on many Midwestern cup plates appears rather infrequently on larger plates and bowls, so it can be disregarded for the time being. A late toddy plate with stippling that almost does not deserve the name uses cinquefoils, scroll dots, and stylized flowers on the shoulder (*277*). Practically the same design with four fleurs-de-lis surrounds a four-pointed star in the center. The stippling is dull, which to a collector of Eastern lacy means that it must be a Midwestern piece. The favorite Midwestern figures are a more valid evidence. Probably the rope edge was used on toddy and cup plates rather than on larger pieces.

If we counted all known lacy pieces, Eastern and Midwestern, we should undoubtedly find the even-scalloped cap ring most widely used. To establish characteristic Midwestern cap rings is more the province of this book. The bull's-eye rim, clear or stippled, unequivocally belongs, as does its cousin, the flat roundels, both large and small. The rare scrolls and six-pointed star have not appeared elsewhere. The alternating large and small scallops also stand out. The large scallop–point–small scallop–point–large scallop design has just as much right to be identified as Midwestern. The rim of the Sandwich heart tray for the well-known casket has a long flattened scallop and point (*278*). The small scallop and point — a standard Midwestern rim — was also used on cup plates (*American Glass Cup Plates*, Nos. 124 and 145). James Rose, however, assigned No. 146 with a perfect Midwestern scallop and point to Eastern Pennsylvania. We must watch for Midwestern design characteristics as well as depend on established cap rings. And we must be guarded in attributions.

Character of Midwestern Design

The second point of identification, after the cap ring, is design. The entire field offers unequivocal examples of Midwestern taste, at the same time

278 The Sandwich heart tray, ca. 1835, is included to show the Eastern scallop and point rim. The intricate and stiff center design contrasts with the simplicity of the hearts on the shoulder. L. 7¹⁄₁₆″. W. 4½″. *The Corning Museum of Glass.*

279 This sugar bowl, 1856–1875, was advertised by Curling, Robertson & Company of Pittsburgh in the 1856–1857 Directory of Pittsburgh. It is also shown in the New England Glass Company catalogue, ca. 1868, at the Corning Museum of Glass. Sandwich claims the bowl too. It has appeared in so many different colors that they may be justified. It is a good example of the end of lacy. Stippling is weak or missing. Design panels are unrelated and some are overdecorated. Had this bowl been made only in the Midwest it would have come in for some harsh criticism. H. 5¾″. *The Henry Ford Museum.*

indicating the common practice in the glass industry of pirating as well as adapting patterns and shapes. At the very end of the lacy period, the fairly common sugar bowl (*279*) was advertised pictorially by Curling, Robertson of Pittsburgh in the 1856–1857 Directory. Sandwich manufactured the same bowl in a wide range of colors. The New England Glass Company catalogue (1868–1869) proves that that factory also produced it. All three claims are undoubtedly valid; what we have is a good example of borrowing and copying. The Roman Rosette pattern represents another Eastern and Midwestern duplication.

The 8-inch Scotch plaid plate with large stippling (*280*) was also made in both the East and the Midwest. No formula has yet been found to limit a plaid plate to a particular area. This plate appears with flat shoulders reminiscent of some of the cup plates from the Fort Pitt factory. It is also pictured in the 1868–1869 catalogue of the New England Glass Company.* Baccarat and St. Louis used the plaid design too, as shown in the 1840–1842 Launay, Hautin catalogue. No careful study has yet been made of relationships between the French and Midwestern lacy.

Both East and Midwest apparently made the Industries bowl (*281*). Even experienced collectors would be hard put to distinguish between Eastern and Midwestern examples. Such is not the case with the Princess Feather (Rochelle) pattern. The East achieved a fineness of execution not found in the coarser and bolder lines of the Midwestern counterparts. That is a fairly safe

* Lura W. Watkins, "Pressed Glass of the New England Glass Company," *Corning Journal of Glass Studies* 12, 1970, 149.

generalization for many Midwestern copies of Eastern patterns. The oak leaf in both areas cannot be as significant, because when it appears as the center of a plate or bowl it frequently has little or no stippling surrounding it. Nor did the East have a monopoly on the Nectarine patterns.

A rare oval dish with crossed peacock feathers on the ends has been assigned by the McKearins to the Midwest (*American Glass,* Plate 146, No. 2). The major design element is stippled diamonds, which are placed within two large circles and a square on the side of the dish. The base, too, is a series of small stippled diamonds. The rim is heavily ridged like other early large pieces. Because of the peacock feathers, the dish has often been assigned to Sandwich.

Elements for Attribution: Circle and Shell

If this twilight zone seems cloudy, a positive approach to Midwestern design may improve our visibility. The Shell and Circle shown on the three 6-inch plates with different cap rings (*262*) represents what must have been the most popular and the most unassailably Midwestern design. Though usually clear, such plates have turned up in a light blue and a green. The shells bordering the center sunburst and the twelve roundels around the shoulders catch the eye immediately. In the 9-inch versions, the roundels are replaced by 15 small circles with eye-dot centers that become table rests. The center sunburst is surrounded by 15 dots and then the overlapping shells, this time framed by a zigzag line around the shoulder. Between each point a single blossom relieves the linear quality. The relationship of the larger version to the smaller would never be in doubt. A clear sugar bowl in the Metropolitan Museum also has the typical shells and circles (*283*).

The 4⅞-inch tea plate (*261*) retains the dramatic roundels (six in all) but drops the shells around the center sunburst. For contrasting decoration, stiff clusters of five leaves break the mo-

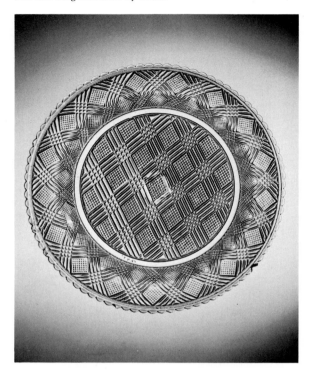

281 The famous Industries bowl, 1840–1850, made at the New England Glass Company, at Sandwich, and in the Midwest. The log cabin and Cincinnatus at the plow indicate the Harrison campaign. The glass factory is clearly meant to be the New England Glass Company in Cambridge. The ship rounds out the symbolism of American life and work. D. 6¼″. *The Henry Ford Museum.*

282 1 — One of the two varieties of Midwestern heart plates, often assigned to Wheeling, 1840–1855. This green plate also occurs with a Pittsburgh cap ring — large scallop, point, small scallop, point. Another variation has the large hearts containing stippled diamonds instead of lines. That version has a different shoulder: circles with diamonds instead of squares, roundels between instead of stylized flowers. D. 5″. 2 —

Large scrolled eye and shell and circle plate, discussed in No. 274–1. 3 — Late, poorly designed blue plate attributed to the Midwest, 1840–1855. The center is interesting: radial ribbons terminate in 16 roundels. The shoulder is overcrowded. This plate appears in several colors. D. 6½″. *The Historical Society of Western Pennsylvania.*

283 A fine example of the circle and shell design in an oval sugar bowl, ca. 1835. Thistles with 2 leaves break the monotony. A circle of large roundels marks the low edge of the bowl. These bowls have been found more frequently in dark blue than in clear. H. of bowl with cover, 5¹¹⁄₁₆″. *Metropolitan Museum of Art, Gift of Mrs. Charles Green.*

notony both in the center and on the shoulders. Looking at the original 6-inch shell plate design, we can see how sometimes the roundel, sometimes the shell, dominate in the variations. A good example of a departure from both, but clearly from the basic source design, is the 9-inch plate at the Historical Society in Pittsburgh (*284*). The center sunburst becomes a five-pointed star; the circles contained within six tangent circles have become a pair of scrolled eyes that stare back piercingly at the observer. They also serve as table rests. On the shoulder, clusters of feathers alternate with cinquefoils. No one would mistake its family line.

The most famous of the shell and circle designs is found on the oval vegetable dish at the Historical Society in Pittsburgh (*274, No. 2*). Eleven touching full moons make a bisecting line across the oval center. Again shells and overlapping circles fill the rest of the space. The center line is repeated by the dramatic roundel cap ring. Though arches, stylized flowers, and thistles

284   1 — Rectangular vegetable dish with bull's-eye cap ring. The bull's-eyes are repeated as borders for the center and for table rests. The center diamond is surrounded by lunettes. Six large cinquefoils grace the shoulders with a lyre at each corner of the dish. Stylized flowers and a triangular diamond appear on the long side. L. 8⅞″. W. 6⅜″. 2 — Scrolled eye plate with a border of plumelike leaves and plain plumes. D. 9½″. Bull's-eye cap ring. The scrolled eyes form table rests. 3 — Peacock eye oval dish with diamond center. The Eastern version of this pattern has a rayed center instead of diamond squares. L. 9½″. W. 7¼″. All pieces 1835–1845. *The Historical Society of Western Pennsylvania.*

285   1 — Round dish with large peacock eye border. Two clear sections separate the stippled forms on the shoulder. Compare with No. 275–1. Rayed center is circled by nine roundels. Between these and the shoulder are circles and shells with 9 small table rests. 2 — Rectangular vegetable dish with bull's-eye cap ring. Similar eyes border the center and form table rests. Shoulders carry 8 Gothic arches, each bisected by a stylized flower. Four thistles with leaves mark the corners. A large sunburst in the center has 16 roundels about it. Shells, circles, and 2 thistles complete the center design. L. 8⅞″. W. 6⅜″. 3 — Small replica of No. 2 except that the stippling on the shoulder ends in small points just below the cap ring. L. 6⅞″. W. 5⅛″. All pieces ca. 1835. 1, *Collection of Dr. E. R. Eller.* 2 and 3, *Collection of the author.*

286 Two Midwestern plates from the Pittsburgh area, ca. 1835–1840. Centers have oak leaf and acorn; shoulders, the lancet and leaf motif found on the Midwestern casket. In the French ring stand, No. 299, and in the Midwestern Hairpin base, none of the lancets is stippled. 1 — Octagonal plate, cap ring of 32 circles separated by stippled points. Similar rims appear on Plate 143, No. 1, McKearins' *American Glass,* and on a ship plate in this series marked "Union." D. 7". *Antiques,* August 1971. 2 — Round plate with bull's-eye cap ring (38 eyes) is an indication of Pittsburgh pressing. D. 5". *Collection of the author.*

cover the shoulder of the dish, the whole feeling is of circle and shell.

One of the octagonal dishes uses the center sunburst, but the pointed rays reach between the oval formed by sixteen good-size roundels (*285*). Around each end of that design appears a single line of stippled circles and shells. Bull's-eye table rests line the two long sides, leaving each end free for an arch and a thistle. Even a clear bull's-eye cap ring is not enough to emphasize the center, since arches and thistle dominate. Nevertheless, this dish belongs to the shell and circle family.

The Lancet and Leaf

The lancet or arrowhead is second to the shell and circle as a solely Midwestern design — a clear pattern beside a stippled one. Surprisingly enough, the design does emphasize stippling; the 7-inch octagonal plate is a brilliant example. Perhaps the contrast, perhaps the stippled border, may produce the brightness and sparkle. A favorite combination — the oak leaf center with lancets around the shoulder of the plate or bowl — is seen in the Grossman compote (*265, No. 2*). A scarce oval pickle or olive dish has eight arches

287 Magnificent Midwestern casket (honey dish), ca. 1835, in the lancet and leaf design. The scrolled edge gives a feeling of classical architecture. The 9-sectional fan on the edge is repeated on the cover, which also carries Gothic arches bisected by stylized flowers. H. 5″ with cover. L. 6⅜″. *The Corning Museum of Glass.*

288 Eastern casket (honey dish), ca. 1835, resting on the heart tray, No. 278. The general effect is Gothic. The arches on the cover are divided into 3 smaller ones with 3 diamonds at the top of the large arch. Those on the sides have bisecting lines with 4 crosses at the top. The rim of the casket consists of a continuous line of stippled ovals with a point between. This is a more traditional and restrained piece than its rival from the Midwest. H. 5¼″. L. 7¹⁄₁₆″. W. 4½″. *The Henry Ford Museum.*

around the shoulder with six fleurs-de-lis in the spandrels. A neat rope edge about the oval center forms a table rest. At each end of the dish appear single thistles and two leaves, replicas of those found on the octagonal dishes. Three unusually large lancets in the oval center set the tone of contrast with the shoulder design. Three roundels at each end of the ellipse enclosing the lancets remind us of the Midwestern predilection for the circle. *Antiques* pictures another tray with lancet center.* With scroll and shell border, the lancets have more authority than the few in the oval dish.

The climax of the lancet design occurs on the sides of the impressive Midwestern casket (*287*). Besides being clear-cut evidence of origin, the lancets individualize the casket and record the designer's perceptive skill.

The Arch

A study of the casket directs the eye to the arch as a design element. The difference between the Eastern and the Midwestern arch, seemingly slight, becomes apparent on close observation. The Midwestern example is bisected by a stem with a large blossom at the inside peak of the arch. The two arches formed on either side of the stem are made up of four small stippled diamonds and four truncated diamonds. That pattern is consistent on octagonal dishes, on the oval dish and trays, and on the casket. The smallest oval tray, 4⁵⁄₁₆ inches by 6 inches (*270*), provides an exception; here the two small arches formed by the bisecting stem and blossom are not subdivided as are those on the larger pieces.

On the side of the Eastern casket, the arches are divided into four slender arcs that do not reach the top (*288*). Four stippled diamonds fill the space between their tips and the inside of the top of the main arch.

* James Rose, "Unrecorded Rarities in Lacy Glass," *Antiques* 55, March 1954, 225.

289 Oval dish with bold mixed designs from church architecture, 1835–1840 (Lee, *Sandwich Glass,* 1947 edition, Plate 97, bottom). Its busyness and large figures suggest the Midwest. The arches are not like those of either area. 1954 Corning Exhibition catalogue, No. 340. L. 9⅜″. W. 6⅛″. *The Henry Ford Museum.*

290 The coarse Princess Feather (Rochelle) bowl on a Midwestern Hairpin base, ca. 1850. Probably Bakewell, Pears, since they produced a set of Princess Feather. H. 3¼″. D. 7⅜″. *The Corning Museum of Glass.*

The arches on the cover of the Eastern casket are arranged much the same as those on the side, except that, being smaller, they need only three slender arcs to support the top decoration of stippled diamonds. These casket arches do not appear often on other shapes, except on salts. Eastern manufacturers apparently did not transfer their chosen arch to other pieces in the way Midwesterners did. The Eastern casket with peacock eye design, made in different colors, did not make use of the arch, and it may therefore be disregarded.

In Ruth Webb Lee's *Sandwich Glass,* 1947 edition (Plate No. 97, bottom), an oval tray carries the same feeling for the arch as does the casket. Because of the design and workmanship, James Rose, in the Corning Museum catalogue, assigned the tray to the Midwest. William Elsholz, however, owns the same tray with stippling so silvery and scintillating that it fits the quality of Eastern rather than Midwestern manufacture. With the spirit of the arch and the sheen of the stippling, the Elsholz tray may well be Eastern.

Arches on three Gothic oblong dishes (Lee, Plate 101) are far away in design from those on the casket — even farther than are the arches on the oval tray. Conventional Gothic arch sugar bowls (Lee, Plate 158, bottom) had both the room and the background to duplicate the casket

arch. They seem instead to be only an echo, with the result that a typical individual arch on Eastern pieces appears less important than in the Midwestern. As incomplete as these comparisons may be, a collector of lacy, using discretion, can rely on the Midwestern arch as an element for attribution.

Thus we have the roundel, the shell, the lancet, and the arch for characteristic parts of Midwestern lacy design. We have already mentioned Princess Feather, or Rochelle (its correct name), a coarsened form of the Eastern version (*290*). Rayed peacock eyes, too, at times emulated the East, the makers handling the copy very well. Thistles, anthemia, lunettes, and acanthuses graced many Midwestern pieces, as did vines, leaves, roses, plumes, fleurs-de-lis, quatrefoils, and cinquefoils.

A Strong Trend to Naturalism

Naturalism was a pronounced element in Midwestern lacy. We expect the eagle and the thistle, the acorn and the oak leaf. We are not astonished by butterflies, roses, anchors, and shields, and we are only mildly surprised when a late piece carries fish or swans. We accept the enthusiastic loyalty that kept using the shield. Situated as they were, Pittsburgh glassmen had long depended on river

291 1 — Smaller replica of No. 284–1. L. 5″, W. 7″.
2 — Rectangular dish featuring the anthemion, 1835–
1840. Coarseness of design and rope edge bespeak the
Midwest. This dish appears in a large size (Lee, *Sandwich Glass,* Plate 103, bottom). L. 7″. W. 5″.
Collection of the author.

292 Unrecorded lacy compote on a heavily ridged
pressed base, ca. 1835. The base is related to that of
No. 244 (a blown celery with copper wheel engraving
set on a pressed base). A Midwestern piece from the
figured design on the bowl as well as from its unusual
base. H. 4″. Diameter of bowl 7⁵⁄₁₆. *The Sandwich
Glass Museum, Tomlinson Collection.*

293 Octagonal ship plate, frigate marked "Union,"
1830–1835. Only one ship after 1830 was named
"Union." This was a steamer with submerged paddles.
Thirteen stars and "Union" evidently refer to an earlier
time. The flag is flying in the wrong direction. Four sets
of stylized oak leaves are on the shoulders of the plate.
The cap ring has roundels with stippled points between.
1954 Corning Exhibition catalogue, No. 362. D. 6⅝".
The Corning Museum of Glass.

freight for receiving supplies and shipping finished
products, and so it is no wonder they designed
octagonal lacy plates depicting Ohio sidewheel
riverboats and the more modern type of steamer,
the so-called Fulton. Another boat plate marked
"Union" (*293*) shows a frigate, possibly the
U.S.S. *Constitution* (Corning Museum Catalogue,
No. 362). The basket of flowers cup plate
(*294*), with its identifiable background, has recently caused James Rose to assign it to the Midwest.

The most naturalistic and exciting tray, present
whereabouts unknown, is a marked Bakewell
& Anderson one. It was photographed by an experienced collector, the late Dr. Henry G. Smith
of Cedar Grove, New Jersey, probably around
1950 (*295*). "The glass plate came out quite
well," Dr. Smith wrote, "considering the condition under which they were made on a dark day
without aid of flash or flood with the camera held
in my hand. Mrs. Kuehn, who had the dish and
book — Bakewell genealogy — would not permit
me to take them to the porch, where the light was
better. Probably thought I would fly away with
them." Alexander Anderson was an active partner with Benjamin Bakewell from 1832 to 1836.
Though this tray lacks stippling, the shell and
scroll border and the four fans at the corners are
typical of lacy designs. This marked piece represents the sort of firsthand historical documentation too often missing from early glass manufacture.

The Forms of Midwestern Lacy

The forms of Midwestern lacy pieces do not
furnish the clear-cut evidence that cap rings and
the character of design have helped to establish.
It is a trite generalization that the area did not
produce in any sizable number the showy large
pieces — platters, compotes, vegetable dishes,
and plates — that have appeared in the East.
Midwestern plates 5 to 7 inches in diameter outnumber the district's other pieces at least three to

294 The Midwestern basket of flowers octagonal plate
with bull's-eye and stippled point cap ring, ca. 1835, has
coarse, dull stippling but is an exceedingly rare piece. The
shoulders carry clusters of grapes and leaves. McKearins'
American Glass, Plate 143, No. 4. D. 7⅜". *Collection
of William J. Elsholz.*

one. Bowls 5⅛ to 8 inches could run second. A few fairly well-known plates, 9⅛ inches in diameter, show how rare the large pieces are (*282*). Oval and rectangular dishes give room for an expression of individuality that is lacking in the smaller plates and bowls; only one Midwestern piece is as long as 10 inches. Rectangular dishes with cut corners and bull's-eye cap rings belong to the Midwest; they come in two lengths: 6⅞ and 8⅞ inches. Covered sweetmeats, decidedly scarce, run from 5¾ to 6¾ inches. Compotes, naturally following the sizes of bowls, are consistently smaller or medium-sized.

The East produced many smaller and lighter pieces in rectangular shape: Gothic Arch, Leaf and Gothic Arch, Pineapple and Gothic Arch, and Nectarine. Of those Eastern examples, only the Nectarine has the sharply turned corners of the Midwestern pieces. Interestingly enough, the Nectarine was also made in the Midwest. Eastern corners usually flow in a slightly rhythmic curve.

Only one lacy creamer, marked "R. B. Curling and Sons, Fort Pitt," has appeared (*257*). Since the basket of flowers was a major design on this pitcher, and since the stippling was brilliant and close, as knowledgeable a collector as Dr. Charles Green kept insisting that Sandwich had made it and labeled it for Curling to sell. The controversy already described on page 254 helped to focus attention on Midwestern lacy and to make it a desirable item for collectors. As compared to this single Midwestern creamer, however, Eastern factories can show several different designs.

Several Midwestern sugar bowls, most of them in the shell and circle pattern, indicate that this form was more in demand than the creamer and more numerous. For every different Midwestern lacy sugar bowl there are at least twice as many Eastern patterns. Midwestern lacy sugars have been found without covers — so many of them that they exceed what might be expected in normal breakage. The theory has been put forward — despite the omnipresent housefly — that functional bowls of this sort were made for sale

without the complication and cost of covers. Use of glass balls as covers, of course, was an early common household practice.

Arguing by analogy, one should assign the Esterly small tumbler to the Midwest (*296*), because the pattern almost matches that of the octagonal plate and its round counterpart (*266*) with identical centers and shoulders. That single tumbler does not help us to solve the puzzle of why American manufacturers of lacy did not produce drinking vessels. Baccarat, St. Louis, and Val St. Lambert still hold center stage with their many handsome lacy goblets and tumblers. American examples of those forms simply do not exist.

The Midwestern Hairpin Base

An accepted American form close to French design is the Midwestern hairpin base — a practical and decorative element — for use on such blown pieces as candlesticks, sugar bowls, lamp fonts, and compotes. A Launay, Hautin & Cie. catalogue from about 1840–1842 poses a question of relationship. Page fifty of the second part shows a saucerlike dish on a pedestal. Its design was called *m a perles* (molded in beads) and its function was called *Baguier f evasée* (flaring ring stand). The decorative quality of the piece justifies its manufacture despite its limited functional value. In America the pattern has long been called the Midwestern Hairpin.

A counterpart of the French ring stand, the 5-inch American nappy (small sauce dish) lacks the smooth brilliance achieved by skillful French fire polishing (*300*). The design of the French piece is on the base mold; in the American it is on the plunger. Another marked difference between French and American pieces lay in the cap ring on the nappy. The serrations of scallop and point occur frequently on Midwestern pieces. French and other Continental manufacturers seemed to prefer to have the design of the rim a border for the whole, as in the ring stand, but they also used

295 Bakewell and Anderson tray, 1832–1836, with a scroll and fan border very much like that found on the Midwestern casket. Note that no stippling exists on the tray. Bakewell and Anderson were partners from 1832–1836. This is an important piece of American glass. *Owner unknown.*

296 1 — Unique lacy tumbler embodying a design not unlike the Pittsburgh plates in No. 266, ca. 1835. American lacy tumblers are hitherto nonexistent. Rose thought this might be a Sandwich piece. H. 2½". 2 — Very rare rectangular dish with hearts and diamonds, probably Midwestern. It shows the influence of cut glass design, ca. 1830. L. 6¾". W. 5³⁄₁₆". 3 — Small lacy mug with pressed handle. This seems more characteristically Sandwich than the tumbler. H. 2". All pieces 1830–1835. Picture courtesy of *Antiques*, February 1957. *Ex Coll. Louise Esterly. The Corning Museum of Glass.*

297 French lacy goblet of fine quality, 1840–1860. The French seemed to specialize in lacy goblets and tumblers. Many were exported to the New World. H. 5⅝". *The Corning Museum of Glass.*

298 Another French lacy goblet showing the possibilities of varying the shape and design, 1840–1860. Both goblets show the influence of Gothic architecture and of earlier cut glass styles. *The Ruth Bryan Strauss Memorial Foundation.*

299 French flaring ring stand made by the St. Louis factory, ca. 1840. Part II of the Launay, Hautin & Cie. catalogue, ca. 1842, owned by the Corning Museum of Glass, shows this stand. Pattern of the bowl matches the Midwestern Hairpin. Graduated diamonds show on the underside of the base. H. 2¾". D. 5". *Antiques,* August 1971. *Collection of the author.*

300 1 — American small bowl or nappy. Cap ring scallop and point is also found on plates and cup plates from the Pittsburgh area, ca. 1840. D. 5⅛". *Antiques,* August 1971. 2 — Bowl of the St. Louis ring stand. This design matches cup plate No. 205 in Lee and Rose, *American Glass Cup Plates.* D. 5". *Collection of the author.*

the cap ring when it suited their purposes. The nappy and the ring stand have a 16-rayed center and 16 bordering lancets, each lancet edged with 34 stippled dots. The outer rim consists of 16 medallions with rayed centers.

In Lee and Rose's *American Glass Cup Plates,* No. 205 seems identical to the French pattern. The cup plate has 16 lancets, 16 rays, and 16 medallions exactly like those on the St. Louis ring stand, and with the same unusual rim. Cup plate No. 205 has a turning pimple in the center, but that need not prevent us from considering the plate French.

William J. Elsholz owns a very rare covered compote on a Midwestern hairpin base (*301*). The terraced cover of his piece carries almost the same design as the hairpin on the French ring stand. The cover has 18 center rays, 18 lancets extending from them, and 18 bordering medallions, where the ring stand has only 16 of each. The terraced line tends to break the eye continuity, but a careful view shows that the curves from the double lancets touch the medallions exactly like those on the French piece. They also include the same starlike blossoms. A marked difference, however, is the series of clear circles

below the medallions. On the French work, it is a series of clear diamonds. As we look down into the bowl we see the same pattern as that on the cover.

The low flaring hairpin on the Elsholz covered dish has been widely used in the Midwest. The hairpin base is a smaller design replica of the French piece and its American counterpart. Twenty rays, lancets, and circle medallions occur instead of the original 16. The stippling is less brilliant, and in examining it one thinks it lacks the artistic strength of the larger examples on the lancet. The plain bull's-eye in the medallion instead of the sunburst on the French design dulls the effect somewhat.

There has been little effort to attribute the Midwestern hairpin base to one factory. On blown and pressed pieces like sugars, candlesticks, and lamps, a variety of styles forbids exact attribution. One pressed compote on the hairpin base is in the Princess Feather pattern — the coarsened form that Bakewell made fairly late. During the 1830s and 1840s at Pittsburgh, the Robinsons, the Curlings, Parke, Campbell & Hanna (Union Glass), and Bakewell were pressing excellent Midwestern lacy. So were the Ritch-

301 Pressed covered sweetmeat on Midwestern Hairpin base, ca. 1835. This is a very rare piece. Both cover and bowl carry a design similar to that on the St. Louis ring stand. H. 7¼". D. 6½". *Antiques,* August 1971. *Collection of William J. Elsholz.*

302 Blown candlesticks with bases pressed in the Midwestern Hairpin, 1830–1835. H. 8" and 8⅛". *Antiques,* August 1971. *The Corning Museum of Glass.*

ies of Wheeling. All could have used the hairpin base on blown and pressed pieces.

From its use on early blown pieces, the Midwestern hairpin base would seem to have preceded the French use. We must admit, however, that if the French copied and refined the hairpin, they also improved it. Their intertwining of circle and lancet makes for unity and grace in the design. The Launay, Hautin & Cie. catalogue of the early 1840s also gives clear evidence of excellent St. Louis workmanship. For the present, the exact relationship between French and American design must remain an enigma.*

Lacy Panes

A Midwestern lacy form that does challenge Eastern and French competition and design is the pane. For many years the Bakewell advertise-

* Lowell Innes, "Lacy Hairpin in French and American Glass," *Antiques* 10, August 1971.

ment of 1836 offering "pressed panes for steamboats" seemed the main evidence that such an article existed; unfortunately, no one came upon a wrecked riverboat of 1830–1850 vintage — at least none with any panes intact. Patient research by Dr. Parke Smith and James H. Rose,* along with discoveries of some panes, has widened our knowledge to include four other uses.

Some panes graced "Picnic," the old Schenley mansion in Stanton Heights, Pittsburgh, bordering the doors between dining room and parlor (*303*). General James O'Hara had built the original part of that house for his daughter, Mary Carson, who married William Croghan, Jr. Their daughter, Mary Croghan, born in 1826, eloped at sixteen to marry a middle-aged widowed British Army officer, Captain Edward W. H. Schenley. Except for a five-year interlude at Picnic, Mrs. Schenley lived the rest of her life in England. She deeded 500 acres to Pittsburgh for two parks. In Picnic there were two different lacy panes. The first and most numerous is pictured (*303*). It fits the size of other marked Pittsburgh and Wheeling panes

* James H. Rose, "Lacy Glass Window Panes, Their Use, Process and Origin," *Antiques* 51, February 1947.

303 Lacy glass panes, 1835–1845. 1 — Lacy glass pane from the old Schenley Mansion in Stanton Heights, Pittsburgh — probably Bakewell. Panes like this formed side panels beside doors between the dining room and parlor. 6⅞″ x 4⅞″. 2 — Lacy glass pane in the Gothic church manner. It is marked "Bakewell" on the un-patterned side. Many of these panes came from a secretary in a house near Wheeling. 3 — Lacy glass pane from the door of a cupboard found near Lisbon, Ohio. Sixteen panes like this have since been reported by Mrs. Rosetta M. Means of Kansas City, Mo. These panes were in a cherry cupboard. On the smooth side they are marked "Bakewell." *Ex coll. John J. Grossman.*

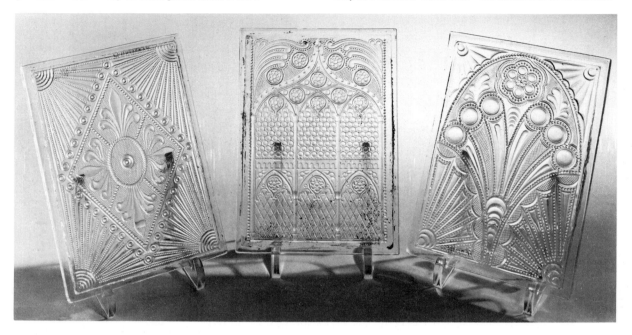

and relates to their design. The second (*304*), owned by the Historical Society in Pittsburgh, is unusual in its size: 6¼ by 4½ inches. The design on this smaller pane is not unlike that on the St. Louis ring stand. The lancets are wider than those on the stand but are less pointed. The looped figure eights on the pane enclosing a blossom and a circle seem very like those on the French piece. At the top and bottom, arches give a cathedrallike style.

A set of 16 panes marked "Bakewell" were found in a cherry cupboard from Lincoln County, Kentucky.* That location, near the Kentucky River and not impossibly far from the Ohio, indicates once again how Pittsburgh glassmen used the riverways for expanding their markets. The same patterned panes, unmarked, were taken from the doors of a corner cupboard in Lisbon, Ohio. The more recent finds, a different Bake-well, marked, and a marked J & C Ritchie (Wheeling), were used in secretaries. The Bakewell panes were found near Uniontown and the Ritchie panes in West Virginia below Wheeling.

Judging from the use of later colored panes, we should expect to find the lacy panes in the small sidelights bordering front doors and the windows in stairways. Amethyst panes were used (*305*), alternating with clear, in the doorway of a brick house built about 1850 in Franklin County, Indiana.* These panes (according to a grandson) had belonged to Dr. William A. Ashton, who had come to America from England in 1834 and settled in Franklin County. A skillful designer of textiles and oilcloth, he operated a flatboat on the Ohio in the thirties and forties when Bakewell was advertising panes for steamboats. He stored these panes in his original log house.

A pane with a feathery design reminiscent of a small Sandwich tray was said to have come from

* "More Lacy Glass Window Panes," editorial note in *Antiques* 51, September 1947. The panes were marked almost invisibly on the smooth side.

* Rose, "Lacy Glass Window Panes."

304 Lacy pane from Schenley house, "Picnic," in Stanton Heights, Pittsburgh, ca. 1840. Design is reminiscent of the marked Bakewell pane, Picture 303, No. 2. It also shows a relationship to that of the St. Louis ring stand, No. 299. It is smaller than the standard-sized lacy pane and measures 6¼″ x 4½″. *The Historical Society of Western Pennsylvania.*

305 Lacy glass pane in amethyst found in the sidelights of the front door of a house in Franklin County, Indiana, 1835–1845. Doctor Wiilliam Ashton settled there in 1834. The panes alternated clear and amethyst. The house was built in 1850. The doctor had brought the panes from the Ohio River Valley. 6⅞″ x 4⅞″. *The Corning Museum of Glass.*

a hall lantern in Wheeling (*306*). Since it is marked "Curlings & Robertson" (Fort Pitt Glass), its residency in Wheeling cannot assign it to that city. The most recently found Ritchie pane depicts a riverboat centered in a small octagon with curving corners. Directly below it stands a huge thistle. Two urns in the classic French manner flank the picture. A vine rises out of each and burgeons into three blossoms, the top flower clearly a rose. From the decorative similarity to the rose-anthemion cup plate, 4-inch plate, and 6½-inch octagonal plate, James Rose raised the question as to whether Wheeling may not have contributed more lacy than it has received credit for.*

* James H. Rose, "Wheeling Lacy Glass," *Antiques* 69, June 1956.

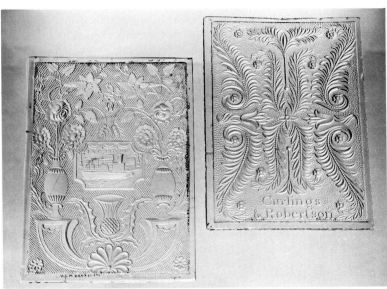

306 1 — Lacy glass pane with a rectangular shield showing an Ohio riverboat. Above the boat is impressed "J. & C. Ritchie." This firm operated in Wheeling probably after 1831. This pane shows more delicacy of design than the others in spite of the naturalistic boat and huge thistle below it. The urns on each side hold graceful flower sprays that rise and entwine at the top of the pane in a manner suggestive of the French.
2 — Lacy glass pane in a feather and scroll design said to have come from a hall lantern in Wheeling. It is marked "Curlings & Robertson" — proprietors of the Fort Pitt Glass House after 1834. *Ex coll. John J. Grossman.*

307 One of a pair of lacy panes, ca. 1840, purchased in Ohio. Approximately 8" x 10", it varies in thickness from ¼" to ⅜". Each pane weighs 2 pounds, 6 ounces. A slightly milky cast makes them almost nontransparent. Similar S scrolls are found on an oval tray — 1954 Corning Exhibition catalogue, No. 196. This type of pane graced a shed in Sandwich, and fragments of like panes have been found in the factory dump. *Collection of Theodore E. Keller.*

308 Fiery opal pane, probably Sandwich, ca. 1845. H. 6⅞". W. 6¼". *Collection of Dorothy Lee Jones.*

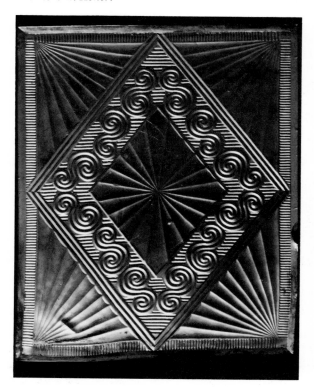

In any case, the two marked Bakewell panes are clearly Pittsburgh, and the likeness of the rayed peacock eye to the unmarked Schenley pane persuades us strongly that it too came from Bakewell. That leaves in doubt only the amethyst pane from Indiana. Dr. Parke Smith, the discoverer, considered it a Pittsburgh piece largely on the basis of the 1836 Bakewell advertisement and the proximity to river trade.*

Of all the panes, the most unusual in design is the Bakewell Gothic church window piece (*303, No. 2*). A barely visible "Bakewell" in block letters is inscribed three quarters of the way up, just below where the top arches begin. It does not appear in the design and would go unnoticed unless one rubbed a finger over the smooth surface.

---

* "Fresh Reflections on American Glass" and "Editorial Notes," *Antiques* 33, February 1938; and "Again Pressed Window Panes," 34, December 1938.

To see it, the viewer must tip the pane and look at the flat surface from a sharp angle.

The bottom arches of this pane, somewhat similar to those found in Eastern lacy, are surmounted by larger arches made up of many tiny roundels. The circles at the top of each arch also contain smaller roundels, and their counterparts on either side of the main peak almost touch what could be abortive peacock eyes. That part of the Gothic piece is clearly related to the other Bakewell panes. All but two panes found have a constant size, 5 by 6⅞ inches.

In 1953, Theodore Keller of Cincinnati bought two lacy panes in Massillon, Ohio. These measured 8 by 10 inches (larger than the standard size and the "Picnic" pane), weighed about two pounds each, and carried beveled edges. Unmistakable evidence gives the Keller panes a Sandwich origin. Similar panes were found in a corn

309 Pittsburgh salts show the persistence of Midwestern design forms as well as a relationship to Eastern and the French patterns. Classification numbers of salts are taken from L. W. & D. B. Neal, *Pressed Glass Salt Dishes of the Lacy Period, 1825–1850.*

OL 24 clear   RD 12 amethyst   DI 6 purple blue   SD 1 clear
BT la clear, "J. Robinson & Son Pittsburgh"   BT 2 blue "Pittsburgh"   BT 2 dark violet "Pittsburgh," 1825–1835 (The BT 2 boat salts are similar to the Lafayette salts made at Sandwich.) *Collection of Kenneth and Ruth Wakefield.*

shed near Sandwich and fragments of them in the factory dump. With the similarity in corner design to the standard Schenley pane (*303,* No. *1*) and with the Ohio purchase by Keller, an eager collector could make a faulty attribution. Undoubtedly the East experimented with lacy panes.

Dorothy Lee Jones of Wellesley Hills, Massachusetts, owns a handsome dolphin pane in fiery opal (6⅞ by 6⅜ inches wide).

In general, scholars of design have felt that French lacy shows more unity of design than American pieces. French design held to the

310   00 3 clear   PP 4 clear   OG 6 clear   OP 23 clear
OG 16 clear
RP 6 clear   SL 10   deep green   PP 1 clear   GA 3

clear, 1825–1845 1, 3, 4, 5, *Collection of L. W. & D. B. Neal.* 6, 7, 8, 9, *Collection of Kenneth and Ruth Wakefield.*

311 All numbers for pictures No. 311–316 inclusive and for No. 318 are taken from Lee and Rose, *American Glass Cup Plates.* Midwestern cup plates in these pictures are *Ex coll. Margaret Grossman.* Cup plate dates are 1830–1845 for illustrations 311–318.*

A stiffness of design as well as variety appears in these six cup plates:

	145B	231	141
132		70	215

classical and traditional, though sometimes it seems overelaborated. Our artisans were inclined to cover a piece at the expense of a major element in the pattern. Except for the Wheeling example, all the Midwestern panes express a concern for geometric configuration highly creditable if compared to sauce dishes, plates, and bowls. Decorative forms were treated in a traditional manner.

Salt Dishes and Cup Plates

Individual and extensive studies have appeared on cup plates and salts of the lacy period. Ruth Webb Lee and James H. Rose on cup plates and L. W. and D. B. Neal on salts will furnish adequate reference for both collector and specialist.

A few generalizations about each group can be in order, with particular attention directed to Pittsburgh factories.

Lacy salts of the Pittsburgh area follow plate, bowl, and compote design in two marked respects: in the Midwestern arch and in the different forms of the peacock eye. In the Neals's *Pressed Glass Salt Dishes of the Lacy Period 1825–1850,* GA3 is a good example of the arch. OG1, OG1a, OG1b, and PP1 are all excellent beaded eyes. 003 with different eyes adds hearts, stars, and small fans. OL9 shows the transition of the rayed peacock eye to the emphasis of the circle. RP5 and RP6, each with a border of beaded eyes, use stiff triangular arches to support them. DD1, OP22, and OP23 adhere to the

* Refer to pages 294–95 for the motifs of the cup plate design.

312 Naturalistic subjects and the symbolic Liberty Torch, No. 159. Roundels and bull's-eyes form the cap rings.

691   693   694
159   133   686

circle, while OG6 and SL10 dramatize it. PP4 and PP4a shape up like the Horn of Plenty, but with blossoms in each circle.

Pittsburgh lacy salts are extremely rare today, and some patterns are unique, but, paradoxically, the Neals found a relatively large number to record. The scarcity and the uncertainty of Pittsburgh salts leave the amateur collector with a feeling of insecurity. Many of the French designs relate closely to salts attributed to Pittsburgh, and so we may question the complete validity of the common generalization that Eastern and French lacy have an affinity for each other that is not found in lacy from beyond the Alleghenies.

The thousands of cup plates manufactured at Pittsburgh and in surrounding areas mirror the characteristics of lacy glass previously discussed. The cap ring analogy, already treated, holds for cup plates. The prevalence of the bull's-eye serrations is impressive; cup plates with 30, 34, 36, 40, 45, and 48 eyes are fairly common. Those with 20 and 24 eyes but with the point between also occur. The real roundel rim as found on the oval vegetable dish does not appear, but Lee and Rose Nos. 233, 234, 691, and 693 express the feeling on a small scale. Scallop and point, large scallop and small scallop, rims can readily be found.

In addition to the cap ring analogy, designs express the Midwestern idiom strongly. The trend to naturalism gives us a Washington bust, eagles, riverboats, a frigate, cabin, anchor, plow, beehive,

313 Naturalistic subjects with interesting cap rings and a
stiff variation of the Midwestern Hairpin, No. 615A.
One plate, No. 614, is marked "Union Glass Works,
Pittsburgh 1836."

593   614   615A

612A   637   605A

314 The eagle as a national bird here retains its savage
power. The marked "Fort Pitt" plate, No. 676, came
from the Curling factory.

656   677B   654A

672   676   670

315 Pittsburgh could handle geometric forms. The cap
ring of No. 183B matches that on the one shown in
No. 266.

	187		216		211
184A		250		183B	

316 The rayed center has always been popular:

	127A		214B		135
180A		128		123	

317 A series of different-sized plates bearing almost the same design, ca. 1840. 1 — Midwestern cup plate, No. 160A (Lee and Rose, *American Glass Cup Plates*). Scalloped rope edge. 2 — Five-inch plate, cap ring large scallop, small scallop. The large plate gives opportunity for expansion of diamonds in both concentric circles. Thirty-one clear ovals (eggs) are introduced at the edge of the inner circle. 3 — The design shows to best advantage on the largest plate. The beads dividing the circular bands emphasize the different patterns enclosed. A 6-pointed star in the center holds a small flower. From the star 3 stems with leaves and blossoms curve into scrolls. *Ex coll. John J. Grossman.*

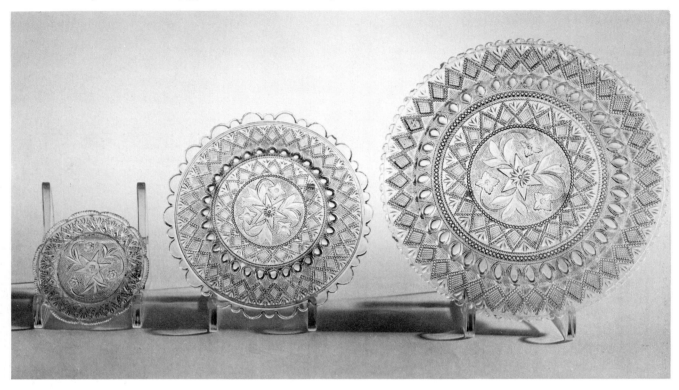

harp, rose, and thistle (*313, 314*). How many of these can be restricted to Pittsburgh proper is uncertain. James Rose attributed to Curling's Fort Pitt factory the Fort Pitt Eagle and Plate Nos. 210 through 217 (Lee and Rose, *American Glass Cup Plates*), relying on serration patterns and relationship to the marked Fort Pitt Eagle. Lacy compotes with cup plate bases have borne out those attributions. Pittsburgh designers acquitted themselves well in geometric patterns (*315*). The ship group of cup plates (Lee and Rose, Nos. 604, 605, 612, and 612-A) fits well with the 7-inch plates that carry the same design. Through economic and geographic background, Pittsburgh would seem to be a logical place of origin, because of its trade dependence on the inland waterways.

No. 129 (Lee and Rose) has a family history. In May 1833, when Hugh Creighton married Jean McPherson in Pittsburgh, a local glassmaker gave as his wedding present one dozen cup plates. Examples of these are found in the museum at Massillon, Ohio, and in the Historical Society in Pittsburgh. By and large, however, Rose made his Pittsburgh attributions not on family history but rather on serration and design. These include Nos. 120–129, 130–137, 197–204, 210–217, 441–445, and 655–656. The rope edge can be found easily in Midwestern cup plates, yet it is seen infrequently on larger plates and dishes. Rose assigned some of these plates tentatively, but he was such a careful scholar that he often leaned over backward in attributing an origin.

Another phase of cup plate design is that in which the same motif is repeated in the 4-inch toddy, the 7-inch plate, and the cup plate (*268*). The rose and anthemion series, possibly Wheeling, exemplifies this repetition. Also the shell and

318 The influence of the roundel can be seen in three
plates. The natural flower becoming stylized and then
abstracted can be seen in the other three plates.
147   148   208
   233A   134A   190

circle, the rayed peacock eye, and the Scotch plaid keep relatively identical patterns in all sizes. Although the center of No. 160-A (Lee and Rose) is somewhat similar to the centers of the 4-inch and 7-inch plates, the larger sizes let the designer add a border of clear eggs where the center joins the shoulder. In the 7-inch version, these become almost the lancet. This series combines a typical Midwestern stylized flower and star with stippled diamonds and trefoils. On the larger plates, the diamonds simulate cut glass patterns.

We also notice the number of Midwestern cup plates that emphasize the circle as an essential facet of design (*318*). Anthemia, the acanthus, the lunette, the shoulder arch, trefoil, quatrefoil, and cinquefoil — all these have been noted on larger pieces of lacy. The lancet leaf seems to have been considered unsuitable for cup plate design, for the centers of Lee and Rose Nos. 204 and 205 are the only examples. The two plates have a sunburst center with the Midwestern treatment and a turning pimple at the center.

The design analogy from Midwestern cup plates to larger lacy pieces is closer and sounder than the cap ring relationship already treated. A

319 Motifs found in Midwestern cup-plate design and on larger lacy pieces. Rose, "Midwestern Cup-Plate Designs," *Antiques,* October 1941.

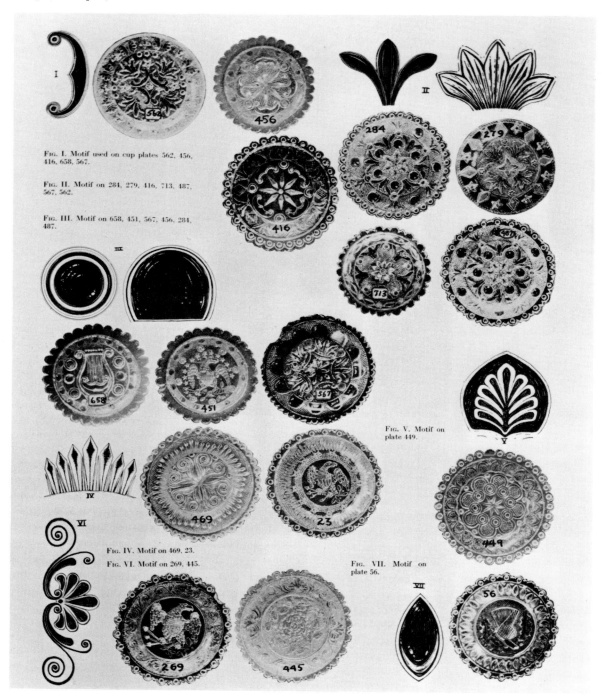

FIG. I. Motif used on cup plates 562, 456, 416, 658, 567.

FIG. II. Motif on 284, 279, 416, 713, 487, 567, 562.

FIG. III. Motif on 658, 451, 567, 456, 284, 487.

FIG. V. Motif on plate 449.

FIG. IV. Motif on 469, 23.

FIG. VI. Motif on 269, 445.

FIG. VII. Motif on plate 56.

pictorial representation seems to be called for. This one gives the forms that have been emphasized here and that also appear on cup plates. James Rose affirmed most of them as early as 1941. He used the numbers from Marble's original listing* (319).

The following cup plates reveal recurring Midwestern patterns in shoulders or in centers. In this outline the numbers are according to Lee and Rose in *American Glass Cup Plates*.

I C — Scroll or Lunette
    126
    126 A
    127 A & B
    176 A & B
    177 A & B
    190

II Trefoil
    127 A & B
    134
    134 A
    150 A & B
    189

Cinquefoil
    129
    197 A
    222

III Plain Circle or Roundel

123 A & B & C	182
124 A & B & C	188
134 A	189
136	381
137	656
180	690

IV Rays
    184 A & B
    185
    669
    670 A & B & C

* James H. Rose, "Midwestern Cup Plate-Designs," *Antiques* 40, October 1941, 222–224.

V Palmette

154 A & B	171
169 A & B	677 A thru G
170	678

VI Anthemion
    201
    202
    203
    672

VII Lancet & Leaf or Egg & Dart

133	216 A & B & C
204	217
205	

Circle & Dot, or Shell & Circle
    136 A
    137
    151 A
    154 A & B

The cap rings, the designs, the presence of table rests, the character of the pieces manufactured — these may be used consistently to identify Midwestern plates. Variants do not upset the generalizations. Hitherto unrecorded pieces broaden our knowledge of stylistic changes, areas of distribution, and techniques of manufacture.

In any list of "One Hundred Best Colored Cup Plates," the Midwest must bow to the East. In fact, cobalt and opal and opal opaque usurp the place of varied colors in the Midwestern group. Green comes next in frequency. Other colors, when and if found, are subjects of special attention.

In any list of "One Hundred Best Clear Plates," the Midwest is artistically competitive in spite of two criticisms: scanting the lead and coarse stippling. Midwest manufacturers were inclined to cut down on the lead they used, the sparseness of which brought disrepute on themselves from the earliest cup plate collectors. By and large, Midwestern stippling on lacy cup plates passes muster, but it is likely to be coarser than that on Eastern plates and sometimes even cloth-

320 An unrecorded lacy plate with bull's-eye cap ring, 1840–1845. Flamboyant forms on the shoulders and a startling center of radial lines going to 7-leafed fans indicate its Pittsburgh origin. Eight table rests complete the design. D. 6″. *Collection of the author.*

like. So much variation in the quality of stippling exists in both East and Midwest, however, that no hard and fast generalization should be laid down, except that the finest, sharpest, most scintillating quality of American stippling has been found in Eastern pieces. A comment once made by Dr. Samuel Johnson is applicable here. Someone asked him whether he thought men or women were smarter. He replied, "Which man? Which woman?" We should follow that cue in assessing lacy cup plates, regardless of where they were made. Cap rings, table rests, and border designs give the collector enough to study without worrying about the character and merits of stippling. And whatever Midwestern designers may have missed in delicacy of design they more than compensated for in the exciting subjects they chose and in the new treatments they gave to stylized forms.

Change and Decay

Present interest in Victorian decoration has led students to build up what are termed substyles in furniture, metals, textiles, and the other arts and crafts, perhaps because of abortive social, political, or artistic movements. The vogue for lacy glass, lasting only two decades, from 1830 to the early 1850s, should not be considered one of these substyles. Its performance in those two decades, and the present high regard in which it is now held, raised this product above the level of a passing fad. Glassmakers, moreover, obviously accepted it, not as a substitute, but more as a partner with other forms of manufacture within the industry. Its decline was clearly caused by the Panic of 1837 and ensuing hard times. Lacy molds chipped by hand were costly. And technical advances in pressing glass offered a practical and economic escape as well as a chance to bring in new styles.

Lacy was cloudy in its birth and undistinguished in its death. Stippling became coarser or was reduced to a mere matlike finish. Glassmen expended less effort on classic and naturalistic design, and they effected economies by using designs that did not require costly handwork in chipping elaborate molds.

Rochelle (Princess Feather) was one lacy design that was carried over to pattern glass. The Bakewell, Pears catalogue of 1875 pictures it and another lacy pattern, Arabesque. Bryce Brothers patented in the 1870s two weak derivatives of lacy: Roman Rosette and Rose in Snow. Loop and Dart of Portland, Maine, was one of the offspring that captured the early lacy quality. Its cousin from Pittsburgh, Leaf and Dart, developed in the Richards & Hartley factory, used the mat finish as its version of stippling.

People often confuse the term "lacy" with a collectible pattern in pressed glass such as those mentioned. Complete sets of such glass came after the 1850s, when lacy was expiring. We must not let the decay and death of lacy glass detract from its originality and beauty. Mrs. John F. Kennedy's selection of the Eastern Providence lacy sugar bowl (eagle and shield) as a gift for

Mrs. Nikita Khrushchev dramatizes the beauty as well as the American quality of the art. That bowl is a magnificent example of craftsmanship.

In its two brilliant and shining decades, lacy glass flashed not only over the American but across the Continental sky as well. Certainly it was a distinct and distinguished contribution to our decorative and industrial arts. French and Eastern lacy employed the widest and most exciting use of color and had the highest unity of design. Midwestern lacy carried the most naturalistic and bold designs, appropriately expressive of an adventurous and young part of the nation.

CHAPTER XIV

The Early Period of Midwestern Pressed Glass

> The most novel article was the pressed glass; which was far superior to anything of the kind I had ever seen either in London or elsewhere. The merit of its invention is due to the Americans, and it is likely to prove one of great national importance.
>
> — James Boardman, on visiting the Fair of the American Institute of the City of New York in 1829, in *America and the Americans*

No unassailably accurate chronological history with documentary support has yet been compiled for early American pressed glass. Students have accepted four fairly sound generalizations as an aid in establishing its characteristics. It has glass with a high lead content. It is likely to have simple geometric patterns. It reveals distinct lines where the molds come together. And one must rely on isolated bits of family history. Students also look for two supplemental techniques of manufacture: the pontil mark, which indicates handling before the perfection of the mold and the snap holder, and fire polishing, which simulated a mold-blown finish and removed the fins left by imperfect joining of the molds.

Students of New England pressed glass believe that all the early pieces were fire polished and that the practice continued during the 1860s. A James B. Lyon catalogue of the O'Hara factory (1861) (see Appendix, page 486) indicates that Pittsburgh manufacturers did not follow the practice. Nappies in the Huber pattern are listed on page four as "Fire polished" and "Not fire polished." By the term "nappies," Lyon meant sauce dishes,

low-footed bowls, bowls with covers but on no standard. Page five shows "nappies on foot"; we should call them covered compotes. Here again we have Huber listed as "Fire polished" and "Not fire polished." Unfortunately, no price is given for the fire-polished pieces. A single sugar bowl in the New Orleans pattern (wide panels) is advertised as fire polished. On page eight, the covers of Huber bowls are specified as fire polished. Out of sixteen pressed patterns pictured and listed in the catalogue, these few references to fire polishing of two patterns persuade me that the practice was on the way out. It could not have been a profitable technique anyway. Besides, glass manufacture and handling had improved considerably by the 1860s.

The difficulties of dating and attributing lacy glass set forth in chapter thirteen mirror the problems that confront any student of early glassware (the trade name for pressed tableware). Because tableware and ordinary functional pieces had less glamour and individuality than lacy glass, their record must be pieced together without factory-marked pieces. The Patent Act of July 4, 1836, which established the American system and its machinery for operating, was followed six years later by the Act of August 29, 1842, which made designs a separate branch. A study of design patents from 1842 to 1864 reveals that glassmen saw little need to use that branch. After 1864, however, when table sets were in great demand and high production flourished, the Patent Office becomes a reliable source of information on who first made certain popular American pressed glass patterns.

During the 1840s and 1850s, our only pictorial help comes from illustrations at industrial fairs and advertisements in directories and trade journals. It is possible after 1860 to find catalogues of pressed patterns of a few American manufacturers. Even the booming Sandwich factory, as far as we can determine, never issued a catalogue before 1875.

To paraphrase Laurence Sterne in *A Sentimental Journey,* they ordered this matter better in France. Launay, Hautin & Cie. of Paris brought out as early as 1840 a very full catalogue depicting models from Baccarat, St. Louis, Bercy, and Choisy le Roi and continued to issue its catalogues approximately every two years. Baccarat issued catalogues of its own during the 1830s, and Val St. Lambert did the same through the following decade.

The first reaction of an American collector to the 1840 Launay, Hautin catalogue is one of amazement that the French factories had such extensive and varied lines of pressed glass so early. The second is how closely the intricacies of a French type of lacy glass paralleled designs in America. In this early period of pressing, the French used the diamond, the flute, and the rays. Less often they used the circle (roundel) and a ridged pattern much like Sandwich and the Pittsburgh plume. Sugars and salts reveal shapes similar to those of American pieces (*323*). French compotes generally have lighter stems and more shapely bowls. Every once in a while, however, square pedestal bases like some on New England

area lamps and vases grace both French sugars and compotes. A classical severity of form lightens the heavy proportions. The influence of earlier cut glass patterns speaks more loudly in the early French catalogues than in the American pressed glass catalogues of the 1860s.

The mystery of the absence of lacy tumblers from American tumblers referred to in the preceding chapter is emphasized when we look at page twelve of the second part of the Launay, Hautin advertisements; it shows 36 different patterns (*324*). True, one pattern (diamond point) dominates or becomes a secondary part of the design on 21 of the tumblers. Even on these, bases and supports are rayed or paneled differently. The pseudo-lacy or mat finish found on a few of the tumblers is superior to decadent American attempts to capture laciness, as in McKee's Ray and Bakewell's Arabesque and Rochelle (Princess Feather).

323 Launay, Hautin & Cie. catalogue, Part II, p. 16. Some American salts are almost copies of the French. *The Corning Museum of Glass.*

324 Launay, Hautin & Cie. catalogue, Part II, p. 12. American nineteenth-century pressed tumblers do not approach the dignity and style of the French. The relationship of several popular American pressed patterns is marked. Again we note the influence of the diamond, the ray, and the panel from earlier cut glass. *The Corning Museum of Glass.*

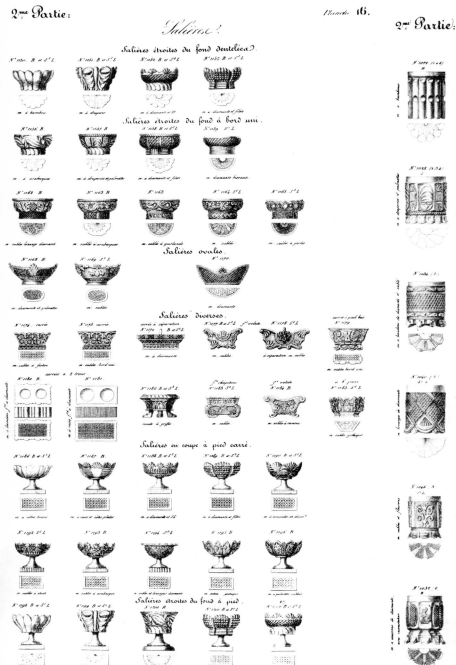

325 King, Son & Co. (Cascade Glass Co.) catalogue, ca. 1875, page 1, shows the types of American tumblers probably made by many American factories. A collector notes immediately how few patterns are represented and how many plain and fluted ones were made. *The Corning Museum of Glass.*

It is surprising that American manufacturers were content in their early pressed tumblers (1860) to repeat the plain six- and eight-paneled whiskeys that flourished in the Pittsburgh District. Not until the 1870s, around the time of the Centennial, could America boast of streamlined pressing in a real tumbler factory. The Rochester (Pennsylvania) Tumbler Company advertised 175 patterns and manufacture of 200,000 tumblers every six days. That, of course, came after pressing had been mechanically improved and a workable lime-soda formula had insured cheap production. No direct comparison should be drawn between the Rochester tumblers and the pressed French tumblers of the forties that simulated cut and lacy glass (*326*). We have many examples of American cut tumblers but none of American lacy. So we continue to deduce that American pressed tumblers, aside from the ubiquitous paneled examples, must originally have been drawn from early patterns like Ashburton, Colonial, Argus, Huber, Diamond Point, and Honeycomb. In those patterns are found various sizes of wines and goblets. Certainly such designs were more conservative and less stylish than the French.

326 French lacy tumbler with 5 arched panels, 1840–1860. Beneath the cross in each panel is a different symbol. Heavy base rayed to a polished pontil. *Collection of the author.*

The scarcity of catalogues in the period 1840–1860 forces us to concentrate on two examples for a discussion of pressed patterns: the so-called Ihmsen sugar bowl and a pictorial advertisement in Curling's 1856–1857 business directory.

The Ihmsen Sugar Bowl

In the late 1930s, Mrs. Jessie McCready of Pittsburgh acquired an unusual pressed sugar bowl (*327*). It was obviously an advertising piece, for each of the nine panels of the bowl carried the impression of a different article of pressed glass. The bowl was bought from an elderly woman who lived on Pittsburgh's South Side only two short blocks from the C. Ihmsen factory site of 1850. Her brother, an employee of that company, told her that experiments had been made to improve wooden molds, which charred

too readily and blurred designs. As she remembers the story, the molds were replaced by pasteboard and papier-mâché (though that would hardly eliminate charring or blurring of the design). Since Ihmsen operated under his own name in 1850 and the owner of the bowl specified 1851 as the year of experimentation, the piece has been given that date.*

The Excelsior pattern dominates in five of the nine panels: on a decanter, a goblet, a covered sugar, an ale, and a spillholder. McKee catalogues of the 1860s feature that pattern, and we do not find the early Excelsior assigned to other rival factories by experts in pattern glass. This is another instance of different factories producing the same design. One cannot fail to note the close relationship of Excelsior to Bigler, a little-known pattern from McKee in the 1860s. The sixth panel — an Ashburton decanter, a pattern from New England Glass Company, Sandwich, and Bakewell — attests the importance of the design. Joseph Magoun of New England Glass applied on October 24, 1848, for a patent for a glass mold; as an example for the mechanical application he used a piece with the Ashburton pattern. Lura Watkins unearthed a bill from the same company indicating that Ashburton pieces had been shipped to California during the 1849 Gold Rush.

The seventh panel, the Flute goblet, sets forth another common pattern of the 1840–1860 period. Both French and American pressed glass manufacturers found Flute panels as attractive, as practical, and as salable as they had been on earlier cut glass. Huber, a prolongation of the flute, remained a steadily popular pattern through the second half of the century. On September 25, 1847, Joseph Magoun applied for a patent for molding and pressing glass; this time a Flute goblet is pictured. So we have evidence of early American origin.

* See Jessie and Delphine McCready, "The Ihmsen Family: Pioneer Pittsburgh Glassmakers," *Antiques* 34, August 1938.

327 Ihmsen sugar bowl in opaque and in clear, used for advertising purposes. Nine panels show pressed pieces; several of them are patterns pictured in the McKee catalogue, ca. 1860. H. 3⅜". *Collection of William J. Elsholz.*

The Star spillholder has the same simplicity of the other patterns, perfectly plain panels alternating with panels containing an elongated eight-pointed star, like the one in Sandwich Star and Buckle. This pattern is not listed or described elsewhere. The ninth panel of the sugar bowl pictures a hexagonal candlestick.

On the rarely found cover of the Ihmsen sugar bowl are depicted an Excelsior compote and footed tumbler, a Flute champagne and goblet, and a six-paneled salt above an inkwell. The bowl and cover of lead glass show the lines of a three-part mold. Faint dots, the kind that sounded the knell of lacy stippling, mark the spandrels and arches between and around the large panels. Pairs of small six-pointed stars decorate the top of each panel. This beading and the starlike medallions set forth the plain ovals that hold the advertised glass examples. The manufacturer evidently considered the sugar bowl an effective advertisement, since several of the bowls have turned up in clear glass, some in milk white. Because the McKee factory made many of the patterns depicted, and because it is difficult to find advertisements of an Ihmsen tableware factory, we inevitably wonder about the attribution of the bowl. Whichever factory made it, one mystery remains: why was a factory mark — a label — omitted on such an obvious attempt to advertise?

The Curling Advertisement

By the year 1856 we have a more accurately documented example of pressed patterns. An advertisement of the Fort Pitt Glass Works appearing in the Pittsburgh and Allegheny Directory for 1856–1857 depicts sixteen pieces of Curling

328 Curling, Robertson & Co. advertisement in the Pittsburgh-Allegheny Directory for 1856–1857. Waffle and Thumbprint was made in the East as well as in the Midwest. Flute and Colonial are two other well-known patterns.

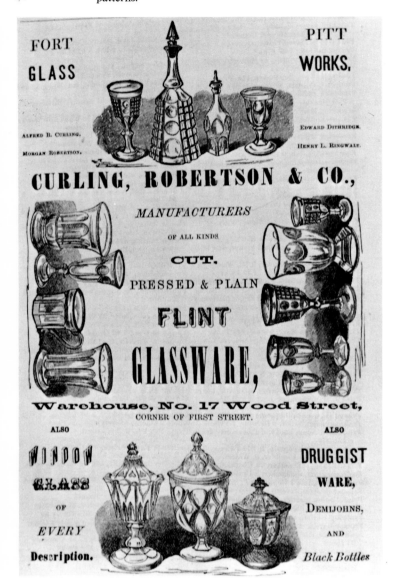

pressed tableware (*328*). The most striking piece is a Waffle and Thumbprint (Palace) decanter with a glass stopper. Beside the decanter is a wine glass of the same pattern; on the right are a goblet and a footed cordial. On the left side, three drinking vessels in the Flute pattern reinforce the previous statement about this pattern. In the Colonial pattern — thought by Ruth Webb Lee to be one of the earliest of pressed patterns — we see a wine at the top, a footed tumbler at the right, and a champagne at the left. Covered sugars and a small covered sweetmeat in this pattern are found in the Tri-State area. Generally they are of heavy, sometimes cloudy metal. Unlike Ashburton, Flute, and Waffle and Thumbprint, Colonial does not belong to several factories. McKee later used the circle-at-the-top-of-the-panel pattern (Colonial) but bordered the top above the circle or bull's-eye with a band that looked like cut diamonds. In an 1864 catalogue McKee called this pattern "Band."

The small bitters bottle beside the decanter seems to be an adaptation of Ashburton in a rather simplified manner. A footed bitters somewhat like it is shown in J. B. Lyon's O'Hara catalogue for 1861. There it is called Saint Nicholas.

The covered sugar in the center of the bottom row remains an unidentified pattern, though it could well be a forerunner of Bryce's Ribbon Candy. Beside it on the left, another sugar reveals an anonymous pattern. The semi-lacy bowl to the right of the center was manufactured by the New England Glass Company and Sandwich. In the East, it comes in beautiful shades of cobalt, green, canary, and opal. An excellent example of coarse stippling and decadent lacy, it shows a certain affinity for the Ihmsen bowl in the character of the dot stippling.

These two instances of Pittsburgh pressing in the 1850s, the Ihmsen bowl and the Curling advertisement, consistently emphasize plainness and heaviness of design, a borrowing or preempting of patterns, and a producing of utilitarian rather than artistic pieces — decanters, goblets, wines, tumblers, sugar bowls.

Later Pressed Patterns

Lura Watkins, speaking of the New England Glass Company catalogue of 1868–1869, has expressed the opinion to me that several of the patterns displayed were probably made at an earlier time and continued to be advertised because of their popularity. Accepting her thesis as sound, we will examine below a hitherto unpublished 1861 catalogue from J. B. Lyon's O'Hara Flint Glass Works. Members of that company besides Lyon were Alexander P. Lyon and William O. Davis, who later became superintendent of the Portland (Maine) Glass Company.

Honeycomb and Huber were evidently two of the most popular patterns around 1860. In Pittsburgh there were two other names for Honeycomb. One, Cincinnati, implied that the combs covered almost the whole surface of the glass; the other, New York, implied that there was a wider band of clear at the top. The New England Glass Company called its narrow-banded version Vernon. Modern collectors too often dismiss Honeycomb because so much of it was made late in the century, and so much of that was of inferior metal. The Lyon product is clear, resonant, and heavy. More pieces of that pattern should be carefully studied, even though many factories made it.

Such a study would open many eyes. Limiting ourselves to extant catalogues, we find pictures of Honeycomb in those of J. B. Lyon, 1861; of McKee, 1864; of New England Glass Company, 1868, 1869; of undated catalogues probably in the 1870s, including King & Son, G. Duncan & Son, Doyle & Company, all of Pittsburgh; of Hobbs, Brockunier and Central of Wheeling; and of Gillinder of Philadelphia. Antique dealers today differentiate pieces by the width of the clear band: New York is wide, Vernon is narrow, and,

theoretically, Cincinnati is Honeycomb running to the top. Nevertheless, the Cincinnati pieces in the J. B. Lyon 1861 catalogue may appear with no clear band, with a narrow band, or with a wide clear band. Fine distinctions of nomenclature and of style obviously became blurred by the competitive commercial goals of pressed glass manufacturers (*329*).

Whereas Honeycomb has no closely related patterns, Huber comes close to several others: Gaines, Hotel, Crystal, Finger Flute, New Orleans, Mioton, and a paneled pressed sugar bowl named for William O. Davis. A logical outgrowth of the Huber panel is the heavy O'Hara loop and the narrower counterpart Genella (*330*). The O'Hara loop was copied at several other factories, Sandwich producing one of the best likenesses. Genella seems to belong only to Pittsburgh. Leaf, an even heavier and possibly earlier version of O'Hara, appears in the later McKee catalogue and in the East as Loop. Perfectly plain panels like Hotel, New Orleans, and Davis can be found in varying degrees of height among the countless tumblers pictured: Mioton, Sage, Western, Gauche, and Mobile. Either for advertising purposes or for style, or both, tumblers and standard drinking vessels were commonly named for well-known cities or regions, including Charleston, Brooklyn, Albany, and Paris.

Diamond and Mitre Diamond, Reeded and Star (*330*) look back to the economy and dignity of early cut glass. Wreath points to approaching popularity of naturalistic motifs. Two different patterns named Crystal predict the heaviness, coarseness, and stiffness of late pressed glass. So here at 1861 we know well the taste of the 1850s, we can expect a transition during the sixties, and we foresee the heavy geometric pieces that were to emerge in the 1880s and 1890s. In the middle sixties we have fewer indications of the strong naturalism that swept the seventies.

The prevalence of molasses cans with both tin and Britannia covers reminds collectors that many covers carry patent marks in the inside

329 James B. Lyon & Co. catalogue, 1861, p. 14. Students of pattern glass are limited by the absence of early catalogues. The Davis pattern was undoubtedly named for William Otis Davis who went from the Lyon factory to superintend the Portland Glass Co. in Portland, Maine. Palace (Bull's-eye and Waffle) was also produced by Fort Pitt (Curling) and Eastern factories. Huber was made in many factories. This is a Lyon version of Crystal. *Collection of the author.*

collars, with dates ranging from the late 1850s through the late 1860s. Mirror and Star and Concave patterns were blown into the mold. Their patterns show a departure from the other designs already discussed. Blown-molded pieces evidently were still in demand, for catalogue captions guide buyers between O'Hara pressed and O'Hara blown.

The Ringwalt Catalogue, 1860

A hitherto unpublished advertising brochure by Henry L. Ringwalt, glass manufacturer and later distributor, throws some illumination on present-day problems of authenticating pressed glass. The brochure bears the legend "2nd Annual Circular, Jany. 1st, 1860," and it contains a map of

330 James B. Lyon & Co. catalogue, 1861, p. 5. Several patterns are not familiar to collectors: Genella, Reeded, Wreath, and Star. Leaf appears in the East as Loop. Diamond and Mitre Diamond are variations. New Orleans, a tumbler pattern, is somewhat like Davis shown in No. 329.

patterns and forms in line drawings. These, in Ringwalt's words, show "a large variety of new and beautiful patterns . . . beautiful designs and superior finish." Should we take that statement with a grain of salt? Perhaps we should when it is applied to such patterns as Huber, Cincinnati (Honeycomb), and O'Hara (Loop or Leaf). At least we have a date (1860), a picture, and a statement from a Pittsburgh glassman.

The first eleven pages of the circular are devoted to pressed and blown tableware. The next two are given to lanterns, candlesticks, lamps, bottles for beverages, and such sundries as fish globes, finger bowls, milk pans, and flasks. Patent fruit jars and cans rival lamps in the space allocation. Glass lamps are distinguished by carbon oil, coal oil, and kerosene, and each classification with an adjectival prefix "fancy" shows gradations

331 See opposite page. H. L. Ringwalt's 2nd Annual Circular, Jan. 1, 1860. Business House Nos. 124 and 125 under the Monongahela House. (155 pieces of pressed glass.) *Collection of the author.*

No.		Per Doz.	No.		Per Doz.	No.		Per Doz.	No.		Per Doz.
1.	6 in. Cincinnati pat. Nappie and cov.	4 00	21. gill. Cincinnati pat. Tumbler.		75	41. 7 in. Cincinnati Bowl and cover—high foot.		12 00	61.	O'Hara pat. Wine Glass.	1 40
2.	6 in. " " on foot.	6 00	22. ½ pt. Cincinnati pat. Tumbler.		1 00	42. 6 in. Cincinnati Bowl and cover—high foot.		9 00	62.	Cincinnati Salt.	1 50
3.	½ pt. Sage 6 flute Tumbler.	1 25	23. ½ pt. Cincinnati pat. Tumbler.		1 75	43.	Cut Wine Bottle.	12 00	63.	Cincinnati Horse Radish.	2 00
4.	pint. 6 flute Soda Tumbler.	1 75	24. ½ pt. Cincinnati pat. Tumbler—handled.		2 00	44. 6 in. N. O. Nappie—on foot and cover.		6 00	64.	Cincinnati Pepper—screw top.	2 00
5.	pint. Heavy 6 flute Tumbler.	1 75	25. ½ pt. Cincinnati pat. Tumbler—handled.		1 50	45. ½ pt. N. O flute bar Tumbler.		1 10	65.	Cincinnati Mustard—metal top.	2 00
6.	½ qt. Mobile 6 flute Tumbler.	1 50	26. gill. Cincinnati pat. Tumbler—handled.		1 25	46. ½ qt. Crosse Tumbler, star bot.		1 50	66.	St. George Salt.	1 50
7.	Cincinnati pat. Sugar and cover.	4 50	27. Cincinnati pat. Spring Glass.		3 00	47. pint. Astor Julep Tumbler.		1 50	67.	Geneva decanter.	9 00
8.	½ pt. 7 flute Tumbler.	80	28. Cincinnati pat. Cellery—small.		6 00	48. ½ qt. Astor Julep Tumbler.		1 50	68.	Genelfa Sugar and Cover.	3 50
9.	½ pt. 8 flute Tumbler.	75	29. Cincinnati pat. Bitter Bottle.		1 50	49. ½ qt. Mobile bar Tumbler.		1 00	69.	Genelia Spoon Glass.	3 00
10.	½ pt. N. B. 9 flute Tumbler.	1 00	30. Cincinnati pat. Goblet—large.		3 00	50. ½ pt. Mobile bar Tumbler.		90	70.	Genelia Cream.	3 00
11.	½ pt. Heavy plain Tumbler.	90	31. Cincinnati pat. Goblet—small.		3 50	51.	Genelia Rice Bottle.	3 00	71. 7 in.	Crystal Nappie and cover.	3 50
12.	½ pt. Heavy plain Tumbler.	1 20	32. Cincinnati pat. Champagne.		2 00	52.	Concave Salt.	50	72.	Crystal Sugar and cover.	4 50
13.	½ pt. Heavy plain Tumbler.	1 60	33. Cincinnati pat. Wines.		1 50	53.	O'Hara Sugar and cover—large.	4 50	73.	Crystal Cellery.	7 50
14.	½ pt. Heavy plain Ale Tumbler.	1 20	34. Cincinnati pat. Cordials.		1 25	54.	Tulip Candlestick.	3 00	74.	Crystal Spoon Glass.	3 00
15.	Cincinnati pat. Cream.	3 50	35. Cincinnati pat. Vinegars.		1 50	55.	Gainer Pillar Tumblers.	1 50	75. 8 in.	Crystal Dish and cove.	4 50
16.	Cincinnati pat. Egg Glass—large.	3 50	36. Cincinnati pat. Beer Mugs.		2 00	56. ½ pt. Gainer Pillar Tumblers.		90	76.	Crystal Cream.	3 50
17.	½ pt. Cincinnati pat. footed Tumbler.	1 75	37. 8 in. Cincinnati Bowl and cover—low foot.		12 00	57.	O'Hara pat. Goblet—large.	3 00	77. 7 in.	Crystal Nappie and cover—on foot	4 50
18.	Cincinnati pat. Egg Glass—small.	1 50	38. 9 in. Cincinnati Bowl and cover—high foot.		16 00	58.	O'Hara pat. Goblet—small.	2 50	78. 7 in.	Crystal Dish and cover.	3 50
19.	Cincinnati pat. Jelly Glass.	1 00	39. 10 in. Cincinnati Bowl and cover—high foot.		18 00	59.	O'Hara pat. Champagne.	2 00	79. ½ pt. Mirror Molasses, brk. top.	3 50
20.	½ pt. Cincinnati pat. footed Tumbler.	2 00	40. 11 in. Cincinnati Bowl and cover—low foot.		9 00	60.	O'Hara pat. Egg Glass.	1 50	80. pint. Mirror Molasses, brk. top.	4 50

No.		Per Doz.	No.		Per Doz.	No.		Per Doz.	No.		Per Doz.
81.	Star and Concave Molasses, brit. top.	4 50	101. 10 in. Huber Bowl—high foot.		18 00	121. No. 1. Huber pat. Wine.		1 50	141. 10 in. Huber Dish and cover—on foot.		21 00
82.	Heavy Gainer Molasses, brit. top.	12 00	102. 8½ in. Huber Bowl—high foot.		12 00	122. No. 1. Huber pat. Egg Glass.		1 50	142. 8 in. Huber Dish and cover—on foot.		18 00
83.	Engraved Water Bottle.	12 00	103. 7½ in. Huber Bowl—high foot.		9 00	123. No. 1. Huber pat. Jelly Glass.		1 75	143. 8 in. Huber Dish and cover.		12 00
84. 12½ in.	Crystal Fruits—high foot.	16 00	104. Huber pat. Bitter Bottle.		3 50	124. No. 1. Huber pat. Champagne.		1 80	144. 10 in. Huber Dish and cover.		15 00
85. 7½ in.	Crystal Bowl—high foot.	7 50	105. Huber pat. Decanter.		9 00	125. No. 1. Huber pat. Ale Glass.		3 00	145. 12 in. Huber Dish and cover.		18 00
86. 7½ in.	Crystal Bowl—low foot.	7 50	106. No. 8. Huber Goblet—large.		3 00	126. No. 1. Huber pat. Goblet.		2 25	146. O'Hara Cellery—small.		6 00
87. 9½ in.	Crystal Bowl—high foot.	16 00	107. No. 8. Huber Goblet—small.		2 50	127. Huber pat. Cream.		3 50	147. O'Hara Cellery—large.		7 50
88. 9½ in.	Crystal Bowl—high foot.	15 00	108. No. 8. Huber Champagne.		2 00	128. Huber Nappie and cover.		3 50	148. Cincinnati Cellery—large.		7 50
89. 9½ in.	Crystal fruits—high foot.	16 00	109. No. 8. Huber Egg Glass.		1 50	129. Huber Sugar and cover.		3 50	149. 6 in. Mitre Diamond Nappie and cover.		3 50
90. 6 in.	Huber Nappie and cover—on foot.	4 50	110. No. 8. Huber Wine.		1 50	130. Huber Molasses, brit. top.		4 50	150. 6 in. Mitre Diamond Nappie & cvr., on foot.		4 50
91.	Huber Jar and cover.	8 00	111. No. 8. Huber pat. Cordial.		1 25	131. Huber Beer Glass.		2 00	151. 8 in. Cincinnati pat. Dish.		6 00
92. 6 in.	Genelia Nappie and cover—on foot.	4 50	112. gill. Huber Tumbler.		75	132. Huber Spoon Glass.		3 00	152. 9 in. Cincinnati pat. Dish.		7 50
93.	Huber Rd. Salt.	12 00	113. ½ pt. Huber Tumbler.		1 00	133. 6 in. Genelia pat. Nappie and cover.		3 00	153. 10 in. Cincinnati pat. Dish.		12 00
94.	Ind. Rd. Salt.	50	114. ½ pt. Huber Tumbler.		1 20	134. Ohio pat. Beer Mugs—small.		2 00	154. 11 in. Cincinnati pat. Fruit—low foot.		18 00
95.	Ind. Sq. Salt.	50	115. ½ pt. Huber Tumbler.		1 50	135. Ohio pat. Beer Mugs—large.		2 25	155. 9 in. Cincinnati pat. Bowl—low foot.		15 00
96. 9½ in.	Huber Fruit—high foot.	12 00	116. ½ qt. Huber Tumbler—handled.		1 75	136. Huber pat. Cellering.		7 50			
97. 10½ in.	Huber Fruit—high foot.	16 00	117. ½ pt. Huber Tumbler—handled.		1 50	137. 8 in. O'Hara Bowl and cover—high foot.		15 00			
98. 12½ in.	Huber Fruit—high foot.	18 00	118. ½ pt. Huber Tumbler—handled.		1 50	138. 9 in. O'Hara Fruit—high foot.		12 00			
99. 13½ in.	Huber Fruit—high foot.	18 00	119. gill. Huber Tumbler—handled.		1 25	139. 7 in. O'Hara Bowl and cover—high foot.		12 00			
100. 11 in.	Huber Bowl—high foot.	18 00	120. No. 1. Huber pat. Cordial.		1 25	140. 12 in. Huber Dish and cover—on foot.		24 00			

in quality and price. Perhaps the top rating was for those with marble bases. The last six pages cover window glass. A small but interesting section here is probably an outgrowth of lacy panes: "Plain and Ornamental Enameled Glass, for churches, Steamboats, etc. Plain White Obscured — Ornamented — Different Patterns." The circular, with its map and price listings, verifies the idea that sets of pressed glass must have begun to flourish in the late 1850s.*

In *The Merchant of Venice*, Portia characterizes her English suitor as one who had bought his several garments in different countries and who had learned his behavior everywhere. After a

perusal of the Ringwalt map, one is tempted to say that about certain patterns of glass.

We know from city directories that Ringwalt was a limited partner in Curling, Robertson & Company at least in the years 1850–1857. That he had parted from that company is attested by the Directory of 1859–1860, which lists "Henry L. Ringwalt, Glass Merchant, 124 and 125 Water Street under the Monongahela House, formerly copartner Curling, Robertson & Co." And yet his brochure, dated January 1, 1860, pictures the main lines offered by J. B. Lyon's 1861 catalogue. Did Ringwalt, now a "manufacturer's agent," break completely with Curling, Robertson and refuse to handle their lines? We may doubt that and believe, instead, that several glasshouses during this era manufactured identical patterns. For example, Lyon's Star and Concave molasses can appears almost as a duplicate in the McKee catalogue of the middle sixties, where it is called

---

* When present-day collectors speak of sets, they mean anywhere from fifteen to fifty different matched pieces. Sales catalogues and retailers' bills of the 1860s and 1870s, however, use the word "set" to mean four pieces: creamer, covered sugar, covered butter, and spoon holder or spillholder.

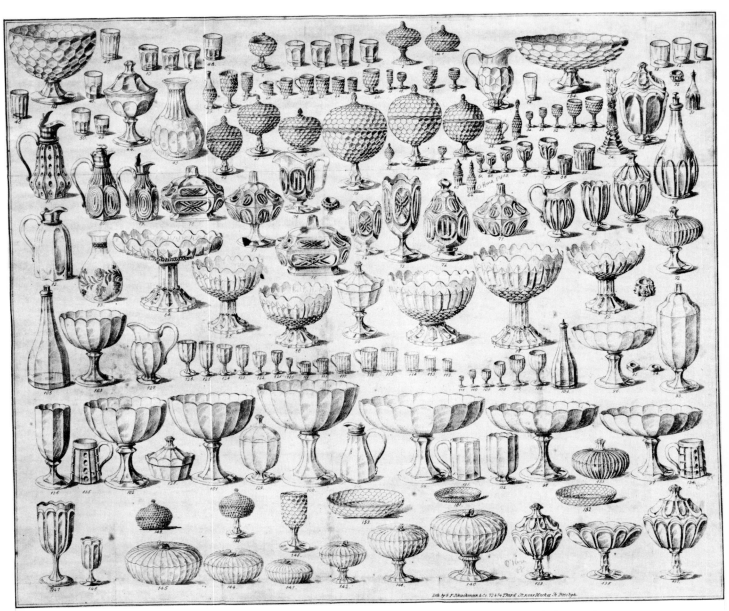

"Diamond." That Ringwalt sold the same item does not prove anything. His only actual tie-up with Curling could have been in the Waffle and Bull's-eye spillholder, which appears in an 1856–1875 Curling ad. Lyon calls it "Palace" and also

pictures an Ashburton line, which keeps the upper sections of design more circular than do Ihmsen, McKee, and Curling.

In any case, we have no Curling-Robertson catalogue for verification. The nearest duplicate

332 Cover of H. L. Ringwalt's 2nd Annual Circular, Jan. 1, 1860.

in pattern to pieces in a Curling advertisement pictured in the Pittsburgh and Allegheny Directory for 1856–1857 are the Aster Tumblers Nos. 47, 48, and 49; the pattern called "N. O. Nappie" No. 44; and the Flute tumblers Nos. 8, 9, and 10. We know, at least, that the J. B. Lyon Company made Huber, Cincinnati, Leaf (Loop), and Mitre Diamond. We also know from pictures in an 1864 catalogue that McKee made Leaf (Loop), Flute (when does Flute end and Huber begin?), Crystal, New York Honeycomb, and Diamond. The three years of difference among Ringwalt (1860), Lyon (1861), and McKee (1864) catalogues emphasize clearly the borrowing of designs. In the early sixties, design patents were few and some of the patterns had been current over a period of time, so that alterations developed. A study of the catalogues, however, will help attributions when variations are pronounced. Otherwise the student will be forced to hedge.

Two other pieces of the Ringwalt catalogue deserve special comment. The Tulip candlestick is as French as it could possibly be. It also favors architecturally fine Belter furniture; it is triumphantly Victorian. The beer mug labeled "Ohio Pat" seems very like the French treatment of the same theme (Launay, Hautin catalogue, page eighteen, No. 1, and page twelve, No. 1).

Henry Ringwalt represents one of the new phases in the distribution of glass. He strengthens the growing opinion among students that, although pressed glass was to usher in big business and mass production, even as late as the 1860s most operations were small and the business largely personalized. Ringwalt undoubtedly was angling for merchants outside of Pittsburgh. One suspects also that the glass companies with their own warehouses and limited sales force were glad that reliable commission men existed.

A Sequence of McKee Catalogues

Three McKee catalogues, two acquired by the Corning Museum of Glass and an unpublished one belonging to the author, throw light on the varied character of glass merchandise, indicate approximate dates for certain patterns, and show a steady progression toward modern advertising. The earliest one, undated, McKee & Brother, has been assigned to 1860 largely on the directory location of the printer, W. S. Haven, Corner of Market and Second Streets. (Haven moved in 1861 to the Corner of Wood and Third.) The second, an unpublished catalogue, McKee & Brothers, is dated July 1, 1864. The third, dated April 1, 1868, is the one Ruth Webb Lee used for illustrations in her *Early American Pressed Glass*.

The 1860 catalogue is smaller in size than the others. It shows more variety and less concentration on individual patterns. In fact, only one page is given over wholly to a single pattern. Thus the McKees were able to show limited forms in many patterns: Excelsior, Mitre Diamond, Eugenie, Comet, Leaf (Loop), Crystal, Ray, Flute, Ashburton. Most pieces shown from one pattern came from Crystal, Excelsior, and Flute. Among the Lamp and Gas Globes twenty-five different items were cut, mostly in the Tulip pattern. In the two later catalogues, cut items were absent. The pressed tableware included all functional pieces familiar to collectors and householders. Two sections, Apothecaries' Shop Furniture and Sundries, run the gamut. The Apothecaries' section takes in everything from Show Globes for window advertising to syringes, breast pipes, and nursing bottles. Of course, mortars and pestles, funnels, graduates, and specie jars with japanned covers were important listings. Among the Sundries we find toys (a neat so-called Sandwich flatiron), bird feeding and bathing holders, fishbowls, pressed rose knobs, butter prints, and white enameled eggs.

The 1864 catalogue reduces the Apothecaries' Shop Furniture section but adds slightly to the Sundries list. In the enlargement of the pressed tableware section, a student gets the feeling that sets were much more important than in 1860. Two pages were devoted to Sprig. Evidently Ribbed Leaf (Bellflower) was being featured: four full pages and one with all pieces carrying a double vine. Therefore we have an approximate date for Bellflower and proof that it was manufactured extensively in Pittsburgh. Other patterns given a single page were Crystal, Excelsior, Stedman, Eugenie, Prism, and Brilliant. In other respects this second catalogue parallels the first, except that we have a whole page and two thirds under a new listing — Carbon Oil Lamps.

It would be invaluable if we had the same catalogue information from other large factories. These three, at least, give documentary evidence of what McKee was making from 1860 through 1868. Eastern collectors may issue claims for certain patterns, but their insistence cannot disprove the clear record of McKee's manufacture. The 1868 catalogue carried on the style of the 1864. It establishes the continued popularity of Excelsior, Eugenie, Sprig, and Crystal. Two pages indicate that N.P.L. (New Pressed Leaf) was the feature. Its similarity to the 1864 catalogue allows us to leave it now with the conviction that collectors and dealers would do well to study all the McKee catalogues to see where the East and the Midwest were duplicating each other and to determine actual dates of pressed patterns.

All these pressed glass comparisons pretty well establish American designs of the 1850s: geometric, coarse, straightforward. Set against the French product, they belong to a young and less sophisticated society. That many factories produced the same line indicates a conservative business approach. The influence of both the Continent and of earlier cut glass has now clearly begun to wane. Designers are waiting for a new idiom. It is strange that they could not find it until the discovery of the lime-soda formula and until pressing techniques lent themselves to streamlined mass production.

CHAPTER XV

Lamps and Chimneys

Thanks to the good gift of petroleum oil and thanks to the inventor of the
student lamp there is no longer any excuse for one's hurting his eyes by
reading at night and thousands of people, who a few years ago were
lauding gas to the skies are now consigning it to its proper place, in halls
and offices and streets, and refusing to allow it in parlors and bedrooms and
replacing the gas fixture with lamps for burning kerosene.
— *The Crockery and Glass Journal,* January 4, 1877

The bread and butter of the Pittsburgh glass trade during the first forty years of the century had been window glass and bottles. With a doubling of the population from 1825 to 1850, an expanding factory system, and around 9000 miles of railroad, the need for improved illumination became pressing.

While the East Coast could depend on whale or sperm oil, the Midwest found lard oil much cheaper and more readily available. In 1840 the packing houses of Cincinnati slaughtered 500,000 hogs. The soapmakers there learned that by heating lard oil with soda alkali they obtained glycerin, stearic acid, and an improved lard oil. Candles made of one part tallow and two parts stearic acid became favorites in the Midwest and the South, supplanting those made of sperm oil. A Solar lamp designed by Robert Cornelius of Philadelphia for any viscous fluid was particularly adapted to the newly improved lard oil. Cornelius introduced a plate with a hole in it to fit across the burner above the wick. This curved draft deflector sent the flame higher and brighter.

Neither lard oil nor sperm oil, however, could compete in price with camphene — the first synthetic oil illuminant used in America. In 1830, Isaiah Jennings' patent for redistilled spirits of turpentine alone or mixed with alcohol for a lamp illuminant emphasized the possibilities of camphene. Though he used vegetable rather than mineral oil, he had shown a way for the transfer of techniques. Volatile camphene needed a strong draft to burn effectively and the wick tubes were angled away from each other and tapered to improve wick security. Though the danger of explosion existed, camphene was light in weight, had low boiling and ignition points, and burned well in cold weather. The cheap conversion of whale oil lamps to camphene tube burners, moreover, could be made for 6 to 12 cents. The shape of bowls for new lamps became more turniplike, less elongated. In fact, McKee Brothers in the 1860s made a font and some pieces of glass in a pattern they called "Turnip." Camphene probably accelerated lamp availability more than the improvement in lard oil and the Solar lamp did. In the 1840s, 69 lamp patents were registered with 28 for lard lamps. In the 1850s, out of 97 patents,

312

only 11 were for lard oil. From 1860 to 1864, 32 out of 206 patents were for coal oil (kerosene) and 30 for vapor lamps.

The fastest-growing source of artificial light during this period was gas, usually manufactured from coal. Though gas light may have been preferred in homes, the city companies had to charge well for services that were available only in large cities and towns. Since a movable unit for gas had not met the economic demand, the search for a more perfect liquid illuminant went on apace. Coal gas illumination pointed the way to other distillations. Coal oil and carbon oil, marketed widely in the last two years of the fifties, became an important manufacturing phase in Pittsburgh. Large companies like Lucesco, Aladdin, and North American flourished. So even before the breakthrough in petroleum, glass manufacturers had the incentive to go ahead with table lamps, shades, and chimneys.

Samuel Martin Kier was a pioneer in using and refining oil. In 1849 he skimmed oil from his father's salt wells near Saltsburg, Pennsylvania. He first sold it as Seneca or Bristol oil, a balsam to cure all ills. By 1854 he advocated and sold this balsam as fuel for lamps. The men in his coal pits were using it as an illuminant and were even trying it at home. Undoubtedly crude oil in burning created black smoke, gave off an offensive odor, and generated a weak yellow light. Kier set up a refinery in the basement of his drugstore at Grant Street and Seventh Avenue in Pittsburgh. He constructed a vessel with a capacity of about five barrels. This same still was shown at Allegheny City in 1876, the Centennial year, with the label, "The first still ever used to refine petroleum."

Kier even experimented with a burner of Britannia consisting of four long tubes of brass, a rather flat oil font, and a circular rim capable of supporting a chimney (333). Kier never patented this lamp, but he obviously meant it for refined petroleum or kerosene. It has been tried today

333 Kier Petroleum Metal Lamp. Samuel Martin Kier, among the first to work on the problems of refining oil, developed this burner, ca. 1855. It will work only with kerosene and carbon oil.

successfully. Lard oil, whale oil, and camphene do not work in it.

From the late 1850s to the early 1860s, many changes and improvements took place in illuminants and lamps. Kerosene from petroleum, in fact, displaced almost every other kind of lamp fuel. Even coal-refining operations were converted to petroleum. In 1861, William Frew and Charles Lockhart completed the first big refinery for petroleum in Pittsburgh. Three big coal-oil refineries were still operating effectively. Within a year they, too, had deserted coal oil for petroleum. Both these illuminants — coal oil and petroleum oil — gave glass manufacturers the stimulus needed to expand production of all kinds of glass lamps and suitable chimneys. The portable lamp had come into its own.

Lamp patents after 1857 show how the market was stimulated. There were 58 such patents in 1858, 58 in 1859, 88 in 1860, and 128 in 1862. High-grade kerosene, sold under such romantic names as Royal Daylight and Tea Rose and soon

334 The Dithridge patent for an oval lamp chimney, Oct. 8, 1861, one of the early chimney patents, showed the possibilities of different shapes.

exported for sale all over the world, retailed at $1 a gallon in 1860; the price dropped to 60 cents within two years.

After trial and error, burners for kerosene lamps were reduced to two types: the Argand lamp with its circular wick and the Vienna burner, in which a flat wick protruded through a metal dome-shaped shield slotted across the top. Both lamps, of course, required chimneys to provide the draft for adequate air supply and a steady flame. Conversion of lamps made to burn heavy oil was often possible simply by fitting a new burner to an old font.

Chimneys

None of the countless lard oil lamps had chimneys to stabilize the flame. Kerosene lamps did, and so a new market was created for a whole new product. Pittsburgh was in an admirable position, geographically and technically, to supply its needs.

Edward Dithridge of the Fort Pitt Glass Company on October 8, 1861 — two years after Colonel Drake brought in the first large well at Titusville — took out Patent No. 33,428 for an oval lamp chimney (*334*). The elliptical body was elongated and the bottom edge flattened to rest on and be locked to the burner. Glass manufacturers had been pressing glass since 1825, and it was inevitable that they would seek a less expensive technique than blowing. The inventive and ingenious Atterburys on October 19, 1875, patented a method of mold pressing that produced a chimney without a seam. It may be assumed that other patents existed before and after that seamless chimney. Adams & Company early in 1875 was advertising a molded (pressed) chimney, and another Atterbury chimney patent followed in November. The eventual goals, of course, were a chimney fashioned wholly by mechanical means, and one so tough that it would not break in a cold draft.

The lamp chimney — cheap, undecorated,

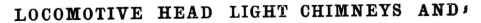

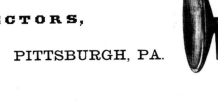

fragile — challenged designers to give their product a distinctive character and chemists to improve the quality of the glass. They varied the shape, frosted the bowl, etched the bowl, and crimped the top (*335*). We find it hard to realize today that an ordinary chimney company, Lindsay Flint Glass of Chartiers Valley, could advertise no fewer than forty different patterns.

Problems arose for management and labor out of increased mechanization of pressing chimneys and the effort to avoid similarity in design. Blowers did not protest the molding and pressing process, for they were called upon to finish the chimney by hand. In fact, the patent opener, which opened and spread the chimney to be worked mechanically, did not infringe greatly on their prerogatives. The patent crimper, however, enabled a green hand to finish off many more chimneys than the blower, and it made him a skilled workman after a few days' practice. On November 11, 1875, Paul Zimmerman patented a machine for fluting or crimping open-ended glassware — a combination centering rest with a tapering tool adapted to both flare and crimp (*336*). A highly paid gaffer with a helper could fashion 300 plain or 250 crimped chimneys in a single move.* An ordinary worker with a patent crimper, without a helper, could make 300, and Edward Dithridge of the Fort Pitt Glass Company foresaw that he could easily make more after he became an expert in the procedure.

That was not to the taste of skilled workmen, and in dealing with management on the 300 plain–250 crimped production sequence they demanded more pay for the extra 50. Blowers knew that many more chimneys would be made with the use of the patent opener and the crimper, and they feared that such a high rate would saturate the market and put them out of work. They disregarded the 30 percent advantage in pay they had over Eastern chimney workers, and they had no conception of a market that expanded endlessly as quality rose and prices dropped. The owners were torn four ways at once — by Eastern price competition, by the need to increase production to meet rising demand, by the need to reduce costs, and now by the workers' demands for more pay and shorter hours.

The chimney blowers went out in 1877 on what was to be a long and painful strike. In August of 1879, Challinor-Hogan paid 36 cents per turn without counting the pieces. Plunkett & Company tried doubling up — that is, requiring blowers to finish the chimneys. Eastern manufacturers supplied the Midwestern market at prices below cost in order to get their chimneys into Pittsburgh packing rooms.† The terms of the settlement in 1880 were that the wage rate was increased to $1.83 a move; a move should include only 300 chimneys; eight instead of six men made up a shop (one working team); and owners could use the crimper and opener as necessary instruments to meet competition (see page 75).

* A turn or move lasted approximately six hours. *The Crockery and Glass Journal* for October 2, 1879, reported that Keystone Glass had carried out eleven turns in a single week — the largest ever accomplished in the glass trade. The price for those chimneys was the lowest ever reached.

† *The Crockery and Glass Journal,* September 11, 1879.

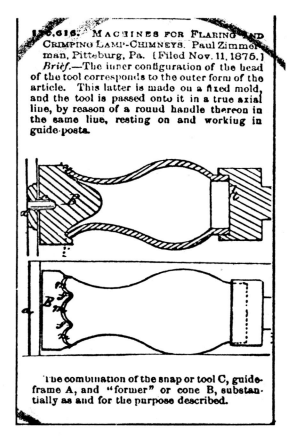

170,616. MACHINES FOR FLARING AND CRIMPING LAMP-CHIMNEYS. Paul Zimmerman, Pittsburg, Pa. [Filed Nov. 11, 1875.] *Brief.*—The inner configuration of the head of the tool corresponds to the outer form of the article. This latter is made on a fixed mold, and the tool is passed onto it in a true axial line, by reason of a round handle thereon in the same line, resting on and working in guide-posts.

The combination of the snap or tool C, guide-frame A, and "former" or cone B, substantially as and for the purpose described.

Glassmakers were conscious of the need for durability, and to obtain it they experimented with techniques to toughen their glass. One diehard glassmaker in Buffalo in 1861 patented a Burner for Lamps without Chimneys; he declared that broken chimneys often exceeded the cost of the oil.

A Frenchman named La Bastie had developed a secret formula for making an almost unbreakable chimney. He tempered the glass at a fierce heat and kept the temperature high in the annealing ovens. Usually lime-soda glass was immersed in paraffin before annealing. La Bastie had bad luck with factory fires in France; England felt his royalty demands were too high and refused to give him financial backing; but America gave him an opportunity. He was highly praised at the 1878 Grand National Exhibition of American Industry (in New York City): "A medal of superiority should be awarded for the exhibit of La Bastie's glass, as it is truly superior to any manufactured before the invention of La Bastie — even twenty times greater and will not Chip or Grizzle."* One cynical manufacturer said of the La Bastie process, "All who are interested in making or selling glass prefer the old style, for to them it is the sweetest music to hear breakages when such do not occur in their own warehouses or factories."

Bakewell, Page had annealed glass in oil as early as 1822, the object then being to toughen the glass so that it would not break on the cutter's stone. Paul Zimmerman had worked on the durability problem during the 1860s; as late as 1876 he was searching for something to add to glass that would bear out his belief that toughness in glass would result from the introduction of a foreign material. Gill Brothers (Acme Glass, Steubenville) advertised that their Non-Breakable Lamp Chimneys were tempered and rendered "Fireproof by Super-Heated Steam." As specialists in lamp chimneys, Gill Brothers claimed they had achieved an effective process for durability. Tests conducted on both Gill's and Zimmerman's chimneys impressed viewers. Their chimneys were dropped on a carpet and from ceiling height to a bare floor and did not break. They were then thrown across a room at a board wall, and while some broke, it was explained to everyone's satisfaction that these had hit knots or nails.

Pittsburgh chimney business in 1878 reached a yearly value of $600,000. Some 790 hands produced 16,200,000 chimneys. To pack the output of just nine chimney factories, 725 tons of straw were required. Pittsburgh boasted that it made all the flint glass chimneys produced in the United States and four fifths of all others. Not far away, Acme Glass of Steubenville persisted in its claim

* The Crockery and Glass Journal, January 3, 1878, October 25, 1875.

that it was the largest chimney house in the country. A. Thierry & Company of South Brooklyn advertised in 1875 that it was the largest; the following year it failed.

It is difficult to winnow the Pittsburgh chimney houses from those that made tableware and various other glass products. Among those companies principally or largely engaged in the manufacture of chimneys were Evans, Sell, Dithridge, Excelsior Flint Glass, Plunkett, Keystone, James Lindsay, Challinor-Hogan, Kunzler, and the Crescent Works. Such well-established companies as Bakewell, Pears, McKee Brothers, King & Son, and McCully turned out chimneys as one line among others, often in very substantial volume. McKee had no fewer than twenty chimney shops working, with crews of at least three men to each shop. That the volume could be tremendous is shown by Evans, Sell's capacity of 600 gross a week and by Keystone's 575 gross (with about 150 hands). That it could be profitable is shown by the value of Keystone's yearly product: $92,000. When the strike shut down Pittsburgh chimney operations, Challinor-Hogan could afford to move its whole factory to Chicago for the duration.

With increase in volume and improvement in production techniques, prices dropped. Ordinary lime glass chimneys sold for 19 cents a dozen. La Bastie chimneys, when well established, sold for 25 cents. Western manufacturers hoped to stabilize their prices between 24 and 28 cents; Eastern groups wanted 30 cents. (A table in the Appendix, page 487, shows a comparison of chimney prices between the 1860s and 1870s and between lime glass and flint.)

Font and Base

The earliest fonts were merely lamp bowls with a short stem called a "peg." These could be fitted into the tops of candlesticks, placed on a metal or wooden stand, or joined to a glass lamp base. By the 1860s, even though illuminating oil had not

337 Lamps and bases from the McKee & Brothers catalogue of 1864. Several popular pressed patterns are represented. Obviously there was little attempt to achieve beauty or symmetry. *Collection of the author.*

been perfected, glassmen were making pressed lamps in standard patterns: Stedman, Sprig, Prism, Bellflower, Ellipse, Star, Chain, Concave, Gaines, Cincinnati, Shell, Tulip, and Vine.

Footed table lamps sold at wholesale from $5.75 to $8.50 a dozen. Peg top fonts brought from $2.75 to $4 a dozen. Both were sold without the burner. Pressed night lamps cost only $1.33 a dozen. Smoke bells for hanging lamps were priced at $8 per dozen in plain white, $9 with a blue edge, $10 with a red edge. A McKee catalogue listed two Bellflower table lamps, one for C. O. (carbon oil), the other for fluid (i.e., any fluid, probably camphene). The sole difference between them appeared in the burner: one with two wicks angled away from each other and the other with the adopted Argand burner that

was to grace hand lamps for several decades.

The early lamps were stiff, heavy, almost crude (*337*), for manufacturers were more preoccupied with mechanical than with artistic improvements. Jacob Reighard of Pittsburgh developed an important improvement: the first glass font with a separate opening for pouring in fuel without unscrewing and lifting the burner and wick. The device had been used on metal fonts, but Hale, Atterbury and Company, to whom Reighard assigned the patent, was the first to apply it to the glass font. A screw collar, fitted with a screw-on cap, was cemented to the neck of the opening. It was neater and it saved the housewife the trouble of unscrewing and lifting the burner and the wick. For some unaccountable reason, this double-vent font was not universally popular with later hand

and table lamps in glass, whereas many elaborate parlor lamps used well into the twentieth century had the separate opening for filling.

During the 1840s and 1850s, the font without a peg and the base were pressed separately and fused by means of a wafer. The operation required three or more steps and still left a weakness in a table lamp. (Every collector has encountered lamps and candlesticks that have parted company at the joining after a sharp blow). Glass manufacturers realized that sales and profits would increase if the font and the base could be joined in one operation. They tried joining the pegged font to the base by means of a metal collar and cement or other adhesive. This was a practical advance but not the final solution. The pegged font, the pedestal or base, and the burner could be sent to the retailer all assembled or they could be sold and shipped separately. Skilled workers would not be needed for joining, and there would be a standardizing of parts.

Patents as late as the 1870s reveal the various ways in which glassmen sought to effect a strong union. During the 1870s and 1880s, the pieces were pressed and then fused by reheating, with no peg on the bowl and often no wafer between them. A popular pressed lamp of the 1880s, Two Panel by Richards & Hartley (*338*), was made in several colors. A light blue example in the author's collection shows three mold lines on both font and stem of the base. No wafer is visible; the top of the base ends in a fold not unlike a collar, so that the lamp appears to have been pressed in one operation. But failure of the mold lines to match by more than half an inch shows that the two parts were pressed separately before the marriage.

An 1863 Atterbury patent pointed the way to a solution. The metal collar on the top of the font, it specified, should be attached to the neck while it was in the act of being blown or molded. It indicated one way eventually used to treat the main joining. The bowl pictured in the patent has a peg base. Five years later D. C. Ripley patented

339 Atterbury's Eureka lamp represented a step forward in joining bowl to base. The parts could be sold separately. Atterbury was more interested in this mechanical development than in showing various patterns in the bowls. Since all Atterbury bowls would fit all bases, we have efficient standardization. Atterbury catalogue, 1872. *Library of the U.S. Patent Office.*

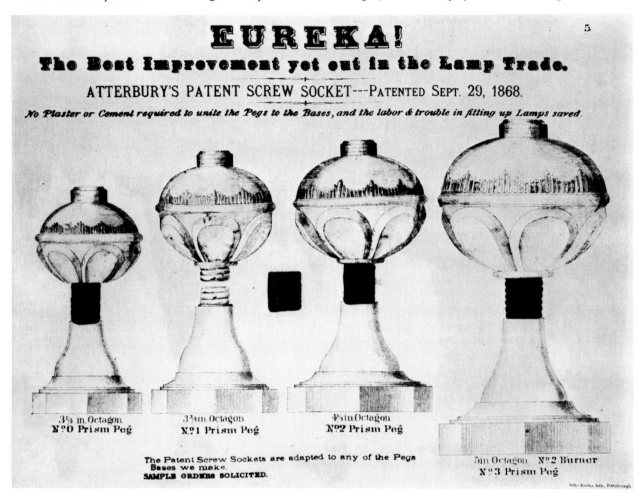

a lamp with a pressed base (one or two handles) and a bowl blown onto it. The Atterburys patented a combined pressing and blowing in the same mold, the handle cast and the bowl blown. The key parts of the patent were probably the successive operations in one mold and the control and direction of the molten glass for the cast handle. The Atterburys may have borrowed the idea from an 1863 D. C. Ripley patent that cast the top and the handle under pressure and used cement to unite the pieces blown separately.

The real breakthrough may have come in 1868 with the Atterbury Eureka Lamp. The Atterburys united the lamp bowl and the pedestal by means of a metal screw connection between the two (*339*). They called this the best improvement yet made in the lamp trade, advertising that no cement or plaster was required to unite peg and base. Thus they saved the labor of assembling the parts and, with the advantage of a screw connection, were able to standardize on pegs and bases. The Atterburys had long been interested in opal

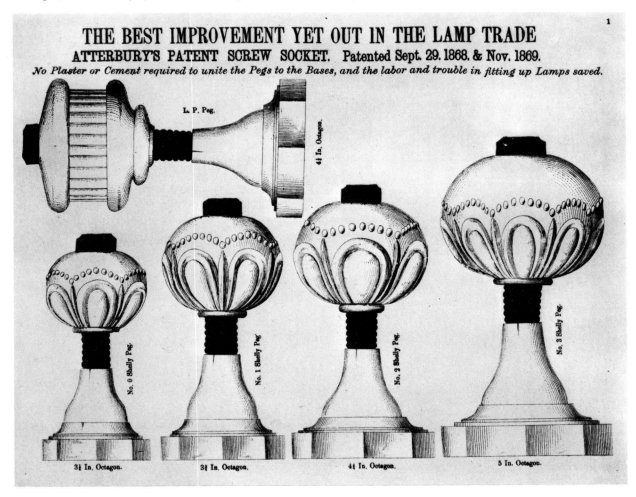

THE BEST IMPROVEMENT YET OUT IN THE LAMP TRADE
ATTERBURY'S PATENT SCREW SOCKET. Patented Sept. 29. 1868. & Nov. 1869.
No Plaster or Cement required to unite the Pegs to the Bases, and the labor and trouble in fitting up Lamps saved.

(white) glass, and the Eureka, with its opal base and clear bowl, became so popular that the company reached annual sales of 15,000 dozen.

The Eureka patent evidently fell short of being the last word in screw sockets, for in 1869 the company bought a patent from a Roland Smith. It reads like an amplification of the Eureka: a screw thread was formed on the peg of the reservoir (bowl) with a corresponding threaded socket on the pedestal (*340*). The company added bosses or knobs on both peg and pedestal and

made a metallic tube with angular grooves for receiving them. In 1870, they devised an apparatus not only for making male and female screws, but for making them in combination with a mold that produced seamless screw-threaded pegs.

If we accept the judgment of *The Crockery and Glass Journal* (December 18, 1879), Atterbury was the largest lamp glass factory in the world. If we reject it, we may still accept a few statistics from its catalogues as evidence that their products

341 The extreme plainness of many of these Atterbury lamps indicates a preoccupation with fast and cheap production. Atterbury catalogue, 1881. *Library of the U.S. Patent Office.*

were indeed widely sold (*341*). Dr. Arthur G. Peterson of De Bary, Florida, who has worked untiringly on glass patents, kindly submitted the following figures. In Atterburys' 1872 catalogue, twenty-two pages in length, no fewer than seventeen pages were devoted to lamps. In the 1874 catalogue, twenty-eight pages in all, twenty were given to lamps. In the 1881 catalogue, thirty-eight pages in all, twenty-two were on lamps. The company was well known for its jelly glasses, jars, seven fairly popular pressed patterns, in opal as well as in colors, and for its opal novelties — it was, in fact, known as the "White House" for its devotion to opal. So high a proportion of its catalogue pages given to lamps, then, is impressive evidence of the volume and value of its lamp sales. It was reported at the Centennial Exposition, "Atterbury Brothers have a grand array of lamps drawn out in line of battle in their case"* (*342*).

* *The Crockery and Glass Journal,* July 5, 1877.

Hand lamps and table lamps lighted every home.
Atterbury catalogue, 1881. *Library of the U.S. Patent
Office.*

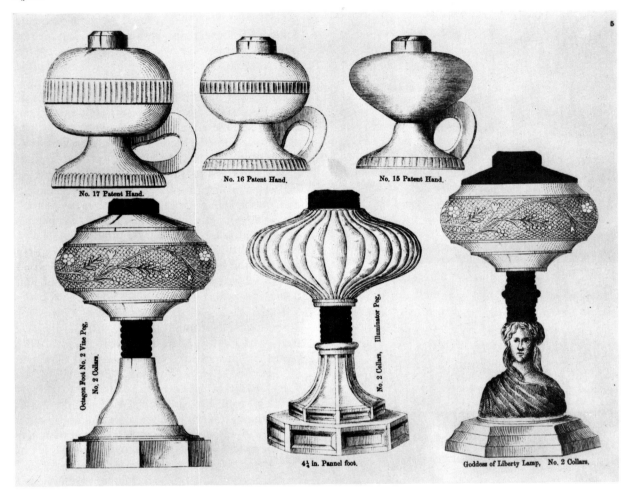

One of the Atterburys' strongest rivals in lamps
was Adams & Company, of whom it was written,
"In all glass lamps, hand lamps, fonts, the patterns of this house will be standard for years to
come."* The company was selling more than
sixty varieties of lamps, from small night lamps to
large and handsome parlor lights. It concentrated
on more pattern glass than the Atterburys. In
November 1876, Adams had twenty-six new

* *The Crockery and Glass Journal,* February 27, 1885.

molds with twenty-six new patterns, which gave
them exceptional opportunity to supplement their
lamp design if they so wished.

John Adams noted an 1870 Ripley patent that
applied a metal handle to a glass lamp, and in
response he took up a patent from C. L. Knecht.
The patentee claimed a new device for united end-
to-end two parts of glass or of glass and metal,
the device being a wire spiral attached to the end
of one part in combination with a threaded stem
or peg in the contiguous end of the other part. In

343 A step toward the lamp that would be completely pressed in one operation is shown in the J. P. Smith, Son & Co. catalogue for 1876, p. 81. The groove top, which prevented oil from leaking over, became popular and remained so for a long time. *Collection of the author.*

344 J. P. Smith, Son & Co. hand lamps with grooved tops, catalogue, 1876, p. 82. *Collection of the author.*

Adams' patented glass lamp with a metallic handle, the key point was not the handle but rather a metal solid eye, or collar, between the bowl and the foot. When the bowl was blown, the peg made a firm union with the glass of the foot. Adams later took up a J. C. Gill patent that embraced the same principle without metal, encompassing the union within the mold itself. The parts were folded together at a welding temperature that caused the glass to unite.

While Adams and the Atterburys were striving for technical improvements, D. C. Ripley caught the public fancy with his "Marriage Lamp." Though the patent reads "two cavities communicating with each other," we should call it two lamp fonts on a center stem. The two bowls were blown in the mold simultaneously. Ripley devised a match holder to fit between the fonts and join them.

Ripley had used the same idea in "Stems for Articles of Glassware" and then had designed a Baptismal Font to fit on this stem. In both these pieces he depended on a metal socket for the joining. In 1876 he improved the metal collar. The shape of his piece was such that it would not interfere with the shrinking of the glass. The socket had a tapering collar with radiating points and belled edges. James Bryce, for his part, devised a pedestal with a socket to receive the peg of the lamp bowl in one piece, a seat being formed on the socket and the socket being strengthened with ribs.

All these minor changes and related techniques were merely attempts to strengthen early lamps and to discover how to reduce operations and costs in pressing. Cement was undoubtedly used more frequently and widely than the patents revealed. The year following the Bryce peg-socket patent, Hobbs, Brockunier of Wheeling believed that it had surpassed Bryce's device and the various Atterbury screw joints. In promoting their product, the owners deplored the use of plaster or cement: "The ordinary socket is fastened on the foot by cement and then the lamp peg is fastened

345 Atterbury's Boss lamp represents the culmination of attempts to solve the problem of joining foot and bowl. Atterbury advertised the strength of such a lamp. The advantage to the industry was cheaper and increased production. Atterbury catalogue, 1881. *Library of the U.S. Patent Office.*

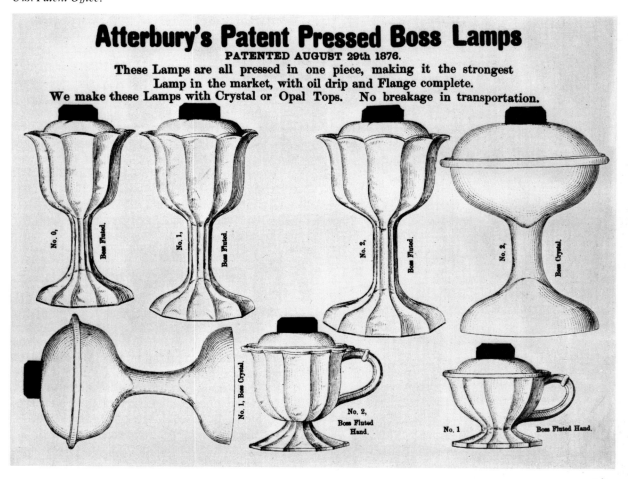

in this socket also by cement. The evaporated oil and constant cleaning and uses of the lamp soon loosens the connections.*

"Foot and Bowl in One Solid Piece"

The next logical step was a one-piece pressed glass lamp. An early example is given in the *Supplement* to the *Illustrated Catalogue of Lamps, Chandeliers & Brackets* published by J. P. Smith, Son & Company, 189 Liberty Street, Pittsburgh, September 15, 1876: "Patent Pressed

* *The Crockery and Glass Journal,* November 18, 1875.

Groove Top — Foot and Bowl in One Solid Piece, Pat'd May 9, 1876." Augustus A. Adams took out this patent and an Adams advertisement in *The Crockery and Glass Journal* for January 4, 1877, uses the same words: "German Flint and Opal Pressed Groove Top Lamps — Foot and Bowl in One Solid Piece." An 1881 Atterbury catalogue advertises a one-piece pressed lamp (*345*) called the "Boss Lamp." This, the Atterburys attested, was "the strongest lamp in the market with oil drip and flange complete. We make these lamps with Crystal or Opal Tops. No breakage in transportation."

346 A good example of a table lamp of the 1870s is the Dewdrop and Star, H. 7½". Campbell, Jones & Co. designed this pattern. *Collection of Mr. and Mrs. Robert Eckhardt.*

The "no breakage" phrase with an assurance of good packing might have helped a salesman, but there was no guarantee of safe arrival. An 1864 McKee catalogue states, "As we have our glass put up by experienced packers, in the most neat and careful manner, We Make no Allowances for Breakage, Bills of Lading being a guarantee of good order when shipped." McKee suggests that shipments be insured and indicates that a low rate is available. Packing was obviously a key element in the distribution of the product. One Ripley & Company packer in the 1870s put through 300 barrels a week at 9 cents a barrel. His $27 received in wages represented substantial pay for glasshouse employees in that decade.*

Patterns, Shapes, and Revolution

A phenomenon not hitherto noted grew out of technical advances in lamp manufacture in the last two or three decades of the century. Lamps were not necessarily made in many of the pressed patterns then currently popular. If a collector thinks of the number of variations found in the Daisy and Button pattern, he will understand why it was more practical to increase the number of table pieces in a set (nappies, drinking vessels, bowls, and compotes) than to worry about lamps. Therefore manufacturers did not produce a lamp or a series of lamps to match each pressed pattern. The scarcity of matching lamps is apparent when one compares the sets of the 1880s with those of the 1850s and the 1860s.

In the 1850s and 1860s, manufacturers completed a number of pressed pattern sets, with two or more lamps for each pattern. The McKee catalogue of 1864 pictures or lists the following patterns used for lamps:

3 Ribbed Leaf (Bellflower)	1 Argus	1 Prism
2 Stedman	1 Star & Concave	1 Ring
2 Tulip	1 Gaines	2 Vine

* *The Crockery and Glass Journal,* December 1879.

2 Sprig	2 Ribbed	1 Turnip
1 Cincinnati (Honeycomb)	2 Shell	
1 Star	1 Ellipse	

Such McKee standby patterns as Excelsior, Eugenie, Leaf, and Brilliant have no lamp pictured or listed, though lamps in those patterns have appeared.

Consider the change that took place over the next decade: the 1875 catalogues of M. W. Sackett & Company, 29 Wood Street, and J. P. Smith, Son & Company do not even name a pattern; the forty-nine page Bakewell, Pears catalogue, undated but about 1875, does not picture a single lamp.

The table below from three McKee catalogues shows the prices of lamps for the years 1860, 1864, and 1868.

In studying comparative prices of the three dated McKee catalogues we observe other points of interest. The twelve patterns listed under Pressed Assorted Large Pegs (1864 and 1868) represent those also used for large lamps and those the McKees considered most salable. Two patterns, Ribbed and Ring, sell for the lowest prices. There is a marked price spread between 4-inch and 5-inch footed lamps. The words "Colored Base" leave us in doubt. It would be easy to say they meant opal and jet. In offering Base and Stem only, the McKees specify by saying White Base and Stem and Black Base and Stem. So we deduce that the word "Colored" is used in its exact meaning. The contradiction is that very few pressed lamps of the 1860s in patterns named have turned up with colored bases.

Increased volume and improved technology account for steadily reduced prices. In the 1864

McKee & Brother 1860

Pressed Gaines for fluid	per Dozen		$6.07
" " " oil	"	"	6.00
" Plain Hand for fluid	"	"	2.75
" " " " oil	"	"	2.10
" Turnip Peg for fluid	"	"	2.00
" " " " oil	"	"	1.50

McKee & Brothers 1864

Carbon Oil Lamps	per Dozen		$3.50 to $11
Pressed R. L. (Bellflower) footed	"	"	6.25
" Argus- 4 inch colored base	"	"	8.50
" Gaines lamps 5 inch colored base	"	"	11.00
" Assorted *Large* Pegs	"	"	2.75
Chain, Cincinnati, Concave, Ellipse, Gaines, Prism, Shell, Sprig, Star, Stedman, Tulip, Vine			
" Assorted *Small* Pegs R. L. (Bellflower) Concave, Argus	per Dozen		1.75
" Assorted Small Pegs-Ribbed and Ring	"	"	1.70
" Ribbed Hand Lamp (no burner)	"	"	2.33

McKee & Brothers 1868

Carbon Oil Lamps	per Dozen		$3.00 to $9.00
R. L. (Bellflower) Footed	"	"	5.50
Argus 4 inch Colored Base	"	"	7.00
Gaines 5 inch Colored Base	"	"	9.00
Pressed Assorted *Large* Pegs (Same list of patterns as 1864)	"	"	2.20
Pressed Assorted *Small* Pegs (Same list of patterns as 1864)	"	"	1.60
Pressed Assorted Small Pegs (Ribbed and Ring)	"	"	1.50
Pressed Ribbed Hand Lamp (no burner)	"	"	2.20

347 The separation of bowl and font gave opportunities for many combinations. Metal bases held sway for a long time. Elaborations were varied. Decorated round shades, frosted and etched, dressed up utilitarian lamps. J. P. Smith, Son & Co. catalogue, 1876, p. 75. *Collection of the author.*

No. 231 B. Height, 9 in.

No. 0162 B. Height, 10½ in.
Hexagon Bronze Base.
No. 232 B. Height, 10½ in.
Square Black Base.

No. 233 B. Height, 11½ in.

No. 234 B. Height, 11 in.

McKee catalogue, standing lamps are clearly made in two sections; the glass wafer joining the font and base protrudes noticeably. In the Atterbury catalogue of 1872, lamps joined in the same way show a less discernible wafer, seeming almost to be folded in. As soon as the methods of fitting pegs to sockets by plaster of paris or by screw sockets became practical, lamps could be assembled by the merchant, and the glass manufacturer was relieved of the two steps requiring a skilled glassworker.

With its separation from the standard patterns, the lamp business came of age economically; it was now a division of its own. Artistically, one

deplores the plainness of complete utility, but utility and one-operation pressing combined to keep costs and prices down and to expand the market for a household article almost as numerous — and as plain — as today's electric light bulb.

Variety and elegance were maintained in the parlor lamps and to some degree in hand lamps in the different sizes and combination of opal and jet bases. *The Crockery and Glass Journal* for July 5, 1877, noted that the Crystal Glass Company had opened an office in New York and that it intended to make a stir in the lamp line, having in readiness *two entirely new styles in five sizes.*

In earlier experiments with collars and joints,

348 The naturalistic tendency in Midwestern design appears in the child, the fox, and the grapes. The Tuscan influence also is still strong. Changes in the shapes of the bowls and shade are forerunners of later tastes. J. P. Smith, Son & Co., 1876, p. 74. *Collection of the author.*

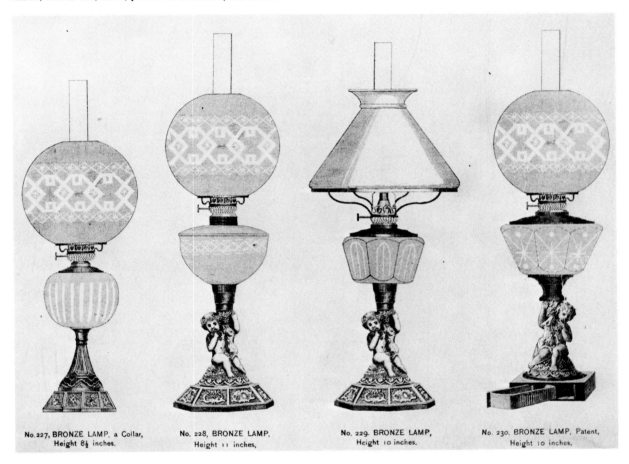

No.227, BRONZE LAMP, a Collar, Height 8¼ inches.

No. 228, BRONZE LAMP, Height 11 inches.

No. 229, BRONZE LAMP, Height 10 inches.

No. 230, BRONZE LAMP, Patent, Height 10 inches.

the use of iron, tin, and copper had a persisting influence (*347*). We have countless forms of metal bases — among them the women's figure, the Infant Samuel Praying (the foot in plain or opal glass, the figure kneeling on a jet base), and the child, fox, and grapes (*348*). Ripley offered a lamp with a blown bowl, the lower part frosted and engraved. The standard was the bust of a knight with helmet, visor raised. The Atterburys patented (February 1876) a glass lamp pedestal of a woman with flowing tresses and robe. Glass, however, could not begin to compete with the many decorative variations and minute details that were possible in metal.

The fact that metals played such an important role in wall brackets, chandeliers, and pendant lamps for library, parlor, and dining room may have influenced decoration of chimneys and shades. The form of the lamp was limited by the metal holders. It almost seems that the geometric designs of earlier pattern glass now imposed an inflexible limitation and severity. What has been considered the bad taste of the 1870s and 1880s freed draftsmen to experiment in metal design, much as they earlier had been freed to introduce naturalism into pattern glass sets.

Diverse artistic forces were at work — Heinrich Schliemann's excavations at Troy and Mycenae,

349 Increased use of metal is shown in these lamps. J. P. Smith, Son & Co., 1876, p. 77. *Collection of the author.*

J. P. SMITH, SON & CO.   77

No. 2. Patent Fount.

No. 238. Patent Extension Chandelier. Spread, 24 inches. Length, 33 inches.

No. 239. Bracket. 1, 2 and 6 Light. To match No. 242 Chandelier.

the stirring of Art Nouveau on the Continent, and waning Victorianism in England — currents from many lands and from the past and the present. The varied influences affected the many patterns of late pressed glass. They brought terra cotta figures and large iron vases and filigreed iron benches to yards and gardens. Glassmakers ordered rococo metal frames for their hanging lamps, and when they were no longer satisfied with metal trimmings, they fashioned enameled pedestals, hand-painted shades, and frosted and engraved fonts. Year after year, however, they held to one product on which they felt safe: plain glass lamps with plain glass chimneys, cheaply produced and widely sold (*342*).

Pittsburgh glassmakers had pretty well taken over the nation's lamp production by 1880. They were not modest about that accomplishment. "Pittsburgh," declared *The Crockery and Glass Journal* for January 1, 1880, "sends out some of the finest lamps to be found anywhere in the country, while, the etched and decorated ware is the wonder of the age." Today collectors of Eastern glass will question this accolade.

Two disadvantages of the kerosene lamp, however, had not been eliminated by the eighties. For example, a lamp explosion on June 2, 1879, at William Maxwell's glass label factory in Pittsburgh caused destruction involving a loss of at least $1500. The other limitation, odor, is clearly emphasized by an enthusiastic front page advertisement in the *Journal* for April 12, 1877:

L.H. Olmsted patentee and sole manufacturer, 81 Nassau Street, New York Little Harry's Odorless Safety Night Lamp.

It costs a fraction of a penny per night. The chimney and shade are combined in one. It is entirely free from odor while burning and is absolutely safe. It weighs 2 ounces. It will hold sufficient oil to burn 12 hours.

I don't wish to seem cynical about advertising, but it seems to me that everything Little Harry's lamp advertised was a phase of kerosene lighting that had not been effectively solved. I am old enough to remember how lamps smelled in the early twentieth century.

Few glassmakers could have known that Thomas A. Edison had been working to overcome these disadvantages. On January 27, 1880, he took out patent No. 223,898 for a lighting device that depended on an electric current. He had developed the first practical incandescent lamp. Its later development and perfection ended the extensive American market for the kerosene lamp.

350 Little Harry's Odorless Night Light. Front page advertisement, *The Crockery and Glass Journal,* April 12, 1877.

Vol. 5. No. 15.   NEW YORK, APRIL 12, 1877. $4.00 per Annum

Little Harry's Odorless Safety Night Lamp

Costs but a fraction of a penny per night to use it.

Chimney and Shade combined in one.

Entirely free from odor while burning, and absolutely safe.

Its weight is two ounces.

Will hold sufficient oil to burn TWELVE HOURS.

The Chimney and Shade are made from Porcelain Glass. The Oil Fount is made from Flint Glass. The remainder of the lamp is made of Brass. There is an aperture in the tube, through which a pin may be used to raise and lower the wick.

My Trade-Mark, LITTLE HARRY'S NIGHT LAMP, is blown in each fount. For sale by the Wholesale Trade generally.

Full size of lamp.

Full size of lamp.

Full size of lamp.

Full size of lamp.   Full size of lamp.

Patented in the United States, England, France, and Canada.

L. H. OLMSTED,

Patentee and Sole Manufacturer,

No. 81 Nassau Street,   NEW YORK.

351 A good lesson in burners. These could be a collectible item to challenge the most persevering and imaginative treasure seeker. *The Crockery and Glass Journal,* Sept. 1876, p. 13.

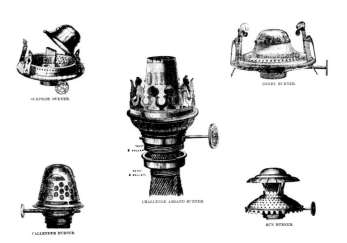

352 Lanterns were just as functional as lamps and considerably more practical. Bakewell, Pears catalogue, ca. 1875, p. 42. *Collection* of *Thomas C. Pears III.*

CHAPTER XVI

Directions of Pressed Glass

With us there is active competition for excellence. It is, however, conceded that James B. Lyon and Co. of Pittsburgh stand first. To such a degree of delicacy and fineness have they carried their manufacture, that only experts in the trade can distinguish between their straw stem wines and other light and beautiful articles made in moulds, and those blown by the most skilled workmen. When we consider the difference in the cost between pressed and blown ware, this rivalry in beauty of the former with the latter becomes all the more important to the public, as it cheapens one of the staple necessaries of civilized life.
— Deming Jarves, *Reminiscences of Glass Making,* 1865

The many technical improvements in pressing glass increased production, reduced costs, and created a strongly competitive market. The lime-soda formula perfected in 1864 by William Leighton, Sr., of Hobbs, Brockunier & Co. in Wheeling was outstanding among these improvements (see pages 42–45). Now the manufacturer had to catch the public fancy in order to sell his wares in volume, and the chemist had to make certain the glass kept its former quality. It was easy for them to compensate for the loss of lead, weight, and resonance by wide use of color, by frosting, by staining, and by etching. And so pressed glass moved into a period of countless patterns and of new kinds of decorations.

The designer took on an added importance. Besides being under the influence of the past, he had to be alert to what was going on around him. Consequently we see in pressed glass a strong kinship to cut glass design and also see attempts to copy, borrow, or adapt rivals' pressed patterns. There was a growing awareness, too, of French and Bohemian workmanship and style. But above all, the Midwestern manufacturer and the designer strove to be original.

The Borrowing of Styles

Two points should be emphasized here so that they need not be repeated in the discussion of the various designs: the competitiveness of Pittsburgh manufacture and the extent to which that competitiveness was expressed in the pirating of designs. The Western Flint and Lime Glass Protective Association promised manufacturers aid in guarding their own, but agreements between manufacturers apparently had little more force than did the authority of the patent office in respect to design patents. Collectors have long been aware of the common habit of borrowing of patterns, sometimes with token changes, sometimes not.

In the East, Sandwich and the New England Glass Company both manufactured Huber and

353 Smith patent, like Adams Plume, May 21, 1878.

DESIGN.

M. SMITH.
Glass-Ware.

No. 10,688.   Patented May 21, 1878.

354 Campbell, Jones & Co., Currant pattern, patented by Mary B. Campbell, April 11, 1871. *Collection of Mr. and Mrs. Robert Eckhardt.*

Flute. The New England Glass Company made a variation of Bakewell's Argus (Thumbprint) and called it Punty. In Pittsburgh Bryce Richards had advertised a heavier version of Punty. Catalogues from McKee and Lyon in the sixties and from Bakewell, Pears & Company and King, Son & Company in the seventies attest the popularity and longevity of Huber, Flute and Argus (Thumbprint).

Almond Thumbprint and Diamond Thumbprint show the free manner in which patterns were copied and altered. The Sandwich Plume clearly antedates Adams' heavier copy in Pittsburgh. Evidently it was a popular pattern, for Matthew Smith of Pittsburgh was granted a design patent of what looks like Plume (*353*). On closer inspection and on reading the patent, we see that the flutes on the plume of Smith's pattern are graduated toward the handles on vessels and toward one side on bowls. Thus Smith could call his a Shell design, as the flutes in the Adams plume are of the same size.

Collectors are always confused by different names for ostensibly the same pattern. Then they try to find marked differences as guides. Unfortunately those differences are often variable: Mc-

355 Campbell, Jones & Co., Currant pattern cake stand. H. 10". *Collection of Mr. and Mrs. Robert Eckhardt.*

356 George Duncan & Sons, Shell and Tassel, square, patented July 26, 1881, by A. H. Heisey. On the patent drawing two designs are shown, the frosted and clear effects being reversed. Shell and Tassel, round, was produced later. Portland Glass Co. also claims Shell and Tassel, ca. 1870. H. 7½". D. 8". *The Henry Ford Museum.*

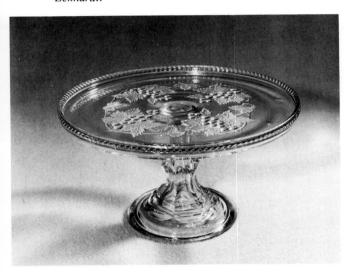

Kee Leaf and the Sandwich Loop and Petal, O'Hara Loop and Sandwich later Loop, McKee Sprig and Sandwich Ribbed Palm, McKee Comet and Sandwich Horn of Plenty, the Eastern Dolphin candlesticks and the Midwestern ones.

John Bryce of East Birmingham (Pittsburgh) patented a raised design of grape leaf, tendril, and grapes in October 1869. Four months later J. H. Hobbs of Hobbs, Brockunier patented a design of leaves, tendrils, and fruit, the word "grape" being omitted. Instead of the grape leaf raised as in the Bryce design, Hobbs planned the figures *in relievo.* Mary B. Campbell, wife of James W. Campbell of Campbell, Jones & Company, on April 11, 1871, patented a design of currants that had obviously sprung from the grape family and looks enough like it to confuse most nongardeners (*354, 355*).

Washington Beck evidently liked the McKee Brothers' Stedman pattern, for in 1874 he patented a design similar to it. The ridges or ribs in his pattern were narrower and more symmetrically related to each other than those in the McKee design. So that there would be no doubt that he had made a change, he added a row of beads as trimming at the top edges.

Shell and Tassel: Portland and Pittsburgh

The longevity of patents varied: design patents could run three and a half years, seven years, or fourteen years; mechanical patents lasted seventeen years. We run into the problem, therefore, of different factories manufacturing the same pattern, perhaps as pirates, perhaps quite legitimately.

For example, we have a mystery centering on two designs, "Tree of Life" and "Shell and Tassel." The first can be readily solved. William O. Davis, superintendent at the J. B. Lyon factory in Pittsburgh, was called to revitalize the Portland Glass Company in Maine in 1867. While there, he designed Tree of Life, afterward produced by Sandwich and by George Duncan and Sons, Pittsburgh. The Portland pattern is often identified by a fanciful "Davis" intertwined among the branches, usually on bowls and compotes, by "P.G.Co." impressed on the bottom of some pieces, and by wide family ownership in the Portland area.

In 1873, after the failure of the Portland venture, Davis returned to Pittsburgh to work for George Duncan and Sons. The bodies of the pieces of Duncan's Tree of Life are ridged like

357 King, Son & Co. (formerly Cascade Glass Co.) catalogue, ca. 1875, p. 12, showing a late version of Argus (Thumbprint). *The Corning Museum of Glass.*

358 Bakewell, Pears's Argus (Thumbprint), the original version, ca. 1845. *Carnegie Museum Exhibition, 1949–1950.*

359 The same pattern shown in the Bakewell, Pears catalogue, ca. 1875, p. 21. *Collection of Thomas C. Pears III.*

melons. Otherwise the pattern is the same. Davis undoubtedly had a hand in the design inception.

Collectors and students of Portland Glass have long claimed Shell and Tassel, though no documentary proof substantiates the claim. The shell in this pattern almost duplicates Davis's Tree of Life, so that there is a possibility that Davis designed it. On July 26, 1881, Augustus H. Heisey, George Duncan's son-in-law, was granted two design patents for Shell and Tassel, the difference being a variation in the frosted effects (*356*). In the second patent the corners are clear, whereas in the first they carry the Tree of Life branches. Much has been made of the polygonal shape of pieces versus the round. Mr. Revi thinks the round shape came much later. He agrees with Mrs. Kamm that an undated Duncan catalogue showing Shell and Tassel belongs to the middle 1880s.

Within the last few years, several Shell and Tassel compotes have been found in Maine with "Duncan & Sons" woven among the branches on the base of the compote in true Davis style. What part did Davis play? What Heisey? We must accept that Pittsburgh made Shell and Tassel, and by family ownership and records from glassmakers' descendants we can also accept the Portland attribution. Arthur G. Peterson in his *Glass Patents and Patterns* states that the official patent record and dates of the Portland factory convince him that the Portland claim is a weak one.

Dates and Attribution

Studying a piece of pressed glass from a pattern that had a long life forces a collector to depend on shaky generalizations. Consistently heavy pieces, those well filled and those whose metal has a strong lead content, are assigned to the late 1840s and 1850s. Such pieces were sometimes handled with a pontil rod, and so roughness marks the base. Sometimes they were even fire polished to smooth the edges or to eliminate fins left by a worn-out or ill-fitting mold. The cream pitcher in

360 Bakewell, Pears's Argus in a variety of forms.
Paneled base indicates earliest Bakewell production.
Decanter H. 11". *Metropolitan Museum of Art, Gift of
Mrs. Emily Winthrop Miles, 1946.*

361 King, Son & Co. catalogue, ca. 1875, p. 9. Bleeding Heart (Floral). On an old set and a new set. *The Corning Museum of Glass.*

Argus advertised by King, Son & Company (*357*) is clearly of the shape of the 1870s, while the Bakewell counterpart (*358, 359*), though it appeared in an 1875 catalogue, has straighter lines and narrower shape. The use of the same mold or of counterparts over a long period confuses us in any attempt to date a piece even approximately. Changes in stems, edges, and shapes, however, could exist simultaneously in the same factory, as attested by King's New Set of Floral and its Old Set advertised on the same page (*361*). These are not clear-cut enough evidence to be trust-

worthy guides to attributions of dates or — when a pattern like Huber is made at several factories — the source. Lura Watkins in one of her searches at the Sandwich dump found at least a dozen different mug and tumbler bases in the Huber pattern alone. Obviously, it is not easy for a collector of pressed glass to set up a generalization supported by irrefutable evidence that such-and-such characteristics of finial or base make a piece belong to the East or the Midwest. In the Pittsburgh area, the widespread acceptance of the lime-soda formula does help considerably in dat-

362 Cut Honeycomb decanter, blown goblet, and blown wine on a baluster stem. *Carnegie Museum Exhibition, 1949–1950.*

ing a piece. Though an article of pressed glass may have brilliance and clarity, if it lacks total resonance and weight we can be almost certain that it was made after 1864.

A standard practice in dating furniture and antiques, as we have said, has always been to attribute to an example the earliest date at which it could have appeared. Advanced students accept the word "circa" wholeheartedly, for they know that cabinet makers and other craftsmen repeated themselves. Between glass and furniture, however, there are quite different phases of evidence.

Suppose, for instance, that a walnut slant-top desk with ogee feet, overlapping drawers, and quarter columns were found in Eastern Ohio. Without specific information as to its origin, a dealer would be eager, and probably justified, to claim a 1780 date, though the piece could well have been made several decades later. We know that so-called Chippendale furniture appeared in the Northwest Territory after 1810, and that more Sheraton and Hepplewhite came still later. Choice of woods and gradations in style require careful study.

In glass, on the other hand, there may be little physical change between pieces made in 1850 and 1880. The Pikes Peak flask designed in 1859 was often identical with the flask McCully advertised in his 1875 price list. The Eastern 1831 eagle cup plate, if undated, would look in design to be of the 1840 period. We can assume that through continued manufacture it was indeed made after 1840. An owner, however, consistently (and understandably) will claim his plate was made in 1831. Changes pictured in the Cascade Glass Company catalogue for Floral (Bleeding Heart) are named the Old Set and the New Set. How can such pieces be dated? They certainly overlap. In standard patterns like Argus, Huber, and Honeycomb, collectors can note applied handles, fire polishing, shaping, and the character of the metal. Nevertheless, the longevity of a pattern causes uncertainty in dating and upsets the method of using the earliest date of production.

Influence of Cut Glass

The pervasive influence of cut glass patterns on pressed glass designs helped to establish early production, but it also pointed the way to the accruing heaviness and the overdecoration of the late 1870s and the 1880s. Huber represented the simplest form of transfer of design from cut to pressed — merely the unadorned panel. It was produced by Bakewell, the McKees, J. B. Lyon, Curling, Ihmsen, and Richards & Hartley. Flute repeated the panel, only here it was not extended to the top edge of the piece. It was produced by Bakewell, Bryce, Campbell, Jones, Curling, Duncan, Ihmsen, Lyon, and McKee (*363*).

Another plain pattern borrowed from cut glass design is Honeycomb (*362*), variously called Cincinnati, Vernon, and New York, depending on the width of the clear band. Bryce, Curling, Duncan, Lyon, and McKee found it consistently

Directions of Pressed Glass   341

363 Celeries from the hitherto unpublished James B. Lyon & Co. Catalogue, 1861, p. 13, showing pressed Cincinnati (Honeycomb). *Collection of the author.*

marketable. Bakewell, using the same design with slightly elongated honeycombs, called it Pitt Diamond. In the East, Gillinder, Sandwich, and New England Glass produced Honeycomb. Related to the Honeycomb design, geometric plain surfaces like Argus (both patterns), Excelsior, Colonial, Mirror, and even the later Oval Mitre indicate the use made of cut patterns. The concentration of more than twenty Pittsburgh factories set against the big three of the East supports the truism that the pressed glass industry had moved west. A Smocking sugar bowl with expanded diamonds and shaped to be larger seems to be a Pitt Diamond.

Panels and honeycombs — merely transfers from the simplest cut designs — admit all sorts of relationships to Ashburton, Bigler, Gaines, Genella, Leaf, New Orleans, O'Hara, Oval Mitre, Concave, and the other Argus. Colonial, Excelsior, and Mirror, also using plain surfaces, emphasize the debt pressed owed to cut glass design. Chasing down designs can be both entertaining and rewarding. Our task, however, is to set forth the main family lines. The next one is clearly the diamond.

The *plain* diamond and the *strawberry* diamond have long attracted artisans in cut glass and have

364 Ashburton, New England Glass Co. Various pieces in this pattern have appeared in the Midwest (Bakewell — Bryce — McKee). The trick pewter stopper is probably later than the decanter. H. 10½".
Metropolitan Museum of Art, Gift of Mrs. Emily Winthrop Miles, 1946.

365 Examples of Ashburton, vase. H. 10½".
Metropolitan Museum of Art, Gift of Mrs. Emily Winthrop Miles, 1946.

366 Excelsior: Creamer, spill holder, goblet, *Collection of J. Nevin Garber.* Eggcup, *Collection of Dr. E. R. Eller.*

367 Excelsior. The sugar bowl on the left, a variant, shows how designers altered their own patterns. Covered sugar, decanter, wine, *Collection of J. Nevin Garber.* Open sugar, candlestick, *Collection of Dr. E. R. Eller.*

competed successfully with the panel and its variation. The *cut* diamond, completely different from the panel, exerted just as strong an influence on pressed design. Called Sawtooth, Diamond, Sharp Diamond, Diamond Point, and Mitre, it was probably produced by nearly every factory. Except for the ware marketed by the New England Glass Company, coarser diamonds are a sign of earlier manufacture. Variations are countless, yet the pieces found in the Pittsburgh District should be more accurately judged according to lead or nonlead content of the metal rather than by the size of the diamonds.

At the J. B. Lyon factory the diamond was combined in 1861 with the panel in a stiff and heavy pattern called Crystal (*372*). The McKee Crystal of the same period does not show the same band of diamonds as that made by Lyon. To confuse the issue still further, Lyon called a pattern Crystal that enclosed a double X in one panel and three parallel upright lines in another.

The principle of using a band of diamonds or segments of diamonds for contrast carried over into the later naturalistic patterns like Adams' Wildflower, Barker's Jumbo spoon holder, and Deer and Pine, Lyon's Hand, Cosmos, and Acorn in Opal, and the very late Mountain Laurel from Wheeling's Central Glass Company (*376*).

We are much more familiar with the combination of Diamond with other geometric forms like

368 Page from the James B. Lyon & Co. catalogue, 1861, p. 11. The popularity of table and bar decanters is clearly shown. *Collection of the author.*

JAS. B. LYON & CO. MANUFACTURERS of FLINT GLASSWARE

Decanters & Bitter Bottles.

Quart Columbus, Plain.

Chicago Bitter.

O'Hara Bitter.

St. Nicholas Bitter.

Pint O'Hara Table, Pressed.

Pint O'Hara Bar Blown.

Columbus Cut & Engraved.

Quart O'Hara Table Pressed.

Quart O'Hara Bar, Pressed.

Pint Table.

Huber Press'd.

Genella Bitter.

Pint Table.

Cinti. Press'd.

Quart Huber Table, Pressed.

Quart Huber Bar, Pressed.

Huber Bitter.

Quart Genella Bar Blown.

Quart Genella Bar Cut Neck.

Quart Cincinnati Bar Pressed.

Cinti Bitter.

Quart Cincinnati Table Pressed.

369 Bigler, an early pattern made in both East and Midwest, ca. 1860. Lamp, H. 11″. Pair of goblets, H. 6⅛″. *Wadsworth Atheneum, Hartford, Edith Olcott van Gerbig Collection.*

370 1 — Pressed, paneled plate, amethyst, with sunburst center. D. 6¾″. ca. 1860. *The Historical Society of Western Pennsylvania, Violet Swem Brendel Fund.* 2 and 3 — Two plates pressed in the Bigler pattern, pale amethyst, ca. 1860. *Ex coll. Robert Carew.*

Directions of Pressed Glass   345

371 Page from the James B. Lyon & Co. catalogue, 1861, p. 15, shows the wide use of syrup jugs. O'Hara pattern, blown and pressed. Star and Concave is very similar to one in the 1864 McKee catalogue and one in the Ringwalt catalogue. The Gaines seems almost a form of pillar-molding. It was undoubtedly fire polished. Mirror shows an unusual design. *Collection of the author.*

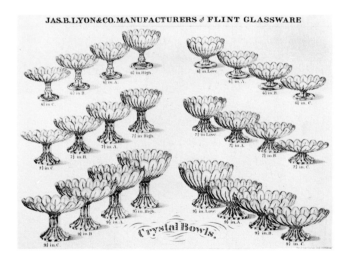

372 Page from the James B. Lyon & Co. catalogue, 1861, p. 9. Lyon called three different patterns Crystal. This page shows the surprising demand for pressed glass in the 1860s, as well as slight variations of stem and base.

373 McKee & Brothers catalogue, 1864. Note the pattern called Argus. Apparently this was never made in an extensive set like the Bakewell Argus (Thumbprint). The McKee Diamond differs from the Lyon version.

374 Campbell, Jones & Co. Dewdrop with Star, covered compote, H. 8″. Jenkins Jones patented this July 17, 1877. *Collection of Mr. and Mrs. Robert Eckhardt.*

375 Campbell, Jones & Co., Dewdrop with Star cake stand. Cake stands were popular forms in pressed sets in the Midwest. H. 9″. *Collection of Mr. and Mrs. Robert Eckhardt.*

Comet or Horn of Plenty and Tulip. Any number of later patterns like Adams' Moon and Star retained the spirit of the diamond design with a few diamonds to contrast with or relieve the main pattern. Bull's-eye with Diamond Point exemplifies the combination of Diamond with geometric forms. Pittsburgh has no right to claim exclusively the borrowing of cut glass patterns. Nevertheless, because of the active operation of so many factories in the Pittsburgh and Wheeling area, they practically set the style for the country's pressed glass during the last quarter of the century.

In addition to the diamond and the geometric figures, cut glass contributed reeding or ridges. No one thinks of Sprig, one of the earliest patented pressed designs, as having any affinity to cut design. McKee's Stedman; Bakewell's Etruscan, Prism, and Icicle (*378*); McKee's Prism and Gaines; Lyon's Star and Reeded — all with narrow panels or reeding like Sprig — emphasize the relationship to cut more clearly. McKee's Bellflower (Ribbed Leaf) (*379–381*), like Sprig, seems not to belong in this relationship, though it may have exceeded others in popularity if one judges by the McKee 1864 catalogue.

376 Adams Wildflower in amber, ca. 1875. One of the most successful of the naturalistic patterns. Produced in clear, amber, canary, blue, and light green. H. syrup jug 8″. *Currier Gallery of Art, Manchester, N.H.*

Directions of Pressed Glass   347

377 Pair of short, early pressed candlesticks. Reeded design on 3-tiered base. Both East and Midwest used this type of base, 1840 and later. H. 6¼". *The Henry Ford Museum.*

378 Bakewell, Pears catalogue, ca. 1875, p. 23. Three typical sets. Note relation of Icicle to McKee's Stedman. *Collection of Thomas C. Pears III.*

379 Three fine examples of double vine Ribbed Leaf (Bellflower). McKee & Brothers catalogue, 1864, featured this pattern. *Privately owned.*

380 Rare Bellflower pieces. Decanter is decorated on its neck with circle cuttings. 2, *Ex coll. Mrs. H. Hughart Laughlin.*

381 Examples of Ribbed Leaf (Bellflower), 1864.
Privately owned.

Influences of French and Bohemian Glass

Pittsburgh manufacturers and those in the East were both influenced by French design as well as by their own cut glass patterns. This is made clear in many of the advertising encomiums appearing in *The Crockery and Glass Journal:* "Duncan & Sons have a new pressed salt which is hard to distinguish from cut," "The Union pattern made by McKee in imitation of French cut glass is substantial and showy," "Duncan & Sons have brought out a plain goblet that will compare favorably with the best French shapes," "The Richards & Hartley new Set goblet and other pieces appear in a very artistic pattern on the cut glass order," "The No. 300 pattern of the Crystal Glass Company is handsome in shape, of a splendid quality, and heavily pressed in imitation of cut glass."*

* The Crockery and Glass Journal, October 28, February 27, September 15, 1875.

From the Centennial we learn that the pressed exhibit of Ripley & Company trod on the toes of cut goods, the glass being pure and of fine color, and that Richards & Hartley imitated cut wine glasses. Pitchers in diamond pattern, closest to cut, came from Crystal Glass Company. The Bryce-McKee Diamond Sunburst, patented December 22, 1874, which was no more nor less than a copy of cut strawberry diamond, was still popular. New York subscribed to the imitation cut idea. The Manhattan Silver Plate Company, large manufacturers of Britannia castor frames, advertised No. 2 and No. 3 five-arch bottles exactly like cut (*382*).*

Bohemian glass was as highly regarded as French. "Duncan & Sons' new set No. 150 is the closest and best imitation of fine Bohemian ware

* The Crockery and Glass Journal, July 5, 1877.

we have seen."* Naturally the real thing was in demand. C. F. A. Hinrichs, who called his building at 29–33 Park Place, New York City, "The Palace of Art," was one of the most active dealers in colorful imported glass. *The Crockery and Glass Journal* gave him its cover on May 6, 1875 (*383*), and wrote on June 10, "Table glassware as well as all kinds of Bohemian and Belgian glassware (of the finest as well as the cheaper class of goods) embracing rich Bohemian — cut and colored vases, toilet sets, coupes, and druggists' and perfumers' fine cut glass vials, a rare collection of antique and imitation glassware." (Hinrichs also had on view a collection of true antique glassware and of pieces made in imitation of antique and eighteenth-century glass.) Jones McDuffee & Stratton — for years the top china and glassware store in Boston — said that 139 cases of Bohemian ware were shipped from Hamburg for Boston via Liverpool and that the freight from Liverpool was less than that from New York to Boston. Thus foreign glass was invading the stronghold of Sandwich and the New England Glass Company. Pittsburgh companies never hesitated to copy the Continent. One article reads, "Large orders for Vienna colognes are being filled by Bryce Walker."†

Pittsburgh's Naturalistic Designs

What Pittsburgh and the Midwest can best claim in this period is that it was originating and popularizing naturalistic designs. Lura Watkins has written,

If one compares these patterns first with the designs of Cambridge and Sandwich, and then with those of the later Western glasshouses, one may observe the transition from the geometrical imitation-of-cutting styles of the Massachusetts flint houses to the naturalistic flower motives of Pittsburgh manufacture. These

* *The Crockery and Glass Journal*, October 18, 1877, p. 17.
† *The Crockery and Glass Journal*, June 10 and October 21, 1875; August 10, 1876.

382 Ripley glass pickle stand, ca. 1875, showing the popularity of using metal with glass. Mrs. Alice Metz in *Early American Pattern Glass* calls this pattern Cube and Diamond. *The Crockery and Glass Journal*, July 29, 1875.

PRESSED GLASS PICKLE STAND,
WITH SILVER-PLATED HANDLE.

MANUFACTURED BY

RIPLEY & CO.,   -   -   PITTSBURGH, PA.

SEND FOR PRICE LIST.

Union patterns partake of both characteristics. Here the elaboration of the earlier seventies arrives at conventionalized flower and leaf forms. When the trend reached a wholly naturalistic expression, the Union Glass Co. along with other Eastern manufactories was no longer interested in pressed tableware.*

"No longer interested in pressed tableware" — the phrase expresses a defeat that the Eastern factories suffered because of Midwestern resources in coal and gas, because of a cheaper and more flexible labor supply, and because of a steadily expanding and near-at-hand market served by better transportation facilities. The essence of that defeat lay in the unwillingness of Eastern manufacturers to accept and adapt the lime-soda formula to their needs, even though it lowered production costs. Lack of taste in Mid-

* Lura Watkins, "The Union Glass Company," *Antiques* 30, November 1936.

383 Advertisement from *The Crockery and Glass Journal,* May 6, 1875. A good chance to make comparisons in form and design between imported and American pieces of the same period. More elaborate etching and engraving are clearly noticeable on the imported.

384 Bakewell, Pears catalogue, ca. 1875, p. 45. Three pressed sets produced in opal. *Collection of Thomas C. Pears III.*

western design may reflect post–Civil War American taste. Even though Eastern manufacturers disapproved of the trend to naturalism, it is surprising they did not compete more actively for the tableware trade.

A critic of art may say that stylistic changes in general arts respond to conditions of civilization with which they come in contact. Glassmen across the Alleghenies were so responding. They were not engaged in abstract study of flowers, fruit, leaves, and animals; they were, rather, seeking a new medium of expression that would appeal to Midwestern families — to their experiences, their emotion of recognition. Natural objects presented through glass — a new medium — took on the charm of novelty. The glassmakers' object was simply to put sets of pressed glass on every table. They wished to overcome the sterility of geometric design. Their new artistic forms would suit an uncomplicated way of living.

Considered from this viewpoint, naturalistic patterns may not deserve the opprobrium accorded them by advanced collectors and students. Bakewell's Cherry, Bryce's Rose in Snow, McKee's Barberry, Adams' Baltimore Pear and Wild-

flower, Bryce-Walker's attractive Thistle and Strawberry, King's Maple and Bleeding Heart (Floral), Campbell, Jones's Currant, Atterbury's Sunflower and Lily — these all sold widely, and they all grace and do credit to the category of naturalistic patterns (*385–390*).

For centuries the grapevine and leaf have attracted artists, designers, architects, metalsmiths.

385 Adams & Co. Baltimore Pear (Gypsy), ca. 1875. A popular pattern produced extensively. Imperial Glass Co. has reissued pieces with the pear stained. *Collection of Mrs. Thomas G. Miller.*

Directions of Pressed Glass   353

386 Adams & Co. Baltimore Pear (Gypsy), ca. 1875. *Collection of Mrs. Thomas G. Miller.*

387 King, Son & Co. Floral (Bleeding Heart), ca. 1875. Covered sugar, H. 7¼". *Collection of Mr. and Mrs. Walter Simmons.*

388 King, Son & Co. Floral (Bleeding Heart), ca. 1875. Covered butter, H. 4". *Collection of Mr. and Mrs. Walter Simmons.*

389 King, Son & Co. Floral (Bleeding Heart), ca. 1875. Unusual variant of the cake stand, probably for desserts, H. 4¹⁄₁₆". *Collection of Mr. and Mrs. Walter Simmons.*

John Bryce took out a patent in 1869 for Grape Band and Curled Leaf and Vine Band. Doyle made Grape and Festoon with Shield and Grape and Festoon with Stippled Grape. King, Son & Company made Paneled Grape Band. In our century the D. C. Jenkins Glass Company of Kokomo, Indiana, and the Westmoreland Company of Grapeville, Pennsylvania, continued to make versions of the Paneled Grape.

A logical advance of naturalism would be the use of animals and persons. In the East, Gillinder carried on the tradition with Westward Ho and Frosted Lion. Thomas Atterbury patented for stemmed glassware a pedestal that held the head and shoulders of a beautiful girl. Perhaps the best known of the Pittsburgh frosted patterns is Three Face, designed by John Ernest Miller for George Duncan & Sons, patented on June 18, 1878. Family tradition — in fact, Mr. Miller's daughter — held that Three Face was designed for the Centennial, though no catalogue record that it was shown there exists. *The Crockery and Glass Journal,* however, praised frosted pieces. Supporting the 1878 date is a passage in *The Journal* of April 18, 1878:

A. Heisey of George Duncan & Sons is in the city. He brings in addition to his cheering presence a very handsome set of crystal tableware. The bowls of the stemware are in clear crystal, while the bases and stems are etched and decorated with female faces (three of them). They are said to be the likenesses of the three chief belles of Pittsburgh.

A correspondent of *The Journal,* in writing of Duncan's new and elegant styles, called his "Three Sisters" set one of the handsomest. Some spoke of Duncan's "Three Graces" (*391–392*). Whatever the name, the actual single model was Miller's wife, Elizabeth Bair of Steubenville, Ohio. In 1880 *The Journal* reported, "Mr. Ernest Miller, foreman of the mold shop of Duncan & Co., is perhaps the finest and most skillful moldmaker in the West. The ware put out by this firm is evidence that the mold shop is engineered by men of

390 Campbell, Jones & Co. compote, Currant pattern, 1871. H. 8½". *Collection of Mr. and Mrs. Robert Eckhardt.*

391 George Duncan & Sons, Three Face, patented June 18, 1878, by J. Ernest Miller. 1 — Biscuit jar is very rare. 2 — Covered compote with etching. 3 — Champagne glass. *Collection of Mrs. Thomas Jones, Jr.*

392 George Duncan & Sons, Three Face. 1 — Goblet with copper wheel engraving. 2 — Goblet with plate etching. 3 — Dessert with acid etching, ca. 1878. *Collection of Mrs. Thomas Jones, Jr.*

more than ordinary merit."* Miller, who lived to be ninety, became the dean of glassmen in the district. One marvels that such a sophisticated, strong design as his Three Face was produced with engraving added to the clear surfaces. In that respect Pittsburgh glassmen should not be blamed for the taste of the period toward over-decoration.

Thomas Bakewell Atterbury patented a classic statue in clear glass on February 29, 1876: a woman's head and bust as a pedestal for stemmed

* *The Crockery and Glass Journal,* January 8, 1880.

glassware. She could be the forerunner of Bakewell's Rebecca at the Well compote (*393*), 1877, a full-length frosted figure supporting the bowl. In 1875 appeared the well-known frosted dolphin balancing a clear shell bowl, long associated with Bakewell's designs. Duncan set a Tree of Life bowl on Frosted Hands. Whether or not these compotes ushered in Three Face, they indicated the rise of frosting and the boldness of pressed glass designers.

The Crystal Glass Company introduced in August 1879 a set No. 350 called Pinafore. An-

393 1 — Bakewell, Pears, Rebecca at the Well, 1877.
2 — Lion desk ornament. 3 — Bakewell, Pears, Frosted
Shell on Dolphin. *Collection of J. Fuller Trump.*

394 Comparative data between modern Fostoria and
early Bakewell — Rebecca at the Well compotes.
Collection of J. Fuller Trump.

COMPARATIVE DATA

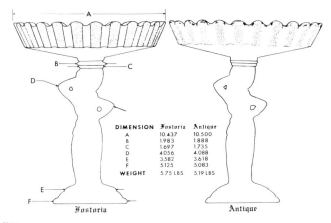

DIMENSION	Fostoria	Antique
A	10.437	10.500
B	1.983	1.888
C	1.697	1.735
D	4.056	4.088
E	3.582	3.618
F	5.125	5.083
WEIGHT	5.75 LBS	5.19 LBS

Fostoria   Antique

Notes
1. The scalloped edge, at the top of the Fostoria reproduction, has a flat and rather sharp edged cross surface, the Antique's scallops are rounded and polished.
2. The frosted ribbons of the Fostoria reproduction, average 0.080" wider than those of the Antique's.
3. The Antique has a concave polished surface in the center of the base. This polished surface is about 1.4" in diameter. The Fostoria reproduction does not have this feature.
4. The openings at the bend of the elbows are quite round in the statue of the Fostoria reproduction. In the Antique they are well defined and conform to the true shape of the arms at the elbows.
5. The frosted surface of the Antique is smoother than that of the Fostoria reproduction. This is perhaps due to the many years of handling while dusting or washing.

other of its sets named Queen of the Night embodies a handsome shape surmounted by a female figure. Dithridge & Company countered three months later with a mug to match Little Bo-Peep. It was known as Little Buttercup with Pinafore pictures inscribed. The La Belle Glass Company of Bridgeport, Ohio, brought out a salable pattern called Actress. In this set they depicted seven of the popular actresses of the day (see page 56). Some of the pieces would carry two pictures: the creamer had Miss Neilson and Fanny Davenport. In the later years of production the names were obliterated.

Blair and Zimmerman, then running Fort Pitt Glass, felt it a new departure to have its pressed tableware etched and embossed with very handsome pastoral views and floral motifs. They obtained from the Washington Beck mold factory a mold for an oval dish decorated with a hunting scene. The interest in stories and art of Greece and Italy had a marked influence on design. Bulfinch's *Mythology*, a standard work of entertainment and education of the period, furnished subject matter. From these influences emerged Gillinder's Classic and Classic Medallion, Atterbury's Medallion, Richards and Hartley's Cupid &

395 Three compotes with frosted bases. 1 — Hand with Tree of Life bowl. George Duncan & Sons. H. 15″. 2 — Rebecca at the Well, with a frosted ribbon bowl. Bakewell, Pears & Co., 1877. H. 16″. 3 — Dolphin with Shell bowl, Bakewell, Pears & Co. H. 10″. *The Historical Society of Western Pennsylvania, 3, Gift of Miss Mary E. Bakewell and Mrs. T. H. B. McKnight.*

Venus and Psyche & Cupid, and Sandwich's Minerva.

Animals, birds, and fish came in for their share of attention. They ushered in the many covered opal dishes of Atterbury, Challinor & Taylor, Richards & Hartley, and Westmoreland that made such themes common. Deer and Pine, of uncertain origin, was made in complete sets. Atterbury, Challinor-Taylor, and Bryce-Higbee used the owl for pitchers. Doyle fashioned it into a mug, and Bakewell into a salt shaker. David Barker, Pittsburgh glassmaker who later worked for the Canton Glass Company, designed Barnum's Jumbo (*396*). The spoon and fork holder carries many of the patterns and devices of pressed glass: frosting for the elephant, stippling under the small shoulders meant to hold the silver, bands of diamonds under the wide apron, and reeding on the stem above the apron and where it joins the base. Such combinations of design, common to the 1880s, indicate attempts to find a new idiom. Quite different from Bake-

396   1 and 3 — Jacob's Ladder (Maltese or Imperial) compotes on Dolphin Stem. These compotes are rare pieces in the set. 2 — Jumbo spoon holder. Patented

Sept. 23, 1884, by David Barker, who assigned it to the Canton Glass Co. H. 11½". *The Metropolitan Museum of Art, Gift of Mrs. Emily Winthrop Miles, 1946.*

well's frosted dolphin was an Atterbury fish plate; it had an opal center with the fish embedded and contrasted with clear glass shoulders. Before this well-executed piece, the Atterburys had patented fish-shaped glassware (June 4, 1872) — primarily for relish dishes. Most of the animal kingdom articles at this time were small, single novelties and remained so until the flood of covered dishes with every creature imaginable — from hens to swans, from frogs to boars.

None of these creatures, however, could claim the scientific accuracy that Charles Ballinger patented for McKee on October 18, 1870. Described as a flying dragon, the pattern employed a finial for covered pieces specified thus in the patent: "Shell of the snail, *conidae,* or *cerites* family or class, which is represented as lying upon another shell of the scallop kind of class." Most Midwestern naturalism achieved popularity more in broad and obvious strokes of a designer's hand than in details of scientific accuracy.

Tumblers and Jelly Glasses

Most factories owed their financial life to the commonplace daily commodities like tumblers and other drinking vessels, decanters, lamp chimneys, bottles, lanterns, drugstore furniture (the trade and catalogue term for apothecary's glass), and standard pattern glass sets. Novelties like female figures, classic statues, menagerie sets, and flying dragons had relatively moderate sales and many faded from the catalogues.

By and large, the design of the practical and commercial tumbler followed the Flute and Huber patterns, probably because Flute had been a standard pattern in cut glass. Every slight variation — the number of flutes and their height —

Directions of Pressed Glass   359

397 The Centennial Medal awarded to the Rochester Tumbler Company. *The Crockery and Glass Journal,* Nov. 16, 1876, p. 25.

called forth a special name. Bakewell, with its long-established Western and Southern trade, named its bar ware for cities and states, obviously in the hope of increasing sales — Richmond, Charlestown, Louisville, and Mobile; Kansas, Montana, and Frisco. As a bow to foreign competition, it gave the names Bohemian, Baccarat Punch, and Dublin Bar. The variation of flutes and grooves alone did not account for differences. The relative heaviness of the bottoms noticeably distinguishes one from another. One tumbler was called a Jigger, another was a specified container for Bitters, while *Schoppens* and *Weissbier* glasses were named among the ales.

One of the standard tumblers, the six or eight flute, has wrongly acquired the generic term Bakewell. Modern dealers and collectors no longer feel safe in applying that name to most cobalt and amethyst tumblers of this sort. The same kind of tumbler, however, is pictured in the McKee catalogue of 1864 and in that of Cascade Glass Company (later King & Son) for 1875. In the James B. Lyon & Company catalogue dated 1861, the first two pages picture tumblers and mugs. Not counting the mugs (merely tumblers with handles), I have found twenty-seven tumblers with flutes of various lengths and widths out of a possible sixty-three. The front cover of *The Crockery and Glass Journal* for May 6, 1875, moreover, shows imported Belgium and Bohemian glass, and ten of the pieces are the so-called

Bakewell tumblers. Finally, a half-page advertisement for the Rochester (Pennsylvania) Tumbler Company in the same issue uses two tumblers: one a Huber and the other a Bakewell Flute (*17*). After the Centennial, Rochester advertised its medal (*397*) and showed the same sort of fluted tumbler erroneously called Bakewell. We must accept in glass manufacture that well-designed and popular pieces in any functional area were copied by other factories.

Unfortunately, we have no Rochester catalogue, though that company turned out an enormous quantity of tumblers and though management spoke pridefully of an 1878 issue. The bulk of their tumblers was undoubtedly pressed, following the plain styles popular for bar ware. Colored patterns and matching patterns to go with sets would find a good market anywhere in the United States. References to cut and blown tumblers exist; some pressed tumblers that had received a good fire polishing could put modern collectors on the wrong track. John Oesterling, president of the Central Glass Company, Wheeling, defending pressed tumblers against those that were blown, warned the public not to be too dogmatic. "They were as thin as a sheet of paper," he said, "and as clear as crystal, also entirely destitute of any mold mark."* That is certainly no description of the ordinary fluted tumbler. It indicates, rather, the variety and the different sort of tumbler from the heavy pieces in patterned sets, and it shows that several lines could stimulate public demand and bring out quality products.

Closely related to tumblers and as commonplace, jelly glasses or cups became a standard product in many factories. Advertisements for these in the 1870s grew as competitive and as assertive as the best (or worst) of present-day advertisements. Atterbury and Company, owning various patents and with the indexical tin cover (*398*), seemed to hold the top position in jelly glasses, mainly because of its successful suit in

* *The Crockery and Glass Journal,* February 22, 1877.

ATTERBURY'S IMPROVED JELLY CUPS,

Patented Oct. 27, 1868, Sept. 1869, May 31st and July 19th, 1870.

THE MOST POPULAR JELLY GLASS IN THE MARKET.

Engravings Half Size of Original.

No. 1. Cup Screw Top.

No. 2. Cup Screw Top.

No. 3. Cup Screw Top.

No. 4. Cup Screw Top.

No, 5. Cup Footed Screw Top.

Index Cover.

With New Index Cover having 17 Different Names on for Jellies.

In using the Index Covers for Jellies, make a mark on the cover opposite the name of the Jelly that you have in the Glass.

To prevent Jelly from moulding, cut a circular piece of paper the size of the mouth of the Jelly Glass, dip the paper in alcohol, and place the paper on the top of the jelly before screwing on the cover.

PATENT

SCREW TOP GLASS COVER JELLIES,

Superior to Anything in Market.

THE ONLY

PERFECT GLASS COVERED JELLIES MADE.

Patented Nov. 22, 1870, and May 31 & July 19, 1870.

No. 1. Tall.
Glass Covered Screw
Top.

1875 against the A. H. Beatty Company of Steubenville. Atterbury claimed that it would immediately challenge other manufacturers of tintop jellies, but apparently it held its fire. A full-page ad in *The Crockery and Glass Journal* for 1875 indicates how important this phase of glass manufacture had become. The ad reveals varieties of form and the number of Atterbury patents in the field.

To suppress or divert other jelly glass manufacturers would have been a labor of Hercules for Atterbury. Adams & Company patented its "Queen Indexical Jelly Glass Tumbler" with a slipcover (May 13, 1873) and found it so popular that it followed with a "King." Doyle & Company patented what it called "The Original Tin Top Jelly" (July 26, 1870) and five years later boasted that it could not begin to fill all its orders. Crystal Glass boasted of an "Air Tight Adhesive Register Label" for its Crystal Jelly Tumbler. Challinor-Hogan advertised "Gem Jelly Tumblers."

In 1877 when the unions were planning their structure and trying their strength, they found jelly tumblers a good target. In the cycles of business, pressers would be discharged; then suddenly new men would be needed. Old employees and boys chose on occasion to embarrass the company by refusing to work. At Adams and Company, jelly pressers tried to establish that no company could make more than a certain number of jellies per week and that no new men could work on jellies.

Fruit and Vegetable Jars

The companion to jelly glasses — fruit and vegetable jars — started just as simply and functionally as the tumbler. Before the advent of pressed tumblers, the early blown jelly glasses with folded rims — sometimes paneled, sometimes with ribbed bases — were light and fragile and had no covers. The first preserving jars were the heavy aqua, green, and amber ones occasionally found at bottle factories, made perhaps merely to be taken to glassblowers' homes. Such jars required skin or parchment covers or a sealer for the contents. The use of tin and glass covers developed naturally to meet the needs of increased production. Before the Mason and the Ball jars were perfected, many Pittsburgh companies pressed a jar with a flat-shouldered neck in which a flat tin cover could be snapped by a ring. The Historical Society owns several marked jars (see page 229).

The Ringwalt catalogue for 1860 listed John L. Mason's pattern quart Glass Jars for $3 per dozen, half gallons at $4. Patent Screw Jars, not Mason's, sold for $2 for quarts, $3 for half gallons. The William McCully 1875 catalogue indicated the lowering of prices with the increase in demand. The McCully Standard Fruit Jar, groove ring with tin cap and wire complete, was listed at $9 per gross for the quart size, $14 for the half-gallon size. The McCully Dictator self-sealing fruit jar with metal tops cost considerably more — $16 per gross for quarts, $22.50 for half gallons. With glass tops the same sizes went for $20 and $28.

McCully advertised "Simplicity! Cheapness! Reliability! No necessity for buying high-priced Screw Top Jars. The Dictator combines all their good points and sells for 25% less." McCully also handled W. W. Lyman's Patent Improved Self-Sealing Fruit Jars with tin caps at $25 per gross for quarts, $30 for half gallons. Two sentences sound familiar: "With the New Opener, which is furnished without charge, any child can Unseal the Jar. We are the Exclusive Manufacturers for the Western Country."

Cunningham & Ihmsen evidently had an agreement to make the "Celebrated Mason Porcelain Lined Queen and Wire-Topped Jar." King & Son stated that it had "the Patent for Glass Covered Jars with gum rings protecting the contents from Loss, Impurities, Vermin, and also covers from breaking." Yet the Mason jar must have been the standard in East and Midwest. Homer Brooke,

399 Geometric pieces, ca. 1850. 1 — Covered amethyst sugar, H. 5″. 2 — Open amethyst salt. 3 — The covered amber sugar looks like a variation of the Ashburton pattern. The heaviness and plainness indicate early pressing. 1 and 2, *The Historical Society of Western Pennsylvania.*

the New York mold maker who received the highest award for excellence of workmanship and construction at the Centennial, estimated that he had made so many molds for Mason jars that they would collectively weigh some hundreds of tons.

Earlier jars with a wire clamp to hold the tin top frequently carried a deep groove, into which sealing wax was to be poured to provide an air-tight cover. One such jar with a circle at one edge bears the name "Beck Phillips & Co. Pitts. Pa." Three oval feet — ⅞ of an inch long and less than ⅛ of an inch high — support the jar. On one side of the body are the words "The Penn," one word below the other and measuring one-half inch in height. This South Side Company produced two other jars: The Pet and No. I. It has been surmised that the Beck member of the company was John Beck, who had originally come

Directions of Pressed Glass   363

400 1 — Loop (Leaf) compote possibly James B. Lyon & Co., ca. 1860, H. 6¼". *The Historical Society of Western Pennsylvania, Gift of Elizabeth Hyde.* 2 — Huber vase, amethyst, J. B. Lyon & Co. *Collection of Fred Mercer.* 3 — Loop (Leaf) covered sweet-meat, ca. 1864, H. 8¼". Both McKee and James B. Lyon in the Pittsburgh District made this pattern. The stem of this covered dish is not pictured in either the McKee 1864 or the Lyon 1861 catalogues. Factories often used several types of stems on the same pattern. Loop (Leaf) was also made in the East. *The Historical Society of Western Pennsylvania, Gift of the Pittsburgh Chapter of the Early American Glass Club.*

from Warren County, New Jersey. It hardly seems possible that he was the Pittsburgher, Washington Beck, inventor and mold maker extraordinary.

In 1884, Daniel C. Ripley, an astute Pittsburgh glassman, declared, "Jelly tumblers and fruit jars are the leaders in glass at the present. Pittsburgh makes comparatively few of the latter." He may have been blowing his own trumpet, for his factory manufactured both lines extensively.

401 Sugar bowl and creamer in Balloon, Heart Lyre pattern, unattributed. Good example of naturalistic design in lead glass, ca. 1875. Creamer H. 4¼".
Collection of Mr. and Mrs. Walter Simmons and Walter Simmons, Jr.

402 King, Son & Co. (Cascade Glass Co.) catalogue, ca. 1875, p. 10. Gothic pattern. *The Corning Museum of Glass.*

CHAPTER XVII

Ornamentation of Pressed Glass

Mention may be made here of a very ingenious American invention by which glass is cut or engraved by means of a jet of sharp sand being blown through a small orifice against the surface of the glass. By this discovery, which is of comparatively recent date, not only glass, but the surface of crystals, of quartz, and even of diamonds, can be cut speedily and at a trifling cost. We are not informed, however, whether this invention, known as *Sand-Blast,* is adapted to the production of very fine and delicate work.
— Industrial Art: The Masterpieces of the Centennial International Exhibition, Walter Smith, 1876–1878

The influences and economic advantages of the lime-soda formula on the glass industry may never be completely analyzed. One obvious but profound effect was the attempt to compensate for increased production of pressed glass in standardized forms by using color, engraving or etching, frosting, and staining. Modern collectors can see the range of colors found in sets like the Wildflower made by Adams and the Thousand Eye made by Adams and by Richards & Hartley. Staining appeared most widely in Adams' Plume set in XLCR (pronounced Excelsior) and in his Block pattern, and in Richards & Hartley's Block with Fan (*403, 404, 405*). Etching and engraving to embellish clear pressed patterns are registered less by the eye than are variations of color and staining. Nevertheless, they are worth more careful study than they have been given.

Feurhake's "Granular Surface"

Though copper wheel engraving has appeared on pressed patterns, it may be dismissed for the moment. The whole purpose of decoration in the last quarter of the century was to ornament the piece in a less costly way than by the work of the single artisan. Henry Feurhake, a publisher of catalogues and a printing engraver in Pittsburgh, epitomized the problem in an 1879 patent called "Improvement in Process of Preparing Glass Molds," issued to himself but assigned to Washington Beck, mold maker and inventor. Actually it reviews the glass industry practices of etching and sets forth a money-saving method of decorating pressed glass. Revived interest in recapturing the effects of stippling and in frosting had helped to direct manufacturers to what was designed as granular surfaces. Feurhake explained that ornamentation produced in the mold could be either over its entire surface or by a raised or depressed design or figure placed in the mold. "The distinguishing characteristic," he said, "is a fine granular surface, which partially obscures and partially reflects light, whereby a new and peculiar effect is produced."

A first response to the word "granular" would

403 Group of canary Thousand Eye glass, Adams & Co., ca. 1875. This appears in clear, canary, amber, blue, and apple green. Knopped finials and stems belong to Adams. Richards & Hartley made the pattern with scalloped edges of base and tops, wherever possible, ca. 1880. Note covered dish at lower right with scalloped edge of base. New Brighton Glass Co. later produced this pattern. Octagonal plate may be a late example. *Metropolitan Museum of Art, Gift of Mrs. Emily Winthrop Miles, 1946.*

404 Group of canary Thousand Eye glass, Adams & Co., ca. 1875. This appears in clear and standard colors. Note knopped stems. *The Metropolitan Museum of Art, Gift of Mrs. Emily Winthrop Miles, 1946.*

405 Excelsior (not the early McKee pattern) was originally made in clear by Adams & Co., ca. 1880. Doyle & Co. also advertised it. Later with red stain, it was named XLCR, Ruby Thumbprint, and King's Crown. It is found in clear with a gilt top, and with gilt, green, or amethyst thumbprints. A very popular pattern, it was often reproduced and is still being made today. 1 — Miniature creamer. 2 — Covered compote, H. 12½". 3 — Marmalade jar, no finial on cover. 4 — Rectangular salt. 5 — Castor set. *Formerly at the Bennington Museum, Bennington, Vermont, C. Kenneth Vincent Collection.*

be to think of the background of Bryce's Roman Rosette and Magic or perhaps of the surface of the Portland Glass Company's Loop and Dart or its oft-debated and much-produced Shell and Jewel. Feurhake probably meant as well a surface akin to our word "frosting," like Bakewell's Frosted Ribbon. The key to his meaning may lie in his specifying a "coarse" or a "finer" granular. He recommended a compound of nitric and fluoric acids for the finer; for the coarser he liked a standard mixture for general etching: pyroligneous acid five parts, alcohol one part, and nitric acid one part. At another time he spoke of engraving the mold by a sandblast when all portions of the mold could be uniformly roughened.

Methods of ornamenting glassware earlier than the Feurhake patent date embodied three general procedures. In the first, a stop-out varnish (asphaltum) or acid resistant was applied to a portion of the article. Then the unprotected portions were etched by application of hydrofluoric acid either in liquid or gaseous state. Dealers and collectors today are likely to assume that pieces roughened or frosted have been decorated in that manner. In the second method, the design formed on glass consisted of raised or sunken figures or a pattern of fine lines. The raised portion of the glass could then be obscured by the brush or wheel. The third way required the article to have a uniformly plain surface so that limited portions could be subjected to the wheel for purposes of ornamentation.

Feurhake admitted that these methods had produced good results but countered with the fact that in each phase of manufacture they required skilled labor, and that they also required treatment of the article after it left the mold. A main purpose of his patent was to eliminate or decrease the amount of such labor.

In mentioning brush and wheel, he accepted the fact that ornamentation would be useful and practical after the piece left the mold. His first step came in the preparation of the mold itself. Heretofore, after the mold had been dressed and polished, the design was cut or engraved on its interior surface by hand labor, much as a metal surface would be engraved. That procedure could produce designs with figures, but no amount of work could bring forth a granular surface. The nearest to a granular surface earlier in the century had been stippling, a main characteristic of lacy. Chipped by hand, lacy eventually gave way to bolder and coarser patterns. Periods of economic strain, the high cost of skilled labor, the steady advance of mechanical improvements, and changing tastes killed off the production of lacy after twenty good years.

In a period given to ornate and heavy design, granular backgrounds and frosting became popular. Whether Feurhake's patent first mechanized the granular surface is uncertain. W. O. Davis of Portland Glass had patented Loop and Dart, similar in its granular quality, in 1869. Bakewell's

Arabesque was marketed earlier than the 1879 of the Feurhake patent. Feurhake's process, however, admirably describes the treatment of the flowers on Adams' Wildflower and the leaves on Baltimore Pear. A. C. Revi assigns those two patterns to around 1874. Since no design patent for them has been found, they could have appeared later. We know that many experiments and trials took place before patents were applied for or were issued. It is entirely possible, therefore, that Feurhake and Beck merely crystallized a technique known to many factories, for in most of the naturalistic patterns of flowers and fruits, granular surfaces were needed — more for contrast with the smooth glass than for realism. As Feurhake describes the process of preparing the mold by the work of acid on metal, we note that the raised effect of figures and objects fits well into the patent specifications.

For the finer surfaces, Bakewell's Ribbon, Duncan's Three Face, and Adams' Moon and Star (Palace) are good examples. Students have always taken for granted that Three Face was etched by hydrofluoric acid, each piece then requiring special treatment. A Dithridge patent indicates how frosting could be done mechanically. A supporting vessel within the mold allowed the piece to be evenly immersed in an acid solution. Ribbon and Moon and Star could well have taken the frosted parts from the mold, as Feurhake advocated. A study of their contours, in fact, supports that conclusion. Augustus H. Heisey patented Shell and Tassel for George Duncan & Sons in 1881. A later version of the Tree of Life, it well exemplifies the coarse granular surface that develops from the mold and requires no treatment outside the mold. Glassmen today are inclined to believe that Feurhake's method of applying a protective coating to the mold fell into disuse; they point out that using paraffin to coat the glass surfaces not to be etched and then using hydrofluoric acid takes little time and probably was less expensive. Nevertheless, in September 1879, Fort Pitt Glass advertised "a beautiful line of ware" called "crystaloid," decorated in an

406 Prism ware. Engraved pattern No. 58. At left, patterns for engraving. Bakewell, Pears catalogue, ca. 1875, p. 43. *Collection of Thomas C. Pears III.*

elaborate manner by a new process called "crystalography." "It possesses the richness of engraved ware and can be sold little above the price of plain ware. Henry Feurhake, lithographer, and Washington Beck, mold maker, obtained the patent for this process."* Within two weeks Fort Pitt received orders from every first-class dealer in New York. Even if Feurhake's process for treating the mold did not supplant acid etching and sandblast, it was at least temporarily profitable. It is too bad that none of the many writers on pressed glass has yet identified *crystaloid*.

Designs in Etched Glass

When we compare etching to treating the surface of the glass in the mold to achieve the desired pattern, we are likely to make invidious comparisons. We envision the earlier, costlier, and undoubtedly more artistic copper wheel engraving, cut or abraded on the finished piece. Frosting, as in Gillinder's Westward Ho and in other all-over

* *The Crockery and Glass Journal,* October 30, 1879.

patterns, is not at all like the small engraved or etched designs applied to many of the pieces of any complete set of pressed glass. Nevertheless, frosting serves the same purpose as engraving or etching. If the effect was gained by the use of acid and not from the surface of the mold, the piece has as much right to the term "etched" as one ornamented with the delicate traceries and figures that embellished many of the otherwise clear-surfaced pressed sets of the 1870s and 1880s. As mentioned earlier, we marvel today that George Duncan & Sons should have thought a pattern as artistically sound as Three Face should need the additional ornament of what, in the narrower sense of the word, we call acid etching. In a collection of that pattern owned by Mrs. Thomas Jones, Jr., of Kennebunkport, Maine, we found four different designs in the etching. Three techniques *(392)* were clearly recognizable: wheel engraving, plate etching, and the use of hydrofluoric acid (see pages 369–70, 379 for definition of terms).

An etched glass set apparently increased an owner's prestige and helped the manufacturer to sell clear glass. George Duncan & Sons, for in-

407 Patterns for engraving at left. King, Son & Co. catalogue, ca. 1875, p. 21. *The Corning Museum of Glass.*

stance, in the spring of 1877 advertised fifty new "engraved" patterns. The Bakewell catalogue circa 1875 pictures eight designs from which the customer or the dealer could choose. The only pressed pattern in the catalogue shown with an etched design is Prism No. 58 (*406*). That design, not one of the eight pictured, is larger and heavier than the others — a sizable bunch of grapes with a leaf on each side, the vine to which they are attached running around the body of the article: a goblet, pitcher, or even a low pickle dish.

At this point, a confusion of terms should be clarified. When catalogues spoke of engraving,

408 Examples of engraving, frosting, and cutting, King, Son & Co. catalogue, ca. 1875, p. 22. *The Corning Museum of Glass.*

FROSTED & CUT
DESIGNATED

PATTERNS.
BY LETTERS.

they did not mean copper wheel engraving only, they also meant etching by acid, plate etching, and probably sandblasting. We must distinguish, therefore, between those methods and copper wheel engraving. Even Feurhake's patent does not clear up the uncertainty, though he did accurately use the terms "wheel engraving" and "etched by hydrofluoric acid."

The Corning Museum of Glass owns a catalogue of the Cascade Glass Company of Pittsburgh. Johnson, King took over that concern in 1869, but glass pictured in the catalogue undoubtedly was still being manufactured after

King absorbed the company, King using the name long after he gained control. Page 21 of the catalogue shows fourteen designs under the caption "Patterns of Engraving" (*407*). Besides these, five additional designs are displayed on various single pieces. Page 22 shows ten pieces with frosted bowls carrying designs wheel-cut through the dull surface (*408*). Above them a series of clear goblets and a covered compote have designs that are bolder but are still like the "engraved" (etched) ones advertised on page 22. Page 24 pictures a set of frosted Ribbon with Double Bars (*409*). Page 25 shows pattern No. 13 (the very

409 Frosted Ribbon, Double Bars. King, Son & Co. catalogue, ca. 1875, p. 24. *The Corning Museum of Glass.*

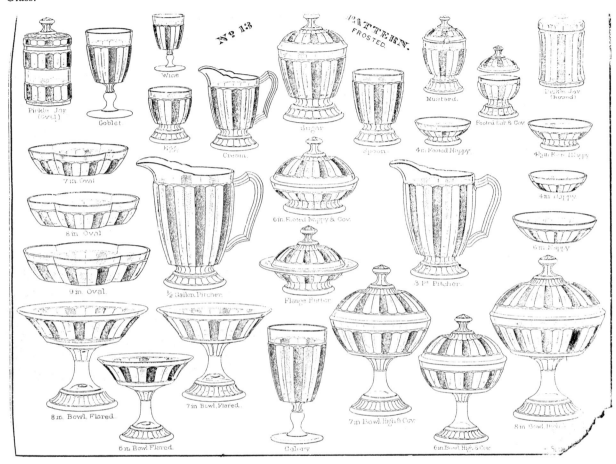

same one without frosting). What was the difference between the manufacturer's terms "engraving" and "frosting"? The answer lies somewhere in obscurity — among wheel cutting after the article was pressed, or etching by acid after the article was pressed, or a completed article from a mold that had been treated by a corrosive acid as intended by Feurhake's patent. The historical importance rests in the widespread use of etched decorations on pressed glass of the 1870s and 1880s and on the anonymity such use creates for plain goblets and compotes. Students try vainly to make attributions on the strength of etched designs that were copied, or were adapted, or came from patterns in other media, or were pirated. (Small designs like these were too numerous to be patented.)

The McKee & Brothers catalogue of July 1, 1864, does not picture a single pressed set with suggested supplementary engraving. True, most of the patterns consist of geometrical designs that pretty well cover the piece. There was little need for ornament; the taste of the period had not become jaded. The only reference to engraving in the whole catalogue occurs on page 12. A dozen Plain Altar Cruets were priced at $12, but en-

410 Table setting of pressed glass, cut and engraved, ca. 1875. Such sets could be ordered with selected decoration and family initials. *The Historical Society of Western Pennsylvania, Gift of Miss Helen Hecker.*

graved ones cost $20. A similar situation existed in an 1861 catalogue of James B. Lyon & Company (O'Hara Flint Glass Works). Water bottles (we would call them carafes) were advertised as Plain, Engraved, and Cut. No prices were given. It is reasonably certain that the engraving spoken of by McKee in 1864 and Lyon in 1861 meant copper wheel.

In an O'Hara Glass Company, Ltd., catalogue that is undated but has to be after July 1876, page 5 is given over entirely to finely etched designs (*411*). As in the Cascade catalogue, they are called "Engraved Patterns." Except for three tumblers, all the articles are goblets, and the twenty-one designs, which relate closely to those in the Cascade catalogue, do not duplicate them. The pressed sets do not offer enough room for etching. Yet Pattern No. 500, consisting of lines

that form rectangles and squares, has a covered sugar with an engraved flower and leaf in one rectangle and a leaf and berries in another.

A later O'Hara Glass Company, Ltd., catalogue, circa 1886, pictures a pattern named for Frédéric Auguste Bartholdi, in the news at this time for his 152-foot statue "Liberty Enlightening the World" placed upon Bedloe's Island in New York Harbor.* The Bartholdi pattern consists of a band of single Daisy and Button at the bottom of cylindrical pieces and another band at the top, with a plain surface in between. Then we see two more pages of the pattern with the plain band etched ("engraved"); a conventionalized spray with berries, blossoms, a realistic leaf, and two

* Bartholdi's statue was completed in Paris and officially given to the United States on July 4, 1884. It was reassembled on its present site in 1886 and dedicated by President Grover Cleveland, October 28, 1886.

wavy fronds. The next two pages picture the same set Cut and Frosted. Thus we have an exact parallel with the Cascade catalogue in nomenclature and product. After this the parallel ceases, since the plain band now appears stained in Topaz and Rainbow, the color a weak green. The same sequence holds for Patterns Nos. 725 and 870 without the Cut and Frosted. In the late seventies and

412 Bartholdi pattern, engraved. O'Hara Glass Co. Ltd. Catalogue, ca. 1885, pp. 24 and 25. *Collection of the author.*

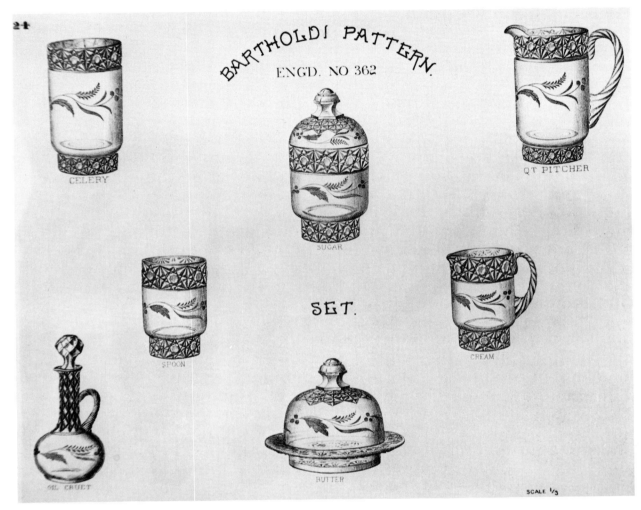

throughout the eighties, etching, frosting, and color were important — so important that sets were designed that needed additional decoration. It seems strange that one of the plainest of the pressed patterns, Mitchell A, B, and C, has not appeared frequently with etched decorations. One would estimate that this pattern was designed for the avowed purpose of using it as a blank for etched decorations.

An eager collector once wrote to the author with this very question of attribution through etched design. From the material she sent, it was clear that her piece would be identified by conformation rather than by the engraving or etching, which had been added. From the crude rubbing of fernlike traceries she supplied, I could find marked similarities to Adams' Saxon, Aetna, Dakota, Empire, Greensburg 20, Iona, Pressed Spray, Sea Shell, and Winona. In that group the design ran around the article. In the fern pendant I found a likeness to Barberry, Delaware, East Liverpool, Flower Pot, Lion with Cable, and

413 Bartholdi pattern, stained. O'Hara Glass Co. Ltd. catalogue, ca. 1885, pp. 28 and 29. *Collection of the author.*

Mosaic (names as listed in the Pitcher Books by Minnie W. Kamm). In both groups the similarities in the etched designs were strong enough to require careful differentiation. Copying and adapting for glass manufacturers were relatively simple. Decorators were not restrained by law or morality, and an accepted design meant a reasonably safe market for anyone who appropriated it. It disturbs me that northern New England collectors, for instance, automatically assume that a plain goblet with fern leaf etched or engraved on

it must necessarily have come from the Portland Glass Company. One of the lessons that advanced collectors, reputable dealers, and glass scholars soon learn is that a single piece of glass was not produced by one factory only at only one specified time. Rather than insist that a piece of glass is Sandwich or Bakewell, they should study the technique of the piece and its pattern, and they then can say, "Well, this type of piece was made in New England and at Pittsburgh." They should comment on the qualities of the specimen rather than lay claim to an attribution that cannot possibly be substantiated.

Henry Feurhake's patent makes us think about decoration added to pressed glass sets and what technique was followed. Certainly his advice on preparing the mold was a forward step. Hidden among the technical directives and chemical formulas for stop-out and corroding agents was this gem for collectors of cup plates, lacy, and early pressed pieces:

It is, of course, evident that in molds for pressing glass the plunger may be prepared in like manner as the mold, and it is here proper to say that it will be observed, in pressing glass, that the design imprinted by the plunger upon the article will, in all cases be much sharper, clearer, and more accurate than that imparted by the mold. This is due to the fact that when the glass is cut into the mold it is slightly chilled when it first comes in contact with the mold, and loses some of its plasticity at that place before the forming pressure is applied, for which reason whenever practicable I prefer in practicing my invention to reverse the usual practice that is, to form the design upon the plunger or its equivalent (pressing upside down) as the more plastic the glass at the time the design is imprinted thereon the better will be the results.

Procedures in Etching

An experienced and inventive glassman, J. E. Miller of George Duncan & Sons, identified the problem of etching and engraving by devising a mechanized way of adding the decoration and by describing his method in the patent explanation. He assigned his 1880 patent on a "Glass Engraving Machine" to the Duncan concern. He described the accepted way of etching — application of a stop-out varnish or beeswax and other substances, then removing a portion of the stop-out in order to trace the design, finally dipping the article so that the acid might act on the exposed design. The acid was neutralized by giving the article a bath in an alkaline solution.

"The operation of forming the figure or design upon the coated article," Miller said, "has generally been done by hand, and such work has involved, necessarily, a large amount of skill and is slow and tedious, and consequently very expensive. Certain machines have been devised for tracing lines up on the coated article, but their usefulness has been limited, owing to the extreme difficulty of obtaining more than a very limited number of movements of said tools."

Miller claimed for his patent an unlimited number of movements for the engraving tools and an even pressure of the tools on the coated surface. His patent represented the steady forward movement toward a mechanical proficiency found in all areas of glassmaking.

Two other forms of etching enabled craftsmen to reach a high degree of artistic proficiency. The procedure in the first, plate etching, was to print the pattern on stone or metal as in lithography and then transfer it to paper so that the inked design would receive the corrosive acid. When the thin paper was pressed against the piece to be etched, the uncovered section of glass was coated inside and out with wax. Sometimes more than one application was needed. The plate method was a quick way to etch intricate patterns needed for family crests and shields and an effective way to affix complicated patterns. Feurhake used the same principle in preparing a mold by fixing French onion skin paper to the mold interior. The inked design could be corroded while the rest of the mold was stopped out.

Needle etching, the other method, required a good draftsman. He traced the design with a needle or an equally thin tool through an all-over wax covering. A vaporized acid was then allowed to attack the glass wherever the thin instrument had registered the fine lines of his design, and the wax or paraffin was melted and washed off. Anyone who has examined the workmanship of one of Joseph Locke's story designs realizes how far removed from the commercial pressed glass etching of the 1880s is the work of a master artisan.

Sandblasting was used for design cutting as early as 1875. A paper with the pattern was affixed to the glass, which had been covered with gelatin or glue. Then through a tube, not unlike a nozzle gun, steam propelled tiny sand particles under strong pressure. The fine spray created equally fine "etched" patterns, but obviously the sandblast was most effective in instances where the all-over etched surface was required. How much the sandblast was used for mold design, as Feurhake implied, has not been determined.

Stained Ware

Pittsburgh in the 1880s was turning out enormous quantities of glass for all kinds of uses — about one half of all the glass produced in the United States. With increasing social niceties and the availability of glass for decorative table use as well as for functional household use, we might expect an improvement in tableware designs over those found in the 1870s. There was no such improvement. Manufacturers increased the number of pieces in sets and went in for units like lemonade sets, a berry bowl and saucers, a series of compotes and saucers of different sizes, and toilet (cologne) and perfume bottles. Harsh geometric lines replaced popular naturalism. Somehow the heaviness that accompanies the revival of severity removes the patterns from a close relationship with the plain but appealing so-called Colonial patterns. Yet Adams' Plume and Moon and Star (Palace), O'Hara's 500, Hobbs' Block, Duncan's Zippered Block, Central's Coin (Silver Age), Challinor & Taylor's Blockade — all these have strength. Perhaps the search for a new idiom and the traditional popularity of cut glass led designers on. Manufacturers cared principally for the popularity of their tableware product.

Even the brilliant cut glass of the eighties was losing its popularity with manufacturers. Ripley and Heisey, for instance, were pressing glass to imitate cut, then staining (painting) the raised surfaces and baking in the color. The cheapness of producing stained ware and its wide use in dressing up otherwise commonplace sets must have accounted for its popularity. The extensive collection of Mr. and Mrs. C. Kenneth Vincent, formerly at the Bennington Museum, attests to the popularity and abundant production of ruby-stained pattern glass. Most of the patterns originated in Pittsburgh and neighboring parts of Ohio and West Virginia; old favorites like XLCR, Red Block, Plume, Crystal, Crystal Wedding, Roman Rosette, and O'Hara Diamond reveal varied forms and indicate constant table use. The Vincents and Richard Barret, who have identified and pictured examples from the best-known patterns,* have done a service to modern collectors.

Less common than ruby, yellow staining as found in Amberette has risen in demand. George Duncan and Sons called it Daisy and Button Single Panel. They had taken up the patent issued to G. W. Blair, dated May 25, 1886. Plain vertical bands stained yellow divided panels of clear Daisy and Button. Later Alexander J. Beatty and Sons of Steubenville and Dalzell, Gilmore & Leighton Company of Brilliant, Ohio, both manufactured it. Amberette (or Klondike), with its vertical panels, is unlike Lyon's Bartholdi, which had a wide clear band running around the center of each piece, with the Daisy and Button above and below. Lyon used Topaz and Rainbow as standard colors, and in another pattern, No. 725 (Van Dyke), showed amber, dark pink, and a greenish blue. With the many Daisy and Button variations, and such patterns as Crossbar and V Panel, the manufacturer had the option of making the set in clear with the ornaments stained in color or of using pot metal (all one color) for the whole set.

The demand for stained ware, which had superseded flashed ware (colorless glass plated with a thin layer of colored glass), had begun to wane and pot metal was again becoming desirable. Streamlined production and improved marketing techniques possibly helped to bring about

* Richard C. Barret, *Popular American Ruby-Stained Pattern Glass* (Manchester, Vt.: Forward's Color Productions, 1968).

414 Ruby stain can be reversed — Crystal Wedding advertised by Adams & Co. and the O'Hara Glass Co. Ltd. in the 1870s. The pattern was reissued by the U.S. Glass Co. in 1891. 1 and 2 — Tumblers. H. 3¾". Pioneer's Victoria pattern was made in the 1880s and 1890s by Pioneer Glass Co. Several other companies named a pattern Victoria. 3 and 4 — Goblets, H. 6⅛".

The Florida pattern ("Sunken Primrose") was made by the Greensburg Glass Co. of Greensburg, Pa., ca. 1893. 5 — Tumbler, ruby stain, clear flowers. 6 — Tumbler, clear top, amber stained flowers. *Formerly at the Bennington Museum, Bennington, Vermont, C. Kenneth Vincent Collection.*

415 1 — "Tacoma" was made by the Greensburg Glass Co. of Greensburg, Pa., in 1894 and by the Central Glass Co. of Wheeling, West Virginia. Syrup pitcher, H. 6". 2 — "Snail" was called No. 360 by Doyle & Co., ca. 1885. George Duncan & Sons also made it, using No. 360. It was continued by the U.S. Glass Co. Tankard pitcher, H. 11½". 3 — "Broken Column with Red Dots" was made by the Columbia Glass Co. of Findlay, Ohio, ca. 1886, and by Richards & Hartley, Tarentum. The Pioneer Glass Co. varied it. Finally it was reissued by the U.S. Glass Co. after 1891 as No. 15021. Covered butter, D. 6". 4 — Adams & Co. made Plume ca. 1874 and continued until the U.S. Glass Co. chose Plume as a popular pattern in 1891 and produced it widely. This is not to be confused with the earlier Sandwich Plume of which only a few forms were made.

We find dated pieces of the Adams Plume in the twentieth century. Usually the plumes are horizontal. Vase, H. 7⅛". 5 — The Co-Operative Flint Glass Co. Ltd. of Beaver, Pa., brought out Ivy-in-Snow, ca. 1890. Around 1937 the Phoenix Glass Co. of Monaca, Pa., made it in clear, calling it Forest Ware. Between the two dates it was produced widely. Goblet, H. 5¾". 6 — Royal Crystal was made in a whole line of tableware. It is a late pattern. Tankard pitcher, H. 9½". 7 — Roman Rosette has been made by many factories. Bryce, Walker & Co. introduced it ca. 1875, though the Portland Glass Co., Portland, Maine, 1863–1873, also claims it. The U.S. Glass Co. capitalized on its popularity in 1892 and 1898, and issued it as No. 15030. Cream pitcher, H. 5¼". *Formerly at the Bennington Museum, Bennington, Vermont, C. Kenneth Vincent Collection.*

this change in taste. *The Crockery and Glass Journal* wrote on February 18, 1886, "Many manufacturers report that imitation cut glass is no longer the sure selling article it was a year ago. During the last few years it has been made in enormous quantities by every tableware house in the country." When Montgomery Ward prolonged the popularity, Woolworth's apparently joined the market. *The Journal* on August 7, 1890: "People who see glassware in a tea store or on a five-cent counter are not disposed to buy such things in a regular store, and many would not have them at any price. (Such sales) have cheapened the best pressed glass in the world."

Dakota: A Representative Pressed Pattern

One particular pattern — Dakota — furnishes us a case history of the last decade of the century: in style, ornamentation, attribution, quality, and technique. The fact that it was called Baby Thumbprint points to a previous relationship with Bakewell's Argus (Thumbprint). Dakota, with its heavier band of thumbprints imposed at the base of each piece, is a far cry artistically from the balanced thumbprints that cover Bakewell's Argus and that reflect a thousand eyes and blend into the whole piece. The influence of Dakota on later designs appears in Adams' Excelsior (Ruby Thumbprint), in McKee's Celtic, in Heisey's No. 120 (Punty Band), and in the Bellaire Goblet Company's Bellaire (No. 91). Ripley used the same principle — heavy band with indentations below a nail — on a show set for the 1893 Chicago Exposition. Bryce had made the original Nail set. Much closer to Dakota in design spirit, however, was Royal, produced by the Co-Operative Flint Glass Company of Beaver Falls.

The late Mr. and Mrs. William Guthrie of Harrisburg who, besides being enthusiastic collectors of Dakota, were eager students, started their collection in 1930. They established that most of the ornamentation on Dakota was copper wheel engraving. They averred that they had not found examples of acid etching on Dakota pieces. They did own examples with the design formed by sandblasting. Since acid etching is a chemical process and sandblasting a mechanical one, we should be careful to apply the term "etching" only to the chemical process of acid etching. The emphasis on color of ten years earlier had now waned. Design and extrinsic decoration were again coming into style.

Dakota has often been attributed to Doyle & Company by writers on pressed glass. Mr. Guthrie's documentary evidence that Doyle made the pattern, unfortunately, rests on a statement about a catalogue, now unavailable, published in 1887 by the Central Lithographing Company of Pittsburgh. Whether he once owned or saw this catalogue, he did not say. He believed, however, that engraved Dakota, Engraving Pattern No. 76, was being produced by 1880.

On the other hand, we have Ripley's advertisement in *The Journal* for December 17, 1885, for "the Celebrated Mascotte and Dakota patterns." No design patent for Dakota exists. That may explain why Ripley & Company was producing Dakota in 1885 and was proclaiming on July 24, 1890, in a full-page ad, "of all the lines in the market in the race for preference Dakota still leads." The featured piece was a 7-inch bowl and cover. How long had Ripley been making Dakota? The ad does not sound as though the product had been on the market for ten years. Changing tastes and the vagaries of a buying public would indicate that 1885 is a closer date than 1880 for the first production of Dakota.

It had been assumed that Ripley was allowed to manufacture Dakota only after the United States Glass Company consolidation in 1891. Under Factory F, which included Ripley & Company, ten pages of the 1891 catalogue were given to Dakota. It is hardly credible that United States Glass Company, because of the consolidation, simply took Dakota away from Doyle and arbitrarily assigned its manufacture to Ripley. Nor is it credible that the failure of Doyle in the middle

416 The three pieces of Amberette have bars stained light amber. Daisy and Button, single panel, patented May 25, 1886, by George W. Blair. On June 29, 1886, August Lang registered a design patent for the same ware and assigned it to George Duncan & Sons. Amberette was also produced by two Ohio firms: Dalzell Brothers and Gilmore and Alexander J. Beatty & Sons. The lamp with a brass stem and stepped marble base is a rare piece. H. covered compote 11⅝″. *Currier Gallery of Art, Manchester, N.H.*

417 Covered compotes in the Dakota pattern, 5″ and 9″. Engraved (or etched) in pattern No. 76. Dakota, long assigned to Doyle, was advertised in *The Crockery and Glass Journal*, Dec. 17, 1885, by Ripley & Co. The U.S. Glass Co. catalogue, 1891, showed Ripley as the manufacturer. *Ex coll. W. M. Guthrie.*

418 Cruet set with condiment bottles, ca. 1884. The side bottles are rare, particularly the one with the stopper. Etching is pattern No. 76. Dakota pattern. *Ex coll. W. M. Guthrie.*

419 Group of table pieces in Dakota etched in the Fern and Berry pattern, No. 76. Creamer, sugar, butter, and spoon holder. The footed spooner has a much shorter stem and a larger knop in the stem than appears on the goblet shown in No. 421. *Ex coll. W. M. Guthrie.*

1880s was responsible for Ripley's success with the pattern. We can agree, in any case, that no one should declare, without careful study, that a pressed pattern belongs only to a single factory. Documentary evidence should always be a starting point.

Ripley may have thought that the names of states carried magic, for in January 1890, he featured Idaho, plain and engraved, at least fifty pieces in a set, and received high compliments for it; and in September and October he followed with Wyoming and Montana. Adams and O'Hara selected Nevada, while Richards and Hartley chose Oregon. Pittsburgh manufacturers concentrated on the Western states, where there was an expanding trade.

When the Guthries were assembling their collection they found a normal flow of pressed glass in Western New York and the Ohio Valley — Kentucky, Indiana, Tennessee. The Dakota pattern was popular also in Wisconsin and Minnesota. The reduction in freight rates to the Northwest and improved rail transportation carried pieces westward rather than eastward where people had long valued traditional styles.

Collectors cannot expect Dakota to have a lead content, since Midwestern glasshouses had capitalized on the lime-soda formula. In general, they had forged well ahead of their Eastern competitors in technology. The clarity and vitality of most Dakota pieces is good. A letter from Frank Challinor to Guthrie would tend to dampen any collector's personal enthusiasm. "You will be floored," he wrote, "when you compare these prices per dozen with today's prices per each. And at these prices today collectors expect perfect pieces. If the truth were told, there aren't any perfect pieces. . . . They were made commercially good. Each piece was inspected and there were 15 or 20 flaws to look out for. As I understand, all those factories were money makers when they were running independently. Challinor

420 Dakota 8-inch cake plate with cover. Dakota was originally made without decoration. *Ex coll. W. M. Guthrie.*

421 Table pieces in Dakota: wine glass, nappy, goblet, tumbler, and footed nappy. Etched in pattern No. 76. *Ex coll. W. M. Guthrie.*

Taylor's dividend was 10% per annum." Under the conditions of mechanical production, management was content with a salable rather than a perfect product.

William Guthrie thought that most of his pieces were decorated by the copper wheel technique, only a few by sandblast. He would have been interested in a note in the March 7, 1889, *Journal:* "At D. C. Ripley's they are decorating by sand blast and then finishing the pattern by the engraving wheel." Guthrie noted that acid etching was not used. That is surprising, for after the Centennial, acid-treated surfaces became popular and economically practical, as Gillinder's Westward Ho and Duncan's Three Face well illustrate. By acid treatment, intricate and delicate tracery bands could be used at will. The Cascade Glass Company catalogue (page 21), the Bakewell catalogue (page 43), and the James B. Lyon–O'Hara Glass catalogue, ca 1876 (page 5) show what a variety of patterns for etching existed.

The so-called standard engraved pattern No. 76 was probably used on table sets and on such smaller pieces as tumblers, goblets, and wines. It consists of a single leaf, tendrils joining it to a spray of three berries. Variations in size of leaf and details can be expected from handwork of copper wheel engraving. According to Guthrie's notes, Doyle employed upward of 50 engravers. A statement in *The Journal* for July 18, 1885, indicates otherwise: "Ripley has the largest engraving department in the country, employing 30-40 skilled engravers." It is amusing how folk tales about Doyle and Dakota also fit documentary evidence about Ripley and Dakota.

Such large pieces as the three Dakota water pitchers (*422*) afforded scope for the imagination of designer and engraver; the swan, the bird, the insect and fern, and the butterfly and rose reflect their skills. A fourth pattern, the fish, appears also on the accompanying goblet. Much rarer than the others, the Fish pattern is listed in the

422 Three pitchers in Dakota with copper wheel engraving, well designed and executed. 1 — Butterfly with flowers and ferns. 2 — Swan with water scene. 3 — Bird and insect with fern and semitropical growth. W. M. Guthrie found catalogue numbers for engraved designs: No. 76 for the frequent fern and berry and No. 80 for the bird and insect on pitcher (3). No. 79 was a fish, not pictured here. So he theorized that butterfly with flower and ferns (1) and the swan (2) might be the missing pattern Nos. 77 and 78. *Ex coll. W. M. Guthrie.*

catalogue as No. 79. We may hazard a guess that the Swan and the Bird could have been Nos. 77 and 78.

The Guthrie collection included other water pitchers with whimsical or individualistic engravings: a stag, a buzzard perched on a dead tree, a spider with insects in its web, a crane wading to catch a small fish. Though engravers testing their expertise and satisfying an urge to create may have decorated these pieces to take home, a parallel explanation exists for such articles: in an increasingly mechanical age, customers may have wished and asked for designs representative of their taste and reminiscent of their own experiences.

This engraved work was superior to the flashed cranberry and ruby souvenirs then being sold at Atlantic City and at the various fairs held throughout the country. The Guthries never found a dated souvenir piece of ruby-stained Dakota later than 1891, though it would be safe to theorize that they must have been made after the U.S. Glass consolidation of that date. Four cranberry goblets with engraving like fern and berry, No. 76, are embellished with a cone or two. In the sandblast method the pattern consisted of a spray of oak leaves. The printed listing of Dakota from the 1891 Factory F (Ripley & Company) shows that engraving could be bought in 1891. We think that engraving ceased in the late 1890s, for the 1903 price list showed only seventeen Dakota items, none engraved. No 1896 list is available, and it seems logical to assume that engraved Dakota was indeed discontinued soon after the cartel was formed. Dakota is not listed at all in 1906. Though it was dropped, its importance should not be underrated.

F. Lloyd Bryant of Tiffin, Ohio, has reported that Doyle used a method of blowing and pressing in the manufacture of Dakota. The discernible mold marks on the base and the unbroken smoothness of the clear upper parts may lend themselves to his view, but obviously molds were used for the upper section of each piece and the

423 Sandwich plate with bail, one of the rarest pieces of Dakota. This piece was reheated and then given scallops. Etched in pattern No. 76. *Ex coll. W. M. Guthrie.*

424 Hotel butter and spooner in Dakota. The scalloped edge of the butter dish distinguishes it from the regular table butter. Etched in pattern No. 76. *Ex coll. W. M. Guthrie.*

Ornamentation of Pressed Glass   387

parts were joined. The top section may have been blown mechanically, for it is unbelievable that Dakota could have been fashioned laboriously by two hand operations. If so fashioned, it simply could not have competed with all the rival sets produced in one pressing operation. A worker may have reported in the early years of manufacture that Dakota was joined laboriously in two parts, but it is a safe wager that Ripley achieved production in one pressing operation.

There is always the possibility that pieces of a pressed set may have been worked over by hand. The very rare sandwich plate with attached bail (*423*) shows a scalloped edge that could have been achieved only by reheating and by fashioning. Ripley had patented a bowl with a bail like this one in 1884. The Hotel Butter and Spooner set (*424*) carries fluted edges to distinguish it from the regular set. It is impossible to predict what unusual variant may turn up in any pressed pattern.

What lessons does Dakota teach us? The answer lies in further questions. By what firm evidence may we claim that a piece of Dakota was made by Doyle rather than Ripley? How can we determine its actual date? What relationship of style does Dakota hold to earlier and later related patterns? Can we prove that it was blown and pressed? Are we sure that it was always engraved by the copper wheel method? Could it have been engraved by stone? Such questions should surely persuade all of us to study more and claim less.

CHAPTER XVIII

The Rise of Opal

The popular favor with which colored glass was received was a godsend to the trade and helped prolong the life of many patterns that would have been shelved long ago.
— *The Crockery and Glass Journal,* April 1, 1886

In the late 1870s, an American general named Alfred Pleasonton, brother to a more famous cavalry general named James, announced a stunning discovery: blue glass had medical and therapeutic value.

Others confirmed his discovery and the news spread. A Frenchman advocated sunbaths of up to five minutes under blue glass, and a citizen of Providence, Rhode Island, who tried it, averred that three baths of five minutes each had cured his rheumatism. A farmer claimed that a chicken hatched under blue glass feathered in two weeks. Florists reported that blue glass hastened the propagation and growth of plants. Graperies used it as an aid to artificial heat.

The blue glass craze swept New York, Philadelphia, Chicago, and even took hold in Boston. The Boston and Sandwich Company advertised, "Those who advocate the blue glass cure will find here lamp shades, tumblers, glasses, etc., of the most cerulean hue and equal in every respect to the rest of the goods." A great deal of the mazarine blue came from France, Belgium, and England. In Pittsburgh, Cunningham & Ihmsen added the blue glass so popular for medical purposes and offered mazarine blue at "extremely low rates." They pointed out that the manager of their colored glass department had served in Bel-gium for thirty years, and they advertised that customers desiring a fair price and a good article could do no better than to trade with such an old, established house.

Blue glass became a commodity to be speculated with, and the price spiraled to 50 cents a square foot, perhaps four times over its previous sales price. The Boston *Transcript,* as quoted in *The Crockery and Glass Journal,* February 22, 1877, editorialized derisively, "Homeopaths are shutting up their little cases, Turkish baths are at a discount, movement cures are waning in popularity, the regular school are generally disgusted, while glaziers and glass dealers are the busiest and happiest men in the community."

This curious minor phase of the glass industry stimulated chemists and designers to seek new directions to catch the buyer's fancy. The lime-soda formula, having lowered the cost of manufacture and debased the quality of glass, had forced glassmen to a wider use of color. Blues, greens, ambers, and yellows in pattern glass sets did not, in themselves, start the craze for the shiny surface of American opaque white glass. Their temporary popularity, however, did convince glassmakers that if they could find the right idiom they would do well to hold to it in spite of the waxing and waning of fashionable demand.

White glass was ready at hand — a vein waiting to be tapped and to lead glassmen to a gold mine called "opal."

A Clarification of Terms

To avoid confusion, writers on early white glass called it "opaque white," sometimes "milk glass." The height of its popularity came in the midnineteenth century with the success of the Bohemians and the French, who created delicate shades of color in it. These they called "opaline" because they were seeking the cloudy milkiness of an opal. In Yolande Amic's study of French opaline (1810–1870), she states: "Beyond 1870 it was devoid of artistic interest."*

American glassmakers of the seventies designated milk glass in their catalogues by the term "opal" (workmen pronounced it *opal'*). We shall use opal synonymously with "opaque white" and "milk glass," the accepted names today.

Collectors and dealers perhaps rightly have reserved "fiery opal" as meaning opaque white that glows when held to the light and shows pale bluish where the glass is thin. Generally "fiery opal" appears in America on heavy early pieces with good lead content. It was not a commercial success. I know of no complete set of pattern glass in fiery opal.†

The English and the French agreed that alabaster glass (*pâte de riz*) had a grayish tone not unlike our off-color white opaques. Sometimes the surface may even seem granular. We have adopted the name "clam-water." From the eighteenth century through the nineteenth collectors and students will note variations in opaque white and will encounter different names for them.

J. Stanley Brothers identifies one such change by the use of cryolite (alumina) to increase the translucence of American opaque white. In speaking of early overlay he says: "The platings of subsequent specimens secured their opacity* from the use of the mineral (cryolite); the softer texture of earlier glass gave way to the *vitreous* appearance of later ware."† By the seventies alumina was hailed in America as making as great a revolution in opaque white as petroleum had made in lighting.

Opaque white had been at hand, in fact, for quite a while. Though Americans produced great quantities of opaque glass in the last quarter of the nineteenth century, they were neither leaders nor sole proprietors. Opal glass had been popular in Venice from the sixteenth century, in Germany from the seventeenth century, and in all of Europe in the eighteenth. Eighteenth-century glassmakers used milk glass in imitation of Chinese porcelain. Glassmen still hoped — vainly — that their opaque glass would replace porcelain tableware and luxury decorative articles.

In seeking to achieve a porcelainlike quality, the English had produced opaque white in the eighteenth and early nineteenth centuries. The big revival, however, came on the Continent from 1820 to 1870, where the Bohemians and the French perfected opaline, merely a slight improvement on and variation of several seventeenth-century formulas for opaque white. With the addition of coloring agents, glassmakers could achieve any shade that would appeal to a buyer's heart. Yolande Amic expresses it well on page 11 of her book on French opaline:

Ladies were given as New Year's gifts lots of colored crystal in milk white called opal; in rose called hydrangea; in blue called turquoise; and in green called emerald. This crystal for the most part was fashioned into vases, baskets without handles (often as in a wicker basket), other baskets, matchholders and vases for violets. The taste for the day, for some time, was settled on objects in opaline crystal.

* Yolande Amic, *L'Opaline Française au XIX Siècle,* Paris, Librairie Grund, 1952, p. 12.
† A dominant French glassmaker, Georges Bontemps, preferred crystal white with orange lights like the opal stone rather than milk white. Accordingly we should be guarded in generalizations about Bristol being milk white and American being fiery opal.

* A seeming contradiction: cryolite to increase the translucence and also to strengthen the opacity.
† "American Opaque White Glass," *Hobbies* 40, July 1936, 69.

The opaline crystal had been prepared from a formula as old as those set forth in Antonio Neri's *L'Arte Vetraria* (1612): twelve pounds of aluminum silicate and alkali, two pounds of lime and lead and tin oxide, and one-half ounce of magnesium oxide. If the mixture was not strong enough in white color, a little lime could be added after the first cooking. Under this early formula, more than one heating of the melt was necessary.

Both English and Continental glassmakers had long used opaque white for air-twist stems on wines, and, of course, had practiced latticinio in moderation. A standard use of opaque white, however, had been for casing, overlay, and lining. American interest in opal had lagged. Trade opinion held that opal glass was extremely hard on the life of clay melting pots. Besides, American glassmakers had been too busy making window glass and bottles for a young country. For a while they had successfully emulated Anglo-Irish cut and engraved. The new country took the lead in pressed technique, and glassmakers soon produced lacy for use on sideboards and for informal entertaining. In general, however, they were not as concerned with nice decorative values as with functional use. Perhaps they felt it was more economical to allow uncontested imports of richly colored Bohemian ware, delicate French opalines, and British pieces with gold traceries and other costly handwork. The moment opal lent itself to pressing, however, the Americans became interested and with their ingenuity made opal serve many purposes: cup plates, salts, and plates. As we look back on nineteenth century glassmaking, we realize that development of the industry rested on a combination of many factors.

American manufacturers had a number of formulas developed to produce a satisfactory white opacity.* We can study at first-hand formulas from three important Pittsburgh factories.

* An undated English catalogue (ca 1870) ostensibly prepared for manufacturers gives twenty-two formulas for opal. Arsenic appears in every one in amounts from 6 ounces to 12 pounds, an average being about 4 pounds. Thirteen other formulas are called white enamel.

425 Atterbury and Bakewell formulas for opal, on Bakewell letterhead. *Collection of Miss Evelyn Evans.*

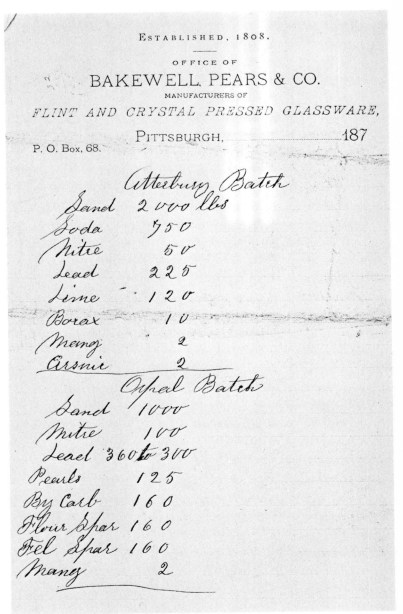

426 Crescent Glass Works, Thomas Evans & Co. formulas. *Collection of Miss Evelyn Evans.*

The Bakewell formula was proved and straight-forward in contrast to those of the Crescent Works, which, varied and glamorous, ushered in the novelty colors of the 1880s. The Atterbury batch probably represents one of the most successful, but may be only what Atterbury released to rival companies (*425, 426*).

Midwestern Cased Glass

It would be wrong to leave a discussion of opal without definitions of "casing" and "overlay" and without showing how vital opaque white has been from pre-Christian glass to the 1870s and 1880s in America. Loops, dragging, and marvering of white in the matrix of another color were popular in the earliest times around the Mediterranean. White and clear in combination have long appealed to glassmakers as being dramatic; the Venetians particularly employed the relationship successfully in their latticinio. The air-twist stems of English and Continental wines and overlay glass represent the most practical combinations of white and clear. All these techniques, however, require free-blowing and reworking.

In his *Curiosities of Glass Making,* Apsley Pellatt describes clearly the steps of casing glass. The gaffer blows a bubble of the lining color but removes it from the metal shell. At the same time, his assistant prepares a bubble of the next color layer, opening the end of his bubble or parison and widening it almost like a bowl. To steady and shape it, the assistant may insert it into the shell, or he may merely rest it on the shell. Now the gaffer blows his lining bubble into the bowllike aperture, and the two layers of glass adhere. The perfect fusion is accomplished by reheating in the glory hole.* Then the cased bubble is worked into its final form. If three or more colors are used, the process is repeated.

On the Continent and among American factories, cased glass is thought of as "overlay." The contrast of color, when the outer layer is cut

* Glass of the same specific gravity must be used to give the parts the capability of harmonizing — contracting and expanding equally.

427 Venetian style latticinio goblet, probably Germany, the Netherlands, or Belgium, late sixteenth or early seventeenth century. H. 8¼". *The Corning Museum of Glass.*

428 Looped white and clear witch ball, vase, pitcher. Possibly Bakewell. Note clear bases and handle. Pitcher is ridged, as some Pittsburgh vases are. 1840–1850. H. of vase 12½". H. of pitcher 6". *Yale University Art Gallery, Mabel Brady Garvan Collection.*

430 Midwestern cased sugar bowl, ca. 1840. Cobalt with bluish white lining. A fine example of early casing. Cover shows lining. H. 7¼". *Yale University Art Gallery, Mabel Brady Garvan Collection.*

429 Pitcher, looped with blue and red. Base and handle clear. Rim of pitcher is folded and threaded. Probably Wheeling, ca. 1850. H. 6⅞". *The Henry Ford Museum.*

431 Opaque white heavy compote with clear casing, ca. 1860. Loops and dragging in pale amethyst. Opaque white stem and base. Pontil is polished. H. 8⅛″. *The Corning Museum of Glass.*

432 Cased compote on clear baluster stem, yellow bowl with opaque white lining. Outer casing is clear glass. Ca. 1850. H. 8¼". *The Historical Society of Western Pennsylvania, David L. Browne Memorial Fund.* Pitcher, clear, cased over opaque white with loopings of pink, blue, and green. Handle and base clear, ca. 1870. *The Historical Society of Western Pennsylvania.*

through and the design figures are cut, makes us forget the basic steps of casing. Overlay glass is made by a process much simpler than the steps in casing. This term should describe the process of "overlaying" one color of glass over another color by dipping the blowpipe on which there is already a gather of one type or color of glass. It is almost impossible to achieve a thin third or fourth layer of glass over the two original ones by this method. This is essentially the difference between overlaying and casing glass.

Much of the midcentury cased glass of the Tri-State Midwestern area, however, was not cut and polished. The Corning Museum owns a compote

of amethyst, white and clear. The Historical Society in Pittsburgh has one of yellow, white, and clear. Other sequences must have been tried. Apsley Pellatt's book may have influenced artisans to experiment.

Since opal or milk white is a preferred color in casing or lining, one naturally thinks of Bakewell's Double Glass with its outer layer of white (see page 414). But Double Glass is mechanically pressed — not blown — and the outer layer of white does not completely encompass the bowl. The technique of casing ensures an enveloping layer of clear or another color.

The early cased sugar bowl with clear cover

433 Free-blown sugar bowl with clear cover and clear wafered stem, ca. 1830. Typically Midwestern in shape and treatment. Bowl is opaque white with clear casing. H. 7½". *Collection of the author.*

and foot (*433*) claims Pittsburgh and the Tri-State through its shape and galleried rim, not simply through its casing. One piece that became a small *tazza* with the rim turned down (*434*) could have been the prototype of the bowl. The heavy drinking vessel (*435*) is much later. The paneled fiery opal celery on the clear baluster stem (*255*) is an early piece, though the vase part is pressed but not cased. Such pressed flutes belong to both the East and the Midwest. Most characteristic of Pittsburgh are the cased pillar-molded celery, compote, cruet, and pitcher. Here cased glass was blown into a ribbed mold, manipulated, and then fire polished.

The technique of casing was used more widely in Eastern America than in the Pittsburgh area. Nor was it limited to white and clear. It persisted through the end of the century in vases, bowls, fancy dishes, and toiletries; we note it in the over-decorated baskets imported from England and copied in America. So we forget that cameo glass is cased, that the fine overlay in the forties and fifties is cased, that pearl satin and Peach Blow are cased. The cased examples from Pittsburgh show restraint and a pleasing simplicity of form untouched by Victorianism.

All Midwestern cased glass was blown, as was much of the European opaline. From 1828 on, we find examples of pressed opal (opaque white) and fiery opal in cup plates, salt dishes, and lacy pieces. Only a few individual pieces from well-known pressed patterns have appeared.

The Ihmsen sugar bowl (pages 302–3) was also made in opal, which fact fortifies the supposition that factories might duplicate their important individual pieces in opal. Fiery opal can be expected in early pressed pieces. In the last quarter of the century, however, it was superseded by opaque white prepared according to the formulas listed in the Appendix, page 483. We may find small pewter-topped perfume bottles, blown into a two-part mold, in fiery opal and in opaque white; paneled bottles of various shapes serving various purposes; and salt dishes — paneled, or lacy, or

434 Blown bowl on elongated clear stem with wafer, ca. 1840. Bowl is opaque white with clear casing. This piece is related to No. 433 and could easily have been fashioned into a sugar bowl. H. 4⅛". *Collection of the author.*

435 Heavy blown goblet on clear cylindrical stem, ca. 1840. Bowl opaque white cased with clear. H. 5¾". *Collection of the author.*

437 Pillar-molded opaque white compote, 8 ribs, on clear cylindrical stem and clear base, ca. 1850. Bowl is cased with clear. Pontil of base is ground. H. 7". *Picture courtesy of* Antiques. *Collection of the author.*

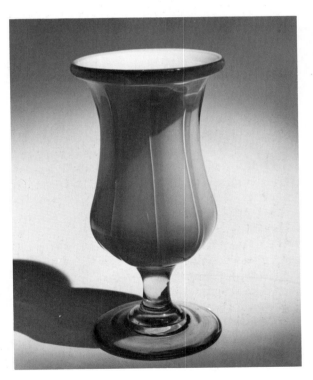

436 Pillar-molded vase, 8 ribs, on clear stem and base, ca. 1850. Opaque white cased with clear. Stem cylindrical. Pontil of base is ground. H. 10⅝". *Picture courtesy of* Antiques. *Collection of the author.*

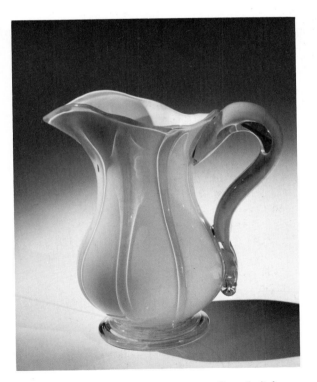

438 Pillar-molded pitcher, 8 ribs. Handle and pitcher, cased, clear over opaque white. Base is clear and pontil is ground, ca. 1850. H. 8". *Ex coll. Crawford Wettlaufer.*

439 Small bowl, clear casing over opaque white with coral lining. Clear baluster stem and base, ca. 1850. H. 4". *Collection of the author.*

440 Cased pitcher, ca. 1870. Lining slate gray, casing dark greenish gray. Handle and base opaque white. Rough pontil. Formation of handle indicates a late piece. H. 8¾". *Collection of the author.*

late lacy — in fiery opal and opaque white. Cup plates, which for the most part came before 1870, are far more often found in fiery opal than in opaque white. The early Pittsburgh market produced no strong demand for opal candlesticks. Religious candlesticks, however, appeared in the eighties in the catalogues of all milk glass manufacturers.

The White House: Atterbury & Company

One of the two great Midwestern names in opaque white glass is that of Atterbury & Company of Pittsburgh, founded around 1858 by Thomas Bakewell Atterbury and James Seaman Atterbury. Though the Atterburys had a reputation for novelty in forms and designs, their begin-

nings in opal were rather modest. An early patent for a lamp, 1861, describes one made in clear glass. Seven years later they patented the Eureka, a screw socket lamp, and in advertising it they described a clear bowl and an opal base comprising pedestal and stem (see pages 320–21). The popularity of the Eureka base brought prestige to pressed milk bases, and the Atterburys were launched on a line that brought them fame and profit. They continued as unusually successful lamp manufacturers, displaying fine hand and stand lamps. The standards for these would be crystal, opal, turquoise, and black.

Atterbury opal (milk glass) products were so extensive that only generalizations can be made. Their catalogues for 1872, 1874, and 1881 presented opal pieces in such well-known tableware

441   Melon with Net. A design patented April 23, 1878. Atterbury catalogue, 1881. *Library of the U.S. Patent Office.*

ATTERBURY'S PATENT MELON WARE.
PAT'D APRIL 23. 1878.
IN OPAL OR FLINT GLASS.

MELON SET.

MELON SUGAR & COVER
OR 4 IN TUREEN.

MELON BUTTER & COVER
OR 6 IN. TUREEN.

8 IN. MELON TUREEN & COVER.

MELON FLANGED BUTTER & COVER.

MELON CREAM.

MELON SPOON HOLDER.

patterns as Crossed Fern, Melon, Melon with Net or Paneled Fern, Lily or Sunflower, Prism, Reeded, Mirror, Basket Weave, and Medallion (*441, 442, 443*). These wares could appear in crystal, amber, blue, turquoise blue, and mosaic, but most certainly they would be produced and advertised in opal. Usually the term "Patent Opal Ware" was used. (Dr. Arthur Peterson, long a careful and thorough student of the Atterburys, believes that the word "patent" had nothing to do with the chemical formula used but referred rather to the design or technique.) Prism and Basket Weave had an Opal designation only. Sometimes only a few pieces of a pattern may have been made, as with the Fish pitchers, platters, and relish dishes.

Atterbury wins more attention in E. M. Belknap's *Milk Glass** than any other manufacturer of opaque white glass. More than forty Atterbury examples are pictured, and Atterbury is praised for the quality of glass and finish of the pieces.

* E. McCamly Belknap, *Milk Glass* (New York: Crown Publishers, 1949).

442 Fern — crossed fern with ball and claw feet. This pattern is also called Paneled Fern. Design patented June 6, 1876. Lily (often called Sunflower) was not patented. Atterbury catalogue, 1881. *Library of the U.S. Patent Office.*

FERN SPOON

FERN SUGAR

FERN CREAM

LILY CREAM

FERN BUTTER & DRAINERS
⅓ SIZE

LILY SPOON

MATCH SAFE WITHCOVER ON

LILY SUGAR

LILY BUTTER

MATCH SAFE WITHCOVER OFF

443 Medallion Pattern, ca. 1870. Fish (not made as a whole set), ca. 1874. Atterbury catalogue, 1874. *Library of the U.S. Patent Office.*

ATTERBURY'S PATENT OPAL WARE

MEDALLION CREAM.

MEDALLION SPOON HOLDER.

MEDALLION SUGAR.

MEDALLION BUTTER & COVER.

3PINT FISH PITCHER.

PINT FISH PITCHER.

MEDALLION MUG.

MOLL'S CAN

444 Atterbury's Prism pattern proved to be popular in opal. Atterbury catalogue, 1874. *Library of the U.S. Patent Office.*

445   Atterbury's Basket Weave as advertised in their 1881 catalogue. Patented June 30, 1874. *Library of the U.S. Patent Office.*

BASKET BREAD PLATE

EGG GLASS

½ GALLON PITCHER

3 IN BASKET NAPPIE

6 IN BASKET BOWL & COVER

INDIVIDUAL HANDLE SALT

8 IN OVAL DISH

7 IN CHEESE PLATE

446 Two rare Fish pitchers in opaque white pictured in the Atterbury catalogue of 1881. 1 — H. 5". 2 — H. 7". *Collection of R. F. Ferson.*

447 The Atterbury Rock of Ages bread plate is an example of inset centers to simulate cameo workmanship. The contrast of opal center and clear shoulders pleased the public. Patented Nov. 23, 1875. *The Corning Museum of Glass.*

Later students are more critical of both. A. C. Revi even uses the word "cheap."

Their novelties were particularly effective. One of these, a series of "Give Us This Day Our Daily Bread" platters, caught the eye with colored centers on such themes as Rock of Ages (*447*), the Three Graces, and the Fish (*448*). At first the shoulder of the plate and the center medallion were pressed separately, then joined by cement or fused at the same temperature. This method did not always produce a firm joining — modern collectors have owned Atterbury platters from which the center medallions have dropped out — and so Atterbury adopted the technique Bakewell had tried the year before in Double Glass. A ring plate placed in the mold created a space where the opal would be pressed to form the center medallion. Any one of the three Daily Bread platters with an opal center and clear shoulders is more dramatic but less artistic than the Bakewell double glass open bowl.

Thomas B. Atterbury seemed always to have the imagination and daring to depart from the conventional. No novelty can be claimed for his Basket Weave platter or ordinary Fish platter, both being completely opaque conventional shapes. In his Basket Weave set, however, he devised an open two-part salt with a pressed glass handle; and his much larger two-section horse-radish and mustard dish, with its separate tin covers, looked very much like a small market basket. Two other companies copied his Twin Fish relish dish. Even as they copied, rival glass-men called Atterbury visionary and distrusted his creations; they feared his novelties would start a trend and harm their sale of more conventional pieces. Atterbury himself was not above borrowing a favorite European pattern, Double Hands with Grapes.

Modern collectors have pursued Atterbury Ducks (*448*) so vigorously that the pieces have been reproduced several times, most recently from an old mold. Many Atterbury pieces carry patent dates, patent applications, or "Patent

448 Atterbury case at the Historical Society of Western Pennsylvania. Fish plate — Give Us This Day, ca. 1875. L. 12″. Ducks, patented Mar. 15, 1887. Boar's Head, Apr. 29, 1889. Bull's Head, July 17, 1888. Frog, ca. 1888. *The Historical Society of Western Pennsylvania, Gift as a Memorial for Sarah Jane Atterbury McGinley.*

449 Combination horseradish and mustard dish in the popular Basket Weave pattern from the Atterbury factory. It bears the patent dates of July 21, 1874, and Feb. 9, 1875. Largest size 9½″ wide by 12″ long. *Collection of R. F. Ferson.*

Pending" marks. On the ducks, even a patent mark or number is no longer absolute proof of early origin. The ducks were made in opaque, amethyst, turquoise blue, and green. Rock of Ages Centennial plates carry patent dates or a patent pending mark. Two table sets — Basket Weave and Melon with Net or Paneled Fern — frequently have patent dates. Pressed sets and novelty pieces were usually made in turquoise blue as well as in opaque white. The Owl, the Covered Rabbit, the Cat, and the Lion (all reproduced) indicated the patent, as did the Boat relish dish and the Double Fish — surprisingly, since it was not customary to bother with patent dates on such pieces. Such marks gave the collector security until the original molds were brought into use or unscrupulous copying began to be practised. The Imperial Glass Company of Bellaire, Ohio, playing fair with the buyer, places "I G" on the base of its Lion dish (made from an old mold). The brown flashed color of that piece, incidentally, never belonged to Atterbury's white or turquoise blue.

Prices of Atterbury opaque white reveal one reason why it traveled over the country. In the Melon set, forty-eight pieces (twenty-four of them with covers) went to dealers for $5.50, or 11½ cents each. Twin Hands and Grapes in opal, pink, or amber cost $1.50 a dozen. Molasses cans (we know them as syrup jugs or cruets today) cost $2.25 a dozen, only $1.50 in crystal. The Sunflower pattern, put up in sets of three designs, cost $7 for a dozen sets. The cheapness of Atterbury's glass is astounding. So is the small difference in price between opal and crystal. The famous Duck bar bottle cost $6 a dozen in clear, $7 in opal.

Certain characteristics of style in Atterbury plates and bowls carried over into bases on the Fox, the Lion, the Cat, and the Hen, Chick and Eggs covered dishes.* The Entwined Fish round dish and the Hand with a Dove square dish were made with lattice bases. For the bowls and bases of the dishes mentioned, the Atterburys designed a series of joined figures almost like little snowmen with arms upraised and tangent to the next figure. Although it looks like an open lattice design, the top consists of closed, inverted V's. Challinor & Taylor used the truly open lattice with tops of X's (*451*). Atterbury undoubtedly found the closed edge lattice as salable an item as did other milk glass manufacturers. The rounded top of the bowl is created by a series of parallel strips with open diamonds (Belknap, Plate 106b). The rounded top made an artistic contrast with the monotonous diamonds of the body. It is unfortunate that we have many examples of the Atterbury animals and so very few complete sets of the bowls and compotes in their five sizes, from 4 to 8 inches.

Challinor & Taylor

Belknap's *Milk Glass* credits Challinor & Taylor with ten important pieces, chief among

* Belknap, *Milk Glass,* Plate 144.

450 Milk Glass Covered Dishes, late 1880s: Ducks with amethyst and blue heads, the Rabbit, and the rare Boar's Head by Atterbury & Co.; the Swan by Challinor, Taylor, Tarentum, Pa. *Ex coll. John J. Grossman.*

them the dramatic Trumpet Vine Pinwheel (Plate 22), an Open Lattice (Plate 25), a Scroll and Eye plate, a Mother Eagle covered dish, and an Owl creamer. That allocation would seem to leave it far behind Atterbury. We know, however, that Challinor-Taylor flooded the market with opaque white plates, bowls, compotes, and novelties, including a variety of animals and birds. Indeed, anyone who studies the U.S. Glass Company catalogues of the period recognizes that the company was the runner-up to Atterbury in number and quality of milk glass produced in the Pittsburgh District. Their section of the 1891 catalogue devotes fourteen pages solely to opal. Two impressive table sets are pictured: Stylized Flower, or Flower and Panel (*452*), and their Number 418, a pattern in which diagonal smooth bars meet to form a herringbone, with four rows of fairly large round dots set in the panels formed by the bars. Both sets reveal an artistic restraint not characteristic of the late 1880s.

Challinor & Taylor's Farm Yard Assortment (*453*) is their best-known work: Duck, Hen,

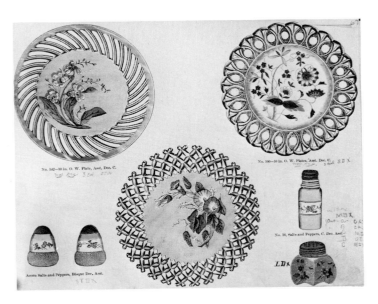

451 Challinor, Taylor & Co., Limited. Trumpet Vine, Pinwheel plate in opal. Morning Glory, Open lattice work plate. Field Flowers, Closed Lattice. U.S. Glass Co. catalogue, 1891. *Carnegie Library of Pittsburgh.*

452 Challinor, Taylor & Co., Limited. Flower and Panel, No. 23 in opal. No. 418 (diagonal smooth bars forming herringbone) in opal, ca. 1885. U.S. Glass Co. catalogue, 1891. *Carnegie Library of Pittsburgh.*

454 Opal novelties from Challinor, Taylor & Co., Limited, 1885–1895. 1 — Owl pitcher — small and large sizes in crystal, opal, and turquoise. Large pitchers in two shades of amber. 2 — Cobb (ear of corn) Pitcher — small size in dark green, large size in crystal, opal, and other colors. 3 — Match safe for large matches. It stood upright with a brace of its own. U.S. Glass Co. catalogue, 1891. *Carnegie Library of Pittsburgh.*

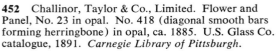

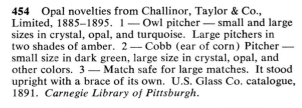

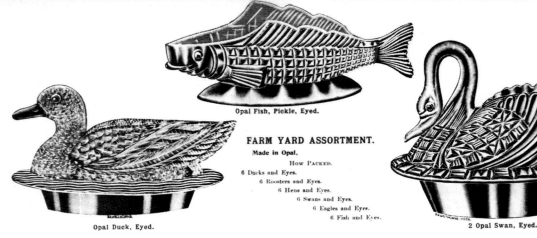

Opal Fish, Pickle, Eyed.

FARM YARD ASSORTMENT.

Made in Opal.

How Packed.

6 Ducks and Eyes.
6 Roosters and Eyes.
6 Hens and Eyes.
6 Swans and Eyes.
6 Eagles and Eyes.
6 Fish and Eyes.

Opal Duck, Eyed.

2 Opal Swan, Eyed.

Opal Hen, Eyed.

Opal Rooster, Eyed.

Opal Eagle, Eyed.

453 Challinor, Taylor & Co., Limited. Farm Yard assortment in opal. U.S. Glass Co. catalogue, 1891. Undoubtedly made before the 1891 merger. *Carnegie Library of Pittsburgh.*

455 Challinor, Taylor & Co., Limited, ca. 1885. 1 — Mother Eagle and Young dish. E. McCamly Belknap in *Milk Glass* considers this one of the ten best pieces of milk glass. 2 — Daisy and Tree of Life bowl. Three panels contain Tree of Life design, 3 others contain the Daisy. D. 8″. 3, 4, and 5 — Varying forms and sizes of Daisy pattern. U.S. Glass Co. catalogue, 1891. *Carnegie Library of Pittsburgh.*

456 Challinor, Taylor & Co., Limited, ca. 1885. 1 — Religious candlesticks in opal and turquoise. 2 — Open lattice footed bowl on funnel base. 3 — Closed lattice, large plate, opal and turquoise. 4 — Closed lattice bowl. U.S. Glass Co. catalogue, 1891. *Carnegie Library of Pittsburgh.*

Rooster, Eagle, and Swan, all covered, and an open Fish pickle dish. (The Swan is almost identical with Atterbury's version.) When these creatures were shipped, the eyes were packed separately. Glassmen never solved the problem of making the eyes of their animals, fowl, and fish stay in place. Consequently, it was more practical to ship them separately and let the merchants assemble them — at least, the merchants could not complain that X number of rabbits had lost their eyes in transit. Modern collectors often find animals with one or two eyes missing. The company was strong in such novelty products as salts and peppers and bureau ornaments. The opal Bull's Head, the Indian Face Match Safe, and the 8-inch Dog Dish (*454*) are typical examples. The base of the Dog Dish forms an interesting architectural pattern: twenty twisted rope bars topped by a narrow rope perpendicular to them, with a series of prisms as the pediment above. The individual Owl Creamer, Eyed, and the Cobb creamer show that a demand existed for two sizes. The large Owl piece, Eyed, is decorated with a cluster of leaves and six cherries. An unusual candlestick in turquoise or opal is a crucifix showing the figure of Christ supporting

the cross, on the top of which rests the socket of a candlestick.

Challinor & Taylor has never received adequate credit for its handsome floral bowls. These are low bowls, ribbed on the inside, one with a diameter of 8 inches, the other a flat-bottom, slope-sided nappy 4½ inches in diameter. The design was usually a daisy with vine and leaves; the best known is the hexagonal Daisy and Tree of Life, with three panels given to each pattern (*455*). Belknap (Plate 106c) does not attribute it, but the bowl appears in the Challinor & Taylor section of the U.S. Glass Catalogue, 1891 (page 49). The indented or crimped sides mitigate the stiffness of a perfectly round edge. Belknap attributes two very similar covered bowls to the Portland Glass Company. Because of copying and adapting forms and designs, attribution must remain uncertain, but in view of the marked similarity to the catalogued bowls, one may question whether the two Belknap bowls may not be Challinor & Taylor pieces.

The Lattice Edge closed bowl (Belknap, Plate 106b), attributed to Atterbury, is also shown in the Challinor & Taylor catalogue (*456*). Both companies, of course, may have produced the

457 Challinor, Taylor & Co., Limited, ca. 1885. Open-work compotes (fruit bowls) in opal. The standards of these compotes represent popular pressed patterns: Basket Weave, Daisy and Button, and Prism or Paneled. Though the base at right looks like a fine cut variant, Alice H. Metz calls it Sequoia. U.S. Glass Co. catalogue, 1891. *Carnegie Library of Pittsburgh.*

458 Challinor, Taylor & Co., Limited, ca. 1885. Open compote and salver. U.S. Glass Co. catalogue, 1891. *Carnegie Library of Pittsburgh.*

same piece. A Lattice Edge open bowl on a funnel base, also latticed, shows the vogue for open work. A series of lattice fruit bowls on patterned bell-shaped bases, though carrying late pressed designs, brings credit to Challinor & Taylor of a kind that has not always been accorded them. The Daisy and Button base and stem is called Diamond Foot (*457*). A similar compote is pictured in another Challinor & Taylor advertisement. The plain center of this bowl is decorated with stylized petals. The Basket Weave and Reeded (on *457*) are not named. Both were made in turquoise as well as in opal. The Shallow Diamond pattern is also called Diamond. An opal salver, plain cakestand with painted decoration comes in 9-inch and 10-inch sizes.

David Challinor, in his search for novelty of forms and for variety of opaque colors, improved the technique of combining colors. Mixing colors and working the parison had always been the job of a single artisan. Gathering a quantity of various colored glasses upon his blowpipe, he mixed them by twisting them together and finally blew the gather into a suitable mold. Challinor changed that procedure with his 1886 patent for the "Manufacture of Variegated Glassware." This called for different pots or tanks for each of the colors to be joined. When the melt reached the same temperature and the batch was in the proper state, the colors were poured into one pot, intermingled, and heated to the proper temperature. The glass was then blown or pressed. This was a forward step both in efficiency of production and in quality of product, especially where white was involved. Workmen had found it difficult to make the white adhere to the other colors.

Challinor's company favored mixtures of purple and white. Articles made showed beautiful wavy lines that resembled those in marble. Such striations, of course, were not original; they can be found in pre-Christian glass. Challinor's method, however, produced a more thoroughly homogeneous surface than anything that had preceded it. In the twentieth century, his product came to be known as Mosaic, Purple Mosaic, Slag, Purple Slag, Marble Calico, and End of the Day. The End of the Day phrase was inaccurate and unfortunate. Legends about workers experimenting with melts that were left over after the day's work have delayed students in learning the actual manufacturing steps Challinor set forth in his patent. These show how carefully he worked and how well he improved the product.

Challinor did indeed catch the fancy of late Victorian housewives and decorators with his Mosaic, and midtwentieth-century collectors have kept interest in his work at a fairly high level. He used Mosaic in many of the molds he had used for opaque white. Lattice edge plates, compotes on high feet, Horn of Plenty vases (459), covered dishes (460), swirled candlesticks, and small oddments for the boudoir table — all these dramatized the new mixture and created a public demand. The writer can remember a small, square Mosaic vase with a rounded pillar at each corner that always rested on the marble washstand in his Grandfather Sawyer's bathroom in Biddeford, Maine. It held toothbrushes.

Few glass collections today can boast an extensive set of Challinor Purple Mosaic pieces in matched pattern. Three such sets, nevertheless, were manufactured: No. 23, Stylized Flower (or Flower and Panel); No. 13, Fluted; and No. 28, Oval Set. Ruth Webb Lee's Sandwich Flute is probably the same as the catalogue's Fluted No. 13. Perhaps the real proof of the popularity of Purple Mosaic lay in the fact that the factory produced a hen sitting on a nest — a standby product in opaque white and turquoise but rather an incongruity in mosaic. Glassmakers wishing to equal the success of Purple Mosaic tried mixing other colors with white. Strangely enough, at that time they did not include turquoise blue, which was advertised as second to white in the opaques. They selected a brown or dark amber that shaded successfully and often weakened to a pleasant molasses color. Without doubt, the famous Holly Amber is a descendant of that marriage.

Sowerby's Ellison glassworks at Gateshead, England, manufactured pressed Mosaic pieces very like the Challinor & Taylor product. Sowerby's registered the patent of its pieces according to the shape of the mold (1877) rather than for the Mosaic metal. The factory had a line of turquoise blue and of cream in opaque. Their pressed opalescent seems much more like our light fiery opal. They brought out many lattice edged plates with basket weave centers both in blue opaque and white. John Ford of Edinburgh tried the Two Hands and Grapes dish that Atterbury and later American makers sold very cheaply. A collector should resign himself to the fact that a pressed form in opaque glass of the eighties and nineties may have had its birth in any one of many places. Since design patents ran out in three and a half to seven years, trade rivals could and did take over popular patterns. In the Tri-State District, many small companies, now nameless, undoubtedly produced milk glass patterns originated by the Atterburys.

Bakewell and Some Others

Other Midwestern factories, though not specializing in opal, found it profitable to make a few of its sets in milk glass or very rarely in colored opaque. Bakewell, Pears produced three handsome sets in opal — Rochelle (Princess Feather), Icicle, and Cherry. They also manufactured ordinary lines like smoke bells with scalloped edges, gas globes, and cone shades, and such apothecary ware as ointment jars, patch boxes, and mortars and pestles. They advertised double eggcups and syrup jugs, which were also made by other local factories. A plain bowl with a top and divider of Britannia ware was evidently a popular product, for Bakewell added to it a ridged bowl with a folding cover and double partition of metal — not unlike the Atterbury two-part basket. Atterbury, besides doing many sets, aimed for table use and novelty. Bakewell's aims in opal were much more limited.

Influenced by the popularity of opal and perhaps striving for novelty, Bakewell patented a new technique called Double Glass. The patent drawing depicts a small, clear, footed ale with pointed petals of opal at the base (named Boquet). In the Bakewell catalogue circa 1875,

459 Challinor, Taylor & Co., Limited, ca. 1886. Variegated or Mosaic glassware in purple and white, patented June 1, 1886, by David Challinor. Though Challinor, Taylor was the largest American producer, Mosaic glass was also made in England and in other American factories. Tall vase H. 7". *The Metropolitan Museum of Art, Gift of Mrs. Emily Winthrop Miles, 1946.*

460 Challinor, Taylor & Co., Limited, ca. 1886. Variegated or Mosaic glassware, patented June 1, 1886. Pitcher and covered butter in fluted pattern, Jenny Lind compote, ruffled bowl in Hobnail pattern. Serving plate may be English. Pitcher H. 9½". *The Metropolitan Museum of Art, Gift of Mrs. Emily Winthrop Miles, 1946.*

461 Rochelle (Princess Feather), ca. 1875. One of the few patterns Bakewell made in opaque white. The Princess Feather pattern is derived directly from lacy glass. Opaque sugar, H. 7½″. *The Historical Society of Western Pennsylvania.*

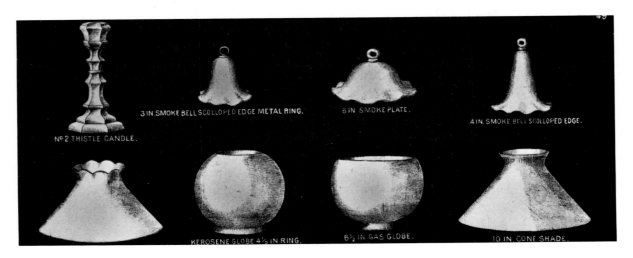

462 Smoke bells from the Bakewell, Pears catalogue, ca. 1875, p. 49. *Collection of Thomas C. Pears III.*

463 Bakewell Double Glass Patent, 1874.

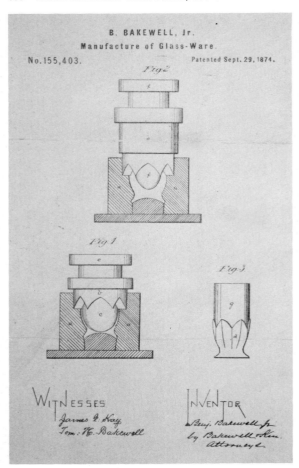

464 Bakewell, Pears, Double Glass bowl, made in three sizes, 8″, 9″, and 10″, clear and fiery opal. D. 9″. Marked on base, "Patd Sept. 29, 1874 B. P. & Co." This bowl was exhibited at the Metropolitan Museum of Art's Centennial Exhibition 1970. *Collection of the author.*

this piece is pictured on page 47 with three fruit bowls of different sizes but made in the same way. The bowls carry "B. P. & Co. Patd. Sept. 29, 1874" on the bottom. Any marked piece of glass is important, but these are doubly so for the way the fiery opal seems to encompass the clear glass and to be an extrinsic decoration. The fluted and gadrooned opal base in this bowl claims kinship with early silver, pewter, and woodcarving forms. It is a relationship often found in superior glass design.*

* Lowell Innes, "Pittsburgh, White and Clear and the Bakewell Patent." *Antiques* 79, June 1961, 557–59.

The Bakewells had undoubtedly followed the technique of an Atterbury and Reddick patent dated June 3, 1862: a device for using two layers of glass, one in petals like those on the Boquet ale. Both the Atterbury and the Bakewell pieces show how smoothly two layers of glass can be fused mechanically into a single piece. The Atterburys had also worked out a method of making the font of a peg lamp with the design on the inside. The plunger of the mold carried the design and the outside of the peg was smooth. If the maker desired, this inner surface could be smoothed also by the introduction of another layer of glass. The principle of Double Glass, then, really depends upon interchangeable and removable rings in the mold. Thus extra glass can be added.

The J. P. Smith supplementary catalogue for Lamps, Chandeliers and Brackets (September 1876) pictures hand lamps with opal feet and fonts, but with clear tops (*344*). These belong most closely to the family of Bakewell's Double Glass — particularly No. 17 on page 82. The Adams factory popularized an opal lamp with a clear top, patented May 9, 1876. Out of the groove top a clear shoulder rose to the brass

465 Double Glass bowls in the Bakewell, Pears catalogue, ca. 1875, p. 47. *Collection of Thomas C. Pears III.*

collar, so that one would think it an example of Double Glass.

The so-called Ihmsen goblet at the Corning Museum (*466*) has a clear bowl blown into a pressed shoulder base of opal, very much as one group of two-part opal lamps was made. In the patent specifications of Double Glass, Bakewell states: "I am aware that bas-relief glass-work has been united to the outer surface of blown glass-ware by first pressing articles of bas-relief and then blowing a glass article so as to unite therewith and do not claim the process." The late Frederick Carder said that the Ihmsen goblet was produced in exactly this way. The process described, he added, was one that he himself had used over many years.*

The other goblet pictured (*468*) with the attractive twisted stem has never been incontrovertibly attributed. Folklore among Pittsburgh collectors had assigned it to McKee before the discovery of the patent for Double Glass. Since it was made by the identical technique of the Boquet ale (*467*), we can logically assign it to

* The Atterbury Rock of Ages bread plate discussed on page 404 is not Double Glass. Cased glass, discussed on pages 392–96, is still a different technique.

466 So-called Ihmsen Goblet, ca. 1850. Clear top blown on opaque white pressed base, H. 6⁵⁄₁₆″. This differs from Double Glass, which is all pressed. *The Corning Museum of Glass.*

467   Double Glass boquet tumbler, ca. 1875. Clear on fiery opal pressed glass. Tumbler is pictured on Bakewell Patent No. 155,403. H. 4½″. *Picture courtesy of* Antiques. *Collection of the author.*

469   Dolphin candlestick in opaque white assigned to the McKee factory, ca. 1886. The 1864 McKee & Brothers catalogue pictures a dolphin candlestick: the base is round and flat; the candleholder is plain and joins the dolphin with a single wafer. The scalloping and petals give this piece a different tone. H. 6½″. *The Corning Museum of Glass.*

468   Double Glass goblet, ca. 1875. Clear and opaque white pressed glass. Bakewell. H. 6″. *Picture courtesy of* Antiques. *Collection of the author.*

Bakewell, Pears. The shoulders of the goblet strongly resemble those on the marked B. P. & Co. bowl. Even allowing for the ordinary pirating of techniques and design, it still seems safe to call it Bakewell. The opal on the goblet is milk white rather than fiery. The scarcity of examples of white and clear in drinking vessels confirms the belief that production was limited.

La Belle Glass Works at Bridgeport, Ohio, turned out work that departed from conservative lines in design and color, experimenting almost entirely in varieties of opaque. Harry Northwood, son of the great John Northwood of England, as manager of La Belle in the middle 1880s, was responsible for taking the factory in this direction. He continued his work after 1887 as manager and part owner of the Buckeye Glass Company at Martins Ferry, Ohio. In July 1890, the trade was talking about the display of richly colored and decorated glassware he was showing at the Monongahela House preparatory to the Pittsburgh

470 King, Son & Co. catalogue, ca. 1875, p. 13. Three pieces in opal. The clear glass molasses jug with Rose Medallion (extreme right) is blown-molded. H. 7¾″ with B. T. (Britannia Top). *The Corning Museum of Glass.* The McKee & Brothers catalogue, 1864, shows a blown-molded can from which this one may have been copied.

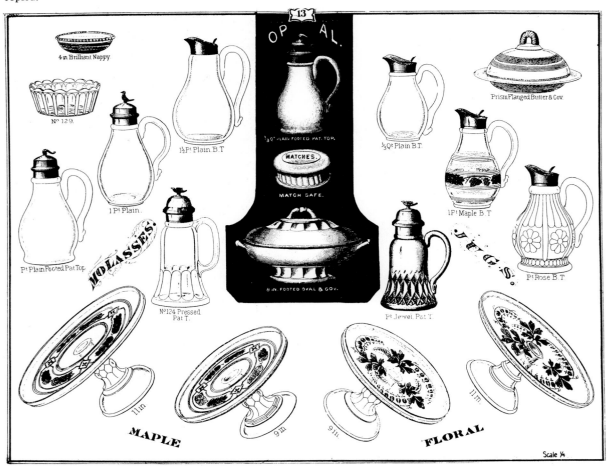

Glass Manufacturers' exhibit. Trained as a designer, mold maker, and chemist, he had a practical background for his work in opalescent, blue, purple, and opaque topaz. In the 1890s he successfully operated factories at Ellwood City and Indiana, Pennsylvania, until he joined the National Glass merger in 1900. By 1902 he had bought the old Hobbs factory at Wheeling, West Virginia, where he turned out iridescent Golden Iris, Pomona (sandblast method), and Florentine glassware. His various operations show how closely related glassmaking in the Tri-State area was. Northwood's influence on the development

and popularity of opaque and iridescent glass in this area can never be overrated.

Other factories tried a few tableware sets in opal. Adams did it with Fleur-de-Lis and Tassel, Pineapple and Fan, and Saxon. Duncan produced Duncan Panel and Swirled Column in opal. Though Ashburton was not a regular McKee pattern, the McKees may have produced single pieces in fiery opal. Belknap pictures a small McKee tray and assigns to that factory covered dishes with the patterns Horse, Turkey, Squirrel, and Lion. He calls these "split ribs" pieces — that is, the ribs do not run down in continuous lines.

The Rise of Opal   417

471 Opaque white mug, ca. 1875. Floral (Bleeding Heart). A good example of a variant that may occur in an extensive pressed set (in this case clear). H. 3¾″. *Collection of Mr. and Mrs. Walter Simmons.*

472 Pressed cruet in fiery opal, ca. 1860. Applied handle, pewter cover. Cruets like this were called molasses jugs or cans in catalogues. Ruth Webb Lee names a pattern almost like this Bull's-eye. H. 5⅞″. *The Henry Ford Museum.*

473 Early pressed pieces in fiery opal, in geometric designs, 1840–1860 — from the Carnegie Museum Exhibition, 1949–1950. 1 — Spillholder — Bull's-eye and Oval. 2 — Goblet — Argus. 3 — Compote — Colonial. 4 — Footed tumbler — Colonial. 5 — Small whiskey. 6 — Footed tumbler — Excelsior. 7 — Tumbler — Charleston.

McKee is also credited with an opaque dolphin compote on a hexagonal base. Twenty-five years ago, collectors generally attributed all opaque Sawtooth table sets to McKee. Most realize now that it is impossible to limit unsigned single or infrequently found forms of pattern glass to a certain factory. How can anyone be certain that a pattern as popular as Sawtooth was made exclusively by McKee?

A catalogue (470) of the Cascade Glass Company (King, Son & Company) shows only three pieces in opal: a reeded syrup jug, a matchbox, and an 8-inch covered bowl. Yet the Walter Simmonses of Grosse Pointe, Michigan, who own an extensive collection of Cascade's Floral (Bleeding Heart), unexpectedly found an attractive Bleeding Heart mug in fiery opal. Odd pieces of opal may turn up in any popular pattern. Individual pieces in these patterns have been found: Argus (Thumbprint), Loop, Bellflower, and Honeycomb; small open compotes and spoon holders in Colonial; tumblers in Flute; and odd pieces in early geometric patterns. A company like Doyle, which manufactured dozens of toy sets, must have varied its output with opal. After 1890, of course, many lines appeared in opal, and factories like Westmoreland and Imperial, subscribing to earlier traditions, did a brisk business.

A Richards & Hartley Thousand Eye bowl in opaque white and light blue makes one wonder why that company did not try opal for the whole set. They constantly advertised perfume and toilet bottles — surely of opal — in *The Crockery and Glass Journal*. When Dithridge Company set up in New Brighton, Pennsylvania, they brought out two sets, Alba and Versailles, the latter in many bureau pieces. Ripley & Company gives us evidence of how varied the formulas for opal must have been. Daniel Ripley patented a "Design for Stems of Articles of Glassware" in 1870. His stem, rather flat and with a cross near the collar, could have been a candlestick just as well as a stem. Seven days later, Ripley was issued a "Design for a Baptismal Font with Candlesticks." The branching arms and the small bowl are joined to the stem for an effective ceremonial article. The opal in these three pieces, however, has almost the translucence of clam-water — a gray white. Ripley's Marriage Lamp in white and turquoise has a stem and base of purer glass, but the web and matchholder connecting the two fonts is like the glass of the candlesticks. The Ripley dates are earlier than those of the Atterbury and Bakewell articles of the late seventies and eighties, but from these dates we should not think Ripley was ignorant of what would make smooth opaque white.

American opal and opaline had their ancestry in Bohemia, France, and England. Europe showed American glassmakers the soft curving shapes that lent themselves to decorative ware, and it stimulated them to follow fashionable trends based on their functional patterns: toiletries, luxury articles, vases, perfumes, jewel boxes, ointment jars, cups, and knickknacks. Limited by the costs of designing and building molds, restrained by the demands of the mass market, American design followed geometric or naturalistic patterns to extremes that lowered the quality and reputation of the product and so brought milk glass into the artistic disrepute from which, to a degree, it still suffers.

474 Atterbury advertisement during the 1876 Centennial, published in *The Crockery and Glass Journal*, Feb. 1876. The "Continental" bread tray pictures the Centennial building. The basket weave salts carry the patent date impressed on the bottom, Mar. 23, 1875. These are usually found in opal.

ATTERBURY & CO.,
MANUFACTURERS OF FLINT GLASSWARE,

CONTINENTAL BREAD PLATE

2 Handle

N?25 Patent Handle Lamps   N? 26 Patent Handle Lamps

2. Handle Salt

The above Engraving represents a Clear Glass Bread Plate.   This Plate has the Centennial Building, of Philadelphia, correctly pressed in the bottom, which produces a very handsome effect from the upper side.

AND EVERY VARIETY OF
PLAIN AND COLORED GLASS LAMPS,
PATENT SCREW TOP JELLIES AND OPAL WARE,
PITTSBURGH, PA.

Manufactory, Corner Carson and Tenth Streets, (South Side.)

475 Atterbury lamps emphasizing the decorative value of opal and the new trend of fusing base to bowl. *The Crockery and Glass Journal,* Oct. 23, 1875.

ATTERBURY & CO.,
MANUFACTURERS OF
EVERY VARIETY OF PLAIN AND COLORED GLASS LAMPS,
PITTSBURGH, PA.

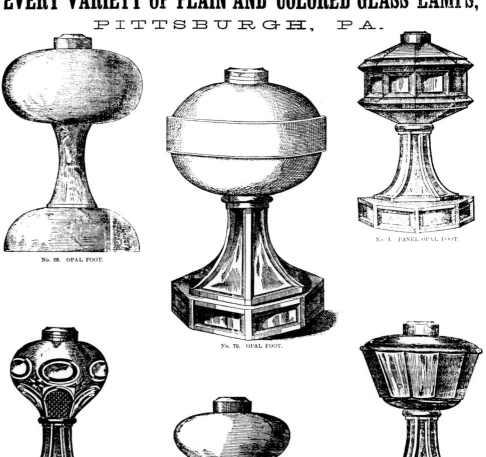

This is a pressed Opal Foot with a clear glass bowl. They are united together in the process of manufacture, no socket or cement being required.

Messrs. ATTERBURY & CO. have procured Letters-Patent, dated June 22, 1875.

The Trade will find this a stronger lamp than any other in the market, and costing much less than the old style of socket lamps. They have a large stock on hand and are ready to fill orders promptly.

SEND FOR CIRCULAR.

476 Looped white and clear witch ball and vase, ca. 1850, H. 10¾″. Cased pitcher clear over white, H. 7½″. *Collection of Dr. E. R. Eller.*

477 Examples of Pittsburgh-Wheeling looped, ca. 1870, from the Carnegie Museum Exhibition, 1949–1950. 1 and 3 — Looped vases in red and white on heavy clear bases. Gauffered rims of cobalt. Attributed to Bakewell, Pears & Co. *The Historical Society of Western Pennsylvania, Gift of Mrs. Frances G. Tracey.* 2 — Milky lined pitcher with loopings of red, white, and blue. Clear handle and base. *Ex coll. Dr. J. H. Neelley.*

478 Bulbous vase, clear with wide loopings of white, ca. 1850. Applied heavy base with rough pontil. A good example of how a blown piece may be attributed to several areas: New Jersey, Pittsburgh, Wheeling. H. 8¼". Diameter of top 4⅞". *Collection of the author.*

479 Spiral applied red on opaque white creamer (not cased), ca. 1840. Undoubtedly a whimsy, one of a kind. H. 5½". *Collection of the author.*

480 Cased opaque salt, cased with clear on the outside and cased with blue lining, blue base. Attributed to Pittsburgh and to New Jersey, ca. 1850. H. 2½". *The Metropolitan Museum of Art, Gift of Mrs. Ernest A. Fairchild, 1920.*

481 Cased creamer with clear handle and base, ca. 1850. Opaque white cased with clear. Probably Midwestern. H. 3⅞". *The Metropolitan Museum of Art, Gift of F. W. Hunter, 1913.*

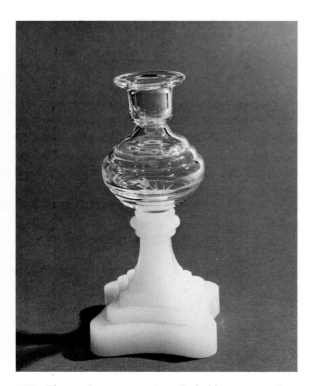

482 Blown, clear, engraved candle holder on pressed clam-water base. Midwestern, ca. 1875. H. 8½". *Collection of the author.*

483 Rare ram's head bowl in opaque yellow, horns gilded. H. 5½". Opaque blue ribbed vase, ca. 1885. Handles and base opaque white, lining light blue. *The Historical Society of Western Pennsylvania, Violet Swem Brendel Fund.*

484 Free-blown creamer with clear handle, ca. 1840. Blue with white loopings. Not cased. The base is drawn out rather than applied. This could be South Jersey. H. 3⅞". *Yale University Art Gallery, Mabel Brady Garvan Collection.*

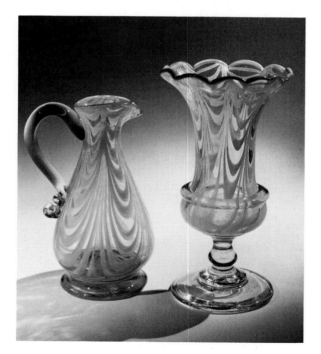

485 Two typically Pittsburgh pieces through heaviness and form, ca. 1850. 1 — Cruet looped in opaque white. Clear heavy handle and base. H. 7⅜". 2 — Vase looped in opaque white with gauffered top, clear baluster stem on clear base. H. 8½". *Collection of the author.*

486 Covered urn, ca. 1860. Not cased. Opaque white with pink and blue loopings. Attributed to Sandwich. H. 10¼". *The Henry Ford Museum.*

487 Urn with red and blue loopings, ca. 1860. On clear cylindrical base. Probably Pittsburgh. Bowl lined with opaque white, cased with clear. H. 12¼". *Wadsworth Atheneum, Hartford, Edith Olcott van Gerbig Collection.*

488 Two-handled cased vase with threaded top, ca. 1850. Handles, heavy baluster stem, and base clear. Loopings pink and blue. *Ex coll. Crawford Wettlaufer.*

489 1 — Free-blown pitcher, clear, upper part of the body looped with white, lower part cobalt over clear with collar joining often found in Pittsburgh vases, ca. 1840. Handle is clear with single veins of red, white, and blue. Base is clear. A rare and fine piece, probably unique. *Collection of Jack Strassler.* 2 — Vase looped in red and blue, ca. 1840. Cased with a thin lining of white. Heavy, clear, double-ringed stem is characteristic of early Eastern work. The shape of the vase and the casing, however, suggest Pittsburgh. *Ex coll. Harriet Carew.* 3 — Powder horn, ca. 1860. Looped in red and blue. *Ex coll. Harriet Carew.*

490 Cased communion cup, opaque white and clear, ca. 1850. Clear heavy baluster stem. Attributed to Pittsburgh and South Jersey. H. 5⅜". *The Metropolitan Museum of Art, Gift of F. W. Hunter, 1913.*

492 Pitcher, ca. 1860. Opaque reddish purple with turquoise swirls, not cased. Handle and base turquoise. Attributed to Wheeling. H. 6⅝". *The Henry Ford Museum. Ex coll. George McKearin.*

491 Collection of powder horns, ca. 1860. 1 — Looped in light red against opaque white. 2 — Clear, looped with opaque white. 3 — Aqua-black powder stain. 4 — Dark red loopings against opaque white. H. 13". *Collection of Dr. E. R. Eller.*

CHAPTER XIX

Glassmaking for the Philadelphia Centennial

The great agony is over. Last evening the whole of the Quaker City was
in a blaze of patriotism, speechmaking and fireworks in spite of the
number of degrees marked by the thermometer. The hot weather seemed
only to act as a stimulant and all nationalities merging into one great
brotherhood joined in doing honor to the anniversary of our birth as
a nation.

There is scarcely an hour when men are not perambulating the aisles with
huge watering pots in their hands, deluging the place, to the detriment
of the exhibits, and to the disgust of the ladies, whose skirts become
woefully bedraggled after a very few minutes promenade.

The glass-men make loud complaints also of a grinding organ in the
French department. It plays all the tunes from the hour of opening to
the close.
— *The Crockery and Glass Journal,* July 6, 1876

As successful as it was, the Pittsburgh Exposition of 1875 (see page 72) was the merest fore-shadowing of Philadelphia's great Centennial, which opened on May 10, 1876, ran through the hottest summer in many years, closed on November 10, and made its impression on American minds, manners, and technology. Exactly 9,910,966 persons passed through the gates of the grounds in Fairmount Park following the Centennial parade, during which glass was blown on one of the floats. President Grant presided over the opening-day ceremonies. The Centennial roused a great deal of patriotic fervor; it also challenged Americans to surpass the artistry and achievement of older nations.

The regulations for qualification and awards were rigorous and specific. The judges were required to make ratings as individuals, then to unite and adjust their decisions collectively, and finally to submit their agreement to the U.S. Centennial Commission. Thus each award passed through three ordeals after acceptance of the product.

Forty-three American glass companies showed their wares. Strong rivalry existed among individual glass firms and among sections of the country, but all united against displays other than glass. Gillinder & Sons of Philadelphia erected for public viewing within the Permanent Exhibition Building a Centennial Glass Works in full operation. The novelties produced there were carried away as souvenirs throughout the world.

Eleven Pittsburgh glass companies* were assigned 880 feet of display space at the Centennial: Adams, Atterbury, Bakewell, Pears, Crystal Glass, George Duncan, Excelsior Flint Glass, Keystone Flint Glass, O'Hara Glass, Ripley, Richards and Hartley, and Rochester Tumbler. Three other companies from the Tri-State area exhibited: Central Glass Company and Hobbs, Brockunier from Wheeling, West Virginia; and La Belle Glass Company from Bridgeport, Ohio.

Only four companies were represented from Massachusetts: New England Glass Company from Cambridge, Smith Brothers and Mount Washington Glass Works from New Bedford, and Boston and Sandwich Glass Company from Sandwich. The East was also represented by such well-known firms as Gillinder and Sons and Whitall Tatum and Company from Philadelphia, and Dorflinger Glass Company from White Mills, Pennsylvania.

The Pittsburgh glassmen had decided in a burst of cooperative zeal to unite their exhibits. A long walnut case fitted with shelves and enclosed on both sides with glass made a dignified window. Space therein was divided equitably without partitions, small signs identifying the wares of each house. The display of pressed tableware attracted a good deal of favorable comment. At this time the Midwesterners were not doing much in cut glass, their specialties besides pressed tableware being lamps, chimneys, molded goods, jelly glasses, and preserve jars.

It was said of Pittsburgh, "Here clustered together may be found a host of glassworks . . . everything from the child's toy mug to the handsomest cut and engraved tableware, — from the common green glass bottle or cheap window glass to those of the most sparkling crystal."† C. W. Elliot proclaimed patriotically in *The Journal* (November 2, 1876), "We may fairly claim that

no better or purer glass can be made than that which we in these U.S. now make, not at Sandwich and Boston only, but at Pittsburgh, Wheeling, and other favored spots." Yet Mr. Elliot admitted that American glass was a bit thicker. It certainly behooved American manufacturers to do their best, for the value of imported glass at the Centennial ran to $43,706, with a duty of $15,178.07.

The Centennial Exposition gave the glass industry a unique opportunity to display its talents. All the methods of production and all the wares manufactured during the season were on view, but many of the products were novelty pieces created for the great occasion, designed to reveal virtuosity and to attract attention. Replicas of the Liberty Bell with different legends served as inkwells, match safes, even paperweights with a pincushion on top. Souvenir hunters found minute statuettes, vases shaped like a hand, a Washington paperweight, and busts of Franklin and Lincoln. The children were not neglected: toy mugs decorated with a Liberty Bell in crystal and opaque white were expected to win smiles of approval from young patriots.

Adams and Company had the largest display among the Pittsburgh houses, and as usual it featured lamps. Three plain ones with the inscription "1776–1876" were an eye-catching novelty, for they each held two gallons of oil and were said to be the largest ever made. Centennial Bread Plate and Liberty Bell fever attacked manufacturers from New York and Philadelphia to Pittsburgh. The Adams version of the Signers' Platter was oval with a long scalloped edge and frosted letters on the underside with the names of the signers of the Declaration of Independence. In the center of the platter the Liberty Bell was placed beneath a ribbon bearing the words "Declaration of Independence 1776–1876." On the shoulders were "100 Years Ago" and John Hancock's signature.* Adams had produced a Lib-

* It is difficult to be certain about the number of glass companies exhibiting, for different editions of the Centennial catalogue vary.
† *The Crockery and Glass Journal,* December 30, 1875.

* The same plate was made with the thirteen states and signers and with the thirteen states only. The so-called

493 Centennial tray (the Signers platter), designed and patented by James C. Gill of Pittsburgh, Sept. 28, 1875, and assigned to Gillinder and Sons of Philadelphia. *The Currier Gallery of Art, Manchester, N.H.*

erty Bell tableware set that was so popular the firm sold 3000 barrels of the set between January 1, 1876, and the second week of May. At the Centennial display Adams pleased the children with toy mugs decorated with a bell in crystal or opaque white.

We can only guess at the pattern of an Adams porcelain tea set. Could it have been Pineapple and Fan? The lower part of each piece was clear, but the upper was ground and decorated with flowers and leaves in gold and brilliant colors. Another set in opal glass fashioned in the style of the eighteenth century was placed beside it for contrast. Though Adams did not qualify for an official award, the judges noted the lampshades of clear and bone glass and tableware of common or fair character.

Bakewell, Pears and Company pointed their Centennial display more in the direction of improvement of their general lines than in manufacture for a temporary market. The Liberty Bell of Benjamin Bakewell, Jr., patented on March 21,

Signers' Platter was manufactured by Gillinder and Sons of Philadelphia. James Gill of Pittsburgh, who took out Design Patent No. 8663 for it, evidently sold his rights.

1876, expressed their only attempt to capitalize on the Centennial. In the patent drawing the bell served as a deep bowl. The cover had as a finial a globe with all the continents marked out. Although Bakewell stated that the design was applicable for glass articles, the absence of collectible items in the pattern indicates its impracticability.

The firm showed lamp chimneys with crimped edges equal, it was said, to any others shown. Its bar goods attracted much attention, as did its druggists' jars with labels containing a photographic center or medallion. Although the Midwest was now more preoccupied with pressed tableware, oil lamps, jelly glasses, and preserving jars, Bakewell could not forget its old debt to cut glass. It displayed a fruit stand of immense size richly cut and a punch bowl cut and engraved with wreaths of grapes and vines about the center. A pressed fruit stand — a charming shell upheld by a dolphin — probably attracted more attention. In pressed ware, a tea service in crystal decorated with gold vines and leaves was highly acclaimed. It is interesting to note that Bakewell avoided the word "lime-glass" used by most of the Pittsburgh manufacturers. Nor did he claim flint as the New England Glass Company and Sandwich did.

The official award to Bakewell read: "Moulded Glass Table Wares, commended for the good quality of thin pieces and for the form of the wares." In a preceding general report, the judges spoke of druggists' bottles, perfumers' wares, etc., of ordinary qualities of form and metal. Yet they praised the Bakewell light tablewares as being well made.

The Crystal Glass Company, David Bennett, president, announced that it had brought out a new pattern for the Centennial but as they did not patent or name it, it remains unidentified. The company advertised dishes and fruit and berry stands in fluted patterns; diamond pattern sets in celeries, pitchers, and stands. Its bar mugs with a U.S. shield were popular. A large pitcher handsomely cut and engraved and wine glasses engraved with ferns topped the display.

The Crystal Glass Company did not earn an official commendation. Nevertheless the judges noted its lime glass tableware as being of fair, ordinary character of metal and forms.

George Duncan and Sons, known for its lime glass pressed tablewares, displayed finely finished goblets and tumblers, some of which imitated cut goods and some of which were engraved with vines and other "ornamentation." Its regular cake and fruit stands also imitated cut pieces. Duncan tried to equal or surpass everything advertised by other companies, from beer mugs and ales to cruets and pitchers and molasses jugs with metal covers. An editorial comment in *The Crockery and Glass Journal* (June 1, 1876) foretold the use of a technique that was to become popular a few years later: "Here also is a fine assortment of frosted glassware in white and colors." The judges generalized in the official award: "commended for good quality of metal and good forms of lime-glass tablewares." In their notes they added "some engraved coarsely but with considerable judgment."

The Excelsior Flint Glass Company manufactured silvered reflectors and lamp chimneys. It decorated its Centennial displays with elegantly engraved flowers, vines, and stars. The headlights for railroad engines, however, were undoubtedly plain. The official award commended the good quality and low price of reflectors. In the judges' general report, they described the lamp chimneys as of ordinary patterns and some coarsely engraved.

The Keystone Flint Glass Company, a large producer of chimneys, also won an award; it was commended for good quality of glass and forms of wares. The general report added that the lamp glasses were of plain, new, and graceful forms.

Atterbury and Company featured Lime Glass Lamps, Lamp Chimneys and Globes, as its main exhibit. The appeal of its table lamps was the variety of color used on the statuesque bases: opal, black, and turquoise. One novelty combined the shade and the chimney so that the cost of a separate shade could be avoided. The Atterburys also displayed a wide assortment of shapes in opaque white in the Basket pattern. They designed and patented an oval Liberty Bell bread platter (No. 8450). It pictured the Centennial Building with the dates "1776–1876" below it. On the under part of the outer rim are pressed the words "Give Us This Day" on one side and "Our Daily Bread" on the other. Hands grasping batons form unusual handles at each end of the plate. For some reason, later plates have the word "Continental" pressed above the Centennial Building. In the patent drawing (1875), this space is clear. In the 1881 Atterbury catalogue, however, the plate carries the word "Continental," a mystery unexplained. The official award to Atterbury read: "Commended for good quality and variety of wares." The judges' notes, though speaking of the many forms of chimneys, shades, and lamps in opal, called them ordinary in character.

James B. Lyon of the O'Hara Glass Company must have taken the Centennial in stride, for ten years earlier, when he had represented the American Manufacturers at the Paris Exposition, he received a commendation and medal. At Philadelphia he displayed sets, wines, salts, and in the words of one observer, "catsup bottles as clear as if cut of purest ice." The wines were so finely made that pressed ones could not be distinguished from those blown and cut. Lyon also produced a beer glass bell from Independence Hall. Among the sets he probably showed Crystal Wedding (patented July 6, 1875), plain and engraved. The pattern carries a scalloped edge with an indented border running just below the rim. Feet and finials are curved shells — a device popularized by King Son and Company. Lyon's Crystal Wedding, a plain ware, should not be confused with the Adams' Crystal Wedding, which carries a

494 Lyon uses the device of foot and finial as that in No. 496. Although the foot is somewhat similar, the finial is quite different. He advertised etching and engraved (cut) designs to relieve the plainness. *The Crockery and Glass Journal*, Jan. 27, 1876.

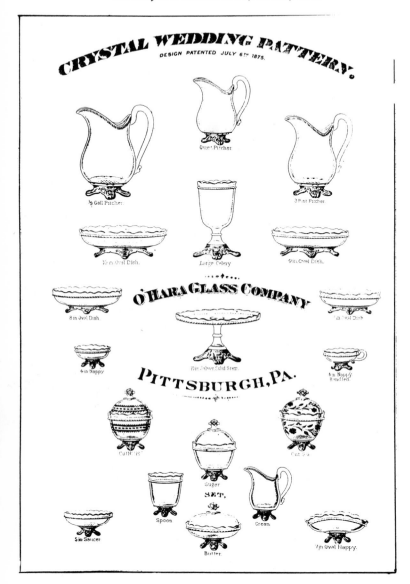

heavy geometric border. The official award merely commended Lyon for good quality of glass and for forms of wares. In their general report, the judges were more complimentary — "metal good and forms light and graceful."

Ripley and Company drew praise for a tableware exhibit that "treads on the toes of cut glass." Lamps and bar goods also graced their exhibit. Its Centennial Bread Plate dramatized Bunker Hill as the "Birthplace of Liberty." The monument was pictured in the center of the oval platter. On the edges were named four heroes — "Prescott, Stark, Warren, Putnam" — with the date "1776." Each of the two handles represented an American shield. Ripley and Company did not earn an official award; the judges wrote of its product: "ordinary character of metal and form."

Richards and Hartley Company, which had sold more than $100,000 worth of its Peerless set since its introduction in 1875, made this pressed set the star of its display. In Peerless, it used one of the standard cut designs (*495*), the strawberry diamond. (Commentators on glass at the Centennial consistently emphasized the excellent imitation of cut glass in pressed pieces.) The company showed pickle jars mounted in silver with alternate panels, plain and diamond. Richards and Hartley seemed to be the only Pittsburgh factory consistently advertising perfume bottles, though, of course, others made them. One of the company's tea sets appeared in the diamond pattern. The company did not win an official award, but the judges noted that the lime glass tablewares were molded of moderate quality of metals and forms.

Rochester Tumbler Company had a well-established reputation before the Centennial. In 1876 it was making 200,000 tumblers every six days in 175 patterns. Eventually it reached 300 patterns, embracing many techniques as well as styles. The official award commended the company for good quality of metal and great variety of forms (*397*). Apparently the glass was brilliant and the forms were considered simple and suitable.

The Centennial Report read:

The eleven foregoing manufacturers all of the city of Pittsburgh are among the largest of that place. They employ in the aggregate about 6,000 persons. The amount of their production is very large and increasing. The prices are exceedingly low.*

Other factories capitalized on the Centennial. Doyle and Company brought out a Centennial salt shaker, the base ingeniously made smaller to prevent caking. "Centennial U.S.," lettered in the lid, allowed the salt to be shaken through the perforations of the letters.

King, Son and Company took a plain set like Mitchell ware, added curved shell feet, handles, and finials on covered pieces, and named it "Centennial." Certainly this was a challenge to patterns with more obvious patriotic symbolism. A year before, King had patented two pieces with ribbed and curved feet. Other glassmen, including J. B. Lyon and David Barker, appreciated the decorative principle and produced similar works. Plain sets were devised to be engraved, etched, or sandblasted. At this time delicate patterns for decoration were advertised in several catalogues. It was all the rage to embellish pressed sets, even with elaborate patterns.

A study of the pieces exhibited reveals that Pittsburgh manufacturers were generally concerned with the practical uses of glass in everyday life, in spite of their adding show pieces for the exhibit. The judges' praise of moderate prices fits in with criticism often leveled at Midwestern mechanically pressed glass. Since increased production was one cause of lowered prices, we should heed a contemporary quotation that defends a second cause.

Of lime glass there are many large and interesting exhibits from Austria and the United States, but more particularly from the latter country. In this descrip-

* *U.S. International Exposition 1876,* Reports and Awards Groups I and II, Washington, 1880. Volume II, p. 110.

495 Richards & Hartley's Peerless pattern, modeled on a cut glass design, was popular before the Centennial and held up in competition with all rival new patterns. *The Crockery and Glass Journal,* Aug. 12, 1875.

tion of glass *great advances have been made in points of brilliance, endurance, and transparency,* and the wares composed of it are sold very *cheaply.** (Italics added.)

It is interesting that the United States should be linked to Austria in manufacturing lime glass, though the best Austrian pieces were undoubtedly of flint. The judges agreed that the J. and L. Lobmeyer exhibit from Vienna was the most important collection of glass in the Exhibition. They noted that the metal was brilliant and of very light texture, much more so than is usual in Bohemian glass. They also praised the artistry

* *U.S. International Exhibition 1876,* Reports and Awards Groups I and II, Washington, 1880, p. 17.

496 Centennial pattern by King, Son & Co. shows how a plain pattern can be dressed up. Ribbed feet and handles. The same ribbing as finials is curved in to look like a snail shell. King, Son and Co. catalogue, ca. 1875, p. 17. *The Corning Museum of Glass.*

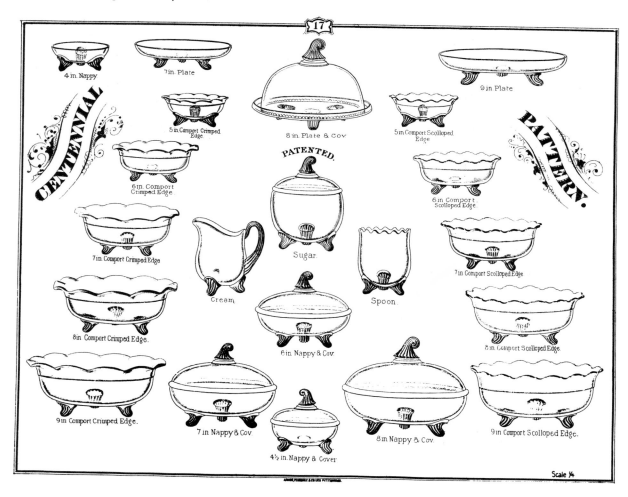

and execution of engraving, even naming Professors Hansen and Storck for their craftsmanship.

The Lobmeyers received the greatest acclaim in *Masterpieces of the Centennial International Exhibition.** Their engraved crystal, Bohemian ware, and opaline in the Venetian style were highly praised for beautiful forms and for variety and

depth of color. Clear pieces cased with transparent red gave their craftsmen a chance to trace marvelous patterns. Out of twenty-seven photographs of glass in the book, Lobmeyer workmanship could claim fifteen.

The Crockery and Glass Journal, at least, had praise for the Americans, though *Masterpieces* had not mentioned them or pictured a single American piece. "The New England Glass Company," *The Journal* wrote (July 27, 1876), "is bearing off the palm at the Centennial by their large and tasteful display of rich and elegant

* Walter Smith, "Industrial Art," *The Masterpieces of the Centennial International Exhibition,* Vol. 2 (Philadelphia: Gebbie-Barrie, 1876–1878).

goods. Their cut glass is so delicately cut and engraved that even the judges were not aware that such work was possible in this country." The reporter had probably read the judges' comments, which generally stressed the quality of metal and excellence of workmanship.

Somehow the Centennial of 1876 seems to have embodied the fruit of the seedling planted by Henry Baldwin and Henry Clay in their American system of domestic manufacture. It was America's first World's Fair and one of its greatest. It gave its exhibitors the chance to catch the eye of the people — an average of 62,350 of them a day for six months. It was no small thing for the Pittsburgh glass manufacturers to have been in the sun of the Great Fair. It was a splendid thing for eleven Pittsburgh manufacturers to be singled out for praise and commendation.

CHAPTER XX

Novelties in Glass

The inquiries are invariably for new designs, specialties and novelties in particular, and the manufacturers are fortunate to occupy a position to meet the demand.
— *The Crockery and Glass Journal,* July 27, 1882

Our definition of a novelty would differ appreciably from that held by a glass manufacturer of the last thirty years of the century. He would be inclined to give more weight to its functional value than to its decorative worth. Consequently he often confused novelty with a variation of design. For example, J. B. Lyon of the O'Hara Glass Company advertised in *The Crockery and Glass Journal* for October 28, 1875, "An elegant bowl (Crystal Wedding) with scalloped edge both cut and pressed is among our novelties." He was simply adding a new piece to an old pattern.

The Journal is filled with references to novelties. We do not know whether these were additions to standard sets or whether they were actually entirely new forms in our meaning of novelty. Others from *The Journal:* "Atterbury & Co. are running on novelties," "George Duncan & Sons were never better prepared, their stock being replete with novelties expressly brought out this season," "George Duncan and Sons' novelties for this season in colored and ornamental glass are some of the finest they have ever produced," "Novelties in color are all the go," "Bryce Brothers' showroom is replete with novelties," "The only thing that has kept life in tableware during the last two years has been the production

of novelties," "Richards & Hartley are showing novelties," "The Phoenix Glass Co. (Philipsburg) have novelties in cut and etched glass." We sense that the editor was reflecting the feeling of glassmen when he wrote, "The designs of today which sell readily will be dead stock a year hence."*

In an active market, a popular novelty, whether functional, semifunctional, or purely decorative, was copied and varied as long as demand flourished. At the same time, a constant effort was made to discard the marginal product and to have other new forms ready to catch the public fancy. Glass shown at the Philadelphia Centennial exemplifies both trends. The many Liberty Bell designs and the bread plates recounting historical events were timely novelties. The bread plate with a religious legend — "Give Us This Day Our Daily Bread" — became an ordinary part of table service for many years after the Centennial. A practical and attractive match holder produced by Bryce Brothers was not equally popular. It copied the hand holding the torch for Bartholdi's statue, *Liberty Enlightening the World.* Unable

* *The Crockery and Glass Journal,* September 21, 1882; October 30, 1879; February 4, 1884; February 25, 1886; March 4, 1886; April 1, 1886; April 25, 1886; March 13, 1890.

to complete the cast in time for the Centennial, Bartholdi had sent over only the hand holding the torch.*

Souvenirs from the Gillinder factory sold readily: small birds, fans, toys, glass resembling porcelain, vases, three-legged kettles, and slippers. With almost endless possibilities of pattern and color, slippers became a fad. Other companies joined in. John Ernest Miller of George Duncan & Sons, Pittsburgh, on October 18, 1886, patented a method of producing pressed glass slippers and assigned the rights to two Pittsburgh companies: Duncan & Sons and Bryce Brothers. On the same day, Henry J. Smith of Pittsburgh patented his own method for pressing slippers. The processes were similar, Smith's slipper having a stubbier toe somewhat folded up. Both were produced in the ubiquitous Daisy and Button pattern; Miller's shoe was commonly called the Daisy Miller after the design and the designer. Thus what had started as a novelty souvenir in 1876 was a sideline product ten years later, and two inventors were able to find two substantial glass companies willing to manufacture the same product simultaneously.

Other novelties striving for originality and heavy sales did not always fare so well:

· Henry J. Smith — he who had patented a slipper — devised a cream pitcher that would pour from lips on two sides and had double loop handles under each spout. It was assigned to Bryce, Walker and Company on March 15, 1881. Apparently it did not catch on.

· James Dalzell designed a salt dish in the form of a wheelbarrow, selling the patent to Campbell, Jones & Company on January 3, 1882.

· William G. Walter patented for Campbell, Jones on April 6, 1886, a whiskbroom relish dish in the Daisy and Button pattern.

· Julius Proeger patented for McKee and Brothers on January 19, 1886, an open-coach

* The Bryce replica, 4½ inches high, is pictured in Ruth Webb Lee's *Victorian Glass,* Plate 103, No. 1.

bowl with wheels, wheel supports, and wagon tongue. (It has been reproduced in our time by the L. G. Wright Glass Company of New Martinsville, West Virginia.)

· Jesse H. Lippincott designed a coal scuttle in Daisy and Button for Duncan & Sons.

· A. H. Heisey of Duncan's designed a vase shaped like a half-opened umbrella, also in Daisy and Button (December 14, 1886).

Other novelty products included a covered dish in the shape of a railway car, a toothpick holder in the shape of an anvil, a glass object of uncertain use that looked like a meerschaum pipe, and a vase that looked like a tree trunk. They included Atterbury's bowl placed on the bowed head of a swan; Bakewell's Liberty Bell covered dish with a globe of the world on top; Campbell, Jones' realistic four-branched twig, the center holding a salt dish; Jonathan Haley's Dog Cart — the list is almost endless. Such objects were made in crystal, amber, canary, and blue, and sometimes in amethyst. Most of them had short lives unless they were reproduced in modern times.

Novelties in Glass   439

498 The Garfield Memorial Plate was made by Campbell, Jones & Co. James W. Campbell patented the design Dec. 20, 1881. Timeliness was often an important factor in planning a novelty. D. 10". *Collection of Mr. and Mrs. Robert H. Eckhardt.*

Thomas B. Atterbury patented on February 29, 1876, a pedestal that was the bust of a woman formalized by a three-layered base on which it rested and by a folded garment over one shoulder and across the breast. Some thought it a likeness of Jenny Lind. Atterbury proposed in his patent that the bust be surmounted with a socket or other suitable means for attaching the peg of a lamp font.

Others evidently also tried the human figure. A *Crockery and Glass Journal* reporter wrote on November 9, 1876, "This is what Pittsburgh manufacturers are now doing; a bouquet holder of a female figure 9 inches high on a 5-inch base, the drapery arranged so as to expose to view one of the lower limbs which is prettily shaped, well defined and prominent. The position of the figure is upright, left hand resting on the thigh, right arm extending upwards over the head, where the hand holds a small bowl, which rests upon the left shoulder into which a bouquet is placed. It is a mantel ornament. A male figure is to be constructed."

The trends of incongruity, variation, and naturalism can be seen in these pieces and throughout glassmakers' efforts to promote sales. The naturalistic strain that had become an integral part of the design of Midwestern pressed tableware was artistically superior to that of the novelties. It reached its zenith in the 1870s and even in its decline persisted as a force. A superficial judgment would depreciate the unattractive novelties by assuming that designers lacked imagination. More careful background study, however, would persuade the modern collector that manufacturers and designers felt certain that familiar household objects presented in a material not used before would hold genuine appeal. Their concern was sales and getting out of old ruts.

Experiments were going on for using glass in a widened variety of products: coffins, sewer pipes, bathtubs, cloth; and if it were not for the development of newer and more suitable materials, we could well be using some of them today. Adams & Company placed glass between the base of a piano and its legs, for the purpose of giving greater resonance and superior musical qualities; it was patented by a Baltimore piano manufacturer. Jonathan Haley patented a method for making ornamental glassware tiles, using a heat-sensitive glass so that a second heating would change and vary the color of the thinner parts. Such oddities rarely developed into workable products with extensive sales, and they can be dismissed.

Novelties with more practical and immediate applications were closely related to technical progress in the industry. Lamp pedestals offered scope for design while technicians were trying to solve the problems of joining pedestal and base. Wheeling offered in February 1877 a lamp — Little Samuel Praying — of which the foot could be in plain or opal glass, with the figure kneeling on a jet base. The seventies ushered in the wide use of metal for figures or for bases of lamps.

Some Representative Pieces

Thomas Cutler of Pittsburgh's Birmingham District took out a design patent in 1868 for

499 Opaque blue Basket Weave covered sectional pickle or relish dish first patented July 21, 1874, by William Kirchner for the Atterburys. Addition of metallic covers was patented February 9, 1875, by T. B. Atterbury. Though covers were usually of tin, this example has pewter ones. *The Brooklyn Museum, Gift of Mrs. Samuel Schwartz.*

500 Base of dish shown on No. 499.

Goblet on a Tripod, the bowl resting on three concave bands of glass. This could well have been a forerunner of Smith's double-handled, double-spouted creamer. Such attempts to join novelty with utility in tableware rarely met with success.

Probably more useful was a perfectly round bread plate patented by McKee Brothers in 1875. The center was decorated by a bunch of grapes; a legend around the shoulders proclaimed, "It's pleasant to labor for those we love." Another table piece, the handled basket divided into two sections, challenged many designers, including those of Atterbury, Bakewell, and Haley. Henry Franz patented for Campbell, Jones & Company on October 21, 1879, a double relish dish, each section looking like an oval tray. The basic idea was embodied in other relish dishes and platters. Atterbury's two fish curling around the top of one of its covered dishes obviously followed the pattern. One double fish relish dish, an opaque white, was patented on June 4, 1872, while the Atterburys patented another similar piece on June 2, 1874.

Bakewell, Pears, generally thought of as a conservative house with limited production, attempted to catch the buyers' fancy with novelty products. They designed a Lion Face as a mantel ornament or paperweight 3¼ inches in diameter. A reviewer said of it that for minuteness of detail, finish, and naturalness, the King of Beasts deserved his title. They fashioned a bust of Washington 11 inches high and 7 inches across the shoulders, the pedestal and chest being hollow. The finish and posture resemble that of a marble statue. To honor Washington again, they pressed his portrait on the under side of a 3¼-inch paperweight; a reporter claimed it was the finest piece of portraiture he had seen, etched to tone down the harsh brilliance of clear flint glass. Yet he felt that Washington looked out as from a mirror. More conservatively, Bakewell brought out an oval salt in a silver-plated holder after the eighteenth-century English fashion.

In July of 1874, William Kirchner patented for Atterbury the Handled Saloon or Pickle Dish (*499*). This has a pressed glass division between the concavities; otherwise it is somewhat like its Campbell, Jones counterpart. Putting sections together may have led D. C. Ripley in 1884 to design a glass holder for castor bottles. The common receptacle for bottles was divided by a central wing piece provided with radially projecting arms. Ripley was ingenious and eager to experi-

ment, and his glass dish or bowl having a pivoted metallic bail-handle secured by metallic lugs had a brief moment of glory. A. H. Heisey of George Duncan & Sons, another experimenter, tried a glass water pitcher with journal bearings in combination with supporting standards.

The Eastern manufacturers were as fully aware as the Midwesterners of the need for novelty. The Mount Washington factory at New Bedford applied in 1890 for a patent for a safety finger and berry bowl. The edges of both bowls were folded under and inward. The patentee claimed that the bowls were 50 percent stronger and safer than the old-style straight edge, that liquids would not slop over the edges, and that the inward curve would force the berries or other contents, when one was serving, into the spoon or back into the dish. As early as July 30, 1878, Ripley had patented a dessert bowl with a drip channel.

Ever since glass balls were blown to cover sugar bowls and creamers to protect the contents against houseflies, flytraps of all sorts had been blown, some of them even decorated with engraving (*501*). *The Crockery and Glass Journal* for September 21, 1876, displayed one of these on its cover — "Fowler's Patent Fly Fan, the Great Home Comfort and Luxury" — with the caption

> Wonder sparkles in the servant's eyes
> At the magic wing o'er the table flies.

Ripley & Company advertised a pressed glass flytrap, the Climax (*502*), declaring that it could not be equaled for a clean and easy method of catching flies; it was, in fact, better than flypaper. The Eureka was another popular trap. Joseph and Frank Brunwasser of Pittsburgh patented a flytrap, the main feature of which was a side opening for the inflow of a suitable liquid, "such as vinegar and water or poison."

Novelties had now crossed the line to become ordinary household gadgets. Ripley made Easley's Patent Lemon Juice extractor. The O'Hara factory brought out a new bouquet holder and

502 Climax flytrap. D. C. Ripley advertisement in *The Crockery and Glass Journal,* May 29, 1890.

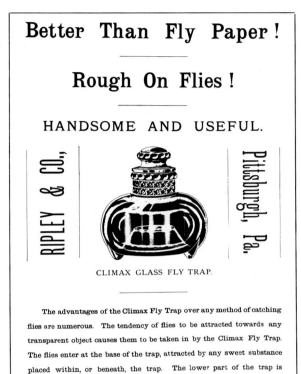

then conceived a glass twine holder that sold widely for several years. Quite in line with these was Washington Beck's hanging match safe, patented on June 13, 1876. It was named The Jolly Jester, since its bowl showed a man's face frozen in a perpetual grin. Challinor & Taylor used the idea many years later, making a match safe in opaque white with the stern face of an Indian chief in feather headdress. Beck's Pressed Door Block (February 13, 1877) portrayed a lion couchant on a pedestal base, to which a ring and chain could be tied for holding it in place.

By the glassman's trade definition and advertising, novelties included pieces added to a regular set or made with any alteration in design, however slight. The milk white mug in Bleeding Heart (Floral) pattern referred to on page 340 is a good example. Collectors of pressed glass frequently find variants or additions in familiar sets, the purpose of which was to stimulate sales. David Barker's Jumbo pattern already discussed (see page 358) had proved to be a white elephant until he added a novelty — a spoon or fork holder with a frosted elephant on a small pedestal at the top (*396*). It was patented on September 23, 1884. It became a popular product in its own time and is a collector's item today. The patent drawing of the spoon holder differs in several respects from the one pictured on Plate 94 of Ruth Webb Lee's *Early American Pressed Glass.* Both have the patent date molded on the bottom edge, but the finial in the patent diagram is plain, the shoulder plate has no design, and there is no reeding above and below the plate.

King, Son & Company altered plain Mitchell ware by adding Shell feet and finials. Their patent, an outgrowth of a joint one issued to King and August Sperber in April 1875 was dated May 25. King called the ware Centennial and offered it for sale throughout the boom of the national celebration. He used the same feet on his Banded Star, though the finials are geometric. Hobbs, Brockunier of Wheeling patented a Centennial pattern on November 21, 1876, with finials and a bearded head on each foot — a Viking, perhaps. John H. Hobbs of the same company tried a pattern on January 8, 1878, with Goat's Head feet and geometric finials. The patent issue pictured a covered sugar, but Hobbs projected the usual pieces of a tableware set.

Glasses, Goblets, and Bottles

Since an important part of glassmaking still centered on drinking, the novelty phase touched serving vessels and containers for liquids. We find many advertisements like that of the Crystal Glass Company: "Novelties in beer mugs, weiss beer glasses, tumblers, schoppens, etc." When George Duncan & Sons advertised "a hot whiskey goblet," we are uncertain what the piece looked like and whether to put the emphasis on "hot" or on "whiskey." Cunningham & Ihmsen declared that no public house should be without their Patent Glass Keg of ruby, green, or blue, holding from one to five gallons. At the same time they praised their bottles for ale, brandy, porter, claret, sarsaparilla, schnapps, bitters, and hock, adding that their hock wine bottles were equal or superior to the imported. (American bottle manufacturers were plagued by an accepted belief that they could not make satisfactory champagne bottles.) McKee Brothers received an accolade from a *Crockery and Glass Journal* writer for a novelty beer mug: "The most taking I have ever seen. The body is clear crystal, oval in shape, while the handle and foot are emerald green. The variety of color gives a peculiarly fine effect when the glass is filled with beer."* The McKees claimed that their glass retained the foam longer than any other and that this would make it popular as a bar glass. The top rim, they said, was similar to that of the imported goods; hitherto, all mugs had been alike.

Glassmakers could practice more extravagance of architecture in their bottles. The Atterbury Duck Bar Bottle, designed by Thomas Atterbury and patented on April 11, 1871, became one of the most famous from the Pittsburgh area. The Atterburys, of course, favored milk glass, but they made their Duck in crystal as well. The word "Whiskey" painted on a round shield on the Duck's breast held great appeal both for bottle buyer and whiskey drinker. William G. Walter, a specialist in novelties, designed a dagger bottle. Charles L. Flaccus patented a boot-shaped bottle for his company. Though no maker is mentioned, a poison bottle deserves attention. "Look for poison when the bell rings. A little glass instrument has been invented to be attached to all bottles in drug stores containing poison. As soon as the bottle is lifted from the shelf a little bell is

* *The Crockery and Glass Journal,* January 6, 1876; February 8, 1877; July 5, 1877.

rung by the instrument, giving notice that the bottle contains poison."* A very elaborate bottle, "The Nevertold Ale — Washington's Hatchet," was shaped like the short-handled ax young Washington used to cut down the cherry tree (503). It held four ounces; the screw top was nickel-plated and cork-lined, and the New Brighton Glass Company advertised it with special pride in 1889.

Unexpected factors could influence or direct production. Of great importance was the new license law of May 1, 1888, that would reduce the number of saloons from 1500 to 223. The same average of reduction prevailed all over Pennsylvania and in Ohio, which was meant to indicate a reduction in demand for bar glassware, tumblers, and goblets. *The Crockery and Glass Journal* for July 31, 1890, stated that the curtailment of number of saloons in Pennsylvania, Ohio, and other states brought a largely increased demand for bottles and flasks, the consumers of liquors in many places being compelled to buy in packages or go without.

Ingenious glassmakers offered the artificial nest egg in opaque glass as a way to elude prohibition. Besides, the egg was a staple article of commerce. "They [eggs] are made to do double duty as both bottle and glass for exhilarating beverages, and it is no uncommon sight to step into a grocery store in a Prohibition town and see a fellow (who cannot succeed in getting a drink elsewhere) suck eggs."†

Judge Ewing of the license court of Pittsburgh made the interesting pronouncement that the man who drinks six glasses of beer in a day is intemperate. It was not known how the judge set his limit. Every one predicted that if his decision carried conviction, the Pittsburgh glassmakers would have to abandon ordinary beer glasses and make schooners. To complicate the glass manu-

* *The Crockery and Glass Journal,* September 23, 1875, p. 17.
† *The Crockery and Glass Journal,* March 29, 1888, p. 22.

facturers' lives, paper bottles were being made for ink, bluing, shoe dressing, glue, etc.

Paperweights

Paperweights attained artistic perfection in France around the middle of the nineteenth century. New England factories emulated the French in the fifties and sixties with some productions of exceptional beauty and virtuosity. New Jersey workmen did not follow the French tradition, but they achieved an equally high standing by virtue of their workmanship and use of color. Midwestern glassmakers were preoccupied with supplying a huge volume of pressed tableware and functional pieces for local, Southern, and Western markets. Pittsburgh manufacturers believed the demand for paperweights was limited. It is not surprising, therefore, that they did not try to distinguish themselves in this art form — though one feels, somewhat regretfully, that if there had been a couple of fine paperweight artists in the area, the story might have been different. By the 1870s, only one Pittsburgh factory had seriously tried the market: W. H. Maxwell of Pittsburgh's South Side. A fire did $1500 in damage to his plant on June 2, 1879, but in September he was advertising a paperweight for official desks with the name of the user encased in the center.

We know that Maxwell was a practical glassman, for he had patented a tool for crimping in 1876. His factory, listed in 1878 on Twenty-Seventh Street, South Side, had a four-pot furnace engaged in the work of producing glass labels and photographic covers in convex shape. Apparently his was the only factory of its kind in Pittsburgh. If the claim was true that New York took all his production* — which seems questionable — his factory would have been one of the few of its kind in the country.

We are indebted to Maxwell for one thing: in Patent No. 263,931, September 5, 1882, he gave

* *The Crockery and Glass Journal,* January 3, 1878.

503 "He Never Told A Lie," a novelty bottle from the New Brighton Glass Co., Pa. *The Crockery and Glass Journal,* May 2, 1889, p. 38.

504 Macbeth (Evans) paperweight advertisement. D. 3¼". *The Corning Museum of Glass.*

a clear exposition of how to place names, monograms, or designs on a thin plate of glass in vitrifiable colors (*504*). Both text and pictures on his patent are exceedingly valuable in understanding how paperweights were made. After the thin plate was put into a base-ring mold, the ring was covered by a cone. Molten clear glass was then dropped into an opening at the top of the cone to cover the design. After the cone mold was removed and the gather attached to the pontil rod, the gaffer proceeded to shape his paperweight. Two other district patents, those of Joseph Reder and Henry Miller, are also illuminating, for they reveal how the air trap or cavity for the contained bubble opened the way for all sorts of floral arrangements.

Maxwell moved to Chartiers some time before 1888; he was still reputed at that date to be the only paperweight manufacturer in the district. The Pittsburgh Novelty Glass Company, an outgrowth of his operation at Chartiers, produced paperweights exclusively. Available Pittsburgh catalogues make no references to paperweights. Such pieces originally had been made by artisans working on their own after hours, and years

passed before the work became an accepted part of factory production.

Campbell, Jones & Company evidently tried the field around 1876, for *The Crockery and Glass Journal* for November 3 of that year reports that their new paperweights did not go off. The designs are of the rudest, crudest, and stiffest sort.

Paul Hollister, an authority on paperweights, reports that Frank Challinor of Challinor & Taylor was trained to make paperweights while working at the Gillinder factory in Philadelphia. Hollister also says that he has had great difficulty in distinguishing between two documented weights that Frank's son, Charles, said were made by his father and some that had been made by Gillinder himself. Perhaps other Challinor weights will be found.*

In *American Glass Paperweights* (1939), Francis E. Smith pictures several Pittsburgh and Ohio weights. He generalizes that the casings were blown into a simple mold and that they were shallow and flat on the inside. Designs were crudely composed of glass dust, small chips of glass, or photographs on a plaque of porcelain composition or other material. A background of flowing glass was often spotted on or colored glass chips were scattered kaleidoscopically. The subjects leaned toward the naturalistic and familiar: holidays, sport, commemorative occasions, and animals like those in the large agates. Some of Maxwell's advertising weights were possibly flat and rectangular; some may even have contained pasted labels or pictures. Pittsburgh concave weights took on a heavy quality; the design was flat and the clear part thick to increase magnification.

The McKearins describe a Masonic weight in *American Glass,* page 413. The square and compass outlined in black enclose a G surrounded by rays. Helen McKearin praises the bordering floral sprays so that we can at least be certain that this was not one of the ill-fated Campbell, Jones

* Frank Challinor, "A Glassman's Collection." *Antiques* 51, April 1947, 254–55.

505 Typical paperweights of the Pittsburgh area. Coarse designs. The weight on the standard is probably by Charles Challinor. Small goblet, fiery pink at rim shading to clear; probably Fry glass, ca. 1888. H. 5". *The Historical Society of Western Pennsylvania, goblet — Gift of Mrs. J. Hanson Rose.*

products. On the underside of the background is inscribed, "Made by Albert Graeser, Pittsburgh, Pa." Graeser must have produced it after hours and have been proud of his work.

The absence of fine weights in the Pittsburgh District was undoubtedly recognized and regretted. *The Crockery and Glass Journal* for May 8, 1890, reported under Pittsburgh factories:

"The Dithridge Flint Glass Co. of New Brighton, Pa., are busy on cut glass, but will add paperweights of a superior design and finish." Few other names in the area are linked to paperweights. After the turn of the century, Aaron Bloom, working in a factory down the Ohio River, carried on the Eastern tradition of paperweight design. He did so in a coarser manner than that of midcentury delicacy, but he was a skilled workman and he taught several worthy pupils.

Walter Smith, giving a preview in 1875 on the quality of work shown at the Centennial Exhibition, sized up the novelty situation amusingly, if rather cynically:

On the breakfast table the boiled eggs are to be found in a porcelain basket which is the model of a setting hen, as though half-hatched eggs were delicacies, and when Mr. Croesus requires some cream for his coffee, he seizes the rampant tail of an earthenware brown cow, and swinging the whole animal in the air, forces the cream through her mouth — cream which had previously been introduced into her body through a skylight in her back . . . To remind Mr. Croesus of his early struggles and to enhance the value by contrast of present wealth are two candlesticks of sea-green glass, which are models of the Crucifixion . . . All this happens when designers forget limitations by which ornamental art for industrial purposes should be bounded — not encroach on the fine arts.*

* Smith, *Industrial Art,* p. 517.

CHAPTER XXI

Art Glass

Just at present, art glass is all the go.
— *The Crockery and Glass Journal,* April 29, 1886

The ambition of eighteenth-century glassmakers — to rival decorative porcelain — was realized in the 1880s. On February 4, 1886, *The Crockery and Glass Journal* reported that for the past six years the market had felt the influence of a really new art in the manufacture of glass — one that resembled porcelain. In color details, glassmen even had the advantage. There were some pieces of glassware on display in New York City that for beauty and attractiveness exceeded anything in the line of modern porcelains — "and that is saying considerable." The article was headed "Artistic Glassware," which was everywhere being shortened to "Art Glass," a name that modern collectors blandly assume our generation originated. *The Journal* wrote of "fine glassware with startling effectiveness . . . once the only flashy vases were Bohemian," and reported, "Just at present art glass is all the go."*

Glass students are familiar with the suit that the New England Glass Company's William L. and Edward D. Libbey instituted against Frederick S. Shirley and the Mount Washington Glass Works, claiming an infringement on their patent for Amberina, an amber-glass mixture containing gold. The settlement is equally well known — a compromise on the name that allowed each com-

pany to continue manufacture of the product, one as Amberina, the other as Rose Amber. *The Journal* for April 3, 1884, carried a full-page New England Glass Company advertisement. It told of special inducements in Amberina art glass, "having revised and greatly reduced the prices covered by Patent No. 282,002, July 24, 1883, to which we have exclusive rights."

Despite the exclusive rights, Challinor & Taylor, lately moved up the Allegheny River to Tarentum, announced that they intended to enter largely the manufacture of "Amberine" and other fancy and colored glassware. They added that they had already procured the molds. There had been an influx of foreign Amberina and price cuts on the product in Eastern cities, but that clearly did not dim the hopes of the glassmakers beyond the Alleghenies. Clearly, too, the manufacture of Amberina during the eighties was widespread, and little-known factories may have experimented with it and produced it in limited quantities.

The Libbeys licensed Hobbs, Brockunier and Company of Wheeling in 1886 to make pressed Amberina. It is difficult to believe that Hobbs, Brockunier did not stretch their license to include more than the technique of pressing. An advertisement they ran in February 1886 contained the words Amberina, Hobnail, and Diamond. Many years ago, after a lecture at Beaver Falls, Pennsylvania, I was shown an expanded diamond

* *The Crockery and Glass Journal,* February 4, April 29, 1886.

creamer in Amberina. In weight, metal, technique, and depth of color it was one of the finest pieces of Amberina I have ever seen. It was said to have come from Wheeling.

Challinor & Taylor became closely associated with Richards & Hartley, which had also left Pittsburgh for Tarentum. In 1886, both companies were using the same agent, D. R. Marshall of 24 Park Place, New York. *The Journal* praised the products in common: "The change from the tawdry lines two short years ago to really delicate and beautiful tints now is really remarkable."* This hardly constitutes proof that Richards & Hartley were also producing Amberina, but it is fairly good circumstantial evidence that they were aiming toward art glass.

One of the most active companies in imported, colorful *nouveau* glass was C. P. A. Hinrichs of New York City. As early as June 1875, *The Crockery and Glass Journal* reported on his importations: all kinds of Bohemian and Belgian glassware (the finest and a cheaper quality), including rich colored vases, toilet sets, druggists' and perfumers' fine cut vials — a rare collection of antique and imitation glassware. In addition to recognizing the influence of these styles on American glassmakers, we should remember that many nineteenth-century American family treasures were imported.

On February 21, 1884, Hinrichs posted a strong full-page ad in *The Journal* for Amberina: "Ruby Amber Glassware — Jugs and Tumblers now in Stock — Bulls Eye or Polka Dot Glass in Amber, Blue and Rose." The Polka Dot glass he advertised had been popular in Western Pennsylvania for the previous nine years. William C. King of King, Son and Company in Pittsburgh brought out the spot motif in 1875 and called it Dot. On this pressed ware, the dots appeared on the inner surface of the glass and represented merely a thickening of color and glass, not the opalescent dots that William Leighton, Jr., perfected in the 1880s. King's tableware pieces fre-

* *The Crockery and Glass Journal,* March 4, 1886.

quently rested on curved, reeded feet. Leighton's began with a parison of opalescent glass introduced into suitable molds so that the dots would be uniform during the chilling and reheating period. Then a piece could be expanded by blowing and finishing in the form desired. Bryce Brothers and Doyle & Company of Pittsburgh used the heavy pressed dot without the Hobbs, Brockunier & Company handwork. Alexander J. Beatty of Tiffin, Ohio, found good demand for the pattern in custard cups. Dewdrop and Hobnail were among the names given this ware.

Collectors today generally call such pieces Shaded Opalescent,* though probably the term should be reserved for pattern-molded pieces that appear in many designs and colors. The original bubble was coated with a heat-sensitive crystal and then blown into a pattern mold to produce raised decoration on the outer surface. After it had been cooled, it was reheated at the glory hole. The raised pattern then took on an opalescent white color, somewhat in the spirit of art glass.

Philip Arbogast of Pittsburgh, who liked the Hobbs, Brockunier–William Leighton method, devised a snap-holding tool that enabled the workmen to expand the piece without interfering with rims or borders of pressed pieces. Though Spot and Dot glass was made in many factories by pressing without additional shaping, the opalescent treatment of spots became more popular because of possible contrasts of color. The chilling and the reheating became standard practice whether a backing or plating of the mother color of glass was used. An outgrowth that has persisted in strongly raised designs is the Opalescent Bar, the Checkered Bar, and the Zig Zag Bar. The swirled and the broken swirl examples of pattern-molding in Opalescent Rib required more skill in shaping and plating than the straight molded. Alexander J. Beatty of Tiffin, Ohio, and J. F. Miller of Martins Ferry, Ohio, gave impetus to this more sophisticated and less obtrusive rib-

* Opalescent means having a milky iridescence: opaline, opal, fiery opal, not opaque.

bing. It lent itself well to water and lemonade sets, to salt and sugar shakers, to barber bottles and lamp fonts, and to vases and small mantel ornaments. In the Tri-State area, widespread production makes for anonymity among the Opalescent Ribbed pieces that have come down to us.

Peach Blow

What may be called the great Peach Blow controversy was touched off in March 1886 by the sale of a Chinese "peach blow" porcelain vase at auction by the estate of Mrs. Mary Morgan, an eccentric collector, for the unheard of price of $18,000. The press ridiculed the vase, and glass manufacturers tried to imitate it. *The Journal* opened its pages to debate and printed such acrimonious readers' comments as "Small fraud, big bait," "Cheaper than the cheapest Whisk Pickle Dish," and "25 cents per dozen in associated colors — we wouldn't have given a dollar for it."

Mount Washington was quick to sense the value of the name Peach Blow and applied for exclusive use of it. Their product was of a homogeneous metal, the color shading from a pale bluish gray to a rosy color under reheating. New England Glass also made a homogeneous Peach Blow, a combination of opal and gold ruby, reheated white to rose. A key point to remember in the experiments with heat-sensitive color is that Thomas Webb and Sons and Stevens and Williams of England had been making Peach Bloom in 1885, the year before the sale of the Morgan vase. The English style was later followed by Hobbs, Brockunier.

Wheeling Peach Blow (Coral) was cased over white, a transparent amber that was sensitive to heat. After the treatment, the top became a vivid dark ox-blood red, while the lower part took on a greenish yellow. First off, Hobbs, Brockunier created a facsimile of the Morgan vase on its gargoyle stand, both in shiny and in satin (or matte) finishes — a creditable accomplishment. They did not limit their product to objects of art but met holiday demand by naturalistic fruit: pears, peaches, apples. Table sets of globular salts, peppers, and mustards, of tumblers, creamers, finger bowls — whatever satisfied utilitarian demand — were turned out in quantities. That is why Hobbs, Brockunier Peach Blow dominated the American market for a long time.

We have no identified examples of Peach Blow in Pittsburgh proper, yet we have reason to believe that such products were made. We read in *The Journal* for April 29, 1886, "Atterbury & Company have just reproduced a facsimile of the Morgan Peach Blow Vase exact in shape, size and other details with the original. The price is $4 a dozen." Was Atterbury transgressing the patent laws? Should we accept the statement as fact? The Atterburys had proved themselves inventive in many other lines. To confuse us still further, *The Journal* for March 11, 1886, credits George Duncan & Sons with "new pieces of the prettiest glassware we have seen," with a peachy ground running into a soft, creamy white like a country girl's cheek.

With the magic word "peach" sweeping the country, it would be strange if Phoenix Glass Company of Philipsburg, Beaver County, Pennsylvania, had not also entered the field legitimately, for Joseph Webb, nephew of Thomas, had been licensed as the sole manufacturer in the United States of the celebrated Webb Glass. One of their advertisements reads, "Etched, Engraved and Decorated Goods in Crystal, Flint, colors — Opalescent, Venetian and Art Effects of every description in Tableware, Kerosene Goods and Shapes of all Kinds" (*508*). Phoenix had reported large orders for its colored and art glassware — much higher than those received a year earlier. *The Journal* praised Phoenix as having had years of experience, being the oldest company engaged in artistic glassware in Pittsburgh, all their products bearing the tokens of skill and educated taste. Yet *The Journal* six years earlier had been more critical in speaking of Phoenix's miscellaneous articles of curious and fancy designs.

506 Free-blown pitcher of Spangled Glass, Hobbs, Brockunier & Co. (Wheeling), patent to William Leighton, Jr., Jan. 29, 1884. A parison of glass is rolled over a marver covered with metallic flakes. Blue with silver flakes and clear handle. H. 5″. *The Henry Ford Museum.*

"On some of the specimens coloured protuberances appear in the most unexpected places, the designer evidently having an eye to the pleasing effect produced by polychromatic decoration even if the general result seems sometimes *outré* and wanting in symmetry."*

There was, of course, a lively importing business in Peach Blow. I. Vogelsang Sons, New York importers, advertised Peach Blow imitation at one-fourth the price of real Peach Blow. A. C. Revi dismisses Continental Peach Blow as being quite different from and inferior to the American product. Whatever the comparative merits of the foreign and the domestic versions, we know the demand in America was heavy.

Crackled . . . and Custard

Crackled and Spangled glass was made in and around Western Pennsylvania, but, unfortunately, we have no way to identify the pieces or to measure the quantity. *The Journal* reported on January 1, 1880, "Genuine crackled glass is among the latest successful productions of George Duncan & Sons." Three years later, Hobbs, Brockunier was advertising its "Craquelle" in Rose, Sapphire, Old Gold, and Marine Green. Since crackled glass is produced by plunging red hot glass into cold water and then reheating and shaping — a technique described by Apsley Pellatt in 1849 — any factory could adopt the process. Duncan had promoted the Tree of Life pattern, which somewhat resembles crackled glass; that factory was a logical manufacturer of Crackled. Certainly other glassmakers in the Tri-State area could have met any demand for it.

Although William Leighton, Jr., patented the process of Spangling glassware, no assurance can be given that Hobbs, Brockunier was its sole producer. Leighton's method consisted merely of rolling the hot bubble of glass over the marver on which was sprinkled a form of copper, or aven-

* *The Crockery and Glass Journal,* July 24, 1890, January 24, 1884.

turine, mica flakes or other colors as desired (*506*). After the bits of decoration had been incorporated in the pot metal, the piece was usually redipped in clear. Finished articles with silver or gold flakes are comparatively rare today, but the numerous vases and bowls in variegated colors without metal flakes show how widely Spangling or Splashing was used and how long it retained its popularity.

Contemporary collectors referring to Custard glass mean the opaque yellow that Northwood fostered when he was experimenting with different colors in opaque. In Indiana, Pennsylvania, and afterward at Wheeling, he made this color in such pressed sequences as punch bowls and cups and bureau sets. Nearly all Custard (opaque yellow)

507 Pearl Satin air trap vase in shaded blue. Phoenix Glass Co., Philipsburg, Pa. Joseph Webb had two patents for manufacturing this product, July 6, 1886, and Mar. 6, 1888. Original lining was mold-blown to establish the design; while still molten it was dipped for outer casing. Thus the original design was trapped by this action. *Smithsonian Institution.*

is pressed. We cannot be at all sure, however, that Ripley & Company meant yellow opaque when it advertised Idaho Custard Engraved and individual cream and sugar pieces. The goods were very lightly pressed and beautifully engraved. Ripley asserted that they were useful in serving desserts and of the greatest convenience for hotel and restaurant service. Ripley had earlier advertised Idaho Pattern, plain and engraved, Nos. 132 and 125, in fifty pieces. It would appear that the cream and sugar was probably an individual issue.

The Westmoreland Company was not only making custard jars two years after its opening but was also furnishing custard powder. Westmoreland had always favored opaque white and turquoise but not yellow; thus one sees how nomenclature can present a problem. The company made glass blacking boxes with blacking and, oddly enough, sold lemon powder in similar boxes. Glass manufacturers in search of novelties certainly widened uses for glass, even if they did so at the sacrifice of artistic design.

Soft Finishes

Because of the many available examples of satin glass (Pearl Satin), modern collectors hardly consider it a novelty. In the eighties and nineties it represented another of the ways glass manufacturers could attract and hold public fancy. The techniques used, the various color combinations, and the soft finishes lent themselves admirably to production of a best-selling product.

The Smithsonian Institution has a beautiful Pearl Satin vase with air trap diamond design (*507*), presented by the Phoenix Glass Company of Philipsburg. Until recently, Phoenix had not been widely credited with quality workmanship in many forms of artistic glass.

The air trap technique, used with two layers of different color, patented by Benjamin Richardson of England in January 1858, was never really discarded by later technicians. It consisted of blowing a bubble, usually of opaque metal, into a cuplike mold with ridges for the intaglio design (crisscross or whatever pattern may have been desired), then casing the original bubble and trapping the air underneath the outer layer of the pattern. Later patents in England, France, and America simply reiterated the Richardson process. William B. Dean and Alphonse Peltier of Brooklyn assigned such a patent in 1881 to the Mount Washington Glass Company, which action later caused a dispute with Phoenix. From its English connection with Webb, Phoenix undoubtedly had been using a similar process.

It remained for Frederick Shirley of Mount Washington to add to this repeated patent. He brought to it in June of 1886 the idea of a lusterless finish achieved by acid dipping, acid vapor, or sandblast. A gradation of different colors could be gained by reheating the sensitive glass. J. Stanley Brothers, writing for *Antiques*,* suggested that additional crystal plating could have been applied after the first coating, which trapped the design. He credits Joseph Webb of Phoenix with such variations as reversing the plating by placing the transparent glass on the interior of the opaque body. Mr. Brothers also surmises that modulations of color like the shaded effect in heat-sensitive glass could be obtained by lightly dipping the partly blown bulb into the desired color. Then the artisan could blow through the end of the bulb for gradations of color intensity. Midwestern manufacturers would have used whatever technique produced salable novelties most cheaply. Webb's third patent (March 6, 1888) related to the use of two molds: one for the design on the inner surface of the piece, the other for the outer casing shell.

Phoenix glassmen were offering new shades in ivory and opal decorated in the most "gorgeous" designs. Their specialties in pearl satin, crystal, ivory, and engraved goods, they admitted, were beyond enumeration. They had a brisk trade in decorated lampshades in bisque and ivory. The character of their decorations reminded people of Royal Worcester and other art pottery. Globes, shades, art and cut glass were decorated with paint, enamel, and etching. With better known names like Sandwich, Stevens & Williams, Mount Washington, and Webb, it was little wonder that Phoenix did not gain big dividends in claiming many pieces of desirable art glass. The small and newly formed Cooperative Flint Glass Company of Beaver Falls, for instance, had come out with a new pattern called Pearl, undoubtedly pressed but using the nomenclature of a neighboring art glass factory. We do not know today how many small factories may have produced glass that has been given famous attribution.

* "American Ornamental Glass," Part I, August 1934; II, March 1936; III, December 1936.

A local historian credited Phoenix with the revival in cut glass, particularly colored.* Yet the Dithridge Flint Glass Company of New Brighton has usually been thought of as a leader in brilliant cutting and engraving in Western Pennsylvania in the years 1885–1900. In January 1890, Dithridge was advertising an impressive list of cut patterns: Elberon, Princess, Persian, Brilliant, Duchess, Gem, Jewel, Peerless, and all the standard patterns. It also made wide claims: Rich Cut and Blown Glassware, the Latest Designs and Shapes, the Newest and Best Patterns, the Most Uniform Color, the Greatest Brilliancy, the Best Workmanship, the Best Finish.† Collectors today are not likely to credit Dithridge with those pat-

* George H. Thurston, *Allegheny County's 100 Years* (Pittsburgh: A. A. Anderson and Sons, 1888), p. 191.
† *The Crockery and Glass Journal,* January 2, 1890.

509 Decanters and wine glass of clear lead glass which has been cut through an overlay of emerald glass. Croesus pattern, Phoenix Glass Co., ca. 1885. *Toledo Museum Exhibition, Collection of Mrs. S. N. Benham. Courtesy of Dorothy Daniel.*

terns and may dismiss it as a small company that produced excellent blanks. The Smithsonian Institution owns a fine example of their work: a cut and engraved goblet with a picture on it of Mount Vernon.

During the Harrison-Cleveland campaign of 1888, the company sent a token of their skill to Benjamin Harrison. In his letter to Edward Dithridge, written October 29, 1888, a few days before his election to the presidency, Harrison expressed his thanks — "The Tankard is certainly a very fine specimen of American skill."

Cameo Glass

The Crockery and Glass Journal for July 24, 1890, spoke of Dithridge as producing cameo glass, and in that month the company advertised that it was making cameo glass in tableware and lamps in several colors and decorations. We may safely assume that these were not the carefully designed and carved forms that had marked the Webb, the Northwood, or the Stevens & Williams English pieces. Tableware and lamps are evidence that the process of manufacture could have been the shallow, acid-etched technique of the

510 Cut and engraved goblet, ca. 1888. View of Mount
Vernon. Dithridge Flint Glass Co., New Brighton, Pa.
H. 6⅝″. *Smithsonian Institution.*

511 Table pieces in pressed amethyst glass. Pattern is S repeat, in a new style. A. C. Revi in *American Pressed Glass and Figure Bottles* assigns this pattern to the National Glass Co. It was undoubtedly produced by one of the companies before the 1899 merger, perhaps by Riverside Glass Co. *The Henry Ford Museum.*

512 Varicolored bell, Inverted Hobnail. *The Historical Society of Western Pennsylvania.* Horn with blue and red loopings, ca. 1875. This actually gives a musical tone. 11½". *Collection of Dr. E. R. Eller.*

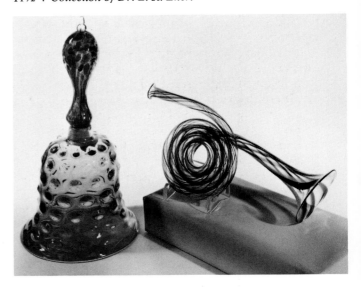

twentieth century, a cheaper method than the English. Perhaps, too, companies were advertising enameled decorations as cameo. Certainly American workmen were not following the techniques of true cameo, which demanded careful and costly hand carving.*

The Journal for July 30 said:

The indications are very bright with the New Brighton Glass Company. Their Cameo glass in tableware and lamps is highly favored by the trade, and they are getting numerous orders for it. They have this in several colors and decorations, and it is a new thing in the market. They have a large line of other decorated goods including lamps and novelties besides a fine assortment of crystal.

Two methods of producing cameo glass more cheaply than by the slow hand-chiseling way had been devised. The English company of Thomas Webb used the following method: the workman painted or printed the design on what we would call the "overlay," frequently opaque white on blue, usually a lighter color over a darker one. Then the chosen design was treated with an acid resist. The cutting wheel could complete the cutting away so that the pattern would be left in bas-

* *The Crockery and Glass Journal,* August 16, 1890.

relief. An elaboration that could be used was tinting those parts that required a shading or a color contrast with a glass color. This was then fixed by subsequent firing and the final polishing. In following this acid-resist procedure the French and the Americans used a darker color for the overlay and could achieve variety from the opaque over blue.

In 1879 William Libbey of the New England Glass Company devised a second way of producing cameo. It combined pressing and blowing. Although the Bakewell Double Glass has been compared to cameo, it merely represents a fusion of two colors mechanically pressed without the bas-relief and configuration of true cameo. Libbey's method, in its simplest essentials, set up a recessed or intaglio portion of the mold that held the eventual design. The recesses were situated on either side of a temporary cone. Two small openings above the cone extended downward to the intaglio portion of the cone-filled chamber. The molten glass could be pressed down from the pressing font above in any desired color. When the temporary cone was removed, the gaffer could insert a bubble of the darker-colored glass and the whole could be reheated and shaped.

That procedure, or some variation of it, would account for the New Brighton Glass Company claim that it could produce cameo glass at a low price. From the Webb technique, a tinting of already existing figures could give a reverse cameo effect on clear pressed pattern glass. Staining the raised design of Baltimore Pear, for instance, would give the darker color over the crystal. Because there are few pattern glass novelty specimens in cameo, we can assume that the New Brighton claims were for a new and short-lived product.

The Midwestern preoccupation with pressing and improved manufacturing techniques limited Pittsburgh glassmakers in joining the true Art Nouveau movement. The ideals of rhythmic naturalism expressed in graceful forms and blended colors demanded individual workmanship like that of Louis C. Tiffany and Arthur Nash. If Pittsburgh failed to set a new style, it did succeed in producing glass that fitted the new movement and sold well. *The Crockery and Glass Journal* wrote in October 1879 that South Side manufacturers were shipping glass to New York that came back to Pittsburgh and was there sold as imported ware. "Some of the importers of foreign ware," *The Journal* said in January 1884, "are Pittsburgh's best customers."

CHAPTER XXII

The Glass Pool—The End of an Era

> The best informed think an arrangement of some kind of combination by tableware manufacturers all but certain, though details have not yet been perfected. Negotiations have reached an advanced stage. . . . The trade is vitally interested. The first result of such a combination will be an increase in prices.
> — *The Crockery and Glass Journal,* August 19, 1889

An American glassman returned from France in 1882 with an enthusiastic report of an organization of glass manufacturers that had succeeded to some degree in defraying and sharing losses during periods of overproduction and of subsequent shutting down.* Glassmakers in the Midwest and elsewhere were deeply interested in such a possibility — in voluntary cooperative association and effort to counter the demands of labor, high cost of materials, and falling glass prices. An inordinate number of small glass concerns had sprung up lately along the Ohio River and were adding to the cutthroat competition and overproduction in the industry. In May 1884, *The Crockery and Glass Journal* laid the key phrase before the industry: Glass Pool. The idea was here, but the manufacturers were not yet ready to unite.

The nucleus for consolidation already existed in the Western Flint and Lime Glass Protective Association of American Flint and Lime Glass Manufacturers, founded in 1875 and now, with fifty-five members, grown much stronger. President Daniel C. Ripley and lesser officers like William McCully, Andrew Bryce, James Gillinder, Thomas Evans, and Paul Zimmerman, sound

* *The Crockery and Glass Journal,* December 28, 1882.

businessmen with an eye to order and progress, were respected throughout the industry. They represented an influence that could put forward the merger idea when the industry was ready for it. President Ripley voiced the manufacturers' sentiments: no businessman should harbor feelings of jealousy or selfishness.

In May 1884, the industry appointed a strong committee on pooling: D. Ripley, A. Bryce, John Adams, A. H. Heisey, James B. Lyon, and Jesse H. Lippincott of Pittsburgh; James Gillinder of Philadelphia; C. W. Brockunier, G. F. Miller, and a Mr. Gorley of the Wheeling District. The talk at that time was of an arrangement whereby a limited number of the larger and more prominent manufacturers would lease all the other factories at a fair rental and run them. Tentative discussion on that theme called forth a critical phrase: A Second Standard Oil Combine.

The big developments began in 1889. On March 21 of that year, *The Crockery and Glass Journal* printed a strong editorial in favor of consolidation of manufacturers. It flatly denied the charge that curbing excessive competition was a menace to society and a violation of the natural law of supply and demand. Combines and trusts, the editors declared, might properly be formed for the benefit and protection of any trade or business threatened with decay and ruin. The public, they said, had been led to think of a trust as a highwayman, but two of the strongest, Standard Oil and American Sugar, had been easy on prices and had stimulated the general use of their products. All talk regarding the monopolistic tendency of corporations was rot. The manufacturing world was "too large to nurse a monopoly of any sort after it becomes oppressive."

The Journal called two months later for consolidation in the sister industry down the Ohio, pottery manufacturing. Operating in unison, it said, would reduce operating costs and lower prices to the public. Then it blasted labor unions. Next to Standard Oil, the most stupendous trust was the Knights of Labor.

In February 1890, the New York *Sun* reported that window glass manufacturers were forming a stock company. When organized, such a company would include the United Glass Company, the Pittsburgh Company, and Chambers and McKee Company, and thus it would be making all the window glass produced in the United States. United would take in factories in Ohio, Indiana, Pennsylvania, and New York; the East and the Midwest would be represented in the new cartel. The name chosen was the American Window Glass Company, central office in Chicago, about sixty concerns participating. Expected capital had been $600,000, but it fell short by a third, Pittsburgh companies subscribing more than $200,000. A committee of five from the central agency allocated stock in the company in amounts relative to the glass sold.

Uniting the major tableware factories presented more intricate problems, and developments proceeded more slowly. These manufacturers, jealous of individual rights and power, had long copied, adopted, even pirated competitors' designs. The O'Hara Company, for example, at one time had as many as 400 molds in storage representing many patterns. When production was reduced under consolidation, each member could be forced to relinquish a favorite pattern to the controlling company.

There had been a few temporary associations before this in the glass trade, mainly to present a unified front against labor, to regulate prices and production, and to seek governmental favors. Several long-lived companies like Bakewell, Pears, the Curlings, and the McKees were family ventures, even though new blood and capital might be injected from time to time. They prized their independence. Partnerships were constantly changing and many companies, because of hard times, failed or reorganized. The background for a pool, therefore, was somewhat weak.

Tableware men of Pittsburgh and the Upper Ohio Valley met twice in October 1889, ostensibly to discuss the scale of wages. By the following July they were talking openly of regulating production, of maintaining prices, of widening the field of operations. They reached a tacit understanding that in the event of a consolidation, output would not be restricted beyond the needs of the trade; there would be no wholesale dismissal of executives; the number of shops (working teams) would be decreased but no factories would be closed; and prices of wares would be maintained at a level that would permit a favorable balance.

The cartel was completed and took effect on July 1, 1891, as the United States Glass Company, with Daniel C. Ripley, Jr., as first president. The cover of the new company's catalogue gave the list of member companies, each carrying an identifying letter by which it was to be known. They were:

Adams & Co., Pittsburgh, Pa.	Factory	A
Bryce Brothers, Pittsburgh, Pa.	"	B
Challinor, Taylor & Co. Ltd., Tarentum, Pa.	"	C
George Duncan & Sons, Pittsburgh, Pa.	"	D
Richards & Hartley, Tarentum, Pa.	"	E
Ripley & Co., Pittsburgh, Pa.	"	F
Gillinder & Sons, Greensburg, Pa.	"	G
Hobbs Glass Co., Wheeling, W. Va.	"	H
Columbia Glass, Findlay, O.	"	J
King Glass Co., Pittsburgh, Pa.	"	K

O'Hara Glass Co., Pittsburgh, Pa.	"	L
Bellaire Goblet Co., Findlay, O.	"	M
Nickel Plate Glass Co., Fostoria, O.	"	N
Central Glass Co., Wheeling, W. Va.	"	O
Doyle & Co., Pittsburgh, Pa.	"	P
A. J. Beatty & Sons, Tiffin, O.	"	R
A. J. Beatty & Sons, Steubenville, O.	"	S
Novelty Glass Co., Fostoria, O.	"	T

Factory catalogues were absorbed and incorporated, often in toto, into the cartel catalogue, though the United States Glass Company undoubtedly did not produce many of the single items and patterns it showed. It soon became apparent that the agreement to keep officers and executives at their posts made for an unwieldy organization; two years after the consolidation there was a purge of vice presidents.

If the cartel was organized in the belief that it could settle the companies' labor troubles, it was wrong. One of the Company's first demands was that the American Flint Glass Workers agree to lift all restrictions on output of their member-workmen. The union, of course, refused to give up a traditional right in the industry, and a three-year strike (1893–1896) followed. Both sides lost. The union gave in on the issues of restrictions on productivity and introduction of new labor-saving machinery and so lost much of its power. A number of companies closed by the strike never reopened, and the United States Glass Company itself never fully recovered from the losses it suffered in the strike.*

In November 1899, nineteen companies merged to create the National Glass Company, under the presidency of Rochester's Henry C. Fry. They were manufacturers of tableware products of lesser variety and excellence; they were strongest in production of tumblers, goblets, and novelties; only one of the nineteen (McKee and Brothers) was located in Pittsburgh and only four others in Pennsylvania. The failure and dissolution of the

* A. C. Revi, *American Pressed Glass and Figure Bottles* (New York: Thomas Nelson and Sons, 1964), p. 308.

combine by 1903 indicated the looseness of its organizational ties.

The cartels mark the end of an era in American glass. Open competition among many small rivals, with all its problems of economy and production, had passed; twentieth-century efficiency and assembly line mass production were being born. Factories lost their identity and managers their freedom to act. What O'Hara, Adams, or Duncan once dared to do in adopting or developing forms and patterns now was subject to committee approval. Old rivalries among members were forgotten. The committee counted on previously successful patterns: Daisy and Button, Dakota, Dewdrop, Honeycomb, Jacob's Ladder, Plume, Red Block, Ribbon Candy, Roman Rosette, Thumbprint, and Wildflower. The directors were interested chiefly in those new ventures where the economic risk was low and the money-making probabilities high.

United States Glass Company catalogues show innumerable patterns which, appearing originally in parent catalogues, now had no birth dates and little evidence or promise of parental care. In fact, many patterns languished and disappeared; some were reissued cheaply and briefly for Montgomery Ward & Company and later mail-order houses.

And thus the rise of the glass giants blunts the interest of the scholar and the collector. We may follow a favorite pattern or form from factory to cartel, from an original design to a gradually altered one, and there our enthusiasm wanes, perhaps dies. Now the attention must shift from a factory to a combine, from a team to a syndicate. It is far more fun to cheer for the Pittsburgh Pirates than for the National League.

In holding a choice piece of early Pittsburgh glass in my hands, I have often thought, "I am holding a miracle." Its fragile perfection has survived the hazards of a century and a half of use. Its beauty was achieved in frontier America, where glassmaking was a new art. Without laboratories for analysis of silica and clays, without thermal gauges for the ovens and lehrs, these craftsmen and artists produced works of beauty and ingenuity in a variety of techniques and design. With nothing but hand and eye to bring the decanter or bowl or vase or goblet into being, they turned out pieces unsurpassed by the generations that followed.

The industry had changed and moved on into an era of lesser interest with its cartelization, but it had left behind a rich national inheritance in glass. This volume has attempted to tell the story of that part of the inheritance created at or near the forks of the Ohio River in the years 1797–1891.

No closing words can conceal the shortcomings or heighten the merits of the work done there. The achievements of the Pittsburgh glassmakers in copying, adopting, and finally individualizing the techniques of blowing, cutting, engraving, and early pressing will never need apologists. Their work belongs to the evolution of fine glass.

Too often in judging a work of art we forget the primary purpose for which it was created, and we surround it with learned and lifeless analysis.

Glassmaking in the Pittsburgh District sprang from a direct need of the settlers beyond the mountains — and from an unspoken promise of the three rivers that they would carry the product to the Great Gulf at the end of the Mississippi Valley or to the Great Lakes and the villages of Canada. Pittsburgh glass, made of silica from the valley creek beds, melted by coal from nearby hills or by natural gas from underlying pools, drew, like a magnet, finer ingredients, and talented workmen from other parts of America.

As quality became refined and production increased, Pittsburgh glass still retained its identity and individuality. In pioneer cabins, on riverboats and in taverns, at the tables of the wealthy and in the homes of the poor, it answered all the demands made of it and added, too, a brightness and cheer. A green flask passing among friendly hands, a deep milk bowl with its layer of cream, a lacy sweetmeat dish on a side table, a dolphin compote filled with berries or fruit — all fitted their natural places and found their natural uses. Today the glass is beyond blame and above praise. It exists. It is there to be looked at and admired, to be studied and enjoyed.

LIST OF ILLUSTRATIONS

APPENDICES

BIBLIOGRAPHY

INDEX

List of Illustrations

XI BOTTLES AND FLASKS

COLOR PLATES

Appendix 1   Patents Referred To

Chapter V   New Companies and Discoveries in Pressing Glass

W. O. Davis	No.	10,470	January 31, 1854	Atterbury and		
		39,698	August 25, 1863	James Reddick —		
Frederick McKee and				join base and font		
Charles Ballinger	No.	42,143	May 29, 1864	of lamp	No. 82,579	September 29, 1868
Jonathan Haley	No.	138,750	May 13, 1873	T. B. Atterbury —		
Washington Beck	No.	162,791	May 4, 1875	Boss lamp	No. 181,618	August 29, 1876
William Gillinder	No.	51,386	December 5, 1865	J. S. and T. B. Atter-		
Washington Beck,				bury — press bowl		
Henry Feurhake,				and handle in one		
William Wuth	No.	221,023	October 28, 1879	mold	No. 79,298	June 30, 1868
Washington Beck,				T. B. Atterbury —		
Henry Feurhake	No.	219,240	September 2, 1879	lamp pedestal of		
D. C. Ripley —				woman's bust	No. 9114	February 29, 1876
pressed tops on				D. C. Ripley — mar-		
blown bodies	No.	75,577	March 17, 1868	riage lamp	No. 104,205	June 4, 1870
D. C. Ripley —				Ripley — stem or base	No. 3834	February 1, 1870
several articles in				Ripley — baptismal		
the same mold	No.	83,210	October 20, 1868	font	No. 3842	February 8, 1870
J. S. and T. B. Atter-				Paul Zimmerman —		
bury and James				flaring and		
Reddick — pressing				crimping machine	No. 170,616	November 30, 1875
and blowing in one				Benjamin Bakewell —		
operation	No.	79,298	June 30, 1868	Double Glass	No. 155,403	September 29, 1874
J. S. and T. B.				J. S. and T. B. Atter-		
Atterbury (similar				bury and James		
process)	No.	139,993	June 17, 1873	Reddick	No. 34,555	March 4, 1862
William King	No.	114,569	May 9, 1871	J. S. and T. B. Atter-		
David Barker	No.	216,134	June 3, 1879	bury — Rock of		
J. S. and T. B.				Ages plate	No. 170,218	November 23, 1875

Chapter XV   Lamps and Chimneys

Edward Dithridge — oval lamp chimney	No. 33,428	October 8, 1861
Paul Zimmerman — flaring and crimping machine	No. 170,616	November 30, 1875
T. B. Atterbury — tools for flaring and crimping chimneys	No. 170,431	November 12, 1875
William H. Maxwell — tools for crimping chimneys	No. 173,801	January 6, 1876
Jacob Reighard — separate opening for fuel assigned to Hale, Atterbury & Co.	No. 32,739	July 2, 1861
J. S. and T. B. Atterbury — metal collar	No. 38,087	April 7, 1863
D. C. Ripley — pressed base and blown bowl	No. 73,122	January 7, 1868
J. S. and T. B. Atterbury and James Reddick — pressing and blowing in one operation	No. 79,298	June 30, 1868
D. C. Ripley — cast top and handle	No. 75,577	March 17, 1868
J. S. and T. B. Atterbury — Eureka lamp	No. 82,579	September 29, 1868
Roland Smith — amplification of Eureka	No. 96,986	November 16, 1869
T. B. Atterbury — added bosses and knobs to joining	No. 102,204	April 26, 1870
D. C. Ripley — design for stems	No. 3834	February 1, 1870
D. C. Ripley — metal handle	No. 101,512	April 5, 1870
C. L. Knecht — wire spiral	No. 110,049	December 30, 1870
J. C. Gill — union within the mold	No. 167,608	July 6, 1875
D. C. Ripley — marriage lamp	No. 104,205	June 4, 1870
D. C. Ripley — baptismal font	No. 3842	February 8, 1870
James Bryce — pedestal with socket for peg	No. 156,669	November 17, 1874
Hobbs, Brockunier — improve joining peg and socket	No.	1874
A. A. Adams — groove top lamp	No. 177,087	May 9, 1876
T. B. Atterbury — Boss lamp pressed in one piece	No. 181,618	August 29, 1876
T. B. Atterbury — lamp pedestal, a woman's bust	No. 9114	February 29, 1876
J. Adams and J. Bonshire — lamp pressed parts joined by cement	No. 183,276	October 17, 1876
A. A. Adams — lamp union of peg and bowl	No. 110,815	June 10, 1871

Chapter XVI   Directions of Pressed Glass

Matthew Smith — design for glassware	No. 10,688	May 21, 1878
John Bryce — Grape Leaf	No. 3716	October 19, 1869
J. H. Hobbs — Leaves and Fruit	No. 3828	February 1, 1870
Mary B. Campbell — Currant	No. 4774	April 11, 1871
Washington Beck — design similar to Stedman	No. 7755	September 15, 1874
A. H. Heisey — Shell and Tassel	No. 12,371	July 26, 1881
Frederick McKee — Sprig	No. 1748	April 21, 1863
Bryce, McKee — Diamond and Sunburst	No. 7948	December 22, 1874
Jenkins Jones — Dewdrop and Star	No. 10,296	November 6, 1877
J. E. Miller — Three Face	No. 10,727	June 18, 1878
Charles Ballinger — Dragon	No. 4419	October 18, 1870

Chapter XVII Ornamentation of Pressed Glass

Henry Feurhake —
preparing glass
molds   No. 219,240   September 2, 1874

Edward Dithridge —
mechanical frosting   No. 206,392   July 30, 1878

J. E. Miller — engrav-
ing machine   No. 239,263   July 14, 1880

W. O. Davis — Loop
and Dart   No.   3494   May 11, 1869

Chapter XVIII The Rise of Opal

J. S. and T. B. Atter-
bury — Eureka
lamp   No. 82,579   September 29, 1868

T. B. Atterbury —
Crossed fern   No.   9324   June 6, 1876

J. S. and T. B. Atter-
bury — Basket
Weave, Basket
Weave salt   No.   7504   June 30, 1874
                        No.   8220   March 23, 1875

J. S. and T. B. Atter-
bury — Rock of
Ages bread plate   No. 170,218   November 23, 1875

T. B. Atterbury —
Duck covered dish   No. 17,192   March 15, 1887

W. G. Walter —
assigned to
Atterburys — Opal
Boar's Head dish   No. 18,358   May 29, 1888

David Challinor —
Variegated glass-
ware   No. 342,898   June 1, 1886

Benjamin Bakewell —
Double Glass   No. 155,403   September 29, 1874

CHAPTER XIX Glassmaking for the Philadelphia Centennial

James Gill — Signers
Platter   No.   8663   September 28, 1875

B. Bakewell, Jr. —
Liberty Bell   No.   9145   March 21, 1876

J. S. and T. B. Atter-

bury — Liberty Bell
platter   No.   8450   July 6, 1875

James B. Lyon —
Crystal Wedding   No.   8464   July 6, 1875

William King — Cen-
tennial pattern   No. 163,787   May 25, 1875

Chapter XX Novelties in Glass

J. E. Miller — Daisy
& Button hat   No. 16,409   December 8, 1885

William G. Walker —
assigned to Camp-
bell Jones & Co.
(whiskbroom relish
dish)   No. 16,607   April 6, 1886

Julius Proeger —
assigned to McKee
& Brothers (Open
Coach Bowl)   No. 16,488   January 19, 1886

A. H. Heisey of Dun-
can's Vase-shaped,
half-opened
umbrella   No. 354,416   December 14, 1886

H. Franz — anvil
toothpick holder   No. 17,345   May 17, 1887

Julius Proeger —
meerschaum pipe   No. 20,079   August 5, 1890

Benjamin Bakewell —
Liberty Bell covered
dish with globe on
top   No.   9145   March 21, 1876

J. Haley — orna-
mental tiles   No.   May 4, 1886

Thomas Cutler —
goblet on a tripod   No.   3154   August 11, 1868

Henry Franz — for
Campbell Jones &
Co. (double relish
dish)   No. 212,208   October 21, 1879

William Kirchner —
for Atterbury's
(handled pickle dish) No. 153,221 July 21, 1874

T. B. Atterbury —
metallic covers No. 159,628 February 9, 1875

D. C. Ripley —
dessert bowl with
drip channel No. 206,617 July 30, 1878

Joseph and Frank
Brunwasser — fly-
trap No. 419,003 January 7, 1890

W. H. Maxwell —
paperweight No. 263,931 September 5, 1882

Washington Beck —
Jolly Jester match
safe No. 178,504 June 13, 1876

David Barker —
spoon holder
(Jumbo) No. 305,498 September 23, 1884

King, Son & Co. —
Mitchell ware shell
feet No. 163,787 May 25, 1875

John H. Hobbs —
goat's head feet No. 10,392 January 8, 1878

Chapter XXI Art Glass

Joseph Webb —
Pearl Satin air
trap No. 345,265 July 6, 1886

Joseph Webb — as-
signed to Phoenix
Glass Co. — Pearl
Satin air trap No. 363,190 May 17, 1887

Joseph Webb —
Pearl Satin air
trap No. 379,089 March 6, 1888

William Leighton, Jr.
(design) No. 14,443 November 27, 1883

Spangled Glass
(Mechanical) No. 292,663 January 29, 1884

William B. Dean and
Alphonse Peltier —
Mother-of-Pearl No. 237,371 February 8, 1887

Appendix 2 Stanger Letters

(SEE CHAPTER III, pp. 38, 48)

Two letters* from Thomas Stanger, glassblower at William McCully's factory in Pittsburgh, to his brother John in Glassboro, New Jersey. The letters are interesting because they come from a family long associated with glassmaking in the East. Thomas describes his work and the conditions of the glass industry and comments on the social aspect of Pittsburgh in 1846 and 1847.

"Pittsburgh August 27th 1846

Dear Brother

   . . . I have no news of an interesting character to write to you from here, there is no use of giving you an elaborate description of this place for you have already read a humdrum description of it and it is about what it is represented to be, there is one street about 1 mile long lined on both sides with quite respectable looking dwellings where the fashionable people of the city live, and about ¼ of the city is well-built though black-looking storehouses the rest is one mass of dirt and smoke completely filled up with furnaces, foundries, factories, mills etc. in almost endless succession, from which clouds of smoke are constantly ascending, there are no less than 19 Glass factories of different kinds within one mile of the centre of this city, and more iron furnaces than you ever heard tell of, the churches here are about

Courtesy of the Corning Museum of Glass

as black outside as glass factories commonly are the people here are pretty much of a church-going people and do not appear to me to be half such barbarians as the[y] are generally represented in the east to be I have no fault to find with anything connected with myself except that I have to change orders so much, there is such a demand for glass out here, that in the summer every thing made of glass is sold, and when the fire begins a complete assortment is immediately wanted, by the way the Glassfactory at Lockport burned down a few days ago, it is to be immediately repaired, our Pots do not stand a great while before they wear out, our first setting were in only 4 weeks when they were all thrown out at one time and a new setting put in,

   . . . I do not know how the weather has been with you, but out here it has been so intensely hot that it has been very uncomfortabl[e] blowing, but now it is a little cooler and I hope we shall have it better, one of McCully's [Wm. McCully & Co. Pittsburgh, Pa] blowers (a western man) has quit and gone to another factory to work, there is plenty of places here for vial blowers yet, and vial blowing is as good as bottle blowing out here, I have a single pit and make no more money than some of the vial blowers,

   I am well at present except that I have a cold which is getting better all the rest of the eastern blowers out here are well and in good spirits, . . .

     . . . Yours Affectionately

     Thomas Stanger"

January 27, 1847

Dear Brother. I received your letter requesting me to give you an answer concerning the Factory as soon as I could but as I could not give an answer just then upon an affair of so much importance, I have delayed writing until now, to obtain all the necessary information I could so that I could give you a decisive answer when I did write. I have at length concluded that if Grandfather and you are willing, I will take a part in the concern with Thos. Stanger and yourself, each of us a third to rent Factory for either 1, 2, 3, 4 or 5 years optional with us, so long as all three or any two of the company should desire to carry it on, to take the Factory about the 15th of June next, that is I think as much the right time to take a Glassfactory as the 25th of March is to take a Farm, and he could occupy the intermediate time between the expiration of the lease of the present company, and the commencement of ours to do those repairs about the houses which he told me last summer he would do.

But I presume it only necessary to mention terms to him for him to object to them, wether they were favourable to him or not, but still I think we ought to endeavor to get the lease on the above terms as nearly as we can, and that would be getting for ourselves a pretty fair scope of liberty, which we should badly want on account of his meddling interferences with everything about there, everything connected with the least must be fully settled before we commence for after that we cannot do it advantageously the other and more ordinary terms of the lease I shall say nothing about for you and and he can arrange them the best way you can with the old man.

I am not so tenacious about the terms above mentioned as to say I will not have it upon any others but I think we should endeavor to get it as favorable to ourselves as we can, I am not extremely anxious to enter the business for I think with a little effort in the summer season I can make 1000$ a year out here and not have to deal with such a troublesome business, and beside that I think in a year or two I could get into business out here at which I could make more than I can there but still I would rather live at home. You can show this to TW Stanger and you and he confer upon the matter and talk with Grandfather about it try to make some arrangement so as to take the Factory. I am well and doing well making the best of wages, . . .

I remain your Brother
Thos Stanger

Mr. J. M. Stanger
Write to me very soon and let me know how you suceed about the Factory.

Appendix 3   Dithridge Formulas

(SEE CHAPTER V, p. 52, AND CHAPTER XVIII, p. 396)

Edward Dithridge, Sr., long a skilled workman at the Fort Pitt factory, became majority stockholder and owner in 1863. Then he changed production, specializing in chimneys as Dithridge & Co., a firm that continued to 1900. On his deathbed in 1873, he urged his sons "never to change the formula."

In 1881, his son Edward purchased a factory at Martins Ferry, Ohio, where he produced blown and pressed ware (The Dithridge Flint Glass Works). In 1887 he moved to New Brighton, Pennsylvania. These formulas* from Edward's notebook, September 24, 1890, show that the factory was also competing in the art glass movement.

Opal for Casing

Sand	100
Lead	120
Pearls	30
Phosphate of Lime	14
Arsenic	4
Borax	4
Oxide of Tin	9

This gives a white enamel for casing inside or outside of flint and may be colored same as opal

* Courtesy of Charles R. Mitchell

Demi opaque or Pat de Riz

Sand	100
Bicarbonate Potash	43
Phosphate Lime	5
Nitrate of Potash	4

This is sometimes called Alabastor and has a milk and water tint. It is in some particulars an imperfect glass. By using oxide or copper oxide of Cobalt and a mixture of iron and copper you can get handsome blues and greens.

This glass should not be submitted to too long a melt as it will become transparent. You can also obtain the above by substituting sulphate of potash for the bicarbonate and bones.

Beautiful Green for Open Pots

Sand	100
Carb Soda	30
Carb Lime	23
Nitrate of Potash	7
Oxide of Copper	6
Oxide of Iron	4

This gives a green, inclining more to a green than blue and gives a color rich and deep enough for a thickness from 1½ millimetres to 2 millimetres the coloring material should be reduced for heavier ware by using

Oxide copper	5
Oxide Iron	3
Bichromate Potash	8½

You have equally a Grass green but more brilliant by using 80 grammes oxide cobalt. You replace the yellow tinge by a blue tint.

Flint Glass rich and heavy for cutting
1C

Sand	1500 lbs
Lead	1000 ”
Pearl	500 ”
Manganese	

No. 2C

Sand	1500
Lead	1000
Pearls	400
Nitrate Potash	100
Manganese	

3C

Sand	1500
Lead	1000
Pearls	300
Soda crystals	80
Nitrate Potash	100
Manganese	

This is virtually the flint or crystal glass of France and England as used for their fine ware both for heavy cut ware and light blown ware including the most delicate

Appendix 4 Niles Register

(SEE CHAPTER VIII, p. 108)

Editorials in *Niles' Weekly Register,* published in Baltimore, for August and September 1819, reveal an increasing pride in American cut glass, the handicap of meeting English competition, and the budding rivalry between the East and the Midwest. An editor indicated his admiration for presentation pieces from the New England Glass Company, which had opened its doors in 1818. He took note of a letter from a correspondent, who knew of trade difficulties in the glass business:

The notice of some handsome articles of American glassware presented to the editor on behalf of the New England Glass Manufacturing Co. with our remarks upon the propriety of protecting home products has induced a gentleman who appears to be well acquainted with the subject to give us information **** to show the difficulties which the American manufacturer has to contend against.

The correspondent in sympathy with the editorial policy of supporting a protective tariff noted the difficulties of glassmen on the East Coast, since the British government paid the whole cost of landing glass in America and added a bounty to the English agent in Boston for his success.

The editor went on to state:

There are establishments at Pittsburgh and other places claiming our regard as much as those at Boston: — the encouragement of productive industry, internal improvement, and individual happiness is just as much an object in one part of the U.S. as in another, for being long accustomed to endeavor to regard himself as a citizen of the republic he has considerably divested himself of local partialities.

In the same year, Bakewell sent to the editor of the *Register* a pair of decanters because of the sympathy and encouragement he had shown manufacturers. Of course the editor echoed his praise in honoring Pittsburgh: "they are equally neat and beautiful. We are pleased to see so much perfection in such distant points of the country."

Appendix 5   James B. Lyon Catalogue, 1861—Outline Analysis

(SEE CHAPTER XIV, p. 298)

Author's outline of the unpublished catalogue of James B. Lyon & Company for 1861. In addition to showing the make-up of an early glass catalogue, it identifies patterns not previously attributed to Lyon and several hitherto unrecorded. These are indicated by asterisks.

The following pictures from the catalogue are in the text: No. 363, No. 329, No. 330, No. 368, No. 371, and No. 372.

O'Hara Flint Glass Works — 1861

Pages 1 and 2 — Tumblers — Some Handled
Sizes ⅓ pint to 1 quart
Patterns
*6 Flute, *7 Flute, *8 Flute, *9 Flute*
    *New York, *Lily, *Crossan, *Genella, *St. Nicholas, *Gaines, *Huber, *Henderson, *Mioton, *Cincinnati, *O'Hara, *New England, *Mobile, *Charleston, *Philadelphia, *Gauche, *Sage

Pages 3 — *Goblets, Champagnes, Wines, Eggs, Jellies, Ales*
    Huber, *Hotel, New York, *Bohemian, *Ashburton, Cincinnati, *St. George (Giant Thumbprint), O'Hara (Loop)

Pages 4 and 5 — *Assorted Nappies and Nappies on Foot*
    Cincinnati, O'Hara, Genella, *Wreath, *Star, Diamond, New Orleans, *Crystal, *Reeded, New York, *Mitre Diamond, *Small Diamond, *Leaf (heavy)

Pages 6, 7, 8, 9, and 10 — *Bowls, covered and open, low and high*
Page 6 — Cincinnati; 7 — O'Hara; 8 — Huber; 9 — *Crystal; 10 — Huber, Cincinnati, *Mirror, Crystal

Page 11 — Decanters and Bitters Bottles: Patent stoppers, pressed ones
    O'Hara, Huber, Genella, Cincinnati, new patterns: *Chicago, *St. Nicholas (footed), *Columbus (cut and engraved)

Page 12 — *Pitchers and Water Bottles: Pint and Quart (plain)*
    O'Hara (cut and engraved), Huber (footed), Genella, Cincinnati

Page 13 — *Celerys* (No new patterns)

Page 14 — *Sugars, Creams, Spoon Holders*
    new patterns: *Davis, *Palace

Page 15 — *Molasses Cans*
    new patterns: Mirror, *Star and Concave

Page 16 — *Salvers* (10 sizes, all Cincinnati)

Page 18 — Huber Bar Sugars — Planished Tin Covers (one and two Hinge) Specie and Squat Jars (1 pint, 1 gallon)
Lightning Rod Insulators

Listed without pictures:
Lamps with Brass Burners (oil or fluid)
Taylor, large; Tulip, medium; Mirror, medium; Cone, handled; Rose, extra large; Palace, large; Night, small

Appendix 6   Table of Chimney Prices

COMPARISON OF CHIMNEY PRICES IN THE
1860s AND 1870s AND BETWEEN LIME GLASS
AND FLINT

(SEE CHAPTER XV, p. 317)

July 1, 1864 McKee & Brothers, 17 Wood St., Corner or First

#3	Coal	Oil		per Dozen	$1.50
2	”	”		” ”	1.20
1	”	”		” ”	.90
1	”	” Frosted		” ”	1.10
0	”	”		” ”	.90

Midsixties McKee & Brothers (undated)

#2	Coal	Oil		per Dozen	.87
1	”	”		” ”	.67
1	”	” Frosted		” ”	.87
0	”	”		” ”	.67

This catalogue also included other chimneys.

2, 2⅛, 2⅜, 2¼ and 2½ inch Solar	per dozen			$1.00
2″	Camphene	”	”	1.75
2¾ and 3 inch	”	”	”	2.00
3¼ and 3½ inch	”	”	”	2.25
3½ inch Turn-over Globes	”	”	”	4.00

McKee & Brothers, 1868

				Flint		Lime
#0	Coal Oil, Net per dozen			$ .70 per doz.		$ .45
1	” ” ”	”	”	.80	” ”	.45
2	” ” ”	”	”	1.10	” ”	.65
3	” ” ”	”	”	1.65	” ”	1.00

May 1, 1875 Wm McCully & Co., 18 and 20 Wood St.

Round and Oval Chimneys		Lime	Flint
#0	per dozen	.40	.65
1	” ”	.45	.70
2	” ”	.65	.95
3	” ”	1.10	1.45

M. W. Sackett & Co. (wholesaler), 29 Wood St.

								Best Flint
#0	Sun Straight, Bulb or Oval, per dozen							.40
1	”	”	”	”	”	”	”	.45
2	”	”	”	”	”	”	”	.60
			Crimp Top					Annealed
#0	Sun Straight, Bulb or Oval, per dozen							.35
1	”	”	”	”	”	”	”	.40
2	”	”	”	”	”	”	”	.55

Nov. 20, 1875 B. L. Fahnestock, 76 Wood St.

Round and Oval-Old Style		Lime	Flint
#0	per dozen	.35	.60
1	” ”	.40	.65
2	” ”	.60	.85
3	” ”	.75	1.25

Bibliography

PAPERS AND DOCUMENTS

Craig, Isaac. His business activities in Pittsburgh, 1790–1804. Carnegie Library, Pittsburgh.

Dick, John, James, and David. Covering the period 1825–1860. Crawford County Historical Society, Meadville, Pa.

Lossing, Benson John. Burton Historical Collection, Detroit Public Library.

O'Hara, General James. Account books and letters, 1790–1819. Denny Papers, Historical Society of Western Pennsylvania, Pittsburgh.

Reynolds, John. Meadville, Pa., merchant, 1816–1855. Historical Society of Western Pennsylvania, Pittsburgh.

Thomson, C. W. "History of Ceredo and Kenova." 1959. Huntington Public Library, Huntington, W. Va.

PRINTED SOURCES

Albert, George Dallas. *History of the County of Westmoreland, Pennsylvania*. Philadelphia: Everts, 1882.

Amic, Yolande. *L'Opaline française au XIX siècle*. Paris: Librairie Gründ, 1952.

Antiques.
 "Again Pressed Window Panes." 34 (Dec. 1938): 294–95.
 "Dated American Glass." 30 (Aug. 1936):55–56.
 "Fresh Reflections on American Glass." 33 (Feb. 1938):80–83.
 "Kenmore." 53 (April 1948):293–96.
 "More Lacy Glass Window Panes." 51 (Sept. 1947): 120–21.

Avila, George C. *The Pairpoint Glass Story*. New Bedford, Mass.: Reynolds–De Walt Printing, 1968.

Bakewell, Mary E. "The Bakewell Glass Factory." *Carnegie Magazine* 21 (July 1947):35–40.

Baldwin, Leland D. *Pittsburgh, the Story of a City*. Pittsburgh: University of Pittsburgh Press, 1938.

———. *Whiskey Rebels*. Pittsburgh: University of Pittsburgh Press, 1939.

Barret, Richard Carter. *A Collector's Handbook of American Art Glass*. Manchester, Vt.: Forward's Color Productions, 1971.

———. *Blown and Pressed American Glass*. Manchester, Vt.: Forward's Color Production, Inc., 1966.

———. *Popular American Ruby-Stained Pattern Glass*. Manchester, Vt.: Forward's Color Productions, 1968.

Begenson, Anne. *Wholesale Prices in Philadelphia 1852–1896*. Philadelphia: University of Pennsylvania Press.

Belknap, E. McCamly. *Milk Glass*. New York: Crown Publishers, 1949.

Bergstron, Evangeline. *Old Glass Paperweights*. 4th ed. New York: Crown Publishers, 1963.

Bining, William. "The Glass Industry of Western Pennsylvania, 1797–1857." *Western Pennsylvania Historical Magazine* 19 (Dec. 1936):255–68.

Birbeck, Morris. *Notes on a Journey in America from the Coast of Virginia to the Territory Illinois*, 3d ed. London: Printed by Severn & Company for James Ridgeway, 1818.

Boardman, James. *America and the Americans*. London: Longman, Rees, Orme, Brown, Green, & Longman, 1833.

Brothers, J. Stanley, Jr. "American Opaque White Glass." *Hobbies* 40 (July 1936):69.

———. "American Ornamental Glass." *Antiques* 26 (Aug. 1934):57–59; 29 (March 1936):11–13; 30 (Dec. 1936):282–83.

————. "Some Interesting Mechanics of the Glass Industry." *Hobbies* 40 (Aug. 1936):76–79.

Centenary Memorial of the Planting and Growth of Presbyterianism in Western Pennsylvania and Parts Adjacent. Pittsburgh: Benjamin Singerly, 1876.

Challinor, Frank. "A Glassman's Collection." *Antiques* 51 (April 1947):254–55.

Coleman, Dorothy S. "Pioneers of Pittsburgh, The Robinsons." *Western Pennsylvania Historical Magazine* 42 (March 1959):55–77.

Covill, William E., Jr. *Ink Bottles and Inkwells.* Taunton, Mass.: Wm. S. Sullwold, 1971.

Cramer, Zadok. *The Navigator; Containing Directions for Navigating the Monongahela, Allegheny, Ohio and Mississippi Rivers; with an Ample Account of These Much Admired Waters.* Pittsburgh: Cramer & Spear, 1811, 1814, 1817.

The Crockery and Glass Journal. New York, weekly publication, issues from 1874–1891 used. In collection of Science and Technology Research Center, The New York Public Library, Astor, Lenox, and Tilden foundations.

Cuming, Fortescue. *Sketches of a Tour to the Western Country.* Pittsburgh: Cramer, Spear & Eichbaum, 1810.

Dambach, L. Earl. "Early Historical Flasks of Pittsburgh and the Monongahela District." *Western Pennsylvania Historical Magazine* 39 (spring 1956):25–34.

Daniel, Dorothy. *Cut and Engraved Glass 1771–1905.* New York: M. Barrows & Co., 1950.

————. "The First Glasshouse West of the Alleghenies." *Western Pennsylvania Historical Magazine* 32 (Sept.–Dec. 1949):97–113.

Davis, Derek C. *English Bottles and Decanters 1650–1900.* New York: The World Publishing Co., 1972.

Davis, Dr. Pearce. *The American Glass Industry and the Tariff.* Cambridge, Mass.: Harvard University Press, 1938.

Di Bartolomeo, Robert E., ed. *American Glass II Pressed and Cut.* Princeton: Pyne Press, 1974.

Donehoo, George P., ed. *Pennsylvania, A History.* New York: Lewis Historical Publishing Co., 1926.

Duss, John S. *The Harmonists, A Personal History.* Harrisburg, Pa.: Pennsylvania Book Service, 1943.

Edwards, Richard, ed. and pub. *Industries of Pittsburgh.* Pittsburgh, 1879.

Egle, William H. *An Illustrated History of the Commonwealth of Pennsylvania.* Harrisburg: Goodrich, 1876. (Article on Allegheny County by William M. Darlington and Thomas J. Bigham, pp. 314–329.)

Fearon, Henry Bradshaw. *Sketches of America.* 2nd ed. London: Longman, Hurst, Rees, Orme and Brown, 1818.

Gest, Neil C., and Smith, Dr. Parke G. "The Glassmaking Kramers." *Antiques* 35 (March 1939):118–21.

Green, Dr. Charles. "Dr. Green Still Champions Sandwich." *American Collector* 2 (Oct. 4, 1934):2, 11.

————. "Sandwich Made First Lacy Glass." *American Collector* 2 (July 26, 1934):1, 7, 11.

Harden, D. B. *Roman Glass from Karanis.* Ann Arbor, Mich.: University of Michigan Press, 1936.

Hinton, John Howard. *The History and Topography of the United States.* Vol. 2. Boston: Samuel Walker, 1846.

Honey, W. B. *Glass, A Handbook & a Guide to the Museum Collection, Victoria & Albert Museum.* London: Published under the authority of the Ministry of Education, 1946.

Hunter, Frederick William. *Stiegel Glass.* Introduction and Notes by Helen McKearin. 1914. Reprint. New York: Dover Publications, 1950.

Innes, Lowell. "Calling All Pittsburgh Glass." *Carnegie Magazine* 14 (Jan. 1941):237–41.

————. *Early Glass of the Pittsburgh District, 1797–1890.* Pittsburgh: Crescent Press, 1949.

————. "First Permanent Glass Collection for Pittsburgh." *Western Pennsylvania Historical Magazine* 37 (fall–winter 1954–1955):199–204.

————. "Forerunners in American Glass — the New Gorley Case." *Western Pennsylvania Historical Magazine* 40 (spring 1957):1–12.

————. "Glass Cut at Pittsburgh." *Carnegie Magazine* 20 (June 1946):42–44.

————. "Glass Pressed at Pittsburgh." *Carnegie Magazine* 15 (Jan. 1942):247–48.

————. "Governor Clinton Comes to Pittsburgh." *Western Pennsylvania Historical Magazine* 44 (Sept. 1961):237–56.

————. "Lacy Hairpin in French and American Glass." *Antiques* 10 (Aug. 1971):228–33.

————. "Pittsburgh Glass." *Antiques* 54 (Dec. 1948):417–19; 55 (Jan. 1949):46–49.

————. "Pittsburgh Glass on Display." *Carnegie Magazine* 23 (June 1949):6–9.

————. "Pittsburgh Pressed Glass." *Antiques* 56 (Sept.–Oct. 1949):168–71, 277–79.

————. "Pittsburgh White and Clear and the Bakewell Patent." *Antiques* 79 (June 1961):557–59.

————. "Studying Pittsburgh Glass." *Carnegie Magazine* 14 (April 1940):13–16.

————. "William Price and the Round Church." *Western Pennsylvania Historical Magazine* 47 (Oct. 1964):317–22.

Jarves, Deming. *Reminiscences of Glass Making.* Boston: Eastburn's Press, 1854, 1st ed. (printed for private circulation); 1865, 2nd ed.

Jefferson, Josephine. *Wheeling Glass.* Mt. Vernon, Ohio: Guide Publishing Co., 1947.

Jones, Samuel. *Pittsburgh in the Year 1826.* Pittsburgh: Johnston and Stockton, 1826.

Kamm, Minnie Watson. *Pitcher Books.* Grosse Pointe Farms, Mich.: privately printed, 1939–1953.

Keyes, Homer Eaton. "Interpreting the Sandwich Fragments." *Antiques* 34 (Sept. 1938):133–36.

————. "Museum Examples of Sandwich Glass." *Antiques* 34 (July 1938):20–22.

Killikelly, Sarah H. *The History of Pittsburgh: Its Rise and Progress.* Pittsburgh: B. C. & Gordon Montgomery Co., 1906.

Knittle, Rhea Mansfield. "American Glass Sugar Bowls." *Antiques* 20 (Dec. 1931):344–48.

————. "Concerning William Peter Eichbaum and Bakewell's." *Antiques* 11 (March 1927):205–6.

————. *Early American Glass.* New York: The Century Company, 1927.

————. "Muskingum County, Ohio, Glass." *Antiques* 6 (Oct. 1924):201–4.

————. "Rex Absolutus of the Monongahela." *Antiques* 13 (April 1928):290–92.

Kramer, LeRoy. *Johann Baltasar Kramer, Pioneer American Glass Blower.* Chicago: privately printed, 1939.

Kumm, Marguerite. "Bakewell Testimony." *Antiques* 44 (Sept. 1943):127–28.

Lagerberg, Theodore and Viola. *British Glass.* A Color Picture Guide to Over 100 Types of Collectible Glass. New Port Richey, Fla., 1968.

Larner, John W., Jr. "The Glass House Boys: Child Labor Conditions in Pittsburgh's Glass Factories, 1890–1917." *Western Pennsylvania Historical Magazine* 48 (Oct. 1965):356–64.

Lee, Ruth Webb. "The Duncan Trio." *Antiques* 23 (April 1933):132–34.

————. *Early American Pressed Glass.* 36th ed. Wellesley Hills, Mass.: Lee Publications, 1960; 1st ed. 1931, privately printed.

————. "Milky and Milk-White Glass." *Antiques* 28 (July 1935):26–29.

————. "Mosaic Glass and Other Types." *Antiques* 31 (Feb. 1937):80–81.

————. "Peachblow Glass." *Antiques* 24 (Aug. 1933):48–50.

————. "Pittsburgh *vs.* Sandwich: Adams & Co." *Antiques* 24 (Aug. 1933):65–67.

————. "Pittsburgh *vs.* Sandwich: Richards & Hartley." *Antiques* 25 (Feb. 1934):57–59.

————. "Rarities in Pattern Glass." *Antiques* 27 (March 1935):92–95.

————. *Sandwich Glass.* Northboro, Mass.: privately printed, 1947.

————. "The Tree of Life and Its Sundry Fruits." *Antiques* 26 (Oct. 1934):141–43.

————. *Victorian Glass.* Northboro, Mass.: privately printed, 1944.

Lee, Ruth Webb, and Rose, James H. *American Glass Cup Plates.* Northboro, Mass.: privately printed, 1948.

McCready, Jessie and Delphine. "The Ihmsen Family: Pioneer Pittsburgh Glassmakers." *Antiques* 34 (Aug. 1938):72–73.

McKearin, George S. "Ohio and Midwestern Glass." *American Collector* 9 (Nov. 1940):12–14.

————. "A Study of Paneled Vases." *Antiques* 36 (Aug. 1939):60–63.

McKearin, George S. and Helen. *American Glass.* New York: Crown Publishers, 1941.

————. *Two Hundred Years of American Blown Glass.* Garden City, N.Y.: Doubleday & Company, 1949.

McKearin, Helen. *Bottles, Flasks and Dr. Dyott.* New York: Crown Publishers, 1970.

————. "The Case of the Pressed Glass Knobs." *Antiques* 60 (Aug. 1951):118–20.

————. "Fictions of Three-Mold Glass." *Antiques* 16 (Dec. 1929):502–5.

McMaster, John Bach. *A History of the People of the United States from the Revolution to the Civil War* Vol. 2. New York: Appleton & Co., 1900.

————. *Manufactures of Pennsylvania.* Philadelphia: Galaxy Publishing Co., 1875.

Mellon, William Larimer. *Judge Mellon's Sons.* Boyden Sparkes, collaborator. Pittsburgh: privately printed, 1948.

Metz, Mrs. Alice Hulett. *Early American Pattern Glass.* Columbus, Ohio: Spencer-Walker Press, 1963.

Michigan Historical Magazine. "Early Travels on the Ohio and Its Tributaries." 20 (spring–summer 1936).

Moore, N. Hudson. *Old Glass, European and American.* New York: Frederick Stokes Company, 1926.

Neal, L. W. and Dorothy B. *Pressed Glass Salt Dishes of the Lacy Period 1825–1850.* Philadelphia: privately printed, 1962.

Neri, Antonio. *L'Arte Vetraria*. London: 1612.

New York State Laws. 50th Session, 2nd Meeting. Rev. Statutes, 1827.

Niles' Weekly Register. Baltimore, 1817, 1819, 1820.

Nixon, Lily Lee. "Three Brothers and a Sister." *Pennsylvania History,* Journal of the Pennsylvania Historical Association XXI, No. 2 (April 1954): 145–52.

Norman-Wilcox, Gregor. "On Attributing American Blown Glass." *Antiques* 36 (Aug. 1939):72–75.

Norris, James. "The Monongahela River." *Western Pennsylvania Historical Magazine* 6 (July 1923): 135–46.

Nuttall, Thomas Green. *A Journal of Travels into the Arkansas Territory During the Year 1819*. Philadelphia: Thomas H. Palmer, 1821.

Parker, Dr. M. *The Arcana of Arts and Sciences or Farmers' and Mechanics' Manual*. Washington, Pa.: J. Grayson, 1824.

Pears, Dr. Thomas Clinton, Jr. "The First Successful Flint Glass Factory in America." *Antiques* 11 (March 1927):201–5.

———. "Visit of Lafayette to the Old Glass Works of Bakewell, Pears & Co." *Western Pennsylvania Historical Magazine* 8 (Oct. 1925):195–203.

Pears, Thomas Clinton, III. "Sidelights on the History of Bakewell, Pears & Co., from the Letters of Thomas and Sarah Pears." *Western Pennsylvania Historical Magazine* 31 (Sept.–Dec. 1948):61–70.

Pellatt, Apsley. *Curiosities of Glass Making*. London: David Bogue, 1849.

Pepper, Adeline. *The Glass Gaffers of New Jersey*. New York: Charles Scribner's Sons, 1971.

Perrot, Paul N. "Glass: English, Irish, or American?" *Antiques* 79 (March 1961):264–68.

Peterson, Arthur G. *Glass Patents and Patterns*. De Bary, Fla.: A. G. Peterson, 1973.

Ramsay, John. "The Fort Pitt Glass Works." *Antiques* 37 (April 1940):190–91.

Reiser, Catherine E. *Pittsburgh's Commercial Development, 1800–1850*. Harrisburg: Pennsylvania Historical and Museum Commission, 1951.

Revi, Albert Christian. *American Cut and Engraved Glass*. New York: Thomas Nelson and Sons, 1965.

———. *American Pressed Glass and Figure Bottles*. New York: Thomas Nelson and Sons, 1964.

———. *Nineteenth Century Glass*. New York: Thomas Nelson and Sons, 1967.

———. ed. *Spinning Wheels' Collectible Glass*. New York: Ottenheimer Publishers, 1974.

Robertson, R. A. *Chats on Old Glass*. New York: Dover Publications, rev. ed., 1969.

Rose, James H. "Lacy Glass Also From Fort Pitt." *American Collector* 2 (Sept. 20, 1934):1, 6–7.

———. "Lacy Glass Window Panes, Their Use, Process and Origin." *Antiques* 51 (Feb. 1947):120–21.

———. "Midwestern Cup-Plate Designs." *Antiques* 40 (Oct. 1941):222–24.

———. "Rims and Reasons." *Antiques* 30 (Aug. 1936): 68–69.

———. *The Story of American Pressed Glass of the Lacy Period, 1825–1850*. Printed in the Netherlands for the Corning Museum of Glass, 1954.

———. "Unrecorded Rarities in American Glass." *Antiques* 71 (Feb. 1957):160–63.

———. "Unrecorded Rarities in Lacy Glass." *Antiques* 55 (March 1954):224–47.

———. "Wheeling Lacy Glass." *Antiques* 69 (June 1956):526–27.

Royall, Anne. *Mrs. Royall's Pennsylvania, or Travels Continued in the United States*. 2 vols. Washington, D.C., privately printed, 1829.

Schwartz, Marvin D., ed. *American Glass, Volume I: Blown and Moulded*. Princeton: Pyne Press, 1974.

Schramm, Eulalia Catherine. "General James O'Hara, Pittsburgh's First Captain of Industry." Master's thesis, University of Pittsburgh, 1931.

Scoville, Warren C. *Revolutions in Glassmaking*. Cambridge, Mass.: Harvard University Press, 1948.

Sicard, Hortense F. "Glassmaker to Two Presidents." *Antiques* 25 (Feb. 1934):56.

Silliman, Prof. Benjamin, and Goodrich, C. R. *The World of Science, Art, and Industry, Illustrated from Examples in the New York Exhibition 1853–1854*. New York: Putnam, 1854.

Smith, Francis E. *American Glass Paperweights*. Wollaston, Mass.: Antique Press, 1939.

Smith, Walter. *Industrial Art*. The Masterpieces of the Centennial International Exhibition, Vol. 2. Philadelphia: Gebbie-Barrie, 1876–1878.

Stow, Charles Messer. "Sandwich Glass that Pittsburgh Made." *Antiquarian* 13 (Oct. 1929):46–47.

Strauss, Jerome. "Another Gallatin Glass." *Antiques* 36 (Aug. 1939):79–80.

Swan, Frank. *Portland Glass*. Providence, R.I.: Roger Williams Press, 1939. Revised and enlarged by Marion Dana. Des Moines, Iowa: Wallace Homestead Books Co., 1972.

Thorpe, W. A. *English and Irish Glass*. London: The Medici Society, 1927.

———. *English Glass*. 2nd ed. London: Adams & Charles Black, 1949.

———. *A History of English and Irish Glass*. 2 Vols. Boston: Hale Cushman & Flint, 1929.

Thurston, George H. *Allegheny County's Hundred Years.* Pittsburgh: A. A. Anderson & Son, 1888.
———. *Pittsburgh As It Is.* 1857.
Toulouse, Dr. Julian. "Empontilling, A History." *The Glass Industry* (March–April 1968).
U.S. Centennial Commission, 1776–1886. *International Exhibition 1876.* Edited by Francis A. Walker. Vol. 3. Washington, D.C.: Government Printing Office, 1926.
U.S. International Exhibition, 1876, Reports and Awards, Groups I and II. Washington, 1880.
Van Rensselaer, Stephen. *Check List of Early American Bottles and Flasks.* Parts 1 and 2. Peterborough, N.H.: Transcript Printing Co., 1926.
Wakefield, Hugh. *Nineteenth Century British Glass.* London: Faber & Faber, 1961.
Warren, Phelps. *Irish Glass.* New York: Charles Scribner's Sons, 1971.
Watkins, Lura W. "An Antecedent of Three-Mold Glass." *Antiques* 36 (Aug. 1939):68–70.
———. *Cambridge Glass 1818–1888.* Boston: Marshall Jones Co., 1930.
———. "Pressed Glass of the New England Glass Company." *Corning Journal of Glass Studies* 12 (1970):149.
———. "The Union Glass Company." *Antiques* 30 (Nov. 1936):222–25.
Weeks, Joseph D. *Report on the Manufacture of Glass, Including a History of Glassmaking in the United States.* 10th Census, 1880. Washington, D.C.: Government Printing Office, 1883.
Westropp, M. S. Dudley. *Irish Glass.* Philadelphia: J. B. Lippincott Company, 1921.
White, Harry Hall. "Early Pittsburgh Glass Houses." *Antiques* 10 (Nov. 1926):363–68.
———. "Glass Monuments to Zebulon Pike." *Antiques* 22 (Sept., Oct. 1932):98–100, 135–38.
———. "The Kentucky Glass Works." *Antiques* 9 (Feb. 1926):85–88.
———. "Migrations of Early Glassworkers." *Antiques* 32 (Aug. 1937):64–67.
———. "New Views of Old Glass, Fins and Rough Surface Appearance on Old Glass." *Antiques* 24 (Nov. 1933):184.
———. "New Views of Old Glass, Patterns and Three-Mold Glass." *Antiques* 23 (May 1933):186.
———. "New Views of Old Glass, Removal of Fins and Mold Marks from Pressed Glass." *Antiques* 24 (Dec. 1933):223.
———. "New Views of Old Glass, Surface Lines and Rounded Edges on Pressed Glass." *Antiques* 23 (April 1933):146.
———. "New Views of Old Glass, What Is a 'Sheared' Neck?" *Antiques* 25 (Jan. 1934):24.
———. "New York State Glasshouses." *Antiques* 16 (July, Sept., Nov. 1929):44–46, 193–96, 394–96.
———. "Pattern Molds and Pattern-Mold Glass." *Antiques* 36 (Aug. 1939):64–67.
———. "The Story of the Mantua Glass Works." *Antiques* 26 (Dec. 1934):212–16; 27 (Feb. 1935): 64–68; 28 (July, Nov. 1935):30–33, 199–203.
Williamson, Harold F., and Daum, Arnold R. *The American Petroleum Industry — The Age of Illumination 1859–1899.* Evanston, Ill.: Northwestern University Press, 1959.
Wilson, Erasmus, ed. *Standard History of Pittsburgh.* Chicago: H. R. Cornell & Co., 1898.
Wilson, Kenneth M. *New England Glass and Glassmaking.* New York: Crowell, 1972.

CATALOGUES

Atterbury and Co. 1872, 1874, 1881.
Bakewell, Pears & Co. ca 1875.
B. L. Fahnestock (later B. L. Fahnestock, Fortune & Co.), 76 Wood St., Pittsburgh. 1875.
King, Son & Co. (The Cascade Glass Company). ca 1875.
Launay, Hautin & Cie (Paris). ca 1840.
W. McCully & Co. (factories: Pittsburgh, Phoenix, Sligo, Empire, and Mastodon), 18 and 20 Wood St., Pittsburgh. May 1, 1875.
McKee and Brother, 23 Wood St., Pittsburgh. Price Lists and Catalogue. ca 1860.
McKee and Brothers. 17 Wood St., Pittsburgh. Price Lists and Catalogue. 1864.
———. Price Lists and Catalogue. 1868.
New England Glass Co., Cambridge, Mass. 1868–1869.
O'Hara Flint Glass Works (James B. Lyon & Co.), 116 Water St., Pittsburgh. 1861.
O'Hara Glass Co. Ltd. ca 1876.
O'Hara Glass Co. Ltd. ca 1885.
Pennsylvania Glassware 1870–1904. American Historical Catalogue Collection, Princeton: Pyne Press, 1972.
H. L. Ringwalt, 124 and 125 under the Monongahela House, Pittsburgh. Second Annual Circular. January 1, 1860.
M. W. Sackett & Co., 29 Wood St., Pittsburgh ca 1875.
J. P. Smith, Son & Co., 189 Liberty St., Pittsburgh. Supplement to Illustrated Catalogue of Lamps, Chandeliers and Brackets. September 15, 1876.
Tibby Brothers, Sharpsburg, Pa. Illustrated Price List. 1893.

U.S. Glass Co. 1891.
  Adams & Co.; Bryce Brothers; Challinor, Taylor &
  Co. Ltd.; George Duncan & Sons; Richards &
  Hartley; Ripley & Co.; Hobbs Glass Co.; Doyle
  & Co.

DIRECTORIES

Pittsburgh:
  Harris Isaac, *Pittsburgh Business Directory,* 1837,
  1839, 1841.
  Pittsburgh & Allegheny Directory, 1856–57,
  1859–60.

NEWSPAPERS

New York:
  Commercial Advertiser. December 1824.
  Sun. February 1890.

Philadelphia:
  Daily Chronicle. July 1831.
Pittsburgh:
  Commonwealth. Issues of 1806, 1809.
  Daily Post. 1875.
  Gazette. Issues of 1793, 1800, 1802, 1809, 1814,
  1824, 1825, 1829, 1833, 1844, 1845.
  Herald. 1875.
  Mercury. Issues of 1814, 1817, 1818, 1830, 1838.
  Morning Post. 1844.
  New Statesman. April 1923.
  Saturday Visiter. 1838.
  Statesman. 1832.
  Tree of Liberty. 1805.
Waterford, New York:
  Reporter, September 9, 1826.
Wheeling, West Virginia:
  Gazette. December 1829.

Index

(All references to photos are in italics. CP refers to color plates.)

118, *11;* Jackson, 118, *64;* Reynolds greyhound, 119, 121, *65, 66;* Father Rapp, 129–31, *81;* Sulphides, 131, 133, *83–85;* American System, 207, 209–10, *12, 13*

VISITORS' COMMENTS: Anne Royall, 31, 41, 92–93, 118–19, 153; M. B. Fearon, 108; Osage chief, 109; English traveler, 111; Lafayette, 118, *63;* Nuttall, 169; *Niles'* editor, 485

GLASS TYPES: engraved, 92, 153–55, *89, 119–23;* cut, 111, 138, 139, *88, 92, 98, 100, 104;* looped, 101, 392, *46, 428;* pattern-molded, 181–85, *151, 160, 161, 163;* pillar-molded, 196, *182*

See also Double Glass

Bakewell family, 196, 279

Baldwin, Henry (U.S. congressman), 25; tariff battles, 28, 39, *12*

Baldwin, Leland D.: *Whiskey Rebels,* 7 n; *Pittsburgh, the Story of a City,* 21 n

Ballinger, Charles, 61, 65, 359, 477

Baltimore, 9, 10, 26, 33, 70; glassworks, 17 n, 19; Pittsburgh glass sold, 47, 74; *Niles' Weekly Register,* 485

Bank of Pennsylvania, 10

Bank of the United States (second), 38

Baptismal font, 64, 478, *22*

Bar goods, 54–55, 360, 432, 486

Barker, Charlotte, *79*

Barker, David, 63, 65; company, 344, 435, 444, 477, 480, *396*

Barker, W. W. (frames), 71

Barnes, Hobbs and Company, 184

Baroque pattern, 155

Barret, Richard Carter, 140, 380

Bartholdi, Frederick Auguste, 375, 380, 438–39, *412, 413*

Beaver River, 58

Beck, John, 363

Beck, Washington, 60, 61, 65, 78, 364; patents, 62, 63, 68, 335, 367, 477, 478; mold factory, 357; granular surface process, 370, 371; novelties, 443, 480

Beck, William, 53

Belgian: crystal, 43; glass, 73, 351, 360, 451, *383, 427*

Belgium, workmen, 54, 76 n

Belknap, E. McCamly, 399, 406 n, 409, 417; on Atterbury, 399, 406 n, 409; Challinor and Taylor, 406, *455*

Bellaire Goblet Company, 382, 462

Belle Vernon, Pa., 8

Bells, *462, 512*

Belton, Dr. Samuel, 52

Beltzhoover, Wendt & Company, 33, 37

Benedum Fund (Historical Society of Western Pennsylvania), *125, 198, 255*

Bennett, David, 55, 56

Bennett, J. N., 56

Bennett, William, 56

Bennington Museum (Vt.), 140, 233, *234, 405;* C. Kenneth Vincent collection, 380, *405, 411, 415*

Bercy factory, 253, 299

Bermuda, 26

Biddle, Nicholas (President of the Second Bank of the United States), 34

Billups, Melvin, 101

Birbeck, Morris (*Journey in America from the Coast of Virginia to the Territory of Illinois*), 15 n

Birmingham (district of Pittsburgh), 73, 74, 76; glasshouses in, 33, 51, 53 n, 54, 55, 56, 69; glass pot factory, 49

Birmingham Flint Glass Company, 36

Birmingham Glass Works, *140*

Bitters bottle, 304, 486, *218*

Black bottle project, 85–86

Blair, George W., 380, *416*

Block pattern, 248

Bloom, Aaron, 448

Blowing, 92–93, 430

Blown glass, 83–85; products, 87–97, *31–38, 46;* use of color, *25, 26, 27, 41, 44. See also* Flasks; Cased glass

Blue glass, 389

Boardman, James (*America and the Americans*), 298

Boat salts, 34. *See also* Salts

Bohemian glass, 73, *383;* influence, 333, 350–51, 360, 435, 451; bar ware, 360

Bonshire, J., patent, 478

Bordentown, N.J., 9

Bosses (knobs), 321

Boston, 17, 47, 74; factories, 173, 389, 431

Boston and Sandwich Glass Company, 13

Boston *Commercial Gazette,* 173

Boston Crown Glass Company, 16

Bottle colors, 83, 196, 204–5; black, 15 n, 53 n; green, *26*

novelties, *497, 499, 505. See also* Aberina; Rose amber; Art glass

Columbia, Ky., 24

Columbia Glass Company, Findlay, O., 461, *415*

Columbian Exposition (1892), 72 n

Columbus, O., 47

Commemorative flasks. *See* pictorial subjects *under* flasks

Commercial wares, 155, 164, 191, 227, *119–28, 222–27;* pillar-molding, 196

Compotes, 34; Bakewell, xvi, 33, 299, 303, *180, 299;* pressed, 243, 248, 282, 338, *234, 252, 330, 374, 390, 395, 400, 405, 416, 417, 473;* cut, *144–45, 58, 94, 110;* engraved, 153–54, 155, 166–68, *116, 122, 139, 146, 417;* pillar-molded, 196, 396, *180, 183, 197, 437;* pressed and blown, 231, 232–33, 247, 248, *230–33;* lacy, 252, 264, 279, 292, *275, 290, 292, 301;* Grossman, 267, 275, *265;* blown, 280, 282; opaque, 407, 410, 419, *457–58;* Mosaic, 410, *460;* pattern-molded, *139, 155;* cased, *431–32, 437, CP1*

Continental glass: characteristics, 95, 105, 121, 134, 168, 169, 252, 392, 419, *383;* cut, 138; influence of, 311, 351; opaque glass, 390–91

Convex glass (for parlor windows), 37

Co-operative Flint Glass Company, Ltd. (Beaver, Pa.), 382, 455, *415*

Copper wheel engraving. *See* copper wheel technique *under* Engraved glass

Cork, Ireland, factory, 238

Corning Journal of Glass Studies, 271 n. *See also* New England Glass Co.

Corning Museum of Glass, special exhibitions, 36, 169, 255; glasshouse catalogues, xvi, xvii n, 50, 54, 310–11, 373, *322–25, 357, 361, 402, 407, 408, 409, 470;* Stanger letters, 481–82

Corning Museum of Glass collection: flasks, 31, 211, 216–17, *12, 13, 206, 210, 213, 215;* engraved, 33, 155, 164–66, 169, *123, 127, 130, 133, 140, 142, 143, 147, 150;* cut, 109, 118, 131–33, 138–39, 142, *57, 83, 87, 92, 100, 107;* pattern-molded, 155, 164, 172, 181, 191, 193, 248, *127, 133, 151, 156, 160, 172, 177, 250;* three-mold blown, 155, *123;* pillar-molded, 196, *184;* pressed and blown, 232, 248, *230, 250, 302;* pressed, 248, 404, 415, *253, 254, 447, 469;* lacy, 254, 255, 261, 267, 269, 276, *257, 263, 272, 278, 280, 287, 290, 293, 296, 297, 302, 305;* blown, 392, 415, *427, 466;* cased, 395, *431,*

CP1; paperweights, 447, *504;* pressed (King, Son & Company catalogue), *357, 361, 402, 407–9, 470, 496*

Corning-Smithsonian excavations, 166

Corrugations. *See* Rib-molding

Coventry, Conn., 175

Covers (sugar bowls), 97, 101–2

Crabtree, Lotta (actress), 56

Crackled glass, 453

Craig, Major Isaac, 7, 9, 12, 21; papers, xix, 9 n, 10, 21; biographical sketch, 10; O'Hara partnership, 18, 28

Craig, Mrs. Paul, 191, *26, 27, 33, 35*

Cramer, Zadok (*The Navigator*), 3, 15 n, 19 n

Craquelle glass, 453

Crawford County Historical Society, 38 n

Creamers: lacy, xvii, 34, 280, *257;* pressed, 66, 254, 338–40, 486, *23, 329, 357, 361, 366, 401, 405;* free-blown, 91, 166, *29, 40, 42, 54, 174, 484, CP4;* engraved, 155, *188, 129, 147–48;* pattern-molded, 182, 196, *132, 151, 154, 162–63, 198–99, CP5;* pillar-molded, *162, 179, 190, 193;* etched, *419;* opaque, *479;* cased, *481*

Creighton, Pa., 78

Crescent Glass Works, 392, *426*

Crescent Works, 52. *See also* Evans and Co.

Crimping. *See* Patent crimper

Crockery and Glass Journal, The, xix, 33, 43, 48, 70, 330–31; use of gas, 45, 46; pressed glass, 51–52, 382, *382, 495;* glass factories, 52, 53, 55, 56, 58, 60, 72, 321, 323, 325, 328, 436, *17, 335, 398;* colored glass, 70, 389; toast at banquet, 70; glass agents, 74; unions and labor troubles, 74, 75–76; plate glass, 77, 78; tableware (pressed), 78, 360–62, 460; cased, 196, *192, 293;* trade, 230, 326, 385; cut glass, 350–51, 455; foreign wares, 350–51, 459, *383;* crystalography, 371; stained ware, 382; perfume bottles, 419; Centennial, 430, 431, *397, 494;* frosted, 433; novelties, 438, 440, 443, 444–45, *502, 503;* O'Hara Glass Co., 438; paperweights, 447, 448; art glass, 450–51, 452–53; Peach Blow controversy, 452; crackled glass, 453; cameo, 456–58; Glass Pool, 460–61; opal, *474, 475*

Cross Cut Canal (1839), 25

Crossan, Colonel, 69

Crown glass method, 86

Cruets, 186–90, *23, 32, 418;* Bakewell, 28, 91; Doyle, 53; Duncan, 57; cut and shut technique, 66–67;

Duncan, George, and Sons (*cont.*)
    n; payroll, 75; strike, 76; tariff parade, 77 n; engraved, 371–72, 379; staining (Amberette), 380, *416;* opal, 417; Centennial, 431, 433; novelties, 438, 439, 443, 444; Peach Blow, 452; crackled, 453
    PATTERNS: Honeycomb, 305; Tree of Life, 335, 356, *395;* Shell and Tassel, 338, 370, *356;* French and Bohemian influences, 350–51, *383;* Three Face, 355–56, 370, 371, 385, *391, 392;* Zippered Block, 380; Snail, *415*
Duncan and Heisey, 56–57
Duncan and Miller Glass Company, 56
Du Pont, E. I., 134, *90*
Duquesne Glass Company, 52
Duss, John S., 130
Duvall, Isaac, 111
Dyottville Works, 48

Eagle motif, 19, 36, *6, 141, 142;* on flasks, 33, *204, 205, 211, 214, 215, 216;* on cup plates, 34, *314;* lacy, *258, 272, 273*
Early American Glass (Knittle), xv, xvi, 206 n, 224
Early American Glass Club, Pittsburgh Chapter, xviii, *3, 400*
Early American Pattern Glass (Metz), 382. *See also* Metz, Alice
Early American Pressed Glass (Lee), xvi, xvii, 50 n, 248, 304, 311, 444. *See also* Lee, Ruth Webb
Early Glass of the Pittsburgh District, 1797–1890 (Innes), xviii n, 118
Easley's Patent Lemon Juice Extractor, 56
Eckhardt, Robert and Mary C., Campbell, Jones pieces and patterns, *346, 354–55, 374–75, 390, 498*
Economy (Harmony Society), 22. *See also* Old Economy
Eddyville, Ky., 23
Edison, Thomas A., 331
Eggcups, 28, 91, 92, 486, *366*
Eichbaum, Arnold (son of William Peter), 16–17
Eichbaum, William Peter: at Bakewell's, xvi, 16, 83, 110; at O'Hara and Craig, 16–17; and F. Wendt, 16, 28, 204–5; other activities, 16, 23; Dorothy Daniel reference, 140
"Electrical vessels," 87
Ellers, Dr. E. R., 269, *95, 104, 108, 136, 232, 275*
Elliot, C. W., 431

Ellison Glassworks (England), 411
Elsholz, William J., 233, 238–40, 264, *239, 241, 294, CP6, 301*
Empire Glass Works, 38, 53 n
England, clay, 9; trade relations, 3, 38, 168, 485; labor, 15; imported brick, 72; industry, 76 n; machines, 78
English and Irish Glass. See Thorpe, W. A.
English glass, 17, 23, 42–44, 78, 91; Anglo-Irish imports vs. American, 38, 168, 169; definitions of flint and crystal, 43–44; lima-soda formula, 43; Weeks' comparison of Pittsburgh with foreign countries, 73; influence, 106, 108, 128, 131; Anglo-Irish tradition, 109, 134, 138–39, 141–42, 164–68, 173; joke on Englishman, 111; pillar-molding, 194
English tumbler, 128, 129, *78*
Engraved glass: Amelung, 152–53; Stiegel, 152; copper wheel technique, 152–53; Bakewell factory, Anne Royall's account, 153; various forms with engraving, 164–68, *120–22, 126, 128–29, 138–39, 244, 501*
    PATRIOTIC DESIGNS: Hornet and Peacock, 33, *140;* Eagle, 118, 169, *63, 141, 142;* Dithridge Mount Vernon, 456, *510*
    IDENTIFICATION OF PATTERNS: 153, 154, *116, 117;* Bakewell, Three leaf and Daisy, 154, 166, *89, 120, 123;* variations, single leaf and daisy, 155, *124, 126–29;* three circles and leaf, 155–64, *125, 130;* three leaves and berry sprays, 164, *131;* floral sprays and festoons, 164, *133–36*
    ORNAMENTATION OF PRESSED: Three Face, 355, *392;* King, Son and Company, 373, *408;* McKee and Brothers, 374; James B. Lyon, 375; Dakota, 385, *422*
    See also Etching; Frosting; American cut and engraved tumblers
Ensell, Edward, Sr., 12, 111; company, 11; with Bakewell, 28; with Wendt, 33
Erie, Pa. *See* Presque Isle
Erie Canal, 25
Esterly, Louise, 261, 280, *263, 296*
Etching: sandblast, 367, 380, 387; treatment of mold, 367–70; technique, 367, 371–72; clarification of terms (frosting), 373–74; etching as an attribution, 377–78; plate etching, 379–80; needle etching, 379; acid-etched cameo, 385, 456; Phoenix Glass Co., enamel and etching, 452, 455; proce-

Manheim, 173

Mantua, O., 173, 175

Manufactures of Pennsylvania (McMaster), 218 n, 222

Marble, Albert, 254

Maring, Hart & Company, 227, *227*

Marshall, D. R. (agent), 451

Marshall & Brothers, S. S. (specialty firm), 71

Martins Ferry, O., 36, 70 n, 483

Mason, John L., 362

Masonic decanter, 144, *107*

Mason jars, 229, 362

Massachusetts Institute of Technology, 45 n

Massilon, O., 74

Masterpieces of the Centennial International Exhibition, The, 436, 449 n

Mastodon Works, 38, 53 n

Match safe, 409, 480, *454*

Mat finish, 299

Matthews, Charles (specialty firm), 71

Maxwell, J., 41 n

Maxwell, W. H., 65, 445–47, 478, 480

Meadville, Pa., 38 n

Means, Mrs. Rosetta M., *303*

Medallions, 131–33, 168, *83, 84. See also* Sulphides *under* American cut and engraved tumblers

Medicine bottles, 226, *217. See also* Bottles

Mediterranean, 43, 177, *154*

Meissen, 257 n

Mestrezat, Charles A., 90, *31*

Metal, 28 n

Metallic oxides, 8

Metropolitan Museum of Art, 155, 181, 272; cased, 362; engraved, *120;* lacy, *283;* pressed, *360, 364, 365, 396, 403, 404;* Mosaic, *459, 460*

Metz, Mrs. Alice, *382, 457*

Michaux, André, 9

Michigan Historical Magazine, 4 n

Midwest: defined, 7, 45

"Midwestern glass": defined, 7

Miles, Mrs. Emily Winthrop, collection, *360, 364, 365, 396, 403, 404, 459, 460*

Milk Glass, 398–99, 406 n, 409–10, 417, *455, 456. See also* Belknap, E. McCamly

Milk glass (Opal, Opaque white), xvii, 54, 55, 389–90, 398, 406, 419, 444; lining (cased), 196, 392–96, 419, 455, *196, 433–35, 481, 490, 508;* Double Glass, 325–26, 415, *343, 344, 464, 467–68;* formu-las, 392, 398–99, 483; pressed sets, 398–99, 411, 419, *441, 442–45, 452*

Milk pans, 87, 89, 97, *27, 28, 30, 61, CP2, CP3*

Miller, G. F., 460

Miller, Henry, 447

Miller, James, 133

Miller, J. F., 451

Miller, John Ernest, 57, 65–66, 355–56, 379, 439, 478, 479, *391, 392*

Mississippi River, 3, 8, 21, 26, *1*

Missouri clay beds, 9, 58, 77

Mitchell, Charles R., 483

Mitchell ware, 56, 444, 480

Molasses cans, 67–68, 177, 305–9, 419, *152–53, 192, 331, 371, 443, 465, 470, 472*

Mold-blown, 155–56, 172–75, 177, 182, 186, 191, *131, 153, 163, 171, 175*

Molded glass, 34, 50, 53, 55

Molds and mold makers, 53, 58, 60–61, 209, 210; importance, 44, 76, 461; material and construction, 58, 61, 62, 205–6, 215, 229, 253, 255, 257–59, 296

Monongahela House, 69–70

Monongahela Navigation Company, 26

Monongahela River, 4, 7, 9, 17, 26, 71, 108, *1, 26, 29, 173*

"Monongahela River glass," 85

"Monongahela rye," 7

Monroe, James (President), xvi, 28, 114, 118, 152, *61, 62*

Montana sets, 56

Montgomery Ward & Company, 57, 462

Montreal, salesroom, 74

Moore, N. Hudson (*Old Glass: European and American*), 121

Moore family, *30*

Morgan, Mrs. Mary, vase, 452

Morrison, James, 10, 18, 19, 20

Mosaic glass, 55, 410–11, 479, *459, 460*

Mount Oliver Cemetery, 100

Mount Pleasant, Bryce glasshouse, 57

Mount Washington (Coal Hill), 9, 45

Mount Washington Glass Works (New Bedford, Mass.), 431, 443, 450, 452, 454–55; patents, 443, 454

Mugs, 133, 358, 486; pillar-molded, 196, *196;* opaque, 419, *471;* toy, 431; beer, 432, 444

Mulvaney, Patrick, 36

Pot factory, 49

Potash, 8–9, 17–18, 38, 76 n

Powder horn, 101, *47, 489, 491*

Preserving jars, 229, *217, 228*

"President Adams" (armed galley), 4

Presque Isle (Erie), 4, 22, *2*

Pressed glass: Naturalism, xviii, 351–55; production, 22, 27, 34, 37, 47–49, 69–77, *8, 9;* lime-soda, 34, 42–44, 106; characteristics of early pressing, 41, 231–43, 253, 298–99, 311, 333; borrowing styles, 333–38; novelties, 438–39; pressed glass patterns, 486; Patents, 477–80. *See also* Molds and Mold Makers; Chapters XIII, XIV, XVI–XX

Pressed glass patterns:

Acorn 344; Actress, 56 (La Belle Glass Company); Almond Thumbprint, 334 (Bryce); Amberette, "Klondike," 57, 380, *416* (Duncan; Dalzell, Gilmore & Leighton); Arabesque, 299, 370 (Bakewell); Argus, "Thumbprint," 50, 54, 301, 326, 334, 340, 341, 342, 382 (Bakewell), *255, 358–60;* (King, Son & Company) *357;* (McKee) *373, 473* (New England Glass Company); Ashburton, 301, 302, 309, 311, 342, *255, 364–65, CP9* (Bakewell; Bryce; McKee; New England; O'Hara); Aster, 310, *328* (Curling)

Balloon, *401;* Baltimore Pear, "Gypsy", 353, *385, 386* (Adams); Banded Buckle, "Union," 54 (King); Barberry, 353 (McKee); Bartholdi, stained, 380, *412, 413* (O'Hara); Basket Weave, *445, 449, 457, 474, 499, 500* (Atterbury); Bellflower, "Ribbed Leaf," 50, 311, 318, 326, *379–81* (Bryce; McKee); Bigler, 302, 342, *369, 370* (McKee); Bleeding Heart, "Floral," 54, 341, 353, *361, 387–89, 471* (King); Bohemian, 486 (Bakewell; O'Hara; Richards & Hartley); Brilliant, 311, 327 (McKee); Broken Column with Red Dot, *415* (Columbia Glass Company); Bull's-Eye and Oval, *473*

Centennial, 54, 432, 434, 444, 479, *496* (Hobbs, Brockunier; King); Cherry, 353, 384 (Bakewell); Cincinnati, "Honeycomb," 51, 301, 305, 307, 310, 318, 327, 341, 342, 486, *363* (Duncan; Gillinder; Hobbs; McKee; O'Hara; New England); Colonial, 34, 301, 304, 342, *253, 328, 473* (Curling; Heisey; McKee); Comet, 50, 311, 335 (Bryce; Doyle; McKee); Concave, 318, 342 (McKee); Cone, 486 (O'Hara); Cosmos, 344 (Dalzell, Gilmore and Leighton); Croesus, *509*

(Phoenix; Riverside); Crystal, 50, 51, 54, 305, 310, 311, 344, 380, 486, *329, 372* (McKee; O'Hara); Crystal Wedding, 51, 380, 433, *414, 494* (Adams; O'Hara); Cube and Diamond, *382* (Bellaire); Curled Leaf, 57 (Bryce); Currant, 53, 353, 478, *354–55, 390* (Campbell, Jones)

Daisy and Button, 57, 380, 439, 462, 479, *416, 457, 497* (Bryce; Doyle; Duncan; O'Hara); Daisy and Button Single Panel, stained, 380 (Duncan); Dakota, "Baby Thumbprint," 382–88, 462, *417–24* (Doyle; Ripley); Davis, 305, 486, *329,* (O'Hara); Deer and Pine, 344; Dewdrop with Star, 53, 478, *374–75* (Campbell, Jones); Diamond, 305, 309–10, 342–43, 478, 486, *152, 373* (Bryce; McKee; O'Hara); Diamond and Concave (O'Hara); Diamond Point, 301, 344 (Bryce); Diamond Thumbprint, 334 (McKee; Sandwich); Double Bars, "Frosted Ribbon," *409* (King); Dragon, 478 (McKee)

Etruscan, 347, *378* (Bakewell); Eugenie, 50, 311, 327 (McKee); Excelsior, 50, 302, 303, 311, 327, 342, *366–67, 473* (Doyle; McKee)

Fern, *442* (Atterbury); Finger Flute, 305 (McKee); Fish, *446* (Atterbury); Floral. *See* Bleeding Heart; Florida, *414* (U.S. Glass Company); Flower and Panel, *452* (Challinor, Taylor); Flute, 34, 302–4, 310, 311, 334, 341, 359, 360, *328* (Bryce; Campbell, Jones; Duncan; McKee); Forest Ware, "Ivy-in-Snow," *415* (Phoenix); Frosted Ribbon, 54, *409* (Duncan)

Gaines, 305, 318, 326, 342, 347, 486, *371* (McKee; O'Hara); Genella, 51, 305, 342, 486, *330* (O'Hara); Gothic, 54, *402* (McKee); Grape, (McKee); Grape Band, 57, 355, 478 (Bryce); Grape and Festoon with Shield, 355 (Doyle); Grape and Festoon with Stippled Grape, 355 (Doyle); Gypsy. *See* Baltimore Pear

Hand, "Pennsylvania," 51, 344 (O'Hara); Hobnail, *460* (Hobbs; McKee; New Brighton); Honeycomb. *See* Cincinnati; Horn of Plenty, "Comet," 144, 335, 344 (Bryce; McKee; Sandwich); Huber, 51, 54, 298, 301, 302, 305, 307, 310, 341, 359, 360, 486, *329, 400* (Bakewell; McKee; New England; Richards; O'Hara)

Icicle, 347, *378, 384* (Bakewell); Imperial, 57, *396* (Adams; Bryce; McKee); "Ivy-in-Snow." *See* Forest Ware

Pressed glass patterns (*cont.*)
Jacob's Ladder, "Maltese," 57, 462, *396* (Bryce; Portland Glass Co.); Jewel, 54 (King; McKee); Jumbo, 344, *396* (Canton)

King's Crown, "XLCR," *405* (Adams)

Leaf, "Loop," 50, 51, 305, 310, 311, 327, 334–35, 342, 486, *330, 400* (Bakewell; Bryce; McKee; New England; O'Hara; Sandwich); Leaf and Dart, 55 (Richards & Hartley); Lily, "Sunflower," 355 (Atterbury); Lion (Gillinder); Loop. *See* Leaf (O'Hara; Portland); Loop and Dart with Diamond Ornaments, 51, 55 (Richards & Hartley); Loop and Dart with Round Ornaments, 51, 55, 369, 370, 479 (Portland); Lotus, 50 (Bakewell; McKee)

Magic, 369 (McKee); Maltese, "Jacob's Ladder," 57, *396* (Bryce); Medallion, *443* (Atterbury); Mellon, 50 (Bakewell); Melon with Net, *441* (Atterbury); Mioton, 305, 486 (McKee; O'Hara); Mirror, 342 (McKee); Mitchell, 54 (King); Mitre Diamond, 50, 305, 310, 311, 342, 486, *330* (McKee; O'Hara); Moon and Star, "Palace," 51, 370 (Adams)

New Orleans, 298, 305, 310, 342, 486, *330* (O'Hara); New Pressed Leaf, "N.P.L.," 311 (McKee); New York, 54, 305, 310 (Bakewell; Bryce; McKee; O'Hara). *See also* Honeycomb

O'Hara Loop, "Leaf," 305, 306, 310, 335, 486, *371* (O'Hara; Portland; Sandwich); O'Hara Diamond, 380 (U.S. Glass Company); Oval Mitre, 342 (McKee)

Palace, "Moon and Star"; "Waffle and Thumbprint," 51, 304, 486, *328–29* (Curling; O'Hara); Paneled, *457;* Paneled Fern, "Fern," *442* (Atterbury); Paneled Grape Band, 355 (King); Peerless, *495* (Richards & Hartley); Pillar, 53 (Bakewell; McKee); Pitt Diamond, 342 (Bakewell); Plume, 51, 299, 380, 462, *415* (Adams); Prism, 50, 311, 318, 326, 347, 372, *406, 444, 457, CP9* (Atterbury; Bakewell; King; McKee); Princess Feather, "Rochelle," 299, *290, 406, 461* (Bakewell); Punty, 334 (Bryce; New England; Richards & Hartley)

Ray, 311 (McKee); Red Block, 380, 462 (Doyle; Duncan); Reeded, 51, 305, 486, *330* (Atterbury; New England; O'Hara; Union); Ribbed Leaf. *See* Bellflower; Ribbed Palm, "Sprig," 335 (Bryce; McKee); Ribbon Candy, 57, 304, 370, 462 (Bryce); Rochelle. *See* Princess Feather; Roman Rosette, 57, 233, 243, 369, 380, 462, *231, 246, 415* (Bryce); Rose-in-Snow, 353 (Bryce); Royal Crystal, *415;* Ruby Thumbprint, 382, *405* (Adams)

Saint Nicholas, 304, 486 (O'Hara); Sawtooth, 344 (Bryce; Gillinder; McKee; New England); Sharp Diamond, 344 (New England); Shell and Jewel, 369 (New England); Shell and Tassel, 57, 335–38, 370, 478, *356* (Duncan; Portland); Small Diamond, 486 (New England; O'Hara); Snail, *415* (Duncan); Sprig, "Ribbed Palm," 311, 318, 327, 334, 347, 478 (Bryce; McKee; Sandwich); *S* repeat, 388 (National); Star, 51, 303, 305, 318, 326, 347, 486, *330* (O'Hara); Star and Buckle, 23 (Bryce); Star and Concave, 308, 326, 486, *152, 371* (O'Hara); Stedman, 50, 310, 311, 318, 326, 335, 347, 478 (McKee); Strawberry, 57 (Bryce; Sandwich); Sunken Primrose, "Florida," *414* (Greensburg); Sunflower, 355 (Atterbury)

Tacoma, *415* (Greensburg); Thistle, 50, 57, 468, *CP11, CP12* (Bakewell; Bryce); Three Face, 57, 478, *391–92* (Duncan); Thousand Eye, 51, 55, *403, 404* (Adams; New Brighton; Richards & Hartley); Tree of Life, 51, 57, 335–38, 453, *395* (Duncan; Portland; Sandwich); Thumbprint. *See* Argus; Tulip, 310, 318, 326, 347 (Bryce; McKee); Two Panel, *338* (Richards & Hartley)

Union, 54, 350 (King; McKee)

Vernon, 305, 486 (New England; O'Hara); Victoria, *414* (Bakewell; Richards & Hartley)

Waffle and Thumbprint, 51, 304, *328* (Curling; New England; O'Hara); Western, 305; Wildflower, 51, 344, 353, 462, *376* (Adams); Wreath, 51, 305, 486, *330* (Bryce; O'Hara)

XLCR, "King's Crown," 367, 380, *405* (Adams)

See Appendix 5 *and* 305 for pressed patterns of tumblers and drinking vessels (Bohemian, Charleston, Chicago, Columbus, Flute, Gauche, Giant Thumbprint, Henderson, Hotel, Sage, Saint George)

See also American Pressed Glass and Figure Bottles; Pitcher Books

Pressed Glass Salt Dishes of the Lacy Period, 1825– 1850 (Neal), 309, *CP6*

Providence Flint Glass Works, 254

Punch cups, 133–34, 140, *87*
Punty. *See* Kugel.

Queenstown, Canada, 22

Ragot gas furnace, 45, 58
Rapp, Father George, 130–31, *81*
Rebecca at the Well motif, 33, *393*
Reddick, James, 63, 65, 414, 477
Reder, Joseph, 447
Reeding, 50, 233–39, 311, 326–27, 347, 358, 399, *237, 239, 377, 379–81, 396*
Reighard, Jacob, 318, 478
Reiser, Catherine E. (*Pittsburgh's Commercial Development, 1800–1850*), 49 n
Reminiscences of Glass Making (Jarves), 51 n, 231, 232, 333
Renner, Mrs. Lee, 125–29, 131, *76, 77*
Report on the Manufacture of Glass (Weeks), 73, 77, 85 n. *See also* Weeks, Joseph E.
Reppert, George, 17 n
Reppert, Lewis, 17
Revi, Albert Christian (*American Pressed Glass and Figure Bottles*), 50 n, 52, 54, 57, 65, 338, 370, 453, 462 n
Revolutions in Glassmaking. See Scoville, Warren G.
Reynolds, Mrs. John E., 119, *65, 66*
Reynolds, William, 119–21, 131, *65, 66*
Rib-molding. *See* Pattern-molding
Richards, Joseph, 55
Richards and Hartley Glass Company: history, 55, 74, 75–76, 77, 461; exhibitions, 71, 431, 434; glass, 286, 319, 341, 350, 358, 384, 419, 434, 438, 451, *338, 403–4, 415, 495*
Richardson, Benjamin (England), 454
Rims:
    BLOWN GLASS: tooled, 95, *121, 148, 154;* galleried, 97, *100, 101, 120, 125;* folded, 97, 155, *35, 36, 39, 40;* gauffered, 419, *477*
    CUT GLASS: French, 257, 280–82, *299;* notched, *60*
    PRESSED: gauffered (scalloped), 248–52, *255–56;* Eastern, 254, 270, *278, 281. See also* Lacy glass; Cap rings
Ring stand, French, 280–83, *299–300, 301*
Ringwalt, Henry L., 34, 306–10, *331–32. See also* Catalogues
Rio de Janiero, 26

Ripley, Daniel C., 49, 56, 72 n, 460; patents, 56, 63, 419, 477, 478
Ripley, Daniel C., Jr., 56, 461
Ripley and Company, Daniel C.:
    History, 56, 72, 75, 77, 326, 364; glass, Marriage lamp and Baptismal font, 64, 327, 419, 477, *21, 22;* exhibitions, 72, 350, 431, 434, *382;* imitation of cut, 380
    PATENTS: 253, 323–24, 441–43, *502;* lamp, 56, 319, 320, 477, 478, *19*
    PATTERNS: states, 56, 454; Dakota, 382–84, 385, 387–88
Ritchie, John and Craig, 254, 283, 284, *306*
Ritchie and Wheat, 111, 144
Riverside Glass Company, *511*
Roanoke, tankard, 56
Robertson, Morgan, 17, 34
Robertson, R. A. (*Chats on Old Glass*), 128
Robinson, Enoch, 41–42
Robinson, George, 111
"Robinson & Son, J.", salt, 34, *16, CP6*
Robinson, John (wholesaler), 92
Robinson, John, Sr. (Stourbridge Flint Glass Works, 1823; J & T Robinson, 1830), 33–34, 43, 83, 109, 111, 254; cut and engraved tumblers, 129, *79, 80;* cut decanter, 134, 144, *89, 93;* flasks, 209 (Washington, Jackson and scrolls), *203, 210*
    PRESSED: 282; market salts, 34, *16, 309, CP6;* lacy knob, 41 n; marked, 261–62, *264*
"Robinson, T. & J." plate, 34, *264*
Robinson, Thomas, 34
Rochester, N.Y., 76
Rochester, Pa., 58
Rochester Tumbler Company: history, 45, 58–60, 72, 462, *17;* Bakewell's gift to Fry, 118, 139, *92;* production, 301; Centennial, 360, 431, 434, 397. *See also* Fry, Henry Clay
Rockingham ware, 259
Rodgers, J. Robert, collection: free-blown, 101, *50;* engraved, 166, 248, *139, 145, 158;* cut and engraved, *85, 86;* pattern-molded, *163, 166, 201;* pillar-molded, *189*
Rogers Fund, *120*
Roller glass, 86. *See also* Broad (cylinder) glass method
Rolling pin, *3, 25*
Roman collection (Elbert Eli Farman), 89
Roman Glass from Karanis. See Harden, D. B.